Problem Solving with *Java*

Elliot Koffman
Ursula Wolz

▲▲ ADDISON-WESLEY

An imprint of Addison Wesley Longman, Inc.

Reading, Massachusetts • Menlo Park, California • New York • Harlow, England
Don Mills, Ontario • Sydney • Mexico City • Madrid • Amsterdam

Acquisitions Editor: Susan Hartman
Production Editor: Amy Willcutt
Assistant Editor: Julie Dunn
Production Assistant: Brooke Albright
Composition: Jackie Davies
Copyeditor: Roberta Lewis
Proofreader: Roberta Brent
Technical Artist: George Nichols
Cover Designer: Diana Coe

Cover credits
© G. Biss/Masterfile (puzzle pieces)
© Ann Cutting/Photonica (cup)

Access the latest information about Addison-Wesley books from our World Wide Web site:
http://www.awl.com/cseng

Many of the designations used by manufacturers and sellers to distinguish their products are claimed as trademarks. Where those designations appear in this book, and Addison-Wesley was aware of a trademark claim, the designations have been printed in initial caps or all caps.

The programs and applications presented in this book have been included for their instructional value. They have been tested with care, but are not guaranteed for any particular purpose. The publisher does not offer any warranties or representations, nor does it accept any liabilities with respect to the programs or applications.

Library of Congress Cataloging-in-Publication Data

Koffman, Elliot B.
     Problem solving with Java / Elliot B. Koffman, Ursula Wolz.
       p. cm.
     Includes index.
     ISBN 0-201-35743-7
     1. Java (Computer program language) I. Wolz, Ursula. II. Title.
QA76.73.J38K64 1999
005.13'3—dc21
                                                98-24943
                                                CIP

This book was typeset in QuarkXPress 3.32 on a Macintosh Quadra 840AV. The fonts used were Times and Gill Sans. It was printed on New Era Matte.

1 2 3 4 5 6 7 8 9 10-MA-0201009998

Preface

This textbook is intended for a first course in problem solving and program design with Java. It assumes no prior knowledge of computers or programming, and for most of its material, high school algebra is sufficient mathematics background. A limited knowledge of discrete mathematics is desirable for a few sections.

The principles of problem solving and program design are relatively language independent, but Java provides facilities for implementation that are easier to use and more powerful than those available in more traditional languages like Pascal or C++. Our intent is to exploit the best of Java to teach good program design based on the ACM/IEEE-CS Joint Curriculum Task Force1.

Problem Solving and Program Design

The primary focus of this book is problem solving with Java, not a study of the Java programming language per se. We achieve this focus by selecting features of the language that lend themselves to good program design. We also emphasize abstraction and follow a standard five-step approach to program design (problem specification, analysis, design, implementation, and testing). We have modified this time-tested approach for software development to the object-oriented paradigm. We follow it faithfully in the solution of more than 20 case studies throughout the book.

Applets versus Applications

We introduce applets early—in fact our first program in Chapter 1 is an applet, rather than a "Hello world" application. However, we focus on applications in Chapters 2 and 3, where we teach the basics of simple programs that calculate results. We use applications rather than applets because we don't want students to have to struggle with the details of providing a graphical user interface (GUI). However, we do provide a package that enables students to write applications that use GUIs (see the next section). We introduce graphics programming in optional sections in Chapters 4 and 6 and use applets exclusively in these sections. We revisit applets again in Chapters 9 and 10 where we discuss Web programming and study the Abstract Window Toolkit (AWT).

Class SimpleGUI and Package simpleIO

We feel it is very important for students in an introductory programming course to be able to write programs that have the look and feel of windows-based programs that they use on a daily basis. At the same time, we recognize that, even in Java, the design of GUIs is a very complicated task, beyond the capabilities of someone just learning to program. For this reason, we provide a class (SimpleGUI) that enables students to use GUIs in their applications. SimpleGUI has data entry methods (getInt, getDouble, getChar, getBoolean) that display a prompt and return a value using a GUI window. The data entry interaction and program outputs (generated by calls to SimpleGUI method displayResult) are captured in a "User Interaction History" window. Students can print the contents of this window or save it as a file. SimpleGUI also has methods that enable students to generate simple menus or lists of choices and to display arrays.

SimpleGUI is part of package simpleIO which can be downloaded from the Web site for this book. Package simpleIO also has classes SimpleReader, SimpleWriter, and SimpleGraphic. SimpleReader and SimpleWriter facilitate programming with file streams; SimpleGraphic enables students to incorporate user interactivity with graphics programs.

Objects versus Procedural Approach

A textbook in problem solving with Java should utilize the object-oriented paradigm from the beginning. We do this in a gentle manner, introducing classes and objects in Chapter 1. Early programs in Chapters 2 and 3 use a separate application class and support class. Each application class has a small main method that instantiates a support class and calls its methods. All the work is done by the support class methods. In the beginning, the support class data fields are all private, and its methods are all public. We declare data fields sparingly, preferring to calculate results as needed rather than store them in the object.

In Chapter 4 we focus on method details, describing constructors, accessors, and modifiers. We also introduce the Math class and its static methods. We discuss inheritance as a facilitator of class reuse and illustrate inheritance in two simple examples.

In Chapters 5 through 7 we focus on aspects of traditional procedural programming, covering control structures for selection (if and switch) and repetition (while, for, and do-while), and arrays and vectors.

In Chapter 8 we revisit object-oriented design and discuss concepts in detail that have been dealt with in simplified form before. For example, we discuss visibility, packages, encapsulation, polymorphism, inheritance, and multiple inheritance though interfaces.

We continue to emphasize the object-oriented paradigm in Chapters 9 and 10, through more detailed study of applets and web programming, graphical user interfaces, and threads. We take an in-depth look at the Abstract Window Toolkit (AWT) in these chapters and study many examples that illustrate how to use its components to design graphical user interfaces. In the process, we emphasize the importance of input/output abstractions, class reuse, inheritance, and encapsulation.

Chapters 11 and 12 concern themselves with more traditional aspects of procedural programming: recursion (introduced briefly in Chapter 6) and processing linked data structures. We develop classes for stacks, queues, and binary search trees.

Coverage of Advanced Topics

There is sufficient material in the textbook for one-and-a-half semesters or for two quarters. We consider Chapters 1 through 7 the core of the book, and they should be covered by all students in sequence. Coverage of the remaining chapters will vary depending on student ability and faculty interests. Some suggestions are:

1. Focus on object-oriented design and continue with Chapters 8–10. Final student projects can occupy the last few weeks of the semester. Projects based on elaborations of the tic-tac-toe game in Chapter 10, either enhancing the game or using it as a model for other games, have proved successful.
2. Focus on traditional advanced topics, skipping Chapters 8–10 and studying Chapters 11 (recursion) and 12 (linked data structures) in depth.
3. Provide a breadth-first overview of OOD (Chapter 8), skip 9 and 10 and cover recursion and ADTs by selecting topics from Chapters 11 and 12.

Interviews with Computer Scientists

A popular feature of Elliot Koffman's Pascal books was a collection of interviews with notable computer scientists. For this text, we sought out people who have contributed to the development of Java, object-oriented programming, and the Internet. These interviews alert beginning students to the breadth of the subject area, providing them with a description of issues of concern in several fields of computer science and how these issues relate to modern programming. Those interviewed include: Marc Andreessen, Vinton Cerf, Esther Dyson, James Gosling, Laura Groppe, Radia Perlman, Kim Polese, and Anthony Russo.

We are grateful to all of them for their thoughtful and insightful contributions.

Pedagogical Features

We employ several pedagogical features to enhance the usefulness of the book as a teaching tool. Discussion of some of these features follows.

End-of-Section Exercises: Most sections end with a number of Self-Check exercises, including exercises that require analysis of program fragments as well as short programming exercises. Answers to odd-numbered Self-Check exercises appear at the back of the book; answers to other exercises are provided in the Instructor's Manual.

End-of-Chapter Exercises: Each chapter ends with a set of Quick-Check exercises with answers. There are also Chapter Review exercises, with solutions provided in the Instructor's Manual.

End-of-Chapter Projects: There are several projects at the end of each chapter that are suitable for programming assignments. Answers to selected projects appear in the Instructor's Manual.

Definitions of Key Terms: Key terms are in bold in the text and their definitions appear in the margin. To help you find a definition, its page number is in bold in the index.

Examples and Case Studies: The text contains a large number and variety of programming examples. Whenever possible, examples contain complete class or method definitions rather than incomplete fragments. Each chapter contains one or more case studies (22 in all) that are solved following the software development method.

Syntax Displays: The Syntax Displays describe the syntax and semantics of each new Java feature, complete with examples.

Program Style Displays: The Program Style Displays discuss issues of good programming style.

Error Discussions and Chapter Review: Each chapter ends with a section that discusses common programming errors. Chapter Reviews include a table of new Java constructs.

Appendixes and Supplements

Appendixes: The text concludes with several appendixes covering the Java language, HTML, unicode, the textbook Web site, Borland JBuilder and the Java Development Kit, package `simpleIO`, resources for finding out more about Java, the AWT (Abstract Window Toolkit), and other Java class libraries.

The textbook Web site: Further information about the textbook can be found at its Web site:

```
http://www.awl.com/cseng/titles/0-201-35743-7/
```

You will be able to download package `simpleIO` and all the class definitions provided in the textbook, including package `simpleMath` and package `intArray`. You will also be able to download a tutorial for Borland JBuilder.

Instructor's Manual: An Instructor's Manual is available through your Addison-Wesley sales representative. In addition to answers to selected exercises and projects, the Instructor's Manual will contain sample test questions.

Acknowledgments

There were many individuals without whose support this book could not have been written. These include the principal reviewers:

Julia E. Benson, DeKalb College; Richard J. Botting, California State University, San Bernardino; Tom Cortina, SUNY at Stony Brook; Robert H. Dependahl, Jr., Santa Barbara City College; Bill Grosky, Wayne State University; Stanley H. Lipson, Kean University of New Jersey; David Mathias, Ohio State University; Bina Ramamurthy, SUNY at Buffalo; Stuart Reges, University of Arizona; James Svoboda, Clarkson University; John S. Zelek, University of Guelph.

Several students at The College of New Jersey (TCNJ) and Temple University helped with the development of the textbook and package `simpleIO`. They include: Brice Behringer, Greg Bronevetsky, George Drayer, William Fenstermaker, Mark Nikolsky, Brian Robinson, and Michael Sipper (from TCNJ) and Kelly Jones, Lana Kucherovsky, Brian Rubin, and John Salmon (from Temple).

We are also grateful to our colleagues who provided valuable insight and advice. In particular, we want to acknowledge Joseph Turner of Clemson University and Penny Anderson and Shawn Sivy from The College of New Jersey.

There are several individuals at Addison-Wesley who worked very hard to see this textbook completed. They include our Sponsoring Editor Susan Hartman, her very able assistant Julie Dunn, and the Production Editor Amy Willcutt. Among their many contributions, Susan and Julie worked with us and the principal reviewers to help refine our manuscript, and Julie coordinated the interviews of computer scientists.

Finally we would like to acknowledge the help and support of our families. The members of Ursula's household, her husband Jim, son Christopher, and father Henry were all very understanding about her preoccupation with this book over the past year as were Elliot's wife Caryn and his children Deborah, Richard, and Robin and grandson Dustin. We are grateful to them all for their love and support.

EBK
UW

Contents

CHAPTER 1
Introduction to Computers and Programming   1

1.1	Overview of Computers	2
1.2	Computer Components	4
1.3	Computer Networks	11
1.4	Overview of Programming Languages, Then and Now	13
1.5	Processing a High-Level Language Program	18
1.6	Problem Solving and Programming Using Classes	23
1.7	Creating a Program in an Integrated Programming Environment	25
	Chapter Review	26
	Quick-Check Exercises	28
	Answers to Quick-Check Exercises	28
	Review Questions	29
	Interview: James Gosling	30

CHAPTER 2
Problem Solving and Java   33

2.1	The Software Development Method	34
2.2	Applying the Software Development Method	39
2.3	Overview of a Java Program	45
2.4	Reserved Words and Identifiers	49
2.5	Data Types	52
2.6	Class Definitions	56
2.7	Method Definitions	60
	Chapter Review	63
	Quick-Check Exercises	65
	Answers to Quick-Check Exercises	65
	Review Questions	66
	Programming Projects	66
	Interview: Kim Polese	68

CHAPTER 3
Methods, Statements, and Expressions　　　71

3.1	Method Bodies: Where the Action Takes Place	72
3.2	Calling Methods	76
3.3	Assignment Statements	83
3.4	Operations and Expressions	86
3.5	Processing Integers	97
3.6	Processing Strings	102
3.7	Writing Code with Style	106
3.8	Common Errors and Debugging	108
	Chapter Review	113
	Quick-Check Exercises	114
	Answers to Quick-Check Exercises	115
	Review Questions	116
	Programming Projects	117

CHAPTER 4
Program Design with Methods and Graphics　　　119

4.1	Building Programs from Existing Information	120
4.2	Extending a Problem Solution	125
4.3	Extending a Problem Solution through Inheritance	130
4.4	Using Methods in Class `Math`	133
4.5	Accessors, Modifiers, Constructors, and Class Methods	143
4.6	Introduction to Computer Graphics	149
4.7	Common Programming Errors	165
	Chapter Review	167
	Quick-Check Exercises	168
	Answers to Quick-Check Exercises	169
	Review Questions	170
	Programming Projects	170
	Interview: Vinton Cerf	174

CHAPTER 5
Selection Structures　　　177

5.1	Control Structures	178
5.2	Boolean Expressions	179
5.3	The `if` Statement	192
5.4	`if` Statements with Compound Statements	196
5.5	Decision Steps in Algorithms	199

5.6   Hand-Tracing an Algorithm   209
5.7   Nested `if` Statements and Multiple-Alternative Decisions   212
5.8   The `switch` Statement and `SimpleGUI` Menus   221
5.9   Exceptions and `try-catch` Blocks   234
5.10   Common Programming Errors   236
       Chapter Review   237
       Quick-Check Exercises   239
       Answers to Quick-Check Exercises   241
       Review Questions   241
       Programming Projects   242
       Interview: Esther Dyson   244

CHAPTER 6
Repetition Structures   **247**

6.1   Counting Loops and the `while` Statement   248
6.2   Accumulating a Sum   252
6.3   State-controlled Loops   260
6.4   Loop Design and the `do-while` Loop   268
6.5   The `for` Statement   276
6.6   Loops in Graphics Programs (Optional)   283
6.7   Introduction to Recursive Methods (Optional)   289
6.8   Debugging and Testing Methods with Loops   292
6.9   Common Programming Errors   295
       Chapter Review   296
       Quick-Check Exercises   298
       Answers to Quick-Check Exercises   298
       Review Questions   299
       Programming Projects   300
       Interview: Radia Perlman   304

CHAPTER 7
Arrays and Vectors   **307**

7.1   Array Declarations and Indices   308
7.2   Processing Arrays and Array Elements   314
7.3   Operations on Whole Arrays   323
7.4   Searching and Sorting an Array   331
7.5   Analysis of Algorithms: Big-O Notation (Optional)   337
7.6   Arrays of Objects   340
7.7   Vectors   346

7.8   More Input/Output: Using Files and `displayRow` (Optional)   351
7.9   Multidimensional Arrays—Arrays of Arrays (Optional)   360
7.10   Common Programming Errors   367
        Chapter Review   369
        Quick-Check Exercises   371
        Answers to Quick-Check Exercises   372
        Review Questions   373
        Programming Projects   374
        Interview: Anthony Russo   378

CHAPTER 8

Object-Oriented Design   381

8.1   Java Classes Revisited   382
8.2   Modular Programming and Reuse   390
8.3   Encapsulation, Inheritance, Visibility, and Packages   395
8.4   Polymorphism   405
8.5   Another Look at Inheritance   414
8.6   Class Members and Instance Members: `static` and `final`   418
8.7   Abstract Classes   425
8.8   Multiple Inheritance and Interfaces   439
8.9   Common Programming Errors   443
        Chapter Review   443
        Quick-Check Exercises   444
        Answers to Quick-Check Exercises   445
        Review Questions   445
        Programming Projects   446

CHAPTER 9

Applets, Graphical User Interfaces, and Threads   447

9.1   Web Programming and Client/Server Model   448
9.2   Applets, Panels, Containers, Components   455
9.3   The Basic Interactive Applet   462
9.4   Introduction to Threads   477
9.5   Threaded Animation (Optional)   485
9.6   Browser/Applet Interaction   491
        Chapter Review   500
        Quick-Check Exercises   504
        Answers to Quick-Check Exercises   504
        Review Questions   505
        Programming Projects   505

CHAPTER 10
GUIs as a Vehicle for Object-Oriented Design   **507**

10.1	Abstraction Layers for User Input/Output	508
10.2	Output to the User—Label, Canvas, Fonts, and Layout Managers	514
10.3	Discrete User Input: Buttons, Boxes, and Lists	527
10.4	Continuous and Textual User Input	544
10.5	Low-Level User Input	554
10.6	Turn-Taking within the Event Model	560
10.7	Applications and Applets: Menus	571
	Chapter Review	578
	Quick-Check Exercises	581
	Answers to Quick-Check Exercises	582
	Review Questions	582
	Programming Projects	583
	Interview: Marc Andreessen	584

CHAPTER 11
Recursion   **587**

11.1	Recursive Methods	588
11.2	Recursive Mathematical Methods	592
11.3	Use of the Stack in Recursion	595
11.4	Recursive Methods with Arrays, Vectors, and Strings	599
11.5	Binary Search	608
11.6	Solving Towers of Hanoi with Recursion	612
11.7	A Recursive Program with a GUI	619
11.8	Common Programming Errors	627
	Chapter Review	627
	Quick-Check Exercises	628
	Answers to Quick-Check Exercises	628
	Review Questions	628
	Programming Projects	629

CHAPTER 12
Linked Data Structures   **631**

12.1	Linked Lists	632
12.2	Stacks	639
12.3	Queues	648
12.4	Binary Trees	654
12.5	A Binary Search Tree Class	661

12.6   Efficiency of a Binary Search Tree   671
12.7   Common Programming Errors   673
         Chapter Review   674
         Quick-Check Exercises   674
         Answers to Quick-Check Exercises   676
         Review Questions   676
         Programming Projects   677
         Interview: Laura Groppe   680

APPENDIXES

Appendix A   Getting Started, Going Further   683

Appendix B   Java Language Summary   693

Appendix C   Classes for Program Abstraction   713

Appendix D   AWT for Graphical User Interfaces   733

Answers to Self-Check Exercises   789

Index   817

CHAPTER 1

Introduction to Computers and Programming

Since the 1940s, the computer has dramatically changed the way we live and how we do business. Computers provide instructional material in school, print transcripts, prepare bills and paychecks, reserve airline and concert tickets, allow us to bank and shop conveniently, and help us write term papers and even books. Most recently, the Internet and the World Wide Web give us access to information on computers all over the world.

Although we often are led to believe otherwise, computers cannot reason as we do. Basically, computers are devices for performing computations at incredible speeds (more than one million operations per second) and with great accuracy. In order to accomplish anything useful, however, a computer must be provided with a program, that is, a list of instructions. Programs are usually written in special computer programming languages such as Java, which is the subject of this book. The Java programming language is a key component of programming on the World Wide Web.

In this chapter, we introduce you to the computer and its components. We also present an overview of programming languages. Finally, we describe how a Java program is constructed.

1.1 Overview of Computers

1.2 Computer Components

1.3 Computer Networks

1.4 Overview of Programming Languages, Then and Now

1.5 Processing a High-level Language Program

1.6 Problem Solving and Programming Using Classes

1.7 Creating a Program in an Integrated Programming Environment

Chapter Review

1.1   Overview of Computers

In our everyday life, we come in contact with computers frequently, and you may have used computers for word processing or for exploring the **World Wide Web**. You may even have studied programming in high school. But computers weren't always seen as accessible to everyone. Not long ago, most people considered computers to be mysterious devices whose secrets were known only by a few computer wizards.

World Wide Web:
a collection of linked documents stored on many different computers and accessed by computers anywhere in the world.

Categories of Computers

The first electronic computer was designed in the late 1930s by Dr. John Atanasoff at Iowa State University. Atanasoff designed his computer to assist graduate students in nuclear physics with their mathematical computations.

The first large-scale, general-purpose electronic digital computer, called the ENIAC, was completed in 1946 at the University of Pennsylvania. The United States Army funded its design. The ENIAC weighed 30 tons and occupied a 30- by 50-foot space. ENIAC was used to compute ballistics tables, to predict the weather, and to make atomic energy calculations.

These early computers used vacuum tubes as their basic electronic component. Technological advances in the design and manufacture of electronic components led to new generations of computers that were considerably smaller, faster, and less expensive than previous ones.

In the 1970s, the Altair and Apple computer companies manufactured the first microcomputers. The computer processor in a microcomputer is an electronic component called a **computer chip**, which is about the size of a postage stamp. Their affordability and small size enable computer chips to be installed in watches, pocket calculators, cameras, home appliances, automobiles, and, of course, computers.

computer chip:
an electronic component often used as a computer processor.

Today, a common sight in offices and homes is a personal computer; it can cost less than $2000 and fit on a desktop, and yet has as much computational power as one that 15 years ago cost more than $100,000 and filled a 9- by 12-foot room. Even smaller computers can fit inside a briefcase or in your hand (Fig. 1.1).

The microcomputers shown in Fig. 1.1 are used by a single person at a time. Businesses and research laboratories also use larger and faster computers, called minicomputers and mainframes, which can be used by many people simultaneously. Supercomputers, the most powerful mainframe computers, can perform in seconds computations that might take hours or even days on other computers.

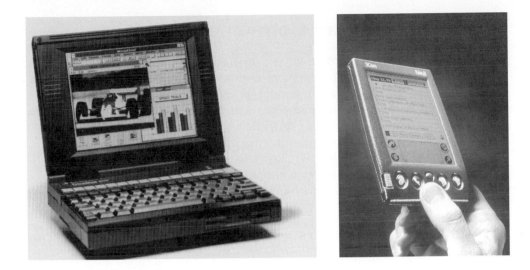

Figure 1.1 Notebook and palmtop computer

Sharing Computer Resources

A technique called **time sharing** is used on mainframe and minicomputers to allow simultaneous access to the computing resources. The problem with time sharing is that you have to wait your turn to use the resources. Usually computer users don't even realize they are taking turns, but during peak periods waiting times can become excessive. Furthermore, if the computer stops working (an event called a crash), all users are affected as they must wait for the computer to be restarted.

Although microcomputers do not have the huge resources of minicomputers and mainframes, they provide their users with dedicated resources. Waiting your turn is no longer an issue. Also, if one machine crashes, others are not affected. The major disadvantage of early personal or workstation computers was that they were isolated from the vast resources of the larger machines. In Section 1.3, we see how computer networks solve this problem.

time sharing:
a technique that allows simultaneous access to a single computer by a number of users.

EXERCISES FOR SECTION 1.1

Self-Check

1. List the different kinds of computers from smallest to largest.
2. Why do you think that, in a time-shared environment, each computer user is unaware that others are also using the computer?

1.2 Computer Components

hardware:

the actual computer equipment.

software:

the set of programs associated with a computer.

program:

a list of instructions that enable a computer to manipulate data in order to perform a specific task.

A computer system consists of two major components. The first is **hardware**, that is, the actual equipment used to perform the computations. The second essential major component is **software**, that is, the **programs**. Programs enable us to communicate with a computer by providing it with the list of instructions it needs to operate.

Despite significant variations in cost, size, and capabilities, modern computers resemble each other in many basic ways. Essentially, most consist of the following hardware components:

- Main memory
- Secondary memory, which includes storage media such as hard disks, floppy disks, and CD-ROM
- Central processor unit
- Input devices, such as a keyboard and a mouse
- Output devices, such as monitors and printers
- Network connection, such as a modem or ethernet interface

Figure 1.2 shows how these components would interact in a computer when a program is executed; the arrows connecting the components show the direction of information flow.

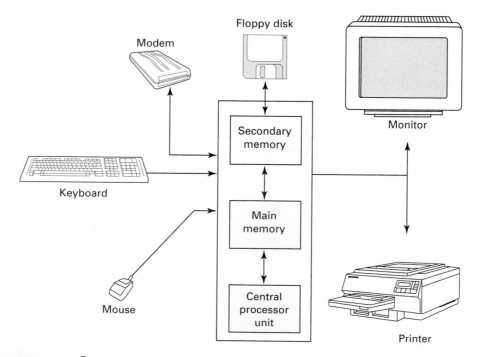

Figure 1.2 Computer components

The program must first be transferred from secondary memory to main memory before it can be executed. Data must be supplied from some source. The person using a program (the program user) may supply data through an input device. Data may also come from a data file located in secondary storage, or it may come from a remote machine via the network connection. The data are stored in the computer's main memory where they can be accessed and manipulated by the central processor unit. The results of this manipulation are stored back in main memory. Finally, the information (results) in main memory may be displayed through an output device, stored in secondary storage, or sent to another computer via the network.

In the remainder of this section, we describe these components in more detail.

Memory

Memory is an essential component in any computer. Before discussing the types of memory—main and secondary—let's first look at what it consists of and how the computer works with it.

Anatomy of memory Imagine the memory of a computer as an ordered sequence of storage locations called **memory cells** (see Fig. 1.3). To store and access information, the computer must have some way of identifying the individual memory cells. Therefore, each memory cell has a unique **address** that indicates its relative position in memory. Figure 1.3 shows a computer memory consisting of 1000 memory cells with addresses 0 through 999. Most computers have millions of individual memory cells, each with its own address.

memory cell:
an individual storage location in memory.

address:
the relative position of a memory cell in the computer's main memory.

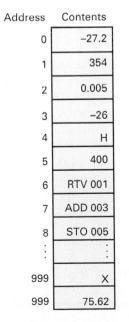

Address   Contents

0	−27.2
1	354
2	0.005
3	−26
4	H
5	400
6	RTV 001
7	ADD 003
8	STO 005
⋮	⋮
999	X
999	75.62

Figure 1.3 1000 memory cells in main memory

contents:
the information stored in a memory cell, either a program instruction or data.

The data stored in a memory cell are called the **contents** of the cell. Every memory cell always has some contents, although the contents may not be meaningful to our program. In Fig. 1.3, the contents of memory cell 3 is the number -26 and the contents of memory cell 4 is the letter H.

A memory cell can also contain a program instruction. Cells 6 through 8 in Fig. 1.3 store instructions to add two numbers (from cells 1 and 3) and store the result in memory cell 5. The ability to store programs as well as data is called the **stored-program concept**: a program's instructions must be stored in main memory before they can be executed. We can change the computer's operation by storing a different program in memory.

stored-program concept:
the idea of storing program instructions in main memory prior to their execution.

byte:
the amount of storage required to store a single character.

bit:
a binary digit, namely a 0 or a 1.

Bytes and bits A memory cell is actually a grouping of smaller units called bytes. A **byte** is the amount of storage required to store a single character, such as the letter H in cell 4 of Fig. 1.3. The number of bytes a memory cell may contain varies from computer to computer.

A byte is composed of even smaller units of storage called bits (see Fig. 1.4). The term **bit** derives from the words **bi**nary dig**it** and is the smallest element a computer can deal with. Binary refers to a number system based on two numbers, 0 and 1; therefore, a bit is either a 0 or a 1. Generally there are eight bits to a byte.

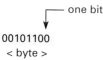

Figure 1.4 Relationship between a byte and a bit

store:
set the individual bits of a memory cell to 0 or 1, destroying its previous contents.

retrieve:
copy the contents of a particular memory cell to another storage area.

random access memory (RAM):
the part of main memory that temporarily stores programs, data, and results.

Storing and retrieving information in memory Each value in memory is represented by a particular pattern of zeros and ones, that is, bits. The pattern can be used to represent a number, a character, such as the letter H, or an instruction such as ADD 003. A computer can either store a value or retrieve a value. To **store** a value, the computer sets each bit of a selected memory cell to either 0 or 1; storing a value destroys the previous contents of the cell. To **retrieve** a value from a memory cell, the computer copies the pattern of 0s and 1s stored in that cell to another storage area for processing; the copy operation does not destroy the contents of the cell whose value is retrieved. The process described above is the same regardless of the kind of information— character, number, or program instruction—to be stored or retrieved.

Main memory Main memory stores programs, data, and results and is made of electronic circuitry in the form of computer chips. In most computers, there are two types of main memory: **random access memory (RAM)**, which offers temporary storage of programs and data, and **read-only memory (ROM)**, which stores programs or data permanently.

RAM temporarily stores programs while they are being executed (carried out) by the computer. It also temporarily stores data such as numbers, names, and even pictures (called graphics or images), while a program is manipulating them. RAM is usually **volatile memory**, which means that when you switch off the computer, you will lose everything in RAM. To prevent this loss, you should store the contents of RAM in secondary memory, which provides for semi-permanent storage of data, before you turn off your computer.

ROM, on the other hand, stores information permanently. The computer can retrieve (or read) information in ROM but cannot store (or write) information in ROM, hence its name, read-only memory. Because read-only memory is not volatile, the data stored in ROM do not disappear when you switch off the computer. Most modern computers contain an internal ROM that stores the **boot instructions** needed to start-up the computer when you first switch it on.

Usually a computer contains much more RAM memory than internal ROM memory; also, the amount of RAM can often be increased (up to a specified maximum), whereas the amount of internal ROM is usually fixed. When we refer to main memory in this text, we mean RAM because that is the part of main memory that is normally accessible to the Java programmer.

RAM is relatively fast memory; however, it is limited in size and is not permanent memory. Next, we introduce secondary memory which, although slower than RAM, is both larger and more permanent.

Secondary memory and secondary storage devices   Secondary memory, through secondary storage devices, provides semi-permanent data-storage capability. Secondary storage usually consists of a magnetic medium such as tape or disk. Audio cassette tapes are an example of a magnetic medium on which music is stored. Computer tapes and disks store digital information instead (sequences of 0s and 1s). Magnetic media can easily be erased and recorded over.

The most common secondary storage device is a **disk drive**; it stores and retrieves data and programs on a disk, transferring the data between secondary memory and main memory. A disk is considered semi-permanent storage because its contents can be changed.

Information stored on a disk is organized into separate collections called **files**. One file may contain a Java program. Another file may contain the data to be processed by that program (a data file). A third file could contain the results generated by a program (an output file).

The two most common kinds of magnetic disks for personal computers are **hard disks** (also called fixed disks) and **floppy disks**. Most personal computers contain one hard disk that cannot be removed from its disk drive; therefore, the storage area on a hard disk can be shared by all users of the

read-only memory (ROM):
the part of main memory that permanently stores programs or data.

volatile memory:
memory whose contents disappear when you switch off the computer.

boot instructions:
program that starts-up a computer.

disk drive:
a device used to store and retrieve information on a disk.

file:
a collection of related information stored on a disk.

hard disk:
a disk with a drive that is built into the computer and normally cannot be removed.

floppy disk:
a personal, portable disk that can be moved easily from one computer to another.

computer. A hard disk can store much more data than can a single floppy disk and the CPU can access that data much more quickly. Normally, the programs that are needed to operate the computer system are stored on its hard disk.

A floppy disk is a small mylar sheet coated with magnetizable material and housed in a hard plastic container. Floppy disks are used primarily to store programs and data for individual users, and to move small amounts of information between personal computers that are not easily networked. A computer user may have several floppy disks that can be inserted into a computer's floppy disk drive. Floppy disks are being replaced by newer technologies (for example, Zip disks). These disks and their supporting drives store more data and access it more quickly, but still have the portability of floppy disks.

An increasingly common storage device is the CD-ROM. A CD-ROM drive accesses information stored on plastic disks that are identical to CDs used in a CD audio player. A computer CD stores data (numbers, characters, graphics, instructions) that can be transferred to the computer's main memory or secondary memory. CD-ROM disks are a convenient way to distribute commercial software products such as word processors. A CD-ROM disk also provides a flexible means of storing data that does not change. For example, images, sound (such as music), and large quantities of text such as encyclopedias are often provided on CD-ROM disks. These disks are also less expensive and more reliable than magnetic media. Newer technologies now enable the user to rewrite CDs.

Central Processor Unit

central processor unit (CPU):
the device that coordinates all computer operations and performs arithmetic and logical operations on data.

The **central processor unit (CPU)** has two roles: coordinating all computer operations and performing arithmetic and logical operations on data. The CPU follows the instructions contained in a computer program to determine which operations should be carried out and in what order. It then transmits coordinating control signals to the other computer components. For example, if the instruction requires getting data from a user, the CPU sends the necessary control signals to the input device.

fetching an instruction:
retrieving an instruction from main memory.

To process a program stored in main memory, the CPU retrieves each instruction in sequence (called **fetching an instruction**), interprets the instruction to determine what should be done, and then retrieves any data needed to carry out that instruction. Next, the CPU performs the actual manipulation, or processing, of the data it retrieved. The CPU stores the results temporarily in main memory, but it can also store them back in secondary memory for later use.

The CPU can perform such arithmetic operations as addition, subtraction, multiplication, and division. The CPU also can compare the contents of two memory cells. For example, it might determine whether two values are equal, and if not, which memory cell has the larger value. The CPU can make decisions based on the results of that comparison.

Input/Output Devices

We use input/output (I/O) devices to communicate with the computer. Specifically, these devices allow us to enter data for a computation and to observe the results of that computation. The most common input device is a keyboard (see Fig. 1.5). The most common output device is a monitor (display screen).

A computer keyboard resembles a typewriter keyboard. When you press a letter or digit key, that character is sent to main memory and it is also displayed on the monitor at the position of the **cursor**, a moving place marker. A keyboard has extra keys for performing special functions. For example, on the computer keyboard shown in Fig. 1.5, the 12 keys in the top row labeled F1 through F12 are **function keys**. The activity performed when you press a function key depends on the program currently being executed; that is, pressing F4 in one program will usually not produce the same results as pressing F4 in another program. Other special keys enable you to delete characters, move the cursor, and enter a line of data you typed at the keyboard.

cursor: a moving place marker that appears on the monitor.

function keys: special keyboard keys used to select a particular operation; the operation selected depends on the program being used.

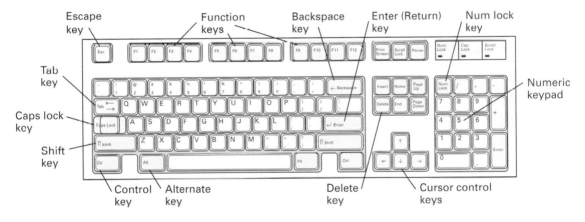

Figure 1.5 Keyboard for IBM-type computers.

Another common input device is a mouse. A **mouse** is a pointing device. Other kinds of pointing devices are touch-sensitive screens (such as used in many ATM machines), and the joy-sticks used with video games. A mouse is a hand-held device containing a rubber ball. When you move the mouse around on your desktop, the rubber ball rotates. As the ball moves, so does the mouse cursor (normally a small rectangle or an arrow) displayed on the monitor's screen. You can use the mouse to select an operation by moving the mouse cursor to a word or picture (called an **icon**) that represents the computer operation you wish to perform. You then press or click a mouse button to activate the operation selected.

mouse: an input device that moves its cursor on the computer screen to select an operation.

icon: a picture representing a computer operation that you can activate by clicking a mouse.

A monitor provides a temporary display of the information that appears on its screen. If you want hard copy (a printed version) of some information, you must send that information to an output device called a **printer**.

printer:
an output device that produces a hard copy of information sent to it.

prompting message:
a message that tells the user to enter information or select from a list of choices.

menu:
a list of choices for actions that may be executed within a program.

Text-based interaction, menu-based interaction, and GUIs Until the mid-1980s most computer input and output were text-based. In this method of interaction, the computer displays a **prompting message** (or prompt) on the screen and the user types in a response on the keyboard, telling the computer what to do next or providing data for a computer program. The computer does something meaningful only if it understands the command or the data that was typed in. In some cases, the computer displays a **menu** with choices for the user; the user selects an operation by typing in one of the alternative choices.

Graphical User Interfaces (GUIs, pronounced "gooeys") changed the nature of text-based interaction (see Fig. 1.6). Pictures, sound, and video could be included in the output presented to the user. The simple turn-taking of text-based systems was replaced by a more open-ended interaction in which the user has more control of what to do next. Visual devices such as icons, **windows**, **pull-down menus**, and **buttons** help the user select the computer operations.

window:
an area on a monitor that displays a view of a software system such as a word processor.

pull-down menu:
a lower-order menu that appears as a result of a user making a selection from a higher-order menu.

button:
an abstraction representing a physical button that is "pushed" by a mouse click.

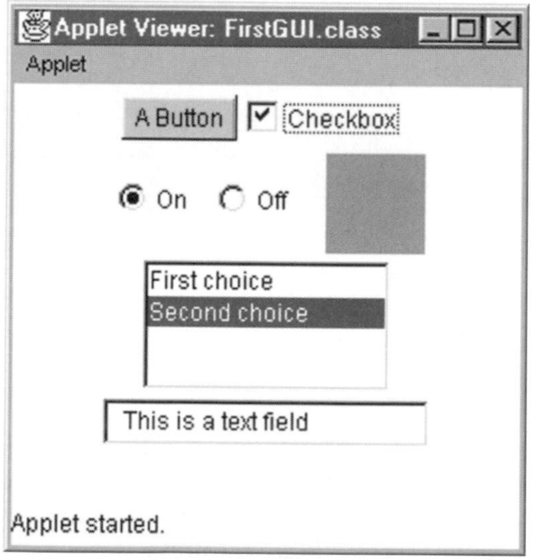

Figure 1.6 Examples of GUI visual devices

GUIs have made it much easier for people to interact with computers; however, compared to older text-based interaction, it is difficult to program

GUIs directly. The object-oriented approach to programming was developed to help manage the complexity of programming with GUIs. Java is an object-oriented programming language that contains a standard set of classes such as windows. The programmer does not have to build GUI objects up from scratch, but can use pre-defined classes to do complicated things like displaying a window with buttons in it.

EXERCISES FOR SECTION 1.2

Self-Check

1. If a computer were instructed to sum the contents of memory cells 2 and 999 and store the result in cell 0, what would be the contents of cells 0, 2, and 999 in Fig. 1.3?

2. One bit can have two values, 0 or 1. A combination of two bits can have four values: 00, 01, 10, 11. List all of the values you can form with a combination of three bits. Do the same for four bits.

3. List the following in order of smallest to largest: byte, bit, main memory, memory cell, secondary memory.

4. Explain the difference in the way a user interacts with a program through text-based interaction, menu-based interaction, and with GUIs.

1.3 Computer Networks

Network technology was invented to connect computers together in order to share resources. Unlike a mainframe, which is a single computer shared by many users, a **computer network** consists of many computers that share resources. Within an organization, a **LAN** (local-area network) allows many personal workstations to access sharable resources from a larger computer called a **server**. The largest network is the **Internet**, which is an interconnection of local networks that connects computers all over the world.

Today, most computers are connected to a network, and the vast majority are connected to the Internet. Computers can be networked with hardware connections and cables that transmit digital signals directly, or through telephone lines and a **modem** (short for modulator/demodulator). The modem at the sending computer converts **digital signals** into **analog signals** that can be sent over telephone lines. The modem at the destination computer converts the analog signals back to digital form, so they can be understood by the destination computer. In the near future most phone lines will support digital as well as analog signals, and modems will become obsolete.

computer network: an interconnected collection of computers that share resources.

LAN: a network of computers in a single organization.

server: computers that provide resources to other computers in a network.

Internet: an interconnected collection of computer networks from all over the world supporting the World Wide Web.

modem: a device that converts digital signals to analog signals and vice versa.

digital signal: a signal used to transmit computer code, sound, and video images.

analog signal: a signal used to transmit sound over telephone lines.

file server: the computer in a network that controls access to the shared disk.

print server: the computer in a LAN that manages a printer or collection of printers.

gateway: a computer that mediates information flow within a network.

Networks typically consist of individual workstations as well as file servers, print servers, and gateways. **File servers** are larger computers that maintain collections of files (programs and data) that many users can access. **Print servers** allow users on a network to share printers, especially expensive high-quality and color printers. **Gateways** are computers that mediate the movement of information between networks of computers. To access the Internet, your personal computer must be connected to a server on the Internet. Colleges and universities as well as commercial service providers such as America Online support such services.

By sharing resources through networking, computer users get the best of both standalone personal computing and large mainframes. For example, many academic computer laboratories arrange their computer hardware in a local-area network, so that students can work on individual machines for word processing or programming tasks and can also retrieve course materials from a central source. If a computer within the network crashes, the users are not all affected, as is the case with time sharing.

A user application such as a programming environment or word processor may be stored on a file server and loaded onto workstations as needed. Programs may store results of a computation in a file on the network server rather than on the local hard drive. Input to a program may come from a user on a computer halfway around the world.

Networks have blurred the boundaries between secondary storage and input/output devices. Streams of data in a program may be moved between an arbitrary collection of devices including keyboards, displays, disks, and printers anywhere on the network.

The World Wide Web The World Wide Web (the Web) was introduced in 1989 and although it is the newest application of the Internet, it is already the most popular feature. The Web was developed at CERN (the European Laboratory for Particle Physics), which was interested in creating an effective and uniform way of accessing all the information on the Internet. You can use the Web to send, view, retrieve, and search for information. You can easily interconnect documents on the Web by inserting **links** in one document that connect it to another.

link:
a connection that allows a user to access related documents while reading another document.

Web browser:
a program that allows you to display and view a Web document and activate links to other documents.

To access the Web, you need a program called a **Web browser**. You use the browser to display the text and graphics in a Web document and to activate the links to other documents. Clicking on a link to a document causes that document to be transferred from the computer where it is stored to your own.

The Web has dramatically transformed not only the way people do business and get entertainment, but it has forced programmers to think about programs in new ways. Because networks consist of many different kinds and sizes of computers, all information and programs on the Web must be usable without modification by a variety of computers. A user of a Macintosh computer should be able to explore the Web in the same way that a Sun, or Intel Microsoft Windows user does. Consequently, there is a need to write programs that can run on any of these machines so that the look and feel doesn't change substantially across computers (creating what is called **platform independence**).

The Web has also intensified the use of **multimedia**, the full integration of text, graphics, sound, video, and animation. For example, people use the Web to listen to music before they buy it, or to view video clips of a news broadcast. The integration of graphics, text, and animation is exploited by advertisers who try to capture the interest of Web surfers. Coordinating the programming of all of this material requires careful analysis of very complex problems involving huge amounts of data. For example a 10-minute video clip requires more storage capacity than that of the entire hard disk of a 1980s personal computer.

One of the reasons for the popularity of Java is that Java is the first programming language to exploit the networked programming environment. Java programs are platform-independent. Also, you can embed special Java programs called applets in Web documents or Web pages. An applet enables a Web document to calculate and display information graphically or to interact with a user through a GUI. We will have more to say about platform independence and applets in Section 1.5.

platform independence: the characteristic of being able to be run on a variety of machines (platforms).

multimedia: software that integrates text, graphics, sound, video, and animation.

EXERCISES FOR SECTION 1.3

Self-Check

1. List some of the roles that a computer can play in a network.
2. Explain in your own words why platform independence is desirable.
3. What features of Java make it desirable for programming on the World Wide Web?

1.4 Overview of Programming Languages, Then and Now

We use programming languages to write computer programs. Although there are many different programming languages, the most commonly used today are called high-level languages. To understand the advantage of high-level languages, you first must understand how a computer communicates.

Machine Language

The native tongue of a computer is **machine language**. Each machine-language instruction is a binary string of 0s and 1s that specifies an operation and identifies the memory cells involved in that operation. For example, if we wanted to compute the cost of an item we can use the algebraic formula

machine language: a computer's native language, containing instructions that are binary numbers.

$cost = price + tax$

To express this formula using machine language, we would assume that the price and tax (the data in our formula) were stored in memory locations. We would need to:

1. Retrieve the price.
2. Add the tax.
3. Store the result in another memory location.

The following three instructions illustrate how instructions appear in a hypothetical machine language.

```
0010 0000 0000 0011
0100 0000 0000 0101
0011 0000 0000 0110
```

operation code:

the part of a machine language instruction that specifies the operation to perform.

In each instruction, the leftmost four digits represent an operation. This part of the instruction is called the **operation code**. The remaining digits represent an address in main memory. The first operation code 0010 tells the computer to retrieve the data from location 0011 and store it in a special memory cell. The operation code 0100 instructs the computer to retrieve the contents of cell 0101, add it to the contents of the special cell and store the result in that special cell, overwriting its prior contents. The operation code 0011 tells the computer to store the new contents of the special cell in location 0110. Note that each instruction involves an operation and a memory location. This interplay of operation and data is a universal property of programming.

Although the computer would have no difficulty understanding the three machine-language instructions above, they are difficult for most people to read even if they know the code.

High-level Languages

high-level language:

a programming language whose instructions resemble everyday language.

When you write programs in a **high-level language**, you use instructions that resemble everyday language. In Java we would use the statement

```
cost = price + tax;
```

which closely resembles the original formula. But the meaning of this statement is not identical to the algebraic formula. In Java it has the following very specific meaning: "Add the value of price to the value of tax and store the result as cost." When you write a program in a high-level language, you can reference data that are stored in memory using descriptive names—for example, price, cost, tax—rather than numeric memory-cell addresses. You can also use familiar symbols (such as +) to describe operations you would like performed.

A computation, whether expressed in machine language or a high-level language, typically consists of getting some data, performing an operation on that data, and then doing something with the result.

A high-level language has a **language standard** that describes the grammatical form (syntax) of the language. Every high-level language instruction must conform to the syntax rules specified in the language standard. These rules are very precise—no allowances are made for instructions that are almost correct. Programs that conform to these rules are portable, which means that they can be used without modification on many different types of computers. A machine-language program, on the other hand, may only be used on one type of computer because it relies on the hardware in the CPU to decode an instruction.

Some common high-level languages are BASIC, C, C++, COBOL, FORTRAN, Java, Lisp, and Pascal. Although each of these languages was designed with a specific purpose in mind (See Table 1.1), they are all used to write a variety of **application software**—software that performs tasks for the computer user. Programmers also use the languages C and C++ to write **system software**—software that performs tasks required for the operation of the computer system.

> **language standard:**
> a description of the syntax and meaning of each high-level language instruction.

> **application software:**
> programs written for a computer user.

> **system software:**
> programs written for the computer system.

Table 1.1 Common high-level languages

High-level language	Original purpose
BASIC	Simple language intended for student use in school work
C	Used for writing system software
C++	Extension of C that supports object-oriented programming
COBOL	For performing business data processing
FORTRAN (**For**mula **tran**slation)	For engineering and scientific applications
Java	A highly portable object-oriented language
Lisp	For artificial intelligence applications that require manipulating abstract symbols
Pascal	For teaching students how to program in a careful, disciplined way

Object-Oriented Languages and Programming

Table 1.1 lists two object-oriented languages: C++ and Java. Object-oriented languages are popular because they can make it easier to reuse and adapt previously written software.

An object is an entity that has a collection of properties. Some of these properties can be encoded into a computer program as data, some can be encoded as **methods** for operating on the data.

As an example of an object, consider a hypothetical automobile. You may visualize wheels, a steering wheel, a body shape, and a color. These are the attributes, or data, of the abstraction for an automobile. You can also imagine

> **method:**
> program code that operates on the data associated with an object.

the actions associated with the automobile, such as starting the engine, or driving it forward or in reverse. These activities are analogous to methods.

The description of an automobile in English provides a loose definition of a hypothetical automobile. It describes any member of the **class** automobile. Not only does the class definition describe an imaginary car, but it can be applied to actual **objects** or instances of the class, such as your car and your parents' car. Both cars have all the attributes of an automobile, but they differ in detail. For example, one may be white and one may be red.

The distinction between the terms class and object sometimes gets a bit blurry. A class definition, or class, describes the properties of the abstract or hypothetical object. Actual objects are instances of the class. An object's data fields provide storage for information, and an object's methods process or manipulate this information. Figure 1.7 shows the relationship between the class `automobile` and two objects of that class.

class:

an entity that defines the attributes of an object; these attributes include data fields and methods.

object:

a member of the class. It is an actual entity that has all the attributes described by the class definition.

Figure 1.7 The relationship between a class and objects within the class

Class `automobile`	**Object** `your car`	**Object** `parents' car`
Properties	Properties	Properties
Color	Red	White
Make	Toyota	Buick
Model	Coupe	Sedan
Year	1989	1998
Has driver's seat	Has driver's seat	Has driver's seat
Has passenger seats	Has passenger seats	Has passenger seats
Can be driven	Can be driven	Can be driven

Classes can have other classes as components. For example, a car has an engine. Some of the properties of a class may be computed using a method. For example, fuel efficiency can be computed from the power of the engine and the weight of the car (along with some other factors.)

Finally, classes can be organized into a hierarchy of **subclasses** and **superclasses**. For example, the class automobile is a subclass of the class vehicle. The class sports car is a subclass of the class automobile. It therefore makes the class automobile a superclass of the class sports car. The class sports car is also a subclass of the class vehicle but not of the class truck. This relationship is shown in Fig. 1.8, in which each arrow points from a subclass to its immediate superclass (called a **parent class**).

Objects in a subclass *inherit* properties (both data and methods) from a superclass. For example, if weight and an engine are properties of the class vehicle, they are properties of all the subclasses shown in Fig. 1.8 (truck,

subclass:

a class that extends another class by adding data or methods or both.

superclass:

a class whose methods and data are inherited by another class.

parent class:

the immediate superclass of a class.

automobile, sports car). The class vehicle and all three subclasses have a driver's seat and method of driving.

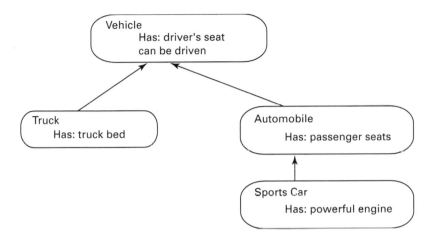

Figure 1.8 A class hierarchy

Typically, subclasses *extend* the properties of the superclass. For example, automobiles extend the notion of seats by including a property called "passenger seats." Sports cars inherit this property, too. Finally, the definition of a sports car extends the general definition of automobiles by including a property that describes the power of its engine.

These basic principles help programmers organize their solutions to problems. In particular, rather than starting each program from scratch, programmers use object-oriented programming because it encourages reuse of code. They can reuse existing classes as components or create subclasses of existing classes.

In Java, the Abstract Window Toolkit (AWT) provides a large hierarchy of classes that help programmers create graphical user interfaces. A portion of that hierarchy is shown in Fig. 1.9. A component is an entity that can be represented on a computer screen. All components have certain properties, such as two dimensions, a background color, and the ability to detect mouse motions and keystrokes.

Simple components such as buttons and checkboxes inherit these properties from the `Component` class and have some that are uniquely their own. The `Container` class is a kind of component that can hold other components (including other containers). `Windows`, `Panels`, and `Applets` are examples. Note that Fig. 1.9 shows only a fraction of the classes in the AWT. Without some simple and consistent rules about how objects behave, it would be impossible to understand and use the AWT. GUI programming is relatively easy in Java because of the AWT. You will learn more about it in Chapters 4, 9, and 10.

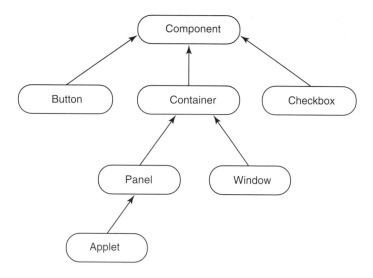

Figure 1.9 A portion of the AWT class hierarchy

EXERCISES FOR SECTION 1.4

Self-Check

1. What do you think the four high-level language statements below mean?

   x = a + b + c;   x = y / z;   d = c - b + a;   z = z + 1;

2. List two reasons why it would be preferable to write a program in Java rather than in machine language.

3. What are the two basic parts of a class?

4. How can existing classes be used by a programmer?

5. Characterize the relationship between mammal, house cat, and feline in terms of superclass and subclass relationships. Find a property that all have and show which class would hold that property.

6. Explain the difference between class and object. Which represents an abstract object? Which represents an actual object?

1.5 Processing a High-level Language Program

Because a computer can only understand programs written in machine language, each instruction in a high-level language program must first be translated into machine language before it can be executed. The original high-level language program is called the **source program**; the machine-language translation is called the **object program** (no relationship to an object of a class).

This simple model applies to languages like C, C++, Pascal, and FOR-TRAN. The problem with this model is that the compile process is dependent upon the underlying machine. The machine language of an Apple computer (for example, a Macintosh) is different from an IBM PC, which is different from a Sun workstation. Therefore, a program written in C must be compiled into a different object program for each different computer as shown in Fig 1.10.

The user of a program is unaware of the compile process. The object code is delivered to the user as the final product. The software developer decides which machines to support and guarantees that the object code works correctly on those machines.

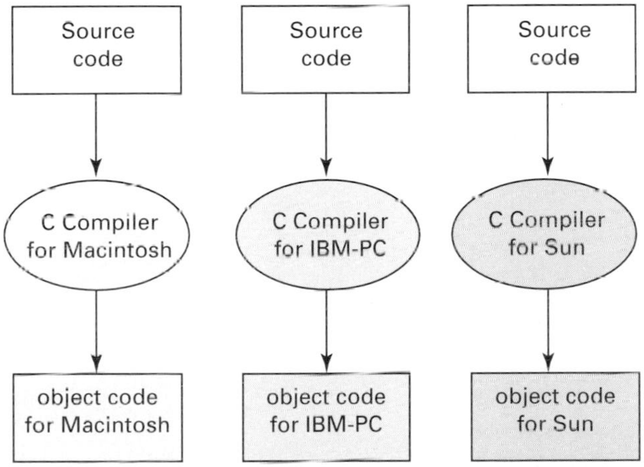

source program: the high-level language program being translated.

object program: the machine-language translation of a source program.

Figure 1.10 A unique C compiler for each computer

Cross-platform Transparency and Virtual Machines

Networks, and especially the World Wide Web, have encouraged the idea of cross-platform transparency. That idea is that, regardless of what machine you use, the application will run correctly. This creates a special burden for the software developer who must verify the correctness of object code for every machine on the network.

The Java language uses a model that relieves the developer of this burden and solves some other network related problems as well. The Java

byte code:
the object code produced
by the Java compiler.

Java Virtual Machine:
a system program that
runs on any platform and
translates byte code into
machine-language instruc-
tions for that platform.

interpreter:
a system program that
translates each instruction
in a program into machine
language and executes the
machine-language instruc-
tion.

compiler does not compile source code into machine language for any particular computer. Instead, the Java compiler creates object code (called
byte code) for the **Java Virtual Machine.** This "machine" is a system program that has been built to run on many different computers. The Java
Virtual Machine is an **interpreter** that translates each byte code instruction
into an appropriate machine-language instruction and executes it. Figure
1.11 shows the new relationship between source code, byte code, and the
Java Virtual Machine (interpreter). The software developer can compile
code once (into byte code for the Java Virtual Machine) and know that it
will run on a variety of computers.

You may be wondering what the difference is between a compiler and an
interpreter since both translate instructions in one computer language to another. The primary difference is that a compiler translates the entire program before it begins to execute individual instructions, whereas an
interpreter interleaves translation and execution. An interpreter translates
the first instruction, executes its machine language equivalent, translates the
second instruction, executes it, and so on.

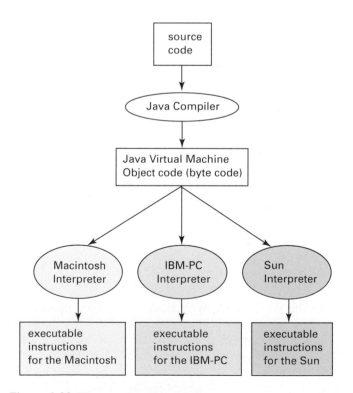

Figure 1.11 The virtual machine model

Applets and Applications

A side benefit of the virtual machine approach is that it supports applets, little application programs that run as part of a World Wide Web page. An applet is stored at a remote site on the Web, but is executed on the user's local computer. Since the Web supports platform transparency, an applet can run on any machine that is able to access its Web page. Without the virtual machine concept, the Web site would have to have object code for the applet available for a variety of computers. When a user requests a program, the Web site would have to identify the type of computer the user has, and send the appropriate object code. Not only is this complicated, it violates the principles of transparency. The Web site should not need to know what kind of machine a particular user has.

With platform transparency the Web site can send the same object code program for an applet to all users regardless of the user's computer. The local machine and its Virtual Machine program worry about the details of executing the application. This kind of compartmentalizing and distribution of responsibility is a fundamental principle of network, GUI, and object-oriented programming.

Because an applet is a program that is intended to be retrieved from a remote site on the World Wide Web, most Web browsers support Java applets, that is, they know how to invoke the virtual machine on the local computer to run the applet. When an applet is compiled, security restrictions are included to protect the local machine from either naive or malicious code that could harm the local machine.

A Java application differs from an applet in that it does not need to be part of a Web page in order to be executed. A Java application is like any other program that runs on a particular computer. The major difference between a Java application and a C program, for example, is that the C program is translated directly into object code for that machine. The Java application is first translated into byte code, which is then interpreted and executed by the Java Virtual Machine. On most machines the user doesn't even notice this process is happening. In this text we will initially focus on applications rather than applets because they are less complicated and permit us to concentrate on the important concepts of programming and problem solving.

In Java, a program consists of a collection of class definitions regardless of whether it is an applet or an application. Class definitions contain data and methods for manipulating that data. Figure 1.12 shows a very simple class definition in Java. Chapters 2 and 3 will cover the details of this class.

The class in Fig. 1.12 is called `FirstProgram`. As shown in Fig. 1.13, activating this class causes a banner and two buttons to appear in a window. When the user clicks on the west button, a line or string of text about `Elliot` appears. In Java, strings of text are surrounded by double quotation marks. When the user clicks on the east button, a string of text about `Ursula` appears.

```
public class FirstProgram extends PeopleInfo {
   public void init() {
      bannerMessage = "Welcome to Problem Solving with Java!";

      westLabel = "Learn about Elliot";
      westMessage = "Elliot's favorite thing about programming " +
                 "is Problem Solving";
      eastLabel = "Learn about Ursula";
      eastMessage = "Ursula's favorite thing about programming " +
                 "is User Interfaces";
      showInfo();
   }
}
```

Figure 1.12 A first program

FirstProgram simply sets up the strings of text that will appear on the banner, within the buttons, and in response to the button clicks. All of the real work occurs in the PeopleInfo class that is the parent of FirstProgram. The FirstProgram class contains one method called init. The method has six program statements. The first five give names to the text strings that will appear. The last statement calls a method showInfo that FirstProgram inherits from PeopleInfo. This method uses these names to set everything up properly.

The amazing thing about object-oriented programming is that a lot of messy detail can be hidden within classes and methods. It allows the programmer to concentrate on the task at hand. In Fig. 1.12 we don't have to know about how method showInfo() works to modify this program. For example, you could change the text strings to create an information window about yourself and a friend.

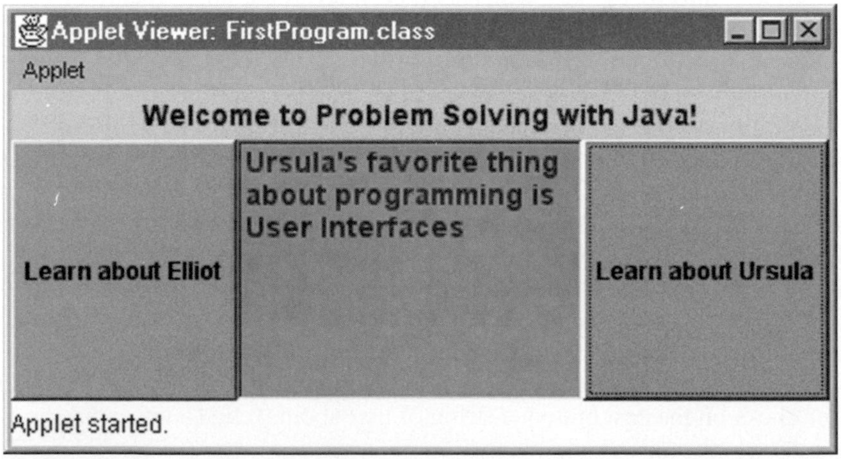

Figure 1.13 Window displayed by FirstProgram

EXERCISES FOR SECTION 1.5

Self-Check

1. Explain the difference between compiling a C program and compiling a Java program.
2. What is the difference between a Java program, byte code, and an executable program? Which do you create, which does the Java compiler create, and which does the Java Virtual Machine create?
3. What are the advantages of a virtual machine?
4. Explain the difference between an applet and an application.

Programming

1. Change the Java class in Fig. 1.12 so that it gives information about you and a friend.

1.6 Problem Solving and Programming Using Classes

Problem Solving and Planning

Because it cannot think, a computer needs a program in order to do any useful work. There is more to programming a computer than simply writing a list of instructions. Problem solving is a crucial component of programming. Before writing a program to solve a particular problem, you must consider carefully all aspects of the problem and then develop and organize its solution. You must do quite a lot of preplanning before you write a program.

You may be tempted to rush to the computer and start writing a Java program as soon as you have some idea of how to approach the problem. Resist this temptation. Instead, think carefully about the problem and its solution before writing any program instructions. When you have a potential solution in mind, plan it out beforehand, using either paper and pencil or a word processor, and modify the solution if necessary before you write the program in a programming language.

Networked computing and the Web have significantly changed the programming landscape in the past five years. However, the idea of disciplined, systematic problem solving and planning is even more crucial now when programming for the Web.

Class Reuse

One revolutionary aspect of programming in an object-oriented language like Java is that you can reuse or modify existing classes of objects to suit your purposes. As a key component of the planning process, you should determine what classes you can use directly, what classes you will modify, and what classes you must construct from scratch. The idea of using "off-the-shelf" components is fairly new to programming, but is one that we will stress in this text.

Desk-Checking

Once you have planned out your solution you should desk-check it by carefully performing each step much as the computer would. To desk-check a solution plan, simulate the result of each step using sample data that are easy to manipulate (for example, small whole numbers). Compare your results with the expected results and make any necessary corrections to the solution plan.

After you have desk-checked your solution plan, you can write it as a program. You should also desk-check your program before you enter it into the computer. Follow the programming strategy summarized in Fig. 1.14. Spending a few minutes to locate and correct errors in your program before you enter it can save you hours of frustration later.

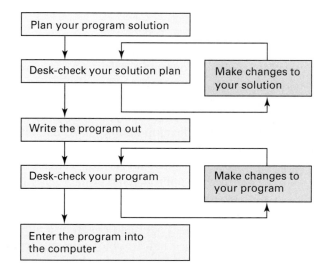

Figure 1.14 Programming strategy

EXERCISES FOR SECTION 1.6

Self-Check

1. If a computer can execute your program quickly and efficiently, what is the purpose of desk-checking the program?

1.7   Creating a Program in an Integrated Programming Environment

Before the computer can process a high-level language program, the programmer must enter the source program into the computer, and the computer must store it in executable form in memory. Several system programs assist with this task. We describe the role of these programs here, but do not show you how to use any particular computer to do it.

In the following discussion, we assume you will be using Java 1.1 and an **integrated programming environment (IPE)**. The IPE coordinates all of the system programs listed below. It keeps track of the status of files, for example, whether you have recently saved the source program, compiled it, or attempted to run it. The IPE also keeps track of the location of libraries of predefined classes.

Appendix A points you toward World Wide Web resources from which you can get Java, install it on your computer, and get support materials. In particular, all the class definitions in this book can be retrieved from the Web site given in Appendix A. Your course instructor may also have information on whether Java and other support resources are available locally at your institution.

integrated programming environment (IPE): a coordinated system for editing, compiling, linking, executing, and debugging a program.

Steps for Preparing a Program for Execution

1. Create a project folder in which you collect all relevant files including predefined classes that you wish to include. Such classes are defined in support libraries. We will discuss libraries in Chapter 2.

2. Use an **editor** program to enter each line of the source program into memory and to save it into the project folder as a source file.

3. Use a **compiler** program to translate the source program into byte code. If there are any **syntax errors** (errors in grammar), the compiler displays these errors in a window.

4. Use the editor program to correct the errors by modifying and resaving the source program. When the source program is error free, the compiler saves its byte-code translation as a file.

5. The Java interpreter (Java Virtual Machine) translates and executes each byte-code instruction.

6. If the code doesn't work correctly, the **debugger** can be used to step through the program and examine the effect of individual instructions.

Besides learning how to use your particular IPE, you will need to learn how to interact with a supervisory program, called the **operating system**. Common operating systems include UNIX (for example, on Sun or Silicon

editor: a program used to create, save, and correct source files.

compiler: a program that translates a high-level language program into machine language.

syntax error: an error in the grammatical form of a line in a Java program.

debugger: a program that helps you to locate errors in another program.

operating system: the program with which the program user interacts in order to specify which application programs and/or system operations the computer should perform.

Graphics Workstations), Microsoft Windows or Windows/NT for computers based on Intel chips (i.e., IBM-compatible computers), and MacOS for Macintosh computers. The operating system provides several essential services to the computer user:

- Loading and running application programs, including the Java IPE
- Allocating memory and processor time
- Providing input and output facilities
- Managing files of information
- Coordinating activities with the network

We expect that your instructor will give you instructions that you need to use your particular operating system and IPE.

EXERCISES FOR SECTION 1.7

Self-Check

1.   Which system program is used to create a source program?
2.   Which system program is used to fix syntax errors?
3.   Which system program is used to fix errors when the program is run?

Chapter Review

1. The basic components of a computer are main and secondary memory, the CPU, and input and output devices.
2. Main memory is organized into individual storage locations—memory cells.
   - Each memory cell has a unique address.
   - A memory cell is a collection of bytes; a byte is a collection of eight bits.
   - A memory cell is never empty, but its initial contents may be meaningless to your program.
   - The current contents of a memory cell are destroyed whenever new information is stored in that cell.
   - Programs *must* be copied into the memory of the computer before they can be executed.

- Data cannot be manipulated by the computer until they are first stored in memory.

3. Information in secondary memory is organized into files: program files and data files. Secondary memory stores information in semi-permanent form and is less expensive and slower than main memory.

4. Mainframe and minicomputers accommodate multiple users through a technique called time sharing. Personal computers can work alone or can access the resources of larger computers if they are connected to a network.

5. A network is a collection of computers that are linked together. Networked computers share resources such as printers and files. A network also provides a way for users on different computers to share information, for example, by sending e-mail (electronic mail).

6. The Internet is an interconnected collection of computer networks. The Internet supports the World Wide Web, a collection of linked documents on computers throughout the world that can be accessed and read using a Web browser.

7. A computer cannot think for itself; you must use a programming language to instruct it in a precise and unambiguous manner to perform a task.

8. Programming a computer can be fun—if you are patient, organized, and careful. We recommend you follow the plan shown in Fig. 1.14.

9. Two categories of programming languages are machine language (meaningful to the computer) and high-level language (meaningful to the programmer). You use several system programs to prepare a high-level language program for execution. You use an editor to enter a high-level language program into memory. A compiler translates a high-level language program (the source program) into machine-language (the object program).

10. The Java compiler translates a Java source program into byte code. The Java Virtual Machine translates byte code into machine language instructions for a particular computer or platform.

11. Applets are small Java programs that can be inserted in Web documents and accessed and run by any computer that has a Web browser or Java Virtual Machine. Applications are standalone Java programs.

12. You can use an Integrated Programming Environment (IPE) to help you manage the details of assembling Java projects and compiling and running Java programs.

13. Through the computer's operating system, you can issue commands to the computer and manage files.

Quick-Check Exercises

1. The _____ translates a(n) _____ program into byte code.
2. The _____ translates byte code into _____.
3. An _____ or _____ provides access to system programs for editing, compiling, and so on.
4. Specify the correct order for these operations: execution, translation to byte code, translation to machine language.
5. A high-level language program is saved on disk as a(n) _____ file.
6. The _____ finds syntax errors in the _____ file.
7. Computer programs are _____ components of a computer system, whereas a disk drive is _____.
8. In a high-level language, you can reference data using _____ rather than memory cell addresses.
9. Determine whether each characteristic below applies to main memory or secondary memory.
   a. Faster to access
   b. Volatile
   c. May be extended without limit
   d. Less expensive
   e. Used to store files
   f. Central processor accesses it to obtain the next machine-language instruction for execution
   g. Provides semi-permanent data storage
10. A _____ converts _____ signals to _____ signals for transmission over _____.

Answers to Quick-Check Exercises

1. Java compiler, Java source
2. Java Virtual Machine, machine language
3. operating system, Integrated Programming Environment
4. translation to byte code, translation to machine language, execution
5. source program
6. compiler, source program
7. software, hardware

8. descriptive names
9. main (a, b, f), secondary (c, d, e, g)
10. modem, digital, analog, telephone lines

Review Questions

1. List at least three kinds of information stored in a computer.
2. List two functions of the CPU.
3. List two input devices, two output devices, and two secondary storage devices.
4. Draw a diagram showing the process that should be used to evaluate a proposed solution to a problem.
5. Why are there two categories of programming languages?
6. Explain the difference between applets and applications.
7. What processes are needed to transform a Java program to a machine language program that is ready for execution?
8. Explain the relationship between memory cells, bytes, and bits.
9. Name three high-level languages and describe their original usage.
10. What are the differences between RAM and ROM?

Interview

James Gosling

James Gosling is a VP and Fellow at Sun Microsystems. He received his BSC in computer science from the University of Calgary, Canada and a Ph.D. in computer science from Carnegie-Mellon University. Mr. Gosling has built satellite data acquisition systems, a multiprocessor version of UNIX, and several compilers. He is perhaps best known for creating the original design of the Java programming language and implementing its original compiler and virtual machine.

What is your educational background? How did you first become interested in computer science?

I have a BSC from the University of Calgary and a masters and Ph.D. from Carnegie Mellon University, all in computer science. My interest in computer science can be traced back to when I was 14 years old and a friend of my dad's gave me a tour of the computer center at UCalgary. I was instantly hooked. From that day forward, I spent most of my waking hours at the university.

What was your first job in the computer industry? What did it entail?

My first job was at the age of 15 working at the University on the ISIS-ii satellite. I had lots of jobs throughout college and did plenty of consulting. My first job after graduation was for IBM Yorktown, working at a joint study institute they had with the CMU Information Technology Center. After that I came to Sun, where I've been ever since.

How did you come to work on the design of the Java programming language? What were your original goals for the language?

It all started as part of a larger project at Sun called the Green project. We were building a prototype, but found that the existing technology couldn't deal with many of the issues. My piece of the project was to deal with programming-language tools. Originally, we wanted a system that was architecture-neutral and would run on any chip. There were also issues with versioning, building robust applications, and security and reliability. Many of the programming languages of the time had security loopholes.

The Java programming language was originally named Oak. Why did its name change and what is the meaning behind the name Java?

I looked out my office window one day, trying to name the language, and saw an oak tree right outside. The name Oak remained for about five years, until the time when we wanted to release the language to the market. When we talked to our lawyers about using the name Oak, they informed us that it was already trademarked and we needed to choose a new name.

We spent a while trying to think of new names for the language. One day, a dozen or so of us gathered together in a room and everyone yelled out suggestions for names. At the end of the day we had a list that we handed to the lawyers. "Java" was the name closest to the top that cleared the trademark search process.

How would you describe a typical day for you at Sun? What is the most challenging part of your job?

I spend about half of the day answering numerous e-mail messages. The other part of my day is divided between going to design reviews and doing the technical work on improving Java and in dealing with implementation issues. I also manage to fit in strategy meetings and traveling to give talks. The biggest challenge is dealing with the politics of working for a large company. I'd love to spend all of my time just working on building great products and shipping them to our customers.

What are some features of Java that have made it such a success in the market?

Java was successful in large part because it was in the right place at the right time. I would also credit its success in part to the original free and open release of the product. People seem to love and use Java for many different reasons. They like that it's architecture-neutral, reliable, it's integrated with the network, it's dynamic, it has a large set of library tools—the list goes on.

How do you see Java evolving and improving over the next few years?

We are actually working very hard to keep the Java language stable. We're very conservative about making changes to the actual language. The biggest action occurs with the libraries. Java's object-oriented facilities make it easy for people to make their own libraries.

What person in computer science has inspired you?

There are so many: Bob Sproull, Ivan Sutherland, Mike Williams, Raj Reddy, Mike Shamos, John Bently, and H. T. Kung, just to name a few. I was really lucky to have fascinating professors who interested and motivated me to continue my studies. H. T. Kung, for example, kept after me to learn numerical analysis even though I hated it at the time. Now, I am glad I stuck with it.

Do you have any advice for computer science students who are learning Java?

Have fun. But also remember to keep a balance in your life. Computers are so much fun that it's easy to spend hours upon hours working on them. Have a great time with your computer, but remember to tear yourself away periodically to experience other joys.

CHAPTER 2

Problem Solving and Java

Programming is a problem-solving activity. If you are a good problem solver, you have the potential to become a good programmer. One goal of this book is to help you improve your problem-solving ability. To accomplish this, we introduce a systematic approach to solving programming problems called the software development method in Section 2.1 and show you how to apply it in Section 2.2.

2.1 The Software Development Method

2.2 Applying the Software Development Method
Case Study: Converting Units of Measurement

2.3 Overview of a Java Program

2.4 Reserved Words and Identifiers

2.5 Data Types

2.6 Class Definitions

2.7 Method Definitions

Chapter Review

This chapter introduces Java, a very new language that was developed by Sun Microsystems and that has only been generally available since 1995. Java is rapidly becoming popular because it has a lot to offer both beginner and more sophisticated programmers. Java is an object-oriented language that facilitates writing reliable programs that are easy for other programmers to read, use, and adapt. Java supports a disciplined approach to solving problems with a computer.

This chapter first introduces the software development method within the context of object-oriented programming and then shows how Java supports this approach. The basic structure of a Java program is described. Within that structure, we discuss classes and objects, and show how they are defined in terms of data and methods.

Although the principles used in writing good programs have not changed since the 1970s, many of the details have. In particular, the way a program user interacts with a program (user input/output) has changed dramatically. We therefore provide a class called `SimpleGUI` that will allow you to do **Simple Graphical User Interface** programming. Our goal is twofold. First, we want to enable you to write some programs that are fun and have the look and feel of applications such as word processors that you may have used. Second, we want you to develop good GUI programming habits right from the start. This chapter and the next introduce some of the methods of `SimpleGUI`. Chapters 9 and 10 go into much more detail about how to "do GUI" properly. Appendix A provides information on how to retrieve the `SimpleGUI` class from the World Wide Web.

2.1   The Software Development Method

The software development method we study in this text grew out of a movement in Computer Science to encourage disciplined programming. To support this, Nicklaus Wirth of Zurich, Switzerland, developed the programming language Pascal. Dr. Wirth promoted an approach to programming in which the programmer writes step-by-step procedures—the **algorithm**—and then verifies that the algorithm solves the problem as intended.

algorithm:
a recipe, or list of steps, for solving a problem.

In 1976 Dr. Wirth published a book called *Algorithms + Data = Programs*. In the preface he says:

> Decisions about structuring data cannot be made without knowledge of the algorithms applied to the data and that, vice versa, the structure and choice of algorithms often strongly depend on the structure of the underlying data. In short, the subjects of program composition and data structures are inseparably intertwined. (Wirth, 1976, xiii)

Around the same time, in Palo Alto, California, researchers at the Xerox Corporation began developing a programming language called Smalltalk that took this idea one step further. Their idea was that all of the components of a program should address the intertwined nature of computational problems. This approach is called **object-oriented programming**, that is, object = data + method, where a method is essentially an algorithm for doing a small task. We will emphasize this idea throughout this book. You may want to review the discussion on object-oriented languages and programming in Section 1.4.

object-oriented programming:
a disciplined approach to programming that supports the idea that data and methods are intertwined.

Object-oriented programming is a disciplined way of solving problems on a computer, and languages such as Smalltalk and Java support this discipline. Java is a good language for students because at every level it encourages you to think about the relationship between data and algorithm in a systematic way.

Problem-solving methods are covered in many subject areas. Business students learn to solve problems with a systems approach, while engineer-

Wirth, N., 1976, *Algorithms + Data = Programs*, Prentice-Hall, Englewood Cliffs, NJ.

ing and science students use the engineering and scientific method. Programmers use the software development method:

Classic Software Development Method

1. Specify the problem requirements.
2. Analyze the problem.
3. Design the algorithm to solve the problem.
4. Implement the algorithm.
5. Test and verify the completed program.
6. Maintain and update the program.

In object-oriented design the focus is on selecting and implementing classes (abstract objects), not designing algorithms. Wherever possible, we want to reuse existing classes as is, or use them as components of new classes, or modify them to create new classes. This approach lets programmers (software designers) use classes as off-the-shelf components to design and build new software systems just as hardware designers use off-the-shelf electronic circuits and components to design and build new computers. Incorporating these ideas in steps 3 and 4 above gives us a new software development method for object-oriented design:

Software Development Method (with Classes)

1. Specify the problem requirements.
2. Analyze the problem.
3. Design the classes to solve the problem by:
    a. Locating relevant classes in existing libraries.
    b. Modifying existing classes where necessary.
    c. Designing new classes where necessary.
4. Implement the new and modified classes.
5. Test and verify the completed program.
6. Maintain and update the program.

We discuss these steps next.

PROBLEM

Specifying the problem requirements forces you to state the problem clearly and unambiguously and to gain a clear understanding of what is required for its solution. Your objective is to eliminate unimportant aspects and zero in on the root problem. This is not as easy as it sounds. You may find you need more information from the person who posed the problem.

ANALYSIS

Analyzing the problem involves identifying the problem (a) *inputs*, i.e., the data you have to work with; (b) *outputs*, i.e., the desired results; and (c) any additional requirements or constraints on the solution.

At this stage it is important to identify the classes that will participate in solving the problem. Sometimes the description of a class will be obvious, other times it will feel somewhat contrived, especially for very small problems that involve simple arithmetic calculations. Typically, for larger problems, when you really understand the problem, the classes you have identified make a lot of sense.

At this stage, you should also determine the required format in which the results should be displayed (for example, as a table with specific column headings) and develop a list of problem variables and their relationships. These relationships may be expressed as formulas.

If steps 1 and 2 are not done properly, you will solve the wrong problem. Read the problem statement carefully, first, to obtain a clear idea of the problem and second, to determine the inputs and outputs. You may find it helpful to underline phrases in the problem statement that identify the inputs and outputs, as in the problem statement below:

Determine the <u>total cost of apples</u> given the <u>number of pounds of apples purchased</u> and the <u>cost per pound of apples</u>.

Look for commonalties in what was underlined. Note that here we keep referring to apples. This is a good indicator that the class to which we are referring is "apple."

Next, summarize the information contained in the underlined phrases:

Data Requirements

Problem Inputs

pounds of apples purchased
cost per pound of apples (in dollars per pound)

Problem Output

total cost of apples (in dollars)

The problem inputs are good candidates for data to be stored in an apple object. Once you know the problem inputs and outputs, develop a list of formulas that specify relationships between them. Some or all of these will be the basis for methods of the "apple" class. The general formula

total cost = unit cost × number of units

computes the total cost of any item purchased. Substituting the variables for our particular problem, yields the formula

total cost of apples = cost per pound × pounds of apples

In some situations, you may have to make certain assumptions or simplifications to derive these relationships. This process of extracting the essential problem data and their relationships from the problem statement is called **abstraction**.

abstraction:
the process of extracting the essential data and relationships of a problem.

DESIGN

Designing the classes to solve the problem requires you to identify existing classes that you can use as is, to identify classes you wish to modify, and to identify classes that you will write from scratch.

This is often the most difficult part of the problem-solving process. Many programmers are tempted to write all of their classes from scratch. This is because it is more fun to solve small problems on your own than to try to find existing solutions elsewhere.

Don't attempt to solve every detail of the problem at the beginning; instead, discipline yourself to use top-down design. In **top-down design**, you first list the major steps, or subproblems, that need to be solved. Then you solve the original problem by solving each of its subproblems. Typically in object-oriented design many of the subproblems will be solved by identifying new classes.

top-down design:
breaking a problem into its major subproblems and solving it by solving the subproblems.

Top-down design is the process you use to create an outline for a term paper. Your first step is to create an outline of the major topics, which you then refine by filling in subtopics for each major topic. Once the outline is complete, you begin writing the text for each subtopic.

For each class you have identified you want to identify the data for which it is responsible and the methods it has for operating on its data. For each class you also want to identify what inputs it needs to execute its methods properly and what outputs its methods produce. Most computer algorithms, and consequently the methods of a class consist of at least the following subproblems.

Algorithm

1. Get the data (input), typically asking a user.
2. Perform computations that are required.
3. Return the results (output), typically displaying the results in a meaningful way.

Once you know the subproblems, you can attack each one individually. For example, step 2, perform the computations, may need to be broken down into a more detailed list of steps called **algorithm refinements**.

algorithm refinements:
a detailed list of steps needed to solve a particular step in the original algorithm.

Desk-checking is an important part of object design that is often overlooked. As described in Section 1.6, to desk-check an algorithm, you must carefully perform each algorithm step (or its refinements) just as a computer would and verify that the objects' methods work as intended. You'll save time and effort if you locate errors early in the problem-solving process.

A final component of the object-oriented design process is to ask how your solution can be generalized so that the classes you create can be adapted by other programmers. In your initial solution you should not get bogged down by this question. Instead, make notes on what could be modified in your design to make it more flexible and general. Later case studies will illustrate this step.

IMPLEMENTATION

Implementing the solution (step 4 in the software development method) involves writing the classes you have defined in a programming language. You must also identify the libraries of classes you will use directly or those you have modified. You must indicate which classes you are modifying and write code that describes your modifications.

TESTING

Testing and verifying the program requires testing the completed program to verify that it works as desired. Don't rely on just one test case—run the program several times using different sets of data, making sure that it works correctly for every situation provided for in your solution.

MAINTENANCE

Maintaining and updating the program involves modifying a program to remove previously undetected errors and to keep it up to date. For example, changes in government regulations or company policies may require modifications to existing systems. Maintenance may also involve adapting the code to integrate it with new kinds of computers and operating systems. Twenty years ago no one thought that programs would remain in use more than five years. As we approach the year 2000 many older programs are still in use and show little signs of becoming obsolete in the near future.

the year-2000 problem: a problem that will manifest itself in year 2000, caused by the fact that some older programs use less than four digits to represent the year in a date.

structured program: a program created by a disciplined approach that is easy to read, understand, and maintain.

Although we will still be using programs written many years ago in the twenty-first century, some of this code may need major updating before the year 2000. The software problem that has required this update is called **the year-2000 problem.** Many of these older programs were written when computer storage space was at a premium, at a time when program designers stored only the last two digits of a year instead of all four digits. These programs represent the year 1999 using the digit pair 99 and the year 2000 using the digit pair 00, which is smaller, not larger, than any other two-digit pair. This discrepancy can lead to errors in calculations that are based on the current date or on the elapsed time in years. This points out that it is generally not wise to introduce inaccuracies in a program just to save some memory space or computer time, and that programs should be written with the future in mind.

For these reasons, the principles of **structured programming**—following a disciplined approach to programming that results in programs that are easy to read and understand and less likely to contain errors—are as important today as they were when first introduced over 20 years ago. The emphasis is on following accepted program style guidelines (which will be stressed in this book) to write code that is clear and readable. Obscure tricks and programming shortcuts are strongly discouraged. Government organizations and industry are strong advocates of structured programming because structured programs are much easier to design in the beginning and easier to maintain over the long term.

EXERCISES FOR SECTION 2.1

Self-Check

1. List the steps of the software development method.
2. What is an algorithm? Contrast it with a class method.
3. In which phase are algorithms developed? In which phase do you identify the problem inputs and outputs?
4. Why is software maintenance important?

2.2 Applying the Software Development Method

Throughout this book, we use the first five steps of the software development method to solve programming problems. These problems, presented as Case Studies, begin with a *problem statement*. As part of the problem *analysis*, we identify the data requirements for the problem, indicating the problem inputs and the desired outputs. Next, we *design* and refine classes that constitute the solution. Finally, we *implement* the classes using Java. We also provide a sample run of the program and discuss how to *test* the program.

We walk you through a sample case study next. This example includes a running commentary on the process that you can use as a model in solving other problems.

Case Study

Converting Units of Measurement

PROBLEM

You work in a store that sells imported fabric. Most of the fabric you buy is measured in square meters, but your customers want to know the equivalent amount in square yards. Write a program to perform this conversion.

ANALYSIS

The first step in solving this problem is to determine what you are asked to do. You must convert from one system of measurement to another, but are you supposed to convert from square meters to square yards, or vice versa? The problem states that you buy fabric measured in square meters, so the problem input is *fabric size in square meters*. Your customers want to know the equivalent amount in square yards, so the problem output is *fabric size in square yards*. To write the program, you need to know the relationship between square meters and square yards. Consulting a metric table shows that one square meter equals 1.196 square yards. The data requirements and relevant formulas are listed below.

Data Requirements

Problem Input

the fabric size in square meters

Problem Output

the fabric size in square yards

Relevant Formula

1 square meter = 1.196 square yards

Everything in the problem refers to a fabric. This makes `PieceOfFabric` a good candidate for a class definition. A characteristic of a piece of fabric object is its size in square meters, and that value should be stored in a data field. Every piece of fabric object must be able to convert its size in square meters to square yards, so we need a method (method `toSqYards`) that performs the conversion.

We have identified one data field and one method that performs a computation. Next, we consider methods that might enable a user to enter data into a `PieceOfFabric` object and to display the results in a meaningful way (method `displayFabric`). Because we need to read a measurement in square meters, we call the data entry method `readSqMeters`.

Our analysis leads to the following specification:

Specification for `PieceOfFabric` class

Data Fields

`sqMeters`—the fabric size in square meters (a data item)

Methods

`toSqYards`—converts a measurement in square meters to square yards
`readSqMeters`—reads a measurement in square meters
`displayFabric`—displays the information in a meaningful way

Figure 2.1 shows a sketch of an object of class `PieceOfFabric`; it indicates that each object of this class has storage for one data item, `sqMeters`.

Also each object has the methods shown in the dark blue area. We will explain the methods in the gray area in Section 2.3.

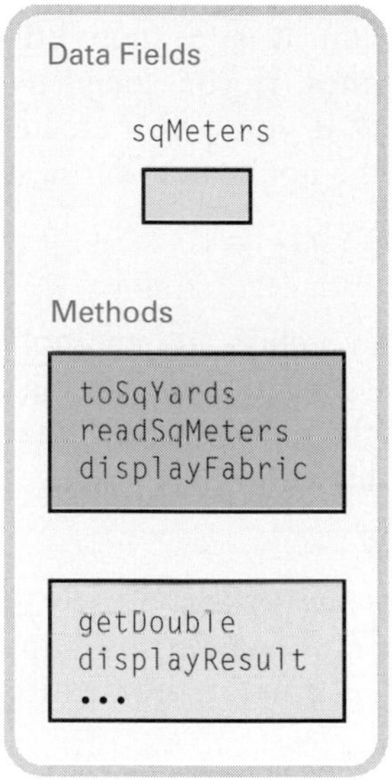

Figure 2.1 An object of class `PieceOfFabric`

The next question to ask is, How will our object be used? In Java there is a special class that we call the **application class**. It must contain a method called `main` that is used by the Java interpreter as a starting point for program execution. Typically, `main` creates object instances of the classes that actually solve the problem. It then activates the methods of those objects in a sequence that solves the problem. In most of our applications `main` will be the only method of the application class.

application class:
the class in a Java application program that has a `main` method—the starting point for the program execution.

Specification for the application class

Methods

`main`—A method that activates the methods of a piece of fabric object in order to solve the problem.

DESIGN

Next, use a top-down strategy to identify the classes needed to implement the solution. We decide what objects in existing libraries can be used, which should be adapted or modified, and which must be written from scratch. We will therefore:

1. Identify the classes.
2. Identify the data and methods of each class.
3. Refine the methods of each class, perhaps identifying new classes.

Notice that we do not dive into one class in great detail. It is far more efficient to break the problem down in stages. Sometimes, if you spend too much time on a detail, it is hard to discard your work if you find it creates unforeseen problems for other classes. We illustrate the application of these three steps next.

Identify the Classes

Our analysis identified two classes: a `PieceOfFabric` class and an application class we will call `ConvertFabric`. Both classes are pretty specialized, and also rather simple. It will be easier to build them from scratch than to spend a lot of time searching libraries for similar classes.

Identify the Data and Methods of Each Class

In the analysis phase, we specified the data fields for the `PieceOfFabric` class and listed three methods: `readSqMeters`, `toSqYards`, and `displayFabric`. We also listed one method, `main`, for the application class.

Refine the Methods of Each Class, Perhaps Identifying New Classes

Methods `readSqMeters` and `displayFabric` interact with the program user to get data and also to show results. Rather than build these methods completely from scratch, we can use methods in our `SimpleGUI` class (discussed in Sections 3.1 and 3.2) if we make class `PieceOfFabric` an extension, or modification, of class `SimpleGUI`. The algorithms for the three methods of class `PieceOfFabric` follow.

Algorithm for `toSqYards` (class `PieceOfFabric`)

1. Multiply the value of `sqMeters` by the conversion factor.

Algorithm for `readSqMeters` (class `PieceOfFabric`)

1. Apply method `getDouble` (defined in `SimpleGUI`) to read a real number into data field `sqMeters`.

Algorithm for `displayFabric` (class `PieceOfFabric`)

1. Apply method `toSqYards` to compute the size in square yards and method `displayResult` (defined in `SimpleGUI`) to display the result in a meaningful way.

Notice that method `displayFabric` must use method `toSqYards` to convert the fabric size to square yards.

Finally, we turn our attention to the application class. From our discussion of this class in the analysis phase, we know that its `main` method must create an object instance for a piece of fabric object and apply that object's methods in the proper sequence to solve the problem. Its algorithm follows.

Algorithm for `main` (class `ConvertFabric`)

1. Create an object instance for a piece of fabric object.
2. Use the object's `readSqMeters` method to get the data (the size in square meters) from the user.
3. Use the object's `displayFabric` method to display the result for the user.

IMPLEMENTATION

To implement the solution, you must specify all of this as a Java program. To do this, you must define each of the classes you have identified. A stepwise refinement process works well here, too. Define the data for each class and declare its methods without writing all the code for each method. Then tackle each method you've defined by describing its data requirements. Next write each step of a method as one or more Java statements.

Figures 2.2 and 2.3 show the Java class definitions created for this solution. A sample execution (Fig. 2.4) is shown as two scenes. The top scene shows the user interacting with a dialog box to give data to the program. The bottom scene shows the display of the object's information. Don't worry about understanding the details of this program yet. We explain the programming in the next several sections and in the next chapter.

TESTING

How do you know the sample run is correct? You should always examine program results carefully to make sure that they make sense. In this run, a fabric size of 2 square meters is converted to 2.392 square yards, as it should be. To verify that the program works properly, enter a few more test values of square meters. You don't need to try more than a few test cases to verify that a simple program like this is correct.

```
/*  File: PieceOfFabric.java
    Developed for Problem Solving with Java, Koffman & Wolz
    Appears in Figure 2.2
*/
import simpleIO.*;
```

Figure 2.2 *continued*

Figure 2.2 *continued*

```java
public class PieceOfFabric extends SimpleGUI {
    // Data fields
    private double sqMeters;   //input - measurement in sq. meters

    // Methods
    // Converts a measurement in square yards to square meters.
    public double toSqYards() {
        double conversionFactor = 1.196;
        return conversionFactor * sqMeters;
    }

    // Reads a measurement in square meters.
    public void readSqMeters() {
        sqMeters = getDouble("Enter the fabric area in sq. meters:");
    }

    // Calculates and displays the result.
    public void displayFabric() {
        displayString("The fabric size is " + sqMeters +
                    " square meters or " + toSqYards() +
                    " square yards.");
    }
} // Class PieceOfFabric
```

Figure 2.2 Class `PieceOfFabric`

```java
/*  File: ConvertFabric.java
    Developed for Problem Solving with Java, Koffman & Wolz
    Appears in Figure 2.3
*/
public class ConvertFabric {
    // Methods
    public static void main(String[] args) {

        // Create an instance of a PieceOfFabric object.
        PieceOfFabric aPiece = new PieceOfFabric();

        // Get the object's data from the user.
        aPiece.readSqMeters();

        // Display the result in a meaningful way.
        aPiece.displayFabric();
    }
} // Class ConvertFabric
```

Figure 2.3 Class `ConvertFabric`

Enter the fabric area in sq. meters:

2.0|

Cancel Input   Clear Input   Accept Input

User Interaction History

File

Enter the fabric area in sq. meters:
2.0
The fabric size is 2.0 square meters or 2.392 square yards.

Figure 2.4 Sample execution of application `ConvertFabric`

EXERCISES FOR SECTION 2.2

Self-Check

1. Consider how you would modify the `PieceOfFabric` class if a user provides a fabric measurement in square yards and a `PieceOfFabric` object converts it to square meters. What data fields and method would you need to provide in the class?

2. List the data requirements, formulas, objects, and methods for a program that converts a weight from pounds to kilograms. (*Hint:* 1 pound is equal to 0.453592 kilograms.)

2.3   Overview of a Java Program

One advantage of Java is that Java programs resemble everyday English. Even though you do not yet know how to write your own programs, with some help, you can probably understand parts of the program in Fig. 2.2 and 2.3. The figures show two files, and each file has the same name as the class definition that it contains. Also, each file name has an extension `.java` that identifies it as a Java class definition.

Reading a Program

Reading code is a skill that beginning programmers should develop. You can learn a lot by studying good code. One thing to realize is that you don't necessarily read code from top to bottom, left to right as you would English text. Instead, look at a program as you would a graphic or picture.

comments:
text in a program that is meant to provide information to the program reader, but that is ignored by the compiler and is not translated into executable code.

delimiters:
a pair of punctuation marks that surround or delimit a part of a program. For example, `/*` and `*/` are delimiters for multiline comments.

Comments The first thing to notice is that a lot of text looks like English. The lines that begin with `//` are **comments**. So is the text at the top that begins with `/*` and ends with `*/`. Comments provide supplementary information to the person reading the program, but they are ignored by the Java compiler. Double bar comments only extend to the end of the line. Bar and star comments may extend over many lines, but it is important to make sure that the **delimiters** `/*` and `*/` match up.

Studying class definitions There are two viewpoints for studying a program. You can try to determine what will happen when the program executes, or you can look for the parts of the program. It is easier to see what a Java program will do after you have identified the major parts.

A Java program is a collection of class definitions. You can identify the role of each class by looking for the class in which program execution begins. In the case of a Java application, this is the class that contains a `main` method (see `ConvertFabric` in Fig. 2.3). Other class definitions, such as `PieceOfFabric` (see Fig. 2.2), are supporting classes that typically do most of the work.

In point of fact, you can write an application class that does all the work without calling on support classes. In our experience, it is easier for beginners to develop good design habits if the application class and support classes are kept separate.

In reading through the methods for class `PieceOfFabric`, you should be aware that you are reading method definitions that describe what the method does—when, and if, it actually executes. However, these methods don't perform an action until they are called into execution by the `main` method, or some other method called by the `main` method. For this reason, the order of the method definitions doesn't matter.

In even the simplest Java program many classes come into play. For example, in Figure 2.2 and 2.3 close to 30 classes will be used to produce the display and get input from the user. To understand our example you don't have to know *how* they all work. You only need to understand *what* one of them does, namely `SimpleGUI`. The other supporting classes are conveniently hidden.

Class Libraries, Packages, and Import Statements

When supporting classes are referenced within a program, the compiler and interpreter must be able to find their corresponding files. Either the files must exist in the same folder as the class file, or the **classpath** must point to folders that contain the files. Setting the classpath is system dependent as described in Appendix A.

Collections of classes that are standardized can be found in file structures called **libraries**. For example, the Abstract Window Toolkit (AWT) is a library that contains hundreds of classes that support graphical user interfaces. To keep things organized, subgroups of those classes are organized into collections called **packages**. A library may consist of just one package. For example the `simpleIO` library that we use in the next few chapters consists of a single package with the same name. By the way, it uses classes from the AWT!

Depending on how your Java environment is configured, the `simpleIO` package folder should be placed in your current working folder or your classpath must point to the `simpleIO` package. (See Appendix A.)

You can refer to a class by using its full name, which consists of its package name and its actual name separated by a period:

packageName.ClassName

For example, the full name of the `SimpleGUI` class is `simpleIO.SimpleGUI`. If you **import** the package into your source file (by placing an **import statement** at the top of the file), you can refer to a supporting class directly, using just the class name. For example, the first line of file `PieceOfFabric.java` (Fig. 2.2) specifies that the package `simpleIO` will be imported or used by our program, so we can refer to class `SimpleGUI` directly. In Chapter 8 we show you how to create packages and decipher complicated package names.

Every class must reside in a package. If a package is not declared for a class, then the Java compiler assigns one (called the **default package**). Until Chapter 8, we will let the compiler package our classes. All we have to do is make sure that all supporting files we create reside in the same folder.

classpath:
system-dependent information that specifies where to find supporting classes.

library:
a file structure that contains definitions for standardized classes.

package:
a named collection of classes.

import:
to allow a package's classes to be referenced directly by the class name without using the package name.

import statement:
lists a package of classes defined elsewhere that will be used by this program.

default package:
the package assigned for a class by the Java compiler.

Viewing What a Program Does

We can view what the program does by reading the sequential steps of the `main` method in the application class (file `ConvertFabric.java`). The first step:

```
// Create an instance of a piece of fabric object.
PieceOfFabric aPiece = new PieceOfFabric();
```

says that we will create an instance of a `PieceOfFabric` object called `aPiece`. The second step:

```
// Get the object's data from the user
aPiece.readSqMeters();
```

says that the `aPiece` object will read data from the user. The third step

```
// Display the result in a meaningful way.
aPiece.displayFabric();
```

says that the `aPiece` object will display its information.

As you can see, there is a lot going on in these three steps. We can determine what will happen without knowing the details of how the methods in class `PieceOfFabric` or `SimpleGUI` work. This is the key to reading and writing programs in an object-oriented language like Java. You don't have to know all the details. You can write application classes that rely on well-designed and properly tested support classes. You may write some of the support classes yourself, or you may rely on classes that others provide to you in libraries. The key is to keep things simple and well organized.

Input, Output, and the `simpleIO` Package

Every application gets data from somewhere and puts data somewhere. The data that it gets are input to the program. The data that it puts somewhere are the program output. Reading data into memory is called an **input operation**. Displaying results or putting them somewhere outside the program is called an **output operation**.

input operation:

an instruction that reads data into memory.

output operation:

an instruction that displays information stored in memory.

As we said in Chapter 1, data may come from a user, from a secondary storage device, or from a network. You may display program output on a screen, store it on a secondary storage device, or broadcast it on a network.

A program needs methods for getting input data and putting output data someplace. Graphical user interfaces and their supporting operating systems have decreased the complexity of these tasks for a program user, but they have made it more difficult for the programmer. To help you, we supply the package `simpleIO` that allows you to do very basic input/output programming. `simpleIO` includes:

`SimpleGUI`   for very basic user interactivity

`SimpleWriter`, `SimpleReader`   for writing and reading text streams

Like any well-designed class, these classes encapsulate the complexity of what they do. In other words, they hide it from you. Chapter 3 introduces `SimpleGUI` methods that get input from and send output to a human user. Class `PieceOfFabric` (Fig. 2.2) uses two of these methods, `getDouble` and `displayResult`. We list the `SimpleGUI` methods used by a `PieceOfFabric` object in the gray area of Fig. 2.1.

EXERCISES FOR SECTION 2.3

Self-Check

1. Where should you begin reading a Java program?
2. What does an `import` statement do?
3. What is a library? What is a package?
4. What is the default package?
5. Explain what input and output statements do.

2.4 Reserved Words and Identifiers

The Java statements in Fig. 2.2 and 2.3 contain one or more words, mathe-matical symbols (+ and =), and punctuation symbols (such as . , ;). Some words have special meaning in Java and are called **reserved words**. Table 2.1 describes the reserved words so far. Later sections will explain their meaning in more detail. Appendix B summarizes all the reserved words in Java.

reserved word:
a word having special meaning in Java.

Table 2.1 Reserved words in Figures 2.2 and 2.3

Reserved word	Meaning
class	Indicates the start of a class definition.
double	Indicates that the variables listed next are storage reposito-ries for double-precision floating point numbers.
extends	Indicates that a class (subclass) extends another class (su-perclass).
new	Creates a new object instance.
private	Accessibility is restricted to the class defining this item.
public	Accessibility is unrestricted.
return	Returns the result that follows to the method caller.
static	There is exactly one method or data field with this identifier for the class. (The method `main` is `static` to guarantee ex-actly one entry point into an application.)
void	Returns no value.

The other words in Fig. 2.2 and 2.3 are identifiers. An **identifier** is a word in a Java program that the compiler recognizes as the name of a datum (data field or variable), a method, a class, or an object. All identifiers must be declared somewhere, either in this class, or in one of its support classes.

identifier:
a name of a datum, method, class, or object.

Identifiers

You have some freedom in selecting identifiers. The syntax rules and some valid identifiers follow. Table 2.2 shows some invalid identifiers. Java is case sensitive, that means R is not the same letter as r.

Syntax rules for identifiers
1. An identifier must begin with a letter, the underscore (_), or the dollar sign ($).
2. An identifier must consist only of a combination of letters, digits, underscore symbols, and dollar signs.
3. A Java reserved word cannot be used as an identifier.
4. An identifier can be any length.

Valid identifiers
Letter1, _letter, $inches, ForEver,
ThisIsAVeryLongOneButItisVALID

Table 2.2 Invalid identifiers

Invalid identifier	Reason invalid
1Letter	Doesn't begin with a letter
new	Reserved word
final	Reserved word
Two*Four	Character * not allowed
Joe's	Character ' not allowed

We generally follow well-established conventions in choosing identifier names. Table 2.3 shows some common conventions used by Java programmers.

Table 2.3 Java conventions for identifiers

Identifier type	Convention	Examples
Variables (data fields), methods, and packages	Start with lowercase; begin a new word with an uppercase letter.	sum sqFeet toSqMeters simpleIO
Class names	Start with uppercase; begin a new word with an uppercase letter.	ConvertFabric Bank SimpleGUI

In Fig. 2.2 and 2.3, we named our classes `PieceOfFabric` and `ConvertFabric`. Each word in a class name, including the first, begins with an uppercase letter. We used the names `sqMeters`, `toSqYards`, `readSqMeters`, and so on, for data fields and methods. These identifiers start with lowercase letters, but each new word begins with an uppercase letter.

A second convention we follow is to use noun phrases for data item names (for example, `sqMeters`) and verb phrases (for example, `getData`, `readSqMeters`, `displaySqYards`) for method names. This guideline makes sense because a data item name represents some information and a method usually performs an action. Following these conventions will make your code easier for human beings to read, but they are not rules imposed by the Java compiler. To differentiate between a method reference and a data field reference in Java code, you should know that parentheses must follow a method name but not a data name (for example, `toSqYards()` references a method and `sqMeters` references a data field).

If you mistype an identifier, the compiler detects the mistake as a syntax error and displays an error message during program translation. It will complain that you have an `unidentified variable`, a `missing method`, or a `missing object`, depending on how it interpreted the identifier. Because mistyped identifiers sometimes resemble other identifiers, avoid picking similar names.

Program Style: *Selecting names in a Java program*

We discuss program style throughout the text in displays like this one. A program that "looks good" is easier to read and understand than one that is sloppy. Most programs will be examined or studied by someone other than the original programmers. In the real world, only about 25 percent of the time spent on a particular program is devoted to its original design or coding; the remaining 75 percent is spent on maintenance (i.e., updating and modifying the program). A program that is neatly stated and whose meaning is clear makes everyone's job simpler.

The Java compiler differentiates between uppercase and lowercase. This means that you cannot write `CLASS` when you mean `class`.

Try to pick meaningful names for identifiers. For example, the identifier `salary` would be a good name for a variable used to store a person's salary, whereas the identifier `S` or `Bagel` would be a bad choice.

It is difficult to form meaningful names with fewer than three letters. On the other hand, typing errors become more likely when identifiers are too long. A reasonable rule of thumb is to use names having 3 to 10 characters.

EXERCISES FOR SECTION 2.4

Self-Check

1.   What are reserved words?
2.   Why shouldn't you use a reserved word as an identifier?

3. Which of the following identifiers are (a) Java reserved words, (b) valid identifiers, and (c) invalid identifiers?

```
new    private   Bill    program   Sue's   Rate
Start   extends   static   XYZ_123   123_XYZ
ThisIsALongOne   Y=Z   Prog#2   'MaxScores'
```

4. Review the class definitions in Figs. 2.2 and 2.3. Find all the reserved words. These classes contain many identifiers. For each identifier, determine whether it refers to a package, a class, a method, or a data field.

2.5 Data Types

data type:
a set of values and operations that can be performed on those values.

primitive type:
one of the eight Java data types used to represent simple values.

A **data type** is a way to represent a particular set of values and to determine what operations can be performed on those values. Java provides eight **primitive types** that are used to represent four kinds of simple values:

1. Integers—simple numbers that do not contain fractional parts such as 5, 4,343,222 (written in Java as 4343222), and –52. The primitive types used to represent integers are `byte`, `short`, `int`, and `long`.

2. Real numbers—numbers that can include fractional parts such as 2.5, 3.66666666, –.000034, and 5.0. The primitive types used to represent real numbers are `float` and `double`.

3. Boolean[1] values—the values false and true. The primitive type used to represent Boolean values is `boolean`.

4. Characters—all of the symbols that can be produced by pressing keys on a keyboard. Characters are used to produce human readable text such as English sentences. The primitive type used to represent characters is `char`.

Although Java has four types to represent integers, we will use type `int` exclusively in this book. Table 2.4 shows the differences between the four integer types. We will use type `double` to represent real numbers as this will ensure we have a sufficient range of values (15 significant digits) to represent any numerical quantity likely to appear in a program. Type `double` values use twice the amount of storage as type `float` values (eight bytes versus four bytes).

Table 2.4 Java integer types

Type	Storage requirement	Range
int	4 bytes	–2,147,483,648 to 2,147,483,647
byte	1 byte	–128 to 127
short	2 bytes	–32,678 to 32,767
long	8 bytes	–9,223,372,036,854,775,808 to . . .

[1] The Boolean data type is named after the English mathematician George Boole (1815–1864) who invented a two-valued algebra.

Primitive Type `int`

In mathematics, integers are positive or negative whole numbers. A number without a sign is assumed to be positive.

Because of the finite size of a memory cell, not all integers can be represented. In Java, you write integers (and all other numbers) without commas. Some valid integers are

```
-10500     435     15     -25
```

We perform the common arithmetic operations (add, subtract, multiply, and divide).

Primitive Type `double`

A real number has an integral part and a fractional part that are separated by a decimal point. Some valid real numbers are

```
-10.5     .435     15.     -25.1234
```

We can use scientific notation to represent very large and very small values. In normal scientific notation, the real number 1.23×10^5 is equivalent to 123000.0 where the exponent 5 means "move the decimal point 5 places to the right." In Java scientific notation, we write this number as `1.23e5` or `1.23e+5`. If the exponent has a minus sign, the decimal point is moved to the left (e.g., `0.34e-4` is equivalent to `0.000034`). Table 2.5 shows examples of both valid and invalid double values. We can perform the common arithmetic operations (add, subtract, multiply, and divide).

Table 2.5 Valid and invalid `double` values

Valid	Invalid
`3.14159`	`-15e-0.3` (`0.3` invalid exponent)
`0.005`	`12.5e.3` (`.3` invalid exponent)
`.12345`	`.123E3` (needs lowercase e)
`12345.0`	`e32` (doesn't start with a digit)
`16.`	`a34e03` (doesn't start with a digit)
`15.0e-04` (value is `0.0015`)	
`2.345e2` (value is `234.5`)	
`1.15e-3` (value is `0.00115`)	
`12e+5` (value is `1200000.0`)	

Primitive Type `boolean`

Unlike the other data types, the `boolean` data type has just two possible values: `true` and `false`. We can use this data type to represent conditional values so that a program can make decisions. Boolean operators allow you to manipulate boolean values. These are presented in Chapter 5.

Primitive Type `char`

Data type `char` represents an individual character value—a letter, a digit, or a special symbol. Each character is unique, for example, the character for the digit zero (`'0'`) is distinct from the character for the letter "oh" (`'O'`), even though they might look identical. In a class definition, each type `char` value is enclosed in apostrophes (single quotes) as shown below.

```
'A'    'z'    '2'    '9'    '*'    ':'    ' '
```

The last value represents the blank character, which is typed by pressing the apostrophe key, the space bar, and the apostrophe key.

Characters are used primarily in strings, a topic that will be introduced shortly. Although there are some simple operators for manipulating characters, we don't use them often in this book because strings are more flexible and convenient. But to understand strings you first need to know some details about characters.

Java uses a coding scheme for characters called Unicode, which has 65,536 unique characters. This allows symbols from languages around the world to be represented in a Java program. (See Appendix B.)

escape sequence:
a two-character sequence beginning with \ that represents a special character.

Java uses a special set of symbols, called **escape sequences**, to represent special characters. Each escape sequence is written as a type `char` value consisting of a backslash \ followed by another character. Table 2.6 shows some common escape sequences. The first four escape sequences represent characters that control the appearance of text that is displayed. The last row shows that Java uses two backslash characters to represent the backslash character.

Table 2.6 Java escape sequences

Escape sequence	Meaning
`'\n'`	Linefeed
`'\b'`	Backspace
`'\r'`	Carriage return
`'\t'`	Tab
`'\"'`	Double quote
`'\''`	Single quote
`'\f'`	Formfeed
`'\\'`	Backslash

`String` Class

Besides the primitive types, Java also supports a `String` class that is used to store sequences of characters. In a class definition, a string is enclosed in quotation marks:

```
"ABCDE"    "1234"    "True"    "Enter the fabric size:"
```

Note that the string `"1234"` is not stored the same way as the integer 1234 and cannot be used in a numerical computation. The string `"true"` is also stored differently from the `boolean` value `true`. Finally, the string `"A"` is not the same thing as the `char 'a'`.

A string can contain any number of characters, but all must be on the same line in a Java program. In Java, strings can be stored, compared, joined together (concatenated), and taken apart. See Appendix C for a full summary of the methods of the `String` class.

Purpose of Data Types

Why have different data types? The reason is that they allow the compiler to know what operations are valid and how much memory space a value will require. For example, a value of type `double` takes more space than an `int`. A `string` will also take up more space than a `double` under most circumstances.

If you try to manipulate a value in memory in an incorrect way (for example adding two `boolean` values), the Java compiler displays an error message telling you that this is an incorrect operation. Similarly, if you try to store the wrong kind of value (for example, a `string` in a data field that is type `int`), you get an error message. Detecting these errors keeps the computer from performing operations that don't make sense.

You might wonder whether you can convert from one primitive type to another. The answer is yes, sometimes. For example, it is obvious how an integer can be converted into a real number. But if you convert a real number into an integer do you truncate (remove) the fractional part or do you round it to the nearest integer? We introduce the rules for conversion between primitive types and between primitive types and strings in the next chapter.

EXERCISES FOR SECTION 2.5

Self-Check

1. List the four major kinds of data.
2. **a.** Write the following numbers in normal decimal notation:

    ```
    103E-4 1.2345E+6 123.45E+3
    ```

    b. Write the following numbers in scientific notation:

    ```
    1300 123.45 0.00426
    ```
3. Indicate which of the following values are legal in Java and which are not. Identify the data type of each valid value.

    ```
    15    'XYZ'    '*'    $ 25.123   15.    -999    .123
    'x'    "X"    '9'    '-5'    true    'True'
    ```

4. What would be the best data type for storing the area of a circle in square inches? How about the number of cars passing through an intersection in an hour? Your name? The first letter of your last name?

5. Distinguish between character (`char`) and integer (`int`) types.

6. Distinguish between a `char` and a `String`.

7. Explain why `char` and `String` types are needed.

8. Why is type `boolean` needed?

2.6 Class Definitions

In Java, we can create and use our own data types. We do this by defining new classes. For example, the data type `String` is a class rather than a primitive type. Someone defined the methods and data fields of the object for us so that we can create objects of this type and use them in our programs. This is very convenient compared to being forced to always manipulate characters directly. The power of Java is that, with a few exceptions, objects can be used in a manner remarkably similar to primitive types. This advantage will become evident in the next few chapters.

A class definition describes the kind of object we are defining. Mathematicians say we are describing a class of objects. This is why Java programmers refer to the definition of an abstract object as its class. During the execution of the program, members or object instances of classes will be used. These object instances will be the values assigned to an identifier of that type, just like the value 5 can be assigned to an identifier of type `int`. Java therefore supports two kinds of data types:

- Primitive types
- Classes

You should be aware that there are classes that capture the abstractions of the primitive types. For example, the class `Integer` allows you to manipulate integer data as objects rather than primitive types. Right now this may not seem very useful. We will discuss these classes in Chapter 7.

Overview of a Class Definition

A class definition tells the compiler what an object is all about. Objects can be almost anything a programmer can imagine. Consequently, there must be a form in which to describe a new class to the compiler. A class definition has three parts:

1. A header declaration
2. The data field declarations of the class
3. The method definitions of the class

These parts are identified for the class `PieceOfFabric` in Fig. 2.5.

```
Header ──▶ public class PieceOfFabric extends SimpleGUI {
              // Data fields
  Data   ──▶  private double sqMeters;   //input - measurement in
declaration                              //square meters

              // Methods
              // Converts a measurement in square yards to square meters.
              public double toSqYards() {
                  double conversionFactor = 1.196;
                  return conversionFactor * sqMeters;
              }

              // Reads a measurement in square meters.
              public void readSqMeters() {
                  sqMeters =
                      getDouble("Enter the fabric area in sq. meters:");
 Method           }
definitions
              // Calculates and displays the result.
              public void displayFabric() {
                  displayString("The fabric size is " + sqMeters +
                                " square meters or " + toSqYards() +
                                " square yards.");
              }
          } // Class PieceOfFabric
```

Figure 2.5 Parts of class PieceOfFabric

The header declaration tells the compiler that this is a class definition. The compiler recognizes that it is a header declaration because it contains the reserved word class. The header identifies the name of the class. It declares the visibility of the class, that is, who will be allowed to use it and how. The header may also declare what class this object extends. The header is followed by the body of the definition, which is surrounded by the delimiters { and }.

Reading a class header requires reading from the middle out in both directions. At the center of the header is the phrase

class *name*

where *name* is the class name such as ConvertFabric or PieceOfFabric.

Visibility The visibility of the class appears to the left of the class name. Reserved words such as public and static appear here. Until Chapter 4, we will specify the visibility of a class as **public**. This means that each class can be referenced by other classes that we create. We will specify the visibility of a data field as **private**. This means that the data field name can appear only inside the class that declares it.

public: a name can appear outside the class that declares it.

private: a name can appear only inside the class that declares it.

inheritance:
the ability to extend the definition of a class and use its methods in the class that extends it.

subclass:
the class that extends another class.

superclass:
the class that is extended by another class, the subclass.

Extending a Class   The ability to extend an object is one of the basic properties of an object-oriented language. It is called **inheritance**. In the phrase

```
PieceOfFabric extends SimpleGUI
```

`PieceOfFabric` is sometimes referred to as the child class (or **subclass**), and `SimpleGUI` is referred to as the parent class (or **superclass**). `PieceOfFabric` is said to inherit from `SimpleGUI`. In practical terms this means `PieceOfFabric` is a kind of `SimpleGUI` object and can do everything a `SimpleGUI` object can do, and more. In our case `PieceOfFabric` can manage the complex problem of putting up GUI windows as well as reading, displaying, and converting fabric sizes. Later chapters provide case studies that show the real power of inheritance.

Introduction to Syntax Displays

The syntax of a language defines the rules for expression in the language. For each new Java construct introduced in this book, we provide a *syntax display* that describes and explains its syntax and shows examples of its use. In the following syntax display, the italicized element, *name*, is discussed in the interpretation section. Here we illustrate a syntax display by describing a simplified form of a class definition.

Syntax Display

Simplified Class Definition

Form: [*visibility*] class *class-name* [extends *parent*] {...}

Example: public class PieceOfFabric
                        extends SimpleGUI{...}

Interpretation: The visibility of class *class-name* may be determined by the reserved word that precedes `class`. Class *class-name* may extend its superclass *parent*. The square brackets indicate that specification of the visibility and extended class are optional. The symbols {...} mean that the body of the definition appears as a sequence of steps delimited by curly braces.

Declaring Data Fields

A class definition body contains a declaration of the data fields and methods of that class. Data fields are used to store data in memory while the program is executing. The data fields store input data, intermediate results of calculations, and perhaps results that will be delivered as output elsewhere.

In the definition of `PieceOfFabric` in Figure 2.2 one data field is declared:

```
// Data fields
private double sqMeters;
```

The data field `sqMeters` is used to store input data. Each time the program executes it will hold different data, depending on what the user gives as input.

A data field declaration is a kind of **data declaration.** Others will be shown in Section 2.7 and in Chapter 3. A data declaration defines the type of an identifier, and may provide an initial value. A data field declaration may also include a visibility for the identifier. For now, we will use `private` as the visibility for all data fields. In most cases it is good programming practice to allow access to data fields only from within an object. Other objects may access data fields through `public` methods. This ensures that data can only be modified in a predictable way.

The declaration for `conversionFactor`

```
double conversionFactor = 1.196;
```

shows that data can be written within a line (in-line) of a Java program. The value of data (in this case, `1.196`) that appears in-line in a program is called a **literal**. As mentioned before, mathematicians use the word "value" to designate the amount or quantity that a number represents. Numbers and boolean values (`true` and `false`) are inherently literal. Characters and strings must be delimited by single and double quotes, respectively, to distinguish them from reserved words and identifiers. For example:

`int age = 15;`	`age` identifies an integer with initial value `15`.
`double gpa = 3.8;`	`gpa` identifies a double with initial value `3.8`.
`boolean enrolled = true;`	`enrolled` identifies a `boolean` with initial value `true`. `true` and `false` are reserved words.
`String name = "John Doe";`	`name` identifies a string with initial value `"John Doe"`. Literal strings are delimited by double quotes.
`char cs1Grade = 'A';`	`cs1Grade` identifies a character with initial value `'A'`. Note that a literal character is delimited by a single quote.

A data field declared with a literal value has that value only until some method changes the value. The literal value is said to be its initial value, and the process of setting an initial value is called **initializing the data field**.

data declaration:
a declaration that defines the type of an identifier and that may provide an initial value. In the case of a data field, it may also specify visibility.

literal:
a value that appears in-line in a program.

initializing a data field:
the process of giving a variable a specific initial value.

Syntax Display   *Data Declaration*

Form: [*visibility*] *dataType dataItem* [= *initialValue*] ;

Example: String myName = "Elliot";
             private int numKids;
             private double maxSalary = 10000.0;

The identifier *dataItem* is a storage repository for information of the specified *dataType*, where *dataType* is either a primitive type or is the name of a class. For now, we will specify the *visibility* of all data fields as private. That means that these data fields can only be accessed by the methods defined within the same class as the data fields. The *initialValue* of a data field, if present, follows the symbol =. This value may change as a result of program execution.

EXERCISES FOR SECTION 2.6

Self-Check

1. List the parts of a class definition.
2. What is the difference between public and private visibility? Why do you think this is important?
3. What does it mean to initialize a data field?
4. What is a literal?
5. Why must character and string literals be quoted, but reals, integers, and booleans are not?

Programming Project

1. Write the definition for a class Mine that has data fields pi (3.14159), radius, area, and circumf defined as double, data field numCirc as an int, and data field circName as String. Do not write the method bodies.

2.7   Method Definitions

A method definition describes a process or action in Java. Methods operate on the information stored in an object's data fields. A method may receive input from an external source and store that information in the object (for example, SimpleGUI's getDouble method). A method may present results to some external destination (for example, SimpleGUI's displayResult method). A method may produce an output or result. For example, in class PieceOfFabric, method toSqYards (Fig. 2.2) calculates a result that depends on the value of the data field sqMeters.

A method may get input through an **argument list**, and it may produce an output through its **return value.** A method must declare what kinds of input it can receive through its argument list, and it must declare the type of its return value.

A method definition may also contain its own variables. Other objects, or even other methods within the method's class, cannot directly access these variables.

A method definition contains a header and a body, just like a class definition. The header identifies the method, the return value, and the argument list. The body of the method, enclosed in braces { }, consists of program statements. These will be introduced in the next four chapters.

argument list:
a list consisting of data declarations that provide input to a method.

return value:
a value whose data type is specified and that is the output of a method.

Method Definition

Syntax Display

Form: [*visibility*] *resultType methodName* ([*argumentList*]) {...}

Examples:
```
private double toSqYards() {...}
public static void main(String[] args) {...}
public int vectorLength(int newXcor, int newYcor) {...}
```

Interpretation: Method *methodName* returns a value of type *resultType*. Arguments to the method may appear in the *argumentList*. This list contains individual data declarations (data type, identifier pairs) separated by commas. The method definition may declare visibility with reserved words (for example, public, private) that precede the *resultType*. The square brackets indicate that specification of the visibility and argument list are optional. The symbols {...} mean that the body of the definition appears as a sequence of statements delimited by curly braces.

The result type can be a primitive type such as double or it can be a class. If a method does not return a result (for example, method main in Fig. 2.3), the result type must be declared as **void**.

The argument list consists of argument declarations separated by commas. An argument declaration specifies the argument's data type and name, for example int n. The argument list is optional; however, the parentheses that enclose it are required. An empty pair of parentheses signifies that the method has no arguments.

Figure 2.6 shows the method header for toSqYards from the PieceOfFabric class definition (Figure 2.2). The visibility is public, which means that method toSqYards can be used outside this class. The empty parentheses indicate that the method has no arguments. It uses the data fields of the object to calculate a result, which it returns as a type double value.

void:
the return type for a method that does not return a result.

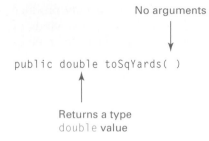

Figure 2.6 Input and output declarations for `toSqYards` (from Figure 2.2)

A method may also be declared as a class method through the keyword `static`. The `main` method in `ConvertFabric` is an example. Don't forget that the `main` method of an application object must be declared `public static`.

Passing Arguments to Methods

The arguments of a method provide a means for other objects to give data to the method. We will not define our own methods with arguments for quite some time, but we have already used methods defined by others that include arguments. For example, in Fig. 2.2 the method `readSqMeters` includes a reference to the `SimpleGUI` method `getDouble`:

```
sqMeters =
    getDouble("Enter the fabric area in sq. meters:");
```

passing an argument:
the process in which a method is called and is given data through its argument list.

Notice the literal string within the parentheses. This method call is **passing an argument** (the string) to method `getDouble`. The string is displayed as a prompt to the user. Because the prompt is an argument to the method, `getDouble` can be used anytime a `double` value is expected from a user. The argument provides the flexibility for `getDouble` to be used to display a different prompt in other contexts.

A method may or may not receive input via its argument list before executing the statements in its body. The declaration of the argument list tells the compiler what the input will look like and how many data items must be given to the method when it is called by other objects. The compiler ensures that the number and type of the arguments are correct when a method is called.

In the declaration of the `main` method for `ConvertFabric`, the input is an array of strings called `args`. You can tell `args` is an array because `string` is followed by square brackets. For now, don't worry about what this means—we discuss arrays in Chapter 7.

EXERCISES FOR SECTION 2.7

Self-Check

1. What is an argument list?
2. What is a return value?
3. Explain what it means for an object to pass an argument.
4. What does the following method definition tell you?

   ```
   int myMethod(String name, int a) {}
   ```
5. What does the reserved word `void` signify?

Chapter Review

This chapter has covered a lot of ground. You have seen how the software development method is used to design, implement, and test a program. You have been introduced to the basic structure of a Java application and have seen how classes, data fields, and methods are declared. The next chapter spends some time on the basic building blocks of methods and continues to use the fabric conversion problem as an example.

The major points of this chapter follow:

1. Follow the software development method to solve programming problems. It consists of the following steps: (1) specifying the problem, (2) analyzing the problem, (3) designing the classes, (4) implementing the program, (5) testing and verifying the solution, (6) maintaining and updating the program. Use a disciplined approach to write error-free code that is easy to read and maintain.

2. Every Java program is made up of one or more classes. An application is a class definition that contains a `main` method. The declaration for the `main` method must be:

   ```
   public static void main(String[] args)
   ```

3. Every Java class resides in a package. If a package is not specified, the default package is assigned. Until Chapter 8, we will use the default package.

4. Packages organize classes. Packages in turn may be organized into libraries. The full name of a class is *packageName.ClassName*. To refer to a class directly by its class name, you must import the package using an `import` statement.

5. Programs typically get data from an external source and place data in some external destination. Input operations provide a means for getting data in. Output operations provide a means for placing data outside of main memory. The package `simpleIO` is used in this text to make some standard input/output operations easier for you.

6. You must declare each identifier and its type. All identifiers begin with a letter, _, or $. The remaining characters may be letters, _, $, and digits. A reserved word cannot be used as an identifier.

7. Java is case sensitive; thus, the identifier `Hello` is not the same as `hello`.

8. We follow the Java conventions for naming: verb phrases for methods, nouns for data fields. Methods, data fields, and packages start with lowercase, classes start with uppercase.

9. Java's types enable the compiler to determine how to store a particular value in memory and what operations can be performed on that value. A type can be either a class or a primitive type. The four primitive types we will use are `double`, `int`, `boolean`, and `char`. The type of each data field in a class and each variable in a method must be declared.

10. New data types are created by defining classes. A class definition includes header, data field, and method declarations. A class may include a declared visibility and may extend another class.

11. The visibility of a class, method, or data field describes who may have access to it. Until Chapter 4 we declare classes as `public`, data fields as `private`, and methods as either `public` or `private`. Public visibility means any object in the package may have access. Private members (data fields and methods) may only be accessed by other members of the class in which they are defined.

12. A method definition specifies its visibility, its return value, its name, its argument list (all in the header), and the statements that make up its body.

New Java Constructs

Construct	Effect
import Statement `import simpleIO.*;`	Placed at the top of a class definition file, it declares that all classes within the package `simpleIO` may be identified by class name only, and do not require the package name.

Class Definition
`public class MakeFabric {...}`
`public class Fabric`
`  extends SimpleGUI {...}`
	Defines a class `MakeFabric` and a class `Fabric` that extends the definition of class `SimpleGUI`. Until Chapter 8 classes are declared `public`, available to any other class in the same folder.

Data Declaration
`private double sqMeters;`
`double pi = 3.14159;`
	Declares `sqMeters` and `pi` to be of type `double`. `sqMeters` has `private` visibility and `pi` has an initial value of `3.14159`.

Method Definition
`public double doIt() {...}`
`public void displayChar(char ch) {...}`
	Defines `doIt` as a method with no arguments that returns a type `double` result. Defines `displayChar` as a method with one type `char` argument that returns no result. Both methods have `public` visibility.

Quick-Check Exercises

1. How can you tell whether a class is the application class or a support class?

2. What does the following statement do?

   ```
   import simpleIO.*;
   ```

3. Identify which of the following gets data from an external source and which one places data at an external destination:

   Input operation

   Output operation

4. List four categories of primitive data types of Java and their names in Java.

5. Explain why different data types are necessary.

6. Write the declaration header for a class called `FunnyObject` that extends `SadObject` and will be visible to all objects in the package.

7. In which step of the software development method are the following operations performed?

   a. finding out the units of measurement that should be used

   b. writing assignment statements in Java

   c. identifying relevant formulas

   d. deciding which classes to use

   e. verifying that a program is correct for several sets of data

   f. specifying the data and methods for a class

   g. determining the problem inputs and outputs

   h. specifying the algorithm for a method

Answers to Quick-Check Exercises

1. The application class is the only one that contains exactly one definition of the method `main`.

2. It declares that all classes in the `simpleIO` package may be referred to directly by their class name.

3. An input operation gets data, an output operation puts data.

4. Integer (`int`), real (`double`), Boolean (`boolean`), and character (`char`).

5. Data types tell the compiler what kind of storage space to allocate and what kinds of operations are allowed for a particular data item. In this way, the most space efficient data type can be selected and memory allocation can be efficient. Data type conflicts that are detected by the compiler tell the programmer about possible coding errors.

6. `public FunnyObject extends SadObject`

7. **a.** problem specification

  b. implementation

  c. analysis

  d. analysis

  e. testing

  f. design

  g. analysis

  h. design

Review Questions

1. List the six steps in the software development method. Briefly explain what happens in each.

2. Create an algorithm for shopping for groceries; that is, list the steps that are necessary to determine what supplies you need and the steps needed to purchase them. What kind of "data" does a problem like this one have?

3. What kind of information should be specified in the comments that appear at the beginning of a program?

4. Check the identifiers that you can use in a program:

___ income	___ two fold	___ Hours*Rate	___ MyProgram
___ 1time	___ C3P0	___ readLine	___ public
___ new	___ income#1	___ void	___ Program
___ tom's	___ item	___ variable	___ pi

5. List four categories of primitive data types of Java.

6. Name two reserved words for visibility. Explain how each impacts on a class, method, or data field. Which reserved words will we use for classes? Which for class methods? Which for class data?

7. Explain the difference between a class definition and a data declaration.

Programming Projects

For each project listed here, use the software development method to identify the data requirements, formulas, and classes needed to solve the problem. Then write each class definition including the class declaration, data field declarations, and method definitions, but excluding the method bodies. If you simply leave the method bodies empty (e.g., { }), you can use your compiler to check your syntax. But of course, since the method bodies are not defined, it is useless to attempt to run the programs.

Problem, Analysis, Design

1. The formula for converting from Fahrenheit to Celsius is

    Fahrenheit = 1.8 × Celsius + 32

    Write a program that will convert from Celsius to Fahrenheit. Write a second program that will convert from Fahrenheit to Celsius. Use the same support class for both applications.

2. Write a program that converts a number of seconds into the equivalent hours, minutes, and seconds.

3. Write a program that reads two data items and computes their sum, difference, product, and quotient.

4. Given the length and width of a rectangular yard, and the length and width of a rectangular house situated in the yard, compute the time required (in minutes) to cut the grass at the rate of 2.3 square meters a second.

5. Write a program that calculates the cost of an automobile trip given the distance traveled, the average cost of a gallon of gas, and the EPA mileage rating for your car in miles per gallon.

Interview

Kim Polese

Kim Polese is president and CEO of Marimba, Inc., a recognized leader in application distribution and management solutions for the Internet. Prior to Marimba, Ms. Polese worked at Sun Microsystems as the product manager for Java (known then as Oak). She holds a B.S. in biophysics from the University of California, Berkeley and studied computer science at the University of Washington, Seattle.

What is your educational background? Why did you decide to study computer science?

I was always interested in science as a child, I even had my own chemistry set. I studied biophysics at the University of California at Berkeley, and while there I started taking courses in computer science. I enjoyed my coursework so much that I decided to teach others about computer science. After my courses, I would teach programming at a local museum. After Berkeley, I realized that I still wanted to learn more about computer science, so I spent a year at the University of Washington, then moved out to Silicon Valley.

What was your first job in the computer industry? What did it entail?

My first job was at IntelliCorp, a company that creates expert systems-building tools. Expert systems are systems that mimic human reasoning; for example, one might automate the movement on a factory floor. The technology was a bit ahead of its time, however, because the AI technology ran on expensive machines and was too complex. In 1989, after spending three years there, I left to become the product manager for C++ at Sun. This was a great experience because I had both technical responsibilities (giving presentations/talks, working closely with the engineers) and creative responsibilities (working on the branding of the product, business development, pricing). I learned so much in that job and was actively involved in the creation of a product.

You worked as the product manager for Java (then known as Oak) at Sun Microsystems for several years. What are some of the advantages that Java offers over other programming languages that have made it so successful?

I worked for three years at a small spinout of Sun called FirstPerson, which was designed to commercialize the new Oak language. I was the only nonengineer on the team, so I learned a lot. I had a number of responsibilities including marketing and charting the strategy for Oak. It was a challenge because I had no one above me telling me what to do.

Java was designed for a networked world. The Internet was just beginning to explode when Java was created. Web pages weren't interactive then, they were just text with no animation. Using Java, we created live spreadsheets that would calculate financial changes based on the stock market. This technology blew people away. The two great things about Java are that it is designed for a networked world with a simple, familiar syntax and it has a "killer app." When Sun built the interactive Web browser hotJava it allowed people to see Java's real potential.

How would you describe a typical day for you now that you're at Marimba? What is the most challenging part of your job?

At Marimba, we work on using Java to enable application distribution and management over the Internet with the simplicity of the "click and run" of a URL. We want to provide a full interactive multimedia experience with ease. I meet with many different people during the day. Typically, I spend some time meeting with our sales team and discussing the status of our accounts (how deals are coming, what the next step might be). I also meet one on one with our executives and employees. I have an open door policy—I'll listen to anyone with an idea. I also hold weekly staff meetings, give talks on our products, meet with our customers, work out our vision for the Internet, and go over internal operations such as the budget.

The biggest challenge for me is plotting a chart in the market. The market is moving so fast that its difficult to listen to customers' needs while also anticipating the next change. It's like driving a car at a very high speed and needing to see what lies around the corner. To help me anticipate changes in the market, I meet with some very smart people. I seek out research analysts, venture capitalists, and others to learn more about where the market is going and develop a strategy for our company.

What person in the computer industry has inspired you?

Scott McNealy, the founder and CEO of Sun Microsystems. He has guided Sun from its infancy to the multi-billion dollar company it is today. Through all of their growth, he has managed to successfully recreate the company. I also admire his attitude towards work. He places an emphasis on getting work done while also having fun. Sun employees know how to beat the competition and still enjoy themselves.

Do you have any advice for students who are currently learning Java and/or anyone entering the field of computer science?

Stay in touch with the market and its changes. Go on the Internet and search out interesting new products, and get on newsgroups for new companies. Technology is changing so fast that it's crucial to keep up with the pace of change. Find a need in the market and create an idea to meet that need.

Methods, Statements, and Expressions

Chapter 2 discussed how to design a Java program, focusing on how to declare the parts of a program, including classes, data fields, and methods. You learned that data fields store an object's information, and that methods process the object's information.

We begin by looking at the methods for the `ConvertFabric` program in Chapter 2. First, we introduce statements for performing arithmetic computations. Next, we introduce statements for manipulating strings. We show how to use method calls as statements by themselves, and how to embed them in expressions.

The chapter's case studies show you how to define operations in methods. The first case illustrates arithmetic operations, and the second case illustrates string processing. We also discuss some issues of good programming style and introduce program debugging.

3.1 Method Bodies: Where the Action Takes Place

3.2 Calling Methods

3.3 Assignment Statements

3.4 Operations and Expressions

3.5 Processing Integers
Case Study: Evaluating Coins

3.6 Processing Strings
Case Study: Pig Latin

3.7 Writing Code with Style

3.8 Common Errors and Debugging

Chapter Review

3.1 Method Bodies: Where the Action Takes Place

By way of review, a method takes some data as input, operates on that data, and outputs a result. Figures 3.1 and 3.2 show the classes defined for the fabric conversion program (Figs. 2.3 and 2.4). These classes illustrate different ways that a method gets input data and returns output data.

```java
/*  File: PieceOfFabric.java
    Developed for Problem Solving with Java, Koffman & Wolz
    Appears in Figure 2.2 and 3.1
*/
import simpleIO.*;

public class PieceOfFabric extends SimpleGUI {
    // Data fields
    private double sqMeters;  // input - measurement in sq. meters

    // Methods
    // Converts a measurement in square yards to square meters.
    public double toSqYards() {
        double conversionFactor = 1.196;
        return conversionFactor * sqMeters;
    }

    // Reads a measurement in square meters.
    public void readSqMeters() {
        sqMeters = getDouble("Enter the fabric area in sq. meters:");
    }

    // Calculates and displays the result.
    public void displayFabric() {
        displayString("The fabric size is " + sqMeters +
                    " square meters or " + toSqYards() +
                    " square yards.");
    }
} // Class PieceOfFabric
```

Figure 3.1 Class PieceOfFabric

```java
/*    File: ConvertFabric.java
      Developed for Problem Solving with Java, Koffman & Wolz
      Appears in Figure 2.3 and 3.2
*/
public class ConvertFabric {
```

Figure 3.2 *continued*

Figure 3.2 *continued*

```
    // Methods
    public static void main(String[] args) {

        // Create an instance of a piece of fabric object.
        PieceOfFabric  aPiece = new PieceOfFabric();

        // Get the object's data from the user.
        aPiece.readSqMeters();

        // Display the result in a meaningful way.
        aPiece.displayFabric();
    }
} // Class ConvertFabric
```

Figure 3.2 Class **ConvertFabric**

Statements

This chapter introduces two important concepts: statement and expression. A **statement** is an instruction that causes the computer to perform an operation. An **expression** is Java code that produces a result. At first glance these ideas may seem the same, but they are not. For example, expressions may be part of statements, but the converse is not true.

The **method body** is the part of the method declaration enclosed in braces { }. A group of statements enclosed in braces is called a **block**. The statements in a block are executed in sequence, one after the other. Each statement ends with a semicolon.

Methods contain two kinds of statements: data declarations and executable statements. The **data declarations** tell the Java compiler what kind of storage locations to allocate and what kinds of operations can be performed.

The **executable statements** instruct the computer how to process the information in storage. The Java compiler translates the executable statements into byte code; the Java interpreter converts these statements into machine-executable code when we run the program. Table 3.1 lists the basic kinds of Java statements.

statement:
an instruction that performs an operation.

expression:
Java code that produces a result.

method body:
the part of the method enclosed in braces { }.

block:
a sequence of statements executed in order and enclosed in braces { }.

data declarations:
statements that tell the Java compiler what kind of storage locations to allocate and what kinds of operations can be performed.

executable statements:
statements that tell the computer how to process the information in storage.

Table 3.1 Java statements

Statement kind	Chapters that cover
Data declaration	2, 3
Object instance creation (a kind of data declaration)	3
Method call	3
Assignment	3
Block	3, 4
Selection	5
Repetition	6

Program, Methods, and Statements

An executable statement does something. Under most circumstances it takes input values, performs an operation, and does something with a result. Does this sound familiar? A program uses objects, objects use methods, and methods use statements to refine the algorithm defined in the software development method. You might wonder why we need all the intermediate baggage. You could just write a program as a sequence of statements. However, when programs get very large it becomes hard to manage the organization of the statements without some kind of intermediate structure. Classes and methods provide that structure.

Data Declarations

variable:
a storage location whose contents can change during program execution.

You saw the general form of data declarations in Chapter 2. Recall that a data declaration tells the compiler to allocate storage space for a value of a particular type. When the contents of that storage space can change during the execution of a program, we refer to that space as a **variable**. The type of a variable can be a class type or one of the primitive types. The declaration provides a name or identifier for the variable. It also establishes its visibility and may provide an initial value.

Data declarations can be used to declare the data fields of a class, or to declare data that is private to a block. For example, in Fig. 3.1, the statement

```
private double sqMeters;
```

declares a data field for a `PieceOfFabric` object. Field `sqMeters` stores a value of type `double` that is visible or accessible only to the object in which it appears.

Creating an Object Instance

object instantiation:
creation of an instance of a class (an object) and assigning that instance to a particular variable of that

The `main` method of class `ConvertFabric` (Fig. 3.2) must process an object of class `PieceOfFabric`, so we need to create a variable whose type will be class `PieceOfFabric`. An **object instantiation** creates an instance of a class and declares a variable of that type. In method `main`, the statement

```
PieceOfFabric aPiece = new PieceOfFabric();
```

creates the object instance `aPiece`. The words to the right of the equal sign tell the Java compiler to create a new `PieceOfFabric` object. The words to the left tell the compiler that the type of the variable `aPiece` is the class `PieceOfFabric`. The equal sign tells the compiler to assign the object just created to the variable `aPiece`.

Notice that the data declaration above does not include a visibility modifier. It doesn't need to. The visibility of data declared in a method is always restricted to the block that declares it; that is, only statements within method `main` may refer to the variable `aPiece`. No other method or object may refer to this variable.

Default Constructors

You may wonder why the identifier `PieceOfFabric` appears twice, once at the beginning and once at the end of the statement. The first reference tells the compiler the data type (`PieceOfFabric`) of variable `aPiece`. The second reference `PieceOfFabric()` includes parentheses because it is a method reference—it invokes or calls a special kind of method called a **constructor**. The constructors (there can be more than one) for an object have the same name as the object class. The constructor method tells the compiler how much space the object instance will need and the initial values of its data fields.

When you define a class, you can also define the constructors for that class. If you neglect to do this (the case in Fig. 3.2), the Java compiler creates a **default constructor**. The default constructor sets the initial values of object data fields using the rules in Table 3.2.

constructor:
a method of a class used to create an instance of the object class. The constructor initializes the data fields of the object instance.

default constructor:
the constructor that is automatically created by Java in the absence of programmer-defined constructors.

Table 3.2 Default initialization for data fields

Type	Default initialization
Integers or real numbers	0
Boolean values	false
Characters	The first character in the Unicode character set
Objects	The "null" or "empty" object

When you create the object instance `aPiece`, you invoke the default constructor. The default constructor sets the initial value of `sqMeters` to 0 (See Fig. 3.3).

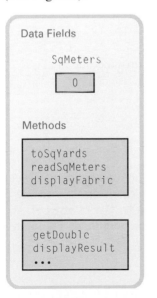

Figure 3.3 Initial state of object `aPiece`

Syntax Display

Creating an Object Instance

Form: *className variableName* = new *classConstructor*([*arguments*]);

Example: PieceOfFabric aPiece = new PieceOfFabric();
Automobile myCar = new Automobile(4, "Neon");

Interpretation: Object *variableName*, an instance of class *className*, is created. The constructor classConstructor is invoked and initializes the data fields of *variableName*. If there are no *arguments*, the default constructor is invoked. If *arguments* are passed to the constructor, a programmer-defined constructor with a matching argument list is invoked instead.

EXERCISES FOR SECTION 3.1

Self-Check

1. What are the two basic kinds of statements?
2. Explain the difference between an expression and a statement.
3. What will be the initial values of the data fields of an object of type MyClass.

   ```
   public class MyClass {
       // Data fields
       private int x;
       private double y;
       private char z = 'a';
       private boolean testResult;
   ```

4. Explain what happens in the following statement:

   ```
   MyClass x = new MyClass();
   ```

5. What is a constructor and why don't we need to provide one in class PieceOfFabric?

3.2 Calling Methods

To process object aPiece in method main (Fig. 3.2), we must be able to access the information in its data fields. However, the data fields of object aPiece have private visibility, so we cannot access them directly inside a method defined in another class (main is defined in ConvertFabric). We can only access this data by using aPiece's public methods. The statements

```
aPiece.readSqMeters();
aPiece.displayFabric();
```

apply the `readSqMeters` method and the `displayFabric` method (defined in class `PieceOfFabric`) to object `aPiece`. When you apply a method to an object instance, the statements in the method body execute and process the information stored in that object instance.

To apply a method to an object instance, you write the object name, a period or "dot," and the method name followed by its arguments (if any) in parentheses:

objectName . methodName (arguments)

An empty pair of parentheses indicates that a method does not have arguments. Notice that there are no spaces around the dot.

If you look at the definitions of methods `readSqMeters` and `displayFabric` in class `PieceOfFabric` (Fig. 3.1), you will see that they are declared as returning `void`, which means they do not return a result

```
public void readSqMeters() {...}
public void displayFabric() {...}
```

A method that doesn't return anything typically gets or puts data somewhere. For example, `readSqMeters` gets data from a user and stores the result in the data field `sqMeters`, and method `displayFabric` reports a result to the user.

Argument List for `displayResult`

Just as method `main` calls `displayFabric`, method `displayFabric` calls upon the `SimpleGUI` method `displayResult` to provide an informative display to the user.

```
public void displayFabric() {
    displayResult("The fabric size is " + sqMeters +
                " square meters or " + toSqYards() +
                " square yards");
}
```

Recall from Chapter 2 that a method can get input from its argument list. When this list exists, it appears inside the parentheses. Method `displayResult` takes a single argument of type `String`. You can pass a string literal, or you can pass an expression that produces a `String` value:

```
"The fabric size is " + sqMeters +
" square meters or " + toSqYards() +
" square yards"
```

There is a lot going on in this expression. We will look at it in detail in Section 3.4. The key point is that `displayFabric` is supposed to informatively show the user the state of object `aPiece`. To do this, it passes a single argument (in the form of an expression) to `displayResult`. Method `displayResult` does the actual work of displaying in the GUI window the string that results from the expression.

Referencing an Object's Data and Methods Inside Its Class

The references to data field `sqMeters` in method `displayFabric` is not preceded by an object name. Recall that the data fields and methods of a class belong to each object instance. The Java compiler assumes that the data fields being referenced belong to the object to which `displayFabric` was applied (`aPiece` in this case). Methods that belong to an object may refer to each other and to the data fields of that object without specifying the object.

For the same reason, method `displayResult` (defined in class `SimpleGUI`) is not preceded by an object name. Recall that class `PieceOfFabric` extends `SimpleGUI`, so it inherits all of `SimpleGUI`'s methods. Therefore, all of `SimpleGUI`'s methods belong to each object instance of class `PieceOfFabric` as well. In Fig. 3.3, we list the `SimpleGUI` methods actually used by object `aPiece` in the gray box; we use the ellipses to indicate that the other `SimpleGUI` methods also belong to `aPiece`.

Using methods inside other methods reduces the effort of the programmer. Instead of having to specify each detail of a task, the calling method relies on the method it calls to implement the details. For example, the `SimpleGUI` method `displayResult` knows how to display its argument string inside a window. This is a fairly complicated task. Instead of doing all these steps ourselves, we let `displayResult` do it for us.

Syntax Display   *Method Call*

Form: [*objectName* .]*methodName* ([*argumentList*])

Examples: `toSqYards()`
     `aPiece.readSqYards()`
     `displayResult("The value of x is " + x)`

Interpretation: Method *methodName* is applied to object instance *objectName* and the statements in the method body start to execute. You should specify *objectName* only if method *methodName* is called by another method that does not belong to the object instance. Otherwise, *methodName* is applied to the same object instance as was the method that called it.

Arguments are passed to a method through its *argumentList*. The arguments consist of a list of expressions, variables, or values separated by commas. The number of arguments in the method call should be the same as the number of arguments in the method definition. The data type of each argument in the call should be compatible with the data type of its corresponding argument in the method definition. Argument correspondence is determined by position in each list (that is, the first argument in the call corresponds to the first argument in the method definition, and so on).

Methods That Return Values

All the methods defined in Figs. 3.1 and 3.2 (except for toSqYards) are type void, which means they do not return a result. Methods can also return values, and calls to such methods can appear in expressions. For example, the body of method readSqMeters:

```
public void readSqMeters() {
   sqMeters =
       getDouble("Enter the fabric area in sq. meters:");
}
```

contains a call to method getDouble (defined in class SimpleGUI) which returns a type double value provided by the user. This value is then stored in data field sqMeters of object aPiece. Notice that method getDouble (like displayResult) takes a type String argument—the prompting message that it displays to the program user.

The statement in the body of method readSqMeters is an assignment statement. We discuss assignment statements in detail in Section 3.3. However, you can probably guess that the value returned by method getDouble is assigned to (or stored in) data field sqMeters of object aPiece.

The only method definition left to consider is that of method toSqYards:

```
public double toSqYards() {
   double conversionFactor = 1.196;
   return conversionFactor * sqMeters;
}
```

The method header says that toSqYards will return a value of type double. The data declaration sets the value of conversionFactor (type double) to 1.196. This variable is visible only within method toSqYards. The **return statement** tells the compiler that the expression following return should be used to calculate the return value or method result. In this example, the result will be the product (* means multiply) of the values of conversionFactor and sqMeters.

return statement: a statement that returns a result from a method.

Syntax Display

Return Statement

Form: return *expression*;

Example: return x + y;

Interpretation: The keyword return tells the compiler that the expression that follows calculates the return value of the method. The data type of the expression must match the type specified for the return value in the declaration of the method.

The expression in the return statement can be any valid expression of the correct type. A syntax error occurs if the expression does not match the type of the return value as declared in the method header. For example, method demo1 below attempts to return a string, instead of a type double value, and causes the error indicated.

```
// incorrect method definition
public double demo() {
    return "This is a string not a double";
}
```

```
Error: Incompatible type for return. Can't convert
java.lang.String to double.
```

The last statement in a method that returns a value must be a return statement. If it is not, you will see a message of the form

```
Error: Return required at end of ... .
```

SimpleGUI Methods

So far we used methods getDouble and displayResult from class SimpleGUI. Table 3.3 describes all the SimpleGUI methods that we use in this book. The first, displayResult, is type void and must be called with a single argument that is displayed in the output area of a GUI window. The argument may be a String, as shown in the sample call, or any primitive type. Each method whose name begins with get displays a prompt (the string passed as its first argument) and returns a value that the program user enters in the GUI window. The data type of the returned value must be the same as the second half of the method name (for example, type int for method getInt). If the user enters an incorrect type data item, it will not be accepted and the user must try again. For methods getChar and getString, the user types in the character or characters without enclosing them in quotation marks.

Table 3.3 `SimpleGUI` methods

Sample call	Description
`displayResult("Value of x is " + x)`	A `void` method that displays its output argument in a GUI window. The output argument may be any primitive type or type `String`.
`getInt("Number of pennies:")`	A type `int` method that displays a prompt (type `String`) in a GUI window and returns as its result the type `int` data item entered by the user.
`getInt("Number of kids:", min, max)`	The type `int` data entered must lie between `min` and `max`, inclusive.
`getDouble("Size in yards:")`	A type `double` method that performs data entry for type `double` data.
`getDouble("Volts:", -12.5, 12.5)`	The type `double` data entered must lie between `-12.5` and `12.5`, inclusive.
`getChar("Enter a character:")`	A type `char` method that performs data entry for type `char` data.
`getChar("Enter lowercase:", 'a', 'z')`	The data entered must be a lowercase letter (between `'a'` and `'z'`, inclusive).
`getChar("Enter uppercase:", 'A', 'Z')`	The data entered must be an uppercase letter (between `'A'` and `'Z'`, inclusive).
`getChar("Enter a digit:", '0', '9')`	The data entered must be a digit character (between `'0'` and `'9'`, inclusive).
`getString("Enter your name:");`	The data entered may be any sequence of characters excluding the double quote character.
`getBoolean("Are you single?", "yes", "no")`	Returns a value of `true` or `false`.

Note that methods `getInt`, `getDouble`, and `getChar` can be called with either one argument or three arguments. In the latter case, the last two arguments represent the range of a valid data item. If the user enters data that is outside of this range, they will not be accepted and the user must try again. The method call `getChar("Enter a small letter", 'a', 'z')` returns a character value between `'a'` and `'z'` that must be a lowercase letter. This method relies on the fact that the lowercase letters are an increasing sequence of characters (as are the uppercase letters and the digit characters). We explain method `getBoolean` in Section 5.2.

EXERCISES FOR SECTION 3.2

Self-Check

1. Explain why methods `displayFabric` and `readSqMeters` in Fig. 3.1 don't end with a `return` statement but method `toSqYards` does.

2. What does the word `void` mean in a method definition?

3. Explain why the statement

   ```
   return true;
   ```

   cannot appear in method `toSqYards` shown in Fig. 3.1.

4. Explain what each of the method calls below does.

   a. `n = getDouble("Enter your age:", 21, 100);`

   b. `ch = getChar("Enter your choice", 'a', 'e');`

   c. `s = getString("Enter your name");`

   d. `x = getDouble("What is your salary?":);`

5. Write a statement to do each of the following:

   a. Enter a number between –5.5 and 7.7.

   b. Enter a person's first initial (uppercase letter).

   c. Enter a positive integer less than 100.

   d. Enter your astrological sign.

Programming

1. For class `PieceOfFabric`, write method `toSqMeters` which converts the value in data field `sqYards` to square meters.

2. For the class that begins with

   ```
   public class MyClass extends SimpleGUI {
       private int x;
       private int y;
       private int z;
   ```

   write a method `readData` that reads and stores data typed in by a program user into the data fields shown. *Hint:* Call `SimpleGUI` method `getInt` to read each data item.

3. For the class in Exercise 2 above, write method `displayData` that displays the values of the three data fields. *Hint:* Call `SimpleGUI` method `displayResult`.

4. Write method `readSqYards` that gets a measurement in square yards from the user and stores it in a `PieceOfFabric` object.

3.3 Assignment Statements

Method `readSqMeters` (discussed in the last section) reads the fabric size in square meters. Although `getDouble` does all the work of actually displaying a prompt in a GUI window and checking that the value the user enters is type `double`, `readSqMeters` actually stores in data field `sqMeters` the data that `getDouble` got from the user. To do this, `readSqMeters` uses the assignment statement

```
sqMeters =
        getDouble("Enter the fabric area in sq. meters:");
```

An **assignment statement** stores a value or a computational result in a variable. This assignment statement says to store the result returned by `getDouble` in the data field `sqMeters`. In Java, the symbol = is the **assignment operator**. Read = as "becomes," "gets," or "takes the value of" rather than "equals."

Let's look at what happens when the assignment statement above executes. Figure 3.4 shows the initial value of `sqMeters` is zero. After the return from `getDouble`, the value (2.0) that was entered by the user replaces the initial value.

> **assignment statement:**
> an instruction that stores a value or a computational result in a variable.
>
> **assignment operator:**
> the symbol =, which means "becomes," "gets," or "takes the value of."

sqMeters
0.0 2.0   ← 2.0   Enter ... meters:
                      2.0
result of
getDouble

Figure 3.4 Effect of assignment statement in `readSqMeters`

Assignment Statement

Form: *variable = expression;*

Example: x = y + z + 2.0;

Interpretation: The *variable* before = is assigned the value of the *expression* after it. The previous value of *variable* is lost. The *expression* can be a variable, a constant, a literal, or a combination of these connected by appropriate operators (for example, +, -, /, and *). The data type of *expression* and *variable* must be the same. The one exception is that *expression* can be an integer type when *variable* is a real type.

EXAMPLE 3.1

In Java you can write assignment statements of the form

```
sum = sum + item;
```

where the variable `sum` appears on both sides of the assignment operator. This is obviously not an algebraic equation, but it illustrates a common programming practice. This statement instructs the computer to add the current value of `sum` to the value of `item`; the result is then stored back into `sum`. The previous value of `sum` is overwritten, as illustrated in Fig. 3.5. The value of `item`, however, is unchanged.

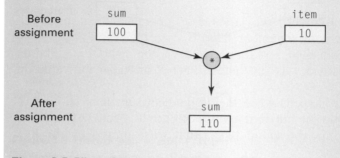

Figure 3.5 Effect of `sum = sum + item;`

EXAMPLE 3.2

You can also write assignment statements that assign the value of one variable to another variable. If `x` and `newX` are type `double` variables, the statement

```
newX = x;
```

copies the value of variable `x` into variable `newX`. The statement

```
newX = -x;
```

instructs the computer to get the value of `x`, negate that value, and store the result in `newX`. For example, if `x` is 3.5, `newX` is –3.5. Neither of the assignment statements above changes the value of `x`.

EXAMPLE 3.3

Assuming `ch` is type `char`, `boolVar` is type `boolean`, and `name` is type `String`, the three assignment statements that follow are all valid in Java.

```
ch = 'C';
boolVar = true;
name = "Alice";
```

Next, we show memory after these statements execute. Note that the quotation marks are not stored with character or string data. The `boolean` value `true` is stored in `boolVar`, not the string `"true"`.

```
ch        boolVar      name
C           true         Alice
```

Because Java represents the values of each data type differently, the value being assigned must be **assignment compatible** with the variable receiving it. For now, this means that the variable and value must be the same type, unless the value is one of the integer types (such as `int`) and the variable receiving it is one of the real types (such as `double`). The assignment statements below are invalid for the reasons given.

assignment compatible: an expression value on the right of the assignment operator that can be assigned to the variable of

`ch = name;`	Error: Incompatible type for =. Can't convert `java.lang.String` to `char`.
`name = ch;`	Error: Incompatible type for =. Can't convert `char` to `java.lang.String`.
`boolVar = "false";`	Error : Incompatible type for =. Can't convert `Java.lang.String` to `boolean`.

Object Creation as Assignment Statement

Is an object creation statement a data declaration or an assignment statement? The answer is both. You can write the first statement in our `main` method as:

```
PieceOfFabric apiece;
apiece = new PieceOfFabric();
```

In fact, all declarations that include an initialization could be written this way. We write them as single statements to make it clear that an initial value is being stored.

EXERCISES FOR SECTION 3.3

Self-Check

1. Indicate whether each assignment below is valid and indicate the result of each valid assignment. Assume `r` is type `double`, `i` is type `int`, `b` is type `boolean`, `c` is type `char`, and `s` is type `String`.

   a. `r = 3.5 + 5.0;`   **f.** `s = c;`

   b. `i = 2 * 5;`   **g.** `c = s;`

   c. `c = 'my name';`   **h.** `r = i;`

   d. `s = your name;`   **i.** `i = r;`

   e. `b = boolean;`   **j.** `r = 10 + i;`

Programming

1. Write statements that ask the user to enter three integers and that read the three user responses into `first`, `second`, and `third`.

2. **a.** Write a statement that displays the line below with the value of x at the end.

    ```
    The value of x is _____ .
    ```

    b. Assuming `radius` and `area` are real data fields containing the radius and area of a circle, write a statement that will display this information in the form:

    ```
    The area of a circle with radius _____ is
    _____ .
    ```

3. Write a program that asks the user to enter the radius of a circle and then computes and displays the circle's area. Use the formula

    area = pi × radius × radius

    where *pi* is the constant `3.14159`.

3.4 Operations and Expressions

Most of the assignment statements in Section 3.3 were not very complicated because the expressions on the right-hand side of the assignment operator = were pretty straightforward. But expressions can be very complex, involving a number of operations, variables, and method calls.

Arithmetic Operations

To solve most programming problems, you will need to write arithmetic expressions that manipulate integer or real data. This section describes the operators used in arithmetic expressions and rules for writing and evaluating the expressions.

Table 3.4 shows all the arithmetic operators. Each operator manipulates two operands that may be variables, methods that return numeric results, or other arithmetic expressions. The operators may be used with both real and integer types. The +, −, and * operators behave as expected. When the operands are integers, an integer result is produced. When the operands are reals, a real result is produced.

The division operator behaves differently depending on whether its operands are integers or reals. If one or both operands are reals, the division operator gives the result of the real division. If both operands are integers, the division operator gives the integer part of the real division as its result. Consider the following variables:

```
int x = 5;
double r = 5.0;
```

The expression r / 2 gives the result 2.5. The expression x / 2 gives the result 2 which is the integer part of 2.5. The fractional part (0.5) is lost.

The % operator is the remainder operator. It returns the integer remainder of the division. For example x % 2 returns 1, which is what is "left over" after the integer division.

Table 3.4 Arithmetic operators

Arithmetic operator	Meaning	Example
+	Addition	5 + 2 is 7. 5.0 + 2.0 is 7.0.
−	Subtraction	5 - 2 is 3. 5.0 - 2.0 is 3.0.
*	Multiplication	5 * 2 is 10. 5.0 * 2.0 is 10.0.
/	Division	5.0 / 2.0 is 2.5. 5 / 2 is 2.
%	Remainder operator	5 % 2 is 1.

Data Type of an Operation

We indicated earlier that an expression that gives an integer result could be assigned to a variable of type double, but not vice versa. A **mixed-type expression** has operands of more than one type. For example, it may have both int and double operands.

mixed-type expression: an expression having operands of different types.

How does Java determine the data type of an arithmetic operation? The following rule applies:

> The type of the result of an arithmetic operation will be double if an operand is type double. If both operands are type int, then the result will be type int.

This means that if i is type int and x is type double, any expression involving i and x as operands gives a type double result. For example, the expression i * x gives a type double result. To calculate this result, Java multiplies the type double equivalent of i (a real number with a fractional part of zero) by the type double value stored in x.

Mixed-Type Assignment Statement

When an assignment statement is executed, the expression is first evaluated and then the result is assigned to the variable preceding the assignment operator =. Either a type double or a type int expression may be assigned to a type `double` variable. Thus, if `m` and `n` are type `int` and `x` and `y` are type `double`, all the following assignment statements are valid:

```
m = 3;
n = 2;
y = m + n;        //assigns 5 to y -
                  //stored as a real number
x = y + m / n;    //assigns 6 to x -
                  //stored as a real number
```

mixed-type assignment: an assignment of an expression of one type to a variable of another type. The only valid mixed-type assignment is one that assigns a type `int` expression to a type `double` variable.

The last two statements are examples of **mixed-type assignment** statements because the variable being assigned and the expression have different data types. The only valid mixed-type assignment in Java, is assignment of a type `int` value to a type `double` value. The type `double` equivalent of the value is actually stored in the variable.

In the last statement, the expression `m  /  n` involves two integers and gives an integer result (1). This value is converted to its type `double` equivalent before being added to `y` (type `double`). Notice that the type conversion is done after the two integer values are divided and not before. If it were done before, the value `6.5` would have been stored in `x`, not `6.0`. (Why?)

Java does not allow a type `double` expression to be assigned to a type `int` variable because the fractional part of the expression cannot be represented and will be lost. This means that the following mixed-type assignment statements are invalid if `count` is type `int` and `average` is type `double`.

`count = 3.5;`	Invalid—assignment of `double` value to `int` variable
`count = count + 1.0;`	Invalid—`1.0` is `double`, so result is `double`
`count = average / count;`	Invalid—result of division is `double`

Each statement above causes this error message:

```
Error: Incompatible type for =. Explicit cast needed to
convert double to int.
```

Casting Operations for Type Conversion

type casting: creating a value of one type from an expression of another type.

You can use **type casting** to create a value of one data type from another. For example, if `x` (type `double`) is `7.8`, the expression

```
(int) x
```

evaluates to `7`, the type `int` value formed by truncating or removing the fractional part of `x`. If `m` is type `int`, the assignment statement

```
m = (int) x;
```

is valid and assigns the integer value `7` to `m`.

Similarly, you can use type casting to create a type `double` value from a type `int` value. If m (type `int`) has the value 6, the result of the expression

`(double) m`

is the real number equivalent to 6, or 6.0, which has a fractional part of zero.

Expressions with Multiple Operators

In our examples so far, most expressions had a single operator; however, expressions with multiple operators are common. To understand and write expressions with multiple operators, we must know the Java rules for evaluating expressions. For example, in the expression 10 + 5 / 2, is + performed before /, or vice versa? In the expression 10 / 5 * 2, is / performed before *, or vice versa? Verify for yourself that the order of operator evaluation does make a difference. In both expressions, the / operator is evaluated first; the reasons are explained in the Java rules for expression evaluation that follow. These rules are based on familiar algebraic rules.

Rules for Evaluating Expressions

a. *Parentheses rule:* All expressions in parentheses must be evaluated separately. Nested parenthesized expressions must be evaluated from the inside out, with the innermost expression evaluated first.

b. *Operator precedence rule:* Operators in the same expression are evaluated in the order determined by their precedence (from highest to lowest):

Operator	Precedence
Method call	Highest precedence
– (unary minus)	
new, type cast	
*, /, %	
+, –	
=	Lowest precedence

c. *Left associative rule:* Operators in the same expression and at the same precedence level (such as + and –) are evaluated in left-to-right order.

These rules will help you understand how Java evaluates expressions. Use parentheses as needed to specify the order of evaluation. Often it is a good idea in complicated expressions to use extra parentheses to document clearly the order of operator evaluation. For example, the expression

`x * y * z + a / b - c * d`

can be written in a more readable form using parentheses:

```
(x * y * z ) + (a / b) - (c * d)
```

The formula for the area of a circle

$$a = \pi r^2$$

can be written in Java as

```
area = pi * radius * radius;
```

where `pi` is the constant 3.14159. Figure 3.6 shows the evaluation tree for this formula. In this tree, which you read from top to bottom, arrows connect each operand with its operator. The order of operator evaluation is shown by the number to the left of each operator; the letter to the right of the operator indicates which evaluation rule applies.

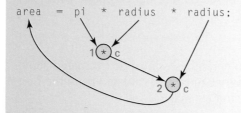

Figure 3.6 Evaluation tree for `area = pi * radius * radius;`

The formula for the average velocity, *v*, of a particle traveling on a line between points p_1 and p_2 in time t_1 to t_2 is

$$v = \frac{p_2 - p_1}{t_2 - t_1}$$

This formula can be written and evaluated in Java as shown in Fig. 3.7.

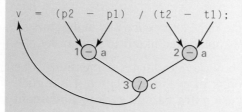

Figure 3.7 Evaluation tree for $v = (p_2 - p_1) / (t_2 - t_1)$

Consider the expression

```
z - (a + b / 2 ) + w * y
```

containing int variables only. The parenthesized expression (a + b / 2) is evaluated first (rule a) beginning with b / 2 (rule b). Once the value of b / 2 is determined, it can be added to a to obtain the value of (a + b / 2). Next the multiplication operation is performed (rule b), and the value for w * y is determined. Then the value of (a + b / 2) is subtracted from z (rule c). Finally the result is added to w * y. The evaluation tree for this expression is shown in Fig. 3.8.

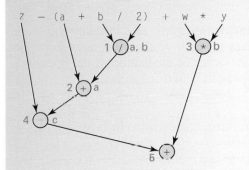

Figure 3.8 Evaluation tree for *z − (a + b / 2) + w * y*

If x (value is 7.8) and y (value is 3.6) are both type double, the expression

```
(int) (x + y)
```

forms the sum x + y (result is 11.4) and then uses casting to create the type int result 11. If m is type int, the assignment statement

```
m = (int) (x + y);
```

is valid and assigns 11 to m.

The parentheses around (x + y) are required in the above statement. If you remove them, the type cast operation (highest precedence) occurs before the addition, so the expression

```
(int) x + y
```

adds the result of the casting operation (int) x (value is 7) to y (value is 3.6). Therefore, the above expression gives the type double result 10.6.

Writing Mathematical Formulas in Java

You may encounter two problems in writing a mathematical formula in Java. First, multiplication often can be implied in a formula by writing the two items to be multiplied next to each other, for example, $a = bc$. In Java, however, you must always use the * operator to indicate multiplication, as in

```
a = b * c;
```

The other difficulty arises in formulas with division. We normally write the numerator and the denominator on separate lines:

$$m = \frac{y - b}{x - a}$$

In Java, however, the numerator and denominator are placed on the same line. Consequently, we use parentheses to separate the numerator from the denominator and to clearly indicate the order of evaluation of the operators in the expression. The above formula would be written in Java as

```
m = (y - b) / (x - a);
```

Table 3.5 shows several mathematical formulas rewritten in Java.

Table 3.5 Mathematical formulas as Java expressions

Mathematical formula	Java expression
1. $b^2 - 4ac$	b * b - 4 * a * c
2. $a + b - c$	a + b - c
3. $\dfrac{a + b}{c + d}$	(a + b) / (c + d)
4. $\dfrac{1}{1 + x^2}$	1 / (1 + x * x)
5. $a \times [\text{-}(b + c)]$	a * (-(b + c))

The points illustrated in these examples can be summarized as follows:

- Always specify multiplication explicitly by using the operator * where needed (formulas 1 & 4).
- Use parentheses when required to control the order of operator evaluation (formulas 3 & 4).
- Never write two arithmetic operators in succession; they must be separated by an operand or an open parenthesis (formula 5).

Unary minus The fifth Java expression in Table 3.5 uses a unary minus to negate the value of (b + c) before performing the multiplication. The unary minus has only one operand and has higher precedence than the subtraction operator.

Expressions Involving Strings

Strings are objects in Java. There is only one string operator: +. As you've probably realized from the fabric conversion program, the operator + **concatenates** or joins two strings together. You can perform other operations on strings using Java's `String` methods (defined in class `String`).

concatenate:
to join two string operands by the operator +.

EXAMPLE 3.8

The argument in the call to `displayResult` (in method `displayFabric`) is a string expression with three + operators and five operands—three are string literals, one is a type `double` variable, and one is a method call.

```
"The fabric size is " + sqMeters +
" square meters or " + toSqYards() + " square yards"
```

The concatenation operations create one long string from the values of the five operands. For example, if the value of `sqMeters` is 2, then the argument string passed to `displayResult` is:

```
"The fabric size is 2 square meters or 2.388 sq. yards"
```

Note that the string concatenation operator accepts a primitive type, such as `double` or `int`, as an operand, as well as type `String`. Java actually creates a string value for each primitive type operand and uses it in the concatenation.

Don't forget to include a space at the beginning or end of a string literal if you want a space to appear between it and a number that is joined to it. You cannot split a string literal in the middle and continue it on the next line.

EXAMPLE 3.9

The string expression below ends with the arithmetic expression x * y.

```
"The value of " + x + " * " + y + " is " + x * y
```

If x is 4.5 and y is 5.2, the string expression evaluates to

```
"The value of 4.5 * 5.2 is 23.4"
```

where 23.4 is the value of x * y. Note that the + operations are evaluated in left-to-right order and that * has higher precedence than +. If we change the * operator to + in the expression

```
"The value of " + x + " + " + y + " is " + x + y
```

we get the string

```
"The value of 4.5 + 5.2 is 4.55.2"
```

which is not what we expected. The characters `4.55.2` at the right are the concatenation of `"4.5"` and `"5.2"`, not the sum of `4.5` and `5.2`. Because the + operators are evaluated in left-to-right sequence, each + operator has at least one string operand and its meaning is interpreted as "concatenate." If we write the expression at the end as `(x + y)`

```
"The value of " + x + " + " + y + " is " + (x + y)
```

the last + has two type `double` operands and its meaning is interpreted as "add," so we get the desired result

```
"The value of 4.5 + 5.2 is 9.7"
```

String Methods

Java provides methods in the `String` class (See Appendix A) to perform other common string operations. Table 3.6 describes three of them: `substring`, `charAt`, and `length`. Method `substring` returns part of a string, and method `charAt` returns a particular character in a string. Neither method changes the string to which it is applied. The arguments for these functions are type `int`, and they represent character positions in the string to which they are applied. The first character in the string is at position 0 (returned by `charAt(0)`), the second character is at position 1, and so on. Method `length` returns the number of characters in a string. We show how to use these methods in a case study (Section 3.6).

Table 3.6 String methods

Method call	Description
`"This string".charAt(6)`	Returns the character in string `"This string"` at the position indicated by its argument, where the first character is at position 0. Returns `'t'`.
`"This string".substring(5)`	Returns the part of the string `"This string"` starting at position 5 through the end of the string. Returns `"string"`.
`"This string".substring(5, 7)`	Returns the part of the string `"This string"` starting at position 5 up to, but excluding, position 7. Returns `"st"`.
`"This string".length()`	Returns the length of the string `"This string"`. Returns 11.

EXERCISES FOR SECTION 3.4

Self-Check

1. **a.** Assuming 7 and 22 are integers, evaluate the following expressions with 7 and 22 as operands.

   ```
   22 / 7    7 / 22    22 % 7    7 % 22
   ```

   Repeat the exercise for these pairs of integers:

   b. 15, 16

   c. 3, 23

   d. -4, 16

2. Given the declarations

   ```
   double pi = 3.14159;
   double maxI - 1000;
   double x;
   double y;
   int a;
   int b;
   int i;
   ```

   indicate which statements are valid and find the value of each valid statement. Also indicate which statements are invalid and explain why. Assume that a is 3, b is 4, and y is -1.

   a. `i = a % b`

   b. `i = (990 - maxI) / a`

   c. `i = a % y`

   d. `x = pi * y`

   e. `i = a / b`

   f. `x = a / b`

   g. `x = a % (a / b)`

   h. `i = b / 0`

   i. `i = a % (990 - maxI)`

   j. `i = (maxI - 990) / a`

   k. `x = a / y`

   l. `i = pi * a`

   m. `x - pi / y`

   n. `x = a / b`

   o. `i = (maxI - 990) % a`

   p. `i = a % 0`

   q. `i = a % (maxI - 990)`

3. Draw evaluation trees for the following expressions. What is the value of the last one?

   ```
   1.8 * celsius + 32.0
   (salary - 5000.00) * 0.20 + 1425.00
   10 % 4 + 1 / 2
   ```

4. Write an assignment statement to implement the following equation in Java.

   $$q = \frac{kA(T_1 - T_2)}{L}$$

5. Assume that you have the following variable declarations:

```
int color, lime, straw, yellow, red, orange;
double black, white, green, blue, purple, crayon;
```

Evaluate each of the following statements given these values: `color` is 2, `black` is 2.5, `crayon` is –1.3, `straw` is 1, `red` is 3, `purple` is 0.2e+1.

a. `white = color * 2.5 / purple;`

b. `green = color / purple;`

c. `orange = color / red;`

d. `blue = (color + straw) / (crayon + 0.3);`

e. `lime = red / color + red % color;`

f. `purple = straw / red * color;`

6. Let a, b, c, and x be the names of four type `double` variables and let i, j, and k be the names of three type `int` variables. Each of the following statements contains a violation of the rules for forming arithmetic expressions. Rewrite each statement so it is consistent with the rules.

a. `x = 4.0 a * c;`   **d.** `k = 3(i + j);`

b. `a = ac;`   **e.** `x = 5a / bc;`

c. `i = 2 * -j;`   **f.** `i = 5j3;`

7. Evaluate the string expressions and method calls below.

a. `"value of x is " + 5 * 7`

b. `"value of x is " + 5 + 7`

c. `"value of x is " + (5 + 7)`

d. `"This string".charAt(0);`

e.
```
String test = "This string";
test.charAt(0);
test.charAt(test.length());
test.substring(0);
test.substring(4, test.length() - 1);
```

8. Assuming x is type `double`, n is type `int`, and ch is type `char`, write the assignment statements described below. Use type casting where necessary:

a. Assign x * 1.5 to n.

b. Assign n + 1 to ch.

c. Assign ch to x.

d. Assign the sum of n and ch to x.

9. Write statements to do the following:

a. Assign to `word2` the first through fifth characters of string `word1`.

b. Assign to `word2` the string consisting of the letter A, the substring of `word1` consisting of the third through fifth characters inclusive, and the letter Z.

c. Assign to `word2` the substring of `word1` starting with the fifth character and ending with the last character.

d. Assign to `word2` the last half of string `word1`.

Programming

1. Write an assignment statement to implement the equation below involving $k, a, b, c, q, t_1,$ and t_2.

$$q = \frac{ka(t_1 - t_2)}{b - ac}$$

2. Write a program that reads three numbers and displays their sum and product.

3.5 Processing Integers

This case study demonstrates the manipulation of type `int` data and shows how the steps in the algorithm refinement process become statements in methods.

Case Study

Evaluating Coins

PROBLEM

Your little sister, who has been saving nickels and pennies, is tired of lugging her piggy bank with her when she goes shopping. She wants to exchange the coins for dollar bills and change. To do this, she needs to know the value of her coins in dollars and cents.

ANALYSIS

To solve this problem, you need to get a count of nickels and a count of pennies in the collection (problem inputs). From those counts, you can determine the total value of the coins in cents and the equivalent amount in dollars and change.

Data Requirements

Problem Inputs

the count of nickels
the count of pennies

Problem Outputs

the number of dollars she should receive
the loose change she should receive

Relevant Formulas

1 dollar = 100 pennies
1 nickel = 5 pennies
total cents = 5 × nickels + pennies
dollars = total cents / 100
change = total cents

DESIGN

Two classes are needed. A `Bank` class reads coin quantities and displays the equivalent amount in dollars and change. An application class actually executes these two steps using a `Bank` object. The algorithm for the application class `PiggyBank` is straightforward. Its `main` method creates and uses a single `Bank` object, `sisters`.

Algorithm for `main`

1. Create a `Bank` object.
2. Read in the count of nickels and pennies.
3. Display the equivalent amount in dollars and change.

A `Bank` object needs to store the number of pennies and nickels it contains. It needs two methods (`readCoins` and `displayBank`) to respond to the calls from the application object. A `Bank` object also needs methods to compute the total value in cents (`computeCents`) and to calculate the equivalent amount in dollars (`toDollars`) and change (`toChange`).

Specification for `Bank` class

Data Fields

`int pennies`—the number of pennies in the bank
`int nickels`—the number of nickels in the bank

Methods

readCoins—asks the user for the amount of pennies and nickels
displayBank—shows the resulting dollars and change
computeCents—calculates the total value in cents
toDollars—calculates the amount in dollars
toChange—calculates the amount of change

Algorithm for readCoins

1. Use SimpleGUI method getInt to read the number of pennies.
2. Use SimpleGUI method getInt again to read the number of nickels.

Algorithm for computeCents

1. Calculate the total value in cents.

Algorithm for toDollars

1. Calculate the amount in dollars by dividing the total amount in cents (from method computeCents) by 100.

Algorithm for toChange

1. Calculate the leftover change as the remainder of the total amount in cents (from method computeCents) divided by 100.

Algorithm for displayBank

1. Use methods toDollars, toChange, and SimpleGUI method displayResult to report the results.

IMPLEMENTATION

The program is shown in Figs. 3.9 and 3.10. In method toDollars, the statement

```
return computeCents() / 100;
```

returns the integer part of the result obtained by dividing the total number of cents by 100, which is the number of dollars. Similarly, in method toCents, the statement

```
return computeCents() % 100;
```

returns the remainder of this division as an integer. This result is the change amount. Figure 3.11 shows a sample run.

```java
/* File: Bank.java
   Developed for Problem Solving with Java, Koffman & Wolz
   Appears in Figure 3.9
*/
import simpleIO.*;

public class Bank extends SimpleGUI {
    // Data fields
    private int pennies; // input - the number of pennies
    private int nickels; // input - the number of nickels

    public void readCoins() {
        private pennies = getInt("How many pennies: ");
        private nickels = getInt("How many nickels: ");
    }

    // Calculates the total amount in cents
    public int computeCents() {
        return 5 * nickels + pennies;
    }

    // Calculates the amount in dollars
    private int toDollars() {
        return computeCents() / 100;
    }

    // Calculates the amount of change
    private int toChange() {
        return computeCents() % 100;
    }

    public void displayBank() {
        displayResult("Pennies: " +  pennies);
        displayResult("Nickels: " + nickels);
        displayResult("Dollars: " + toDollars());
        displayResult("Change: " + toChange());
    }

} // Class Bank
```

Figure 3.9 The Bank object

```
/* File: PiggyBank.java
   Developed for Problem Solving with Java, Koffman & Wolz
   Appears in Figure 3.10
*/
public class PiggyBank {
    public static void main(String[] args) {
        // Create a bank object
        Bank sisters = new Bank();

        // Get the coin's in the sister's bank
        sisters.readCoins();

        // Show the equivalent amounts
        sisters.displayBank();
    }
} // Class PiggyBank
```

Figure 3.10 The application object `PiggyBank`

Figure 3.11

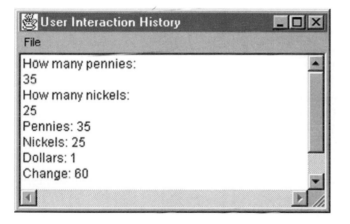

Figure 3.11 Execution of `PiggyBank`

TESTING

To test this program, try running it with a combination of nickels and pennies that yields an exact dollar amount with no change left over. For example, 35 nickels and 25 pennies should yield a value of 2 dollars and no cents. Then increase and decrease the amount of pennies by one (26 and 24 pennies) to make sure that these cases are also handled properly.

Program Style: *Storing Only Essential Data in an Object*

Those of you who are familiar with programming in other languages might wonder why we didn't introduce a third data field in the Bank class for storage of the total amount in cents. This would enable us to calculate it once and store it instead of calculating it each time we need it (in methods toDollars and toChange). The reason is that this value is not an essential characteristic of a Bank object. If we stored it, then we would have to make sure that each time we changed nickels or pennies we also changed the total amount in cents; otherwise, the information stored in the object would not be accurate or consistent. For these reasons, object-oriented programmers prefer to allocate storage only for essential data fields. We recommend that you follow this convention and use methods to calculate intermediate results as you need them rather than storing them in an object.

EXERCISES FOR SECTION 3.5

Programming

1. Modify class Bank to include dimes and quarters.
2. Modify class Bank to dispense the change using the minimum number of coins. For example, if the change is 90 cents, the change should be dispensed as three quarters, one dime, one nickel, and no pennies.

3.6 Processing Strings

This case study illustrates how strings can be used in expressions. Many children enjoy speaking "Pig Latin." This is a play on English in which each word in a sentence is modified as follows: If the first sound is a consonant sound, put it at the end of the word and add "ay" to it. For example, "cat" becomes "atcay".

Case Study

Pig Latin

PROBLEM

Our task is to create an object that will translate a single word. We also simplify the task for now by making the rule more general. We take the first letter of the word, put it at the end of the word, and add "ay" to it.

ANALYSIS

To solve this problem, you need to get a word from the user. To have a little fun, we will ask and translate twice. The input to the program will be the word to translate, the output is the translated word.

Most of the work in this example is building the formula that does the translation. The relevant formula can be expressed in English this way: We construct a string from the second letter to the end of the input word, the first letter of the input word, and the literal `"ay"`. We can rewrite this formula using the concatenation operator as

second letter to the end of input word + first letter of the input word + `"ay"`

We can use methods `substring` and `charAt` (see Section 3.4) to get the indicated parts of the string. If the variable `word` contains the input word, we can rewrite the above formula as:

```
word.substring(1) + word.charAt(0) + "ay"
```

Remember, the first letter is at position 0, not 1.

Data Requirements

Problem Inputs

`String word`—the word provided by the user

Problem Outputs

`String translatedWord`—the pig Latin equivalent of the English word

Relevant Formulas

```
word.substring(1) + word.charAt(0) + "ay"
```

DESIGN

Two objects are needed. A PigLatin object gets the word and translates it. An application object actually executes these two steps using a PigLatin object. The algorithm for the application object is straightforward. Its main method does all the work, requiring a single block variable to create a PigLatin object.

Algorithm for `main`

1. Create a `PigLatin` object to do the work.
2. Read in a word.
3. Display the resulting translation.
4. Do steps 2 and 3 again.

The `PigLatin` object is also straightforward. It needs to store the word to be translated. It needs methods to respond to the calls from the application object. It also needs a method to do the translation.

Specification for `PigLatin` class

Data

`String word`—the English word to be translated

Methods

`translateWord`—converts a word from English to Pig Latin
`getEnglish`—gets an English word from the user
`displayPigLatin`—shows the translation in Pig Latin

Algorithm for `getEnglish`

1. Use `SimpleGUI` method `getString` to read the English word.

Algorithm for `displayPigLatin`

1. Use `translateWord` to translate the word to pig Latin and
   `SimpleGUI` method `displayResult` to show the translation.

IMPLEMENTATION

The program is shown in Figs. 3.12 and 3.13. A sample run is shown in Fig. 3.14.

```
/* File: PigLatin.java
   Developed for Problem Solving with Java, Koffman & Wolz
   Appears in Figure 3.12
*/
import simpleIO.*;

public class PigLatin extends SimpleGUI {
    // Data Fields
    private String word; // input - the word given by the user

    // Methods
    // Converts a word from English to Pig Latin
    public String translateWord() {
        return word.substring(1) + word.charAt(0) + "ay";
    }

    public void getEnglish() {
        word = getString("Enter a word of at least 1 character: ");
    }

    public void displayPigLatin() {
        displayResult(word + " translates to " + translateWord());
    }
} // Class PigLatin
```

Figure 3.12 Simplified version of `PigLatin translator`

```
/* File: SimpleTranslator.java
   Developed for Problem Solving with Java, Koffman & Wolz
   Appears in Figure 3.13
*/
import simpleIO.*;

public class SimpleTranslator {

    public static void main(String[] args) {
        // Create a PigLatin object.
        PigLatin aPig = new PigLatin();

        // Get the English word and translate it.
        aPig.getEnglish();
        aPig.displayPigLatin();

        // Do it again.
        aPig.getEnglish();
        aPig.displayPigLatin();
    }
} // Class SimpleTranslator
```

Figure 3.13 Application object SimpleTranslator for Pig Latin

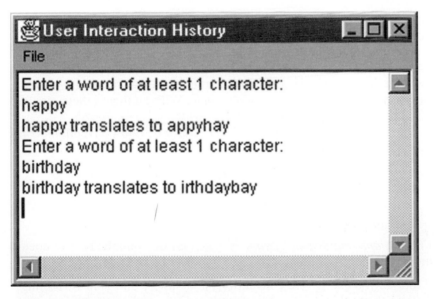

Figure 3.14 Execution of Pig Latin program

TESTING

To test this program, try running it with a number of different words. Try running it with a word that is a single character. Does it work? Try running it with consonant pairs such as "th" at the beginning. Try it with words that begin with vowels.

EXERCISES FOR SECTION 3.6

Programming

1. A silly picture can be created by "rotating right" the letters of a word, and printing each rotation on a separate line. Write a program that does this kind of rotation. Assume words are exactly four letters long. For example, the word `"help"` is displayed as:

    ```
    help
    phel
    lphe
    elph
    ```

3.7 Writing Code with Style

Throughout the discussion so far, you saw that the Java compiler imposes rules on what you may do. The syntax of the language creates a discipline for expressing solutions. But programmers also use **conventions** to make code more readable for humans. The compiler does not concern itself with conventions. You do not need to follow these rules to make the program run, however they are critical to maintenance. Without them others may not be able to read your code easily.

convention:
a coding style that programmers agree to follow.

In your initial programming experience you will find conventions coming from at least three sources:

1. *Java community conventions from the originators of the language.* Examples: how to name objects, data fields, and methods.

2. *Conventions established in this text.* For example: how to lay out the spacing in your code.

3. *Conventions established by your instructor.* For example: how to document your programs; that is, how to identify the class definition files.

Of course, you can ignore conventions and simply "do your own thing." In practical terms this creates more work for you and other programmers. You may be asked to rewrite code, or others may require more time to understand your unique style. Also, ignoring conventions may lead to lower grades on programming assignments.

Line Breaks in Programs

Java ignores line breaks so a Java statement can extend over more than one line. A statement that extends over more than one line cannot be split in the middle of an identifier, a reserved word, or a literal.

Also, we can write more than one statement on a line. For example, the line

```
int x = 5;  double y = 5.3;
```

contains two statements that declare and initialize values. A semicolon follows each statement. We recommend that you place only one statement on a line because it improves readability and makes it easier to maintain a program.

Blank Spaces and Lines in Programs

The consistent and careful use of blank spaces can improve the style of a program. A blank space is required between words in a program line.

The compiler ignores extra blanks between words and symbols, but you may insert space to improve the readability and style of a program. You should always leave a blank space after a comma and before and after operators such as *, -, and =. However, do not insert blanks before or after the dot symbol (.). Be careful not to insert blank spaces where they do not belong. For example, the identifier startSalary cannot be written as start Salary.

The case study files provide examples of how to make class definitions and methods easy to read. Place the open brace { at the end of a header for a class definition or method definition. Indent each line of a method body or class body. Align the close brace } under the first letter of the header. If a body is particularly long, follow the closing delimiter with a comment. Finally, use blank lines between sections of a program, between methods, and between subproblems in a method.

Comments in Programs

Programmers use comments to make a program easier to understand. Comments may describe the purpose of the program, the use of identifiers, or the purpose of a program step. Comments are part of the **program documentation** because they help others read and understand the program. The compiler, however, ignores comments, and they are not translated into machine language.

A comment can appear by itself on a program line, at the end of a line following a statement, or even embedded in a statement. In the following variable declarations, the comment follows the declaration statement.

program documentation: information that enhances the readability of a program.

```
private double sqMeters;     //input - fabric size in
                            //        sq. meters
```

We document most variables in this way. In the chapters to come, we discuss program style in special side bars such as the one here on Using Comments.

Program Style: *Using Comments*

Each class should begin with a header section that consists of a series of comments specifying

- The programmer's name
- The date of the current version
- A brief description of what the class does

If you write the class for a course assignment, you should also list the course identification and your instructor's name.

```
/* File: MyFirstObject.java;

   Programmer: William Bell      Date completed: May 9, 1998
   Instructor: Janet Joseph      Course: CS1
   This program reads a value in square meters and
   converts it to square yards.
*/
```

You should also precede a method definition with a comment describing what the method does unless the method is very simple and its name is self-explanatory. For example, method `readCoins` does not need a comment. Also, if a method definition implements multiple algorithm steps, you should precede the Java code for each step with a comment describing the step:

```
// Get the English word and translate it.
aPig.getEnglish();
aPig.displayPigLatin();
```

3.8 Common Errors and Debugging

As you begin to program, soon you will discover that a program rarely runs correctly the first time it executes. Murphy's Law, "If something can go wrong, it will," seems to have been written with the computer program in mind. In fact, errors are so common that they have their own special name—*bugs*—and the process of correcting them is called **debugging** a program. (According to computer folklore, the first hardware error was caused by a large insect found inside a computer component.) To alert you to potential problems, we will provide a section on common programming errors at the end of each chapter.

debugging:
removing errors from a program.

When Java detects an error, an error message is displayed indicating that you have made a mistake and describing what the likely cause of the error might be. Unfortunately, the error messages are often difficult to interpret and are sometimes misleading. As you gain experience, you will become more proficient at locating and correcting errors. Depending on the IPE you are using, you may have a lot of support in tracking down errors or virtually none. Many IPEs contain a "debug" mode that lets you walk through the steps of your program step by step, run the program to a particular point and then stop, or mark particular variables for viewing. Even without a fancy debugger, there is a lot you can do to view your program using simple tools.

There are three kinds of errors: syntax errors, run-time errors, and logic errors. Depending on which one you have encountered, you use different techniques to determine exactly what is wrong and to fix it.

Syntax Errors

A **syntax error** occurs when your code violates one or more grammar rules of Java. Syntax errors are detected and displayed by the compiler as it attempts to translate your programs. If a statement has a syntax error, it cannot be translated and your program cannot be executed. Finding and removing syntax errors, one at a time, can be time-consuming. Desk check your program carefully before compiling it the first time. Table 3.7 describes some syntax errors you may encounter and some possible error messages.

syntax error:
a violation of the Java grammar rules, detected during program translation.

Table 3.7 Some common syntax errors

Syntax error	Sample message
Using an operator with an incorrect data type (for example, using arithmetic operator * with `char` or `String` data).	`Incompatible type for *`
Forgetting to declare a variable or data field or misspelling its name.	`Undefined variable`
Using an expression type in an assignment statement that is not assignment compatible with the variable type.	`Incompatible type for =`
A missing string delimiter.	`String not terminated at end of line` or `';' expected`
Referencing a private data field from outside the class that declares it.	`Invalid expression statement`
Forgetting to define a method or misspelling its name.	`Method not found`
Using an argument of the incorrect type in a method call.	`Incompatible type for method`
A method returning a value of the wrong type.	`Incompatible type for return`
Missing `return` at end of a method whose result type is not `void`.	`Return required at end of method`
Calling a `private` method of a class from a class in which the method is not defined.	`No matching method found in class`
Omitting an object name before a call to a `public` method from a class in which the method is not defined.	`Method not found` or `Can't make static reference to method`

Incorrect data types The table shows that improper use of a data type often causes a syntax error. Some examples are:

- Use of arithmetic operators with character or string data, except that + (concatenate) can be used with string data.
- Assigning a value of one type to a variable of another type, except that a type int value can be assigned to a type double variable.
- Returning a result from a method that is the wrong data type or not returning a result (missing return).

Incorrect use of quotation marks Improper use of quotation marks with a character or string literal also causes a syntax error. Make sure you always use a pair of single quotes or apostrophes to delimit character literals and a pair of double quotes to delimit strings. Also, a string literal must fit on one line.

Errors in use of comments Beware of dangling comments. If the compiler seems to have lost large segments of your code, you probably began a /* comment and didn't end it properly or didn't end it in the right spot.

Beware of dangling comments of another sort. Make sure that a comment following // does not end up on the next line. For example:

```
// This is a very long and involved comment that
accidentally ended up here too.
```

The accidentally will be viewed as part of your code and confuse the compiler.

Run-Time Errors

run-time error:
an attempt to perform an invalid operation detected during program execution.

Run-time errors are detected and displayed by the computer during the execution of a program. A **run-time error** occurs when the user directs the computer to perform an invalid operation, such as dividing a number by zero or manipulating undefined or invalid data.

EXAMPLE 3.10

When the following class is instantiated, the data field x is automatically set to 0.

```java
public class RunTimeError {
  private int x;

  public void doIt() {
    x = 10 / x;
  }
}
```

If method `doIt` is called, a run-time error occurs when the assignment statement executes. The error message

`java.lang.ArithmeticException: / by zero`

indicates an attempt to divide by zero (value of x), an invalid operation.

No object file error One common error occurs when the application object class and the file containing it have different names. Sometimes this is due to case sensitivity. Make sure that the name of each class exactly matches the name of the file in which it resides.

Class path errors Class path errors are also quite common. The class path tells the compiler where to look for a file if it is not stored in the same folder as the application class. Make sure all files that you create for a particular application are in the same folder. (See Appendix A.)

Data entry errors Data entry errors are common run-time errors. They are caused by reading data of the wrong type into a variable, for example, reading a real number or a character into a type `int` variable. `SimpleGUI` methods were designed to overcome these errors. Make sure you follow the instructions when responding to `SimpleGUI` messages.

Arithmetic overflow Another common run-time error is **arithmetic overflow**. This error occurs when a program attempts to store in a variable a value that is too large.

arithmetic overflow: a run-time error caused by an attempt to store in a variable a value that is too large.

Logic Errors

Logic errors occur when a program follows an incorrect algorithm. Because logic errors usually do not cause run-time errors and do not display error messages, they are very difficult to detect. The only sign of a logic error may be incorrect program output. You can detect logic errors by testing the program thoroughly, comparing its output to calculated results. You can prevent logic errors by carefully desk-checking the algorithm and the program before you type it in.

logic error: an error caused by following an incorrect algorithm.

Because debugging can be time-consuming, plan your program solutions carefully and desk check them to eliminate bugs early. If you are unsure of what a statement does or its syntax, look it up in reference material or in relevant appendixes of this book. Following this approach will save time and avoid trouble.

Debugging

One simple technique for debugging involves inserting diagnostic output statements in a method to display intermediate results. You can do this very easily in Java by using method `println`. You call method `println` by applying it to object `System.out` (the console window associated with a Java application). Like method `displayResult`, its argument is a string.

EXAMPLE 3.11

Figure 3.15 shows a new version of method `computeCents` (see Fig. 3.10). Method `computeCents` calculates the coin collection value in cents and stores it in a local variable `totalCents`. If the value of `totalCents` is incorrect, later calculations based on it will also be incorrect. The statement

```
System.out.println("Total cents is " + totalCents);
```

allows us to view the value of `totalCents` before we return it. Method `println` evaluates its string argument and displays its value in the console window.

```
// Calcuates the total amount in cents
public int computeCents() {
    int totalCents = 5 * nickels + pennies;

    // Display in console window for
    //    debugging purposes.
    System.out.println("Total cents is " + totalCents);
    return totalCents;
}
```

Figure 3.15 Revised method `computeCents`

EXERCISES FOR SECTION 3.8

Self-Check

1. Indicate why each of the statements below would not be valid in method `main` of class `ConvertFabric`. (See Fig. 3.1 and 3.2).

   a. `aPiece.toSqYards();`

   b. `aPiece.displayResult();`

   c. `aPiece.sqMeters = 5.5;`

   d. `aPiece.sqMeters =`
   `         getDouble("Enter square meters:");`

   e. `aPiece.readSqMeters;`

   f. `Piece.readSqMeters();`

   g. `readSqMeters();`

2. Indicate why each of the statements below would not be valid in a method of class `PieceOfFabric`.

    a. `toSqYards(sqMeters);`

    b. `displayResult(sqYards * sqMeters);`

    c. `sqMeters = getChar("Enter a measurement");`

    d. `sqYards = getDouble("Enter a measurement");`

    e. `toSqYards() = SqMeters;`

Chapter Review

1. A Java class definition contains data declarations and method definitions. Method definitions may contain their own block data declarations and executable statements.

2. Method `main` must create an object instance to process using a statement of the form

    className objectName `= new` *className*`();`

    which calls the default constructor to allocate storage for an object and initialize its data field. Method `main` applies this object's methods to the object instance using statements of the form

    objectName`.`*methodName*`(`*arguments*`);`

    Method `main` can reference only `public` methods of this object instance.

3. In methods that belong to an object instance, you should use the data field name or the method name to reference the object's data fields or to call other methods. You can reference `public` and `private` data and methods.

4. Type `void` methods do not return a result. Other methods return a result whose type is specified in the method header. The last statement of a method that returns a result must be a `return` statement.

5. Assignment statements perform computations and store results in memory. The data type of the expression being assigned and the variable receiving the expression value must be the same type, except that a type `int` expression may be assigned to a type `double` variable.

6. Arithmetic operators with type `int` and type `double` data produce a type `double` result. The operators `*`, `/`, and `%` have higher precedence than + and – (subtraction). Operators at the same precedence level are evaluated left to right. Division of two type `int` operands always yields a type `int` result, the remainder is lost. The operator `%` gives the remainder of an integer division.

7. String expressions are formed using string literals and objects and the operator + (concatenate). If the operands of + are a string and a primitive type, the string equivalent of the primitive type data is concatenated with the string.

New Java Constructs

Construct	Effect
Creating an Object Instance	
`Piece aPiece = new aPiece();`	Creates object instance `aPiece` of class `Piece`.
Method Call	
`aPiece.readSqMeters();`	Applies method `readSqMeters` to object `aPiece`.
`displayResult("This");`	Applies method `displayResult` from class `SimpleGUI` to the object instance to which the method belongs. Method `displayResult` displays the string `"This"`.
Assignment Statement	
`x = y * z;`	Assigns the product of `y` and `z` as the value of `x`.
`x = toSqYards();`	Assigns the result returned by method `toSqYards` as the value of `x`.
String Concatenation	
`"The value of x is " + x`	Joins the left operand (a string literal) to the string created from the right operand.

Quick-Check Exercises

1. What value is assigned to x (type `double`) by the following statement?
   ```
   x = 25 * 3 / 2.5;
   ```
2. What value is assigned to x by the following statement, assuming x is 10?
   ```
   x = x - 20.0;
   ```
3. In the following statement, list the sequence of operator evaluation: `x = a + b / c * d;` . Assume a (type `double`) is `5.5`, b (type `int`) is `6`, c (type `int`) is `4`, d (type `double`) is `2.5`, x (type `double`) is `0`.
4. Indicate which data type you would use to represent the following items: number of children at school, a letter grade on an exam, the average number of school days absent each year, your name, whether or not you are single.

5. Explain why method `main` needs to create an instance of a support class. How does the constructor method for the support class enter into this.

6. What is the syntactic purpose of the semicolon in a Java program?

7. Explain why the expression below is incorrect and correct it. If x is 5 and y is 7.5, what is its value before and after the correction?

   `"The sum is " + x + y`

8. When would you declare a method as `private`?

9. Does Java require you to use type casting if you want to assign a type `int` expression to a type `double` variable? What about assigning a type `double` expression to a type `int` variable? Does either operation lead to a loss of accuracy?

10. Write an expression that forms a string consisting of the first and last letters of string `word` with a star between them.

Answers to Quick-Check Exercises

1. `30`

2. `-10`

3. `/, *, +, =.` `6 / 4` is `1`, `1 * 2.5` is `2.5`, `5.5 + 2.5` is `8`, `8` is assigned to `x`.

4. `int, char, double, String, boolean`

5. In order to use the support class methods, method `main` needs to create an object of the support class type. It does this using a statement of the form

   ClassType objectName = new *ClassType* `()` ;

   This statement declares the type of *objectName* to be *ClassType* and also creates the object instance by calling the default constructor (method call is *ClassType* `()`). The constructor allocates storage space for the new object and initializes the data fields using default values if none are specified (`0` for `int` or `double`, `false` for a `boolean`, and so on).

6. It terminates an expression and must appear at the end of each statement.

7. The expression x + y must be in parentheses because otherwise both + operators mean concatenate. The value before correction is

   `"The sum is 57.5"`.

   The value after correction is

   `"The sum is 12.5"`.

8. Declare a method as private when the method is only to be used by methods of its own class.

9. A type `int` expression is assignment compatible with a type `double` variable so type casting is not required. This is not the case for a type `double` expression and a type `int` variable. Type casting would truncate the fractional part of the type `double` value being assigned to a type `int` variable.

10. `word.charAt(0) + "*" + word.charAt(word.length() - 1)`

Review Questions

1. What kind of information should be specified in the comments that appear at the beginning of a program?

2. List and describe the rules for order of evaluation of arithmetic expressions.

3. If the average size of a family is 2.8 and this value is stored in the variable `familySize`, provide the Java statement to display this fact in a readable way in a GUI window. What assumption are you making?

4. Which of the following expressions evaluate to the same value?

   a. `a + b * c`

   b. `(a + b) * c`

   c. `a + (b * c)`

5. Assuming a (value is 6) and b (value is 5) are type `int`, what are the values of the following expressions? Evaluate them if the values of a and b are switched.

   a. `a / b`

   b. `a % b`

   c. `a * b`

6. Differentiate between syntax errors, run-time errors, and logic errors.

7. If you were writing a class `Barrel` to be used in a program that calculates the time it takes to fill a barrel with a fluid, indicate how you would use each of the following items in this class.

   a. The barrel radius in inches

   b. The fill time in minutes

   c. The rate at which liquid enters the barrel in gallons per minute

   d. The steps used to calculate barrel volume

   e. The barrel volume

   f. The number of cubic inches in a gallon

   g. The steps used to calculate the number of gallons the barrel holds

   h. The steps used to calculate the time it takes to fill the barrel.

Programming Projects

1. Write a program to convert a temperature in degrees Fahrenheit to degrees Celsius.

    Problem Input

    temperature in degrees Fahrenheit

    Problem Output

    temperature in degrees Celsius

    Relevant Formula

    $celsius = (5.0 / 9.0) \times (fahrenheit - 32.0)$

2. Write a program to read two data items and print their sum, difference, product, and quotient.

    Problem Inputs

    two numbers

    Problem Outputs

    sum of two numbers
    difference of two numbers
    product of two numbers
    quotient of two numbers

3. Write a program to read in the weight (in pounds) of an object and compute and print the weight in kilograms and grams. (*Hint:* 1 pound is equal to 0.453592 kilogram and 453.59237 grams.)

4. Write a program to solve Review Question 7. There are 231 cubic inches in a gallon.

5. Write a program that prints your first initial as a block letter. (*Hint:* Use a 6 × 6 grid for the letter and read in six strings, each of which represents a different row of the grid. Each string should consist of asterisks (symbol *) interspersed with blanks. For example, if the letter E is your first initial, the first string would consist of six asterisks and the second string would begin with one or two asterisks and the rest blanks. After reading the six strings, display them in sequence to show the block letter.

6. Write a program that reads in the name of a dinosaur and the number of years ago that the dinosaur lived and computes the number of months and days ago that the dinosaur lived. (Use 365.25 days per year). Test your program with Eric, a Triceratops who lived 145 million years ago and Alfred, a Brontosaurus who lived 182 million years ago.

7. Write a program that reads in the length and the width of a rectangular yard and the length and the width of a rectangular house situated in the yard. Your program should compute the time required (in minutes) to cut the grass at the rate of 2.3 square meters a second.

8. Arnie likes to jog in the morning. As he jogs he counts the number of strides he makes in the first minute of his jogging and the last minute. Arnie then averages these two and calls this the average number of strides he makes in a minute when he jogs. Write a program that accepts these averages and the total time Arnie spends jogging in hours and minutes and outputs the distance Arnie has jogged in miles. Assume Arnie's stride to be 2.5 feet. (There are 5280 feet in a mile.)

9. Write a program that inputs a number of seconds up to 18,000 (5 hours) and outputs the hours, minutes, and seconds equivalent.

10. The Pythagorean theorem states that the sum of the squares of the sides of a right triangle is equal to the square of the hypotenuse. For example, if two sides of a right triangle have lengths 3 and 4, then the hypotenuse must have a length of 5. The integers, 3, 4, and 5 together form a Pythagorean triple. There is an infinite number of such triples. Given two positive integers, m and n, where $m > n$, a Pythagorean triple can be generated by the following formulas:

$side_1 = m^2 - n^2$
$side_2 = 2mn$
$hypotenuse = m^2 + n^2$

Write a program that reads in values for m and n and prints the values of the Pythagorean triple generated by the above formulas.

CHAPTER 4

Program Design with Methods and Graphics

Programmers who use the software development method to solve problems seldom tackle each new program as a unique event. Information contained in the problem statement and amassed during the analysis and design phases helps the programmer plan and complete the finished program. Programmers also use segments of earlier program solutions as building blocks to construct new programs.

In the first part of this chapter, we demonstrate how you can tap existing information and code in the form of predefined methods to write programs. In addition to using existing information, programmers can use top-down design techniques to simplify the development of algorithms and the structure of the resulting programs. To apply top-down design, the programmer starts with the broadest statement of the problem solution and works down to more detailed subproblems. In this chapter, we demonstrate top-down design and show how to use inheritance to develop new classes from existing ones.

We conclude the chapter with a section that introduces computer graphics. Computer graphics, in advanced forms, is used to make science fiction movies and cartoons and to create video games. In Java, you can also use graphics programming to create applets (small applications) that can be inserted in Web pages. Our intention is to introduce you to Java's capabilities for doing graphics programming, not to make you a graphics expert.

4.1 Building Programs from Existing Information
Case Study: Finding the Area and Circumference of a Circle

4.2 Extending a Problem Solution
Case Study: Finding the Most Pizza for Your Money

4.3 Extending a Problem Solution through Inheritance

4.4 Reuse of Methods in Class `Math`

4.5 Accessors, Modifiers, Constructors, and Class Methods

4.6 Introduction to Computer Graphics

4.7 Common Programming Errors

Chapter Review

4.1 Building Programs from Existing Information

Programmers seldom start off with a blank slate (or empty screen) when they develop a program. Often some—or all—of the solution can be developed from information that already exists or from the solution to another problem, as we demonstrate in this section and the next.

Before you even begin to code a program you can generate important system documentation by carefully following the software development method described in the previous chapters. This system documentation, consisting of class specifications and algorithms for methods (developed during the Design phase), summarizes your intentions and thought processes.

You can use this documentation as a starting point in coding your program, as we show in the next case study. For example, you can begin by editing the class specification to conform to the Java syntax for class definitions.

To code a method, first use the method algorithm and any refinements as comments in the method body. The comments provide documentation that guide your Java code. After the comments are in place in the method body, you can begin to write the Java statements. We illustrate this process in the next case study.

Case Study

Finding the Area and Circumference of a Circle

PROBLEM

Read the radius of a circle. Compute and display the circle's area and circumference.

ANALYSIS

Clearly, the problem input is the circle's radius. Two outputs are required: the circle's area and circumference.

Data Requirements

Inputs

radius of a circle

Outputs

area of a circle
circumference of a circle

Relevant Formulas

area of a circle $= \pi \times radius^2$
circumference of a circle $= 2\pi \times radius$

DESIGN

We need a `Circle` class with data field `radius` (type `double`). The class should contain methods for reading a `Circle` object's radius and for computing a `Circle` object's area and circumference. We also need a method for displaying the results. The class specification follows:

Specification for Circle class

Data fields

`double radius`—radius of a circle

Methods

`readRadius`—reads circle radius
`computeArea`—computes area
`computeCircumf`—computes circumference
`showCircle`—displays circle area and circumference

We also need an application class that contains one method, `main`. Next, we list the algorithm for the `main` method and the methods of class `Circle`.

Algorithm for main (class CircleStats)

1. Create a circle object.
2. Read the circle radius.
3. Compute and display the circle area and the circumference.

Algorithm for readRadius (class Circle)

1. Read the circle radius.

Algorithm for computeArea (class Circle)

1. Compute π `* radius * radius`.

Algorithm for computeCircumf (class Circle)

1. Compute `2 *` π `* radius`.

Algorithm for `showCircle` (class `Circle`)

1. Display the circle radius.
2. Compute and display the area.
3. Compute and display the circumference.

IMPLEMENTATION

Figure 4.1 shows the outline for class `Circle`. Class `Circle` is an edited version of the class specification and method algorithms. Figure 4.2 shows the final version of class `Circle`, with Java code for all methods.

```
/*    File: Circle.java
      Developed for Problem Solving with Java, Koffman & Wolz
      Appears in Figure 4.1
*/
import simpleIO.*;

public class Circle extends SimpleGUI {
    // Data fields
    protected double radius; // input - circle radius

    // Methods
    // Reads circle radius.
    public void readRadius() {
        // Read the circle radius.
    }

    // Computes area.
    public double computeArea() {
        // Compute pi * radius * radius.
    }

    // Computes circumference.
    public double computeCircumf() {
        // Compute 2 * pi * radius.
    }

    // Displays the area and circumference
    public void showCircle() {
        // Display the circle radius.
        // Compute and display the area.
        // Compute and display the circumference.
    }
} // Class Circle
```

Figure 4.1 Outline of class `Circle`

```
/*    File: Circle.java
      Developed for Problem Solving with Java, Koffman & Wolz
      Appears in Figure 4.2
*/
import simpleIO.*;

public class Circle extends SimpleGUI {
    // Data fields
    protected double radius;  // input - circle radius

    // Methods
    // Reads circle radius.
    public void readRadius() {
        radius = getDouble("Circle radius:");
    }

    // Computes area.
    public double computeArea() {
        return Math.PI * radius * radius;
    }

    // Computes circumference.
    public double computeCircumf() {
        return 2 * Math.PI * radius;
    }

    // Displays the area and circumference.
    public void showCircle() {
        displayResult("Radius is " + radius);
        displayResult("Area is " + computeArea());
        displayResult("Circumference is " + computeCircumf());
    }
} // Class Circle
```

Figure 4.2 Class Circle

In Fig. 4.2, we represent π as Math.PI, a constant value defined in class Math. We discuss this class further in Section 4.4. Note that the data field radius in Fig. 4.2 has a **protected** rather than a private visibility. Private data fields may only be accessed within the class itself. Protected data fields may be accessed by subclasses. In Section 4.3 we extend the Circle class, and we will need to access the data field radius from a subclass.

protected visibility: allows access to data fields and methods of a class by a subclass.

Figure 4.3 shows the outline for class CircleStats (the application class), which is based on the algorithm for method main. Figure 4.4 shows the Java code.

```
/*    File CircleStats.java
      Developed for Problem Solving with Java, Koffman & Wolz
      Appears in Figure 4.3
*/
public class CircleStats {

    public static void main (String[] args) {
        // Create a Circle object.

        // Read the circle radius.

        // Compute and display the area and circumference.
    }
} // Class CircleStats
```

Figure 4.3 Outline for class `CircleStats`

```
/*    File CircleStats.java
      Developed for Problem Solving with Java, Koffman & Wolz
      Appears in Figure 4.4
*/

public class CircleStats {

    public static void main (String[] args) {
        // Create a Circle object.
        Circle circ = new Circle();

        // Read the circle radius.
        circ.readRadius();

        // Compute and display the area and circumference.
        circ.showCircle();
    }
} // Class CircleStats
```

Figure 4.4 Class `CircleStats`

TESTING

The sample output in Fig. 4.5 provides a good test of the program because it is relatively easy to compute by hand the circle area and circumference for a radius value of 5. The radius squared is 25 and π is approximately 3, so the value of the area appears correct. The circumference should be 10 times π, which is also an easy number to compute by hand.

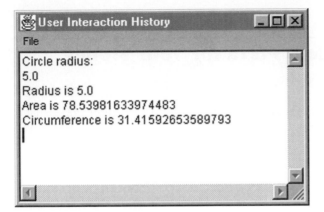

Figure 4.5 Sample run of `CircleStats`

Program Style: *Use of Color to Highlight New Constructs*
In Fig. 4.2, program lines that illustrate new Java constructs are in color, so that you can find them easily. We will continue to use color for this purpose in figures that contain programs.

EXERCISES FOR SECTION 4.1

Self-Check

1. Explain the value of creating an outline of your solution before you begin coding.

2. Critique the documentation in Figs. 4.2 and 4.3. Does the documentation tell you just the right amount about what the code does. Is there too much or too little documentation?

3. Redesign the case study so that it calculates the radius from the diameter entered by a user.

4. What does `protected` visibility do? Contrast it with `public` and `private` visibility.

Programming

1. Implement the solution for Self-Check Exercise 3.

2. Add to the design of the case study so that the volume of a cylinder is calculated. This requires an additional input: the height of the cylinder. The formula is: *volume = area of the base * height*.

4.2 Extending a Problem Solution

Another way in which programmers use existing information is by extending the solution for one problem to solve another. For example, you can easily solve the next problem by building on the solution to the previous one.

Case Study

Finding the Most Pizza for Your Money

PROBLEM

You and your college roommates frequently order a late-night pizza snack. Many pizzerias in the area deliver. Since you are on a tight budget, you want to know which pizza is the best value.

ANALYSIS

To find which pizza is the best value, you must be able to compare pizza costs. One way to do this is to compute the unit price of each pizza. You can find the *unit price* of an item by dividing the total price of that item by a measure of its quantity. A good measure of quantity would be the pizza weight, but pizzas are not sold by weight; they are sold by size (diameter) measured in inches. Consequently, the best you can do is to use some meaningful measure of quantity based on pizza diameter. One such measure is pizza area. Using pizza area, you can define the unit price of a pizza as its price divided by its area.

Data Requirements

Inputs

size (diameter) of a pizza
price of a pizza

Outputs

unit price

Relevant Formulas

$radius = diameter / 2$
$area = \pi \times radius^2$
$unit\ price = price / area$

DESIGN

We can specify a new class, `PricedCircle`, which is similar to `Circle` but has one more data field: `price`. It also has three new methods: `readPCircleData` (replaces `readRadius`), `computeUnitPrice`, and `showPricedCircle` (replaces `showCircle`). The class specification follows:

Specification for `PricedCircle` class

Data

double `radius`—radius of a circle
double `unitPrice`—cost per square inch

Methods

readPCircleData—reads diameter and price of circular item and up-
            dates all its data fields

computeArea—computes area

computeUnitPrice—computes unit price

showPricedCircle—displays priced circle data

The algorithm for method main is like that in the previous case study. The algorithms for main and the new methods of class PricedCircle follow.

Algorithm for main (class PricePizza)

1. Create a type PricedCircle object.
2. Read the pizza diameter and price.
3. Compute and display the pizza area and unit price.

Algorithm for readPCircleData (class PricedCircle)

1. Read the circle diameter and store its radius.
2. Read the circle price.

Algorithm for computeArea (class PricedCircle)

1. Compute π * radius * radius.

Algorithm for computeUnitPrice (class PricedCircle)

1. Compute price / area (result of computeArea).

Algorithm for showPricedCircle (class PricedCircle)

1. Display the diameter.
2. Display the price.
3. Compute and display the unit price (result of computeUnitPrice).

Notice that method computeUnitPrice computes the area (using method computeArea) as an intermediate step in the calculation of unit price.

IMPLEMENTATION

Figure 4.6 shows class PricedCircle. Figure 4.7 shows class PricePizza, and Fig 4.8 shows a sample run of this program.

In method readPCircleData, the statement

```
radius = getDouble("Diameter:") / 2;
```

uses method getDouble to read the circle diameter and then stores half of that value in data field radius.

```
/*    File: PricedCircle.java
      Developed for Problem Solving with Java, Koffman & Wolz
      Appears in Figure 4.6
*/
import simpleIO.*;

public class PricedCircle extends SimpleGUI {
    // Data fields
    private double radius;   // input - circle radius
    private double price;    // input - circle price

    // Methods
    public void readPCircleData() {
        // Enter diameter and price.
        radius = getDouble("Diameter or size:") / 2;
        price = getDouble("Price $:");
    }

    public double computeArea() {
        return Math.PI * radius * radius;
    }

    public double computeUnitPrice() {
        return price / computeArea();
    }

    public void showPricedCircle() {
        displayResult("Size is " + 2 * radius);
        displayResult("Price is $" + price);
        displayResult("Unit price is $" + computeUnitPrice());
    }
} // Class PricedCircle
```

Figure 4.6 Class `PricedCircle`

```
/*    File: PricePizza.java
      Developed for Problem Solving with Java, Koffman & Wolz
      Appears in Figure 4.7
*/
public class PricePizza {

    public static void main (String[] args) {
        // Create a PricedCircle object.
        PricedCircle pizza = new PricedCircle();
```

Figure 4.7 *continued*

Figure 4.7 *continued*

```
            // Read the pizza diameter and price.
            pizza.readPCircleData();

            // Compute and display the area and unit price.
            pizza.showPricedCircle();
    }
} // Class PricePizza
```

Figure 4.7 Class `PricePizza`

```
User Interaction History                    _ □ ×
File
Diameter or size:
12.0
Price $:
20.0
Size is 12.0
Price is $20.0
Unit price is $0.17683882565766149
```

Figure 4.8 Sample run of `PricePizza`

TESTING

To test this program, run it with a few different pizza sizes. You can verify that the program is working correctly by multiplying the unit price by the area. The product should equal the price of the pizza.

EXERCISES FOR SECTION 4.2

Self-Check

1. Describe the problem inputs and outputs and write the class specifications and method algorithms for a program that computes an employee's gross salary given the hours worked and the hourly rate.

2. Write a preliminary version of the program from your solution to Self-Check Exercise 1. Show the data declarations and the program comments corresponding to the algorithm and its refinements.

3. What changes should you make to enable the classes in Self-Check Exercise 1 to include overtime hours? When you compute the employee's gross salary, assume that overtime is paid at 1.5 times an employee's normal hourly rate. Assume also that overtime hours are entered separately.

Programming

1. Add refinements to the program outline that follows and write the final Java program, including an application class.

```
public class SumAndAverage {
    // Find and dislay the sum & average of two numbers.

    // Data Fields
        private int one;    // input - numbers to process
        private int two;

    // Get two numbers from the user.
    public void getData() {
        // Read first number into one.
        // Read second number into two.
    }

    // Display the sum and average.
    public void displayResults() {
        // Display the two numbers.
        // Compute and display the sum.
        // Compute and display the average.
    }
}
```

2. Write a complete Java program for Self-Check Exercise 1.

3. Write a complete Java program for the revised payroll algorithm developed in Self-Check Exercise 3.

4.3 Extending a Problem Solution through Inheritance

Although the solution in the previous section works, it is far from ideal. We have not taken advantage of one of the fundamental properties of object-oriented programming—inheritance. Next, we show how to extend a problem solution using inheritance.

Because a PricedCircle object is a kind of Circle object, we can define class PricedCircle as an extension of class Circle. Now to write class PricedCircle, we need to declare only those variables and methods that are new to it; all protected or public data fields and methods of class Circle (and, therefore, of class SimpleGUI) are automatically inherited and can be used with objects of the new class. Recall from Section 4.1 that the data field radius of the class Circle was declared protected. Figure 4.9 shows the definition of PricedCircle as an extension of class Circle.

```
/*    File: PricedCircle.java
      Developed for Problem Solving with Java, Koffman & Wolz
      Appears in Figure 4.9
*/
import simpleIO.*;

public class PricedCircle extends Circle {
    // Data fields
    private double price;   // input - circle price

    // Methods
    public void readPCircleData() {
        radius = getDouble("Diameter or size:") / 2;
        price = getDouble("Price $");
    }

    public double computeUnitPrice() {
        return price / computeArea();
    }

    public void showPricedCircle() {
        displayResult("Size is " + 2 * radius);
        displayResult("Price is $" + price);
        displayResult("Unit price is $" + computeUnitPrice());
    }
} // Class PricedCircle
```

Figure 4.9 Class `PricedCircle` extends class `Circle`

Notice how much easier it is to write this new, improved version of class `PricedCircle`. Figure 4.10 shows a class diagram, listing the data fields and methods for a `PricedCircle` object. The color screens show data and methods defined in the class; the gray screens show inherited data and methods. We list just the `SimpleGUI` methods used by class `PricedCircle`.

Surprisingly, class `PricePizza` (Fig. 4.7) does not change at all. As far as the application is concerned, it makes no difference that we used inheritance to implement class `PricedCircle`. Figure 4.10 does not show data fields or methods for class `SimpleGUI`, the parent of class `Circle`. Just as in earlier programs, objects of type `Circle` or `PricedCircle` can access methods (e.g., `getDouble`, `displayResult`) defined in class `SimpleGUI`.

As you can see, inheritance is a very powerful tool. It enables us to easily extend one class (the parent class) to create a more specialized one (the child class) without having to duplicate variables and methods defined in the parent class. Objects of the child class provide storage for data fields de-

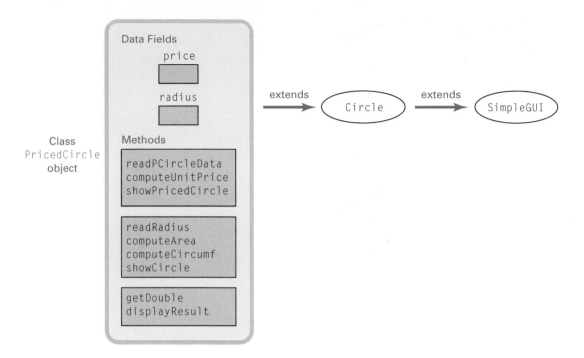

Figure 4.10 Object of class `PricedCircle`

clared in either class. Also, these objects can be used with methods defined in either class. Objects of the parent class are not affected by the fact that the child class exists.

EXERCISES FOR SECTION 4.3

Self-Check

1. The implementation in Fig. 4.9 relies on the definition of `Circle` in Fig. 4.2 having `protected` visibility for data field `radius`. Explain what would happen if the visibility for `radius` was `private`. What would the impact on the overall design be if the visibility were `public`?

2. Modify the solution to Self-Check Exercise 3 of Section 4.2 to use inheritance. Extend the class derived as the solution to Self-Check Exercise 1.

Programming

1. Write a complete Java program for the revised payroll problem developed in Self-Check Exercise 2.

4.4 Using Methods in Class Math

Predefined Methods and Reusability

A primary goal of structured programming is to write error-free code. One way to accomplish this goal is to reuse whenever possible code that has already been written and tested. This feature is called *reusability*. Stated more simply, "Why reinvent the wheel?"

Java promotes reusability by providing many predefined methods that can be used in your programs. We have already done this by using the constant Math.PI, which is defined in class Math. You will learn how to create your own constants in Chapter 8. In this section, we introduce some methods of the class Math that are used for mathematical computations. We start with the method sqrt, which performs the square root computation. The expression part of the assignment statement

activates the code for method sqrt, passing the argument x to the method.

The prefix Math. indicates that method sqrt is defined in the Math class. In earlier method calls, we used an object name, not a class name, as a prefix. These earlier methods are called **instance methods** because you can only refer to them from an instance of a class. Here, we use the class name instead because Java does not permit users to declare instances (objects) of class Math. Therefore, the methods of class Math are defined as **class methods**, and the class name must appear as a prefix in each class method call. After method sqrt executes, the method result is assigned to variable y. (Chapter 8 discusses class methods in more detail.)

If x is 16.0, the assignment statement above is evaluated as follows:

instance method:
a method that can be applied to a class instance (an object). These are the methods we typically use.

class method:
a method that is called by prefixing it with a class name, not an object name.

1. x is 16.0, so method sqrt computes the square root of 16.0, or 4.0.

2. The method result, 4.0, is assigned to y.

A computational method can be thought of as a "black box" that is passed one or more input values and automatically returns a single output value. Figure 4.11 illustrates this process for the call to method sqrt. The value of x (16.0) is the method input, and the method result, or output, is the square root of 16.0 (result is 4.0).

```
x is 16.0     ┌──────────┐     result is 4.0
──────────────│  method  │────────────────────▶
              │   sqrt   │
              └──────────┘
```

Figure 4.11 Method sqrt as a "black box"

If w is 9.0, the assignment statement

```
z = 5.7 + Math.sqrt(w);
```

is evaluated as follows:

1. w is 9.0, so method sqrt computes the square root of 9.0, or 3.0.
2. The values 5.7 and 3.0 are added together.
3. The sum, 8.7, is stored in z.

EXAMPLE 4.1

The application in Fig. 4.12 calls on the class in Fig. 4.13 to display the square root of two numbers as well as the square root of their sum. We store the numbers entered by the user in data fields data1 and data2. To display their square roots as well as the square root of their sum, Math.sqrt must be called three times:

```
displayResult("Square root of " + data1 + " is " +
            Math.sqrt(data1));
displayResult("Square root of " + data2 + " is " +
            Math.sqrt(data2));
displayResult("Square root of their sum is " +
            Math.sqrt(data1 + data2));
```

For the first two calls, the method arguments are variables (data1 and data2). The third call shows that a method argument can also be an expression (data1 + data2). For all three calls, the result returned by method Math.sqrt is displayed. Fig. 4.14 shows an example of the results displayed for input data: 9 and 16.

```
/*    File: SquareRootDemo.java
      Developed for Problem Solving with Java,
        Koffman & Wolz
      Appears in Figure 4.12
*/
public class SquareRootDemo {
    public static void main (String[] args) {

          // Create a type SquareRootSum object.
          SquareRootSum tester = new SquareRootSum();

          // Get two numbers.
          tester.readData();
```

Figure 4.12 *continued*

Figure 4.12 *continued*

```
            // Display square root of each number and of
            //   their sum.
            tester.showResults();
    }
} // Class SquareRootDemo
```

Figure 4.12 An application for showing the sum of the square roots

```
/*    FILE: SquareRootSum.java
      Developed for Problem Solving with Java,
        Koffman & Wolz
      Appears in Figure 4.13
*/
import simpleIO.*;

public class SquareRootSum extends SimpleGUI {
    // Data fields
    private double data1;  // input - 1st number
    private double data2;  // input - 2nd number

    // Methods
    void readData() {
        data1 = getDouble("Enter the first number");
        data2 = getDouble("Enter the second number");
    }

    void showResults() {
        displayResult("Square root of " +
                        data1 + " is " +
                        Math.sqrt(data1));
        displayResult("Square root of " +
                        data2 + " is " +
                        Math.sqrt(data2));
        displayResult("Square root of their sum is " +
                        Math.sqrt(data1 + data2));
    }
} // Class SquareRootSum
```

Figure 4.13 Illustrating method Math.sqrt

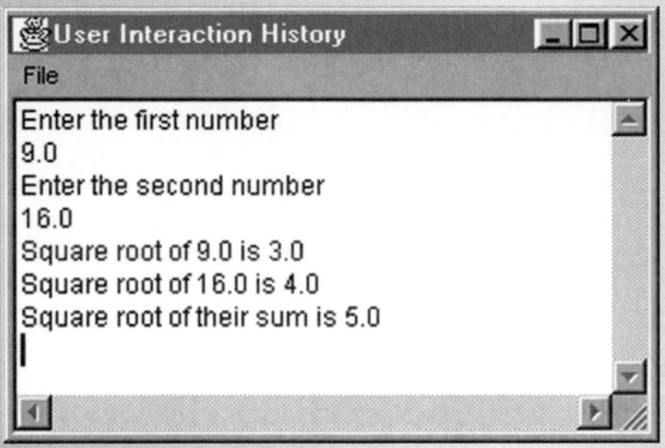

Figure 4.14 Sample run of SquareRootDemo

Methods in Class Math

Table 4.1 lists the names and descriptions of some of the methods in class Math. Most of them perform common mathematical computations. You may recognize several methods (sin (sine), cos (cosine), tan (tangent), asin (arcsine), acos (arccosine), atan (arctangent)) from an earlier course in trigonometry.

Table 4.1 Methods in class Math

Method	Purpose	Argument	Result type
abs(x)	Returns the absolute value of x	any numeric type	same as argument
acos(x)	Inverse cosine—Returns the angle y in radians satisfying $x = \cos(y)$; $-1 \leq x \leq 1; 0 \leq y \leq \pi$	double	double (radians)
asin(x)	Inverse sine—Returns the angle y in radians satisfying $x = \sin(y)$; $-1 \leq x \leq 1; -\pi/2 \leq y \leq \pi/2$	double	double (radians)
atan(x)	arctangent—Returns the angle y in radians satisfying $x = \tan(y)$; $-\pi/2 < y < \pi/2$	double	double (radians)
ceil(x)	Returns smallest whole number $\geq x$	double	double

continued

Table 4.1 *continued*

Method	Purpose	Argument	Result type
cos(x)	Returns the cosine of angle x	double (radians)	double
exp(x)	Returns e^x where $e = 2.71828...$	double	double
floor(x)	Returns largest whole number $\leq x$	double	double
log(x)	Returns the natural logarithm of x (base e) for $x > 0.0$	double	double
max(x, y)	Returns the larger of x and y	any numeric type	same as argument
min(x, y)	Returns the smaller of x and y	any numeric type	same as argument
pow(x, y)	Returns x^y. An error will occur if $x = 0$ and $y \leq 0$, or $x < 0$ and y is not a whole number.	any numeric type	double
random()	Returns a pseudorandom number between 0.0 and 1.0	double	double
rint(x)	Returns the closest whole number to x	double	double
round(x)	Returns the type int value closest to x	double	int
sin(x)	Returns the sine of angle x	double (radians)	double
sqrt(x)	Returns the positive square root of x for $x > 0.0$	double	double
tan(x)	Returns the tangent of angle x	double (radians)	double

Methods abs, max, and min can take arguments of any numeric type; they return a value of the same type as the argument. Method round takes a type double argument and rounds it to the nearest type int value. The remaining methods take type double argument(s) and return a type double value.

The argument for `log` and `sqrt` must be positive. The argument for `sin`, `cos`, and `tan` must be expressed in radians, not degrees. Methods `acos`, `asin`, and `atan` express their results in radians. Methods `min`, `max`, and `pow` take two arguments.

EXAMPLE 4.2

We can use the `Math` method `sqrt` to compute the roots of a quadratic equation in x of the form

$$ax^2 + bx + c = 0$$

The two roots are defined as

$$\text{root}_1 = \frac{-b + \sqrt{b^2 - 4ac}}{2a}$$

$$\text{root}_2 = \frac{-b - \sqrt{b^2 - 4ac}}{2a}$$

when the *discriminant* $(b^2 - 4ac)$ is greater than zero. If we assume that this is the case, we can use the following assignment statements to assign values to `root1` and `root2`:

```
// Compute two roots, root1 and root2, for disc > 0.0.
disc = b * b - 4 * a * c ;
root1 = (-b + Math.sqrt(disc)) / (2 * a);
root2 = (-b - Math.sqrt(disc)) / (2 * a);
```

EXAMPLE 4.3

If we know the length of two sides (b and c) of a triangle and the angle between them in degrees (*alpha*) (see Fig. 4.15), we can compute the length of the third side (a) by using the formula

$$a^2 = b^2 + c^2 - 2bc \cos alpha$$

To use class `Math` cosine method (`cos`), we must express its argument angle in radians instead of degrees. To convert an angle from degrees to radians, we multiply the angle by $\pi/180$. The following Java assignment statement computes the unknown side length:

```
a = Math.sqrt(b * b + c * c -
      2 * b * c * Math.cos(alpha * Math.PI / 180.0));
```

This statement uses the constant `PI` (value of π) defined in class `Math`.

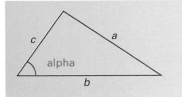

Figure 4.15 Triangle with unknown side *a*

The method `random` generates a random number. A *random number* is a number that is selected from a specified range of numbers (the range is `0.0` to `1.0` for method `random`). Each of the numbers in the range is equally likely to be selected. Random numbers can be used to simulate the toss of a coin (two possible values) or the throw of a die (six possible values). (Technically, method `random` returns a *pseudorandom* number because, unlike real random numbers, the numbers it generates will eventually repeat.)

EXAMPLE 4.4

Figure 4.16 shows a Java application that provides drill and practice in multiplication. In method `setQuestion` (class `Question`), the statement

```
factor1 = (int) (limit * Math.random() + 1);
```

assigns a random integer between `1` and `limit` to `factor1`. The result returned by `Math.random()` (a real number between `0.0` and `1.0`) is multiplied by `limit`, yielding a real number between `0.0` and `limit`. We add `1` to this number and use the typecasting operator `(int)` to extract the integral part of the result (an integer between `1` and `limit`). If `limit` is `10` and `0.712` and `0.875` are the values returned by `Math.random()`, method `getAnswer` displays the prompt

```
Enter the value of 8 x 9
```

and stores the user's answer in `answer`. Method `showResult` computes and displays the actual product, so the user can check the answer.

In a more complete drill and practice program, the program would compare the value of `factor1 * factor2` to the user's answer and would display an appropriate message. You will learn how to do this in the next chapter. Figure 4.17 shows an application object that displays two `Question` sessions. Figure 4.18 shows a sample run.

```
/*    File: Question.java
      Developed for Problem Solving with Java,
         Koffman & Wolz
      Appears in Figure 4.16
*/
import simpleIO.*;
```

Figure 4.16 *continued*

Figure 4.16 *continued*

```java
public class Question extends SimpleGUI {
    // Data fields
    private int factor1;  // multiplicand (0 - 10)
    private int factor2;  // multiplier (0 - 10)
    private int answer;   // input - student's answer


    // Methods
    public void setQuestion() {
        private int limit = 10;
        factor1 = (int) (limit * Math.random() + 1);
        factor2 = (int) (limit * Math.random() + 1);
    }

    public void getAnswer(){
        setQuestion();
        answer = getInt("Enter the product of " +
                        factor1 + " * " + factor2);
    }

    public void showResult() {
        displayResult("You said the product of " +
                      factor1 + " * " + factor2 +
                      " is " + answer);
        displayResult("The correct answer is " +
                      factor1 * factor2);
    }
} // Class Question
```

Figure 4.16 Multiplication practice program

```java
/*   File: Quiz.java
     Developed for Problem Solving with Java,
       Koffman & Wolz
     Appears in Figure 4.17
*/
public class Quiz {

    public static void main (String[] args) {
```

Figure 4.17   *continued*

Figure 4.17 *continued*

```
        // Create a Question object.
        Question quest = new Question();

        // Ask a question based on one pair of
        // random numbers.
        quest.getAnswer();
        quest.showResult();

        // Ask a second question based on new
        // pair of numbers.
        quest.getAnswer();
        quest.showResult();
    }
} // Class Quiz
```

Figure 4.17 The Quiz application asks two Questions

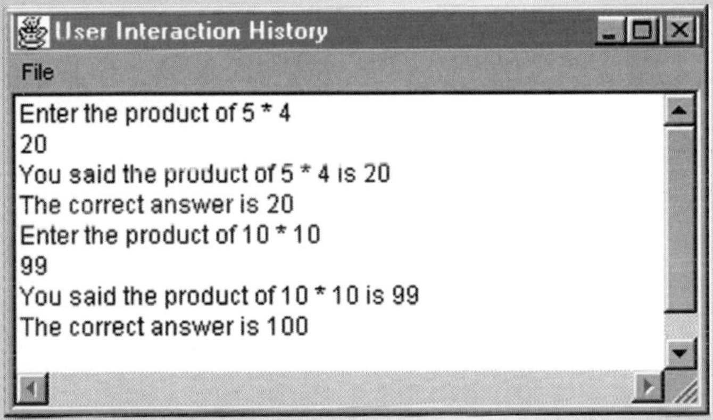

Figure 4.18 Sample run of Quiz application

Methods that Return Whole Numbers

Table 4.1 lists three methods, floor, ceil, and rint, that return a type double whole number based on their type double argument. You can think of methods floor and ceil as returning the whole numbers (type double) that bracket a type double value: floor(x) returns the largest whole number less than or equal to x and ceil(x) returns the smallest whole number greater than or equal to x. Figure 4.19 shows the relationship between a real value and the whole numbers that bracket it. The *x*-axis shows the whole numbers from –3 to 3 in increasing order.

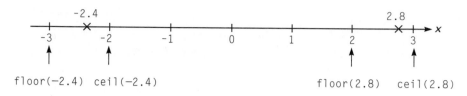

Figure 4.19 Methods floor and ceil with arguments –2.4 and 2.8

Method rint (round integer) returns the nearest whole number corresponding to its type double value. If the fractional part of the argument is
0.5 or larger, rint rounds up; otherwise, it rounds down (e.g., rint(7.4)
is 7.0 and rint(7.5) is 8.0). Method round performs the same operation as rint; however, it returns a type int value instead of a type double
value (e.g., round(-7.4) is –7 and round(-7.5) is –8).

EXERCISES FOR SECTION 4.4

Self-Check

1. Rewrite the following mathematical expressions using Java methods:
   a. $u + v \times w^2$
   b. $\log_e (x^y)$
   c. $(x - y)^3$
   d. $|xy - w/z|$
   e. $\sqrt{x^2 + y^2}$

2. Evaluate the following method calls and indicate the type of the result:
   a. Math.floor(-15.8)
   b. Math.round(-15.8)
   c. Math.round(6.8) * Math.sqrt(3)
   d. (int)-15.8 * Math.sqrt(3)
   e. Math.sqrt(Math.abs(Math.round(-15.8)))
   f. Math.round(3.5)
   g. Math.sqrt(3.0)
   h. Math.floor(22.1) * Math.sqrt(3)
   i. Math.floor(3.2)
   j. Math.ceil(3.2)

3. What is a class method? What is an instance method? How do you reference a class method? How do you reference an instance method?

Programming

1. Write statements that read values into *x* and *y* and compute and display the absolute difference (e.g., if *x* is 7 and *y* is 9, the absolute difference is 2).

2. Using the `round` method, write a Java statement to round any real value *x* to the nearest two decimal places. *Hint:* You will have to multiply the value by 100 before rounding, round the result, and then divide by 100.

3. Write a complete Java program that prompts the user for the Cartesian coordinates of two points, (x_1, y_1) and (x_2, y_2), and displays the distance between them computed by using the following formula:

$$distance = \sqrt{(x_1 - x_2)^2 + (y_1 - y_2)^2}$$

4. The trigonometric functions expect their input to be in radians rather than degrees. Write a class that converts between radians and degrees. *Hint:* 2π radians = 360 degrees.

4.5 Accessors, Modifiers, Constructors, and Class Methods

Until now, all our methods, except for `main`, have had no arguments or inputs. This section shows how to write your own Java methods with arguments. First, we explain how to write some simple methods that return an object's private data. We end the section with a discussion of class methods.

Accessor and Modifier Methods

We have stressed that it is good programming practice for the data fields of a class to be private or protected. If the class is used to support another object such as an application, there is no way for that object to reference the support object's data directly. For example, a user of class `Circle` (Fig. 4.2) might want to use the circle's radius in some special calculation. Currently, the only way to do this would be to extend class `Circle` and include a new method that performs the special calculation in the subclass. A better approach is to provide `public` **accessor methods**, or methods that return the values stored in an object's data fields.

Just as we need to access an object's private or protected data from another object, we sometimes need to store data in an object's private or protected data fields. We use **modifier methods** to do this.

Figure 4.20 shows a new class `Circle` with an accessor method and a modifier method at the bottom. The accessor method returns the type `double` value stored in data field `radius`. The modifier method stores its argu-

accessor method:
a method that returns the value stored in an object's data field to another object.

modifier method:
a method that is used by an object to store a value in another object's data field.

ment value in data field `radius`. Because these methods are available, we changed the visibility of `radius` from `protected` to `private`. We discuss constructors in the next section.

EXAMPLE 4.5

Assume `aCircle` is a `Circle` object declared in another class. In this class, you can use the statement

`aCircle.setRadius(diameter / 2);`

to store half the value of `diameter` in data field `radius` of object `aCircle`. Similarly, you can use the expression

`Math.sqrt(aCircle.getRadius())`

to calculate the square root of data field `radius` of object `aCircle`.

```
/*    File: Circle.java
      Developed for Problem Solving with Java,
        Koffman & Wolz
      Appears in Figure 4.20
*/
import simpleIO.*;

public class Circle extends SimpleGUI {
     // Data fields
     private double radius;   // input - circle radius

     // Methods
     // Constructors
     public Circle() {}   // Don't do anything special
                          //    here.

     public Circle(double rad) {
          radius = rad;
     }

     // Reads circle radius.
     public void readRadius() {
          radius = getDouble("Circle radius:");
     }

     // Computes circle area.
     public double computeArea() {
          return Math.PI * radius * radius;
     }
```

Figure 4.20 *continued*

Figure 4.20 *continued*

```
    // Computes circle circumference.
    public double computeCircumf() {
        return 2 * Math.PI * radius;
    }


    // Computes and displays circle area and
    //    circumference.
    public void showCircle() {
        displayResult("Radius is " + radius);
        displayResult("Area is " + computeArea());
        displayResult("Circumference is " +
                        computeCircumf());
    }


    // Accessor
    // Returns the value in the radius field.
    public double getRadius() {
        return radius;
    }


    // Modifier
    // Stores a value in the radius field.
    public void setRadius(double rad) {
        radius = rad;
    }
} //class Circle
```

Figure 4.20 Class `Circle` with accessors, modifiers, and constructors

Defining Constructors

Sometimes an application object needs to specify certain data field values when it creates a support object. Recall that every class has a constructor method that is called when an object is created. So far the default constructor has been built automatically for us by the compiler. We now show how you can define the constructor method yourself.

EXAMPLE 4.6

You need to process a circle object with radius 1 (a unit circle). The application object can create a new `Circle` object, `unitCircle`, using the statement

```
Circle unitCircle = new Circle(1.0);
```

which passes the value 1.0 as an argument to a constructor method for class Circle.

Figure 4.20 shows two constructor methods, each with the class name Circle. The first one is the default constructor and has no argument list and an empty method body. The default constructor automatically initializes all data fields to zero when it is called by the expression new Circle(). The argument list in the second constructor indicates that it has one type double argument, rad. When the expression new Circle(1.0) executes, it creates a new Circle object with all data fields set to the default value of zero. Then the statement

```
radius = rad;
```

resets the value of data field radius to the argument value, or 1.0. Notice that we do not specify a result type in a constructor header. A constructor always returns an object of the class type.

The compiler creates a default constructor only if you don't. If you define a constructor, you must also define the default constructor, even if you don't want it to do anything special. Although this approach may seem strange now, in Chapter 8 you will see the flexibility it actually provides. Without the default constructor, you will not be able to create new objects using the expression new circle(). If you attempt to do so, you will get the message: build failed—no constructor circle() found in class circle.

Defining Class Methods

We mentioned that class Math has class methods that you call by using the prefix Math. Class methods are convenient because they allow you to call a method without having to create an instance of the class. You may want to create your own mathlike class to perform some common computations. The modifier static preceding a method definition makes the method a class method.

EXAMPLE 4.7

Often, we want to determine a random integer within a specified range of values. We can use method randIntRange defined in class MyMath (Fig. 4.21) to accomplish this. Method randIntRange takes two integer arguments, low and high, and returns a random integer in the range low through high, inclusive. The expression returned is a generalization of the expression in Example 4.4 which calculates a random integer between 1 and limit, inclusive.

Class MyMath also contains a method, aveTwo, which returns the average value of its two type double arguments. Notice that both of these methods are declared as static, so you can call them with the prefix MyMath instead of attempting to apply them to an object of type MyMath.

```
/*    File: MyMath.java
      Developed for Problem Solving with Java,
        Koffman & Wolz
      Appears in Figure 4.21
*/
import java.io.* ;

public class MyMath {

      // Returns a random integer in range low to high,
      //    inclusive.
      public static int randomIntRange(int low,
                                        int high) {
            return (int) ((high - low + 1) * Math.random()
                      + low);
      }

      // Returns the average of its two arguments.
      public static double aveTwo (double first,
                                    double second) {
            return (first + second) / 2.0;
      }
} // Class MyMath
```

Figure 4.21 Class MyMath with methods randomIntRange and aveTwo

Next, we show a sample call for each method. The first assignment statement simulates the tossing of a die, storing a value between 1 and 6 in nextToss. The next statement displays the average of two data fields passed as arguments to method aveTwo. We leave it as an exercise to create an application that includes these statements.

```
//Store the result of "tossing a die" in nextToss.
nextToss = MyMath.randIntRange(1, 6);

//Display the average of data fields x and y.
displayResult("The average of " + x +
              " and " + y + " is " +
                 MyMath.aveTwo(x, y));
```

EXERCISES FOR SECTION 4.5

Self-Check

1. What is an accessor?
2. What is a constructor?

3. Why is it worthwhile to create constructors with arguments?

4. Under what circumstances is it better to define a class method rather than an instance method?

5. Design a class `Box` that calculates the volume and surface area of a box given its height, width, and length. The volume is defined as the product of the height, width, and length. The surface area can be calculated by summing the areas of the six sides. (*Hint:* There are actually only three unique sides!). Include the following constructors:

    ```
    Box() // unit box (height,width,length = 1)
    Box(int s) // cube, height = width = length = s
    Box(int squareBase, int h) // width = length
    Box(int h, int w, int l)
    ```

    Include accessors for each of the data fields you define.

6. Design a class that has class methods for converting between radians and degrees. 2π radians = 360 degrees.

7. If data fields are declared public, do you need accessors and modifiers? How does this affect the reliability of code? List the pros and cons of the two approaches: `public` data fields vs. `private` data fields with accessors and modifiers.

8. Both modifiers and constructors enable you to store data in an object. How are they different?

9. At first it is rather annoying that the default constructor is no longer automatically built if you define any other constructor. There is, however, a good rationale for this. Come up with an example in which you might not want a default constructor, but do want other constructors.

Programming

1. Implement a solution to Self-Check Exercise 5.

2. Implement a solution to Self-Check Exercise 6.

3. Use your solution in Programming Exercise 2 to write an application object that displays the radians that correspond to the following values in degrees: 0, 30, 60, 90, 180.

4. Use your solution in Programming Exercise 2 to write an application object that displays degrees that correspond to the following values in radians: 0, $\pi/2$, π, $3\pi/2$, 2π.

5. Design and implement a class with class methods that finds the integer bounds of a type `double` value. *Hint:* Use `Math.floor` and `Math.ceil`.

4.6 Introduction to Computer Graphics

So far all our output has been in the form of GUI windows that contain textual information. Java provides a collection of graphics methods that enable you to draw pictures or graphical patterns (**computer graphics**) on a **drawing surface** such as a computer screen. You can draw lines and various geometric shapes (e.g., rectangles, circles, ovals) with a **graphics context**. You can specify the position of each shape and also its color. In Java, a graphics context, or object used for drawing, is accessed through the Graphics class.

Composition of Drawing Surface

In graphics programming, you control the location on a drawing surface of each line or shape that you draw. Consequently, you must know the size of your drawing surface and how to reference the individual picture elements (called **pixels**) on it.

You can visualize a drawing surface as an *x–y* grid of pixels. Assume that your surface has the dimensions 400 × 300. Figure 4.22 shows your surface and the coordinates for the four pixels at the corners. The pixel at the top-left corner has *x–y* coordinates (0, 0), and the position at the top-right corner has *x–y* coordinates (400, 0).

computer graphics:
the drawing of pictures or graphical patterns on a drawing surface.

drawing surface:
a device such as a computer display or printer that has the capability for drawing graphics.

graphics context:
an object used for painting or drawing graphics.

pixel:
a picture element on a computer screen.

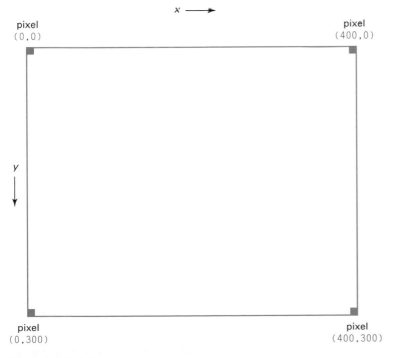

Figure 4.22 Referencing pixels in a window

Notice that Java numbers the pixels in the *y*-direction in a different way than we are accustomed to. The pixel (0, 0) is at the top-left corner of the screen, and the *y*-coordinate values increase as we move down the screen. In a normal *x–y* coordinate system, the point (0, 0) is at the bottom-left corner.

The easiest way to get a drawing surface in Java is through an applet. In this section you will see how to display various shapes in an applet; in Chapters 9 and 10 you will see how to create your own windows with scroll bars, buttons, and the like.

The AWT Class Library

Chapter 1 mentioned that Java provides a class library called the Abstract Window Toolkit (AWT) to facilitate graphics and GUI programming. When you wish to draw, you must import the AWT package `java.awt`. The AWT contains a hierarchy of classes for displaying windows and GUI components. Figure 1.9 shows a portion of the component hierarchy that includes the `Applet` class. Every component (`Window`, `Frame`, `Button`, `Panel`, `Applet`, and so on) has an associated drawing surface that can be accessed through its `paint` method. In this chapter we will extend the `Applet` class, inheriting its ability to draw graphics.

We will explain applets in detail in Chapter 9. For now, recall from Chapter 2 that an application object contains a method `main` that tells the Java interpreter where to start processing. An application class is a completely self-sufficient entity that may rely on support objects to do its job. An applet is not self-sufficient. It is intended to be a support object in a larger context such as a Web browser like Netscape or Internet Explorer. You can therefore start up an applet from a browser, or you can use the program `appletviewer` (see Appendix A). The Java interpreter expects to process a compiled class file (a file with extension `.class`). In contrast, a browser or the appletviewer, expects an HTML file, which is a sequence of instructions in the **HyperText Markup Language** (a file with extension `.html`).

Figure 4.23 shows a small HTML file that starts up an applet. More elaborate HTML files will be shown in Chapter 9. For now, look at the text in the HTML file that is in color. These are the parts that change depending on the applet you wish to view in the browser. The text on the first line surrounded by `title` will appear on the browser's frame header (see Figure 4.24). The file that must be loaded to start the applet follows the directive `code=`. The filename (file `Intersection.class` in this case) must be inside double quotes, and it must be a compiled Java `.class` file. You must also specify a width and height (in pixels) for the applet drawing surface. Finally, we follow a convention of applet developers and include a link to the source code (after `href=`). In Fig. 4.23 the text `The source` is highlighted. If you click on this text in a browser, you will be taken to the source file for the applet (file `Intersection.java`).

Three files play a role in the HTML page defined in Fig. 4.23. All of them must reside in the same directory for the HTML file to work properly.

- *htmlFileName*.html   specifies the HTML page that is displayed by the browser
- *className*.class   specifies the compiled applet that is to be executed
- *className*.java   specifies the source file that may be viewed through a link

```
<title>Class Intersection</title>
<hr>
<applet code="Intersection.class" width=300 height=200>
</applet>
<hr>
<a href="Intersection.java">The source.</a>
```

Figure 4.23 An HTML file for the Intersection applet

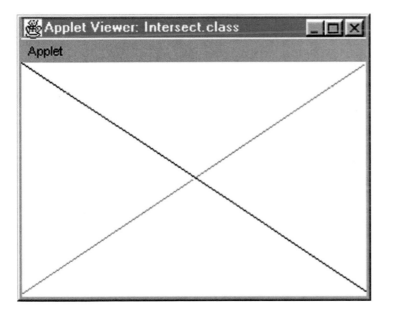

Figure 4.24 Viewing applet Intersection in a browser

Figure 4.25 shows class Intersection, which draws the black and blue intersecting lines shown in Fig. 4.24. Class Intersection extends Applet. Notice that Intersection must import both java.awt.* and java.applet.Applet. Class Intersection defines a single method, paint. Method paint has a single argument, object g of class Graphics. This object will be called upon to do the actual drawing using methods defined in class Graphics (setColor, drawLine, and so on).

Each call to method `setColor` sets the color to be used by all drawing methods until the next call to `setColor` occurs. Therefore, the first call to `drawLine` draws a black line and the second call to `drawLine` draws a blue line. Table 4.2 shows the standard color values defined as constants in class `Color` (indicated by the prefix `Color.`). Although we will not go into details here, you can "mix" your own colors if these are not satisfactory.

```
/*    File: Intersection.java
      Developed for Problem Solving with Java, Koffman & Wolz
      Appears in Figure 4.25
*/
import java.awt.*;
import java.applet.Applet;

public class Intersection extends Applet {

    public void paint(Graphics g) {

        // Draw a black line from (0,0) to (300, 200).
        g.setColor(Color.black);
        g.drawLine(0, 0, 300, 200);

        // Draw a blue line from (300, 0) to (0, 200).
        g.setColor(Color.blue);
        g.drawLine(300, 0, 0, 200);
    }
} // Class Intersection
```

Figure 4.25 Class `Intersection`

Table 4.2 Color constants (defined in class `Color`)

black	gray	magenta	red
blue	green	orange	white
cyan	lightGray	pink	yellow
darkGray			

Method `drawLine` has four arguments. The first two are the x–y coordinates of the line's starting point and the last two are the x–y coordinates of its ending point. It "draws a line" by changing the color of all pixels in the line defined by its arguments to the current color (as set by `setColor`).

Drawing Rectangles

You can use method `drawRect` (defined in class `Graphics`) to draw a rectangle on the screen. The statement

```
g.drawRect(x1, y1, 100, 50);
```

draws a rectangle that has point (x1, y1) as its top-left corner and has a width of 100 pixels and a height of 50 pixels (Fig. 4.26).

Figure 4.26 Rectangle with (x1, y1) as top-left corner

EXAMPLE 4.8

Class House (see Fig. 4.27) draws a house. The variables define four corner points of the house (points (x1, y1) through (x4, y4)). The two calls to drawLine draw the roof as a pair of lines meeting at point (x2, y2). The first call to drawRect draws the rest of the house. The second call to drawRect draws the door with top-left corner at point (x5, y5) and bottom-right corner at point (x6, y6).

We specified two corner points for the rectangular part of the house and the door; however, method drawRect requires the width and height of a rectangle as its third and fourth arguments. We account for this by passing the difference between the *x*-coordinates as the third argument and the difference between the *y*-coordinates as the fourth argument.

Figure 4.28 shows the HTML file that loads the applet (House.html), and Fig. 4.29 shows the applet in a viewer. This HTML file begins with a four-line comment. We laid out the house assuming a window size of 600 × 500. For different window dimensions, you may want to redefine the coordinates of the corner points. Next, we explain the purpose of the calls to method drawString at the end of the class.

```
/*    File: House.java
      Developed for Problem Solving with Java,
         Koffman & Wolz
      Appears in Figure 4.27
*/
import java.awt.*;
import java.applet.Applet;
```

Figure 4.27 *continued*

Figure 4.27 *continued*

```java
public class House extends Applet {

    // 4 corner points for the house
    int x1 = 100;   int y1 = 200;   // lower-left
                                    //    corner of roof
    int x2 = 300;   int y2 = 100;   // peak of roof
    int x3 = 500;   int y3 = 200;   // lower-right
                                    //    corner of roof
    int x4 = 500;   int y4 = 400;   // bottom-right
                                    //    corner of house


    // Corner points for door
    int x5 = 275;   int y5 = 325;   // top-left
                                    //    corner of door
    int x6 = 325;   int y6 = 400;   // bottom-right
                                    //    corner of door


    public void paint(Graphics g) {
        g.setColor(Color.black);

        //Draw the roof.
        g.drawLine(x1, y1, x2, y2);
        g.drawLine(x2, y2, x3, y3);

        //Draw the house as a box.
        g.drawRect(x1, y1, x4 - x1, y4 - y1);

        //Draw a door.
        g.drawRect(x5, y5, x6 - x5, y6 - y5);

        //Label the corner points.
        g.drawString("(x1,y1)", x1, y1);
        g.drawString("(x2,y2)", x2, y2);
        g.drawString("(x3,y3)", x3, y3);
        g.drawString("(x4,y4)", x4, y4);
        g.drawString("(x5,y5)", x5, y5);
        g.drawString("(x6,y6)", x6, y6);
    }
} // Class House
```

Figure 4.27 Class House

```
<!    File: House.html
      Developed for Problem Solving with Java,
        Koffman & Wolz
      Appears in Figure 4.28 >

<title>Class House</title>
<hr>
<applet code="House.class" width=600 height=500>
</applet>
<hr>
<a href="House.java">The source.</a>
```

Figure 4.28 HTML file for the House applet

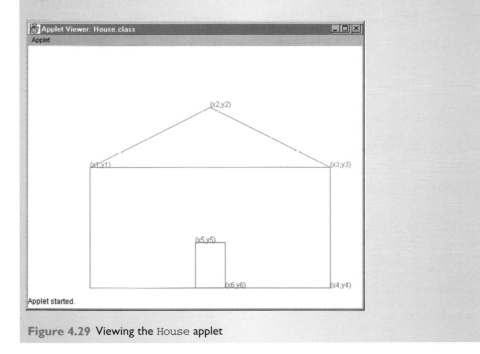

Figure 4.29 Viewing the House applet

Adding Text to Drawings

In graphics mode, you must draw characters just as you draw other shapes. Java provides a method, drawString, to do this. In Fig. 4.27, the method call

```
g.drawString("(x1,y1)", x1, y1);
```

draws each character in a string (its first argument) starting at the point whose *x*–*y* coordinates are specified by the last two arguments. The string "(x1,y1)" starts at the pixel whose *x*-coordinate is x1 and whose *y*-coordinate is y1.

Hence, the calls to method `drawString` draw labels at the corner points of the house and door (Fig. 4.29).

Drawing Arcs and Circles

Method `drawArc` draws an arc. The method call

```
g.drawArc(x, y, 100, 100, 0, 90);
```

draws an arc (see Fig. 4.30) bounded by a rectangle 100 pixels in width and height whose top-left corner is point (x, y). The arc begins at an angle of 0 degrees and extends for 90 degrees in a counterclockwise direction. If you imagine a clock on the screen, 0 degrees is at 3 o'clock (horizontal direction) and 90 degrees is at 12 o'clock (straight up).

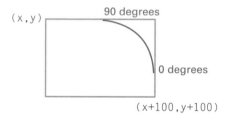

Figure 4.30 Arc drawn by `g.drawArc(x, y, 100, 100, 0, 90)`

You can use this method to draw a circle as an arc of 360 degrees. However, the `Graphics` class also has a method `drawOval` that draws a 360 degree arc within a rectangle. The method call

```
g.drawArc(x, y, 100, 100, 0, 360);
```

is equivalent to

```
g.drawOval(x, y, 100, 100);
```

Usually we specify a circle's center and radius, rather than its bounding rectangle. A circle with center at point (x1, y1) and radius r could be drawn inside a square whose top-left corner is at point (x1-r, y1-r). The length of each side of the bounding square would be the same as the circle's diameter. Therefore, use the method call

```
g.drawOval(x1-r, y1-r, 2 * r, 2 * r);
```

to draw this circle (see Fig. 4.31).

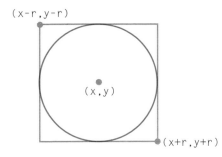

Figure 4.31 Drawing a circle inside a square

EXAMPLE 4.9

Method `paint` in class `HappyFace` (Fig. 4.32) draws an outer circle first (radius `headRadius`). Next it draws three smaller circles representing the eyes (radius `eyeRadius`) and nose (radius `noseRadius`). Finally, it draws the smile as an arc of 120 degrees staring at 210 degrees (8 o'clock). The arc has the same center as the outer circle but its radius is three-fourths as large. Figure 4.33 shows the applet. The `.html` file is left as an exercise.

```
/*    File: HappyFace.java
      Developed for Problem Solving with Java,
        Koffman & Wolz
      Appears in Figure 4.32
*/
import java.awt.*;
import java.applet.Applet;

public class HappyFace extends Applet {

    // window dimensions
    int maxX = 500;    int maxY = 400;

    // center of head and radius of head
    int headX = maxX / 2;   int headY = maxY / 2;
    int headRadius = maxY / 4;

    // position of eyes and radius of eyes
    int leftEyeX = headX - headRadius / 4;
    int rightEyeX = headX + headRadius / 4;
    int eyeY = headY - headRadius / 4;
    int eyeRadius = headRadius / 10;
```

Figure 4.32 *continued*

Figure 4.32 *continued*

```
    // position of nose and radius of nose
    int noseX = headX;
    int noseY = headY + headRadius / 4;
    int noseRadius = eyeRadius;

    // radius of smile
    int smileRadius =
            (int) Math.round(0.75 * headRadius);

public void paint(Graphics g) {
    g.setColor(Color.black);

    // Draw head.
    g.drawOval(headX - headRadius,
                headY - headRadius,
                2 * headRadius, 2 * headRadius);

    // Draw left eye.
    g.drawOval(leftEyeX - eyeRadius,
                eyeY - eyeRadius,
                2 * eyeRadius, 2 * eyeRadius);

    // Draw right eye.
    g.drawOval(rightEyeX - eyeRadius,
                eyeY - eyeRadius,
                2 * eyeRadius, 2 * eyeRadius);

    // Draw nose.
    g.drawOval(noseX - noseRadius,
                noseY - noseRadius,
                2 * noseRadius, 2 * noseRadius);

    // Draw smile.
    g.drawArc(headX - smileRadius,
                headY - smileRadius,
                2 * smileRadius, 2 * smileRadius,
                    210, 120);
    }
} // Class HappyFace
```

Figure 4.32 Class HappyFace

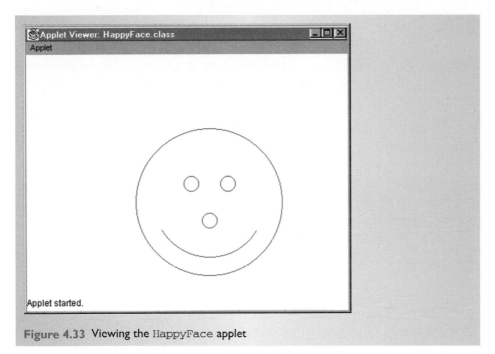

Figure 4.33 Viewing the HappyFace applet

Program Style: *Writing General Graphics Programs*
Method paint in Fig. 4.32 is general, so you can easily expand and shrink the
happy face by changing the values of maxX and maxY. On the other hand, the
size and position of the house drawn by method paint in Fig. 4.27 cannot easily
be changed. As you can see, it is generally easier to draw graphical images that
are fixed in size; however, with a little practice you should be able to write general graphics programs. To generalize the program in Fig. 4.27, you could base
the coordinates of the house corners on the screen dimensions (for example,
maxX = 600, maxY = 500) as shown below (see also Self-Check Exercise 4 in
this section).

```
int x2 = maxX / 2;      // peak of roof - middle of x-range and
int y2 = maxY - 20;     // just below top of y-range
```

Drawing Filled Figures

So far all our graphics figures have been line drawings. You can fill in sections of the screen using different colors. Use method fillRect to actually
fill in a rectangle. The method call statement

```
g.drawRect(x1, y1, 100, 50);
```

fills the rectangle shown earlier in Fig. 4.27 by changing the color of all
pixels inside the rectangle to the current drawing color.

EXAMPLE 4.10

The class `PaintedHouse` (see Fig. 4.34) extends class `house` (see Fig. 4.27). Class `PaintedHouse` calls method `fillRect` to color the pixels in the rectangular portion of the house blue and to color the pixels in the door gray (see Fig. 4.35). The statement

```
super.paint(g);
```

draws the outline of the house shown earlier (Fig. 4.29). The next program style display explains the meaning of this statement.

```
/*    FILE: PaintedHouse.java
      Developed for Problem Solving with Java,
        Koffman & Wolz
      Appears in Figure 4.34
*/
import java.awt.*;

public class PaintedHouse extends House {

    public void paint(Graphics g) {

        // Draw the house.
        super.paint(g);

        // Paint the house blue.
        g.setColor(Color.blue);
        g.fillRect(x1, y1, x4 - x1, y4 - y1);

        // Paint the door gray.
        g.setColor(Color.gray);
        g.fillRect(x5, y5, x6 - x5, y6 - y5);
    }
} // Class PaintedHouse
```

Figure 4. 34 Class `PaintedHouse`

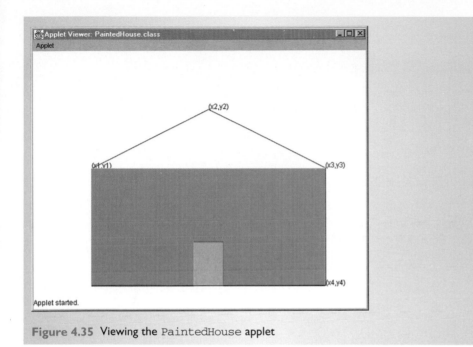

Figure 4.35 Viewing the PaintedHouse applet

Program Style: *Use of Prefix super*

In the statement

```
super.paint(g);
```

the prefix super. represents the parent class (House) of the class being defined (PaintedHouse). Therefore, the above statement calls the paint
method for class House, which draws the outline of the house.

Pie Slices

Java provides methods to draw pie slices. A *pie slice* is a filled segment of a
circle. The method call

```
g.fillArc(x-r, y-r, 2 * r, 2 * r, 20, 30);
```

draws the 30-degree pie slice shown in Fig. 4.36. Method paint in class
Pirate (see Fig. 4.37) uses a similar method call to draw a pirate's eye-
patch (a 50-degree pie slice) over the right eye of the happy face (Fig. 4.38).
The call to method drawString draws the text shown under the face.

Table 4.3 provides a summary of all the methods discussed in this section.

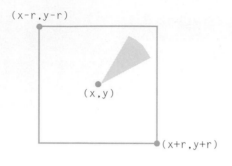

Figure 4.36 A pie slice

```
/*    File: Pirate.java
      Developed for Problem Solving with Java, Koffman & Wolz
      Appears in Figure 4.37
*/
import java.awt.*;

public class Pirate extends HappyFace {

    public void paint(Graphics g) {

        // Draw a happy face.
        super.paint(g);

        // Add an eye patch.
        g.fillArc(headX - smileRadius, headY - smileRadius,
                2 * smileRadius, 2 * smileRadius, 20, 50);

        // Draw a label at the bottom.
        g.drawString("Pirate with an eye patch",
                headX - headRadius, maxY - 20);

    }
} // Class Pirate
```

Figure 4.37 A pirate with an eye patch

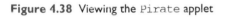

Pirate with an eye patch

Figure 4.38 Viewing the `Pirate` applet

Table 4.3 Summary of graphics methods

Method Call	Effect
`drawArc(x, y, w, h, a1, a2);`	Draws an arc inside the rectangle with top-left corner at (x, y) and bottom-right corner at (x+w, y+h). The arc extends from angle a1 to angle (a1+a2), measured in degrees.
`drawOval(x, y, d, d);`	Draws a circle with diameter d inside the square with top-left corner at (x, y) and bottom-right corner at (x+d, y+d).
`drawLine(x1, y1, x2, y2);`	Draws a line with end points (x1, y1) and (x2, y2).
`drawRect(x, y, w, h);`	Draws a rectangle with top-left corner at (x, y) and bottom-right corner at (x+w, y+h).
`drawString(s, x, y);`	Displays string s starting at (x, y).
`fillOval(x, y, d, d);`	Draws a colored circle with diameter d inside the square with top-left corner at (x, y) and bottom-right corner at (x+d, y+d).
`fillArc(x, y, w, h, a1, a2);`	Draws a colored pie slice inside the rectangle with top-left corner at (x, y) and bottom-right corner at (x+w, y+h). The slice extends from angle a1 to angle (a1+a2), measured in degrees.

Table 4.3 *continued*

Table 4.3 *continued*

Method Call	Effect
`fillRect(x, y, w, h);`	Draws a colored rectangle with top-left corner at (x, y) and bottom-right corner at (x+w, y+h).
`paint(g);`	Draws a graphical image in a window.
`setColor(Color.red);`	Sets the drawing color to `red`.

EXERCISES FOR SECTION 4.6

Self-Check

1. In Fig. 4.32, what is the reason for basing the head radius on `maxY` and not on `maxX`?

2. Explain the relationship between a browser and an applet. Which one is the supporting object?

3. The method paint has an argument g of type `Graphics`. Explain what this object does in the `paint` method.

4. Show the drawing produced by the following fragment. Assume a 640×480 drawing surface.

```
public void paint(Graphics g) {
    g.drawOval(200, 50, 25, 25);
    g.drawLine(200, 75, 100, 100);
    g.drawLine(200, 75, 300, 100);
    g.fillArc(200, 75, 245, 295, 100);
    g.drawLine(200, 150, 100, 250);
    g.drawLine(200, 150, 300, 250);
}
```

5. Write statements to add two windows to the second floor of the house in Fig. 4.29.

6. Modify the program in Fig. 4.27 so that it draws the house in the center of the screen and with the same relative size regardless of the actual drawing surface dimensions.

7. What impact does the `setColor` method have? How long is it in effect?

Programming

1. Write the statements to draw a tennis racket. Use a circle at the end of a thin rectangle. Color the circle yellow.

2. Write a graphics program that draws a rocket ship consisting of a triangle on top of a rectangle. Draw a pair of intersecting lines under the rectangle. Color the rectangle red.

3. Write a program that draws a pair of nested rectangles at the center of the screen. The inner rectangle should be red and the outer rectangle should be white. The outer rectangle should have a width that is one-fourth of the *x*-dimension and a height that is one-fourth of the *y*-dimension of the screen. The height and width of the inner rectangle should be half that of the outer rectangle.

4. Write a program that draws a male and female stick figure side by side.

5. Write an HTML file for the `HappyFace` class. You will need to determine the height and width of the drawing surface ahead of time.

4.7 Common Programming Errors

We have introduced three kinds of visibility. Make sure you declare an explicit visibility for each of your data fields, methods, and classes. Remember that data fields declared with `private` visibility in a superclass cannot be accessed by a subclass of that superclass. If you extend a class, make sure any data fields you need in the subclass have `protected` visibility in the superclass.

`Math` is a special kind of class that only contains class methods (indicated by modifier `static`). You cannot declare an instance of this class. Attempting to do so will cause a compiler error.

Remember that if you define any constructor, then the default constructor will not be automatically built for you. If you want to have the default constructor included, then you must define it as follows in your class definition:

```
public class MyClass {
    . . .
    public MyClass() {} // the default constructor
    . . .
```

Be careful about the data types of arguments you pass to methods, both those in libraries and those you create yourself. If you provide the wrong type argument, the compiler will tell you that the method does not exist. For example, given the method declaration

```
myMethod(String x) {...}
```

the method call:

```
someObject.myMethod(15);
```

causes the compiler to tell you that method `myMethod(int)` is not defined.

Avoid defining classes that have both class methods and instance methods. If you do this and define a class with a data field and a class method, the class method may not be able to access the data field. If you want a class that will preform general operations on its arguments (such as the `Math` methods) without accessing data fields, then use the `static` modifier to define the methods as class methods.

We introduced applets and graphics. Remember that you must import two libraries for applets to work properly:

```
import java.awt.*;
import java.applet.Applet;
```

You cannot define a class that uses both `Applet` and `SimpleGUI` methods because Java only allows you to extend one class. Furthermore, `SimpleGUI` was designed with applications in mind. For now, don't try to write programs that mix interactivity with graphics.

Remember that an applet may only be executed within the context of a Web browser or the `appletviewer` program. If you load an HTML file and the applet doesn't run, or doesn't seem to load, check the following:

- Check to make sure that the `.html` file and the `.class` file reside in the same folder.

- Make sure the applet referenced in the HTML is the one you compiled.

- Check the bounds of the display area. If the bounds are too big or too small, the browser may give up and do nothing.

- Verify that the HTML syntax is correct. Even the slightest mistake will cause the browser to ignore your applet entirely. Use the examples in this chapter as a guide.

- Verify that you are actually drawing within the field you expect to see. Make sure your drawing points are not negative numbers.

- Make sure that your background color and foreground color are not the same. If they are, you will not be able to see what you draw.

- Drawing may only occur within the `paint` method, or by `Graphics` methods that are called by `paint`. If method `paint` calls support methods to do the drawing, you must pass the `Graphics` object `g` to the support methods:

```
public void paint(Graphics g) {
      drawHead(g);
      drawBody(g);
      drawHat(g);
}
```

Make sure you include an argument of type `Graphics` in each support method definition. Remember, it is the `Graphics` object that does the actual drawing. The method `paint` receives the graphics context from the browser.

Chapter Review

1. Develop your program solutions from existing information. Use the system documentation derived from applying the software development method as the initial framework for the program.

   • Edit the data requirements to obtain the data declarations.

   • Use the refined algorithm as the starting point for each method body.

2. If a new problem is an extension of a previous one, modify the previous program rather than starting from scratch. Inheritance allows you to use existing methods and data fields of classes you defined earlier.

3. Using `protected` visibility allows a subclass to access the methods and data fields of the superclass, but prohibits access by other classes.

4. Java includes a package of predefined methods in class `Math` that can simplify mathematical computations. Use the prefix `Math.` in a call to any of the class methods defined in class `Math`.

5. An accessor method retrieves the value of a `private` or `protected` data field. If you include accessor methods in a class definition, you will enable methods declared in other classes to access these data. You control this access because it can occur only through a call to the appropriate accessor method.

6. An application object can set the initial values for the data fields of an object it creates by passing these values through a constructor's argument list. The object's class must define a constructor with a matching argument list. If you define a constructor with an argument list, the compiler will not build a default constructor and you must supply your own default constructor.

7. Each applet (small application) that you write must extend `Applet` and contain a call to method `paint`, which does the actual drawing. The `Graphics` class provides several methods that you can call in method `paint` to draw simple graphical patterns (see Table 4.3). Use a Web browser or appletviewer to view a Java applet. You must include in the same folder as the applet a `.html` file which you can load to start up the applet. Figure 4.23 shows a sample `.html` file which you can modify for your particular applet.

New Java Constructs

Construct	Effect
Visibility Protected	
`protected double area;`	Allows access to data field `area` by methods of a subclass of its class and by methods of its own class.
Modifier `static`	
`double public static do_it(int n) {`	Defines method `do_it` as a class method that can be called by prefixing it with its class name.
Class Constructors	

`public MyClass(int n) {`
`    count = n;`
`}`
	Creates an instance of class `MyClass` and assigns to data field `count` the value of the argument passed to the constructor.

`public MyClass() {}`	Defines a default constructor that you may need if other constructors are defined.
Accessor Method	

`public double getCount() {`
`    return count;`
`}`
	Defines an accessor method that enables methods defined in other classes to retrieve the data in a `private` or `protected` data field.

Quick-Check Exercises

1. Explain how the software development method can be used to develop documentation as you go.
2. Explain how you can use the solution of one problem to extend another.
3. Fill out the following table by describing the word at the left.

visibility	Tells who is allowed access to data fields and methods
`public`	_____
`private`	_____
`protected`	_____

4. The class `Math` contains only class methods. State whether the Java statements below are allowed. Explain each answer.

    ```
    Math mt = new Math();
    x = Math.cos(2 * Math.PI);
    return mt.sqrt(4);
    ```

5. Explain why explicit constructors are useful.
6. Explain why accessors are needed.

7. Under what circumstances should a method be declared as static?

8. What is a drawing surface and which object can draw upon it?

9. What purpose is served in creating an HTML file for an applet?

Answers to Quick-Check Exercises

1. During the design phase of the software development method, you describe the purpose of methods in English. These can be used as comments that precede the method definitions. Similarly, you form an outline of the algorithm during design. These statements can clarify the purpose of Java statements in the actual code.

2. Often a problem solution is adaptable. For example, some methods, especially those that calculate intermediate results, may apply to a new problem.

3. visibility   Tells who is allowed access to data fields and methods

   public   Accessible by any method defined in any class

   private   Accessible only by methods defined in the same class

   protected   Accessible by methods defined in the same class or in any subclass of this class

4. `Math mt = new Math();`   not allowed; you cannot create instances of class `Math`

   `x = Math.cos(2 * Math.PI);`   allowed

   `return mt.sqrt(4);`   not allowed; you must prefix `sqrt` with `Math`.

5. Explicit constructors for a class are useful when the method creating an object instance needs to initialize its data fields.

6. Accessors allow a method defined in another class to retrieve the values of private and protected data fields.

7. A method should be declared as `static` when its actions are not tied to the data fields of an object. An example would be a method that does a calculation based only on values of its arguments.

8. A drawing surface is a device such as display screen or printer that can accept graphics directives and create corresponding images. In the Java AWT, the `Graphics` class is capable of drawing on such surfaces.

9. An applet is a support object for a program such as a browser. The HTML file associated with an applet contains an HTML directive specifying which applet to load and the size of the applet drawing surface.

Review Questions

1. Why is it important to document as you implement. How can the design phase assist in developing documentation?
2. What does it mean to extend an existing solution?
3. Why is `protected` visibility necessary? Explain why `public` and `private` do not provide sufficient flexibility.
4. What is a class method? What is an instance method? What are the advantages and disadvantages of each?
5. Explain the role of constructors, accessors, and modifiers. Under what circumstances do you need each of them?

Programming Projects

1. Write a program that computes the duration of a projectile's flight and its height above the ground when it reaches the target.

> **Problem Inputs**
>
> angle (radians) of elevation
> distance (ft) to target
> projectile velocity (ft/sec)
>
> **Problem Output**
>
> time (sec) of flight
> height at impact
>
> **Relevant Formulas**
>
> *time = distance / (velocity × cos theta)*
> *height = velocity × time − (g × time²)/2*, where *g* = 32.17

2. Four track stars have entered the mile race at the Penn Relays. Write a program that will read in the race time in minutes (`minutes`) and seconds (`seconds`) for a runner and compute and display the speed in feet per second (`feetPS`) and in meters per second (`metersPS`). (*Hint:* There are 5280 feet in one mile, and one kilometer equals 4282 feet.)

Minutes	Seconds
3	52.83
3	59.83
4	00.03
4	16.22

3. In a new computer-assisted board game moves are determined by selecting a random number. However, the player can influence his move by taking a risk. The player selects a number *n* from 1 to 10. The computer then generates a random integer *r* from 1 to 10. The players move

is then $(r - n + 1) * n$. A cautious player selects 1 and always moves forward. The ambitious player selects higher numbers and may move more forward, or may move backward. Write a program to determine one move in the game. Display the computer's integer selection and the move.

4. In shopping for a new house, you must consider several factors. In this problem the initial cost of the house, the estimated annual fuel costs, and the annual tax rate are available. Write a program that will determine the total cost of a house after a five-year period and run it with the following sets of data.

Initial house cost	Annual fuel cost	Tax rate
$67,000	$2,300	0.025
$62,000	$2,500	0.025
$75,000	$1,850	0.020

To calculate the house cost, add the initial cost to the fuel cost for five years, then add the taxes for five years. Taxes for one year are computed by multiplying the tax rate by the initial cost.

5. The first two verses of the song "99 Bottles of Beer on the Wall" are:

> 99 bottles of beer on the wall.
> 99 bottles of beer.
> Take one down and pass it around.
> 98 bottles of beer on the wall.
>
> 98 bottles of beer on the wall.
> 98 bottles of beer.
> Take one down and pass it around.
> 97 bottles of beer on the wall.

Write a program that will display the first five verses of this song.

6. A class with 100 students took an exam in which grades A, B, C, D, and F were assigned. The table lists the number of students who received each grade.

Grade	Number of students
A	20
B	30
C	35
D	10
F	5

You can create a bar graph of this data by using the `Graphics` method `fillRect`. Each bar has a standard width. Each height is dependent upon the number of students with that grade. Draw a bar graph of this data in which each grade is represented in a different color, and each bar is labeled with the corresponding grade and total number of people.

7. Use the data in Programming Project 6 to create a line graph. Use the Graphics method drawLine to plot the points corresponding to the number of students with each grade.

8. Use the data in Programming Project 6 to create a pie chart. In a pie chart, the size of each "slice" should be proportional to the quantity it represents. You may find it useful to create a method that can take a percentage of a circle and return the number of degrees. For example, 25% of a circle is 90 degrees, 50% of a circle is 180 degrees.

9. A horizon effect occurs when objects get progressively smaller along a line. Write a method that draws a figure of your choosing (a house, a flower, a person, an animal). The dimensions of the figure must be variable, like the HappyFace in Fig. 4.32. Start in the lower-left corner of a drawing surface and draw smaller and smaller versions of the figure on a diagonal line toward the upper-right corner of the surface. The visual effect should be of a row of your figures fading into the distance.

10. How do the artists draw three-dimensional figures on a two-dimensional surface? They play tricks on your eyes. You can experiment with this phenomenon by drawing a series of ovals with the same center but with decreasing width. Try to draw the series of ovals in the following diagram.

11. Create some abstract art. Create a few figures of your own choosing that have variable dimensions (see Programming Project 9). Create a class with class methods that randomly select points within a display area as well as figure dimensions. Place figures of random sizes at random positions on the screen.

12. You can use lines to draw any kind of polygon. You simply draw lines from point to point in the figure. For example, you can draw a triangle using three pairs of *x,y* coordinates with lines drawn between them. Design a class that can draw three-, five-, and six-sided polygons. *Hint:* Methods in your class must accept a Graphics object as an argument. Otherwise the paint method cannot call them. Implement the class for triangles.

13. Programming Project 12 required methods with as many as 12 arguments. If you limit yourself to equilateral figures (those whose sides are all the same size) where one side falls along the horizontal axis, you can define any of these figures in terms of a starting point and the length of the side. Implement a class that draws such figures.

Vinton Cerf

Vinton G. Cerf is senior vice president of Internet Architecture and Engineering for MCI Communications Corporation. Cerf holds a Bachelor of Science degree in mathematics from Stanford University and a Masters of Science degree and Ph.D. in computer science from the University of California at Los Angeles. While working on the ARPANET project, Cerf co-designed the TCP/IP protocols of the Internet. He served as president of the Internet Society from 1992–1995.

You majored in mathematics at Stanford. What made you decide to pursue computer science instead?

I had been introduced to computers by my best friend, Steve Crocker, and got a chance to use a Bendix G-15 at UCLA before coming to Stanford. Stanford had a Burroughs 5000, as I recall, and I learned BALGOL on it—a great language. In any case, I took every computer course available and found, by my senior year, that I was more interested in programming than I was in Riemannian geometry.

What was your first job in the computer industry?

I was the systems engineer for IBM's QUIKTRAN time-sharing service operating out of the Los Angeles Data Center on Wilshire Boulevard. I was responsible for maintaining the system software and making upgrades to it. It taught me a lot and also showed me that I knew too little about operating systems and how they worked. Eventually I persuaded myself to return to school for an advanced degree.

How did you come to be involved with ARPANET and the development of the Internet?

Steve Crocker and I, along with Jon Postel, Dave Crocker (Steve's brother) and a number of others at UCLA were part of a crowd of programmers hired by Prof. Len Kleinrock to help build his Network Measurement Center, which he proposed to build as part of the ARPANET project. Our job eventually centered on the design of the computer protocols and implementation of software to realize the designs to aid in resource sharing on the ARPANET. Bob Kahn was one of the chief architects of the ARPANET working at Bolt Beranek and Newman in Cambridge, MA. He visited UCLA to test the fledgling ARPANET, which had about four nodes at the time, the first at UCLA, the second at SRI-International, the third at UC Santa Barbara and the fourth at University of Utah. We met at UCLA and worked together as I had responsibility for programming the applications of the Network Measurement Center. Later, Bob joined ARPA and I went to Stanford. Bob was pursuing packet radio and packet satellite in addition to ARPANET, and he came to Stanford where I had gone after finishing my Ph.D. at UCLA. Eventually, we realized that we would have to find standard ways of linking disparate packet networks together. We invented the "gateway" to link the nets and a new protocol suite, now called TCP/IP (Transmission Control Protocol/Internet Protocol).

Bob and I published a paper in 1974 titled "A Protocol for Packet Network Interconnection" in *IEEE Transactions on Communication*. My research group at Stanford then undertook to do detailed specification and testing of the new protocols.

How would you describe a typical day for you at MCI? What is the most challenging part of your job?

I have no typical days! I travel a great deal—I'm responding to these questions from Madrid at 0420 in the morning. I'm on the Net for hours every day, answering a lot of e-mail. I have meetings with staff, vendors of new hardware and software. I might brief senators, congressmen and their staff on one day, and meet with special interest groups on the next. I have an Internet design and engineering group that builds the MCI Internet systems so I might meet with some of them on a typical day. I might take a video or audio conference call every other day on the average. I even have a chance, now and then, to meet with my own people!

Where do you see the communications industry heading over the next few years?

It is all becoming a data-oriented set of services with packet switching as its primary basis. Rapid growth in Internet applications— audio, video, telephony, online commerce. Internet-enabled appliances such as TV or VCR.

Why did you found the Internet Society in 1992? How do you see its role changing or expanding in the future?

I thought it was important to find ways to support critical administrative infrastructure of the Internet with nongovernmental funding. And I thought it was time that we focus on the societal as well as the technical and business aspects of Internet. I hope it will expand its support role from IETF and annual conferences to helping to shape the administrative structure of the domain name system, copyright and patent laws, privacy and integrity enforcement. Eventually, I hope ISOC can really represent an "Internet" society.

What person in computer science has inspired you?

Bill Wulf with his collaboratory concept; John McCarthy with his work on artificial intelligence topics; J. C. R. Licklider with his vision of networked futures.

Do you have any advice for computer science students today?

Get very involved in networking and distributed processing systems. Everything is going to be connected to everything else!

C H A P T E R 5

Selection Structures

In this chapter you begin studying statements that control the flow of program execution. You will learn to use Java `if` and `switch` statements to select one group of statements to execute from several alternative groups. Through the use of these control statements, you enable your program to evaluate its data and to select a path of execution to follow based on the data.

The chapter begins with a discussion of Boolean expressions because the `if` statement relies on them. Next we discuss the `if` and `switch` statement. In the last section, we discussed exceptions and `try-catch` blocks. Exceptions are potential sources of error in a program, and you can use `try-catch` blocks to detect exceptions and take corrective action when they occur.

We also discuss additional features of class `SimpleGUI`. We show how to enter a `Boolean` value using method `getBoolean`. We also introduce a feature of `SimpleGUI` that enables a program to display a list of choices in a dialog window and get the user's selection.

The text editor case study illustrates common text editing operations, such as string deletion, insertion, replacement, and search. It incorporates all the selection statements discussed in the chapter and illustrates the use of a menu.

5.1 Control Structures

5.2 Boolean Expressions

5.3 The `if` Statement

5.4 `if` Statements with Compound Statements

5.5 Decision Steps in Algorithms
Case Study: Payroll Problem

5.6 Hand-Tracing an Algorithm

5.7 Nested `if` Statements and Multiple-Alternative Decisions

5.8 The `switch` Statement and `SimpleGUI` Menus
Case Study: Simple Text Editor

5.9 Exceptions and `try-catch` Blocks

5.10 Common Programming Errors

Chapter Review

5.1 Control Structures

control structures:
combinations of individual instructions into a single logical unit with one entry point and one exit point.

Structured programming utilizes **control structures** to control the flow of execution in a program or method. The Java control structures enable us to combine individual instructions into a single logical unit with one entry point and one exit point. We can then write a program as a sequence of control structures rather than as a sequence of individual instructions (Fig. 5.1).

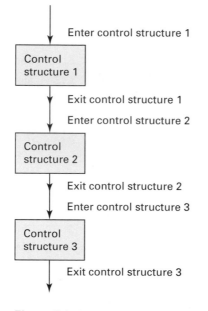

Enter control structure 1

Control structure 1

Exit control structure 1

Enter control structure 2

Control structure 2

Exit control structure 2

Enter control structure 3

Control structure 3

Exit control structure 3

Figure 5.1 A program as a sequence of three control structures

compound statement:
a group of statements bracketed by { and } that are executed sequentially.

There are three kinds of control structures for controlling execution flow: *sequence*, *selection*, and *repetition*. Until now we have been using only sequential flow. A **compound statement** or block, written as a group of statements bracketed by { and }, is used to specify sequential flow.

```
{
        statement₁;
        statement₂;
        . . .
        . . .
        . . .
        statementₙ;
}
```

Control flows from *statement₁* to *statement₂*, and so on. You have been using blocks all along—a method body consists of a single compound statement.

This chapter describes the Java control structures for selection. Some problem solutions require that choices be made between alternative algorithm steps. Depending on the input data, only one of these steps will execute. A **selection control structure** chooses the alternative to execute.

selection control structure:
a control structure that chooses among alternative program statements.

5.2 Boolean Expressions

A program chooses among alternative steps by testing the value of key variables. For example, since different tax rates apply to various salary levels, an income tax program must select the rate appropriate for each worker by comparing the worker's salary to the salary range for a particular income tax bracket. In Java, Boolean expressions, or conditions, perform such comparisons. Each Boolean expression has two possible values, `true` or `false`, where `true` indicates a successful test and `false` indicates an unsuccessful test.

Boolean Variables

The simplest Boolean expression is a `boolean` variable. The variable declarations

```
boolean leapYear = true;
boolean switch;
boolean flag;
```

declare `leapYear`, `switch`, and `flag` to be `boolean` variables—variables that may be assigned only the values `true` and `false`. Further, the `boolean` variable `leapYear` has the value `true`.

Given these declarations, these simple assignment statements are valid.

```
switch = leapYear;      //switch gets true
flag = false;           //flag gets false
```

After these statements execute, both `switch` and `leapYear` have the value `true` and `flag` has the value `false`.

Reading and Writing Boolean Values

You can use the `SimpleGUI` method `displayResult` to display Boolean values just like any other values. You can read a Boolean value by using `SimpleGUI` method `getBoolean`. If `flag` is a `boolean` data field in an object that has method `getBoolean`, the statement

```
flag = getBoolean("The flag position is up");
```

causes the dialog window below to pop up.

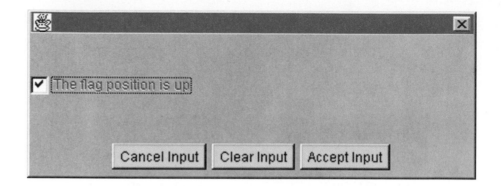

You can change the checkbox value by clicking on it with the mouse. If the box has a check mark, clicking the mouse clears it. To set the value of `flag` to `true`, make sure the checkbox is marked, then click the "Accept Input" button. To set the value of `flag` to `false`, clear the checkbox before you click on "Accept Input."

You can also use the statement

```
flag = getBoolean("The flag position is:",
                  "up", "down");
```

to set the boolean value of `flag`. This statement causes the dialog window below to pop up. Instead of a single checkbox, it contains two radio buttons.

If you click on one button, the other will be turned off, like the old buttons on pre-digital car radios. To set the value of `flag` to `true`, make sure the "up" button is set, then click on "Accept Input." To set the value of `flag` to `false`, click on the "down" button before you click on "Accept Input." When you call method `getBoolean` with three `String` arguments, the second argument represents `true` and the last argument represents `false`.

Boolean Expressions with Relational Operators

Boolean expressions that perform comparisons often have one of these forms:

variable	*relational-operator*	*variable*
variable	*relational-operator*	*literal*

Relational operators are the following symbols:

< (less than)	> (greater than)
<= (less than or equal)	>= (greater than or equal)
== (equal)	!= (not equal)

These symbols should be familiar, except for the equal operator (==) and not equal operator (!=), sometimes called the **equality operators**. The items being compared, called operands, are often two variables or a variable and a literal. If i is type int, the condition i < 3 is true when i is negative or 0, 1, or 2.

equality operators: the symbols == and !=.

The two operands of a relational operator should be the same data type (both type int, float, double, char, or boolean), although Java does allow some mixing of types. As you will see shortly, operands can also be more complicated expressions.

EXAMPLE 5.1

An individual's tax rate depends on his or her salary. Single persons who earn less than $18,550 are taxed at a rate of 15%, and those who earn between $18,550 and $44,900 pay 15% of the first $18,550 earned and 28% of the rest. If taxable income is stored in the type double variable income, the boolean expression corresponding to the question "Is annual income less than $18,550?" is

```
income < 18550.00
```

This expression evaluates to true when the answer is "Yes," and it evaluates to false when the answer is "No."

EXAMPLE 5.2

Table 5.1 lists the relational operators and some sample conditions. Each condition is evaluated assuming the variables have the following values:

x	power	maxPow	y	item	minItem	momOrDad	num	sentinel
-5	1024	1024	7	1.5	-999.0	M	999	999

Table 5.1 Java relational operators and sample conditions

Operator	Condition	Meaning	Boolean value
<=	x <= 0	x less than or equal to 0	true
<	power < maxPow	power less than maxPow	false
>=	x >= y	x greater than or equal to y	false
>	item > minItem	item greater than minItem	true
==	momOrDad == 'M'	momOrDad equal to 'M'	true
!=	num != sentinel	num not equal to sentinel	false

Boolean Operators

We can form more complicated Boolean expressions by using the three boolean operators—`&&` (and), `||` (or), `!` (not)—which require type boolean operands. Two examples of boolean expressions formed with these operators are

```
(salary < minimumSalary) || (dependents > 5)
(temperature > 90.0) && (humidity > 0.90)
```

The first boolean expression determines whether an employee is eligible for special scholarship funds. It evaluates to true if *either* condition in parentheses is true. It will be true for an employee with a low salary or a large family or both. The second boolean expression describes an unbearable summer day, with temperature and humidity both in the nineties. The expression evaluates to true only when *both* conditions are true.

In Java boolean variables are boolean expressions, so they also can be operands of boolean operators. The boolean expression

```
winningRecord && (!probation)
```

manipulates two boolean variables (winningRecord, probation). A college team for which this expression is true has a winning record and is not on probation so it may be eligible for the post-season tournament. Note that although the expression

```
(winningRecord == true) && (probation == false)
```

is logically equivalent to the prior one, we prefer the prior one because it is more concise and more readable.

Table 5.2 shows that the `&&` (and) operator yields a true result only when both its operands are true. Table 5.3 shows that the `||` (or) operator yields a false result only when both its operands are false. The `!` (not) operator has a single operand; Table 5.4 shows that the `!` operator yields the logical *complement*, or *negation*, of its operand (that is, if switch is true, `!switch` is false, and vice versa).

Table 5.2 The && (and) operator

operand1	operand2	operand1 && operand2
true	true	true
true	false	false
false	true	false
false	false	false

Table 5.3 The || (or) operator

operand1	operand2	operand1 || operand2
true	true	true
truc	false	true
false	true	true
false	false	false

Table 5.4 The ! (not) operator

operand	!operand1
true	false
false	true

An operator's precedence determines its order of evaluation. Table 5.5 lists all Java operators introduced so far in decreasing precedence order. After method calls and type casts, the operator ! and unary + and – have the highest precedence. They are followed by the arithmetic, relational, equality, and then the binary logical operators. The assignment operator has the lowest precedence. To prevent errors and to clarify the meaning of expressions, use parentheses freely.

Table 5.5 Operator precedence

Operator	Description
Method call	
Type cast	
!, + (unary), – (unary)	Logical not, unary plus, unary minus
*, /, %	Multiplication, division, modulus
+, –	Addition, subtraction
<, <=, >=, >	Relational inequality
==, !=	Equal, not equal
&&	Logical and
||	Logical or
=	Assignment

EXAMPLE 5.3

Java interprets the expression

```
x + a < y + b
```

correctly as

```
(x + a) < (y + b)
```

because + has higher precedence than <. Java also interprets the expression

```
min <= x && x <= max
```

correctly, but you can insert parentheses to make its meaning clearer to human readers:

```
(min <= x) && (x <= max)
```

If you remove the parentheses in the expression

```
(flag || leapYear) && switch
```

you change its meaning because `&&` has higher precedence than `||` and would be performed first.

EXAMPLE 5.4

Expressions 1 to 4 below contain a variety of operators. Each expression's value is given in the comment assuming x, y, and z are type `double`, `flag` is type `boolean`, and the variables have the values:

```
x     y     z     flag
3     4     2     false
```

1. `!flag`   `//not false is true.`
2. `(x + y / z) <= 3.5`   `//5 <= 3.5 is false.`
3. `(!flag) || ((y + z) >= (x - z))`   `//true or true is`
                                           `//   true.`
4. `!(flag || ((y + z) >= (x - z)))`   `//not (false or`
                                           `//   true) is false.`

Figure 5.2 shows the evaluation tree for expression 3.

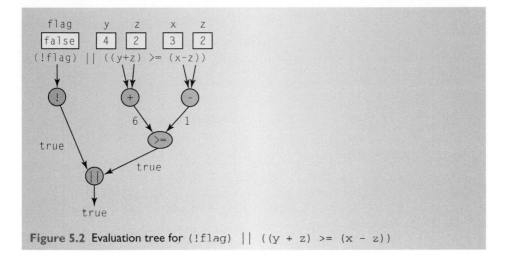

Figure 5.2 Evaluation tree for (!flag) || ((y + z) >= (x - z))

Writing Conditions in Java

To solve programming problems, we must convert conditions expressed in English to Java. Many algorithm steps test whether a variable's value is within a specified range of values. For example, if min represents the lower bound of a range of values and max represents the upper bound (min is less than max), the expression

(min <= x) && (x <= max)

tests whether x lies within the range min through max, inclusive. In Fig. 5.3 this range is shaded. The expression is true if x lies within this range and false if x is outside the range. The expression

(min < x) && (x < max)

excludes the endpoints min and max from the range of x-values for which the expression is true.

Figure 5.3 Range of true values for (min <= x) && (x <= max)

EXAMPLE 5.5

Java expressions 1 to 5 below (left) implement an English condition shown in the comment on the right. You can remove the parentheses without changing the expression value.

```
    // Assume x = 3.0, y =4.0, z = 2.0
1.  (z > x) || (z > y)        // z greater than x or y—false
                              //    or false is false.
2.  (x == 1.0) || (x == 3.0)  // x equals 1.0 or 3.0—false
                              //    or true is true.
3.  (x > z) && (y > z)        // x and y are greater than z—
                              //    true and true is true.
4.  (z < x) && (x < y)        // x is in the range z to y—true
                              //    and true is true.
5.  (x <= z) || (x >= y)      // x is outside the range z to y—
                              //    false or false is false.
```

Expression 1 is the Java code for the English condition "z greater than x or y". You may be tempted to write this as z > x || y. However, this expression causes a syntax error because the type `double` variable y cannot be an operand of the logical operator ||.

If you use the assignment operator = instead of the relational operator == in expression 2, you also will get a syntax error because the expression x = 1.0 is not type `boolean` and, therefore, cannot be an operand of the logical operator ||.

Expression 4 is the Java code for the mathematical relationship $z < x < y$. The boundary values, 2.0 and 4.0, are excluded from the range of x-values that yield a result of `true`.

Expression 5 is `true` if x lies outside the range bounded by z and y. In Fig. 5.4 the shaded areas represent the values of x that yield a `true` result. Both y and z are included in the set of values that yield a `true` result.

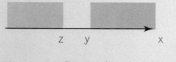

z   y   x

Figure 5.4 Range of `true` values for (x <= z) || (x >= y)

Comparing Characters

Besides comparing numbers, you can compare characters and strings using the relational and equality operators. Several examples of such comparisons are shown in Table 5.6.

The order of `char` comparisons is based on the Unicode position of each character (see Appendix A). Within Unicode, the uppercase letters appear in alphabetical order, lowercase letters also appear in alphabetical order, and the digit characters are ordered as expected: `'0' < '1' < '2' < ... < '9'`. See Appendix C for the relationships among other characters (such as `'+'`, `'<'`, `'!'`) or between two characters not in the same group (for example, `'a'` and `'A'`, or `'B'` and `'b'`, or `'c'` and `'A'`).

Table 5.6 Examples of character comparisons

Expression	Value
`'a' < 'b'`	true
`'X' <= 'A'`	false
`'3' > '4'`	false
`'3' <= '4'`	true
`'a' > 'A'`	true
`('A' <= ch) && (ch <= 'Z')`	true if ch contains an uppercase letter; otherwise false.

Comparing Strings for Equality

You can also compare `String` objects; however, you must use methods in class `String`, not the relational operators. Use the `String` method `equals` (not the relational operator `==`) to compare two strings for equality. The value of the expression

```
string1.equals(string2)
```

is `true` if `string1` is equal to `string2`. Two strings are equal if they contain the same characters and are the same length. Either string may be a variable or a literal.

For the declarations

```
String first = "ace";
String second = "aces";
```

Table 5.7 shows some string comparisons. The next-to-last entry uses the concatenation operator to form the string `"aces"`, and the last entry uses the `substring` method to create the string `"ace"`.

Table 5.7 `String` comparison with method `equals`

Expression	Value
`first.equals(second)`	false
`second.equals("aces")`	true
`first.equals("aces")`	false
`"aces".equals("ACES")`	false
`"ace".equals(first)`	true
`second.equals(first + "s")`	true
`first.equals(second.substring(0, 3))`	true

Table 5.7 shows that the expression `"aces".equals("ACES")` is false. You can use method `equalsIgnoreCase` to compare two strings for equality, ignoring case differences between corresponding characters. The expression

`"aces123*+".equalsIgnoreCase("ACes123*+")`

has the value `true`.

Lexicographic Comparisons

lexicographic order:
the order in which strings would appear in a dictionary.

Java provides a method, `compareTo`, that you can use to compare strings lexicographically. The **lexicographic order** of two strings is the order in which they would normally appear in a dictionary. The expression

`string1.compareTo(string2)`

- Has a negative value if `string1` is lexicographically less than `string2`
- Has the value `0` if `string1` is lexicographically equal to `string2`
- Has a positive value if `string1` is lexicographically greater than `string2`

The result returned by `compareTo` depends on the relationship between the first pair of different characters in the strings being compared. For the method call

`"acts".compareTo("aces")`

the result depends on the relationship between characters `t` and `e` (`'t'` > `'e'`). Therefore, `"acts"` is lexicographically greater than `"aces"` and the above expression has a positive value. (Its actual value is `15`, which is the difference between the character codes for `'t'` and `'e'`.) Table 5.8 shows the result of several other string comparisons. For `"1234"` and `"56"`, the result depends on the first character in each string (`'1'` < `'5'`), not on the strings' numeric values. The last two comparisons involve a string (`"aces"`) that begins with a shorter *substring* (`"ace"`). The substring `"ace"` is lexicographically less than the longer string `"aces"`.

Table 5.8 Method `compareTo`

Expression	Value	Reason
`"XYZ".compareTo("ABC")`	Positive	`'X' > 'A'`
`"XYZ".compareTo("XYZ")`	Zero	`"XYZ"` equals `"XYZ"`
`"XYZ".compareTo("xyz")`	Negative	`'X' < 'x'`
`"1234".compareTo("56")`	Negative	`'1' < '5'`
`"acts".compareTo("aces")`	Positive	`'t' > 'e'`
`"aces".compareTo("ace")`	Positive	`"aces"` begins with `"ace"`
`"ace".compareTo("aces")`	Negative	`"aces"` begins with `"ace"`

Boolean Assignment

You can write assignment statements to assign a `boolean` value to a `boolean` variable. If `same` is type `boolean`, the statement

```
same = true;
```

assigns the value `true` to `same`. Since assignment statements have the general form

variable = expression;

You can use the statement

```
same = (x == y);
```

to assign the value of the `boolean` expression (`x == y`) to `same`. The value of `same` is `true` when `x` and `y` are equal; otherwise, `same` is `false`.

EXAMPLE 5.6

The following assignment statements assign values to two `boolean` variables, `inRange` and `isLetter`. Variable `inRange` gets `true` if the value of `n` is in the range `-10` through `10`; variable `isLetter` gets `true` if `ch` is an uppercase or a lowercase letter.

```
inRange =   (n > -10) && (n < 10);
isLetter = (('A' <= ch) && (ch <= 'Z')) ||
           (('a' <= ch) && (ch <= 'z'));
```

The expression in the first assignment statement is `true` if `n` satisfies both the conditions listed (`n` is greater than `-10` and `n` is less than `10`); otherwise, the expression is `false`. The expression in the second assignment statement uses the `boolean` operators `&&`, `||`. The subexpression on the first line is `true` if `ch` is an uppercase letter; the subexpression on the second line is `true` if `ch` is a lowercase letter. Consequently, `isLetter` gets `true` if `ch` is a letter; otherwise, `isLetter` gets `false`.

EXAMPLE 5.7

The next statement assigns the value `true` to `isEven` (type `boolean`) if 2 is a divisor of n (type `int`):

```
isEven = (n % 2 == 0);
```

Because all even numbers are divisible by 2, the value assigned to `isEven` indicates whether n is even (`isEven` is `true`) or odd (`isEven` is `false`).

Short-Circuit Evaluation of `boolean` Expressions

When evaluating `boolean` expressions involving the operators `&&` and `||`, Java employs a technique called short-circuit evaluation. This means that Java stops evaluating a `boolean` expression as soon as its value can be determined. For example, if the value of `flag` is `true`, the expression in Fig. 5.5 must evaluate to `true` regardless of the value of the parenthesized expression following the `||` operator (that is, `true || (...)` must always be `true`). Consequently, there is no need to evaluate the parenthesized expression following `||` when `flag` is `true`. Similarly, we can show that `false && (...)` must always be `false`, so there is no need to evaluate the parenthesized expression following the `&&` operator.

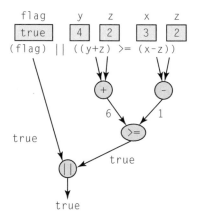

Figure 5.5 Evaluation tree for `flag || ((y + z) >= (x - z))`

EXAMPLE 5.8

If x is zero, the condition below

```
(x != 0.0) && (y / x > 5.0)
```

is `false`, because `(x != 0.0)` is `false`, so `false && (...)` must be `false`. Consequently, there is no need to evaluate `(y / x > 5.0)` when x is zero. However, if you reverse the order of the subexpressions:

```
(y / x > 5.0) && (x != 0.0)
```

Java will evaluate (y / x > 5.0) first, leading to a division-by-zero run-time error because the divisor x is zero. This result points out that the order of subexpressions in a condition can be critical.

EXERCISES FOR SECTION 5.2

Self-Check

1. Assume x is 15 and y is 25. What are the values of the following conditions?

   a. x != y

   b. x < x

   c. x >= y - x

   d. x -- (y + x   y)

2. Draw evaluation trees for the following:

   a. a == (b + a - b)

   b. (c == (a + b)) || !flag

   c. (a != 7) && (c >= 6) || flag

   d. !(b <= 12) && (a % 2 == 0)

   e. !((a > 5) || (c < (a + b)))

3. Evaluate each expression above if a is 5, b is 10, c is 15, and flag is true.

4. Evaluate the following expressions, assuming short-circuit evaluation, if x is 6 and y is 7. Would the results be any different without short-circuit evaluation?

   a. (x > 5) && (y % x <= 10)

   b. (x <= 10) || (x / (y - 7) > 3)

5. Evaluate the following expressions assuming ch is 'c', digit is '7', and string1 is "happy".

   a. 'a' <= ch && ch <= 'z'

   b. '0' <= digit && digit <= '9'

   c. digit < '0' || digit > '9'

   d. string1.equals("Happy")

   e. string1.equalsIgnoreCase("HAPPY")

   f. string1.compareTo("Happy")

   g. string1.compareTo("happyer")

   h. string1.compareTo("HAPPY") == 0

   i. '0' < digit && string1.compareTo("happyer") < 0

Programming

1. Write a `boolean` expression for each of the following relationships.

    a. `age` is from `18` to `21` inclusive.

    b. `water` is less than `1.5` and also greater than `0.1`.

    c. `year` is divisible by 4 (*Hint:* Use `%`).

    d. `speed` is not greater than `55`.

    e. `ch` is an uppercase letter.

    f. `ch` is not a letter.

2. Write `boolean` assignment statements for the following.

    a. Assign a value of `true` to `between` if `n` is in the range `-k` and `+k`, inclusive; otherwise, assign a value of `false`.

    b. Assign a value of `true` to `upperCase` if `ch` is an uppercase letter; otherwise, assign a value of `false`.

    c. Assign a value of `true` to `divisor` if `m` is a divisor of `n`; otherwise, assign a value of `false`.

5.3 The `if` Statement

In Java, the primary selection control structure is an `if` statement that always contains a `boolean` expression. An `if` statement may either have two alternatives or a single consequent. An `if` with two alternatives determines which alternative statement group will be executed. An `if` with a single consequent determines whether the consequent statement will be executed.

`if` Statement with Two Alternatives

The `if` statement

```
if (gross > 100.00)
        net = gross - tax;
else
        net = gross;
```

selects one of the two assignment statements. It selects the first one if the `boolean` expression is `true` (i.e., `gross` is greater than `100.00`); it selects the second one if the `boolean` expression is `false` (i.e., `gross` is not greater than `100.00`).

flowchart:
a diagram that shows the step-by-step execution of a control structure or a program fragment.

Figure 5.6(a) is a **flowchart** of the preceding `if` statement. In a flowchart, boxes and arrows give a diagram of the step-by-step execution of a control structure or program fragment. A diamond-shaped box in a flowchart represents a decision, for which there is always one path in and two paths out (labeled `true` and `false`). A rectangular box represents one or more statements.

Figure 5.6(a) shows that the condition (gross > 100.00) is evaluated first. If the condition is true, program control follows the arrow labeled true, and the assignment statement in the right rectangle is executed. If the condition is false, program control follows the arrow labeled false, and the assignment statement in the left rectangle is executed.

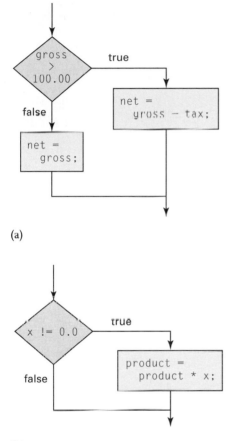

(a)

(b)

Figure 5.6 Flowcharts of if Statements with (a) two alternatives and (b) one consequent

if Statement with One Consequent

The if statement in the last section has two alternatives but executes only one for a given value of gross. You also can write if statements with a single consequent that executes only when the condition is true.

The if statement diagrammed in Fig. 5.6(b),

```
// Multiply product by a non zero x only
if (x != 0.0)
        product = product * x;
```

has one consequent, which is executed only when x is not equal to 0. It causes product to be multiplied by x and the new value to be saved in product, replacing the old value. If x is equal to 0, the multiplication is not performed.

EXAMPLE 5.9

The if statement

```
if (momOrDad == 'M')
        displayResult("Hi Mom");
else
        displayResult("Hi Dad");
```

has two alternatives. It displays either "Hi Mom" or "Hi Dad", depending on the character stored in the variable momOrDad (type char).

EXAMPLE 5.10

The following if statement has one consequent: It displays the message "Hi Mom" only when momOrDad has the value "M". Whether "Hi Mom" is displayed or not, the message "Hi Folks" is always displayed.

```
if (momOrDad == 'M')
        displayResult("Hi Mom");
displayResult("Hi Folks");
```

Syntax Display **if *Statement (One Consequent)***

Form: if (*condition*)
            statement$_T$;

Example: if (x > 0.0)
                posProd = posProd * x;

Interpretation: If *condition* evaluates to true, then *statement*$_T$ (the true task) is executed; otherwise, *statement*$_T$ is skipped.

Syntax Display **if *Statement (Two Alternatives)***

Form: if (*condition*)
            statement$_T$;
        else
            statement$_F$;

Example: `if (x >= 0.0)`
                 `displayResult("Positive");`
         `else`
                 `displayResult("Negative");`

Interpretation: If *condition* evaluates to `true`, then *statement*$_T$ (the `true` task) is executed and *statement*$_F$ is skipped; otherwise, *statement*$_T$ is skipped and *statement*$_F$ (the `false` task) is executed.

Program Style: *Format of the* if *Statement*

All `if` statement examples in this text indent *statement*$_T$ and *statement*$_F$. The word `else` is typed on a separate line, aligned with the word `if`. The format of the `if` statement makes its meaning apparent and is used solely to improve program readability; the format makes no difference to the compiler.

EXERCISES FOR SECTION 5.3

Self-Check

1. What do these statements display?

    a. `if (12 < 12)`
                 `displayResult("Less");`
         `else`
                 `displayResult("Not less");`

    b. `var1 = 25.12;`
         `var2 = 15.00;`
         `if (var1 <= var2)`
                 `displayResult("<=");`
         `else`
                 `displayResult(">");`

2. What value is assigned to x when y is `15.0`?

    a. `x = 25.0;`
         `if (y != (x - 10.0))`
                 `x = x - 10.0;`
         `else`
                 `x = x / 2.0;`

    b. `if ((y < 15.0) && (y >= 0.0))`
                 `x = 5 * y;`
         `else`
                 `x = 2 * y;`

3. What do these statements display when `name` is `"Chris"`?

a. `if (name.compareTo("Chris") == 0)`

  `displayResult("Hi Kiddo");`

 `displayResult("How was your day?")`

b. `if (name.equals("Chris"))`

  `displayResult("Hi Kiddo");`

 `else`

  `displayResult("How was your day?");`

Programming

1. Write Java statements to carry out the following steps.

a. If `item` is nonzero, then multiply `product` by `item` and save the result in `product`; otherwise, skip the multiplication. In either case, display the value of `product`.

b. Store the absolute difference of `x` and `y` in `y`, where the absolute difference is `(x - y)` or `(y - x)`, whichever is positive.

c. If `x` is `0`, add `1` to `zeroCount`. If `x` is negative, add `x` to `minusSum`. If `x` is greater than `0`, add `x` to `plusSum`.

5.4 if Statements with Compound Statements

Some `if` statements have compound statements as `true` or `false` tasks. When the symbol `{` follows the `if` condition or the reserved word `else`, Java treats the statements between the `{` and the `}` as a compound statement.

EXAMPLE 5.11

In many programming problems you must order a pair of data values in memory so that the smaller value is stored in one variable (say, `x`) and the larger value in another (say, `y`). The `if` statement in Fig. 5.7 rearranges any two values stored in `x` and `y` so that the smaller number is in `x` and the larger number is in `y`. If the two numbers are already in the proper order, the compound statement is not executed. Variables `x`, `y`, and `temp` should all be the same data type, where the variable `temp` is used to store a copy of the original value of `x`.

```
if (x > y) {
      // Switch x and y
      temp = x;                    // Stores old x in temp.
      x = y;                       // Stores old y in x.
      y = temp;                    // Stores old x in y.
} // end if
```

Figure 5.7 if statement to order x and y

Table 5.9 traces the execution of this if statement when x is 12.5 and y is 5.1. The table shows that temp is initially undefined (indicated by ?). Each line shows the part of the if statement that is being executed, followed by its effect. If any variable gets a new value, its new value is shown on that line. If no new value is shown, the variable retains its previous value. The last value stored in x is 5.1, and the last value stored in y is 12.5.

Table 5.9 Step-by-step trace of if statement

Statement part	x	y	temp	Effect
	12.5	5.1	?	
if (x > y)				12.5 > 5.1 is true.
temp = x;			12.5	Stores old x in temp.
x = y;	5.1			Stores old y in x.
y = temp;		12.5		Stores old x in y.

EXAMPLE 5.12

As manager of a clothing boutique, you keep records of your checking transactions. When transType is 'C', the compound statement following the if condition processes a transaction (transAmount) that represents a check you wrote to pay for goods received; otherwise, the compound statement following else processes a deposit made into your checking account. Both compound statements display an appropriate message and update the account balance (balance).

```
if (transType == 'C') {
        // Process check.
        displayResult("Check for $" + transAmount);
        // Deduct check amount.
        balance = balance - transAmount;
} else {
        // Process deposit.
        displayResult("Deposit of $" + transAmount);
        // Add deposit amount.
        balance = balance + transAmount;
} // end if
```

Program Style: *Writing if Statements with Compound true or false Statements*

Each if statement in this section contains at least one compound statement bracketed by { }. Each compound statement is indented. The purpose of the indentation is to improve our ability to read and understand the if statement; indentation is ignored by the Java compiler. The comment after the last symbol } makes the if statement more readable, but it is optional.

In this text, we write `if` statements using the style below:

```
if (condition) {
        trueStatements;
} else {
        falseStatements;
}
```

Many programmers prefer the alternate style:

```
if (condition)
{
        trueStatements;
}
else
{
        falseStatements;
}
```

Neither form is "better"; it is a matter of personal preference. And, of course, it makes no difference to the Java compiler which form you use.

EXERCISES FOR SECTION 5.4

Self-Check

1. Rewrite the `if` statement below to improve its readability, but don't change its meaning. When does the last line execute?

```
// messy if statement
if (x > y)
{
x = x + 10.0;
displayResult("x bigger");
}
else
displayResult("x smaller");
displayResult("y is " + y);
```

2. Explain the effect of removing the braces in Exercise 1?

3. What is the effect of placing braces around the last two lines in Exercise 1?

4. Find and correct the errors in the `if` statement below. Assume `add` is type `boolean` and the other variables are type `int`.

```
if (add == 'A') {
        product = num1 * num2 * num3;
        displayResult("product is " + product);
} else {
        sum = num1 + num2 + num3;
        displayResult("sum is " + sum);
```

Programming

1. Write an `if` statement that, given two real values x and y, will negate the two values when both are negative or both are positive.

2. Write a program that computes the area of a rectangle (`area = base × height`) or a triangle (`area = 1/2 base × height`) after prompting the user to type the first character of the figure name (R or T).

3. Write a program that asks for the last names of three people and displays their names in alphabetical order.

5.5 Decision Steps in Algorithms

Algorithm steps that select from a choice of actions are called **decision steps**. The algorithms in the following problems contain decision steps that are coded as Java `if` statements.

decision step: an algorithm step that selects one of several actions.

Searching a String

Earlier we discussed comparisons of characters and strings. In the next example, we show several different ways of determining whether a string begins with a vowel. In the process, we illustrate that there may be more than one good way to solve a problem.

EXAMPLE 5.13

Figure 3.12 showed a simple translator that converts each data word to pig Latin by a simple rule: strip off the first character, add `"ay"` to it, and join it to the end of the word. You may have noticed that this rule is incorrect when a word begins with a vowel or the letter y. For example, the word `"example"` should not be changed to `"xampleeay"`, but should remain untranslated. Our revised rule becomes:

```
if the first letter is a vowel
        don't translate
else
        translate the word to pig Latin in the normal way
```

We can determine whether the first letter in a word is a vowel by comparing it to the letters a, e, i, o, u, y and A, E, I, O, U, Y. Figure 5.8 shows a method that does this.

```
private boolean firstLetterIsAVowel() {
        // Set first to the first letter of word.
        char first = word.charAt(0);
```

Figure 5.8 *continued*

Figure 5.8 *continued*

```
        if (first == 'a' || first == 'e' ||
            first == 'i' || first == 'o' ||
            first == 'u' || first == 'y' ||
            first == 'A' || first == 'E' ||
            first == 'I' || first == 'O' ||
            first == 'U' || first == 'Y')
            return true;
    else
            return false;
}
```

Figure 5.8 Method firstLetterIsAVowel, version 1

The condition in method `firstLetterIsAVowel` compares the value of `first` (type `char`) to each of the vowels. The declaration

```
char first = word.charAt(0);
```

calls the `String` method `charAt`, which returns the character at position 0 (the method `argument`) in string `word`. Recall that Java uses 0, not 1, to designate the first character in a string. If the condition is `true`, the `if` statement sets `isVowel` (type `boolean`) to `true`; otherwise, it sets `isVowel` to `false`.

Figure 5.9 shows another way to write method `firstLetterIsAVowel`. This version directly returns the value (`true` or `false`) of the condition used in the `if` statement of the first version.

```
private boolean firstLetterIsAVowel() {
        // Set first to the first letter of word.
        char first = word.charAt(0);

        return (first == 'a' || first == 'e' ||
                first == 'i' || first == 'o' ||
                first == 'u' || first == 'y' ||
                first == 'A' || first == 'E' ||
                first == 'I' || first == 'O' ||
                first == 'U' || first == 'Y');
}
```

Figure 5.9 Method firstLetterIsAVowel, version 2

If you examine the `String` class you may notice there is a method `indexOf` that returns the first position of its character argument in a string, and returns `-1` if its argument is not part of the string. For example, if we declare

```
String example = "hello";
char c1 = 'e';
char c2 = 'l';
char c3 = 'w';
```

then

```
example.indexOf(c1)    // returns 1, e is 2nd character
                       // in "hello"
example.indexOf(c2)    // returns 2,  the position of the
                       // first l
example.indexOf(c3)    // returns -1, no w in "hello"
```

Figure 5.10 shows the final version of method firstLetterIsAVowel. It uses indexOf to search for the first letter in the string "aeiouyAEIOUY". Method firstLetterIsAVowel returns true if the search is successful.

```
private boolean firstLetterIsAVowel() {
        String vowels = "aeiouyAEIOUY";
        char first = word.charAt(0);

        return (vowels.indexOf(first) > -1);
}
```

Figure 5.10 Method firstLetterIsAVowel, version 3

Now that we know how to determine whether a string begins with a vowel, we can write a new version of method displayPigLatin (Fig. 5.11) that implements our improved algorithm:

if the first letter is a vowel
        don't translate
else
        translate the word to pig Latin in the normal way

```
public void displayPigLatin() {
        if (firstLetterIsAVowel())
                displayResult(word +
                        " starts with a vowel or y, " +
                        " so it stays the same");
        else
                displayResult(word + " translates to " +
                        translateWord());
}
```

Figure 5.11 Method displayPigLatin, version 2

The next case study uses several decision steps and if statements.

Case Study

Payroll Problem

PROBLEM

Your company pays its employees time and a half for all hours worked over 40 hours a week. Employees who earn more than $100.00 a week pay union dues of $25 per week. Write a program to compute an employee's gross pay and net pay.

ANALYSIS

The relevant employee information includes the input data for hours worked and hourly pay. The problem outputs are gross pay and net pay.

Data Requirements

Problem Inputs

hours worked
hourly rate

Problem Outputs

gross pay
net pay

Relevant Formulas

gross pay = hours worked × hourly rate
gross pay = 40 × hourly rate + 1.5 × overtime hours × hourly rate
net pay = gross pay – union dues

DESIGN

Next, we specify the `Employee` class. We need data fields to store the payroll data and methods to read the employee data, compute the gross pay and net pay, and show the employee information.

Specification for *Employee* Class

Data Fields

`double hours`—hours worked
`double rate`—hourly rate

Methods

`enterEmpData`—enters hours worked and hourly rate
`computeGross`—computes gross pay
`computeNet`—computes net pay
`showEmp`—displays employee information

Algorithm for `enterEmpData` (class `Employee`)

1.   Enter hours worked and hourly rate.

Algorithm for `computeGross` (class `Employee`)

1.   `if` no overtime

Compute gross pay without overtime pay.

`else`

Compute gross pay with overtime pay.

Algorithm for `computeNet` (class `Employee`)

1.   `if` no union dues

net pay is gross pay

`else`

net pay is gross pay – union dues

Algorithm for `showEmp` (class `Employee`)

1.   Compute and display gross pay.
2.   Compute and display net pay.

pseudocode:
a combination of English phrases and Java constructs to describe algorithm steps.

The decision steps above are expressed in **pseudocode**, which is a mixture of English and Java used to describe algorithm steps. The indentation and reserved words `if`, `then`, and `else` show the logical structure of each decision step. Each decision step has a condition (following `if`) that can be written in English and Java; similarly, the `true` and `false` tasks can be written in English and Java.

Next, we provide the algorithm for the `main` method of the application class.

Algorithm for `main` (class `PayAmounts`)

1.   Create an `Employee` object.
2.   Enter `hours worked` and `hourly rate` (call `enterEmpData`).
3.   Compute and display `gross pay` and `net pay` (call `showEmp`).

IMPLEMENTATION

Figure 5.12 shows class `Employee` and Fig. 5.13 shows the application class. Method `computeGross` uses the following `if` statement to implement the decision step shown earlier in pseudocode.

```
//Compute gross pay.
if (hours <= maxNoOvertime)
        return hours * rate;
else {
        double regularPay = maxNoOvertime * rate;
        double overtimePay = (hours - maxNoOvertime) *
                                overtimeRate * rate;
        return regularPay + overtimePay;
}
```

If the employee works overtime, the compound statement after `else` computes `regularPay` and `overtimePay` separately and stores their values in local variables before computing their sum.

The net pay computation depends on the value of gross pay. Consequently, we must compute gross pay first and pass gross pay as an argument to method `computeNet`. The header for method `computeNet` shows that it has a single argument:

```
public double computeNet(double gross) {
```

Method `showEmp` uses the statement

```
double gross = computeGross();    // Store gross pay.
```

to compute and store gross pay in a local variable (`gross`). The call to method `displayResult`

```
displayResult("Net salary is $" + computeNet(gross));
```

passes this value to method `computeNet`.

```
/*    File: Employee.java
      Developed for Problem Solving with Java, Koffman & Wolz
      Appears in Figure 5.12
*/
import simpleIO.*;

public class Employee extends SimpleGUI {
        // Data fields
        private double hours;    // input-hours worked
        private double rate;     // input-hourly rate

        // Methods
        // Enters employee data
        public void enterEmpData() {
                // Enter hours and rate.
                hours = getDouble("Hours worked:");
                rate = getDouble("Hourly rate $");
        }
```

Figure 5.12 *continued*

Figure 5.12 *continued*

```
        // Computes gross pay.
    public double computeGross() {
            // Local constants
            double maxNoOvertime = 40;    // hours in work week
            double overtimeRate = 1.5;    // overtime rate

            // Compute gross pay.
            if (hours <= maxNoOvertime)
                    return hours * rate;
            else {
                    double regularPay = maxNoOvertime * rate;
                    double overtimePay = (hours - maxNoOvertime) *
                                        overtimeRate * rate;
                    return regularPay + overtimePay;
            }
    }


        // Computes net pay.
    public double computeNet(double gross) {
            // Local constants
            double maxNoDues = 100;    // max earnings before dues
            double dues = 25;          // dues amount

            // Compute net pay.
            if (gross <= maxNoDues)
                    return gross;
            else
                    return gross - dues; // Deduct dues amount.

    }


        // Shows employee information.
    public void showEmp() {
            // Local variables
            double gross = computeGross();  // Store gross pay.

            displayResult("Hours worked are " + hours);
            displayResult("Hourly rate is $" + rate);
            displayResult("Gross salary is $" + gross);
            displayResult("Net salary is $" + computeNet(gross));
    }
} // Class Employee
```

Figure 5.12 Class Employee

```
/*    File: PayAmounts
      Developed for Problem Solving with Java, Koffman & Wolz
      Appears in Figure 5.13
*/
public class PayAmounts {

      public static void main (String[] args) {
            // Create an Employee object.
            Employee programmer = new Employee();

            // Get employee data.
            programmer.enterEmpData();

            // Compute and display employee information.
            programmer.showEmp();
      }
} // Class PayAmounts
```

Figure 5.13 Class PayAmounts

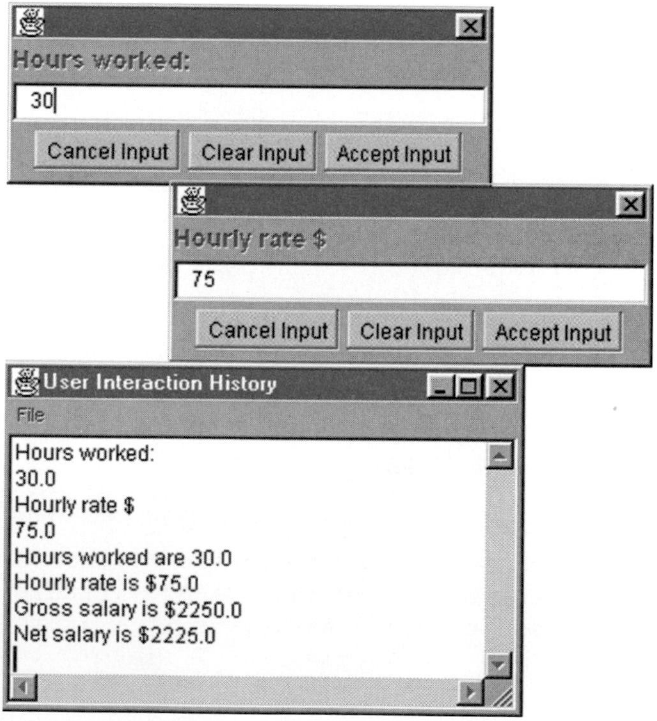

Figure 5.14 Sample run

TESTING

Figure 5.14 shows a sample run. To test this program, run it with several data sets that yield all possible combinations of values for the two if statement conditions (true/true, true/false, false/true, false/false). As an example, to get the condition values true/true, hours worked should be less than 40 and gross pay should be less than $100. Also test the program with a data set for which hours worked is exactly 40 and one for which gross pay is exactly $100.

Program Style: *Choosing Variable Scope*

You might be puzzled about our decisions about variables and their placement in the implementation. In particular:

Why did we use local variables rather than data fields?

Why did we create a local variable gross in showEmp?

When choosing the **scope of variables** (where they are accessible) we follow these principles:

scope of a variable: a description of where a variable is accessible or visible.

1. Keep variables as local as possible.
2. Avoid making a calculation more than once.
3. Use variables sparingly.

Following principle 1, in the methods of class Employee we declare variables only within the block in which they are needed. For example, regularPay and overtimePay are only needed in the else block of the method computeGross, so that is their scope. In Java, the scope of a variable is determined by the closest pair of braces that encloses that variable's declaration. If we declared them as local variables within the entire method, or worse, as class data fields, then their scope would be far larger than necessary. This could expose them to misuse. Following principle 3, both computeGross and computeNet do not declare local variables gross and net, respectively, to store the method result. For example, we could have written computeNet as:

```
public double computeNet(double gross) {
            // Local constants
            double maxNoDues = 100;   // Max earnings before dues
            double dues = 25;         // Dues amount
            double net;               // Method result

            // Compute net pay.
            if (gross <= maxNoDues)
                  net = gross;
```

```
        else
                net = gross - dues; // Deduct dues amount.
            return net;
    }
```

Instead, in Fig. 5.12, each branch of the `if` statement returns the computed result directly. Some argue that there should only be one exit from a method to ensure that the proper type is always returned. This rule isn't necessary in Java. When a method is declared with a return value, the Java compiler guarantees that all paths through the method return a value of the proper type. Consequently, we can avoid introducing an unnecessary variable such as `net`.

Although we try to use variables sparingly, it sometimes makes sense to use them just for efficiency. In `showEmp`, the local variable `gross` is computed and stored because it will be used twice within this method. We choose principle 2 over principle 3. Self-Check Exercise 3 explores why using a local variable is better than making `gross` a data field of `Employee`.

Program Style: *Using Constants to Enhance Readability and Maintenance*

Four constants appear in the `if` statements in Fig. 5.12. For method `computeGross`, we could just as easily have placed literals directly in the `if` statements, as shown next.

```
if (gross <= 100)
        return gross;
else
        return gross - dues; // Deduct dues amount.
```

However, using constants rather than literals has two advantages. First, the original `if` statement is easier to understand because it includes the descriptive names `maxNoDues` and `dues` rather than numbers that have no intrinsic meaning. Second, a program written with constants is much easier to maintain than one written with literals. For example, to change the dues amount to $50, you need to change only the constant declaration. However, if you had inserted the literal 25 directly in the `if` statement, you would have to change the `if` statement and any other statements that manipulate that literal.

EXERCISES FOR SECTION 5.5

Self-Check

1. Change the algorithm for method `computeNet` so that it uses a decision step with one consequent. *Hint:* Assign `gross` to `net` before the decision step and use the decision step to change `net` when necessary.

2. Predict the payroll program output when

    a. hours is 30.0, rate is 5.00

    b. hours is 20.0, rate is 4.00

    c. hours is 50.0, rate is 2.00

    d. hours is 50.0, rate is 6.00

3. In class Employee, method showEmp has a local variable gross. Would the implementation be correct if gross was declared as a data field of the Employee class? Would computeNet need gross as an argument in that case? Consider what would happen if someone wrote an application that bypassed showEmp and used computeNet and computeGross directly. What would happen if computeNet was called before computeGross?

Programming

1. Modify method computeNet to deduct union dues of 10% for gross salary over $100.00 and 5% otherwise. Also, deduct a 3% city wage tax for all employees.

5.6   Hand-Tracing an Algorithm

A critical step in algorithm design is to verify the algorithm's correctness before you spend extensive time coding it. These few extra minutes often save hours of coding and testing time.

A *hand trace*, or desk check, is a careful, step-by-step simulation on paper showing how the computer would execute the algorithm. The results should show the effect of each step's execution using data that are relatively easy to process by hand. In Section 5.4, we traced the execution of an if statement that switches the values of two variables. Now we will trace the execution of the algorithm for the payroll problem solved in Section 5.5.

Table 5.10 is a trace of the program, beginning with step 1 of method main. Each step is listed at the left in the order of its execution, and the effect of each step is given in the last column. If a step changes the value of a data field or variable, then the table shows the new value. If no new value is shown, the variable retains its previous value. For example, the table shows that the step

1. Enter hours and rate (in method enterEmpData).

stores the data values 30 and 10 in data fields programmer.hours and programmer.rate.

Table 5.10 Trace of algorithm for payroll problem

Algorithm Step	programmer. hours	programmer. rate		Effect
In main: **1.** Create an Employee object.	0	0		
In main: **2.** Get employee data (trace method enterEmpData).				
In enterEmpData: **1.** Enter hours and rate.	30	10		Reads the data.
In main: **3.** Compute and display employee information (trace method showEmp).				
In showEmp: **1.** Compute and display gross pay (trace method computeGross).	30	10	gross undefined	
In computeGross: **1.** if no overtime Return hours * rate to showEmp.	30	10		hours <= 40 is true. Compute gross with no overtime. Return 300.
In showEmp: Display hours. Display rate. Display gross. **2.** Compute and display net pay (trace method computeNet).	30	10	gross 300	Display 30. Display 10. Display 300.

Table 5.10 *continued*

Table 5.10 *continued*

Algorithm Step	programmer. hours	programmer. rate	Effect
In computeNet:	30	10	gross 300
1. if no union dues			gross <= 100 is false.
Return gross – dues to showEmp.			Return 275.
In showEmp:			
2. Display value re- turned.			Display 275.

The trace in Table 5.10 shows that the values 300 and 275 are computed and displayed for gross pay and net pay, respectively. To verify that the algorithm is correct, you would need to select other data that cause the two conditions to evaluate to different combinations of their values. Since there are two conditions and each has two possible values (true or false), there are two times two, or four, different combinations that should be tried. (What are they?) An exhaustive hand trace of the algorithm would show that it works for all combinations.

Besides these four cases, you should verify that the algorithm works correctly for unusual data. For example, what would happen if hours were 40 (value of maxNoOvertime) or if gross were 100 (value of maxNoDues)? Would the algorithm still provide the correct result? To complete the hand trace, you would need to show that the algorithm handles these special situations properly.

Take care when tracing each case, making sure to execute the algorithm exactly as the computer would. Often programmers assume how a particular step will be executed and don't explicitly test each condition and trace each step. A trace performed in this way is of little value.

EXERCISES FOR SECTION 5.6

Self-Check

1. Provide sample data that cause the condition in computeGross to be false and the condition in computeNet to be true, and trace the execution for these data.

2. If hours is equal to maxNoOvertime and gross is equal to maxNoDues, which assignment steps in the algorithm would be performed? Provide a trace.

Nested if Statements and Multiple-Alternative Decisions

Until now we have used if statements to code decisions with one or two alternatives. In this section we use **nested if statements** (one if statement
inside another) to code decisions with multiple alternatives.

EXAMPLE 5.14

The following nested if statement has three alternatives. It increases one of
three variables (numPos, numNeg, or numZero) by 1, depending on
whether x is greater than zero, less than zero, or equal to zero, respectively.
The boxes show the logical structure of the nested if statement: the second
if statement is the false task (following else) of the first if statement.

```
// increment numPos, numNeg, or numZero depending on x
if (x > 0)
        numPos = numPos + 1;
else
        if (x < 0)
                numNeg = numNeg + 1;
        else   //x is 0
                numZero = numZero + 1;
```

The execution of the nested if statement proceeds as follows: the first
condition (x > 0) is tested; if it is true, numPos is incremented and the
rest of the if statement is skipped. If the first condition is false, the second condition (x < 0) is tested; if it is true, numNeg is incremented; otherwise, numZero is incremented. It is important to realize that the second
condition is tested *only* when the first condition is false.

Table 5.11 traces the execution of this statement when x is -7. Because x
> 0 is false, the second condition (x < 0) is also tested.

Table 5.11 Trace of if statement in Example 5.14 for x = -7

Statement part	Effect
if (x > 0)	-7 > 0 is false.
if (x < 0)	-7 < 0 is true;
numNeg = numNeg + 1;	add 1 to numNeg.

Comparison of Nested if and Sequence of ifs

Beginning programmers sometimes prefer to use a sequence of if statements rather than a single nested if statement. The nested if statement for Example 5.14 is logically equivalent to the following sequence of if statements:

```
// Inefficient sequence of if statements
if (x > 0)
      numPos = numPos + 1;
if (x < 0)
      numNeg = numNeg + 1;
if (x == 0)
      numZero = numZero + 1;
```

The nested if statement is more readable because the sequence doesn't clearly show that one and only one of the three assignment statements is executed for a particular x, as the nested if does. With respect to efficiency, the nested if statement executes more quickly when x is positive because the first condition (x > 0) is true, so the part of the if statement following the first else is skipped. In contrast, all three conditions are always tested in the sequence of if statements. When x is negative, two conditions are tested in the nested if versus three in the sequence of if statements.

Java Rule for Matching else with if

We use indentation to convey the logical structure of a nested if statement to the program reader. The indentation in Example 5.14 clearly shows an if statement with an if-else statement as its false task. The Java compiler disregards this indentation, however, and uses its own rule for matching elses with corresponding ifs: Java matches each else with the closest preceding if that is not matched with a closer else. This is analogous to the rule for matching left and right parentheses in an expression, in that an if is like a left parenthesis and an else is like a right parenthesis.

EXAMPLE 5.15

In the nested if statements below

```
if (x > 0)
      if (y > x)
            displayResult("y > x > 0");
      else
            displayResult("(x > 0) and (y <= x)");
```

Java matches the `else` with the second `if`. Therefore, Java translates this statement as an `if` statement whose `true` task (following the first condition) is an `if-else` statement.

If you want the else to go with the first `if`, not the second, then you must place braces around the inner `if` statement.

```
if (x > 0) {
        if (y > x)
                displayResult("y > x > 0");
} else
        displayResult("x <= 0");
```

Java translates this statement as an `if-else` statement whose true task is an `if` statement.

Multiple-Alternative Decision Form of Nested `if`

multiple-alternative decision:
a nested if statement in which each `false` task (except possibly the last) is an `if-else` statement.

Nested `if` statements can become quite complex. If there are more than three alternatives and indentation is not consistent, it may be difficult to determine the logical structure of the `if` statement. In situations like Example 5.14 in which each `false` task is an `if-else` statement, you can code the nested `if` as the **multiple-alternative decision** described in the next display.

Syntax Display

Multiple-Alternative Decision

Form: `if` (*condition*$_1$)
        statement$_1$;
    `else if` (*condition*$_2$)
        statement$_2$;
    `else if` (*condition*$_3$)
        statement$_3$;
            .
            .
            .
    `else if` (*condition*$_n$)
        statement$_n$;
    `else`
        statement$_e$;

Example:

```
// Increment numPos, numNeg, or numZero depending on x.
if (x > 0)
        numPos = numPos + 1;
```

```
else if (x < 0)
      numNeg = numNeg + 1;
else  // x is 0
      numZero = numZero + 1;
```

Interpretation: The *condition*s in a multiple-alternative decision are evaluated in sequence until a true *condition* is reached. If a *condition* is true, the *statement* following it is executed, and the rest of the multiple-alternative decision is skipped. If a *condition* is false, the *statement* following it is skipped and the next *condition* is tested. If all *condition*s are false, the *statement*$_e$ following the last else is executed.

   Note: It is not necessary to have an else *statement*$_e$. In this case, nothing happens if all *condition*s are false.

EXAMPLE 5.16

Suppose you want to assign letter grades based on exam scores.

Exam Score	Grade Assigned
90 and above	A
80–89	B
70–79	C
60–69	D
below 60	F

The following multiple-alternative decision displays the letter grade assigned according to this table. For an exam score of 85, the first true condition is score >= 80, so B would be displayed and program control would pass to the call to method displayResult after the multiple-alternative decision.

```
if (score >= 90)
      displayResult("Grade is A");
else if (score >= 80)
      displayResult("Grade is B");
else if (score >= 70)
      displayResult("Grade is C");
else if (score >= 60)
      displayResult("Grade is D");
else
      displayResult("Grade is F");
displayResult("Score is " + score);
```

Program Style: *Writing a Multiple-Alternative Decision*

In the multiple-alternative decision, the reserved words else if and the next condition appear on the same line. All the words else align, and each task is indented under the condition that controls its execution.

Order of Conditions in a Multiple-Alternative Decision

When more than one condition in a multiple alternative decision is true, only the task following the first true condition executes. Therefore, the order of the conditions can affect the outcome.

The following multiple-alternative decision assigns grades incorrectly. All passing exam scores (60 or above) would be categorized as a grade of D because the first condition would be true and the rest would be skipped. The most restrictive condition (score >= 90) should come first.

```
// incorrect grade assignment
if (score >= 60)
        displayResult("Grade is D");
else if (score >= 70)
        displayResult("Grade is C");
else if (score >= 80)
        displayResult("Grade is B");
else if (score >= 90)
        displayResult("Grade is A");
else
        displayResult("Grade is F");
```

EXAMPLE 5.17

You could use a multiple-alternative decision to implement a decision table that describes several ranges of values for a particular variable and the outcome for each range. For instance, let's say you are an accountant setting up a payroll system based on Table 5.12 that shows five different ranges for salaries up to $15,000.00. Each table line shows the base tax amount (column 2) and tax percentage (column 3) for a particular salary range (column 1). Given a person's salary, you can calculate the tax due by adding the base tax to the product of the percentage times the excess salary over the minimum salary for that range. For example, the second line of the table specifies that the tax due on a salary of $2,000.00 is $225.00 plus 16% of the excess salary over $1,500.00 (i.e., 16% of $500.00, or $80.00). Therefore, the total tax due is $225.00 plus $80.00, or $305.00.

The if statement in Fig. 5.15 implements the tax table. If the value of salary is within the table range (0.00 to 15000.00), exactly one of the statements assigning a value to tax will execute. Table 5.13 shows a hand trace of the if statement when salary is 2000.00. Verify for yourself that the value assigned to tax, 305.00, is correct.

Table 5.12 Decision table for Example 5.17

Salary range	Base tax	Percentage of excess
0.00–1,499.99	0.00	15%
1,500.00–2,999.99	225.00	16%
3,000.00–4,999.99	465.00	18%
5,000.00–7,999.99	825.00	20%
8,000.00–15,000.00	1425.00	25%

```
if (salary < 0.00)
      displayResult ("Error!  negative salary $" +
                      salary);
else if (salary < 1500.00)
// First range
      tax = 0.15 * salary;
else if (salary < 3000.00)
// Second range
      tax = (salary - 1500.00) * 0.16 + 225.0;
else if (salary < 5000.00)
// Third range
      tax = (salary - 3000.00) * 0.18 + 465.00;
else if (salary < 8000.00)
// Fourth range
      tax = (salary - 5000.00) * 0.20 + 825.00;
else if (salary <= 15000.00)
// Fifth range
      tax = (salary - 8000.00) * 0.25 + 1425.00;
else
      displayResult ("Error!  too large salary $" +
                      salary);
```

Figure 5.15 if statement for Table 5.12

Table 5.13 Trace of if Statement in Fig. 5.15 for salary = $2000.00

Statement part	salary	tax	Effect
	2000.00	?	
if (salary < 0.0)			2000.0 < 0.0 is false.
else if (salary < 1500.00)			2000.0 < 1500.0 is false.
else if (salary < 3000.00)			2000.0 < 3000.0 is true.
tax = (salary - 1500.00)			Evaluates to 500.00.
* 0.16			Evaluates to 80.00.
+ 225.00		305.00	Evaluates to 305.00.

Program Style: *Validating the Value of a Variable*

If you validate the value of a variable before using it in a computation, you can avoid processing invalid or meaningless data. Instead of computing an incorrect tax amount, the `if` statement in Fig. 5.15 displays an error message if the value of `salary` is outside the range covered by the table (`0.0` to `15000.00`). The first condition detects negative salaries; an error message is displayed if `salary` is less than zero. All conditions evaluate to `false` if `salary` is greater than `15000.00`, so the task following `else` displays an error message.

Nested `if` Statements with More Than One Variable

In most of our examples, the use of nested `if` statements to test the value of a single variable has enabled us to write each nested `if` statement as a multiple-alternative decision. When several variables are involved, we cannot always use a multiple-alternative decision. Example 5.18 contains a situation in which we can use a nested `if` statement as a "filter" to select data that satisfy several different criteria.

EXAMPLE 5.18

The Department of Defense would like a program that identifies single males between the ages of 18 and 26, inclusive. One way to do this is to use a nest of `if` statements whose conditions test the next criterion only if all previous criteria tested were satisfied. In the following nest of `if` statements, assume that all variables have initial values and that the `boolean` variable `single` has been set previously to indicate whether the individual is single (`single` is `true`). Recall that the condition `single` is preferable to `single == true`. Method `displayResult` is called only when all conditions are `true`.

```
// See whether all criteria are met.
if (single)
      if (gender == "M")
            if ((age >= 18) && (age <= 26))
                  displayResult("Current person " +
                              "satisfies the criteria.");
```

Another approach to solving this problem is to write a `boolean` expression that combines all the individual conditions that must be true by using the `&&` operator. This expression appears on the right side of the following `boolean` assignment. The `if` statement executes after the `boolean` assignment, and it displays an appropriate message based on the value assigned to `allMet`.

```
// Set allMet to true if all criteria are met.
allMet = single && (gender == 'M') &&
        (age >= 18) && (age <= 26);

// Display the result of the filtering operation.
if (allMet)
        displayResult("Current person " +
                      "satisfies the criteria.");
else
        displayResult("All criteria are not satisfied.");
```

Could we have placed the `boolean` expression directly in the `if` condition? Yes. In this case we used the variable `allMet` for readability.

EXAMPLE 5.19

In a discussion with your parents about your options for college, your parents told you that you could apply to your first-choice school if your SAT scores were above 1300 and you earned more than $2000 over the summer. If your SAT scores were not over 1300 but you still earned over $2000, then your parents suggested you apply to their alma mater and live at the dorm. If you could not earn the necessary $2000, your parents wanted you to live at home and commute to a less-costly local college. The following nested `if` statement summarizes this decision process.

```
if (earnings > 2000.00)
   if (SAT > 1300)
      displayResult("Apply to first-choice college");
   else
      displayResult("Apply to parents alma mater");
else
   displayResult("Apply to local college");
```

The first call to `displayResult` executes when both conditions are `true`; the second call to `displayResult` executes when the first condition is `true` and the second is `false`; the third call to `displayResult` executes when the first condition is `false`.

We could also use the multiple-alternative decision below to implement this decision.

```
if ((earnings > 2000.00) && (SAT > 1300))
        displayResult("Apply to first-choice college");
```

```
else if (earnings > 2000.00)
      displayResult("Apply to parents alma mater");
else
      displayResult("Apply to local college");
```

The first call to `displayResult` executes when both summer earnings and SAT scores are sufficient. The condition following `else if` is tested only when the first condition fails, so it can be `true` only when summer earnings are sufficient but SAT scores are not. Note that it is not necessary to test the value of `SAT` in that condition. The third call to `displayResult` executes when summer earnings are insufficient.

EXERCISES FOR SECTION 5.7

Self-Check

1. Trace the execution of the nested `if` statement in Example 5.17 when `salary` is `13500.00`.

2. In Example 5.19, how many comparisons are required to execute the first `if` statement when `earnings` is `2500.00` and `SAT` is `1250`? What about the second? Which `if` statement is more efficient? Which is more readable?

Programming

1. Rewrite the `if` statement for Example 5.16 using only the relational operator < in all conditions. Test for a failing grade first.

2. Implement the following decision table using a nested `if` statement. Assume that the grade point average is within the range `0.0` through `4.0`.

Grade point average	Transcript message
0.0–0.99	Failed semester—registration suspended
1.0–1.99	On probation for next semester
2.0–2.99	(no message)
3.0–3.49	Dean's list for semester
3.5–4.0	Highest honors for semester

3. Write a Java program to roll a dice. Use a random-number generator to generate the six possible values of each die and display "You Win!" if a 7 or 11 is rolled, "Snake Eyes!" if a 2 is rolled, or "Try Again.", otherwise. (*Hint:* Use `(int)(6 * random () + 1)` to determine a dice roll.)

5.8 The switch Statement and SimpleGUI Menus

In addition to the `if` statement, you can use the Java `switch` statement to select one of several alternatives. The `switch` statement is especially useful when the selection is based on the value of a single variable or a simple expression (called the *switch selector*). The `switch` selector must be an **ordinal data type**, that is, a primitive data type whose values may all be listed. Data types `int`, `boolean`, and `char` are ordinal types. Data type `double` is not an ordinal type—if you tried to list the real numbers between 3.1 and 3.2 as 3.11, 3.12, 3.13, …, you would be leaving out 3.111, 3.112, 3.113, ….

ordinal data type:
a data type having a finite set of values that can always be listed in order from the first to the last.

EXAMPLE 5.20

The `switch` statement

```
switch (momOrDad) {
      case 'M':
      case 'm':
            displayResult("Hello Mom - " +
                        "Happy Mother's Day");
            break;
      case 'D':
      case 'd':
            displayResult("Hello Dad - " +
                        "Happy Father's Day");

}  // end switch
```

behaves the same way as the following `if` statement when the character stored in `momOrDad` is one of the four letters listed (M, m, D, or d).

```
if (momOrDad == 'M' || momOrDad == 'm')
      displayResult("Hello Mom - Happy Mother's Day");
else if (momOrDad == 'D') || (momOrDad == 'd')
      displayResult("Hello Dad - Happy Father's Day");
```

The message displayed by the `switch` statement depends on the value of the `switch` selector `momOrDad` (type `char`). If the `switch` selector value is `'M'` or `'m'`, the first message is displayed. If the `switch` selector value is `'D'` or `'d'`, the second message is displayed. The lists `'M'`, `'m'` and `'D'`, `'d'` are called *case labels*.

The reserved word `break` passes control out of the `switch` statement to the first statement following the `switch` statement. Otherwise, execution flows through to the statements following the next case label. For this reason, you should place a `break` statement before each new set of case labels unless you want the statements after them to execute, too.

EXAMPLE 5.21

The following switch statement sets the price for an incandescent light bulb. The selector expression, watts, is the wattage of the bulb. The statements after the case label default assign zero to price and displays an error message when the value of watts does not match the wattage of bulbs in stock (40, 60, 75, 100, or 150). 100-watt and 150-watt light bulbs both cost $1.

```
// Set price for a light bulb.
switch (watts) {
      case 40:
              price = 0.50;
              break;
      case 60:
              price = 0.69;
              break;
      case 75:
              price = 0.85;
              break;
      case 100:
      case 150:
              price = 1;
              break;
      default:
              price = 0;
              displayResult("No bulb in stock.");
} // end switch
```

One common error is using a string such as "Saturday" or "Sunday" as a case label. This usage causes a syntax error. Remember that only ordinal values (i.e., single characters, integers, or boolean values) may appear in case labels.

Syntax Display   **switch *Statement***

Form: switch (*selector*) {
         case *label*$_1$:
                 statements$_1$;
                 break;
         case *label*$_2$:
                 statements$_2$;
                 break;
                 . . .

```
        case labelₙ:
                statementₙ;
                break;
        default:
                statement_d;
} // end switch
```

Example:
```
switch (n) {
        case 1:
        case 2:
                displayResult("1, 2, " +
                                "Buckle my shoe");
                break;
        case 3:
        case 4:
                displayResult("3, 4, " +
                                "Shut the door");
                break;
        case 5:
        case 6:
                displayResult("5, 6, " +
                                "Pick up sticks");
                break;
        default:
                displayResult(n + " +
                                " is out of range");
} // end switch
```

Interpretation: The *selector* expression is evaluated and compared to each *label*. Each *label* is a single, constant value, and each *label* must be different from the others. If the value of the *selector* expression matches a *label*, then execution begins with the first statement following that *label*. To prevent executing the statements associated with another *label*, you must place a `break` statement before each new set of *labels*. Control passes out of the `switch` statement when a `break` statement executes.

Note 1: If the value of the *selector* does not match any *label*, no *statement* is executed unless a `default` case is provided. If present, the `default` statements (*statement_d*) are executed.

Note 2: Each *label* must be a unique value.

Note 3: The type of each *label* must correspond to the type of the *selector* expression.

Note 4: Any ordinal data type is permitted as the *selector* type.

Note 5: If a `break` statement is missing, execution "falls through" to the statements associated with the next set of *labels*.

A Warning About Missing break Statements

The last note in the syntax display above indicates what happens if a break statement is not the last statement in a particular statement group: the next statement group is also executed even though no label for that group matches the selector value.

Using return Statements in a switch Statement

A return statement following a case label will not only exit the switch statement but will return from the method call as well. If you use return statements, you must use them for all cases, and the Java compiler will guarantee that all cases return the proper type value. Example 5.21 is rewritten here as a method that returns the price of a bulb or returns zero as a default:

```java
public double bulbPrice(int watts) {
      switch (watts) {
            case 40:
                  return 0.50;
            case 60:
                  return 0.69;
            case 75:
                  return 0.85;
            case 100:
            case 150:
                  return 1;
            default:
                  return 0;
      } // end switch
} // bulbPrice
```

Comparison of Nested if and switch

You can use nested if statements, which are more general than a switch statement, to implement any multiple-alternative decision. A switch statement, however, is more readable and should be used whenever practical. Remember not to use type double values or strings as case labels.

If the same statements execute for a long list of values of the switch selector, you should use an if statement instead of a switch. For example, use an if statement with the condition (num >= 1 && num <= 9) instead of the statement sequence beginning with:

```java
switch (num)
{
      case 1:   case 2:   case 3:   case 4:   case 5:
      case 6:   case 7:   case 8:   case 9:
      ...
```

SimpleGUI Menus

A very common use for the `switch` statement is to select a method for execution based on a selection made by the program user from a list of possible choices, called a **menu**. To facilitate this process, `SimpleGUI` supports the creation of menus, or lists of choices. We see how to create and use menus in the next example.

menu:
a list of choices provided to a program user.

EXAMPLE 5.22

Method `buildEditMenu` (Fig. 5.16) uses `SimpleGUI` methods `createMenu` and `addChoice` to create a list of choices for a text-editor program. Method `createMenu` sets up a menu dialog window with no choices. Each call to method `addChoice` adds a choice to the list of choices (five in all). To display the menu dialog window, use method `getChoice` as shown next.

```
buildEditMenu();  // Build the menu dialog window
editOp = getChoice("Select an edit operation:");
```

When method `getChoice` executes, the dialog window in Fig. 5.17 appears. To display the choices in order to make a selection, the user clicks on the small button at the right of the first bar.

```
public void buildEditMenu() {
      createMenu();     // Create an empty menu.

      // Define the list of choices.
      addChoice("Search");
      addChoice("Insert");
      addChoice("Delete");
      addChoice("Replace");
      addChoice("Quit");
}
```

Figure 5.16 Building a menu

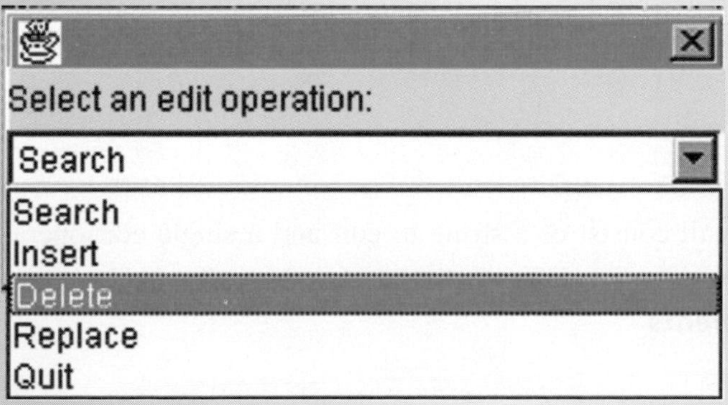

Figure 5.17 Menu created by `readEditOperation`

Method `getChoice` displays the prompt shown in the line above the list of choices. Once the user makes a selection and presses the "Accept Input" button (hidden by the list of choices in Fig. 5.17), `getChoice` returns an integer value corresponding to the user's selection, starting with 0 for the first choice. For the menu above, `getChoice` returns 0 if the user selects `Search` and 4 if the user selects `Quit`. Table 5.14 lists the methods discussed in this section.

Table 5.14 `SimpleGUI` methods for menus

Method call	Description
`createMenu();`	Creates a menu with an empty list of choices.
`addChoice("Column A");`	Adds `Column A` to the list of choices in the menu.
`getChoice("Select a column")`	Displays the menu dialog window with the prompt shown and returns an integer value corresponding to the user's choice (0 for the first choice listed, 1 for the second choice, and so on).

Because method `getChoice` returns an integer between 0 and 4, it makes sense to follow its execution with a `switch` statement that uses the value returned as a selector. We illustrate this in the next case study; it shows how to perform some common string processing operations.

Simple Text Editor

PROBLEM

You would like to be able to build a text editor that performs some common edit operations such as string insertion, deletion, replacement, and search. As a precursor, you need to investigate how to perform these operations on a string in Java.

ANALYSIS

Your problem input will consist of a string to edit and a single edit operation to perform.

Data Requirements

Problem Inputs

a string to edit
the edit operation

Problem Outputs

the edited string

DESIGN

We will store the string to edit and the edit operation as data fields in an `EditableString` object. Because we expect to get the edit operation through a menu selection, we represent it using a type `int` variable. We need methods to perform each of the editing operations: `search`, `insert`, `delete`, and `replace`, and a method that calls the appropriate one of these based on the user's choice. We also need methods to read the string, build the menu, and display the result of the editing operation.

Specification for EditableString *class*

Data Fields

`String text`—string to edit
`int editOp`—the edit operation

Methods

`readEditString`—enters the string to edit
`buildEditMenu`—builds the edit operation menu
`doEditOperation`—performs the requested edit operation
`search`—searches for a substring of a string
`insert`—inserts a new substring into a string
`delete`—deletes a substring of a string
`replace`—replaces one substring of a string with another
`showEditOperation`—reads and performs the edit operation and displays the edited string

We show the method algorithms next.

Algorithm for readEditString (class EditableString)

1. Read and store the editable string.

Algorithm for doEditOperation (class EditableString)

1. Call the appropriate method based on `editOp`.

Algorithm for search (class EditableString)

1. Read the string to be found.
2. Search for the string.
3. `if` the string was found
       display its starting position
   `else`
       display a "string not found" message.

Algorithm for `insert` (class `EditableString`)

1. Read the string to be inserted.
2. Read the index of the string to be inserted.
3. Store in `text` the string formed by joining the substring up to the insertion point, the string to be inserted, and the substring that starts at the insertion point.

Algorithm for `delete` (class `EditableString`)

1. Read the string to be deleted.
2. Find the position in text of the string to be deleted.
3. `if` the string was found

    store in `text` the string formed by joining the substrings that precede and follow the string being deleted.

Algorithm for `replace` (class `EditableString`)

1. Read the string to be replaced (the out string).
2. Read the replacement string (the new string).
3. `if` the out string was found

    store in `text` the string formed by joining the substring that precedes the out string, the replacement string, and the substring that follows the out string.

Algorithm for `showEditOperation` (class `EditableString`)

1. Read the edit operation.
2. Perform the edit operation.
3. Display the edited string.

Algorithm for `main` (class `TextEditor`)

1. Get the string to edit.
2. Read and perform the edit operation and display the edited string (using `showEditOperation`).

IMPLEMENTATION

Figure 5.18 shows class `EditableString` and Fig. 5.19 shows the application class `TextEditor`. Method `doEditOperation` contains a `switch` statement that selects an edit method to execute based on the value (0 through 4) stored in `editOp`.

Each edit method reads the local data it needs to perform its operation. All of the edit methods, except `insert`, call `indexOf` to search for a substring in string `text`. Recall that we used method `indexOf` in Fig. 5.10 to search for a character in a string. If its argument is a string, method indexOf returns the starting position of the string being searched for in its argument string. If the argument string is not found, indexOf returns -1. For example:

```
"This is a string".indexOf("is")
                // returns 2, location of "is" in "This"
"This is a string".indexOf("is a")
                // returns 5, location of "is a"
"This is a string".indexOf("this")
                // returns -1, "this" not found
```

Let's look at each of the edit methods. The if statement in method search displays the result of the call to indexOf.

Method insert begins by reading the insertion point, index, of the new string (newString). The statement

```
text = text.substring(0, index) + newString +
       text.substring(index);
```

builds a new string by joining three substrings. The first is the part of string text up to, but excluding, the insertion point (index); the second is the new string; and the third is the part of string text from the insertion point to the end of the string. The resulting string is stored back in text.

Method delete first finds the position of the string to be deleted (posOut). The statement

```
text = text.substring(0, posOut) +
       text.substring(posOut + out.length());
```

builds a new string by joining two substrings. The first is the part of string text up to, but excluding, the character at posOut. The second is the part of string text that follows string out. We compute its starting point as posOut + out.length().

We illustrate this with the string below in which we are trying to delete the five-character substring "darn ". The value of posOut is 15, so the last character in the first substring would be the space at position 14. The first character in the second substring would be the letter s at position 20 (15 + 5). This means that the characters at positions 15 through 19 would be deleted as desired.

```
        Let's get this darn string edited!
        _____/      _____/
text.substring(0, posOut) ↑  text.substring(posOut + out.length()]
                  posOut
                   15
```

Method replace works similarly to delete, except it inserts a new string in between the two substrings shown in color in the diagram above. ▼

```
/*    File: EditableString.java
      Developed for Problem Solving with Java, Koffman & Wolz
      Appears in Figure 5.18
*/
import simpleIO.*;

public class EditableString extends SimpleGUI {
      // Data fields
      private int editOp;    // input - edit operation
      private String text;   // input - text being edited

      // Methods
      public void readEditString() {
            text = getString("Enter string to edit:");
      }

      public void buildEditMenu() {
            createMenu();    // Create an empty menu.

            // Define the list of choices.
            addChoice("Search");
            addChoice("Insert");
            addChoice("Delete");
            addChoice("Replace");
            addChoice("Quit");
      }

      public void doEditOperation() {
            switch (editOp) {
                  case 0:
                        search();
                        break;
                  case 1:
                        insert();
                        break;
                  case 2:
                        delete();
                        break;
                  case 3:
                        replace();
                        break;
                  case 4:
                        displayResult("All done");
                        break;
```

Figure 5.18 *continued*

Figure 5.18 *continued*

```
                    default:
                            displayResult("Invalid operation.");
            }
    }


    // Searches text for a target string.
    public void search() {
            String target = getString("Enter string to find:");
            int index = text.indexOf(target);

            if (index >= 0)
                    displayResult("String '" + target +
                                            "' starts at position " + index);
            else
                    displayResult("String not found");
    }


    // Inserts a substring in text.
    public void insert() {
            String newString = getString("Enter string to insert:");
            int index = getInt("Enter index of insertion point:",
                                    0, text.length());

            // Join string before index, newString, and
            //       string after index.
            text = text.substring(0, index) + newString +
                    text.substring(index);
    }


    // Deletes a substring of text.
    public void delete() {
            String out = getString("Enter string to delete:");
            int posOut = text.indexOf(out);  // Find starting position

            if (posOut >= 0)
                    // Join string before out and string after out
                    text = text.substring(0, posOut) +
                            text.substring(posOut + out.length());
            else
                    displayResult("String not found " +
                                            "- no deletion performed");
    }
```

Figure 5.18 *continued*

Figure 5.18 *continued*

```
        // Replaces one substring of text with another.
        public void replace() {
                String out = getString("Enter string to replace:");
                String newString = getString("Enter replacement string:");
                int posOut = text.indexOf(out);   // Find starting position

                if (posOut >= 0)
                        // Join string before out, newString,
                        //      and string after out
                        text = text.substring(0, posOut) + newString +
                                text.substring(posOut + out.length());
                else
                        displayResult("String not found " +
                                                "- no replacement performed");
        }

        public void showEditOperation() {
                buildEditMenu();
                editOp = getChoice("Choose an edit operation");
                doEditOperation();
                displayResult("Edit string is: " + text);
        }
}
```

Figure 5.18 Class EditableString

```
                /*    File: TextEditor.java
                        Developed for Problem Solving with Java,
                          Koffman & Wolz
                        Appears in Figure 5.19
                */
                import simpleIO.*;
                public class TextEditor {

                        public static void main(String[] args) {
                                // Create an EditableString object.
                                EditableString edString =
                                                        new EditableString();
                                // Read a string to edit.
                                edString.readEditString();

                                // Show the result of the edit operation.
                                edString.showEditOperation();
                        }
                }
```

Figure 5.19 Class TextEditor

TESTING

Figure 5.20 shows a sample run of the text editor program. You should try each edit operation for substrings at various positions in string text and with substrings not found in text.

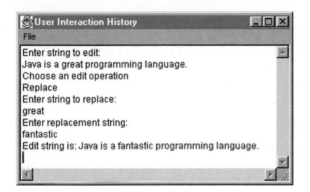

Enter string to edit:
Java is a great programming language.
Choose an edit operation
Replace
Enter string to replace:
great
Enter replacement string:
fantastic
Edit string is: Java is a fantastic programming language.

Figure 5.20 Sample run of the text editor program

Program Style: Defensive Programming

We admit it—after years of programming we are still overly cautious! You may have noticed that the default case for method doEditOperation (Fig. 5.18) should never execute because method getChoice can only return a value between 0 and 4. However, every now and then, "impossible" events occur. Rather than let them go unnoticed, we prefer to watch out for unexpected situations and display warning messages when they occur. The cost for this extra diligence is not great—just adding a default case and an error message display. But our efforts will certainly pay off if someone adds another choice to the edit operation menu and forgets to modify method doEditOperation!

EXERCISES FOR SECTION 5.8

Self-Check

1. Write an if statement that corresponds to the following switch:

```
switch (x) {
    case 2:
        displayResult("Snake Eyes!");
        break;
    case 7:
    case 11:
        displayResult("Win!")
        break;
    default:
        displayResult("Try again.")
} // end switch
```

2. Write a `switch` statement that corresponds to the following `if`:

```
if ((grade >= 'A') && (grade <= 'C'))
        displayResult("Passing");
else if ((grade == 'D') || (grade == 'F'))
        displayResult("No credit");
else
        displayResult("Invalid grade");
```

3. Rewrite your `switch` in Exercise 2 to return the string from a method rather than display it.

4. Can the nested `if` statements in Examples 5.16 through 5.20 be rewritten using `switch` statements? If not, why not?

Programming

1. Write a `switch` statement that displays a message indicating whether `nextCh` (type `char`) is an operator symbol (+,-,*,=,<,>,/), a punctuation mark (comma, semicolon, parenthesis, brace, bracket), or a digit. Your statement should display the category selected.

2. Write a nested `if` statement that is equivalent to the `switch` statement described in Programming Exercise 1.

5.9 Exceptions and `try-catch` Blocks

In the text editor case in the last section, we used `if` statements to test for unusual conditions that could cause our program to fail. For example, methods `delete` and `replace` use the condition (`posOut > 0`) to verify that the substring `out` is in string `text` before attempting to delete or replace it. If you omit that test, you might get the error message

```
java.lang.StringIndexOutOfBoundsException: String index
out of range: -1
```

This happens when Java references `text.substring(0, posOut)` and `posOut` is `-1` (the case when `out` is not found in string `text`). The error message indicates that there is no character in the string with an index of `-1`. (The first character in a string is always at position 0.) .

exception:
an unusual, potentially harmful, situation that can occur in a program.

A string `index` that is out of bounds is an **exception**, or unusual situation that can cause your program to fail. You can often use `if` statements to prevent exceptions from occurring, as we did in Fig. 5.18. But there are some exceptions that are beyond the programmer's control. Also, sometimes you might want to detect an exception and incorporate the fact that the exception occurred in your program. For this reason, Java provides a mechanism that detects or catches exceptions and allows your program to handle them and continue program execution when they occur.

To use exceptions, you must do the following:

1. Create a `try` block containing *statements* that may cause an exception. A `try` block has the form:

```
try {
        // Statements that may cause an exception
        statements;
}
```

2. Follow the `try` block by one or more `catch` blocks. Each `catch` block contains *statements* that handle a particular exception. A `catch` block has the form:

```
catch (exceptionType exceptionIdentifier) {
        // Statements that handle an exception
        statements;
}
```

where the part in parentheses is like an argument list. The first item is the type of the exception being handled. The second item is a name that can be used to refer to the exception by the statements that handle it. Later chapters provide other examples of exception handling.

EXAMPLE 5.23

In Fig. 5.21 we rewrite method `delete` using `try-catch` blocks. The `catch` block handles the exception `StringIndexOutOfBoundsException` by calling method `displayResult` to display an error message. We placed the data declarations before the `try` block, but they may appear inside it.

```
public void delete() {
        String out =
            getString("Enter string to delete:");
        int posOut = text.indexOf(out);

        try {
                text = text.substring(0, posOut) +
                        text.substring(posOut +
                                        out.length());
        } catch (StringIndexOutOfBoundsException e) {
                displayResult("String not found " +
                                " - no deletion performed");
        }
}
```

Figure 5.21 Method `delete` with `try-catch` blocks

Programming

1.   Rewrite methods `insert`, `replace`, and `search` using `try-catch` blocks.
2.   Write a class method `percent` for class `MyMath` (Fig. 4.21) that returns a percentage corresponding to its two type `int` arguments. For example, if its arguments are 2 and 4, method `percent` should return 50 (for 50%). Use a `try-catch` block to detect and handle a divide-by-zero error (exception type `ArithmeticException`). Your method should display an error message if this exception occurs.

5.10 Common Programming Errors

You can use the `boolean` operators, `&&` (and), `||` (or), and `!` (not), only with `boolean` expressions. In the expression

```
flag && (x == y)
```

the variable `flag` must be type `boolean`. The expression would be valid without the parentheses because `==` has higher precedence than `&&`; however, the parentheses make the meaning clearer. Make sure you do not use `=` instead of `==`; this would cause a Java syntax error.

Don't forget to bracket a compound statement used as a `true` task or a `false` task with braces { , }. If the braces are missing, only the first statement will be considered part of the task, and a syntax error might occur. In the following example, the braces around the `true` task are missing. The compiler assumes that the `if` statement ends with the assignment statement. You will get a syntax error after the line `else` because a statement cannot begin with `else`.

```
// if with missing { , }
if (x > 0)
        sum = sum + x;
        displayResult("X is positive");
else
        displayResult("X is not positive");
```

When writing a nested `if` statement, try to select the conditions so that you can use the multiple-alternative format shown in Section 5.7. If more than one condition can be `true` at the same time, place the most restrictive condition first.

Remember that the Java compiler matches each `else` with the closest unmatched `if`. If you are not careful, you may get a pairing that is different from what you expect. This may not cause a syntax error, but it will affect the outcome. Desk-checking your code is a good way to catch these errors.

In `switch` statements, make sure the `switch` selector and case labels are of the same ordinal type (`int`, `char`, or `boolean`, but not `double` or `string`). Remember that no value may appear in more than one `switch` label. Use a `default` label to display a warning message if the selector evaluates to a value not listed in any of the case labels.

Remember that the Java compiler will catch any selection paths that do not return the proper value. It will only complain that a return is required at the end of the method. It will not necessarily tell you where you are missing a return.

Make sure you use = and == properly. An assigment statement such as:

```
int x ;
x == 5;          // should be =, not ==
```

causes the compiler error "Invalid declaration". A condition such as (x = 5) in

```
int x = 3;
if (x = 5)       // should be ==, not =
    x = 7;
```

causes a more obscure error message: `Error: Incompatible type for if. Can't convert int to boolean.` The statement `x = 5` implicitly returns an integer (5). The integer cannot be converted to a boolean.

Chapter Review

1. Use control structures to control the flow of execution through a program. The compound statement is a control structure for sequential execution.

2. A `boolean` expression can appear in an `if` statement and can be written
   - Using `boolean` variables
   - Using the relational operators (`<`, `<=`, `>`, `>=`, `==`, `!=`), to compare variables and literals of the same data type
   - Using the logical operators (`&&`, `||`, `!`) with `boolean` operands

3. Use selection control structures to represent decisions in an algorithm and write them in algorithms using pseudocode. We use the `if` statement to code decision steps in Java.

4. A hand trace of an algorithm verifies whether it is correct. You can discover errors in logic by carefully hand-tracing an algorithm. Hand-tracing an algorithm before coding it as a program will save you time in the long run.

5. Nested if statements are common in Java and are used to represent decisions with multiple alternatives. Programmers use indentation and the multiple-alternative decision form to make nested if statements easier to read and understand.

6. A second selection structure, the switch statement, implements decisions with several alternatives. The particular alternative chosen depends on the value of a variable or simple expression (the switch selector). The switch selector can be type int, char, or boolean, but not type double or string.

7. You can use try-catch blocks to detect errors and recover from them. The try block contains the statements that you want to execute. Each catch block recovers from a particular exception. It consists of an exception type and statements to execute when an exception of that type occurs.

New Java Constructs

Construct	Effect
if Statement	
One Consequent	
`if (x != 0.0)` `    product = product * x;`	Multiplies product by x only if x is nonzero.
Two Alternatives	

`if (x >= 0.0)`
`    displayResult(x + " is positive");`
`else`
`    displayResult(x + " is negative");`
	If x is greater than or equal to 0.0, displays "is positive"; otherwise, displays the message "is negative".

Several Alternatives	

`if (x < 0.0) {`
`    displayResult("negative");`
`    absX = -x;`
`} else if (x == 0.0) {`
`    displayResult("zero");`
`    absX = 0.0;`
`} else {`
`    displayResult("positive");`
`    absX = x;`
`}`
	Displays one of three messages depending on whether x is negative, positive, or zero. absX is set to represent the absolute value or magnitude of x.

Construct	Effect
`switch` Statement	

<table>
<tr><td>

```
switch (nextCh) {
  case 'A':  case 'a':
    displayResult("Excellent");
    break;
  case 'B':  case 'b':
    displayResult("Good");
    break;
  case 'C':  case 'c':
    displayResult("Fair");
    break;
  case 'D': case 'd':
  case 'F': case 'f':
    displayResult("Poor, on probation");
    break;
  default:
    displayResult("No grade of " + nextCh);
} // end switch
```

</td><td>

Displays one of five messages based on the value of nextCh (type char). If nextCh is 'D', 'd' or 'F', 'f', the student is put on probation. If nextCh is not listed in the case labels, displays the message "No grade of ".

</td></tr>
</table>

`try-catch` Blocks

<table>
<tr><td>

```
try {
    percent = part / whole * 100;
} catch (ArithmeticException e) {
    displayResult("Can't divide by 0");
```

</td><td>

Computes the percentage equivalent of the ratio of part divided by whole. Displays an error message if whole is zero.

</td></tr>
</table>

Quick-Check Exercises

1. An `if` statement is a control statement for _____ .
2. What is a compound statement?
3. A `switch` statement is often used instead of _____ .
4. Rewrite the `if` statement condition below to prevent a possible run-time error. What error is prevented? What feature of Java keeps the error from occurring?

   ```
   if ((j / i == 0) && (i > 0))
       displayResult("i is a factor of j");
   ```

5. The relational operator `! =` means _____ .

6. Will the expression

```
!(j * i == x + y && i > 0)
```

compile without error? List the operators in this expression in precedence order, from highest to lowest. List the operators in the order in which they will be evaluated.

7. Correct the syntax errors in the following statement:

```
if (x > 25.0) {
        y = x - 25.0;
else
        y = x
}
```

8. What value is assigned to `fee` by the nested `if` statements on the left and right when `speed` is 75? Which is correct?

```
if (speed > 35)                 if (speed > 75)
        fee = 20.00;                    fee = 60.00;
else if (speed > 50)            else if (speed > 50)
        fee = 40.00;                    fee = 40.00;
else if (speed > 75)            else if (speed > 35)
        fee = 60.00;                    fee = 20.00;
```

9. What output is displayed by the following statements when `grade` is `'I'`? When grade is `'B'`? When grade is `'b'`?

```
switch (grade) {
        case 'A' :  points = 4;  break;
        case 'B' :  points = 3;  break;
        case 'C' :  points = 2;  break;
        case 'D' :  points = 1;  break;
        case 'E': case 'I': case 'W' :
                    points = 0;  break;
        default:  displayResult("Bad grade");
} // end switch
if (('A' <= grade) && (grade <= 'D'))
        displayResult("Passed, points earned = " +
                        points);
else
        displayResult("Failed, no points earned");
```

10. Explain the difference between the statements on the left and the statements on the right. For each, what is the final value of `x` if the initial value of `x` is 0?

```
if (x >= 0)                     if (x >= 0)
        x = x + 1;                      x = x + 1;
else if (x >= 1)                if (x >= 1)
        x = x + 2;                      x = x + 2;
```

Answers to Quick-Check Exercises

1. selection or decision making

2. A compound statement consists of one or more statements bracketed by `{ , }`.

3. nested `if` statement or a multiple-alternative decision

4. `if ((i > 0) && (j / i == 0))`
   A division-by-zero error is prevented because of short-circuit evaluation.

5. not equal

6. Yes, the operators listed in decreasing precedence are: `!, *, +, >, ==, &&`. The operators listed in the order of their evaluation are: `*, +, ==, >, &&, !`.

7. Remove `{ , }` and insert a semicolon after the last statement.

8. `20.00` (first condition is `true`), `40.00` (second condition is `true`); `40.00` is correct.

9. When grade is `'I'`: Failed, no points earned; when grade is `'B'`: Passed, points earned = 3; when grade is `'b'`: Bad grade.

10. A nested `if` statement is on the left; a sequence of `if` statements is on the right. x becomes 1 on the left; x becomes 3 on the right.

Review Questions

1. Place the following operators in precedence order (highest first):
   `&&, ||, !, >=, !=, +, *`

2. How does a relational operator differ from a `boolean` operator?

3. What is short circuit `boolean` evaluation?

4. Which method will be called in the following case if `temp` is `27.34`?
   ```
   if (temp > 32.0)
           notFreezing();
   else
           iceForming();
   ```

5. Write a nested `if` statement to display a message that indicates the educational level of a student based on her number of years of schooling: 0–None, 1 through 5–Elementary School, 6 through 8–Middle School, 9 through 12–High School, > 12–College. Display a message to indicate bad data as well.

6. Redo Review Question 5 using a `switch` statement.

7. Write a `switch` statement to select an operation based on the value of inventory. Increment `totalPaper` by `paperOrder` if inventory is `'B'`

or `'C'`; increment `totalRibbon` by 1 if inventory is `'E'`, `'F'`, or `'D'`; increment `totalLabel` by `labelOrder` if inventory is `'A'` or `'X'`. Do nothing if inventory is `'M'`.

8. Redo Review Question 7 using a multiple-alternative `if` statement.

Programming Projects

1. Write a program that reads a letter C, S, or T and, depending on the letter chosen, displays the message circle, square, or triangle.

2. Write a program that reads in four words and displays them in increasing alphabetic sequence and also in decreasing alphabetic sequence.

3. While spending the summer as a surveyor's assistant, you decide to write a program that transforms compass headings in degrees (0 to 360) to compass bearings. A compass bearing consists of three items: the direction you face (north or south), an angle between 0 and 90 degrees, and the direction you turn before walking (east or west). For example, to get the bearing for a compass heading of 110.0 degrees, you would first face due south (180 degrees) and then turn 70.0 degrees east (180.0 − 70.0 is 110.0). Therefore, the bearing is South 70.0 degrees East. Be sure to check the input for invalid compass headings.

4. Write a program that reads in a room number, its capacity, and the size of the class enrolled so far and displays the classroom number, capacity, number of seats filled, number of seats available, and a message indicating whether the class is filled. Test your program with the following classroom data:

Room	Capacity	Enrollment
426	25	25
327	18	14
420	20	15
317	100	90

5. Write a program that determines the additional state tax owed by an employee. The state charges a 4% tax on net income. Determine net income by subtracting a $500 allowance for each dependent from gross income. Your program will read gross income, number of dependents, and tax amount already deducted. It will then compute the actual tax owed and show the difference between tax owed and tax deducted, followed by the message `"Send check"` or `"Refund"`, depending on whether the difference is positive or negative.

6. Write a program to control a bread machine. Allow the user to input the type of bread (white or sweet). Ask the user if the loaf size is double and if the baking is manual. Use `getBoolean` to read these data into

`boolean` data fields. The following table details the time chart for the machine for each bread type. Display an output line for each step. If the loaf size is double, increase the baking time by 50%. If baking is manual, stop after the loaf-shaping cycle and instruct the user to remove the dough for manual baking.

Bread time chart

Operation	White bread	Sweet bread
Primary kneading	15 mins	20 mins
Primary rising	60 mins	60 mins
Secondary kneading	18 mins	33 mins
Secondary rising	20 mins	30 mins
Loaf Shaping	2 seconds	2 seconds
Final rising	75 mins	75 mins
Baking	45 mins	35 mins
Cooling	30 mins	30 mins

7. Write a program that determines the day number (1 to 366) in a year for a date that is provided as input data. As an example, January 1, 1994 is day 1. December 31, 1993 is day 365. December 31, 1996 is day 366 because 1996 is a leap year. A year is a leap year if it is divisible by four, except that any year divisible by 100 is a leap year only if it is divisible by 400. Your program should accept the month, day, and year as integers.

Interview

Esther Dyson

Esther Dyson is president of EDventure Holdings, a company that focuses on emerging information technology and on the computer markets of Central and Eastern Europe. Esther travels frequently to meet with people in the industry and to learn more about the development of new technology oversees. In addition, EDventure publishes a newsletter, Release 1.0, and holds an annual PC Forum and East-West High-Tech Forum. Esther also serves as the chairman of the Electronic Frontier Foundation, an organization dedicated to online civil liberties.

You studied economics as an undergraduate at Harvard. What led you to become interested in information technology?

I pretty much fell into it at Forbes, when I wrote some stories about computer companies (stories about Data General, the Japanese as a threat in hardware but not software, Datapoint and so on). Then I started working as a security analyst covering high-tech start-ups such as Cray, Tandem, and ultimately Apple. Of course, I probably would have come to it one way or another, but it seemed random at the time. I liked the technology itself as an intellectual challenge, and its utility and effect on people.

How would you describe a typical work day for you? What is the most challenging part of your job?

I have no typical workday. I spend most of my time talking with people, which means I travel a lot because I prefer face-to-face to over the phone. I sit in board meetings, give speeches, meet with companies, and go to lunches and dinners a lot when I travel.

For those students who are not familiar with it, what is the Electronic Frontier Foundation? How did you first become involved with the EFF?

In 1991 Mitch Kapor invited me to join the board of his new group, the Electronic Frontier Foundation, an organization devoted to online civil liberties. The EFF works to ensure that the government does not interfere with citizens' freedom of speech and privacy rights online. I wasn't sure I would agree with all of their work, but he assured me that he wanted my participation precisely because of my different views. The focus of the EFF has changed over the last few years from keeping the government out of the Net, to figuring out ways to build appropriate governance from within. In the fight for freedom of speech, we now argue not only against censorship, but also for the right of individuals to control the content that they and their children receive.

Every day technology such as the Internet is bringing people from around the world closer together. In your opinion, how is this new way of interacting going to change our lives?

The marketplace will get much more competitive, and good ideas will spread more quickly. The Internet is causing a shift in power from nation-states to commercial entities. Even small businesses and organizations that use the Internet are gaining power and recognition. The Internet allows people to reach a wide audience and make a difference in the world without the overhead concerns that past generations have had to deal with.

What person in the computer industry has inspired you?

Mitch Kapor. He was the person who introduced me to the EFF and got me involved with the Internet. Until we worked on the EFF together, I hadn't even had much experience with using e-mail to communicate!

Do you have any advice for computer science students today?

Do something you enjoy, because otherwise you will never do it with enough persistence and passion. And assume that you will have several jobs over your career, so don't be afraid to take risks and try new things.

Repetition Structures

Each statement in a method executes at most one time whenever the method is called. There are many situations when we would like to be able to execute the statements in a method multiple times. For example, the text editor in Section 5.8 can perform only a single edit operation on a string. Compare that with the text editor you may be using. In most text editor programs, you can perform as many edit operations as you need to.

Repetition, you'll recall, is the third type of program control structure (*sequence*, *selection*, *repetition*), and the repetition of steps in a program is called a loop. In this chapter we describe loop forms that occur frequently in programming such as counting loops, sentinel-controlled loops, flag-controlled loops, and menu-driven loops. Also, we describe the three Java loop control statements, `while`, `for`, `do-while`, and we show how to write the common loop forms using these statements.

We also discuss recursion—a problem-solving technique that is an alternative to repetition. Finally, we discuss how to debug and test programs with loops.

6.1 Counting Loops and the `while` Statement

6.2 Accumulating a Sum
Case Study: Computing Company Payroll

6.3 State-controlled loops
Case Study: A Checking Account Program

6.4 Loop Design and the `do-while` Loop

6.5 The `for` Statement
Case Study: Displaying a Temperature Table

6.6 Loops in Graphics Programs (Optional)

6.7 Introduction to Recursive Methods (Optional)

6.8 Debugging and Testing Methods with Loops

6.9 Common Programming Errors
Chapter Review

6.1 Counting Loops and the while Statement

Counting Loops

loop:
the repetition of steps in a program.

In programming, we frequently encounter situations in which we use a **loop** to repeat a sequence of steps a prespecified number of times. For example, you may want to display a particular pattern in a graphics program four times, each time in a different position. If you employ your six siblings to help you with a task, you need to repeat the pay computations six times, once for each of your siblings. A loop that executes a prespecified number of times is called a **counting loop** (or **counter-controlled loop**). The repetition is controlled by a variable called a **counter**, whose value represents the number of loop iterations performed so far.

counting loop:
a loop that repeats a pre-specified number of times.

counter:
the variable that controls the repetition in a count-ing loop.

The while Statement

We first show how to implement a counting loop in Java using a while statement, the most versatile loop control statement. A while statement begins with the word while and has the form:

```
while  (condition)
        statement;
```

loop body:
the instructions that are re-peated in the loop.

loop-repetition condition:
the condition following while that controls loop repetition.

where *statement* represents the **loop body**, or instructions to be repeated. Loop repetition is controlled by the **loop-repetition condition** in parentheses. Its value (true or false) indicates whether more repetitions are required.

The program fragment in Fig. 6.1 contains a loop that processes seven employees. The loop body (enclosed in braces { }) calls methods from Fig. 5.12 that read a single employee's payroll data (into object programmer) and compute and display that employee's gross pay and net pay. The last statement in the loop body adds 1 to countEmp, which is a count of the employees processed. After seven employees are processed, the loop body is exited.

```
          Employee programmer = new Employee();
          int countEmp = 0;          // No employees processed.

          while (countEmp < 7) {   // Test value of countEmp.
              // Get employee data
              programmer.enterEmpData();

              // Compute and display employee information.
loop body     programmer.showEmp();

              // Add one to count of employees processed.
              countEmp = countEmp + 1;
          }
```

Figure 6.1 Program fragment with a while loop

The three color lines in the above fragment control the looping process. The statement

```
int countEmp = 0;          // No employees processed.
```

declares a type int variable, countEmp, with an initial value of 0, which is the count of employees processed so far. The next line

```
while (countEmp < 7) { // Test value of countEmp.
```

evaluates the boolean expression countEmp < 7. If it is true (countEmp is 0, 1, 2, 3, 4, 5, or 6), the loop body is executed. If it is false (countEmp is 7), the loop body is exited. The last instruction in the loop body

```
countEmp = countEmp + 1;
```

adds 1 to the value of countEmp. After this statement executes, control returns to the line beginning with while, and the boolean expression countEmp < 7 is reevaluated for the next value of countEmp.

The loop body is executed once for each value of countEmp from 0 to 6. Eventually, countEmp becomes 7, and the boolean expression evaluates to false. When this happens, the loop is exited. We could just as easily have started the count at 1 and gone to 7. We prefer starting at 0 so that when the loop ends, the value of countEmp contains the number of employees processed.

Syntax Display

The `while` Statement

Form: `while` (*repetitionCondition*)
      loop-body

Example:
```
// Display n asterisks.
countStar = 0;
while (countStar < n) {
    displayResult("*");
    countStar = countStar + 1;
}
```

Interpretation: The *repetitionCondition* is tested; if it is `true`, the *loop-body* is executed and the *repetitionCondition* is retested. The *loop-body* is repeated as long as the *repetitionCondition* is `true`. When the *repetitionCondition* is tested and found to be `false`, the loop is exited, and the next program statement after the `while` statement is executed.

Note: If *repetitionCondition* evaluates to `false` the first time it is tested, *loop-body* is not executed.

Program Style: *Formatting the `while` Statement*
For clarity, indent the body of a `while` loop. If the loop body is a compound statement, bracket it with braces { }. You should align the closing brace under the w of `while`. Sometimes programmers place the comment `// end while` after the closing brace to indicate the end of a `while` loop.

Comparison of `if` and `while` Statements

The flowchart of the `while` loop in Fig. 6.2 illustrates the execution of a `while` loop. The condition in the diamond-shaped box is evaluated first. If it is `true`, the loop body is executed, and the process is repeated. The `while` loop is exited when the condition becomes `false`.

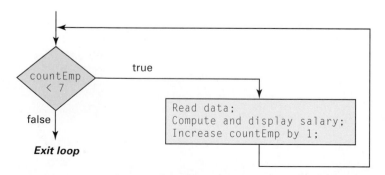

Figure 6.2 Flowchart of a `while` loop

Make sure you understand the difference between the while statement in Fig. 6.1 and the if statement

```
if (countEmp < 7) {
    . . .
}
```

The compound statement after the if condition executes at most one time. In a while statement, the compound statement after the condition may execute more than one time.

Loop-control Variable

In Fig. 6.1 the variable countEmp is called the **loop-control variable** because its value determines whether the loop body is repeated. The loop-control variable countEmp must be (1) initialized, (2) tested, and (3) updated for the loop to execute properly.

- *INITIALIZATION*—countEmp is set to an initial value of 0 (initialized to 0) before the while statement is reached.
- *TESTING*—countEmp is tested before the start of each loop repetition (called an *iteration* or a *pass*).
- *UPDATING*—countEmp is updated (its value increased by 1) during each iteration.

Similar steps must be performed for every while loop. Without the initialization, the initial test of countEmp is meaningless. The updating step ensures that the program progresses toward the final goal (countEmp >= 7) during each repetition of the loop. If the loop-control variable is not updated, the loop will execute endlessly ("forever"). Such a loop is called an **infinite loop**.

loop-control variable:
the variable whose value controls loop repetition.

infinite loop:
a loop that executes forever.

EXERCISES FOR SECTION 6.1

Self-Check

1. How many times is the following loop body repeated? What is printed during each repetition of the loop body and after exit?

```
x = 3;
count = 0;
while (count < 3) {
    x = x * x;
    displayResult(x);
    count = count + 1;
}
displayResult(x);
```

2. Repeat Exercise 1 when the last statement in the loop body is

```
count = count + 2;
```

3. Repeat Exercise 1 when the last statement in the loop body is omitted.

Programming

1. Write a `while` loop that displays each integer from 1 to 5 on a separate line together with its square.

2. Write a `while` loop that displays each even integer from 4 down to −6 on a separate line. Display the values in the sequence 4, 2, 0, and so on.

6.2 Accumulating a Sum

Loops often accumulate a sum by repeating an addition operation. Figure 6.3 shows the program from Fig. 6.1 with a new local variable `payroll`. We accumulate in `payroll` the sum of all employee gross salaries.

```
Employee programmer = new Employee();
double payroll = 0;
int countEmp = 0; // No employees processed yet.

while (countEmp < 7) {  // Test value of countEmp.
    // Get employee data.
    programmer.enterEmpData();

    // Compute and display employee information.
    programmer.showEmp();

    // Add gross salary to company payroll.
    payroll = payroll + programmer.computeGross();

    // Add one to count of employees processed.
    countEmp = countEmp + 1;
}
```

loop body

Figure 6.3 Accumulating gross salary amounts in `payroll`

Prior to loop execution, the data declaration

```
double payroll = 0;
```

accumulator:
a variable used to store a value being computed in increments during the execution of a loop.

sets data field `payroll` to zero, where `payroll` is an **accumulator**, a variable used for accumulating the total payroll value. In the loop body, the assignment statement

```
payroll = payroll + programmer.computeGross();
```

adds the current employee's gross salary to the sum being accumulated in `payroll`. Consequently, the value of `payroll` increases with each loop iteration. Figure 6.4 traces the effect of repeating this statement for three employees.

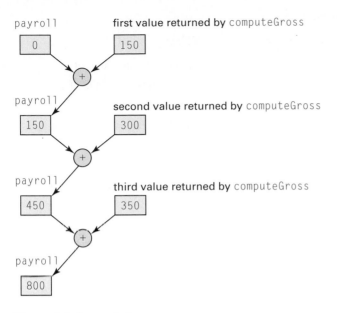

Figure 6.4 Accumulating a sum

Increment, Decrement, and Compound Operators

Figure 6.3 contains two statement forms that frequently appear in loops:

```
countEmp = countEmp + 1;
payroll = payroll + programmer.computeGross();
```

Because they are so common, Java provides special operators that you can use to write these statements in a more compact form. The first statement below uses the operator ++ (increment), and the second statement uses the compound operator += (first add and then assign).

```
countEmp++;     // Increment countEmp by 1.
// Add result of computeGross to payroll.
payroll += programmer.computeGross();
```

Java also provides a decrement operator:

```
countDown = countDown - 1;          |          countDown--;
```

You can write a compound assignment operator consisting of a binary arithmetic operator (+,-,*,/,%) followed by the assignment operator = with no spaces between them. Java interprets a compound operator as shown next where *op* represents any of the five arithmetic operators.

x *op*= y; | x = x *op* y;

As shown above, Java evaluates x *op* y before performing the assignment. Table 6.1 summarizes these operators.

Table 6.1 Increment, decrement, and compound assignment operators

Operator	Example	Equivalent statement	Effect
++	n++;	n = n + 1;	Increments the value of n.
--	i--;	i = i - 1;	Decrements the value of i.
+=	sum += score;	sum = sum + score;	Adds score to sum.
-=	balance -= payment;	balance = balance - payment;	Subtracts payment from balance.

In the next case, we solve a problem for payroll computation. The method used to compute payroll totals will contain a loop similar to the one in Figure 6.3. We will also reuse class Employee from Section 5.5.

Case Study

Computing Company Payroll

PROBLEM

Your summer landscape maintenance company has grown and you need a program to do your payroll computation. The program should display the net and gross pay paid to each employee and also compute and display the total gross salary and net salary paid to all employees.

ANALYSIS

The problem inputs are the total number of employees and the hours worked and hourly rate for each employee. The outputs are each employee's gross pay and net pay and the total gross pay and net pay.

Data Requirements

Problem Inputs

number of employees
hours worked for each employee
hourly rate for each employee

Problem Outputs

gross pay for each employee
net pay for each employee
total gross pay
total net pay

Relevant Formulas

total gross pay = summation of all individual gross pay amounts
total net pay = summation of all individual net pay amounts

DESIGN

We can use an object of the Employee class created in Section 5.5 to store the data (hours worked and hourly rate) for each employee. This class has methods for reading the employee's data and for computing the employee's gross pay and net pay. We need a new class, Company, to store the total information for the company. This class should have data fields for the number of employees and the total gross pay and total net pay.

Specification for Company Class

Data Fields

int numberEmp—number of employees
double totalGross—total gross pay
double totalNet—total net pay

Methods

readNumberEmp—reads number of employees
computePayTotals—computes total gross pay and net pay
displayPayTotals—displays total gross pay and net pay

Next we show the algorithms for the methods of class Company and the main method for the application class.

Algorithm for computePayTotals (class Company)

1. Create an Employee object.
2. Set totalGross and totalNet to zero.
3. for each employee in the company
    4. Read the employee's pay data.
    5. Compute gross pay, display it, and add it to totalGross.
    6. Compute net pay, display it, and add it to totalNet.

Algorithm for displayPayTotals (class Company)

1. Calculate pay totals (call computePayTotals).
2. Display total gross pay.
3. Display total net pay.

Algorithm for main (class Payroll)

1. Create a Company object.
2. Get number of employees from user.
3. Compute total gross pay and total net pay and display them.

Step 1 in method `computePayTotals` (class `Company`) creates an `Employee` object that is used to store and process the data for each `Employee`. Method `main` (class `Payroll`) must create a `Company` object.

IMPLEMENTATION

We show class `Company` in Fig. 6.5. Method `computePayTotals` has a `while` loop similar to the loop in Fig. 6.3. The loop body applies methods from class `Employee` to object `gardener`. The counter variable `countEmp` controls the repetition of the loop.

TESTING

We show the application class `Payroll` in Fig. 6.6 and a sample run in Fig. 6.7. Notice that there are two history windows. The one on the right shows all the calls to `SimpleGUI` methods for object `gardener`; the one on the left shows all the calls to `SimpleGUI` methods for object `myCompany`.

Notice that the escape sequence `\n` appears in one string literal and one string expression in Fig. 6.5. This sequence represents the line-feed character, and "displaying it" causes a blank line to appear in the history display.

```
/*    File: Company.java
      Developed for Problem Solving with Java, Koffman & Wolz
      Appears in Figure 6.5
*/
import simpleIO.*;

public class Company extends SimpleGUI {
    // Data fields
    private int numberEmp;      // input - number of employees
    private double totalGross;  // output - total gross pay
    private double totalNet;    // output - total net pay

    // Methods
    public void computePayTotals() {
        //Local data
        double gross;    // gross pay for an employee
        double net;      // net pay for an employee
```

Figure 6.5 *continued*

Figure 6.5 *continued*

```
        // Create an Employee object
        Employee gardener = new Employee();

        totalGross = 0;
        totalNet = 0;

        // Compute each employee's gross pay & net pay
        //    and add it to totals.
        int countEmp = 0;              // no employees processed
        while (countEmp < numberEmp) {

            // Get employee data.
            gardener.enterEmpData();

            // Compute gross pay and net pay.
            gross = gardener.computeGross();
            net = gardener.computeNet(gross);

            // Display gross pay and net pay.
            gardener.displayResult("Employee gross pay is $"
                                        + gross);
            gardener.displayResult("Employee net pay is $" +
                                        net + "\n");

            // Add gross pay and net pay to totals.
            totalGross += gross;
            totalNet += net;

            // Add one to count of employees processed.
            countEmp++;
        }
    } // computePayTotals


    public void readNumberEmp () {
        numberEmp = getInt("Enter number of employees:");
    }

    public void displayPayTotals() {
        // Compute total gross pay and total net pay.
        computePayTotals();

        displayResult("\nNumber of employees is " + numberEmp);
        displayResult("The total gross pay is $" + totalGross);
        displayResult("The total net pay is $" + totalNet);
    }
} // class Company
```

Figure 6.5 **Class** Company

```
/*    File: Payroll.java
      Developed for Problem Solving with Java, Koffman & Wolz
      Appears in Figure 6.6
*/
public class Payroll {

    public static void main(String[] args) {

        // Create a Company object.
        Company mine = new Company();

        // Read the number of employees.
        mine.readNumberEmp();

        // Display total gross pay and total net pay.
        mine.displayPayTotals();
    }
} // class Payroll
```

Figure 6.6 Class Payroll

User Interaction History ▭ ◻ ✕

File

```
Enter number of employees:
2

Number of employees is 2
The total gross pay is $1025.0
The total net pay is $975.0
```

User Interaction History ▭ ◻ ✕

File

```
Hours worked:
20.0
Hourly rate $
10.0
Employee gross pay is $200.0
Employee net pay is $175.0

Hours worked:
50.0
Hourly rate $
15.0
Employee gross pay is $825.0
Employee net pay is $800.0
```

Figure 6.7 Sample run of Payroll application

Program Style: *Design Considerations in the `Payroll` Problem*
This case provides another example of reuse of a class written to solve an earlier
problem in the textbook. Class `Company` uses an object of type `Employee`.
Because class `Company` creates an instance of class `Employee` (object gardener), methods in class `Company` can apply `public` methods of class `Employee`
to object gardener. For example, in method `computePayTotals`, the statements

```
gardener.enterEmpData();
gardener.displayResult("Employee gross pay is $" + gross);
```

apply methods `enterEmpData` and `displayResult` to object gardener. Class
`Company` and class `Employee` must be in the same folder.
    Once again notice the scope of variables and data fields. Method
`displayPayTotals` must first calculate values for `totalGross` and `totalNet`
using method `computePayTotals`. Two results are calculated and then displayed. The simplest way to complete this transaction between the two methods
is to store the results as data fields.

EXERCISES FOR SECTION 6.2

Self-Check

1. What output values are displayed by the following `while` loop for a
   data value of 5?
   ```
   int x = getInt("Enter an integer:");
   int product = 1;
   int count = 0;
   while (count < 4) {
       displayResult(product);
       product = product * x;
       count = count + 1;
   }
   ```

2. What values are displayed if the call to `displayResult` comes at the
   end of the loop instead of at the beginning?

3. Rewrite the fragment in Exercise 1 using compound operators and the
   increment operator.

4. What mathematical operation does the following segment compute?
   ```
   int x = getInt("Enter x:");
   int y = getInt("Enter y:");
   int product = 1;
   while (y > 0) {
       product *= product;
       y--;
   }
   displayResult("result = " + product);
   ```

5. How would you modify class `Company` in Fig. 6.5 to display the average gross salary and net salary in addition to the totals?

Programming

1. Write an application class that allocates storage for a `Company` object and calls method `computePayTotals` to compute and display the company payroll. Execute and test the completed application class.

2. When Robin's new baby was born, she opened a savings account with $1000.00. On each birthday, starting with the first, the bank added an additional 4.5% of the balance and Robin added another $500.00 to the account. Write a loop that will determine how much money was in the account on the child's 18th birthday.

6.3   State-controlled Loops

state-controlled loop:
a loop whose repetition stops when a particular state is reached that causes the loop-repetition condition to become false.

We can categorize most loops as either counter-controlled loops or state-controlled loops. In the former, repetition is controlled by a counter variable and the loop repeats a specified number of times. In a **state-controlled loop**, or general conditional loop, repetition stops when a particular state is reached that causes the loop-repetition condition to become `false`. We illustrate a state-controlled loop in the next case study.

Case Study

A Checking Account Program

PROBLEM

Assume you have a stack of bills and are sitting down to write monthly checks. You don't know beforehand how many bills you can pay with your limited funds, but you do know you can't pay them all. Your bills are arranged in order of the payment due date. You will simply pay bills until your money runs out.

ANALYSIS

You will pay each bill in order and stop writing checks when you run out of money. In other words, you should continue writing checks as long as your account balance is positive (greater than zero). The state at which to stop is when the "account balance is equal to zero or there is a negative balance." The problem inputs are your initial account balance and the amount of each bill. Since the bills are already arranged in order, you do not need to worry about the due date. The problem outputs are the amounts paid on each bill and the final account balance.

Data Requirements

Problem Inputs

initial account balance
each bill amount

Problem Outputs

amount paid on each bill
final account balance

Relevant Formulas

account balance = account balance – amount paid

DESIGN

There are really two classes in this problem. One is the class `Bill` and one is the class `CheckingAccount`. Class `CheckingAccount` has a data field for the account balance and methods to read the initial balance, pay all bills, and display the balance. Class `Bill` has a data field for the bill amount and methods to read the bill, to pay the bill, and update the account balance. We provide the class specifications next.

Specification for CheckingAccount class

Data Fields

`double balance`—account balance

Methods

`readBalance`— reads the initial account balance
`payAllBills`—pays as many bills as possible
`displayBalance`—displays the account balance

Relevant Formulas

balance = balance – amount paid

Specification for Bill class

Data Fields

`double amount`—amount of current bill

Methods

`readBill`—reads the bill
`payBill`—pays the bill in full or part and updates the balance

We show algorithms for methods `payAllBills` and `payBill` next. We also show the algorithm for method `main` in the application class.

Algorithm for `payAllBills` (class `CheckingAccount`)

1. Create a `Bill` object.
2. `while` the account balance is positive
    3. Get the next bill.
    4. Pay the next bill and update the account balance.

Algorithm for `payBill` (class `Bill`)

1. `if` the account balance >= bill amount
    2. Pay the full amount of the bill and deduct it from the account balance.

    `else`

    3. Pay the amount of the account balance and set balance to zero.

Algorithm for `main` (class `BillPayer`)

1. Read the initial account balance.
2. Pay all the bills showing the amount paid for each bill.
3. Display the final balance.

Table 6.2 traces the loop in the algorithm for `payAllBills` assuming an initial account balance of $100 and bills for $15, $25, $50, and $60. You can pay all bills in full except for the last one. The account balances after each payment are the decreasing sequence: $85, $60, $10, and $0. Loop exit occurs when the balance becomes zero.

Table 6.2 Trace of bill-paying algorithm

Step	balance	amount	Effect
	100		
Is balance positive?			Yes, execute loop.
Get the next bill		15	
Pay it in full.			100 >= 15, pay $15.
Deduct payment from balance.	85		
Is balance positive?			Yes, execute loop.
Get the next bill		25	
Pay it in full.			85 >= 25, pay $25.
Deduct payment from balance.	60		
Is balance positive?			Yes, execute loop.
Get the next bill		50	
Pay it in full.			60 >= 50, pay $50.

Table 6.2 *continued*

Table 6.2 *continued*

Step	balance	amount	Effect
Deduct payment from balance.	10		
Is balance positive?			Yes, execute loop.
Get the next bill.		60	
Make a partial payment.			10 < 60, pay $10.
Set balance to zero.	0		
Is balance positive?			No, exit loop.

Just like the counter in a counting loop, the loop-control variable (data field `balance` in class `CheckingAccount`) for a state-controlled loop must be *initialized, tested,* and *updated* for the loop to execute properly.

- *INITIALIZATION*—`balance` must be set to the initial account balance (entered by the user) before the loop is reached.
- *TESTING*—`balance` must be tested before each execution of the loop body.
- *UPDATING*—`balance` must be updated (reduced by the amount paid) during each iteration.

Remember that similar steps must appear in *every* loop that you write.

IMPLEMENTATION

Next we write the code for class `CheckingAccount` (Fig. 6.8) and class `Bill` (Fig. 6.9).

```
/*    File: CheckingAccount.java
      Developed for Problem Solving with Java, Koffman & Wolz
      Appears in Figure 6.8
*/
import simpleIO.*;

public class CheckingAccount extends SimpleGUI {
    // Data fields
    private double balance;    // Account balance

    // Methods
    public void readBalance() {
        balance = getDouble("Starting balance $");
    }
```

Figure 6.8 *continued*

Figure 6.8 *continued*

```
    // Pays all bills.
    public void payAllBills() {

        // Create a bill object.
        Bill nextBill = new Bill();

        // Pay each bill as long as account balance is positive.
        // Update balance after each bill is paid.
        while (balance > 0) {
            nextBill.readBill();
            balance = nextBill.payBill(balance);
        }
    }

    public void displayBalance() {
        displayResult("Balance is $ " + balance);
    }

} // class CheckingAccount
```

Figure 6.8 Class CheckingAccount

```
/*    File: Bill.java
      Developed for Problem Solving with Java, Koffman & Wolz
      Appears in Figure 6.9
*/
import simpleIO.*;

public class Bill extends SimpleGUI {

    // Data fields
    private double amount;        // Input - amount of bill

    public void readBill() {
        amount = getDouble("Bill amount $");
    }
    // Pays the bill.
    public double payBill(double balance) {
        if (balance >= amount) {
            // Pay bill in full
            balance -= amount;
            displayResult("Pay bill in full, " +
                          "new balance is $" + balance + '\n');
```

Figure 6.9 *continued*

Figure 6.9 *continued*

```
        } else {
            // Make partial payment.
            displayResult("Make partial payment of $" + balance);
            balance = 0;
        }

        return balance;
    } // payBill

} // class Bill
```

Figure 6.9 Class Bill

TESTING

Figure 6.10 shows an application class to test method payAllBills and Fig.
6.11 shows a sample run. The window on the left is for object myChecks; the
window on the right is for object nextBill.

```
/*    File: BillPayer.java
      Developed for Problem Solving with Java, Koffman & Wolz
      Appears in Figure 6.10
*/
public class BillPayer {

    public static void main(String[] args) {

        // Create a checking account object.
        CheckingAccount myChecks = new CheckingAccount();

        // Enter the initial account balance.
        myChecks.readBalance();

        // Pay all the bills until you run out of money.
        myChecks.payAllBills();

        // Display the final balance.
        myChecks.displayBalance();
    }
} // class BillPayer
```

Figure 6.10 Class BillPayer

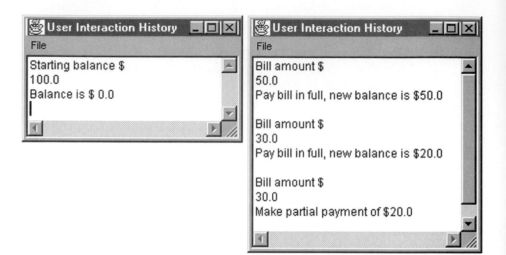

Figure 6.11 Sample run of `BillPayer` application

Checking for a Zero-Iteration Loop

Although we expect a loop body to be repeated more than once, it is possible for a loop body not to execute at all (called a **zero-iteration loop**). The loop body will not execute if the loop-repetition condition evaluates to `false` when it is first tested. Because the loop initialization step is always performed, even for zero-iteration loops, it should be written to ensure that a program with a zero-iteration loop generates meaningful results.

The bill-paying method has a zero-iteration loop if the initial account balance is zero or negative. If the user incorrectly enters `-100` as the initial account balance, the loop body would be skipped and the message "Insufficient funds to pay any more bills!" would be displayed immediately.

MAINTENANCE

Recall that the sixth phase of the software-development method is maintenance. During this phase, you consider enhancements or improvements to programs. After you graduate from college and get your first programming job, you may notice that you don't always run out of money before paying all your bills. An obvious enhancement, would be to modify the program so that it stops paying bills when either your balance is less than or equal to zero or you have no more bills to pay. One of the basic tenets of object-oriented programming is that a well-designed program is easy to maintain. Let's put that goal to the test.

A nice way to solve this maintenance problem would be to add a one-statement `boolean` method `moreChecks` to class `CheckingAccount` that asks the user whether there are any more bills to pay:

```
public boolean moreBills()
        return getBoolean("Any more bills?",
                            "Yes", "No");
}
```

When this method executes, the dialog window below pops up.

Any more bills?
● Yes   ○ No
Cancel Input   Clear Input   Accept Input

Where is the proper place to call this method? You should make it part of the loop-repetition condition. Because we want the loop to repeat if the balance is positive and there are more checks to pay, the while loop in method payAllBills should begin with the line

```
while (balance > 0 && moreBills())
```

Notice that the logical operator is && not ||. We repeat the loop when both conditions are true and we exit the loop when either condition is false.

EXERCISES FOR SECTION 6.3

Self-Check

1. What is the least number of times that the body of a while loop can be executed?

2. **a.** Make the change suggested in the maintenance phase and rerun the program.
   b. How would you modify the loop in payAllBills in Fig. 6.8 so that it also determines the number of bills paid (countBills)?
   c. How would you modify the loop if it is possible for all bills to be paid before the account becomes overdrawn? Assume that the number of bills to pay (numberBills) as well as the initial account balance are provided as data. *Hint:* Use the loop repetition condition ((balance > 0) && (countBills < numberBills)).

3. Trace method payAllBills in Fig. 6.8 for bills: 75.00, 50.00, 25.00, 30.00. Assume the intial balance is $150.00.

Programming

1. There are 9,870 people in a town whose population increases by 10% each year. Write a loop that determines how many years (`countYears`) it would take for the population to go over 30,000.

6.4 Loop Design and the `do-while` Loop

It is one thing to analyze the operation of a loop and another to design your own loops. There are two ways to design loops. One approach is to analyze the requirements for a new loop to determine what initialization, testing, and updating of the loop-control variable are needed. A second approach is to develop templates for loop forms that frequently recur and to use a template as the basis for a new loop.

Analyzing Requirements for Loop Control and Loop Processing

To gain some insight into the design of the loop needed for the bill-paying program, we study the comment lines below that summarize the goals of the loop.

```
// Pay each bill as long as account balance is positive.
// Update balance after each bill is paid.
```

To accomplish these goals, we must focus our attention on loop control and loop processing. Focusing on loop control means making sure that the loop exit occurs when it is supposed to; focusing on loop processing means making sure that the loop body performs the required operations.

To formulate the necessary loop-control and loop-processing steps, we start by listing what we know about the loop. In this example, if `balance` is the loop-control variable, we can make four observations:

1. We must read the initial account balance before the loop begins.
2. If the account balance is greater than or equal to the bill amount, we make a full payment on the current bill; otherwise, we make a partial payment equal to the account balance.
3. The account balance during the next pass must be less than the account balance during the current pass by the payment amount.
4. We stop paying bills when the account balance is no longer positive.

Requirement 1 tells us what initialization must be performed. Requirement 2 tells us when to make a full payment (if the condition `balance >= amount` is `true`). Requirement 3 tells us how to update `balance`. Requirement 4 tells us that the loop should be exited when the condition `balance <= 0` is `true`. These requirements form the basis for the algorithm shown earlier. The *loop-repetition condition*, `balance > 0`, is the opposite of the *loop-exit condition*, `balance <= 0`.

Using Templates to Design Loops

The structure just defined is the most general case of loop structure. Any looping problem can be analyzed as a state-controlled loop. But many loop solutions have general structures that are a bit more specific, so we can create general frameworks—or templates—to use in designing these common loops. For example, we used counters to control the loops in Figs. 6.3 and 6.4. We standardize the steps of a counter-controlled loop in the following template:

Template for counter-controlled loop
1.   Set *counter variable* to 0.
2.   `while` *counter variable* < *final value*
     `//Do the loop processing ...`
           Increase *counter variable* by 1.

Three other common loops are sentinel loops, loops controlled by `boolean` flags, and menu-driven loops. These loops, too, can be standardized into templates to help with their design.

Sentinel-controlled Loops

Many programs with loops read one or more additional data items each time the loop body is repeated. Often we don't know how many data items the loop should process when it begins execution. Therefore, we must find some way to signal the program to stop reading and processing new data.

   One traditional way to do this is to signify the end of the input data with a **sentinel value**. This last value does not count as input data. It occurs after the last "real" data item. The loop-repetition condition tests each data item and causes the loop exit when the sentinel value is read.

sentinel value:
an end marker that follows the last data item.

Template for a sentinel-controlled loop
1.   Read the first value of *input variable*.
2.   `while` *input variable* is not equal to the sentinel
     `// Do the loop processing ...`
           Read the next value of *input variable*.

   Choose the sentinel value carefully; it must be a value that could not normally occur as data. For program readability, you should store the sentinel value in a constant.

   A method, `sumScores`, that calculates the sum of a collection of exam scores is a candidate for using a sentinel value. If the course section is large, the instructor may not know the exact number of students who took the exam being graded. The method should work regardless of the section size. The algorithm below follows our template. It reads each data value into variable `score` (the loop-control variable). It also uses `sum` as an accumulator variable. The loop processing step adds the current score to the accumulating sum.

Algorithm for Method sumScores

1. Set sum to 0.

2. Read the first score into score.

3. while score is not the sentinel

    4. Add score to sum.

    5. Read the next score into score.

6. Return the value of sum.

Step 2 reads the first data value into score before the loop is reached. In the loop body, step 4 adds each score to sum (initial value is 0). Step 5 reads each data value in turn including the sentinel value. The loop repeats as long as the previous data value read is not the sentinel. Each iteration causes the previous data value to be added to sum and the next data value to be read into score. Because the loop exit occurs right after the sentinel value is read, the sentinel is not added to sum.

There are two steps that read data into score, steps 2 and 5. The initial read before the loop (step 2) reads only the first score and is called the *priming read*. This is analogous to priming a pump, which is done by pouring a cup of water into the pump chamber before the pump can draw water out of a well.

Figure 6.12 shows method sumScores. We use -1 as the sentinel value (stored in constant sentinel), because all exam scores should be nonnegative.

```
public int sumScores() {
   // Local data
   int sentinel = -1;     // Sentinel value
   int score;             // Each exam score - input data

   //Read each score and add it to the accumulating sum.
   int sum = 0;
   score = getInt("Enter an exam score or -1 to stop:", -1, 100);
   while (score != sentinel) {
      sum += score;
      score = getInt("Enter an exam score or -1 to stop:", -1, 100);
   }

   return sum;
}
```

Figure 6.12 Method sumScores

Although it may look strange at first to see the statement

```
score = getInt("Enter an exam score or -1 to stop:",
               -1, 100);
```

at two different points in the program, this repetition is perfectly normal with sentinel-controlled loops and causes no problems. Typically, the sentinel value should be one less than the smallest possible real data value, or one more than the largest.

Checking for a zero-iteration loop We should verify that the program is correct if there are no data items to process. In that case, enter the sentinel value as the first score. The loop exit would occur right after the first (and only) test of the loop repetition condition, so the loop body would not execute (zero-iteration loop). Variable sum would retain its initial value of 0, which would be correct.

Loops Controlled by Boolean Flags

Another common state-controlled loop is one whose execution is controlled by a boolean variable. A **program flag**, or **flag**, is a boolean variable whose value (true or false) signals whether a particular state has been reached. Traditionally, the flag value is initially set to false to indicate the state has not been reached. A flag-controlled loop continues to execute as long as the flag value is still false (!flag is true). The loop body should test whether the state being monitored has been reached and reset the flag to true when it does.

flag:
a boolean variable whose value signals whether a particular state has been reached.

Template for a traditional flag-controlled loop
1. Initialize *flag* to false.
2. while (!*flag*)
    // Do the loop processing ...
    3. Reset *flag* to true if the state being monitored has been reached.

For example, assume method getDigit displays a prompt (its argument) and returns the first digit character typed as data. Consequently, method getDigit should ignore any blanks, letters, punctuation symbols, and so on, and return the first digit character that it reads. A boolean variable, say, digitRead, could be used as a flag to monitor whether a digit character has been read.

Method variable

boolean digitRead—program flag whose value changes from
                   false to true after a digit character is read

Because no characters have been read before the data entry loop begins, we should initialize digitRead to false. The while loop must continue to execute as long as digitRead is false, because this means that the state "digit character read as data" has not yet been reached. Therefore, the loop-repetition condition should be !digitRead, because this condition is true when digitRead is false. Within the loop body, we will read each data character and set the value of digitRead to true if that data character is a digit. Figure 6.13 shows method getDigit.

```
public char getDigit(String prompt) {
    // Local data
    char nextChar;                  // Input - each data character

    boolean digitRead = false; // No digit character was read.
    while (!digitRead) {
        nextChar = getChar(prompt);

        //Reset digitRead to true if nextChar is a digit
        digitRead = ('0' <= nextChar) && (nextChar <= '9');
    }

    return nextChar;
}
```

Figure 6.13 Method getDigit

Inside the loop body, the boolean assignment statement

```
digitRead = ('0' <= nextChar) && (nextChar <= '9');
```

assigns a value of true to digitRead if nextChar is a digit character (within the range '0' through '9'); otherwise, digitRead remains false. If digitRead becomes true, loop exit occurs and nextChar is returned; if digitRead remains false, the loop continues to execute until a digit character is read.

We said that traditionally the flag was initially false and was reset to true when the state being monitored was reached. Sometimes an implementation is expressed more naturally as one in which a state is no longer true.

Template for an alternative flag-controlled loop

1. Initialize *flag* to true
2. while (*flag*)
    // Do the loop processing ...
3. Reset *flag* to false if the state being monitored is no longer true

Figure 6.14 shows the getDigit method expressed this way.

```java
public char getDigit(String prompt) {
    // Local data
    char nextChar;                  // Input - each data character

    boolean noDigitSoFar = true; // No digit read so far.
    while (noDigitSoFar) {
        nextChar = getChar(prompt);

        //Reset noDigitSoFar to false if nextChar is a digit.
        noDigitSoFar = (nextChar < '0') || (nextChar > '9');
    }

    return nextChar;
}
```

Figure 6.14 Method getDigit with flag initially true

Menu-driven Loop

The menu-driven loop is the last loop form we consider. During each repetition of a menu-driven loop, the user views a menu and chooses one of the selections (see Section 5.8). When done, the user selects quit to exit the loop.

The template for a menu-driven loop follows:

Template for a menu-driven loop
do
   1.   Display the menu and read the user's choice.
   2.   Perform the selected option.
while choice is not quit

do-while Loop

A menu-driven loop terminates when the user selects the option to quit the loop. Unlike the other loop forms in this section, a menu-driven loop must always execute at least once, so the user can view the menu and select an option. Java provides a loop form, the do-while loop, in which the loop-repetition test follows the loop body, so the loop body executes at least once, as required for a menu-driven loop.

Syntax Display

The *do-while* Statement

Form: do {
         loop-body
       } while (*repetition-condition*);

Example:
```
do {
    ch = getChar("Enter a digit");
} while (ch < '0' || ch > '9');
```

Interpretation: After each execution of *loop-body*, the *repetition-condition* is evaluated. If the *repetition-condition* is `true`, the *loop-body* is repeated. If the *repetition-condition* is `false`, loop exit occurs and the next program statement is executed. The *loop-body* always executes at least once.
Note: If the loop body contains a single statement, you do not need to enclose it braces.

The loop shown in the syntax display reads a sequence of data characters into `ch`, stopping with the first data character that is a digit. The repetition condition is `true` if `ch` is either less than `'0'` or is greater than `'9'`. Therefore, the loop repeats when `ch` is not a digit character and loop exit occurs after the first digit character is read. We show another example of the `do-while` loop next.

EXAMPLE 6.1

You can modify the text-editor program from Section 5.8 to perform multiple text-editing operations. Method `buildEditMenu` creates a menu for class `EditableText` that includes a `Quit` option (see Fig. 5.17). Method `showAllEdits` (see Fig. 6.15) contains a loop that enables multiple text-editing operations. Insert method `showAllEdits` in class `EditableString`. The application class can apply this method to an `EditableString` object (see Programming Exercise 6).

```
public void showAllEdits() {

    buildEditMenu();

    do {
        editOp = getChoice("Select an edit operation:");
        doEditOperation();
        displayResult("Edit string is :" + text);
    } while (editOp != 4);
}
```

Figure 6.15 Method `showAllEdits`

Method `showAllEdits` builds the menu for the text editor problem (using `buildEditMenu`) before entering the loop. The loop body gets an edit operation from the menu, performs it, and displays the resulting edited string. After each execution of the loop body, the loop-repetition condition compares the value read into `editOp` (0 through 4) to the value (4) associated with the menu selection `Quit`. The loop body repeats only if the selection was not `Quit`.

Loop Templates in Event-driven Programming

As you will see in Chapters 9 and 10, very little "looping" is needed to manage user input when you program GUIs directly. There is an event model that manages the complex interaction between the user and the GUI to control the repetition for you. Keep this in mind as you use SimpleGUI to implement solutions based on the templates just presented. In a sense we are teaching you the "old fashioned way" of doing things. Often, as you solve one of the programming exercises you may find that your user interface simply isn't as friendly and naturally interactive as you would like. Think about its limitations. This will help prepare you for problem solving in more open-ended GUI environments.

So why did we show you these templates? First, templates have historical significance. They do indeed model standard forms of looping that occur in today's complicated programs. For example, loops controlled by boolean flags are intrinsic to most operating systems. Menu-driven loops are still at the core of most GUI event models. Sentinel-loops help move data around networks. We've given you models that enable a beginner to program some relatively simple interactive applications. Bear in mind that this isn't necessarily the best way to do the user interface, but the templates still are tremendously useful for more complicated, nonuser interactive problems.

EXERCISES FOR SECTION 6.4

Self-Check

1. Why would it be incorrect to move the assignment statement in the sentinel-controlled loop of Fig. 6.12 to the end of the loop body? Trace the execution of the original loop and the modified loop for exam scores of 60, 50, 45, 95, 70, -1.

2. Rewrite the sentinel-controlled loop in Fig. 6.12 as a flag-controlled loop. In this case the state being monitored would be "sentinel value was read."

3. Another approach to maintaining the checking account program so that it stops execution when you run out of checks would be to modify the loop so that it acts like a sentinel-controlled loop. In this case the next bill would be the loop-control variable. The user can enter a bill amount of 0 (sentinel value) to stop loop execution as an alternative to running out of funds. Rewrite the loop in Fig. 6.8 so that it is exited when either the state "account balance <= 0" or the state "bill amount is 0" occurs.

4. When would a flag-controlled loop be a better choice than a sentinel-controlled loop?

Programming

1. Write a program to maintain a checkbook. It should first ask for a balance. Then, it should ask for transactions, with deposits entered as positive values, and checks entered as negative values. After each check or deposit, the new balance should be printed. Use 0 as a sentinel value.

2. Write a program segment that allows the user to enter values and prints out the number of positive values entered and the number of negative values entered. Use 0 as the sentinel value.

3. Write the `while` loop that displays all powers of an integer, *n*, less than a specified value, `maxPower`. On each line of a table, show the power (0, 1, 2,...) and the value of the integer *n* raised to that power.

4. Write a loop that prints a table of angle measures along with their sine and cosine values. Assume that the initial and final angle measures (in degrees) are available in `initDeg` and `finalDeg` (type `double`), respectively, and that the change in angle measure between table entries is given by `stepDeg`. *Hint:* Don't forget to change degrees to radians.

5. Write a flag-controlled loop that continues to read pairs of integers until it reads a pair with the property that the first integer in the pair is evenly divisible by the second.

6. Write a new application class `TextEditor` that uses method `showAllEdits` to perform multiple text-editing operations.

6.5 The for Statement

Java provides a third loop control statement, the `for` statement. The `for` statement allows you to condense the code for a counter-controlled loop, as you can see by comparing the pseudocode forms below.

while loop pseudocode
```
counter = initial;
while (counter <= final) {
    //Insert loop-processing steps here.
    . . .
    counter++;
}
```

for loop pseudocode
```
for (counter = initial;  counter <= final;  counter = counter++) {
    //Insert loop-processing steps here.
    . . .
}
```

The `for` loop header (the first line) specifies all manipulation of the counter variable. These three operations are as follows:

1. Initialize *counter* to *initial*.
2. Test if *counter* <= *final*. If so, repeat the loop body. If not, exit the loop.
3. Increment *counter* by 1 after each repetition of the loop body.

As shown in the next example, programmers usually combine the declaration and initialization of the counter variable.

EXAMPLE 6.2

The for loop

```
//Display 5 asterisks.
for (int countStar = 1; countStar <= 5; countStar++)
    displayResult("Showing star " + countStar + ": *");
```

displays five output lines in the history window.

```
User Interaction History                        _ □ X
File
Showing star 1: *
Showing star 2: *
Showing star 3: *
Showing star 4: *
Showing star 5: *
```

The loop body executes once for each value of `countStar` in the range 1 through 5, inclusive. During each pass, the loop displays `countStar` followed by an asterisk.

The for Statement   **Syntax Display**

Form: for (*initialization statement; repetition condition;*
              update statement)
          loop body

Examples: sum = 0;
          for (int n = 0; n < 5; n++) {
              nextNum = getInt("Enter an integer:");
              sum += nextNum;
          }

```
for (int i = 10; i >= 0; i--)
    displayResult(i);
```

Interpretation: The `for` loop header summarizes the loop-control operations. The *initialization statement* executes when the `for` statement begins execution. Prior to each loop repetition, including the first, the *repetition condition* is tested. If it is `true`, the *loop body* executes. If it is `false`, loop exit occurs. The *update statement* executes right after each repetition of the *loop body*. If you declare a variable in the *initialization statement*, the variable is visible only within the loop.

The syntax display examples show two counting loops. In the first, the loop control variable n goes from 0 through 5, inclusive, and loop exit occurs when n is 5. During the last iteration of the loop body, n is 4. In the second example, the loop control variable i gets the values 10, 9, 8, ... , 2, 1, 0, -1 and loop exit occurs when i is -1. During the last iteration of the loop body, i is 0.

The loop-control statements in these examples manipulate a counter variable, but you can use the `for` statement to implement general conditional loops by writing more general loop-control statements. In this textbook we use the `for` statement primarily for implementing counting loops.

Program Style: *Declaring Counter Variables in the `for` Loop Header*
In the `for` statement examples above, we declare and initialize the loop control variable in the `for` loop header. This is common practice in Java and results in the loop-control variable being visible (accessible) only in the block consisting of the loop. If you attempt to reference the loop-control variable outside of the loop, you will get an "Undefined variable" syntax error.

EXAMPLE 6.3

The `for` statement below displays each uppercase letter and its Unicode value on a line.

```
for (char ch = 'A'; ch <= 'Z'; ch++)
    displayResult(ch + " " + (int) ch);
```

The update step ch++ changes the contents of ch to the next uppercase letter. The output lines would have the form:

```
A 65
B 66
. . .
Z 90
```

In the next case study we use a loop to display a table of values by repeating the computation and display steps to generate a sequence of output lines.

Case Study

Displaying a Temperature Table

PROBLEM

Many situations call for displaying output in tabular form. An example would be a table of equivalent Celsius and Fahrenheit temperatures for a specified range of values (say, for -10 degrees Celsius to +10 degrees Celsius in increments of 2 degrees).

ANALYSIS

The table display program should read the minimum and maximum values for the range of Celsius temperatures and the increment value in degrees. The program displays on each output line a Celsius temperature in the range and its corresponding Fahrenheit value.

Data Requirements

Inputs

minimum Celsius temperature
maximum Celsius temperature
change in Celsius temperature for each table line

Outputs

a table of equivalent Celsius and Fahrenheit temperatures

Relevant Formulas

fahrenheit = 1.8 * *celsius* + 32

A temperature table class might have the following specification.

DESIGN

Class TempTable has the specification below. Method showTempTable displays the table of corresponding values.

Specification for *TempTable class*

Data Fields

int minCelsius—minimum Celsius temperature
int maxCelsius—maximum Celsius temperature
int stepCelsius—change in Celsius temperature for each table line

Methods

`readTableLimits`—enters table limits

`toFahrenheit`—converts a Celsius temperature to Fahrenheit

`showTempTable`—shows a table of equivalent Celsius and Fahrenheit temperatures

Algorithm for `showTempTable` (class `TempTable`)

1. Display a heading for the table.
2. `for` each Celsius temperature in the range
    3. Show the Celsius temperature and its corresponding Fahrenheit value.

IMPLEMENTATION

Figure 6.16 shows class `TempTable`. Method `showTable` first displays a description of the table followed by a blank line. The statement

```
displayResult("Celsius" + "\t" + "Fahrenheit");
```

displays a line containing two column labels (`"Celsius"` and `"Fahrenheit"`). The string `"\t"` inserts a Tab character between these values; this insertion has the same effect as pressing the Tab key on your keyboard in a word processor or editor program. Next, the `for` statement in `showTable` displays one table line for each value of the counter variable `celsius`, starting with `minCelsius` and increasing by `stepCelsius`. The statement

```
displayResult(celsius + "\t" + toFahrenheit(celsius));
```

displays the value of `celsius` and its equivalent Fahrenheit temperature separated by a Tab character.

TESTING

You need to write a small application class to test class `TempTable` (see Programming Exercise 3). Figure 6.17 shows the output table for `minCelsius = -10`, `maxCelsius = 10`, and `stepCelsius = 5`.

```
/*    File: TempTable.java
      Developed for Problem Solving with Java, Koffman & Wolz
      Appears in Figure 6.16
*/
import simpleIO.*;

public class TempTable extends SimpleGUI {
    //Data fields
    private int minCelsius;  // smallest Celsius temp value
    private int maxCelsius;  // largest Celsius temp value
    private int stepCelsius; // change in Celsius values

    //Methods
    public void readTableLimits() {
        minCelsius = getInt("Enter min Celsius temperature:");
        maxCelsius = getInt("Enter max Celsius temperature:",
                           minCelsius, 1000);
        stepCelsius = getInt("Enter change in Celsius temp " +
                            "between table lines:");
    }


    public double toFahrenheit(int celsius) {
        return 1.8 * celsius + 32;
    }


    public void showTempTable() {
        // Display table heading and blank line.
        displayResult("\nTable of Celsius and " +
                     "Fahrenheit temperatures\n");
        displayResult("Celsius" + "\t" + "Fahrenheit");

        // Display the table rows.
        for (int celsius = minCelsius; celsius <= maxCelsius;
            celsius += stepCelsius)
                displayResult(celsius + "\t" + toFahrenheit(celsius));
    }
} // class TempTable
```

Figure 6.16 Class TempTable

```
┌─────────────────────────────────────────────────────┐
│ 🖼 User Interaction History              _ ☐ ✕        │
├─────────────────────────────────────────────────────┤
│ File                                                 │
├─────────────────────────────────────────────────────┤
│ Enter min Celsius temperature:                    ▲ │
│ -10                                                 │
│ Enter max Celsius temperature:                      │
│ 10                                                  │
│ Enter change in Celsius temp between table lines    │
│ 5                                                   │
│                                                     │
│ Table of Celsius and Fahrenheit temperatures        │
│                                                     │
│ Celsius   Fahrenheit                                │
│ -10          14.0                                   │
│ -5           23.0                                   │
│ 0            32.0                                   │
│ 5            41.0                                 ▒ │
│ 10           50.0                                 ▼ │
├─────────────────────────────────────────────────────┤
│ ◀                                              ▶  ▓ │
└─────────────────────────────────────────────────────┘
```

Figure 6.17 Sample temperature table

EXERCISES FOR SECTION 6.5

Self-Check

1. Trace the program fragment below.

    ```
    j = 10;
    for (i = 1; i <= 5; i++) {
        displayResult(i + "\t" + j);
        j -= 2;
    }
    ```

2. What is the minimum number of times the statements that comprise a `for` loop body can be executed? Give an example program fragment that will execute that minimum number of times.

3. Write `for` loop headers that process all values of Celsius (type `int`) in the following ranges assuming a temperature of 1 degree Celsius:

   a. `-10` through `+10`

   b. `100` through `1`

   c. `15` through `50`

   d. `50` through `-75`

4. Variables of which data types can be declared as `for` loop counter variables?

Programming

1. Write a `for` statement that computes the sum of the odd integers in the range `0` to `100`, inclusive.

2. Write a program fragment with a `for` statement that accumulates the total number of days for the years 1950 to the year 2000. Remember, any year divisible by 4 is a leap year and has 366 days.

3. Write an application class to test class `TempTable`.

6.6 Loops in Graphics Programs (Optional)

You can form many interesting geometric patterns on your screen by using a loop in a graphics program to draw the same shape in different sizes, colors, and starting positions.

EXAMPLE 6.4

Method `paint` in Fig. 6.18 draws a "quilt" with 15 nested colored rectangles (see Fig. 6.19). It first draws a large black rectangle that fills the output window. Each subsequent rectangle is drawn inside the previous rectangle, overwriting its pixels in a new color, so only a border from the previous rectangle remains on the screen. The statements

```
//   Change in x-coordinate
int stepX = maxX / (2 * numRecs);
//   Change in y-coordinate
int stepY = maxY / (2 * numRecs);
```

define the change in x- and y-values for the top-left corners of each rectangle and these corners are computed so that there will be room to display all the rectangles.

Within the loop, the statement

```
// Select the next color
g.setColor(defineColor(i % numColors));
```

calls method `defineColor` to determine the color of the *i*th rectangle, based on the value of counter variable `i`. Method `defineColor` returns one of 11 color values, which is passed as an argument to `setColor`. After method `fillRect` draws a rectangle, the statements

```
x1 += stepX;            // Increment x-coordinate.
y1 += stepY;            // Increment y-coordinate.
width -= 2 * stepX;     // Decrement width of rectangle.
height -= 2 * stepY;    // Decrement height of rectangle.
```

change the top-left coordinates (point x1, y1) and dimensions of the next smaller rectangle. For interesting effects, try changing the values assigned to `stepX` and `stepY`.

```
/*    File: Quilt.java
      Developed for Problem Solving with Java,
         Koffman & Wolz
      Appears in Figure 6.18
*/
import java.awt.*;
import java.applet.Applet;

public class Quilt extends Applet {
    //Data Fields
    int maxX = 600;             // Window size in
                                // horizontal direction
    int maxY = 500;             // Window size in
                                // vertical direction
    int numRecs = 15;           // Number of rectangles
    int numColors = 10;         // Number of colors

    //Methods
    // Returns one of 11 standard colors.
    private Color defineColor(int i) {
        switch (i) {
            case 0: return Color.black;
```

Figure 6.18 *continued*

Figure 6.18 *continued*

```
        case 1: return Color.blue;
        case 2: return Color.cyan;
        case 3: return Color.gray;
        case 4: return Color.green;
        case 5: return Color.magenta;
        case 6: return Color.orange;
        case 7: return Color.pink;
        case 8: return Color.red;
        case 9: return Color.white;
        default: return Color.yellow;
    }
}

public void paint(Graphics g) {
    int x1 = 0;  //starting x-coordinate
    int y1 = 20; //starting y-coordinate
    // Change in x-coordinate
    int stepX = maxX / (2 * numRecs);
    // Change in y-coordinate
    int stepY = maxY / (2 * numRecs);

    // Width of outermost rectangle
    int width = maxX;
    // Height of outermost rectangle
    int height = maxY - 20;
    for (int i = 0; i < numRecs; i++) {
      // Select the next color
      g.setColor(defineColor(i % numColors));
      // Draw a filled rectangle
      g.fillRect(x1, y1, width, height);
      x1 += stepX;        // Increment x-coordinate
      y1 += stepY;        // Increment y-coordinate
      width -= 2 * stepX;    // Decrement width
                            // of rectangle
      height -= 2 * stepY;    // Decrement height
                            // of rectangle

    }
  }
}
```

Figure 6.18 Class Quilt

Figure 6.19 Nest of rectangles

Graphics in SimpleGUI

You may have noticed that you can't use SimpleGUI in an applet, and it seems you can't do graphics in SimpleGUI. Does this mean that you can't control a drawing based on user input? Well, you can, but it is a little harder to do because you must understand how the objects interact.

Recall that when you created a user menu you had to create an instance of a menu object (using method createMenu) and then call its addChoice method. To create a graphic display in a SimpleGUI window, you must create an instance of a class that extends the class SimpleGraphic, and you must also define the class. Within the class definition you need a paint method that will do the drawing. Your class definition must also contain data field modifiers so that your SimpleGUI object can set the data fields based on user input.

Figures 6.20–6.22 show how the quilt drawn in Fig. 6.18 as an applet can be adapted so that user input controls the number of squares that will be drawn. Figure 6.20 is an application class that creates an instance of the VariableBoxes class, gets user input, and then draws the graphics.

```
/*      File: DrawingDemo.java
        Developed for Problem Solving with Java, Koffman & Wolz
        Appears in Figure 6.20
*/
public class DrawingDemo {

        public static void main(String[] args) {
             VariableBoxes demo = new VariableBoxes();
             demo.getNumberOfRectangles();
             demo.showQuilt();
        }

}
```

Figure 6.20 An application that draws a quilt with variable boxes

Figure 6.21 shows the definition of the class `VariableBoxes` that extends `SimpleGUI`. In method `showQuilt`, we create an instance of a `VaryingQuilt` object (Fig. 6.22). You must set the size of any drawing, otherwise it will not appear. We also use the modifier `setNumRects` to set the number of rectangles that will be drawn in the quilt. Finally, the `SimpleGUI` method `showGraphic` is called with the `VaryingQuilt` object `aDrawing` as its argument. Method `showGraphic` adds the drawing to the `SimpleGUI` window.

```
/*      File: VariableBoxes.java
        Developed for Problem Solving with Java, Koffman & Wolz
        Appears in Figure 6.21
*/

import simpleIO.*;

public class VariableBoxes extends SimpleGUI {
        private int rectNumber;    // Input - number of rectangles

        public void getNumberOfRectangles() {
             rectNumber = getInt("How many rectangles (1 to 15)",1,15);
        }

        public void showQuilt() {
             VaryingQuilt aDrawing = new VaryingQuilt();
             aDrawing.setSize(600, 500);

             aDrawing.setNumRects(rectNumber);
             showGraphic(aDrawing);
        }

}
```

Figure 6.21 A `SimpleGUI` class that draws graphics

This is the new part. Just as you previously created an extension of an applet to draw, you extend the class SimpleGraphic to draw to a SimpleGUI window. The class VaryingQuilt is almost identical to the class Quilt in Fig. 6.18. The differences are highlighted in color. First, VaryingQuilt extends SimpleGraphic instead of Applet. Second, it includes the method setNumRects that allows the VariableBoxes class to modify the number of rectangles that can be drawn.

```java
/*    File: VaryingQuilt.java
      Developed for Problem Solving with Java, Koffman & Wolz
      Appears in Figure 6.22
*/
import simpleIO.*;
import.java.awt.*;

public class VaryingQuilt extends SimpleGraphic {
    // Data Fields
    int maxX = 600;        // Window size in horizontal direction
    int maxY = 500;        // Window size in vertical direction
    int numRecs = 15;      // Default value for number of rectangles
    int numColors = 10;    // Number of colors

    // Methods
    // Modifier for data field numRecs
    public void setNumRects(int rn ) {
        if  (rn < 1 || rn > 20)
            numRecs = 15;
        else
            numRecs = rn;
    }

    // Returns one of 11 standard colors
    private Color defineColor(int i) {
        // Same as Quilt, see Fig. 6.18
    }

    public void paint(Graphics g) {
        // Same as Quilt, see Fig. 6.18
    }
}
```

Figure 6.22 Class VaryingQuilt

EXERCISES FOR SECTION 6.6

Self-Check

1. What would be drawn by the following fragment?

    ```
    radius = 40;
    x = radius;          y = 300;
    for (i = 0; i < 10; i++) {
          g.setColor(defineColor(i % numColors));
          g.fillOval(x - radius, y - radius,
                     2 * radius, 2 * radius;
          x = x + radius;
    }
    ```

2. Experiment by changing numRecs and numColors in Fig. 6.18 to see what different patterns get displayed.

Programming

1. Draw a series of small squares of different colors but fixed size that move from the bottom-left corner to the top-right corner of your screen.

6.7 Introduction to Recursive Methods (Optional)

Java allows a method to call itself. A method that calls itself is a **recursive method**. Sometimes it is simpler to implement a repeated operation using recursion instead of iteration. A recursive method calls itself repeatedly, but with different argument values for each call. We describe one recursive method in this section.

recursive method:
a method that calls itself.

Just as we did for a loop, we need to identify a situation (called a **stopping case**) that stops the recursion; otherwise, the method will call itself forever. Usually a recursive method has the following form:

stopping case:
a condition that stops recursion.

Template for a recursive method

if the stopping case is reached

> Return a value for the stopping case

else

> Return a value computed by calling the method with a different argument.

The if statement tests whether the stopping case is reached. When it is reached, the recursion stops and the method returns a value. If the stopping case is not reached, the method calls itself with different arguments. The arguments in successive calls should bring us closer and closer to reaching the stopping case.

The recursive function we describe returns an integer value representing the factorial of its argument. The factorial of n is defined as the product of all integers less than or equal to n and is written in mathematics as $n!$. For example, 4! is the product $4 \times 3 \times 2 \times 1$ or 24. We provide a recursive definition for $n!$ next.

$$n! = 1 \qquad \text{for } n = 0 \text{ or } 1$$
$$n! = n \times (n-1)! \qquad \text{for } n > 1$$

Next, we translate this definition into pseudocode using the template shown earlier:

if n is 0 or 1

    Return 1

else

    Return $n \times (n-1)!$

Figure 6.23 shows method `factorial` rewritten as a recursive method. When n is greater than 1, the statement

```
return n * factorial(n - 1);
```

executes, which is the Java form of the second formula. The expression part of this statement contains a valid method call, `factorial(n - 1)`, which calls method `factorial` with an argument that is 1 less than the current argument. This function call is a *recursive call*. If the argument in the initial call to `factorial` is 3, the following chain of recursive calls occurs:

```
factorial(3) → 3 * factorial(2) →
                         3 * (2 * factorial(1))
```

In the last call above, n is equal to 1 so the statement

```
return 1;
```

executes, stopping the chain of recursive calls.

```java
// Returns the product 1 * 2 * 3 * ... * n for n > 1;
// Returns 1 when n is 0 or 1
public int factorial(int n) {
   if (n <= 1)
      return 1;
   else
      return n * factorial(n - 1);
}
```

Figure 6.23 Recursive factorial method

When it finishes the last function call, Java must return a value from each recursive call, starting with the last one. This process is called **unwinding the recursion**. The last call was `factorial(1)` and it returns a value of 1. To find the value returned by each call for n greater than 1, multiply n during that call by the value returned from the next call. Therefore, the value returned from `factorial(2)` is 2 times the value returned from `factorial(1)` or 2; the value returned from `factorial(3)` is 3 times the value returned from `factorial(2)` or 6 (see Fig. 6.24).

unwinding the recursion:
the process of returning a value from each recursive call.

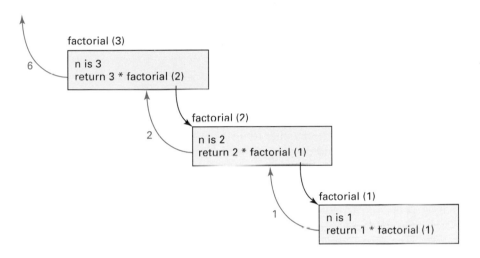

Figure 6.24 Returning from recursive calls

For comparative purposes, Fig. 6.25 shows an iterative factorial method that uses a loop to accumulate partial products in local variable `productSoFar`. The `for` statement repeats the multiplication step when n is greater than 1. If n is 0 or 1, the `for` statement does not execute, so `productSoFar` retains its initial value of 1. After loop exit, the last value of `productSoFar` is returned as the method `result`.

```
// Returns the product 1 * 2 * 3 * ... * n for n > 1;
// Returns 1 when n is 0 or 1.
public int factorial(int n) {
   int productSoFar = 1;    //accumulated product so far

   // Perform the repeated multiplication.
   for (int i = n; i > 1, i--)
     productSoFar *= i;

   return productSoFar;
}
```

Figure 6.25 Iterative factorial method

EXERCISES FOR SECTION 6.7

Self-Check

1. Show the chain of recursive calls to method `mystery` when m is 4 and n is 3. What do you think `mystery` does?

```
public int mystery(int m, int n) {
    if (n == 1)
        return m;
    else
        return m * mystery(m, n-1);
}
```

Programming

1. Write a recursive method that, given an input value of n, computes n + n − 1 + ... + 2 + 1.

2. Write a method c(n, r) that returns the number of different ways *r* items can be selected from a group of *n* items. The mathematical formula for c(n, r) follows. Test c(n, r) using both the recursive and the nonrecursive versions of `factorial`.

$$c(n,r) = \frac{n!}{r!(n-r)!}$$

6.8 Debugging and Testing Methods with Loops

In Section 2.9 we described the three general categories of errors: syntax errors, run-time errors, and logic errors. Sometimes the cause of a run-time error or the source of a logic error is apparent and the error can be fixed easily. Often, however, the error is not obvious and you may have to spend considerable time and energy to locate it.

The first step in locating a hidden error is to examine the program output to determine which part of the program is generating incorrect results. Then you can focus on the statements in that section of the program to determine which are at fault. To help you find problem areas during debugging, insert extra `System.out.println` statements to display intermediate results at different points in your program. For example, if the loop in Fig. 6.12 is not computing the correct sum, the diagnostic output statement in color below will display each value of `score` and `sum`. The asterisks highlight the diagnostic output in the debugging runs and the diagnostic output statements in the source program.

```
score = getInt("Enter the next score or -1 to stop:",
                -1, 100);
while (score != sentinel) {
    sum += score;
    System.out.println("***** score is " + score +
                       ", sum is " + sum);
    score = getInt("Enter the next score or -1 to stop:",
                    -1, 100);
}
```

Be careful when you insert diagnostic output statements. Sometimes you must add curly braces if a single statement inside an `if` or a `while` statement becomes a compound statement when you add a diagnostic output statement.

After it appears that you have located the error, you will want to take out the diagnostic output statements. As a temporary measure, turn the diagnostic statements into comments by prefixing them with `//`. If the same errors crop up again in later testing, it is easier to remove the `//` than to retype the diagnostic statements.

Off-by-One Loop Errors

A fairly common logic error in programs with loops is caused by a loop that executes one more time or one less time than it is supposed to. If a sentinel-controlled `while` loop performs an extra repetition, it may erroneously process the sentinel value along with the regular data.

If a `while` loop performs a counting operation, make sure that the initial and final values of the loop-control variable are correct. For example, the loop body below executes n + 1 times instead of n times. If you want the loop body to execute exactly n times, change the `while` condition to `count < n`.

```
count = 0;
while (count <= n) {
    sum += count;
    count++;
}
```

Checking Loop Boundaries

You can determine if a loop is correct by checking the loop boundaries, that is, the initial and final values of the loop-control variable. Determine the initial and final values of the loop-control variable and make sure that these values make sense. Next, substitute these values everywhere the loop-control variable appears in the loop body and verify that you get the expected results at the boundaries. As an example, in the for loop

```
sum = 0;
for (i = k; i <= n - k; i++)
    sum += (i * i);
```

check that the first value of the counter variable i is supposed to be k and that the last value is supposed to be n - k. Next check that the assignment statement

```
sum += (i * i);
```

is correct at these boundaries. When i is k, sum gets the value of k squared. when i is n - k, the value of $(n - k)^2$ is added to the previous sum. As a final check, pick some small value of n and k (say, 3 and 1) and trace the loop execution to see that it computes sum correctly for this case.

Testing

After you have corrected all errors and the program appears to execute as expected, test the program thoroughly to make sure that it works. In Section 5.6 we discussed tracing an algorithm and suggested that you provide enough sets of test data to ensure that all possible paths are traced. The same is true for a completed program. Make enough test runs to verify that the program works properly for representative samples of all possible data combinations.

EXERCISES FOR SECTION 6.8

Self-Check

1. For the while loop in the subsection entitled "Off-by-One Loop Errors," add debugging statements to show the value of the loop-control variable at the start of each repetition. Also, add debugging statements to show the value of sum at the end of each loop repetition.

2. Why does the following code fragment fail? What are the loop boundaries for this code fragment?

```
x = 10;
do {
    x--;
    displayResult(x + "\t" + Math.sqrt(x));
} while (x >= 0);
```

6.9 Common Programming Errors

Beginners sometimes confuse `if` and `while` statements because both statements contain a condition. Make sure that you use an `if` statement to implement a decision step and a `while` statement to implement a loop.

Be careful when you use tests for inequality to control the repetition of a `while` loop. For instance, the following loop is intended to process all transactions for a bank account while the balance is positive.

```
while (balance != 0)
    balance = update(balance);
```

If the bank balance goes from a positive to a negative amount without being exactly 0, the loop will not terminate (becoming an infinite loop). This loop would be safer:

```
while (balance > 0)
    balance = update(balance);
```

You should verify that the repetition condition for a `while` loop will eventually become `false`. If you use a sentinel-controlled loop, remember to provide a prompt that tells the program user what value to enter as the sentinel. Make sure that the sentinel value cannot be confused with a normal data item.

If the loop body is a compound statement, remember to bracket it with `{` and `}`. Otherwise, only the first statement will be repeated, and the remaining statements will be executed when and if the loop is exited. The loop below will not terminate because the step that updates the loop-control variable is not considered part of the loop body. The program will continue to print the initial value of `power` until you instruct the computer to terminate its execution.

```
power = 1;
while (power <= 10000)
    displayResult("Next power of n is " + power);
    power = power * n;   // Never executed!
```

Be sure to initialize to 0 an accumulator variable used for accumulating a sum by repeated addition. Be sure to initialize to 1 a variable used for accumulating a product by repeated multiplication. Omitting this step may lead to incorrect results.

A `do-while` loop always executes at least once. Use a `do-while` statement only if you are certain that there is no possibility of zero loop iterations; otherwise, use a `while` loop instead.

Be careful about the visibility of data. A variable declared in a block is only visible within that block. So if you declare a variable in a loop, you cannot reference that variable outside the loop. If you attempt to do so, you will get an undeclared variable error.

Chapter Review

1. Use a loop to repeat steps in a program. Four kinds of loops occur frequently in programming: counting loops, sentinel-controlled loops, flag-controlled loops, and menu-driven loops. For a counting loop, the number of iterations required can be determined before the loop is entered. For a sentinel-controlled loop, repetition continues until a special data value is read. For a flag-controlled loop, repetition continues until a state being monitored has been reached. A menu-driven loop executes at least once and loop repetition stops when the user selects the quit option.

Template for Counter-controlled Loop

1. Set *counter variable* to 1.
2. `while` (*counter variable* <= *final value*)
   ```
   //Do the loop processing ...
   ```
   Increase *counter variable* by 1.

Template for a Sentinel-controlled Loop

1. Read the first value of *input variable*.
2. `while` (*input variable* is not equal to the sentinel)
   ```
   //Do the loop processing ...
   ```
   Read the next value of *input variable*.

Template for a Flag-controlled Loop

1. Initialize *flag* to `false`.
2. `while` (!*flag*)
   ```
   //Do the loop processing ...
   ```
   Reset *flag* to `true` if the state being monitored has been reached.

Template for a Menu-driven Loop

`do`
   1. Display the menu and read the user's choice.
   2. Perform the selection.
`while` (user's choice is not quit) ;

2. Java provides three statements for implementing loops: `while`, `for`, and `do-while`. Use the `for` statement to implement counting loops and the `do-while` statement to implement loops that must execute at least once (such as menu-driven loops). Write all other conditional loops using the `while` statement.

3. In designing a loop, focus on both loop control and loop processing. For loop processing, make sure that the loop body contains steps that perform the operation that must be repeated. For loop control, you must provide steps that initialize, test, and update the loop-control variable. Make sure that the initialization step leads to correct program results when the loop body is not executed (zero-iteration loop).

4. Two groups of Java operators affect variable values: the increment/decrement operators and the compound assignment operators. You can use the former to implement the update step in a counting loop; you can use the latter to accumulate a total value.

New Java Constructs

Construct	**Effect**
`while` Statement	

`sum = 0;`
`while (sum <= maxSum) {`
 	
`    next = getInt("Next item:");`
`    sum += next;`
`}`
	A collection of input data items is read, and their sum is accumulated in `sum`. This process stops when the accumulated `sum` exceeds `maxSum`.

`for` Statement	

`for (curMonth = 3;`
`    curMonth <= 9;`
`    curMonth++) {`
 	
`    String prompt =`
`        "Sales for month ";`
`    monthSales =`
`        getDouble(prompt + curMonth);`
`    yearSales += monthSales;`
`}`
	The loop body is repeated for each value of `curMonth` from 3 to 9, inclusive. For each month, the value of `monthSales` is read and added to `yearSales`.

`do-while` Statement	

`sum = 0;`
 	
`do {`
 	
`    nextInt = getInt("Next:");`
`    sum += nextInt;`
`} while (nextInt != 0);`
	Integer values are read, and their sum is accumulated in `sum`. The process terminates after the first zero is read.

Quick-Check Exercises

1. If the loop condition is a `boolean` variable, what type of loop is this?
2. It is an error if a `while` loop body never executes. True or false?
3. The priming step for a sentinel-controlled loop is what kind of statement? Where is this statement placed? What is the purpose of a similar statement in the loop body? Where would it occur?
4. The sentinel value is always the last value added to a sum being accumulated in a sentinel-controlled loop. True or false?
5. Which loop form (`for`, `while`, `do-while`) is described in each of the following?

   a. Executes at least one time

   b. Is the most general

   c. Condenses the code for a counting loop

   d. Should be used in a sentinel-controlled loop
6. What does the following fragment display?

   ```
   int product = 1;
   int counter = 2;
   while (counter <= 5) {
       product += counter;
       counter++;
   }
   displayResult(product);
   ```
7. An erroneous loop in a program that always executes one too many times has a problem at the _____ . This is called an _____ error.
8. What will be displayed by the following fragment?

   ```
   n = 10;
   for (int i = 1; i <= 10; i++) {
       displayResult(i);
       n -= i;
   }
   displayResult(n);
   ```

Answers to Quick-Check Exercises

1. flag-controlled loop
2. False
3. The priming step is an input operation; it is placed just before loop entry and as the last statement in the loop body. The input operation in

the loop body reads all but the first data item, which is read by the input operation before loop entry. The input operation occurs at the end of the loop body.

4. False—the sentinel should not be processed.

5. **a.** `do-while`

   b. `while`

   c. `for`

   d. `while`

6. the value of `1 * 2 * 3 * 4 * 5`, or `120`.

7. loop boundary, off-by-one

8. `1 2 3 4 5 6 7 8 9 10 -45`

Review Questions

1. How does a sentinel value differ from a program flag as a means of loop control?

2. For a sentinel value to be used properly when data is read in, where should the input statements appear?

3. Write a program fragment that allows a user to input several pairs of values for x and y and, for each pair, computes x raised to the y power by repeated multiplication. The program should keep obtaining values from the user until a sentinel value of 0 is entered for x.

4. Hand trace the following program fragment given these data:

```
4 2 8 4    1 4 2 1    9 3 3 1    -22 10 8 2    3 3 4 5

int y2 = getInt("Enter an integer:");
int y1 = getInt("Enter an integer:");
int x2 = getInt("Enter an integer:");
int x1 = getInt("Enter an integer:");

while (x2 != x1) {
        double slope = (y2 - y1) / (x2 - x1);
        displayResult("Slope is " + slope);
        y2 = getInt("Enter an integer:");
        y1 = getInt("Enter an integer:");
        x2 = getInt("Enter an integer:");
        x1 = getInt("Enter an integer:");
}
```

5. Can you always replace a `while` loop with a `for` or a `do-while` loop? Why or why not?

6. Consider the program fragment

```
int count = 0;
for (int i = 1; i <= n; i++) {
    int x = getInt("Enter an integer:");
    if (x == i)
        count++;
}
```

a. Write a `while` loop equivalent to the `for` loop.

b. Write a `do-while` loop equivalent to the `for` loop.

Programming Projects

1. Write a program that will find the smallest, largest, and average values in a collection of *n* numbers. Read in the value of *n* before reading each value in the collection of *n* numbers.

2. Modify Programming Project 1 to compute and display both the range of values in the data collection and the standard deviation of the data collection. To compute the standard deviation, accumulate the sum of the squares of the data values (`sumSquares`) in the main loop. After loop exit, use the formula

$$standard\ deviation = \sqrt{\frac{sumSquares}{n} - (average)^2}$$

3. Bunyan Lumber Co. needs to create a table of the engineering properties of its lumber. The dimensions of the wood are given as the base and the height in inches. Engineers need to know the following information about lumber:

cross-sectional area = base × height
moment of inertia = (base × height³)/12
section modulus = (base × height²)/6

The height sizes are 2, 4, 6, 8, and 10 inches. Produce a table with appropriate headings to show these values and the computed engineering properties. Do not duplicate a 2-by-6 board with a 6-by-2 board.

4. Write a program to generate a calendar for a year. The program should accept the year and the day of the week for January 1 of that year (1 = Sunday, 7 = Saturday). Remember, February has 29 days if the year is divisible by 4. The calendar should be printed in the following form (for each month).

```
January
                      1
 2   3   4   5   6   7   8
 9  10  11  12  13  14  15
16  17  18  19  20  21  22
23  24  25  26  27  28  29
30  31
```

5. **a.** Write a program to read in a collection of exam scores ranging in value from 1 to 100. Your program should count and print the number of outstanding scores (90–100), the number of satisfactory scores (60–89), and the number of unsatisfactory scores (1–59). It should also display the category of each score. Test your program on the following data:

```
63   75   72   72   78   67   80   63   75
90   89   43   59   99   82   12   100
```

b. Modify your program to display the average exam score (a real number) at the end of the run.

6. Write a program to process weekly employee time cards for all employees of an organization. Each employee will have three data items: an identification number, the hourly wage rate, and the number of hours worked during a given week. Each employee is to be paid time-and-a-half for all hours worked over 40. A tax amount of 3.625 percent of gross salary will be deducted. The program output should show the employee's number and net pay. Display the total payroll and the average amount paid at the end of the run.

7. Suppose you own a beer distributorship that sells Piels (ID number 1), Coors (ID number 2), Bud (ID number 3), and Iron City (ID number 4) by the case. Write a program to do the following:

   a. Read in the case inventory for each brand for the start of the week.

   b. Process all weekly sales and purchase records for each brand.

   c. Print out the final inventory.

   Each transaction will consist of two data items. The first item will be the brand identification number (an integer). The second will be the amount purchased (a positive integer value) or the amount sold (a negative integer value). The weekly inventory for each brand (for the start of the week) will also consist of two items: the identification number and the initial inventory for that brand. For now you may assume that you always have sufficient foresight to prevent depletion of your inventory for any brand. (*Hint:* Your data entry should begin with eight values representing the case inventory, followed by the transaction values.)

8. Revise Programming Project 7 to make it a menu-driven program. The menu operations supported by the revised program should be Enter Inventory, Purchase Beer, Sell Beer, Display Inventory, and Quit Program. Negative quantities should no longer be used to represent goods sold.

9. Before high-resolution graphics displays became common, computer terminals were often used to display graphs of equations using only text characters. A typical technique was to create a vertical graph by spacing over on the screen, then drawing an *. Write a program that displays

the graph of an increasing-frequency sine wave this way. The program should ask the user for an initial step size in degrees and the number of lines of the graph to display. A sample output begins as:

```
                                        *
                                            *
                                                *
                                                    *
                                                        *
                                                          *
                                                            *
                                                              *
                                                               *
                                                            *
                                                          *
                                                        *
                                                    *
                                                *
                                            *
                                        *
                              *
                      *
            *
      *
    *
```

10. A horizon effect occurs when objects get progressively smaller along a line. Write a method that draws a figure of your choosing (a house, a flower, a person, an animal). The dimensions of the figure must be variable. Start in the lower-left corner of a drawing surface and draw smaller and smaller versions of the figure on a diagonal line toward the upper-right corner of the surface. The visual effect should be of a row of your figures fading into the distance.

11. How do the artists draw three-dimensional figures on a two-dimensional surface? They play tricks on your eyes. You can experiment with this phenomenon by drawing a series of ovals with the same center but with decreasing width. Try to draw the series of ovals in the following diagram.

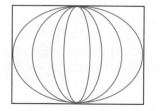

12. Create some abstract art. Create a few figures of your own choosing that have variable dimensions (see Programming Project 10). Create a class with class methods that lets you randomly select points within a display area as well as figure dimensions. Place figures of random sizes at random positions on the screen.

Interview

Radia Perlman

Radia Perlman is employed at Sun Microsystem's Boston Center for Networking. She holds a Ph.D. in Computer Science from the Massachusetts Institute of Technology. While at Digital Equipment Corporation, Radia designed the spanning tree algorithm, which became the IEEE standard for bridge technology. Radia is highly regarded in the networking community for her work with networks and network security.

What is your educational background? Why did you decide to study computer science?

I went to MIT and majored in math. I went to graduate school there in math also. I wound up dropping out (with a master's) and working in industry designing computer network protocols and loved it. After becoming an expert in a field, I returned to grad school at MIT in computer science (I wanted to see what, if anything, I'd missed by having not taken computer science courses) and got a Ph.D.

What made you pursue networking over other areas of computer science?

It was purely luck. At the time I'd done all the straightforward stuff in grad school but had no idea how to start on a thesis. Just at that time an old friend asked me how I was enjoying grad school and I said I was having trouble finding an advisor and a research topic and he said, "Well, how about joining our group at BBN?" So I did. And it happened to be the group designing protocols for the packet radio network.

While employed at Digital Equipment Corporation, you designed the spanning tree algorithm that was later adopted as the IEEE standard for bridge technology. Tell me a little about the algorithm and how it has affected the industry.

First of all, bridges were a kludge invented because people mistakenly thought that it was reasonable to consider the Ethernet a network rather than a link in a network. So they left out the network layer (protocols like IP, DECnet, IPX are network-layer protocols). Bridges were a simple idea for moving packets around without the cooperation or knowledge of the end systems. Basically, bridges just forward packets from the port they hear a packet on to their other ports. They learn station addresses to cut down on unnecessary forwarding. This idea does not tolerate loops. The spanning tree algorithm is a simple protocol that the bridges run amongst themselves to find a subset of the topology that has no loops but yet connects everything together.

How would you describe a typical day for you at the Boston Center for Networking? What is the most challenging part of your job?

My typical day involves reading lots of email and documents like Sun internal documents, IETF drafts, or academic papers. Design work is lots of fun. Sometimes I do this alone, but at some stage in the process I discuss it with someone else while drawing pictures on whiteboards and making lists of advantages of method A versus method B. I also really enjoy explaining things to people and do a lot of talks or tutorial documents (including books).

How has Java affected the field of networking?

It revolutionized the way people could use the Web. Things could be interactive and you could send executables with reasonable security.

What are some of the top security issues that affect networks today? Do you see network security as a growing field for students to become involved with?

Network security is definitely a fascinating field with lots of employment opportunities. One difficult problem is "denial of service." For example, a system might be secure enough to prevent an unauthorized person from reading or destroying information, but it might take more time for a server to make the decision to deny access to someone than it takes for them to make the request. In that case, unauthorized people can completely tie up a system by attempting access.

The ugliest problem is political. Various governments (e.g., the U.S.) are afraid for systems to be too secure because they want to be able to seize your computer and figure out what you've been doing, or wiretap. It's hard enough to build a secure system without having to also attempt to satisfy vague and sometimes impossible governmental demands.

What person in the computer industry has inspired you?

Mischa Schwartz. He came along at a crucial point in my career. I had written my first paper and submitted it to a journal. It was on problems with a particular routing protocol. The paper was rejected and received one very negative review. I was discouraged and would never have attempted to publish anything else. But a few months later Mischa Schwartz called me and asked for a bibliographic reference for that paper since he wanted to reference it himself. I told him it was rejected. He was shocked. I sent him what the negative reviewer said. He said, "Oh, that's no problem. Want it in *Computer Networks*"? (a journal he was on the editorial board of)? I said sure, and it got published there, and is considered a very important paper.

Do you have any advice for students who are currently learning Java and/or anyone entering the field of computer science?

Keep things simple. Don't design what I call "meta-architectural frameworks", which are content-free things that don't actually do anything. Find real problems and solve them in the simplest possible way.

Don't let insecurity hold you back. You don't have all the answers, but then again nobody does. Most of the people around you are as insecure as you are. Asking the right questions is probably even more valuable than knowing the answers.

Most of all, have fun with everything you do and make sure everyone around you is having fun.

CHAPTER 7

Arrays and Vectors

Primitive data types (int, double, boolean, char) use a single memory cell to store a variable. For many programming problems, it is more efficient to group data items together in main memory than to allocate an individual memory cell for each variable. A program that processes exam scores for a course, for example, would be easier to write if all the scores were stored in one area of memory and could be accessed as a group. Java allows a programmer to group such related data items together into a single composite data structure: the array.

Arrays enable us to store in memory all the values in a collection of data we are processing, rather than just the most recent one. For example, in the payroll program in Section 6.2, we could only store one employee at a time. After we finish with the current employee, we overwrite its storage area with the data for the next employee. If we store the employee data in an array, we can go back and access the first employee's data at any time. The case study in Section 7.6 illustrates this approach.

We also discuss vectors, a Java data structure that simplifies some array operations. We also show how to use arrays with two or more dimensions to represent information in the form of tables. Finally, we discuss how to use data files as a source of program input and how to save program output in data files.

7.1 Array Declarations and Indices

7.2 Processing Arrays and Array Elements
Case Study: Computing Statistics

7.3 Operations on Whole Arrays

7.4 Searching and Sorting an Array

7.5 Analysis of Algorithms: Big-O Notation (Optional)

7.6 Arrays of Objects
Case Study: Payroll Problem with an Employee Array

7.7 Vectors

7.8 More Input/Output: Using Files and displayRow (Optional)

7.9 Multidimensional Arrays— Arrays of Arrays (Optional)

7.10 Common Programming Errors
Chapter Review

7.1 Array Declarations and Indices

array:
a collection of data items of the same type.

data structure:
a composite of related data items stored under the same name.

The **array** is a **data structure** in which we store a collection of data items of the same type (for example, all the exam scores for a class). By using an array, we can associate a single variable name (for example, `scores`) with the entire collection of data (see Fig. 7.1). We can also reference individual items in the array. The naming process is like the one used to describe families and their members. The Clinton household refers to all three members of President Bill Clinton's immediate family, and individual names—Hillary Clinton, for example—designate individuals in his family.

Array `scores`

88	95	33	67	85

Figure 7.1 Array scores

Java stores an array in consecutive storage locations in main memory, one item per memory cell. We can perform some operations, such as passing the array as a method argument, on the whole array. We also can access individual items stored in the array (called **array elements**) and process them like other simple variables. In this section we describe how to declare arrays in Java programs and how to reference individual array elements.

array element:
a data item that is part of an array.

Declaring Arrays

We allocate storage for arrays in Java using *array declarations* that specify the array element type, array name, and array size (number of elements):

```
Array        Array                    Array
type         name                     size
 ↓            ↓                         ↓
double[]  salary  =  new double[50];
```

This declaration begins with the type of the array being declared, `double[]`, an array of type `double` elements. Next, comes the array name, `salary`. The rest of the declaration specifies that a new storage area for 50 type `double` values should be allocated.

You can also declare and initialize an array at the same time. The statement

```
Array        Array                  Array
type         name                   values
 ↓            ↓                       ↓

int[]  coinValues  =  {1, 5, 10, 25, 50};
```

allocates storage for an array, `coinValues`, containing five integers. Each integer represents the number of pennies in one of the U.S. coins (`1` for a penny, `5` for a nickel, `10` for a dime, `25` for a quarter, and `50` for a half-dollar). Notice that you do not need to use the `new` operator nor do you need to specify the array size in this form of array declaration. Java allocates one array element to store each value listed, so array `coinValues` has five elements:

Array `coinValues`

1	5	10	25	50

Array Declaration

Form: *elementType* `[]` *arrayName* `=` `new` *elementType* `[size]`;
         elementType `[]` *arrayName* `=` `{`*list-of-values*`}`;

Example: `double[] salary = new double[50];`
         `int[] coinValues = {1, 5, 10, 25, 50};`

Interpretation: The identifier *arrayName* represents a collection of array elements; each element can store an item of type *elementType*. The array *size*, or number of array elements, may be specified in the array declaration. In the second form, the array size is not explicitly specified, but is implied by the size of the *list-of-values* enclosed in braces. These values are stored sequentially (one after the other) in the array elements and their data type must be *elementType*.

Note 1: The *elementType* can be any primitive type or class. If the element type is a class, the array elements contain references to objects of the class and storage must be allocated separately for each of these objects (discussed in Section 7.6).

Separating Array Declaration and Storage Allocation

You can also declare an array and allocate storage for it in separate steps. For example, you could write the declaration for array `salary` as

```
double[] salary;
salary = new double[50];
```

where the first statement declares `salary` as an array of type `double` values, and the second statement allocates storage for 50 type `double` elements. Or you can ask the program user to specify the array size during runtime:

```
double[] salary;
salary = new double[getInt("How many salaries?")];
```

The value returned by method `getInt` determines the number of elements allocated to array `salary`. This approach has the advantage that the array will contain exactly as many elements as there are salary data values, no more and no less.

Array Index

array index:
a value or expression enclosed in brackets after the array name, specifying which array element to access.

To process the data stored in an array, we must be able to access its individual elements. We access an array element by the array name (a variable) and the array index (historically called a *subscript*, from matrix algebra notation). The **array index** is enclosed in brackets after the array name (e.g., `coinValues[2]`). The array index may be an integer or an integer-valued expression.

A curious fact of Java is that we use the index 0, not 1, to reference the first element of an array, just as we use 0 as the index of the first character in a string. Therefore, we use the indices 0 through 4 to reference the five elements of array `coinValues` (see Fig. 7.2).

Counting from 0 rather than 1 is an artifact of computer architecture, where there actually is a memory location 0. Although it may seem counter-intuitive at first, many computer solutions involving relative locations turn out to be easier to implement when you start at 0 rather than 1. If you continue studying computer science you will see many examples of how this technique is used.

Array `coinValues`

indices [0] [1] [2] [3] [4]

Figure 7.2 Array `coinValues` with indices

indexed variable:
a variable followed by an index in brackets.

We call a variable followed by an index in brackets (e.g., `coinValues[1]`) an **indexed variable**. An indexed variable has the same data type as the array element it references. An indexed variable can be used just as a regular variable can. Because the elements of array `coinValues` are type `int`, we can manipulate `coinValues[1]` like any other `int` variable. Specifically, we can use `coinValues[1]` with the arithmetic operators, the relational operators, and the assignment operator. We can pass `coinValues[1]` to a method that is expecting a type `int` argument.

To store a value in an array element, we write an assignment statement of the form

indexed variable = expression;

To retrieve or access a value stored in an array element, just write the corresponding indexed variable in an expression.

EXAMPLE 7.1

Let x be the array of real values shown in Fig. 7.3. Some statements that manipulate elements of this array are shown in Table 7.1.

Array x

x[0]	x[1]	x[2]	x[3]	x[4]	x[5]	x[6]	x[7]
16.0	12.0	6.0	8.0	2.5	12.0	14.0	−54.5

First   Second   Eighth
element element   element

Figure 7.3 The eight elements of array x

Table 7.1 Storing and retrieving values in array X

Statement	Explanation
`displayResult(x[0]);`	Displays the value of x[0], or 16.0.
`x[3] = 25.0;`	Stores the value 25.0 in x[3].
`sum = x[0] + x[1];`	Stores the sum of x[0] and x[1], or 28.0, in the variable sum.
`sum = sum + x[2];`	Adds x[2] to sum. The new sum is 34.0.
`x[3] = x[3] + 1.0;`	Adds 1.0 to x[3]. The new x[3] is 26.0.
`x[2] = x[0] + x[1];`	Stores the sum of x[0] and x[1] in x[2]. The new value of x[2] is 28.0.

The contents of array x after execution of these statements are shown in Fig. 7.4. Notice that only array elements x[2] and x[3] have changed because they are the only ones that are assigned new values.

Array x

x[0]	x[1]	x[2]	x[3]	x[4]	x[5]	x[6]	x[7]
16.0	12.0	28.0	26.0	2.5	12.0	14.0	−54.5

First   Second   Eighth
element element   element

Figure 7.4 Array x after execution of statements in Table 7.1

Each index in Table 7.1 is a literal enclosed in square brackets (e.g., [4]). In Example 7.2, we show that an array index may be an integer expression.

EXAMPLE 7.2

The statements in Table 7.2 manipulate elements in array x (Fig. 7.4) where i is a type int variable with value 5.

Table 7.2 Using index expressions with array x

Statement	Effect
`displayResult(x[7]);`	Displays -54.5 (value of x[7]).
`displayResult(i + "\t" + x[i]);`	Displays 5, and 12 (value of 5, and x[5]).
`displayResult(x[i + 1]);`	Displays 14 (value of x[6]).
`displayResult(x[i + i]);`	Illegal attempt to display x[10].
`displayResult(x[2 * i - 4]);`	Displays 14 (value of x[6]).
`x[i] = x[i + 1];`	Assigns 14 (value of x[6]) to x[5].
`x[i - 1] = x[i];`	Assigns 14 (new value of x[5]) to x[4].
`x[i] - 1 = x[i - 1];`	Illegal assignment statement.

When i is 5, the indexed variable x[i + i] references element x[10], which is not in the array. Java would display a message, "Out of bounds error."

Two different indices are used in the last three assignment statements in the table. The first assignment statement copies the value of x[6] to x[5] (indices i + 1 and i); the second assignment statement copies the value of x[5] to x[4] (indices i and i - 1). The last assignment statement causes a syntax error because x[i] - 1 is an expression, not a variable.

Syntax Display

Array Element Reference

Form: *array* [*index*]

Example: x[3 * i - 2]

Interpretation: The *index* must be an integer expression. If the expression value is not in the allowable range of values, an Out of bounds error occurs during run-time.

EXERCISES FOR SECTION 7.1

Self-Check

1. Given the statements y = x3 and y = x[3], supply declarations such that these statements are valid. Assume y is type double.

2. For the following declarations, how many memory cells are reserved for data and what type of data can be stored there?

a. `int[] scores = new int[10];`

b. `char[] grades = new char[100];`

c. `boolean[] quizAnswers = new boolean[50];`

d. `int[] primes = {2, 3, 5, 7, 11, 13,`
`                    17, 19, 23, 29};`

e. `String[] choices = {"Delete", "Insert", "Replace",`
`                    "Search", "Quit"};`

f. `double[] checks;`
`checks = new double [getInt("How many checks?")];`

3. Provide array declarations for representing the following:

   a. The area in square feet for each of the rooms in your house

   b. The number of students in each grade of an elementary school with grade levels (1 through 6)

   c. The color used to paint the 30 offices in a building with letter values assigned according to the first letter of their name (e.g., `'B'` for blue)

   d. The same as part c, but store Java's standard colors instead (see Section 4.6).

   e. The names of the days of the week

   f. The names of the people in your immediate family

4. For the array in Question 2, part d, indicate the effect of each statement below if it is valid. Rewrite the statements that are not valid.

   a. `int sum = (primes[1] + primes[4]) / 2;`

   b. `primes[0] = primes[9];`
   `primes[9] = primes[0];`

   c. `displayResult("The last prime number < 30 is " +`
   `                primes[10]);`

   d. `if (primes[3] == 5)`
   `    displayResult("Gotcha!");`
   `else`
   `    displayResult("Couldn't fool you.");`

   e. `primes[1 + 4] = primes[1] + primes[4];`

Programming

1. For the array declared in Self-Check Question 2, part a, write statements that do the following:

   a. Store `0` in the first and last elements.

   b. Display a message indicating whether the value of the third element is positive or negative.

   c. Store the sum of first three elements in the last element.

7.2 Processing Arrays and Array Elements

We discuss how to process arrays and array elements in this section. Many programs require processing all the elements of an array in sequence, starting with the first element. To enter data into an array, to display its contents, or to perform other sequential processing tasks, use a `for` loop whose loop-control variable is also the array index.

The three steps for loop control are:

- *Initialize the loop control variable*: Because the first array element has an index of 0, initialize the loop-control variable to 0.
- *Test the loop-control variable*: Compare the loop-control variable to the size of the array. If the loop-control variable is smaller, repeat the loop body.
- *Increment the loop-control variable:* Increase it by one after each element is processed to advance to the next element.

Data Field `length`

To accomplish the loop-control variable test, we take advantage of the fact that Java automatically allocates a data field `length` for each array and stores the array's size in that data field. For example, if `x` is an array, you can use `x.length` to determine its size. Notice that `length` is a data field for an array, not a method as it is for a string (i.e., if `name` is a `String` object, `name.length()` gives its size). The next example illustrates sequential access to the elements of an array.

EXAMPLE 7.3

For the array `cubes` declared as:

```
int[] cubes = new int[10];
```

you can use the `for` statement

```
for (int i = 0; i < cubes.length; i++)
    cubes[i] = i * i * i;
```

to store the `cubes` of the first 10 integers in this array. The condition

```
i < cubes.length
```

compares the loop-control variable `i` to data field `length` of array `cubes`.

Array cubes

[0]	[1]	[2]	[3]	[4]	[5]	[6]	[7]	[8]	[9]
1	8	27	64	125	216	343	512	729	1000

You can use the statements

```
int sumCubes = 0;
for (int i = 0; i < cubes.length; i++)
    sumCubes += cubes[i];
```

to accumulate the sum of all element values of array cubes (stored in sumCubes). Similarly you can use the statements

```
for (int i = 0; i < cubes.length; i++)
    displayResult(i + "\t" + cubes[i]);
```

to display each element of array cubes on a separate line; each line begins with the element's index.

Figure 7.5 shows a class ArrayCubes with an array data field cubes. Method askArraySize asks the user to set the size of the array. Method showCubes contains the for statements discussed in this section. Fig. 7.6 shows an application class and Fig. 7.7 shows a sample run.

```
/*   File: ArrayCubes.java
     Developed for Problem Solving with Java, Koffman & Wolz
     Appears in Fig. 7.5
*/
import simpleIO.*;

public class ArrayCubes extends SimpleGUI {
   // Data fields
   private int[] cubes;   // An array of integers

   // Methods
   public void askArraySize() {
      cubes =
           new int[getInt("How many numbers should be cubed?")];
   }

   public void showCubes() {
      // Fill array cubes.
      for (int i = 0; i < cubes.length; i++)
         cubes[i] = i * i * i;

      // Find sum of cubes.
      int sumCubes = 0;
      for (int i = 0; i < cubes.length; i++)
         sumCubes += cubes[i];

      // Display each cube and the sum of all cubes.
      displayResult("i" + "\t" + "cube" + "\n");
      for (int i = 0; i < cubes.length; i++)
         displayResult(i + "\t" + cubes[i]);
```

Figure 7.5 *continued*

Figure 7.5 *continued*

```
        displayResult("\nSum of cubes is " + sumCubes);
    } // showCubes

} // class ArrayCubes
```

Figure 7.5 Class ArrayCubes

```
/*    File: ArrayCubesTest.java
      Developed for Problem Solving with Java, Koffman & Wolz
      Appears in Fig. 7.6.
*/
public class ArrayCubesTest
{
      public static void main (String[] args) {
            ArrayCubes ac = new ArrayCubes();
            ac.askArraySize();
            ac.showCubes();
      }
}
```

Figure 7.6 Class ArrayCubesTest

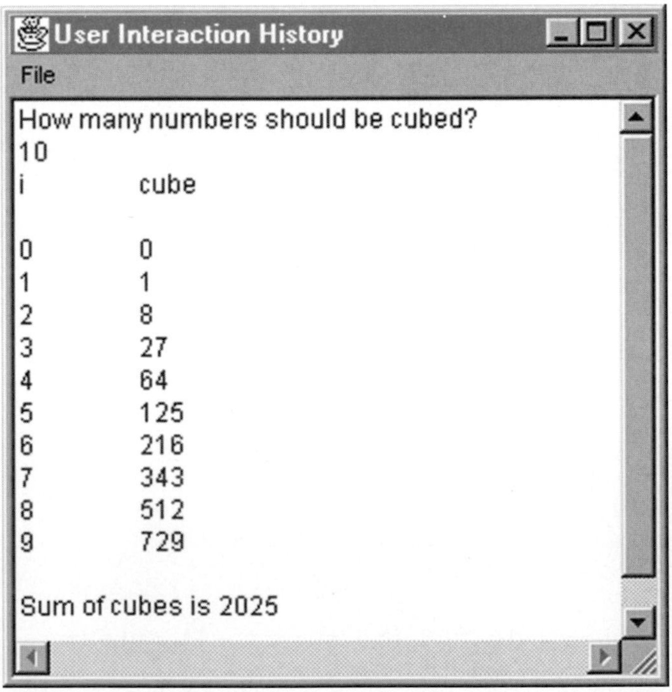

Figure 7.7 Sample run of class ArrayCubesTest

Reading Data into an Array

You can read data into an array by reading and storing one array element at a time. Figure 7.8 shows method readCubes; it reads data values into array cubes and could be inserted in class ArrayCubes. When i is 0, the statement

```
cubes[i] = getInt("Enter element " + i);
```

displays the prompt Enter element 0 and stores the data value entered in cubes[0].

```
public void readCubes() {
    for (int i = 0; i < cubes.length; i++)
        cubes[i] = getInt("Enter element " + i);
}
```

Figure 7.8 Method readCubes

Case Study

Computing Statistics

PROBLEM

Your computer science instructor needs a simple program for computing exam statistics. This program should read the scores for an exam and then compute and display various exam statistics such as the mean score, median score, standard deviation, low score, and high score for the exam.

ANALYSIS

The problem inputs consist of the count of scores and the exam scores. The outputs are all the exam statistics.

Data Requirements

Problem Inputs

count of scores
exam scores

Problem Outputs

the exam statistics

Relevant Formulas

mean = sum of array values / count of elements

$$\text{standard deviation} = \sqrt{\frac{\text{sum of squares of array values}}{\text{count of elements}} - (\text{mean})^2}$$

▼

DESIGN

Class Exam contains storage for an array of student scores. Notice that we don't need to store the size of this array because it is automatically saved in the array data field length. Method showStats computes all the exam statistics by calling separate methods to compute each statistic (for example, computeMean to compute the mean score). Our application class (see Programming Exercise 1) consists of a main method that allocates an Exam object and calls methods getExamData (reads the count of students and exam scores) and showStats (computes and displays the statistics). The class specification and method algorithms follow.

Specification for Exam *Class*

Data Fields

int[] scores—array of scores, size determined by user

Methods

getExamData—reads exam data
showStats—computes and displays exam statistics
findMin—finds and displays the smallest score
findMax—finds and displays the largest score
computeMean—computes and displays the mean score
computeMedian—finds and displays the median score
computeStandDev—computes and displays the standard deviation

Since the standard deviation is dependent upon the mean, we must ensure that the calculation of the standard deviation has a proper value for the mean.

Algorithm for getExamData

1. Get number of exam scores and create the array
2. for each student who took the exam
        Read the next score

Algorithm for showStats

1. Find and display the low score.
2. Find and display the high score.
3. Compute and display the mean score.
4. Compute and display the standard deviation.
5. Find and display the median score.

Algorithm for `findMin`

1. Set `minSoFar` to the first exam score.
2. `for` each student who took the exam after the first one
       `if` the current score is less than `minSoFar`
          Set `minSoFar` to the current score.

Algorithm for `computeMean`

1. Set sum of scores to zero.
2. `for` each student who took the exam
       Add the current score to sum.
3. Divide sum by the number of students who took the exam.

Algorithm for `computeStandDev`

1. Set sum of squares to zero.
2. `for` each student who took the exam
       Add the current score squared to sum of squares.
3. Divide sum of squares by count of students, subtract the mean squared, and take the square root of the result.

IMPLEMENTATION

Method `getExamData` (Fig. 7.9) begins with the statement

```
scores =
    new int[getInt("How many students took the exam?")];
```

which customizes the array `scores` to fit the class. Next, the `for` statement reads the exam data into array `scores`.

Method `findMin` returns the smallest exam score stored in the array. Because we have no idea what the smallest score might be, we begin by assuming that it is the first exam score and save that as the initial value of `minSoFar`, the smallest score so far. In step 2, we compare each value in the array field to `minSoFar`. If the next score is smaller than `minSoFar`, then we reset `minSoFar` to the next score. When we're finished checking the array of scores, we return the last value assigned to `minSoFar` as the smallest exam score. We can easily modify this algorithm to design method `findMax`.

Methods `computeMean` and `computeStandDev` involve accumulating a sum. For `computeMean`, we accumulate the sum of exam scores, and for `computeStandDev` we accumulate the sum of the exam scores squared. Because the mean score is needed in the computation of the standard deviation, method `computeStandDev` expects to receive the mean score as its argument when it is called.

In Section 7.4, we develop a general method (`IntArray.findMedian`) for finding the median value in an array. `ComputeMedian` calls that method and simply returns its result.

```
/*    File: Exam.java
      Developed for Problem Solving with Java, Koffman & Wolz
      Appears in Fig. 7.9
*/
import simpleIO.*;
import simpleMath.*;    // For computeMedian

public class Exam extends SimpleGUI {
   // Data Fields
   private int[] scores;   // scores is an array of ints.

   // Methods
   public void getExamData() {
      // Allocate storage for the array.
      scores = new int[getInt("How many students took the exam?")];

      // Read the scores.
      for (int i = 0; i < scores.length; i++)
         scores[i] = getInt("Score for student " + i +":");
   }

   public void showStats() {
      // Compute statistics if array is created.
      if (scores.length > 0) {
         displayResult("student" + "\t" + "score");
         for (int i = 0; i < scores.length; i++)
            displayResult("" + i + "\t" + scores[i]);

         displayResult("\n" + "Minimum score:       " + findMin());

         displayResult("\n" + "Maximum score:       " + findMax());

         // Save mean for standard deviation.
         double mean = computeMean();
         displayResult("\n" + "Mean score:          " + mean);

         displayResult("\n" + "Median score:        " + computeMedian());

         displayResult("\n" + "Standard deviation: " +
                                      computeStandDev(mean));
```

Figure 7.9 *continued*

Figure 7.9 *continued*

```
      } else
         displayResult("No students entered, so no stats!");
   } // showStats

   public int findMin() {
      int minSoFar = scores[0];
         for (int i = 0; i < scores.length; i++)
             if (scores[i] < minSoFar) minSoFar = scores[i];
      return minSoFar;
   }

   public int findMax() {
      int maxSoFar = scores[0];
         for (int i = 0; i < scores.length; i++)
             if (scores[i] > maxSoFar) maxSoFar = scores[i];
      return maxSoFar;
   }

   public double computeMean() {
      int sum = 0;
      for (int i = 0; i < scores.length; i++)
         sum += scores[i];
      return (double)sum / (double)scores.length;
   }

   // Computes standard deviation.
   // Requires the mean score as its argument.
   public double computeStandDev(double mean) {
      // Compute sum of scores-squared
      double sumSquares = 0;
      for (int i = 0; i < scores.length; i++)
         sumSquares += scores[i] * scores[i];

      return Math.sqrt(sumSquares / (double)scores.length - mean * mean);
   }


   // Computes the median value.
   // Uses method findMedian (Fig. 7.19) in class IntArray.
   public int computeMedian() {
      return IntArray.findMedian(scores);
   }
}
```

Figure 7.9 Class Exam

TESTING

An application class must create an `Exam` object and call methods `getExamData` and `showStats`. Figure 7.10 shows a sample run.

```
User Interaction History                    _ □ ×
File
How many students took the exam?
5
Score for student 0:
100
Score for student 1:
90
Score for student 2:
90
Score for student 3:
80
Score for student 4:
70
student    score
0          100
1          90
2          90
3          80
4          70

Minimum score:    70

Maximum score:    100

Mean score:       86.0

Median score:     90

Standard deviation: 10.198039027185569
```

Figure 7.10 Sample run of statistics program

EXERCISES FOR SECTION 7.2

Self-Check

1.   The following sequence of statements changes the contents of array x displayed in Fig. 7.4. Describe what each statement does to the array and show the final contents of array x after all statements execute.

```
i = 3;
x[i] = x[i] + 10.0;
x[i - 1] = x[2 * i - 1];
x[i + 1] = x[2 * i] + x[2* i + 1];
for (i = 5; i <= 7; i++)
    x[i] = x[i + 1];
```

```
for (i = 3; i >= 1; i--)
    x[i + 1] = x[i];
```

2.   Write program statements that do the following to array x shown in Fig. 7.4:

   a. Replace the third element with `7.0`.

   b. Copy the element in the fifth location into the first one.

   c. Subtract the first element from the fourth and store the result in the fifth element.

   d. Increase the sixth element by 2.

   e. Find the sum of the first five elements.

   f. Multiply each of the first six elements by 2 and place each product in an element of the array `answerArray`.

   g. Display all elements with even indices on one line.

Programming

1.   Write a loop to compute the product of all elements of an array of real numbers. Write a suitable type for this array.

2.   Write an application that uses class `Exam`.

7.3   Operations on Whole Arrays

In our examples so far, we process one array element at a time by specifying the array name and index. In this section, we show how to perform operations on a whole array. Our examples include passing an array as a method argument, assigning the values in one array to another, and copying the data in one array to another.

   For the examples in this section, we consider a class `ThreeArrays` that begins as follows:

```
public class ThreeArrays extends SimpleGUI {
    // Data fields
    private int[] x = new int[5];
    private int[] y = new int[5];
    private int[] z = new int[5];
```

Class `ThreeArrays` declares three arrays of integer elements, x, y, and z, with 5 elements in each array.

Array Assignment

You can assign one array to another. In class `ThreeArrays`, the effect of the array assignment statement

```
x = y;
```

is to make `x` and `y` identical arrays that occupy the same storage area. After the array assignment, array elements `x[i]` and `y[i]` contain the value stored in `y[i]` before the assignment, and the values stored in `x[i]` before the assignment are no longer accessible.

Because `x` and `y` are identical arrays after the assignment, if you change the element values in one array, you also change them in the other array. Therefore, the following statements

```
x = y; // x and y are identical arrays.
x[0] = 10;
x[1] = 20;
y[2] = 30;
y[3] = 40;
```

set the first four elements of both arrays `x` and `y` to the values 10, 20, 30, and 40.

To understand why this is so, we need to look more closely at how arrays `x` and `y` are stored in memory. The declaration for array `x`

```
int[] x = new int[5];
```

causes the allocation of five storage locations, named `x[0]` through `x[4]`, with an initial value of zero. Java allocates one more storage location named `x`, which references these storage locations (see Fig. 7.11).

Figure 7.11 **Effect of** `int[] x = new int[5];`

The same thing happens when we declare array `y`.

```
int[] y = new int[5];
```

In this case, the cell named `y` references the storage area for the elements of array `y` (`y[0]` through `y[4]` in Fig. 7.12).

The array assignment statement

```
x = y;
```

copies the contents of the cell named y to the cell named x. From this point on, x references the same storage area as y, which is the storage area for the elements of array y (see Fig. 7.12). The effect of this is to make the storage locations for array x in Fig. 7.11 inaccessible. Because x and y both reference the storage area for array y, x[0] and y[0] reference the same storage location (the one named y[0] in Fig. 7.12), x[1] and y[1] reference the same storage location, and so on.

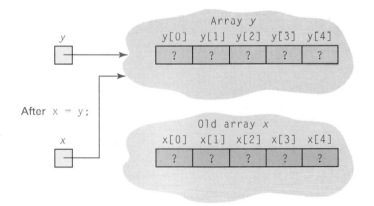

Figure 7.12 Effect of `int[] y = new int[5]; x = y;`

Copying Arrays

You can copy all or some of the values in one array to another using Java's `arraycopy` method. The statement

```
System.arraycopy(y, 0, x, 0, y.length);
```

copies all elements of array y to array x. Now the arrays x and y contain the same values, but they are not identical arrays. Therefore, you can change one without affecting the other.

You can also copy part of one array to another. The statement

```
System.arraycopy(y, 0, x, 2, 3);
```

copies the first three elements of array y (starting with y[0]) to the last three elements of array x (starting with x[2]). This means that y[0] is copied to x[2], y[1] to x[3], and y[2] to x[4].

Syntax Display

Method arraycopy

Form: System.arraycopy(*sourceArray*, *sourcePosition*,
$\qquad\qquad\qquad\qquad\qquad$ *destinationArray*, *destinationPosition*, *count*);

Example: System.arraycopy(y, 0, x, 2, 3);

Interpretation: Copies *count* elements from *sourceArray*, starting with the element at index *sourcePosition,* to the *destinationArray*, starting at index *destinationPosition.*

Array Arguments

In the calls to method arraycopy shown earlier, we pass arrays x and y as actual arguments. Next, we see how to declare arrays as arguments in methods and how to process array arguments.

You have already seen an example of a method with an array argument. The heading for method main

```
public static void main(String[] args)
```

declares its argument args as an array of String objects. We have ignored this array argument in our programming so far. It provides a way for the user of the operating system to provide arguments to the entire program.

In the UNIX operating system, you can provide arguments to a program when you run it. Using the Java Development Kit (JDK) in UNIX, you would start an application called MyApplication by typing the command line:

```
java MyApplication
```

You can provide command-line arguments by typing:

```
java MyApplication this is way cool
```

The interface between the operating system and the Java Virtual Machine recognizes that you have typed four strings (separated by spaces). Notice that double quotes are not needed around these strings. They are stored in the array args (i.e., args[0] is "this", args[1] is "is", args[2] is "way", and args[3] is "cool").

Figure 7.13 provides a sample of what a program such as MyApplication could do with the strings. This program displays the input string in reverse order (in the console window), starting with args[3]. Because strings may be converted into any primitive type, you can pass virtually any kind of data to a program.

```
/*    File: MyApplication.java
      Developed for Problem Solving with Java, Koffman & Wolz
      Appears in Fig. 7.13
*/
public class MyApplication {

    public static void main(String[] args) {
        if (args.length > 0)
            for (int i = args.length - 1; i >=0; i--)
                System.out.println(args[i]);
        else
            System.out.println("No command line args - no fun!")
}
```

Figure 7.13 Application with command-line arguments

In the next example, we show a method that compares its two array arguments. We include this method, along with several others that we develop in this chapter, in class `IntArray` (part of our package `simpleMath`). Because they are class methods, you can use them with any integer arrays. If they were not class methods, you would have to create an object of class `IntArray` and apply them to that object.

EXAMPLE 7.4

Method `sameArray` in Fig. 7.14 determines whether its two array arguments, a and b, contain the same values and are the same length. The first `if` statement returns `false` if the actual array arguments have different lengths.

Within the loop, the `if` condition (`a[i] != b[i]`) compares corresponding pairs of array elements, starting with the first pair, `a[0]` and `b[0]` If a pair is found to be different, an immediate return occurs with a result of `false`. If all array element pairs match, the `for` statement is exited after the last pair is tested, and method `sameArray` returns `true`.

```
/* Part of class IntArray in package simpleMath.
   Developed for Problem Solving with Java,
     Koffman & Wolz.
   Appears in Fig. 7.14.

   Returns true if its array arguments are equal.
   Returns false if they are not.
*/
    public static boolean sameArray(int[] a, int[] b) {
        // Check for unequal lengths.
```

Figure 7.14 *continued*

Figure 7.14 *continued*

```
        if (a.length != b.length)
            return false;

        // Return false if any pair doesn't match.
        for (int i = 0; i < a.length; i++)
            if (a[i] != b[i])
                return false;

        // All pairs matched.
        return true;
    }
```

Figure 7.14 Method sameArray of class IntArray

If class ThreeArrays imports our simpleMath package, the if statement below

```
System.arraycopy(y, 0, x, 0, x.length);
if (IntArray.sameArray(x, y))
    displayResult("Arrays have same values.");
else
    displayResult("Arrays are not the same.");
```

would display the message "Arrays have same values."

Argument Correspondence for Array Arguments

In the method call

```
IntArray.sameArray(x, y)
```

the contents of x is passed to the first method argument, int[] a, and the contents of y is passed to the second method argument, int[] b. Therefore, during the method execution, argument a references the storage area for array x and argument b references the storage area for array y. Furthermore, a[0] references the first element in array x and the value of a.length tells us how many elements are allocated to array x.

Returning an Array of Values

A Java method can return an array of values. We illustrate this idea next.

EXAMPLE 7.5

Method getX shown below is an accessor method that returns the array of values corresponding to data member x for class ThreeArrays. Similarly, method getY returns the array of values corresponding to data member y.

```
      public int[] getX() {
         return x;
      }


      public int[] getY() {
         return y;
      }
```

A class containing the declaration

```
ThreeArrays myArrays = new ThreeArrays();
```

could use the `if` statement below to compare the contents of arrays `x` and `y` in object `myArrays`:

```
if (IntArray.sameArray(myArrays.getX(),
                       myArrays.getY()))
    displayResult("Arrays x and y have same values");
else
    displayResult("Arrays x and y are not the same");
```

EXAMPLE 7.6

The assignment statement

```
z = x + y; // Illegal addition of arrays
```

is invalid because the operator + cannot have arrays as operands. You can use method `addArray` (Fig. 7.15) to add two arrays of integer values.

```
/* Part of class IntArray in package SimpleMath.
   Developed for Problem Solving with Java,
     Koffman & Wolz.
   Appears in Fig. 7.15.

   Returns a reference to an array
     that contains the sum of
     corresponding pairs of elements
     of its array arguments.
   The first element in the result array is a[0] + b[0],
     the second element is a[1] + b[1], ... .
*/
public static int[] addArray(int[] a, int[] b) {
   int[] c = new int[Math.min(a.length, b.length)];
```

Figure 7.15 *continued*

Figure 7.15 *continued*

```
    for (int i = 0; i < c.length; i++)
        c[i] = a[i] + b[i];

    return c;
}
```

Figure 7.15 Method addArray **of class** IntArray

In method addArray, the statement

```
int[] c = new int[Math.min(a.length, b.length)];
```

creates an array whose length is the same as the length of the smaller of its two array arguments. In the for loop, the statement

```
c[i] = a[i] + b[i];
```

adds a pair of elements in the argument arrays with the same index. It stores this sum in the corresponding element of array c. The return statement returns a reference to the storage area for array c.

When the assignment statement below executes

```
z = IntArray.addArray(x, y);
```

the formal arguments a and b in method addArray reference actual arrays x and y, respectively. After the method finishes execution, the reference to the array of sums is stored in z. Because z now references the array of sums, the storage area formerly referenced by z may be inaccessible.

EXERCISES FOR SECTION 7.3

Self-Check

1. Describe the effect of each of the statements below. Show the new values for the array modified by each statement.

```
int[] x = {1, 2, 3, 4, 5, 6, 7, 8, 9, 10};
int[] y = new int[10];
int[] z = new int[10];
System.arraycopy(x, 0, y, 5, x.length / 2);
System.arraycopy(x, 5, y, 0, x.length / 2);
z = IntArray.addArrays(x, y);
```

2. When is it better to pass an entire array of data to a method rather than individual elements?

Programming

1. Write a method that assigns a value of `true` to element i of its result array if element i of one array argument has the same value as element i of the other array argument; otherwise, assign a value of `false`. Assume the two argument arrays have the same length and element type `int`.

2. Write a method that reverses the values in an array. For example, if the array argument is `inArray` and the result array is `outArray`, copy `inArray[0]` to the last element of `outArray`, then copy `inArray[1]` to the next-to-last element of `outArray`, and so on.

7.4 Searching and Sorting an Array

This section discusses two common problems in processing arrays: *searching* an array to determine the location of a particular value and *sorting* an array to rearrange the array elements in numerical order. For example, we might want to use an array search to determine which student, if any, got a particular score. Or we might use an array sort to rearrange array elements so that they are in increasing order by score. This rearrangement would be helpful if we wanted to display the list in order by score or if we needed to locate several different scores in the array.

Array Search

We can search an array for a particular value by comparing each array element, starting with the first, to the *target*, the value we are seeking. If a match occurs, we have found the target in the array and can return its index as the search result. If we test all array elements without finding a match, we return −1 to indicate that the target was not found. We choose −1 because no array element has a negative index.

Algorithm for `search` Method

1. `for` each array element
2. `if` the current element contains the target

    Return the index of the current element.
3. Return −1.

   To make sure we test each array element, we need to use a loop, and the upper limit of the loop-control variable should be the index of the last value stored in the array (`length-1`). In a general method that examines all the elements in an array argument, we can use the array's length attribute as the upper limit. Figure 7.16 shows such a search method. The array to be searched is the method's first argument and the search target is the method's second argument.

```
/* Part of class IntArray in package SimpleMath.
   Developed for Problem Solving with Java,
     Koffman & Wolz.
   Appears in Fig. 7.16.

   Searches for target in its array argument.
   Returns the index of the first occurrence or -1 if
   target is not found.
*/
   public static int search(int[] x, int target) {
      for (int i = 0; i < x.length; i++)
         if (x[i] == target)
            return i;              //index of target

      // All elements tested without success.
      return -1;
   }
```

Figure 7.16 Method search of class IntArray

We can use this general method to search the array of scores described in Section 7.2. The statement

```
index = IntArray.search(scores, 100);
if (index > -1)
   displayResult("Student " + index +
         " is the first student with a perfect score");
else
   displayResult("No student got a perfect score");
```

Sorting an Array

Many programs execute more efficiently when the data they process are sorted before processing begins. For example, a check-processing program executes more quickly when all checks are in order by checking account number. Other programs produce more understandable output if the information is sorted before it is displayed. For example, your university might want your instructor's grade report sorted by student ID number. In this section, we describe one simple sorting algorithm from among the many that have been studied by computer scientists.

The *selection sort* is a fairly intuitive (but not overly efficient) sorting algorithm. To perform a selection sort of an array, we locate the smallest element in the array and then switch the smallest element with the element at index 0, thereby placing the smallest element at index 0. Then we locate the smallest element remaining in the subarray with indices 1 through length-1 and switch it with the element at index 1, thereby placing the second smallest element at index 1. Then we locate the smallest element remaining in the subarray with indices 2 through length-1 and switch it with the element at index 2, and so on.

Figure 7.17 traces the operation of the selection sort algorithm on an array of length 4. The first array shown is the original array. Then we show each step as the next smallest element is moved to its correct position. The subarray in color represents the portion of each array that is sorted. Note that, at most, `length-1` exchanges will be required to sort an array.

Algorithm for Selection Sort

1. For each index, `fill`, in the array up to, but excluding, the last index

    2. Find the smallest element in the subarray starting at `scores[fill]`.

    3. if the smallest element is not at index `fill`

        4. Exchange the smallest element with the one at index `fill`.

```
[0] [1] [2] [3]
```

74	45	83	16

fill is 0   posMin is 3
The smallest element in the subarray starting at scores[0]
is at index 3—exchange scores[0] and scores[3].

```
[0] [1] [2] [3]
```

16	45	83	16

fill is 1
posMin is 1
The smallest element in the subarray starting at scores[1]
is at index 1—no exchange necessary.

```
[0] [1] [2] [3]
```

16	45	83	74

fill is 2
posMin is 3
The smallest element in the subarray starting at scores[2]
is at index 3—exchange scores[2] and scores[3].

```
[0] [1] [2] [3]
```

16	45	74	83

Figure 7.17 Trace of selection sort

Method `selectSort` in Fig. 7.18 implements the selection sort algorithm. The array to be sorted is passed as the method argument. During each pass of the `for` loop, `posMin` stores the index of the next smallest value in the array (returned by method `findPosMin`, which is discussed next). The `if` statement in the `for` loop exchanges the next smallest value in the array

```
/* Part of class IntArray in package SimpleMath.
   Developed for Problem Solving with Java, Koffman & Wolz.
   Appears in Fig. 7.18.

   Sorts the data in its array argument so that the
   values in the array are in increasing order.
   Calls method findPosMin
*/
public static void selectSort(int[] x) {

    int posMin;         // Index of next smallest element
    int temp;           // Temporary value for exchange

    for (int fill = 0; fill < x.length-1; fill++) {
       /* invariant:
             The elements in x[0] through x[fill-1] are in
             their proper place and fill < x.length.
       */
       // Find index of smallest element in subarray
       //   starting at element x[fill].
       posMin = findPosMin(x, fill);

       // Exchange elements with indices fill and posMin.
       if (posMin != fill) {
         temp = x[fill];
         x[fill] = x[posMin];
         x[posMin] = temp;
       }
    }
}


public static int findPosMin(int[] x, int fill) {
    int posMinSoFar = fill;
    for (int i = fill + 1; i < x.length; i++)
       if (x[i] < x[posMinSoFar])
          posMinSoFar = i;

    return posMinSoFar;
}
```

Figure 7.18 Methods findPosMin and selectSort of class IntArray

(at posMin) with the one at fill. After execution of method selectSort, the values in its actual array argument will be in increasing order.

The *loop invariant* for the loop in selectSort

```
/* invariant:
      The elements in x[0] through x[fill-1] are in
      their proper place and fill < x.length.
*/
```

must always be true during execution of the loop. Computer scientists use invariants to help prove that a loop is written correctly. The invariant summarizes the progress of the selection sort: The subarray whose elements are in their proper place is shown in the color part of array x in the sketch below. The remaining elements are not yet in place and are all larger than x[fill-1].

Array x

[0] [1] ... [fill-1]	[fill] ... [x.length-1]
Elements in their proper place	Elements larger than x[fill-1]

During each pass, the portion of the array in color (the sorted subarray) grows by one element, and fill is incremented to reflect this increase. When fill is equal to x.length-1, all the elements will be in their proper place.

Method findPosMin

In method selectSort, the statement

```
// Find index of smallest element in subarray
//   starting at element x[fill].
posMin - findPosMin(x, fill);
```

calls method findPosMin to find the index of the smallest value in the unsorted portion of its array argument, starting at index fill. In findPosMin, local variable posMinSoFar stores the index of the smallest element so far (initially the one at index fill). The for loop control variable, i, selects each element in the rest of the subarray (indices fill + 1 through x.length-1). The if statement resets posMinSoFar to i if the current element at index i is less than the one at posMinSoFar.

Finding the Median Value in an Array

We can use method selectSort to find the median value in an array. If an array is sorted, the median value would be the one in the middle of the array, or the one with index x.length / 2. Figure 7.19 shows method findMedian.

```
/* Part of class IntArray in package SimpleMath.
   Developed for Problem Solving with Java,
     Koffman & Wolz.
   Appears in Fig. 7.19.

   Returns the median value in its array argument.
*/
public static int findMedian(int[] x) {
       // Create a copy of array x.
       int[] copyX = new int[x.length];
       System.arraycopy(x, 0, copyX, 0, x.length);

       selectSort(copyX);   // Sort array copyX

       return copyX[x.length / 2];
}
```

Figure 7.19 Method findMedian of class IntArray

EXERCISES FOR SECTION 7.4

Self-Check

1. For the search method in Fig. 7.16, what happens in each of the following cases?

    a. The last student score matches the target.

    b. Several scores match the target.

2. Trace the execution of the selection sort on the following two lists:

    10   55   34   56   76   5   5   15   25   35   45   45

    Show the arrays after each exchange occurs. How many exchanges are required to sort each list? How many comparisons?

3. How could you modify the selection sort algorithm to get the scores in descending order (largest score first)?

4. Explain why we made a copy of the array argument in Fig. 7.19 before sorting it.

Programming

1. Write a method to find the index of the next to the smallest element of an array. Assume that there are no duplicate entries in the array. Return −1 if the array only has one item.

2. Another way of performing the selection sort is to place the largest value in index x.length-1, the next largest in index x.length-2, and so on. Write this version.

7.5 Analysis of Algorithms: Big-O Notation (Optional)

There are many algorithms for searching and sorting arrays. Because arrays can have many elements, processing an array can be very time consuming. Therefore, it is important to have some idea of the relative efficiency of different algorithms. It is difficult to measure precisely the performance of an algorithm or program, so programmers normally try to approximate the effect on an algorithm of a change in the number of items, n, that the algorithm processes. Programmers can compare two algorithms by seeing how each algorithm's execution time increases with n .

For example, if

$$2n^2 + n - 5$$

expresses the relationship between processing time and n, the algorithm is an $O(n^2)$ algorithm, where O is an abbreviation for order of magnitude. This notation is known as *Big-O notation*. The reason that this is an $O(n^2)$ algorithm instead of an $O(2n^2)$ algorithm or an $O(2n^2 + n - 5)$ algorithm is that the fastest-growing term (the one with the largest exponent) is dominant for large n and we ignore constants.

To search an array of n elements for a target using method search, we have to examine all n elements if the target is not present in the array. If the target is in the array, then we have to search only until we find it. However, the target could be anywhere in the array—it is equally likely to be at the beginning of the array as at the end. So, on average, we have to examine $n/2$ array elements to locate a target value in an array. This means that an array search is an $O(n)$ process, so the growth rate is linear.

To determine the efficiency of a sorting algorithm, we focus on the number of array element comparisons and exchanges that it requires. Performing a selection sort on an array with n elements requires $n - 1$ comparisons during the first pass through the array, $n - 2$ comparisons during the second pass, and so on. Therefore, the total number of comparisons is represented by the series

$$1 + 2 + 3 + \ldots + (n - 2) + (n - 1)$$

The value of this series is expressed in the closed form

$$\frac{n \times (n + 1)}{2}$$

so the number of comparisons performed in sorting an array of n elements is $O(n^2)$.

The number of array element exchanges varies, depending on the initial ordering of the array elements. If an element is already in its correct position, it is not exchanged. If the array happens to be sorted before method `selectSort` is called, all its elements will be in their proper place, so there will be zero exchanges (considered the best-case situation). If no elements are in their correct positions, there will be one exchange at the end of each pass through the array, or a total of $n - 1$ exchanges (the worst-case situation). Therefore, the number of array element exchanges for an arbitrary initial ordering is between zero and $n - 1$, which is $O(n)$.

Because the number of comparisons is $O(n^2)$, selection sort is called a *quadratic sort* (i.e., its growth rate is proportional to the square of the number of elements). What difference does it make whether an algorithm is an $O(n)$ process or an $O(n^2)$ process? Table 7.3 evaluates n and n^2 for different values of n. A doubling of n causes n^2 to increase by a factor of 4. Since n^2 increases much more quickly than n, the performance of an $O(n)$ algorithm is not as adversely affected by an increase in array length as is an $O(n^2)$ algorithm. For large values of n (say, 100 or more), the differences in performance for an $O(n)$ and an $O(n^2)$ algorithm are significant (see the last three lines of Table 7.3).

Table 7.3 Values of n and n^2

n	n^2
2	4
4	16
8	64
16	256
32	1024
64	4096
128	16384
256	65536
512	262144

Other factors besides the number of comparisons and exchanges affect an algorithm's performance. For example, one algorithm may take more time preparing for each exchange or comparison than another. Also, one algorithm might exchange indices, whereas another algorithm might exchange the array elements themselves. The latter process can be more time-consuming.

Another measure of efficiency is the amount of memory required by an algorithm. Often beginning programmers learn to focus on time analysis, disregarding space analysis. There is always a tradeoff between the two. More space often means a solution can run in less time.

The key idea is the growth rate. If you want to process n data items, think about the time–space tradeoffs and assume you have two solutions: one that requires n storage locations but is just a bit slower, and one that requires 2^n

storage locations but that is a bit faster. You will probably have an opportunity to examine these issues in later computer science courses.

EXERCISES FOR SECTION 7.5

Self-Check

1. Table 7.3 showed the rate of growth for n^2. Fill out the following table for other standard growth rates:

n	n^2	n^3	2^n
1			
2			
3			
4			
5			
10			
100			
1000			

2. What does it mean for a term to dominate an equation? To get a feel for the answer, calculate the results for the following equations with these values of n:

n	$n^2 + n - 5$	$n^2 - n + 5$	$2n^2$
1			
10			
100			
1000			
10000			

Which equation always has the highest value? Do you think this trend continues for $n > 10,000$? Can you explain why?

Programming

1. Write a program fragment that displays the values of y_1 and y_2 defined below for values of n from 10 to 100 in increments of 10. Does the result surprise you?

$y_1 = 100n + 10$
$y_2 = 5n^2 + 2$

7.6   Arrays of Objects

In our examples so far, we focused on arrays of integers. You can declare arrays of any element type in Java. In this section, we see how to declare and process arrays of objects.

Arrays of Objects

When you declare an array of objects, you are actually allocating storage for an array of object references. Each of these references is initialized to the value `null` by Java. For example, the declaration

```
Employee[] employees = new Employee[5];
```

allocates storage for an array of five references to `Employee` objects. You also must allocate storage for each individual array element (object) before you can access it. We illustrate this idea in the next examples and case study by using an array of `Strings` and an array of `Employee` objects.

EXAMPLE 7.7

Recall that Java strings are objects, not primitive types. The array declaration:

```
String[] dayNames = {"Sunday", "Monday", "Tuesday",
        "Wednesday", "Thursday", "Friday", "Saturday"};
```

creates an array `dayNames` that stores references to the seven `String` objects listed. The contents of `dayNames[0]` is the string `"Sunday"` and the contents of `dayNames[6]` is the string `"Saturday"`. By listing the `String` literal `"Sunday"`, you are actually creating a `String` object.

EXAMPLE 7.8

The statement

```
Employee[] employees = new Employee[5];
```

declares an array `employees` with storage for five elements, each an object of type `Employee` (see Fig. 5.12). Java actually allocates storage for five storage cells that are references to objects, so each element of the array can reference an object of type `Employee`. However, no storage is allocated as yet for the `Employee` objects. The first statement below

```
employees[0] = new Employee();
employees[0].enterEmpData();
```

allocates storage for a new `Employee` object, and sets array element `employees[0]` as a reference to this object. The next statement calls method `enterEmpData` (See Fig. 5.12) to read data into the employee object just created.

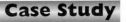

Payroll Problem with an Employee Array

PROBLEM

In Chapter 6, we provided a class `Company` (see Fig. 6.5) with methods to perform payroll computations for the employees of a small landscaping company. In this section, we discuss a new class with a data member that is an array of `Employee` objects. This class will include data members and methods for calculating both the mean and median gross salary for an employee.

ANALYSIS

As before, our problem inputs will be the number of employees and the hours worked and hourly rate for each employee. Our problem outputs will be the total gross pay and the mean and median gross pay.

Data Requirements

Problem Inputs

number of employees

hours worked for each employee

hourly rate for each employee

Problem Outputs

total gross pay

mean gross pay

median gross pay

Relevant Formulas

total gross pay = summation of all individual gross pay amounts
mean gross pay = total gross pay / number of employees
median gross pay = median value of gross pay

DESIGN

Class `NewCompany` needs a data field for the array of employees and for the total gross pay. It does not need to store the number of employees because data field `length` of the employee array stores that information. Next, we specify the `NewCompany` class.

Specification for NewCompany class

Data Fields

`Employee[] employees`—array of employee objects

`double totalGross`—total gross pay

Methods

`readAllEmpData`—reads number of employees and reads and stores all employee data

`computeTotalGross`—computes total gross pay

`computeMeanGross`—computes mean gross pay

`computeMedianGross`—computes median gross pay

`showPayroll`—displays payroll information

Algorithms for several methods follow.

Algorithm for `readAllEmpData` (class `NewCompany`)

1. Read the number of employees in the company.
2. `for` each employee
    3. Create a new `Employee` object, read its data, and save it in the array `employees`.

Algorithm for `computeTotalGross` (class `NewCompany`)

1. Set `totalGross` to zero.
2. `for` each employee
    3. Compute the employee's gross salary and add it to the total gross pay.

Algorithm for `computeMeanGross` (class `NewCompany`)

1. `if` `totalGross` and `numberEmp` are not zero
    divide `totalGross` by `numberEmp`.

Algorithm for `computeMedianGross` (class `NewCompany`)

1. Sort the array of employees.
2. Return the value of the middle element.

IMPLEMENTATION

Figure 7.20 shows class `NewCompany` with the exception of method `computeMedianGross`. We leave this for an exercise (See Programming Exercise 1.)

```
/*    File: NewCompany.java
      Developed for Problem Solving with Java, Koffman & Wolz
      Appears in Fig. 7.20 and Fig. 7.25
*/
import simpleIO.*;

public class NewCompany extends SimpleGUI {
    // Data fields
    private Employee[] employees; // Array of employees
    private double totalGross;

    // Methods
    // Reads employee data.
    public void readAllEmpData() {
        // Create array of Employee references.
        employees = new Employee[getInt("Number of employees")];

        for (int countEmp = 0;
            countEmp < employees.length;
            countEmp++) {
            // Create a new Employee object and reference
            //    it through employees[countEmp].
            employees[countEmp] = new Employee();
            employees[countEmp].enterEmpData();
        }
    }

    // Computes total gross pay.
    public void computeTotalGross() {
        totalGross = 0;
        for (int countEmp = 0;
            countEmp < employees.length;
            countEmp++)
                totalGross += employees[countEmp].computeGross();
    }

    // Computes mean gross pay.
    public double computeMeanGross() {
        if (employees.length != 0 && totalGross != 0)
            return totalGross / employees.length;
        else
            return 0.0;
    }
```

Figure 7.20 *continued*

Figure 7.20 *continued*

```
      // Computes median gross pay.
      // See Programming Exercise 1.
      public double computeMedianGross() {
          displayResult("Method computeMedianGross coming");
          return -1;    // Return a value.
      }

      public void showPayroll() {
          computeTotalGross();
          displayResult("Total gross pay is $" +
                      totalGross);
          displayResult("Mean gross pay is $" +
                      computeMeanGross());
          displayResult("Median gross pay is $" +
                      computeMedianGross());
      }

} // class NewCompany
```

Figure 7.20 Class NewCompany

In `readAllEmpData`, the statement

```
employees[countEmp] = new Employee();
```

allocates a new `Employee` object, referenced by `employees[countEmp]`, and the statement

```
employees[countEmp].enterEmpData();
```

reads data into it (using method `enterEmpData` of class `Employee`). In method `computeTotalGross`, the statement

```
totalGross += employees[countEmp].computeGross();
```

computes the current employee's gross pay (using method `computeGross` of class `Employee`) and adds it to `totalGross`.

TESTING

Figure 7.21 shows a sample run of an application class that uses class `NewCompany`. The window on the left is for the application class; the windows on the right are for the `Employee` objects.

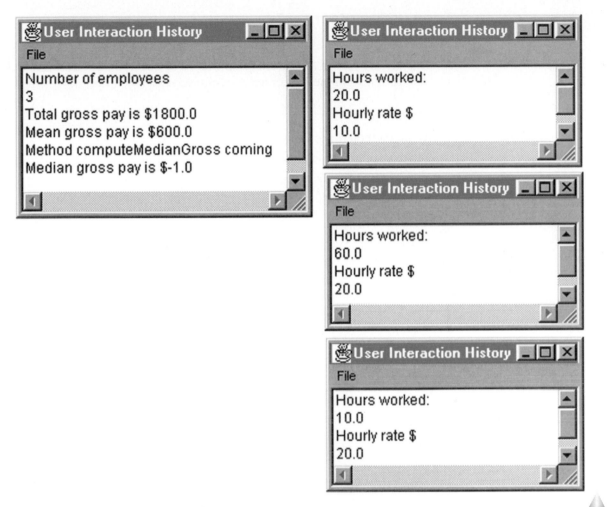

Figure 7.21 Sample run of new payroll program

Program Style: *Algorithm Simplification Due to Use of Arrays*

The data structure used in a program can affect the complexity of the algorithm. Compare the payroll program in this section to the one in Section 6.2. Method `computePayTotals` (in Section 6.2) reads each employee's data and also processes it. Because we could only store one employee's data at a time, we had to process the current employee's data before we could read the next employee's data. The array data structure enables us to save data for all the employees, so we can separate the reading operation (done by method `readAllEmpData`) from the payroll processing operation (done by method `computeTotalGross`). This results in a simplification of the algorithm for method `computeTotalGross`.

EXERCISES FOR SECTION 7.6

Self-Check

1. Explain the reason for checking the values of `employees.length` and `totalGross` in method `computeMeanGross`.

Programming

1. Write method `computeMedianGross`.
2. Write an application class that uses `NewCompany`.

7.7 Vectors

Java provides a class called `Vector` that is like an array but with some additional features. Unlike an array, you don't need to declare the size of a vector, but you can let it grow and shrink as needed. Also, there are methods in the `Vector` class that let you add elements, retrieve elements, insert elements in the middle of a vector, or remove elements. The elements that you place in a vector must be objects, not primitive types. You must insert the statement

```
import java.util.*;
```

before the definition of a class that uses vectors.

EXAMPLE 7.9

In this example, we show how to use the `Vector` class for storing a collection of employees. The data declaration

```
Vector employees = new Vector();
```

is all that is required to allocate storage for a vector named `employees`. We don't need to declare the type of object to be stored in the vector, or the size of the vector, because its size is automatically adjusted as new items are added and removed.

If `employeeA` and `employeeB` are both `Employee` objects, you can store them in vector `employees` (see top of next page) using the statements:

```
employees.addElement(employeeA);
employees.addElement(employeeB);
```

If there were no prior calls to `addElement`, the vector contents would be `employeeA` (at index 0) and `employeeB` (at index 1). The method call `employees.size()` would return 2, the current size of vector `employees`.

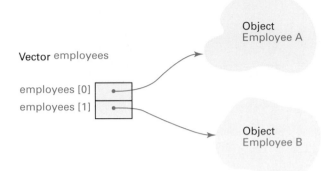

To access an element of a vector, you use method `elementAt`. If `anEmployee` is type `Employee`, the statement

```
anEmployee = (Employee)employees.elementAt(1);
```

assigns to `anEmployee` the second object in vector `employees` (the object at index 1). The type cast `(Employee)` is needed because method `elementAt` always returns a value of type `Object`. Before this value can be assigned to `anEmployee`, it should be converted to type `Employee`.

Three other useful methods for vectors are `setElementAt`, `insertElementAt`, and `removeElementAt`. You use `setElementAt` to change an element of a vector. The statement

```
employees.setElementAt(employeeA, 1);
```

stores `employeeA` at index 1 (formerly occupied by `employeeB`). Now there are two copies of `employeeA` in vector `employees`.

You use `insertElementAt` to insert an element somewhere in the middle of a vector—the elements that follow it are shifted up one position to make room. The statement

```
employees.insertElementAt(employeeB, 1);
```

inserts a new element containing `employeeB` at index 1, the element formerly at index 1 is moved to index 2. The vector contents is now `employeeA` (at index 0), `employeeB` (at index 1), and `employeeA` (at index 2). The vector's size is 3 (see Fig. 7.22).

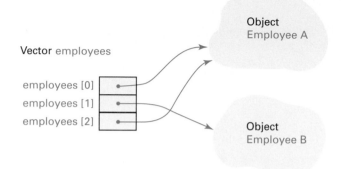

Figure 7.22 New contents of vector `employees`

Similarly, you use `removeElementAt` to remove an element from the vector—the elements that follow it are shifted down one position to fill the vacated space. As you would expect, the vector size automatically adjusts after an insertion or removal. The statement

```
employees.removeElement(0);
```

removes the first element in the vector. The vector contents is now `employeeB` (at index 0) and `employeeA` (at index 1) and its size is 2.

Table 7.4 summarizes the methods for class `Vector`.

Table 7.4 Methods for `Vector` class

Method call	Effect
`Vector()`	Constructs an empty vector.
`employees.addElement(Emp1)`	Appends object `Emp1` (type `Employee`) to vector `employees` and increments its size.
`(Employee)employees.elementAt(0)`	Returns the object at index 0 of vector `employees` and converts it to type `Employee`.
`employees.size()`	Returns the `size` of vector `employees`.
`employees.setElementAt(Emp2, 1)`	Changes the object at index 1 to `Emp2` (type `Employee`).
`employees.insertElementAt(anEmp, 1)`	Inserts object `anEmp` (type `Employee`) at index 1 of `employees`, shifting up the object formerly at index 1. Increments the size of `employees`.

Table 7.4 *continued*

Table 7.4 *continued*

Method call	Effect
`employees.removeElementAt(1)`	Removes the element at index 1 from `employees`, shifting elements above it down one position. Decrements the size of `employees`.
`employees.size()`	Returns the size of vector `employees`.

Wrapper Classes

You can store objects, but not primitive types, in vectors. However, Java provides a **wrapper class** for each primitive type. A wrapper class encapsulates a primitive type value in an object and contains methods for converting back and forth between primitive types and objects. The wrapper classes for Java's primitive types are `Boolean`, `Character`, `Integer`, and `Double`.

Each wrapper class includes the following constructors and methods.

wrapper class:
a class that stores a primitive type value in an object and contains methods for converting back and forth between primitive types and classes.

- A constructor that takes a primitive type value and creates an object of the type class (for example, `new Double(3.14159)` holds the real number `3.14159` in a type `Double` object).

- A constructor that decodes a string argument to get the object's initial value. (For example, `Double w = new Double("3.14159")` holds the real number `3.14159` in the type `Double` object w.)

- A `toString` method that creates a string version of the object's value. (For example, `(w.toString()` creates `"3.14159"`.)

- A *type*`Value` method that gives the primitive *type* value. (For example, `w.DoubleValue()` gives `3.14159`. The other *type*`Value` methods are `intValue`, `charValue`, and `booleanValue`.)

- An `equals` method that compares objects of the same type class for equality. (For example, if x and y are type `Double`, `x.equals(y)` is `true` when they wrap the same real number.)

EXAMPLE 7.10

You can use the statements

```
double x = 5.67;
double y = 7.92;
Vector numbers = new Vector();
numbers.addElement(new Double(x));
numbers.addElement(new Double(y));
```

to insert the values of x and y in vector `numbers`. The vector stores the real numbers `5.67` (at element 0) and `7.92` (at element 1).

The class `Double` has a method `doubleValue` that returns the type `double` value encapsulated in a type `Double` object. In the statement

```
double w = ((Double)numbers.elementAt(0)).doubleValue();
```

the part in the outer parentheses accesses the first type `Double` object in vector `numbers`. Method `doubleValue` returns its type double value (`5.67`), which is assigned to w. The corresponding method for type int is called `intValue`.

EXERCISES FOR SECTION 7.7

Self-Check

1. Complete the `for` loop below that displays the information in vector `employees`. Method `showEmp` is defined in class `Employee`.

   ```
   for (int i = 0; i < _____ ; i++)
                   _____.showEmp();
   ```

2. Write statements to wrap the integer 6, the character `'z'`, and the real number `5.35` in object instances.

3. Explain each statement in the fragment below.

   ```
   Vector n = new Vector();
   n.addElement(new Integer(5));
   n.addElement(new Integer(8));
   n.setElementAt(new Integer(6), 0);
   n.insertElementAt(new Integer(3), 2);
   int k = ((Integer)n.elementAt(2)).intValue();
   n.removeElementAt(1);
   displayResult("Size is " + n.size());
   ```

4. Assume you have a vector of `Employee` objects. Write statements to replace the element at index 1 with `empC`. Insert `empB` at index 2. Then remove the value in the middle of the vector and move it to the end.

Programming

1. Write method `readAllEmpData` (Fig. 7.20). Assume that the data are stored in a vector of `Employee` objects.

2. Rewrite method `computeTotalGross` (Fig. 7.20). Assume that the data are stored in a vector.

3. Rewrite method `computeMeanGross` (Fig. 7.20). Assume that the data are stored in a vector.

7.8 More Input/Output: Using Files and `displayRow` (Optional)

In this section, we discuss two more features of package `simpleIO`. We begin with a discussion of a `SimpleGUI` method that you can use to display an array of data instead of just displaying one element at a time. Then we discuss the use of data files for reading and saving array data.

SimpleGUI Method displayRow

Method `displayRow` will display an array of primitive type data. For example, if you have the following data field declaration in a class that inherits `SimpleGUI`,

```
private int[] x = new int[10];
```

the method call

```
displayRow(x);   // Display all elements.
```

displays all 10 integer values of array `x` across a line of the information history window. If you only want to display the first five elements, use the method call

```
displayRow(x, 4);   // Display elements through x[4].
```

If you want to display array elements, `x[3]` through `x[7]`, inclusive, use the method call

```
displayRow(x, 3, 7); // Display elements x[3]
                     // through x[7].
```

Method displayRow uses the tab character (`'\t'`) as a default spacer between array elements. If you prefer to specify a different spacer (for example, the character `','`), pass it as the fourth argument:

```
displayRow(x, 0, x.length-1, ',');
```

You must use all four arguments if you want to specify a spacer character.

Using Data Files

So far the data entered by the user only exists while the program is running. **Data files** are used to store data between executions of a program, or as a means for programs to share data. Although a full treatment of file processing is beyond the scope of this text, we show you the rudiments of file processing here. The package `simpleIO` contains two classes:

`SimpleWriter`—allows you to store data to a file.

`SimpleReader`—allows you to retrieve data from a file.

data file:
a file that stores data between executions of a program, or provides a mechanism for different programs to share data.

The following three actions must be taken whether you are reading or writing to a file.

1. Inform the operating system that you want to open up a file.
2. Move data either to or from the file.
3. Inform the operating system that you want to close the file.

In this simple model you only can read or write to a file, you can't do both operations. You either open a file for reading (SimpleReader) or for writing (SimpleWriter). Traditionally, a file opened for reading is an **input file**, and one opened for writing is an **output file.**

input file:
a file from which data will be read. The data will be retrieved from the file.

output file:
a file to which data will be written. The data will be saved to the file.

Writing or Saving to a File

If you want to save to a file, you first create an instance of a SimpleWriter object. For example to save a string:

- Create a SimpleWriter object.
- Use the SimpleWriter method putData to save the string.
- Call the SimpleWriter method close to tell the operating system that you are done.

Figure 7.23 shows an application that does this. After you run this application you should notice a file in your directory called "StringFile" that contains the string "This string will be saved."

Notice that the three file operations are in a try block. This is because file operations work correctly almost all the time, but every so often something unanticipated goes wrong. The catch blocks take care of the rare occurrences when something strange happens within the operating system. The FileNotFoundException occurs when the file cannot be opened for some reason. The IOException is a more general error that says something has gone wrong with the operating system. In the event of an IOException, the exception can print a trace of what happened using method printStackTrace.

```
/*    File: WriteStringDemo.java
      Developed for Problem Solving with Java, Koffman & Wolz
      Appears in Fig. 7.23
*/
import simpleIO.*;
import java.io.*;
public class WriteStringDemo {
    public static void main(String[] args) {
        try {
            SimpleWriter outFile =
                    new SimpleWriter("StringFile");
```

Figure 7.23 *continued*

Figure 7.23 *continued*

```
            outFile.putData("This string will be saved.");
            outFile.close();
    } catch (FileNotFoundException e) {
        System.err.println("Can't open StringFile.");
    } catch (IOException e) {
        e.printStackTrace();
    }


    }
}
```

Figure 7.23 Saving a single string to a file

Method `putData` accepts any primitive type or a `String` as an argument. A sequence of `putData` calls will result in the corresponding sequence of data in the file. Each `putData` call adds data to the end of the file. `SimpleWriter` does not allow you to insert data into an arbitrary place in a file.

Each call to `putData` stores the item on a separate line in a text file. You should be able to view the contents of the file from a text editor.

The methods of `SimpleWriter` are summarized in Table 7.5. Notice that there are two constructors. If you provide only a file name, then the current contents of the file (if it exists) will be lost, and a new file is created. If you provide two arguments and the second one is the `boolean` value `true`, then the original data will be preserved and `putData` operations will add to the end of the existing file.

Table 7.5 `SimpleWriter` methods

Method	Purpose
`SimpleWriter("MyFile")`	Creates a `SimpleWriter` object that opens a file named `"MyFile"` into which you may write data. The file will be in the current directory unless you specify a full path name. If the file existed before, then its previous contents are lost.
`SimpleWriter("MyFile", true)`	Creates a file named `"MyFile"` into which you may write data and appends data to the end of the file, if it exists. The file will be in the current directory unless you specify a full path name.

Table 7.5 *continued*

Table 7.5 *continued*

Method	Purpose
putData("This string");	Stores the string "This string" in the file.
putData('a');	Stores the character a.
putData(34.5);	Stores the real number 34.5 in the file.
int i = 10; putData(i);	Stores the number 10 in the file.
putData(true);	Stores the boolean value true in the file.
close();	Closes the file, saving its contents.

Retrieving or Reading from a File

If you want to retrieve data from a file, you can create an instance of a SimpleReader object and use the methods in Table 7.6 to retrieve the kind of data you want. Figure 7.24 shows an application that retrieves the string written in Fig. 7.23. Each call to method getString retrieves the next line of data in the file. You cannot retrieve data from an arbitrary point in the file. If you want the fifth item, then you must first retrieve the four items that precede it, even if you simply discard them.

```
/*    File: ReadStringDemo.java
      Developed for Problem Solving with Java, Koffman & Wolz
      Appears in Fig. 7.24
*/
import simpleIO.*;
import java.io.*;

class ReadStringDemo {
    public static void main(String[] args) {
        try {
            SimpleReader inFile =
                    new SimpleReader("StringFile");
            String str = inFile.getString();
            inFile.close();
        } catch (FileNotFoundException e) {
            System.err.println("StringFile not found");
        } catch (IOException e) {
            e.printStackTrace();
        }

    }
}
```

Retrieving a single string from a file

Table 7.6 `SimpleReader` methods

Method	Purpose
`SimpleReader("MyFile")`	Creates a `SimpleWriter` object that opens a file called `"MyFile"` from which you may read data. The file will be in the current directory unless you specify a full path name.
`getString()`	Retrieves a string from the file.
`getChar()`	Retrieves the next character from the file. `getChar` ignores end of line characters.
`getDouble()`	Retrieves a `double` from the file.
`getInt()`	Retrieves an `int` from the file.
`getBoolean()`	Retrieves a `boolean` value from the file.
`EOF()`	Returns `true` if the end of the file has been reached.
`close()`	Closes the file.

You must take care to call `getInt` and `getDouble` only when you are certain the expected data will be the proper numeric type. Otherwise, the methods will print an error message in the system console window and return 0. For example, if a data file `"ErrorExample"` contains the following data:

```
52
Hello there
```

the following code fragment will display a sum of 52 (52 + 0):

```
SimpleReader inFile = new SimpleReader("ErrorExample");
int i = inFile.getInt();        // Reads 52.
int sum = i + inFile.getInt(); // Attempts to read
                                // string, not number.
System.out.println(sum);
outFile.close();
```

Creating Data Files

Before you can read a data file, you must store some information in it. There are two ways to create data files. The simplest way is to access an editor or word processor, open a new file and type in your data, then save it as a text file just as you would for a file that contains Java statements. The second way is to run a program similar to the one in Fig. 7.23.

Method EOF

Sometimes you may not know how many items are stored in a file. The method EOF (end of file) returns true only if you have reached the end of the file. If you try to retrieve data when the end of the file is reached, the method call will throw an exception.

Saving and Retrieving an Array of Data

When you load data into a large array, you must do a lot of typing. This extra effort can be a nuisance during debugging. It makes much more sense to first save the data in a file and read the data from the file. The java.io package has many sophisticated ways to do this that are beyond the scope of this text. We show you how to use SimpleReader and SimpleWriter to accomplish this task. See Appendix C for more information on the java.io package.

Once a file is open, any method of any object may read data or write data to it, provided the object can refer to the appropriate SimpleWriter or SimpleReader object. We illustrate this by extending the Employee and NewCompany classes from the last case study.

EXAMPLE 7.11

The NewCompany class (Fig. 7.25) contains an array employees of type Employee. In Fig. 7.25, method writeArrayToFile first writes the array size to a file and then uses a for statement to write out the contents of the array.

Method readDataFromFile uses a while statement to read in data from the file. The read method relies on the fact that the write method placed the length of the array at the top of the file. However, just to make sure there was no error, readDataFromFile first checks that it has at least one array element. By checking for the end of file in the loop-repetition condition, it makes sure that it does not attempt to read past the end of the file. The last if statement checks to make sure that it read the correct number of items.

```
/*    File: NewCompany.java
      Developed for Problem Solving with Java,
        Koffman & Wolz
      Appears in Fig. 7.20 and 7.25.
*/
import simpleIO.*;
import java.io.*;
```

Figure 7.25 *continued*

Figure 7.25 *continued*

```java
public class NewCompany extends SimpleGUI {
    // Data fields
    private Employee[] employees;
    ...


    // Methods for file input/output
    // Writes array size and data to a file.
    public void writeArrayToFile() {
        try {
            SimpleWriter outFile =
                    new SimpleWriter("EmployeeData");

            // Save the length of the array.
            outFile.putData(employees.length);

            // Write the array data.
            for (int i = 0; i <= employees.length; i++)
                // tell employee i to put data in
                //   outFile
                employees[i].saveData(outFile);
            outFile.close();

        } catch (FileNotFoundException e) {
            System.err.println
                    ("EmployeeData file not found");
        } catch (IOException e) {
            e.printStackTrace();
        }
    } // writeArrayToFile


    // Reads array size and data from a file.
    public void readDataFromFile() {
        try {
            SimpleReader inFile =
                    new SimpleReader("EmployeeData");

            // Read the length of the array and
            //   the array data.
            int arraySize = inFile.getInt();
            if (arraySize <= 0)
                System.err.println("Bad array size");
```

Figure 7.25 *continued*

Figure 7.25 *continued*

```
                else { // Read the array data.
                    int count = 0;
                    while ((count < arraySize) &&
                            !inFile.EOF()) {
                        employees[count].loadData
                                            (inFile);
                        count++;
                    }

                    // Check for incorrect number of
                    //   values.
                    if (count != arraySize) {
                        // Reached end of file
                        //   unexpectedly
                        System.err.println(
                            "Not all data read!");
                    }
                inFile.close();
                }

        } catch (FileNotFoundException e) {
            System.err.println(
                    "EmployeeData file not found");
        } catch (IOException e) {
            e.printStackTrace();
        }
    } // readDataFromFile

} // class NewCompany
```

Figure 7.25 Class NewCompany

The NewCompany class expects the Employee objects in the array to write out or read in the appropriate data (hours worked and hourly rate). The methods saveData and loadData are defined in the Employee class, as shown in Figure 7.26. These methods are given the file handling object as an argument. They can then reference that object to do their respective jobs.

```
/*    File: Employee.java
      Developed for Problem Solving with Java,
        Koffman & Wolz
      Appears in Fig. 5.12 and 7.26.
*/
```

Figure 7.26 *continued*

Figure 7.26 *continued*

```
import simpleIO.*;
import java.io.*;
public class Employee extends SimpleGUI {
    // Data fields
    private double hours;
    private double rate;

    // Methods
    . . .
    public void loadData(SimpleReader inFile)
                            throws IOException {
        hours = inFile.getDouble();
        rate = inFile.getDouble();
    }

    public void saveData(SimpleWriter outFile)
                            throws IOException {
        outFile.putData(hours);
        outFile.putData(rate);
    }
}
```

Figure 7.26 Saving and retrieving employee data fields

Each method header in Fig. 7.26 ends with the phrase throws IOException. This means that these methods do not provide catch blocks to handle an exception, but just pass the exception back to the method that calls them (to writeArrayToFile or to readDataFromFile). Both these methods contain catch blocks to handle an IOException.

EXERCISES FOR SECTION 7.8

Self-Check

1. Write statements in a try block that open a file "MyStats" for output. Then write your name, age, gender (a character), and social security number to the file.
2. Write statements in a try block to read the data you wrote in Self-Check Exercise 1.

Programming

1. Incorporate the statements you wrote for Self-Check Exercise 1 in a method.

2. Incorporate the statements you wrote for Self-Check Exercise 2 in a method.

3. Write a method for class `Exam` (Fig. 7.9) that reads the count of exam scores and the exam scores from a data file.

4. Write method `writeVectorToFile`. Assume that the `Employee` objects are stored in a vector, not an array.

5. Write method `readDataFromFile`. Assume that the `Employee` objects are stored in a vector, not an array.

7.9 Multidimensional Arrays—Arrays of Arrays (Optional)

multidimensional array: an array with two or more dimensions.

The array data structure allows a programmer to organize information in arrangements that are more complex than the linear or one-dimensional arrays you've seen so far. We can declare and use arrays with several dimensions. Although **multidimensional arrays** give you more flexibility in arranging data than one-dimensional arrays, the rules for element types are the same: the array elements may be simple or structured, but they must all be the same type.

Two-dimensional arrays, the most common multidimensional arrays, store information that we normally represent in table form. An example is a seating plan for a classroom in which you list each student's name in the position (row and seat) where that student's desk is located in the classroom (see Fig. 7.27).

Figure 7.27 Classroom seating plan (11 rows and 9 seats per row)

	Seat 0	Seat 1	. . .	Seat 8
Row 0	Alice	Bill		Gerry
Row 1	Jane	Sue		Groucho
.	.	.		.
.	.	.		.
.	.	.		.
Row 10	Harpo	Sam		Jillian

Declaring Two-dimensional Arrays

The next examples demonstrate how to declare and process two-dimensional arrays. To reference an element of a two-dimensional array, you must specify the array name and provide two index expressions. The first index is the row index, and the second index is the column index.

EXAMPLE 7.12

A familiar two-dimensional object is a tic-tac-toe board. The statement

```
char[][] ticTacToe = new char[3][3];
```

allocates storage for array `ticTacToe` (see Fig. 7.28). Array `ticTacToe` is a two-dimensional array with three rows and three columns. This array has nine elements, each of which must be referenced by specifying a row index (0, 1, or 2) and a column index (0, 1, or 2).

```
                  Column

Row     0       1       2

0       X               0

1       0       X       0    ◄── ticTacToe[1][2]

2       X               X
```

Figure 7.28 A tic-tac-toe board stored as array `ticTacToe`

The indexed variable

```
ticTacToe[1][2]
     ↑        ↑   ↑
   Array    Row  Column
   name     index index
```

selects the array element in row 1, column 2 of the array in Fig. 7.28; it contains the character O.

EXAMPLE 7.13

Your instructor wants to store the seating plan (Fig. 7.27) for a classroom on a computer. The statements

```
String[][] seatPlan = new String[11][9];
```

allocate storage for a two-dimensional array of strings called `seatPlan`. Array `seatPlan` could be used to hold the first names of the students seated in a classroom with 11 rows and 9 seats in each row. The statement

```
seatPlan[5][4] = "Marilyn";
```

places a student named `Marilyn` in row 5, seat 4, the center of the classroom.

Initializing a Two-dimensional Array

Just as for one-dimensional arrays, you can initialize the elements of a two-dimensional array when you declare it. You specify the element values for each row in braces, and enclose all the row values in an outer pair of braces.

EXAMPLE 7.14

The statements

```
double matrix[][] = {{5.0, 4.5, 3.0},
                     {-16.0, -5.9, 0.0}};
```

allocate storage for the array matrix with two rows and three columns. Each inner pair of braces contains the initial values for a row of the array matrix, starting with row 0 as shown next.

```
        col 0 col 1 col2
row 0  |  5.0| 4.5 | 3.0 |
row 1  |-16.0|-5.9 | 0.0 |          matrix[1][2]
```

Displaying a Two-dimensional Array

The next example illustrates that a two-dimensional array is really an array whose elements are references to other array objects. It uses method displayRow from Section 7.8 to display each row of a two-dimensional array. For a two-dimensional array, the length data field stores the number of rows.

EXAMPLE 7.15

The for statement below displays the seating plan array from Fig. 7.27 in table format. Because the for loop initializes row to its largest value, the first row displayed lists the names of the students sitting in the last row of the classroom; the last row displayed lists the names of the students sitting in the first row of the classroom (closest to the teacher).

```
for (int row = seatPlan.length - 1; row >= 0; row--)
   displayRow(seatPlan[row]);
```

Nested Loops for Processing Two-dimensional Arrays

You must use nested loops to access the elements of a two-dimensional array in row-order or column-order. If you want to access the array elements in row-order (the normal situation), use the row index as the loop control variable for the outer loop and the column index as the loop control variable for the inner loop. The general form of such a loop is

for each row r in the array
      for each column c in the array
            Process the element with indices [r][c]

For each value of r (normally from 0 to its maximum), the inner loop executes and cycles through all values of c. This means the nested loops process the elements of array matrix (see Example 7.14) in the sequence:

```
matrix[0][0]  matrix[0][1]  matrix[0][2]
matrix[1][0]  matrix[1][1]  matrix[1][2]
```

EXAMPLE 7.16

Method sumMatrix (part of class IntArray) in Figure 7.29 finds the sum of all elements of the two-dimensional array passed as the function argument (twoDim). To make the method general, we use twoDim.length as the limit value in the outer loop. This is the number of rows in the actual argument array. We use twoDim[row].length as the limit value in the inner for loop, which is the number of elements in the current row of the matrix.

```
/* Part of class IntArray in package simpleMath.
   Developed for Problem Solving with Java,
      Koffman & Wolz.
   Appears in Fig. 7.29.

   Returns the sum of all elements of
      its matrix argument.
*/
public static int sumMatrix (int[][] twoDim) {
   int sum = 0.0;

   for (int row = 0; row < twoDim.length; row++)
      for (int col = 0; col < twoDim[row].length; col++)
         sum += twoDim[row][col];

   return sum;
}
```

Figure 7.29 Method sumMatrix from class IntArray

Arrays with Different Row Lengths

Because a two-dimensional array is an array of array objects, its rows do not have to be of uniform length. The statement

```
int[][] pascalTriangle = {{1}, {1, 1}, {1, 2, 1},
                          {1, 3, 3, 1}, {1, 4, 6, 4, 1}};
```

allocates storage for the array `pascalTriangle` with five rows. Here `pascalTriangle[0]` references the first row, an array with one element (`pascalTriangle[0][0]`); `pascalTriangle[1]` references the second row, an array with two elements (`pascalTriangle[1][0]` and `pascalTriangle[1][1]`).

Figure 7.30 shows a sketch of a Pascal triangle that illustrates the property that the element at indices `[i][j]` (row i, column j) is determined by adding the element values at indices `[i-1][j-1]` and indices `[i-1][j]`. In Fig. 7.30, the values being summed to form each element are above that element and to its left and right. For example, the element at indices `[4][2]` (the value 6 in the last row) is the sum of the elements at indices `[3][1]` and `[3][2]` (the values 3 in the next-to-last-row). In the formation of the sum, an element that is not part of the triangle (i.e., an element with an out-of-bounds index) is considered to be zero.

```
                        1
                 1             1
           1           2             1
      1          3           3             1
1          4           6           4           1
```

Figure 7.30 Pascal's triangle of depth 5

Figure 7.31 shows a method `buildTriangle` that builds a Pascal's triangle of any depth. The statement

```
pascalTriangle = new
    int[getInt("How high should the triangle be?")][];
```

reads in the depth of the triangle and allocates storage for a two-dimensional array with the same number of rows as the triangle depth. Each row is a reference to an array object that must still be created and filled in. The statements

```
pascalTriangle[0] = new int[1];
pascalTriangle[0][0] = 1;
```

allocate storage for row 0 of the triangle, a row of length 1, and store 1 in its only element. Within the `while` loop, the statement

```
int lastRow[] = pascalTriangle[row-1];
```

declares an array `lastRow` that references the same elements as the previous row of the Pascal triangle. The statement

```
int newRow[] = new int[row+1];
```

creates a new array with one more element than the row number. After storing 1 in the first and the last elements of the new array, the `for` statement defines the values in the middle of the array by adding elements in the previous row. Then the statement

```
pascalTriangle[row] = newRow;
```

causes the element in the Pascal triangle with index `row` to reference the new array that was just filled in. We leave method `showTriangle` as an exercise (see Programming Exercise 1).

```
/*    File: PascalTriangle.java
      Developed for Problem Solving with Java,
         Koffman & Wolz
      Appears in Fig. 7.31.
*/
import simpleIO.*;

public class PascalTriangle extends SimpleGUI {
    // Data field
    private int pascalTriangle[][];

    // Methods
    // Builds a Pascal triangle.
    public void buildTriangle() {
        pascalTriangle = new int[getInt
            ("How high should the triangle be?")][];

        // Start with the first row.
        pascalTriangle[0] = new int[1];
        pascalTriangle[0][0] = 1;

        // Build the remaining rows,
        //    one row at a time.
        int row = 1;
```

Figure 7.31 *continued*

Figure 7.31 *continued*

```
            while (row < pascalTriangle.length) {
                int lastRow[] = pascalTriangle[row-1];
                int newRow[] = new int[row+1];

                // Store 1 in the first and last elements
                //    of the row.
                newRow[0] = 1;
                newRow[newRow.length - 1] = 1;

                // Fill in the middle of the row.
                for (int i = 1;  i < newRow.length - 1;
                        i++)
                    newRow[i] = lastRow[i-1] +
                                lastRow[i];

                pascalTriangle[row] = newRow;
                row++;
            }
        }


    // Display Pascal triangle - see Programming Ex. 2
    public void showTriangle() {}

} // class PascalTriangle
```

Figure 7.31 Building a Pascal triangle

Arrays with More Than Two Dimensions

There is no limit to the number of dimensions for Java arrays, but arrays with more than three dimensions occur infrequently. The three-dimensional array declared below can be used to store the monthly sales figures for the last five years for each of 10 salespeople.

```
int salesPeople = 10;
int years = 5;
double[][][] sales = new double[salesPeople][years][12];
```

The array sales has a total of 160 ($10 \times 5 \times 12$) elements. The array element sales[0][4][11] represents the amount of sales made by the first salesperson during the last month of the last year.

EXERCISES FOR SECTION 7.9

Self-Check

1. For the two-dimensional array

    `double[][] matrix = new double[5][4];`

    answer these questions:
    a. How many elements in array `matrix`?
    b. Write a statement to display the element in row 2, column 3.
    c. How would you reference the element in the last column of the last row?

2. List the indices of the elements in the next row of the Pascal triangle in Fig. 7.30 and the value of each element.

Programming

1. Write a method for class `IntArray` to display a matrix using `displayRow`.

2. Write method `showTriangle` that uses method `displayRow` to display a Pascal triangle.

7.10 Common Programming Errors

When debugging programs (or methods) that process arrays, it is best to test them on arrays having a small number of elements. If constants are used in array size declarations, then these constants should be small values. After your program is error free, you can change the constants to their normal values.

The most common error in the use of arrays is an index expression whose value goes outside the allowable range during program execution. Index-range errors most often are caused by an incorrect index expression. If the index is also the loop-control variable and is incremented before each loop iteration, index-range errors can result from nonterminating loops, or from loops that execute one more time than required.

Index-range errors are most likely for index values at the loop boundaries. If these values are in range, it is likely that all other index references in the loop are in range as well. When debugging, you may want to display a variable or expression used as an array index, particularly if the array reference is inside a loop.

As with all Java data types, make sure there are no type inconsistencies. The index type must be an integer expression. The element type must correspond to what is specified in the array declaration. Similarly, the element types of two arrays used in an array copy or assignment statement, or as corresponding arguments for a method, must be the same.

Remember that you must both declare an array and create an instance of it. If you write:

```
int[] a;
a[i] = 10;     // error
```

you will get a null pointer exception because you have declared the array, but have not allocated storage space for it. You may get this error when you want to defer creating an array until after you have read in its size.

You can also get a null pointer exception if you forget to create an object to be stored in an array of objects. For example, the following will properly create an array of references to objects with array length equal to `size`. However, object `a[0]` does not exist, so you will get a null pointer exception when you try to call method `someOperation`.

```
class Demo {
    private SomeObject[] a; // array a will contain
                            //    SomeObjects

    public createArray(int size) {
        a = new int[size];
        a[0].someOperation();   // error
    }
```

Before you can access `a[0]`, you must create it using the statement

```
a[0] = new SomeObject();
```

When using vectors, be careful not to remove more data than are in the vector. Don't forget to perform a type cast on each object that you remove from a vector. Also, don't attempt to store primitive types in a vector without placing their values in a wrapper object.

When you save data in a file or retrieve data from a file, make sure that you always close the file when you are finished. Otherwise, you may end up losing data, particularly if your program quits unexpectedly. If you are working with a data file that took a long time to type in, save a copy of it so that you can recreate it if necessary.

If you use nested `for` loops to process the elements of a multidimensional array, make sure that loop-control variables used as array indices are in the correct order. The order of the loop-control variables determines the sequence in which the array elements are processed.

Chapter Review

1. Arrays are data structures that store collections of data items of the same type.

2. You can reference the entire collection of data using the array name; you can reference individual items using the array name followed by an index (an indexed variable). The index must be an integer constant or expression. The data field `length` gives the size of the array and `length-1` is the index of the last element.

3. You can use a `for` statement to reference the individual elements of an array in sequence. Some common array operations written using `for` loops are: initializing arrays, reading arrays, and printing arrays. You can also reference array elements in arbitrary or random order (called *random access*).

4. You can write methods that have array arguments and return an array of values.

5. You can write methods that search an array for a specific target value and sort the array so that its contents are ordered in an increasing, or decreasing, sequence. You can use Big-O notation to compare the efficiency of two searching or sorting algorithms.

6. You can store a collection of objects in an array that contains references to objects. When you allocate an array that will contain objects, initially all references are null. Make sure you create an object for an array element to reference (using `new`) before you attempt to store its data in the array.

7. You can also store a collection of objects in a vector. Make sure you insert the statement

    ```
    import java.util.*;
    ```

    before a class that uses a vector. The vector size adjusts automatically as new objects are stored and removed from the vector. If you insert an object in the middle of a vector, the ones that follow it are moved accordingly. You can use method `size()` to determine the size of a vector and `size()-1` is the index of the last element.

8. You can save and retrieve data between program runs by using a file. Three steps are essential: opening the file, reading or writing individual data items to the file, and closing the file.

New Java Constructs

Construct	Effect

Array Declaration

```
int[] cube = new int[10];
int[] count = new int[10];
```

Allocates storage for arrays `cube` and `count` with 10 type `int` elements each.

Array Initialization

```
int[] primes = {2, 3, 5, 7, 11};
```

Stores the first five prime numbers in array `primes`.

Array Reference

```
for (int i = 0; i < 10; i++)
    cube[i] = i * i * i;
```

Saves i cubed in the `i`th element of array `cube`.

```
if (cube[5] > 100)
    displayResult(cube[5]);
```

Displays `cube[5]` if it is greater than `100`.

Array Copy

```
System.arraycopy(cube, 0, count,
                 0, 10);
```

Copies contents of array `cube` to array `count`.

Array Assignment

```
count = cube;
```

Makes arrays `count` and `cube` identical arrays. They contain the values stored in array `cube`.

Array of Objects

```
Employee[] people = new
            Employee[10];
```

Allocates storage for an array `people` with references to 10 type `Employee` objects.

```
people[0] = new Employee();
```

Allocates storage for a particular element of array `people` (`people[0]`).

Vectors

```
String[] names = new Vector();
names.addElement("Robin");
```

Creates a vector names used to store string objects.

Stores `"Robin"` at `names[0]`, `names.size()` is 1.

```
names.insertElementAt("Debbie", 0);
```

Inserts `"Debbie"` at `names[0]` and moves `"Robin"` to `names[1]`, `names.size()` is 2.

```
names.setElementAt("Rich", 1);
```

Stores `"Rich"` at `names[1]`, replacing `"Robin"`.

Construct	Effect
`(String)names.elementAt(0)`	Retrieves the string `"Debbie"`.
`names.removeElementAt(0);`	Removes the string `"Debbie"` and places `"Rich"` at `names[0]`, `names.size()` is 1.

Two-dimensional Arrays

Construct	Effect
`int[][] table = new int[3][5];`	Allocates storage for an array `table` with three rows and five columns
`table[0][0] = 5; table[2][4] = 5;`	Stores 5 in the first element and last element of array `table`.

`for (int i = 0; i < 3; i++)`
`    for (int j = 0; j < 5; j++)`
`        table[i][j] *= 2;`
	Doubles each element in array `table`.

Method `displayRow`

Construct	Effect
`displayRow(table[0]);`	Displays row 0 of array `table`.
`displayRow(table[1], 3);`	Displays `table[1][3]` and `table[1][4]`.
`displayRow(table[2], 2, 3, '*')`	Displays `table[2][2]`, a `'*'`, and `table[2][3]`.

Construct	Effect
`Files`	See Tables 7.5 and 7.6.

Quick-Check Exercises

1. What is a data structure?
2. Can values of different types be stored in an array?
3. If an array is declared to have 10 elements, must the program use all 10?
4. Show a way to declare an array of integers named x and define its size during run-time.
5. Explain the difference between assigning one array to another and copying the values of one array into another. Write statements that do both for arrays x and y (assign or copy y to x).
6. Fill in the initialization, repetition test, and update step for the following loop that accesses all elements of array x in sequential order:

   `for (int i = ____ ; _____ ; _____)`
7. Write expressions that access the last character in string x, the last element of array x, and the last element of vector x (a vector of integers).
8. Explain the purpose of the type cast `(Integer)` in the answer to Quick-Check Exercise 7. What exactly is type `Integer` and why do we need it?

9. Why will you get a null pointer reference error if you do the following? How can you fix it?

```
Employee[] employees = new Employee[10];
employees[0].enterEmpData();
```

10. Declare variables `names` and `ages` that can be used to store your friends' names and ages in separate arrays. Assume 50 names and ages need to be stored.

11. Write a `for` statement that reads data into these two arrays. Ask the user for a person's name and then that person's age.

Answers to Quick-Check Exercises

1. A data structure is a grouping of related values in main memory.

2. No.

3. No, there can be some elements at the end whose values are undefined and not used.

4. `int[] x;`
`x = new int[getInt("How many values in array")];`

5. If you assign array x to array x (x = y;), the elements allocated to array x become inaccessible and arrays x and y will always reference the storage locations accessed to array y. If you copy array y to array x (`System.arraycopy(y, 0, x, 0, y.length);`), the values in y are copied over to array x's storage locations, which remain accessible.

6. `for (int i = 0; i < x.length; i++)`

7. `x.charAt(x.length()-1), x[x.length-1],`
`(Integer)x.elementAt(x.size()-1)`

8. `(Integer)` type casts the value returned by `elementAt` (type `Object`) to type `Integer`. Type `Integer` is a wrapper type for an integer value; we need it to represent an integer value as an object.

9. You will get a null pointer reference because there is no object allocated to `employees[0]`. You need to insert the statement

`employees[0] = new Employee();`

between the two listed.

10. `String[] names = new String[50];`
`int[] ages = new int[50];`

11. `for (int i = 0; i < ages.length; i++) {`
`    names[i] = getString("Enter name " + i);`
`    ages[i] = getInt("Enter age " + i);`
`}`

Review Questions

1. Identify the error in the following code segment. When will the error be detected?

```
int[] x = new int[9];
for (int i = 0; i <= 9; i++)
    x[i] = i;
```

2. Indicate which of the assignment statements in the following code segment are incorrect. For each incorrect statement, describe what the error is and when it will be detected:

```
int[] x = new int[10];
int[] y = new int[10];
i = 1;
x(i) = 7.5;
```

3. A method has one argument that is an array and it returns as its result an array of the same type (int[]). The method copies the elements in its argument array to the result array in reverse order. Write the method.

4. Write a method that reads in a collection of strings and stores them in a vector. Assume that the class that defines the method has a vector of strings as a data field.

5. Write a method that displays the collection of strings that were read in for Review Question 4 in the reverse order in which they were read. *Hint:* The last string read in is at index size()-1 in the vector.

6. Write a method that writes the strings in the vector to a data file, starting with the first string in the vector. Write the number of strings as the first item in the data file.

7. Write a method that loads the vector using the data file created in Review Question 6.

8. How many exchanges are required to sort the following list of integers using selection sort? How many comparisons?

```
20 30 40 25 60 80
```

9. What is the Big-O notation for selection sort. Why?

10. Create a two-dimensional array that you can use to store the names of friends that you called on the telephone during each day of the past week. Write a method that reads this data interactively into the array. The number of friends you call each day can vary.

11. Write a method that you can use to display the contents of your array of friends from Review Question 10 in a history window.

Programming Projects

1. Write a program to read data items into two arrays, x and y. Store the product of corresponding elements of x and y in a third array, z. Display a three-column table displaying corresponding elements of the arrays x, y, and z. Then compute and print the square root of the sum of the items in z.

2. Write a program for the following problem. You are given a collection of scores (type `int`) for the last exam in your computer course. You are to compute the average of these scores and assign grades to each student according to the following rule:

    If a student's score is within 10 points (above or below) of the average, assign a grade of `Satisfactory`. If a student's score is more than 10 points higher than the average, assign a grade of `Outstanding`. If a student's score is more than 10 points below the average, assign a grade of `Unsatisfactory`.

    The output from your program should consist of a labeled two-column list that shows each score and its corresponding grade. You will need methods to read the student data, to write the student data, to compute the mean score, and to assign a letter grade based on the exam score and the mean score.

3. Redo Programming Project 2 but this time assume that the data for each student contains a student's ID number (an integer), the student name, and an exam score. Place your data in a data file that begins with a count of students. All the data for a student are in consecutive lines of the file. Your output should also be sent to a data file and should consist of a series of strings, where each string shows the ID, name, score, and grade for a student.

4. If an array is sorted, we can search for an item in the array much more quickly by dividing the array and searching decreasing halves. This technique is called a *binary search*. Given a beginning and an end in an array, the binary search determines a middle index and compares the middle value to the search value. If they are equal, the method can return the middle index. If the middle is less than the search value, we search to the right of the middle, repeating the same process. Write a binary search method for an array of integers and a test program that searches for each value in an ordered array of 1000 numbers (0 to 999). Have the program count the total number of comparisons required. Compare this number to the 5,005,000 comparisons required by the simple search method.

5. The results of a true-false exam given to a computer science class have been coded for input to a program. The information available for each student consists of a student identification number and the student's answers to 10 true-or-false questions. The available data are as follows:

Student Identification	Answer String
0080	FTTFTFTTFT
0340	FTFTFTTTFF
0341	FTTFTTTTTT
0401	TTFFTFFTTT
0462	TTFTTTFFTF
0463	TTTTTTTTTT
0464	FTFFTFFTFT
0512	TFTFTFTFTF
0618	TTTFFTTFTF
0619	FFFFFFFFFF
0687	TFTTFTTFTF
0700	FTFFTTFFFT
0712	FTFTFTFTFT
0837	TFTFTTFTFT

Write a program that first reads in the answer string representing the 10 correct answers (use FTFFTFFTFT as data). Next, read each student's data and compute and store the number of correct answers for each student in one array and store the student ID number in the corresponding element of another array. Determine the best score, best. Then print a three-column table that displays the ID number, the score, and the grade for each student. The grade should be determined as follows: if the score is equal to best or best-1, give an A; if it is best-2 or best-3, give a C. Otherwise, give an F.

6. The results of a survey of the households in your township are available for public scrutiny. Each record contains data for one household, including a four-digit integer identification number, the annual income for the household, and the number of household members. Write a program to read the survey results into three arrays and perform the following analyses:

a. Count the number of households included in the survey and print a three-column table displaying the data. (Assume that no more than 25 households were surveyed.)

b. Calculate the average household income and list the identification number and income of each household that exceeds the average.

c. Determine the percentage of households with incomes below the poverty level. Compute the poverty level income using the formula

$$p = \$6500.00 + \$750.00 \times (m - 2)$$

where *m* is the number of members of each household. This formula shows that the poverty level depends on the number of family members, *m*, and that the poverty level income increases as *m* gets larger.

Test your program on the following data.

Identification Number	Annual Income	Household Members
1041	12,180	4
1062	13,240	3
1327	19,800	2
1483	22,458	8
1900	17,000	2
2112	18,125	7
2345	15,623	2
3210	3,200	6
3600	6,500	5
3601	11,970	2
4725	8,900	3
6217	10,000	2
9280	6,200	1

7. Assume that your computer has the very limited capability of being able to read and write only single-integer digits and to add together two integers consisting of one decimal digit each. Write a program that can read in two integers of up to 30 digits each, add these digits together, and display the result. Test your program using pairs of numbers of varying lengths.

Hints: Store the two numbers in two integer arrays of length 30, one digit per array element. If the number is less than 30 digits in length, enter enough leading zeros (to the left of the number) to make the number 30 digits long.

You will need a loop to add the digits in corresponding array elements starting with index 30. Don't forget to handle the carry digit if there is one! Use a boolean variable to indicate whether the sum of the last pair of digits is greater than 9.

8. A prime number is any number that is divisible only by 1 and itself. Write a program to compute all the prime numbers less than 2000. One way to generate prime numbers is to create an array of boolean values that are true for all prime numbers, false otherwise. Initially, set all the array entries to true. Then, for every number from 2 to 1000, set the array locations indexed by multiples of the number (but not the number itself) to false. When done, output all numbers whose array location is true. These numbers will be prime numbers.

9. Write a program that generates the Morse code for a sentence that ends in a period and contains no other characters except letters and blanks. After reading the Morse code into an array of strings, your program should read each word of the sentence and display its Morse equivalent on a separate line. The Morse code is as follows:

```
A .-   B -...  C -.-.  D -..  E .   F ..-.  G --.
H ....  I ..   J .---  K -.-  L .-..  M --  N -.
O ---  P .--.  Q --.-  R .-.  S ...  T -  U ..-
V ...-  W .--  X -..-  Y -.--  Z --..
```

10. Write a program that plays the game of Hangman. Read the letters of the word to be guessed into array `word`. The player must guess the letters belonging to `word`. The program should terminate when either all letters have been guessed correctly (player wins) or a specified number of incorrect guesses have been made (computer wins).

Hint: Use array `solution` to keep track of the solution so far. Initialize `solution` to a string of symbols `'*'`. Each time a letter in `word` is guessed, replace the corresponding `'*'` in `solution` with that letter.

11. An important data structure in computer science is a stack. A stack is like the dishes in a buffet line—you can only access the element at the top of a stack. You can implement a stack using a vector. In this case, the element at the top of the stack is the one with index `size()-1` in the vector. You insert an item by pushing it onto the stack (using method `push`). Method `push` should be passed the item to be inserted as its argument and should call method `addElement` to do the insertion. You remove an element by calling method `pop`. Method `pop` should return as its result the item removed from the top of the stack. You also need a method `empty` that returns `true` if the stack is `empty` and `false` if it is not.

Write a class that can be used to process a stack of string objects. Then write an application that uses this class to read a collection of strings. Store them on a stack and then display them in the reverse order in which they were read. *Hint:* The element at the top of the stack is the last string read.

Interview

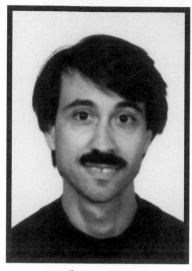

Anthony Russo

Anthony Russo is a senior scientist at Veridicom, a Bell Laboratories company. He is a fingerprint expert who designed and developed the verification algorithm module of Veridicom's fingerprint authentication software. This software measures the "ridges and valleys" of a fingerprint, reconstructs the print in digital form to find unique features, matches the fingerprint to the sample given by the user, and protects fingerprints from unauthorized copying or altering. Mr. Russo has a BSEE from Columbia University and an MSEE from Rensselaer Polytechnic Institute.

What is your educational background? How did you first become interested in computer science?

I have a B.S. in Electrical Engineering from Columbia University (1985) and an M.S. in Electrical Engineering from Rensselaer Polytechnic Institute (1986). My specialties are pattern recognition, image processing, and neural networks. And, of course, they pay me to push the fingerprint processing to the state of the art.

I first became interested in computer science when I took my first programming course in high school. I was writing FORTRAN programs on punchcards and I *still* enjoyed it!

What was your first job in the computer industry? What did it entail?

Well, my first job was a summer position (1984) at Sperry Corporation (now Unisys). My department did automatic test equipment for the military, and so there were a lot of computers around. At first, I was given the busy-work exercise of writing a program to identify all the consecutive prime numbers that the micropreocessor was capable of finding. It was, unfortunately, a boring task for me. I wanted to do something "useful," and this was not it! So I teamed up with a friend of mine and, during lunch hours, wrote a video game called "Space Mantiss" on an HP PC running HP Basic. The engineers were all playing it by the time the summer ended. For all I know, they still are.

How did you become involved with your work on fingerprint authentication?

It's a long story. My first "real" job was at AT&T Bell Laboratories (now Lucent Bell Labs) and back then they had a program to send eligible new hires to school to get a master's degree full time, all expenses paid, while still drawing two-thirds of their salary. It was a very generous deal for me, so I went off to RPI to study control theory. However, control theory wasn't really my love—image processing/pattern recognition were—so I made sure to choose a master's thesis topic that was interesting to me. I was lucky to find one that involved writing fingerprint processing algorithms, which combine image processing and pattern recognition very nicely.

Can you describe how fingerprint authentication works? What are some ways that companies might use this product?

Well, we at Veridicom describe it as "Personal ID." This is using your finger to gain access to personal things such as your laptop computer, or your car, or your file cabinet.

It works by first creating an image of your fingerprint, then processing that image to extract just the features that make it unique. These unique features form a template, and pattern recognition algorithms are used to compare that template against one that's on file. If they match, then your identity is verified and your car door or your PC will open for you.

How would you describe a typical day for you at Veridicom?

Exciting is one way to put it. Frenzied is another. The nature of software, and this is especially true of algorithm design, is that it keeps evolving. Everyone wants more and better, and because it's software, everyone thinks it's possible. So I do some invention and coding, some problem solving for others, and some planning for how the software should evolve in the coming year.

What is the most challenging part of your job?

Keeping customers satisfied, which means making our software extremely accurate, reliable,and easy to use. Sometimes we pull our hair out when we're faced with unreasonable requests and then wind up figuring out how to deliver them the next day. That's a lot of fun.

How do you see fingerprint authentication affecting our daily lives?

In the future—5 to 10 years—the products we use and the items we own will become very personalized. Your garage door will only open for you; the family PC will auto-play some Nine-Inch Nails song when you log on and a Beatles song when your father does. And it will all be very convenient: no more passwords and PINs to remember. Now, it may sound strange to build fingerprint verification into your blender, but if someone steals it, and it won't work for anyone but the owner, well, maybe next time the thief will just raid the refrigerator and go home.

Do you have advice for beginning computer science students?

View the computer as a tool, and concentrate on what it can help you accomplish. PCs can't change the world. You can.

Object-Oriented Design

Throughout the preceding chapters we introduced concepts of object-oriented design (OOD). This chapter re-examines and formalizes those concepts. We consider the four major components of object-oriented design:

- **abstraction**—modeling real-life entities by retaining only essential information

- **encapsulation**—clustering data and methods in a way that creates safe and reliable boundaries

- **polymorphism**—allowing some flexibility in the naming of entities and in expressing abstractions

- **inheritance**—extending abstractions to embrace more detailed knowledge or more refined knowledge

In this chapter, we show how these components interact to make all phases of the software development method more manageable. We focus on the basic mechanisms for object-oriented programming in Java. It is beyond the scope of this text to provide a detailed discussion of object-oriented design. Our intent is to provide you with a basic introduction, highlighting the important techniques for implementing a solution in an object-oriented way using Java.

Within this framework, we will study how to produce modular and reusable code. We review both inheritance and visibility. Much of what we do to maintain object-oriented principles involves creating packages of classes. We show how a method can take a variety of argument types to meet

8.1 Java Classes Revisited
Case Study: A General-Purpose Rectangle Class

8.2 Modular Programming and Reuse

8.3 Encapsulation, Inheritance, Visibility, and Packages

8.4 Polymorphism

8.5 Another Look at Inheritance
Case Study: Is a Square a Rectangle?

8.6 Class Members and Instance Members: `static` and `final`

8.7 Abstract Classes
Case Study: Areas of Different Geometric Figures

8.8 Multiple Inheritance and Interfaces

8.9 Common Programming Errors

Chapter Review

different needs (polymorphism). We will look at how objects interact, expanding our knowledge of inheritance relationships to include the Java concepts of abstract methods and interfaces. We present a case study that uses OOD to build a rather sophisticated program out of fairly simple parts.

Finally, note that with the exception of the final section, most of the class definitions in this chapter are support objects that assume that client objects (applications) will use them. Rather than get bogged down in the details of building `SimpleGUI`-based applications, we show prototype examples using `System.out.println`. These examples actually illustrate a component of the implementation process. We show how parts of the solution work without worrying about the details of the entire implementation.

8.1   Java Classes Revisited

Previous chapters have emphasized that good solutions result from using the software development method. Good design requires identifying the relationship between data and algorithms and then bundling them within class definitions. This is what it means to create abstractions.

Abstraction

abstraction:
a model of a real-life entity that retains only essential information about that entity and excludes extraneous detail.

In the first step of the software development method, we specify the problem requirements. In the analysis phase, we determine what information from the problem requirements is critical to finding a solution. Finding a representation for that information involves creating **abstractions**, or models, for entities in the real world (the design phase). The goal is to capture only what is necessary to solve the problem and to avoid extraneous detail.

Abstractions can provide different perspectives on real-world entities. For example, an abstraction of a person for a medical office might include the person's name, address, age, medical history, and health insurer. An educational institution would need the person's name and academic record, but not the medical history. A mail-order catalog "person" would consist of a name, address, and perhaps a consumer profile. Each of these abstractions provides a different viewpoint, or perspective, on the person entity.

Class definitions in Java provide a mechanism for creating abstractions. The data fields capture the essential attributes of entities being represented. Methods provide a mechanism for manipulating those attributes.

abstract data type:
a representation of an entity that includes both data (information) and methods (operations) for that entity.

An abstraction provides a way of clustering data and methods. Traditionally, computer science views an **abstract data type** as one that collects the essential components of an entity in one place. Classes provide a mechanism for creating abstract data types in Java.

Abstractions Made Real: Communication between Objects

In classic object-oriented programming, objects (which are instances of a class) interact by sending **messages** to one another. A **sender** of a message requests that the **recipient** of the message do some operation for the sender. The request can be to perform an operation (such as reading data or displaying information) or to respond with a value that the sender can use. The next example illustrates these interactions.

We call the class that sends messages the **client class**. The recipient is the **support class**. The client class also creates instances (objects) of the support class.

> **message:**
> a request to an object to perform a particular operation.
>
> **sender:**
> the object that sends the message and waits for a response.
>
> **recipient:**
> the object that receives and responds to a message.
>
> **client class:**
> the class that creates instances of our support class and sends messages to those instances.
>
> **support class:**
> the class whose instances respond to messages from the client class.

EXAMPLE 8.1

Let's revisit the problem of calculating the area and perimeter of a rectangle, but from the perspective of message sending. Assume that a class IntRectangle exists. (We will be defining it shortly.) The class Sender defined in Fig. 8.1 is an application class. It creates two instances of the IntRectangle class, r1 and r2. It tells each one to set its length and width and then requests that each report back its area.

```java
/*    File: Sender.java
      Developed for Problem Solving with Java,
         Koffman & Wolz.
      Appears in Fig. 8.1.
*/
public class Sender {

    public static void main (String[] args) {
        IntRectangle r1 = new IntRectangle();
        IntRectangle r2 = new IntRectangle();

        r1.setLength(10);
        r1.setWidth(20);

        r2.setLength(20);
        r2.setWidth(30);

        if (r1.computeArea() < r2.computeArea())
            System.out.println("R1 is smaller");
        else
            System.out.println("R2 is smaller");
    }
}
```

Figure 8.1 Using Class IntRectangle

In this example the sender and recipient are not on equal footing. First, the sender creates two instances of the recipient class. It can refer to the recipients by name (r1 and r2). The sender can send requests to the recipients. For example the statement:

```
r1.setWidth(20);
```

tells r1 to reset its width to 20.

The recipient only knows that it has received a message. It cannot reference the sender or make a request to the sender; it can only respond to messages from the sender. The recipient implicitly sends messages in response. Either it returns a value or notifies the sender that it has completed the task. For example, object r1 responds to the r1.computeArea() request by returning a value. In response to the r1.setWidth(20) request, it simply notifies the sender that it has completed the task.

Class Definitions Establish the Rules for Message Passing

The methods of the recipient class determine how the sender may interact with the recipient. The programmer must therefore define the class carefully to provide the right level of abstraction. Traditionally, we categorize methods as shown in Table 8.1.

Table 8.1 Categories of methods

Methods	Action
Constructors	Create instances of the class.
Accessors	Return values of an object.
Modifiers	Change the values of data fields of an object.
Destructors	Delete instances of a class.
Operations	Used to calculate output and intermediate results.

In previous chapters we took a less rigid approach to defining methods, and Java does not require you to define methods in these terms. However, categorizing methods in this way helps others understand what your methods do. Attempting to identify all of the methods within a category also helps the analysis process. You can quickly determine which methods are necessary and which are not.

Case Study

A General-Purpose Rectangle Class

Let's define the IntRectangle class that we used in Example 8.1. For simplicity, the client class will be responsible for getting user input and displaying results.

PROBLEM

Write a class that represents the geometric figure "rectangle." A rectangle can be defined by its length and width. There are formulas for calculating its area and perimeter based on its length and width.

ANALYSIS

Analysis of the problem leads us to identify the following data requirements.

Data Requirements

Problem Inputs

length and width of a rectangle

Problem Output

area and perimeter

Relevant Formulas

*area = length * width*
*perimeter = 2 * (length + width)*

DESIGN

In the design phase we focus on the properties and operations for class `IntRectangle`. The following data fields are needed:

Specification for `IntRectangle` class

Data Fields

`int width`—width of rectangle

`int length`—length of rectangle

We don't create data fields for the area and perimeter because they are output values. It doesn't make sense to set them directly. They are **dependent variables** because their values are dependent upon the values of length and width.

Next, we must identify possible methods. We need a way to set the values of the input data fields width and length. We need a way to calculate values of the area and perimeter. You can quickly identify necessary methods by looking at the input and output requirements.

dependent variable: a variable whose value can be calculated from other variables.

Modifiers

We need modifiers for the independent variables, but not the dependent ones. The client of our class should not be allowed to modify dependent variables.

```
setWidth(int w)      // Modifies the width data field.
setLength(int l)     // Modifies the length data field.
```

Accessors

We typically want accessors for each data field:

```
int getWidth()       // Retrieves the value of width.
int getLength()      // Retrieves the value of length.
```

In some class definitions, data fields may exist that store constants or intermediate values that are of little interest to the message sender. We do not need to provide accessors for such fields.

Operations

We need operators to compute the dependent variables:

```
int computeArea()       // Retrieves the value of area.
int computePerimeter()  // Retrieves the value of
                        //  perimeter.
```

These seem similar to the accessors. The only real difference is that unlike the accessors, the values are calculated rather than merely retrieved from data fields.

Constructors

In previous chapters the Java compiler automatically created a default constructor for us. The current problem shows how a constructor that takes arguments would be helpful. In fact, that is the purpose of constructors: to initially load information into newly constructed object instances. In Example 8.1 the `Sender` object took four steps to create `r1` and `r2` and give each the proper value. The statement:

```
IntRectangle r1 = new IntRectangle();
```

created `r1` as an instance of a rectangle and set its data fields to `0`. We can explicitly define a constructor that allows us to set the length and width immediately.

```
// Creates a new object with width w and length l.
IntRectangle r2 = new IntRectangle(int w, int l);
```

Destructors

garbage collector:
the Java mechanism that identifies objects that are no longer in use and makes their storage space available for reuse.

Just as the constructor creates an instance of an object, a destructor should eliminate an object, freeing the space it uses in memory for some other use. In most Java applications the programmer does not have to write an explicit destructor. Java has a **garbage collector** that searches out objects that are no longer being used. The garbage collector is a misnomer, since it is actually a recycler. But it cannot automatically recycle everything. Therefore, in some cases we want to give it some help by creating an explicit mechanism for eliminating objects. Destructors are mentioned here for purposes of completeness, but we don't use them in this book.

Having identified the methods, we would normally write their algorithms. However, they are all easy to code, so we will skip directly to the implementation phase.

IMPLEMENTATION

The implementation is presented in Fig. 8.2. All but the constructor method
should look familiar.

```java
/*    File: IntRectangle.java
      Developed for Problem Solving with Java, Koffman & Wolz.
      Appears in Fig. 8.2.
*/
public class IntRectangle {
    // Data Fields
    private int width;      // input - essential attribute
    private int length;     // input - essential attribute

    // Constructors
    public IntRectangle() {} // Sets data fields to defaults.

    public IntRectangle(int w, int l) {
        width = w;
        length = l;
    }

    // Modifiers

    // Modifies the width data field.
    public void setWidth(int w) {width = w;}

      // Modifies the length data field.
    public void setLength(int l) {length = l;}

    // Accessors:
    // Retrieves the value of width.
    public int getWidth() {return width;}

    // Retrieves the value of length.
    public int getLength() {return length;}

    // Operations:
    // Retrieves the value of area.
    public int computeArea() {
        return length * width;
    }
}
```

Figure 8.2 *continued*

Figure 8.2 *continued*

```
    // Retrieves the value of perimeter.
    public int computePerimeter() {
        return 2 * length * width;
    }

} // class IntRectangle
```

Figure 8.2 A first implementation of the `IntRectangle` class

In Java you declare a constructor by defining a method named after the class itself. The constructor method implicitly returns an instance of the class, so you do not need to give it a return type. More than one constructor may be declared for a class. This is an example of polymorphism and will be explored further in Section 8.4.

In Fig. 8.2, we define two constructors. The first is the default constructor with no arguments and an empty body. It sets the data fields to their default values as explained in Section 8.3. In Java, if you do not define any constructors, the compiler conveniently builds a default for you. But as soon as you define a constructor, you must also define the default (if you want to use it). If you omit the default constructor, the statement

```
new r1 = new IntRectangle();
```

would cause the following error message: `No constructor matching IntRectangle() found in IntRectangle`.

The constructor with arguments in Fig. 8.2 takes `w` and `l` and uses them to set the data fields `width` and `length`.

Syntax Display   ***Constructor Definition***

Form: `public` *ClassName*`() {}`
        `public` *ClassName*`(`*arguments*`) {...}`

Example: `public IntRectangle() {}`
        `public IntRectangle(int w, int l) {`
            `width = w; length = l;`
        `}`

Interpretation: A constructor's *arguments* and body describe how to initialize the data fields of a new object. A default constructor has no arguments and an empty body, and it sets the data fields of a new object to their default values.

TESTING

You should write an application class to thoroughly test the `IntRectangle` class. A requirement of testing is to make sure that all of the `IntRectangle` class methods work correctly (see Programming Exercise 1).

MAINTENANCE

The class defined here has some interesting uses, as you will see in the sections and chapters that follow. Maintenance of this class involves expanding what it does as well as modifying it to fit into a broader context of geometric figure implementation.

Program Style: *When to Declare Data Fields*

In most problems you can identify data that are intrinsic or absolutely necessary to the solution. These are independent variables and should be declared as data fields (`width` and `length` in class `IntRectangle`). They should have accessors and modifiers. Typically, you also want to be able to initialize their values through constructors. Often, you can calculate dependent variables (for example, area and perimeter) directly from independent variables. In most cases, you want to avoid declaring data fields for dependent variables because you must then make sure to update these data fields whenever the independent variables get new values. Otherwise, your object may contain inaccurate or inconsistent information.

Program Style: *Writing Accessors and Modifiers on a Single Line*

Notice that we've changed our formatting conventions just a bit in Fig. 8.2. Accessors and modifiers tend to do very simple tasks, either setting or returning data values. The one-line format is more space efficient, and given the simple nature of the tasks, easier to read.

EXERCISES FOR SECTION 8.1

Self-Check

1. What is the difference between the sender and receiver of a message within the context of object-oriented programming?
2. Explain why the sender can be viewed as the "client."
3. Contrast the activities of accessors, modifiers, constructors, and destructors.
4. Sometimes it pays to explore the ramifications of alternative design choices. Your supervisor insists that you create data fields for area and

perimeter. What accessors and modifiers should you add? If a client modifies length or width, how do you keep all your data fields up to date? Contrast this implementation with the one presented in the section. Decide which implementation is better and make a case for it.

Programming

1. Write an application class `Sender` that tests the `IntRectangle` class.

2. Write a class definition for an ellipse. An ellipse has two radii: a length and a width. Its area can be defined by the formula

   area = π * *length* * *width*

3. Write a cube class. It has three essential characteristics: a height, width, and length. Each face of the cube has an area and perimeter. The cube also has a volume defined as the product of the essential characteristics. It also has a surface area defined by the sum of the areas of each face.

4. Modify the `Employee` class (see Fig. 5.12) so that it creates data fields for `grossPay` and `netPay` (dependent variables).

8.2 Modular Programming and Reuse

modular programming: a technique based on dividing a problem solution into manageable modules or units.

Creating abstractions by defining classes supports the idea of **modular programming**. Rather than having to cope with all the details of a solution at one time, a programmer can concentrate on its separate parts (modules) without worrying about the details of other parts. When solutions require very large systems, teams of programmers can concentrate on their own modules, trusting that the class definitions will provide the necessary structure for communication between code written by different teams.

The idea of reuse is also important in object-oriented programming. Instead of starting each problem solution from scratch, the programmer should be able to adapt existing solutions to new problems. This idea does not apply just to code reuse, but to all phases of the development process. Techniques for solving problems as well as for writing actual code should be adaptable. In large projects, programmers should be able to build from previous problem solutions in a reliable way.

EXAMPLE 8.2

A drawable rectangle is shown in Fig. 8.3. It is a rectangle that has a position in space, a border color, and an internal color. All the other data elements of a drawable rectangle (its length, width, perimeter, and area) are the same as for a rectangle.

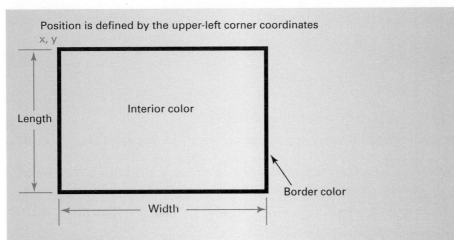

Position is defined by the upper-left corner coordinates

x, y

Length

Interior color

Border color

Width

Figure 8.3 A drawable rectangle

Fig. 8.4 shows a definition of class `DrawableRect` as an extension of class `IntRectangle`. Each `DrawableRect` object inherits `length` and `width` data fields from its superclass, `IntRectangle`, as well as all methods defined in class `IntRectangle`.

The data fields defined directly in `DrawableRect`

```
private Point pos;          // The position of top-left
                            //    corner
private Color borderColor;   // The border color
private Color interiorColor; // The interior color
```

use object types from the Java Abstract Windows Toolkit (the AWT). This is an example of reuse. Rather than creating our own definitions and conventions for representing position in space and object color, we use `Point` and `Color`. You may want to review Section 4.6, which discusses the AWT, or see Appendix C.

We've used `Color` before. A `Point` object holds an x and y coordinate. For example, the point x = 1, y = 15 is constructed as follows:

```
Point myPoint = new Point(1, 15);
```

We also need a way to draw the rectangle. Again, rather than inventing a method for drawing, we use the AWT. A `Graphics` object does the drawing. We pass the `Graphics` object g as an argument to the `drawMe` method. We use its methods `setColor`, `drawRect`, and `fillRect` to draw the figure. First we draw the interior rectangle using method `fillRect`. Then we draw the border on top of it using method `drawRect`. The statements below accomplish this drawing.

```
g.setColor(interiorColor);
g.fillRect(pos.x, pos.y, getWidth(), getLength());
g.setColor(borderColor);
g.drawRect(pos.x, pos.y, getWidth(), getLength());
```

The Graphics methods fillRect and drawRect expect four arguments:

startingXposition, startingYposition, width, length

The starting position, pos, represents the upper-left corner of the figure and would be set by a client of the class. The x and y coordinates of the starting position are stored in the public data fields pos.x and pos.y. The object being drawn uses accessor methods getWidth and getLength to retrieve its width and length values.

```
/*   File: DrawableRect.java
     Developed for Problem Solving with Java,
       Koffman & Wolz.
     Appears in Fig. 8.4.
*/
import java.awt.*;

public class DrawableRect extends IntRectangle {
    // Data fields
    private Point pos;               // Input - the position
                                     //   of top-left corner
    private Color borderColor;       // Input - the border
                                     //   color
    private Color interiorColor;     // Input - the
                                     //     interior color


    // Methods
    // Constructors
    public DrawableRect() {}

    public DrawableRect(int w, int l,
                        Point p, Color b, Color i) {
        // Define width and length fields.
        super(w, l);
        pos = p;
        borderColor = b;
        interiorColor = i;
    }
```

Figure 8.4 *continued*

Figure 8.4 *continued*

```
    // Accessors
    public Point getPos() {return pos;}
    public Color getBorderColor() {return borderColor;}
    public Color getInteriorColor()
      {return interiorColor;}

    // Modifiers
    public void setBorderColor(Color c)
      {borderColor = c;}
    public void setInteriorColor(Color c)
      {interiorColor = c;}
    public void setPoint(Point p) {pos = p;}

    // Operations
    // Draw a rectangle.
    public void drawMe(Graphics g) {
        g.setColor(interiorColor);
        g.fillRect(pos.x, pos.y, getWidth(),
                    getLength());
        g.setColor(borderColor);
        g.drawRect(pos.x, pos.y, getWidth(),
                    getLength());
    }

} // class DrawableRect
```

Figure 8.4 Class DrawableRect

Constructors and the Reserved Word super

The first constructor for DrawableRect is the default. Java automatically creates the code that sets all of the data fields from both DrawableRect and IntRectangle to proper default values. In this case, all integers are set to 0, and all object types are set to a special value null, which means the "empty object." This is the best the compiler can do because it has no idea what initial "shape" objects should have.

When a client class allocates a new DrawableRect object and passes it data, the second constructor in Fig. 8.4 executes. It begins with the statement

```
super(wid, len);
```

which calls the superclass constructor (that is, an `IntRectangle` constructor) with two arguments, `w` and `l`. The `IntRectangle` constructor stores these argument values in the `width` and `length` data fields. Notice that this is the only way you can call a superclass constructor without creating a new superclass object.

Syntax Display

Use of super in a Subclass Constructor

Form: `public subclassConstructor (formalArguments)  {`
         `super (actualArguments);`

Example: `public DrawableRect(int w, int l, Point p,`
                        `Color b, Color i) {`
           `super(w, l);`

Interpretation: The *subclassConstructor* calls its superclass constructor to define the subclass data fields inherited from the superclass.
Note: The call to the superclass constructor must be the first statement in a subclass constructor.

Initializing Default Values for Data Fields

To provide more useful default values we must initialize the data fields. We can do this either in the data field declaration or in the default constructor. By convention in Java, we do it in the data field declaration. For example, assume that the vast majority of times that the `DrawableRect` class is used its position is at `(0, 0)`, its interior color is white, and its border color is black. Figure 8.5 shows the data field declarations.

```
public class DrawableRect extends IntRectangle {
    // Data fields
    private Point pos = new Point(0, 0);
    private Color borderColor = Color.black;
    private Color interiorColor = Color.white;
```

Figure 8.5 Declaring data fields with default values

When to Initialize Data Fields

Data fields should be given explicit initial values only when those values are different from the defaults. Therefore, primitive types are typically not given explicit values and they default to the values 0 for numbers, `false` for `booleans`, and `'  '` for `char`. When a data field is a type of object it should have some kind of default "shape" and shouldn't simply be a `null` or nonexistent object.

Program Style: *Avoiding Public Data Fields*

You may have noticed that data fields x and y of type Point have public visibility, so we didn't need accessors to retrieve them or modifiers to change them in Fig. 8.4. This seems to be a departure from what we have been doing in the text. The reason the Java developers made the coordinates of a point public is that there is a substantial history that says that graphics points are integers. A graphics point is a pair of discrete values. It will never be a real number. Consequently, it makes sense for the Point class to allow any user direct access to the two integers that represent these values.

However, you should continue to avoid making your own data fields public. By forcing the client (the message sender) to use accessors and modifiers, you protect the data field from accidental misuse. You also provide maximum flexibility in case you decide to change the internal representation later (say, from int to long int or double). You may need to modify the accessor or modifier method in your class, but the large numbers of clients of the class will not be affected. We continue this discussion in the next section.

EXERCISES FOR SECTION 8.2

Self-Check

1. Explain why getWidth and getLength are needed in method drawMe. Under what circumstances would you be able to use the field names width and length instead?

2. Explain the actions of the constructor below. Can you give a situation in which you might want to use it?

```
public DrawableRect(int wid, int len) {
    super(wid, len); // Define width and
                     //   length fields.
}
```

Programming

1. Write an applet that will display rectangles of different sizes and colors.

2. Write a default constructor for DrawableRect that stores the default values in its data fields. Assume that the values were not provided in the data field declarations.

8.3 Encapsulation, Inheritance, Visibility, and Packages

In Chapter 2 we stated that all data fields of a class should be private to protect them from inadvertent access. We also stated that most methods should be public, so that objects can communicate with each other through their methods. Java allows considerably more flexibility. The data fields of a class can have any one of four kinds of visibility. The relationship between the class of the sender object and the class of the recipient object determines who can access a data field and how it can be done.

Encapsulation

encapsulation:
a technique for clustering data and methods together in a single program unit.

While abstraction provides a way to capture the essentials of an entity, it does not provide a discipline for maintaining the integrity of the data being represented. For example, a medical office keeps a medical history that should be confidential. The abstraction allows the key parts of the history to be represented, but does not describe how those records are kept nor guarantee that only those with proper authority have access. Rules must be established for how the data can be manipulated and who is allowed to do it. We can provide this control through **encapsulation**, or by clustering the data and methods together.

Encapsulation builds a wall around an object's private data, allowing user's of an object to access its data only through the `public` methods of the object's class. Figure 8.6 illustrates this for an `Employee` object. The object's data (`hours`, `rate`) can be accessed only through its methods (`enterEmpData`, `computeGross`, and so on).

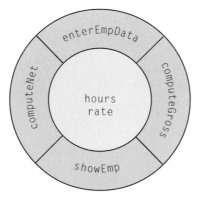

Figure 8.6 Encapsulation of data in an `Employee` object

Encapsulation is essential to very large computer programs. Before object-oriented languages became popular, programmers would develop elaborate conventions for naming variables in a program. They tried to ensure that one programmer didn't write code that would accidentally change values critical to another part of the program. The programmers were responsible for maintaining the integrity of the data.

By encapsulating data and methods in a class, Java does the work for the programming team. It takes responsibility for maintaining the integrity of the data, relieving fallible humans from a tedious detail. Programmers still must agree on how classes communicate with each other. The rules they establish are encoded in the `public` methods declared for a class. Consequently, both the methods that are chosen and their visibility are key ingredients for designing a well-encapsulated object.

Encapsulation not only protects a class from outsiders, but hides the details of the class from users of the class (a process called **information hiding**). For example, rather than reading a medical chart, a patient asks a doctor for an interpretation of the information on the chart. In Java, the visibility assigned to data fields and methods provides a mechanism for hiding detail. The user of a class needs to know only what a class does and how to make it do it. The user does not need to know the coding details for its methods.

information hiding:
a process in which details of class methods are hidden from the clients of the class.

Packages and Default Visibility

In the previous section, even though class `DrawableRect` (Fig. 8.4) extends class `IntRectangle` (Fig. 8.1), `DrawableRect`'s methods cannot access the `private` data fields `width` and `length` defined in class `IntRectangle`. Notice that the `drawMe` method in Fig. 8.4 uses accessors to retrieve these values rather than directly accessing the data fields.

This solution is not good from a design standpoint. `DrawableRect` should be able to directly manipulate its essential data fields. Just as some data should be hidden from the outside, an object should have access to its essential parts. This is a basic principle of encapsulation. But remember, we don't want to make data fields `public` so that any class can access them. Next, we explore two ways to enable certain classes to access data fields defined in other classes.

In Fig. 8.7, we provide a new `IntRectangle` class with data fields that have no explicit visibility; hence, they have default visibility. Default visibility does exactly what we need to support the `DrawableRect` class. Data fields or methods with default visibility can be accessed by any object in the same package. The package to which a class belongs is declared at the top of the file in which the class is defined. The keyword **package** is followed by the package name and a semicolon. Generally, all classes in the same package are stored in the same directory or folder. The directory should have the same name as the package.

```
/*    File: IntRectangle.java (with package-default-visibility)
      Developed for Problem Solving with Java, Koffman & Wolz.
      Appears in Fig. 8.7.
*/
package figures;

public class IntRectangle {
   // Data Fields
   int width;       // input - essential attribute
   int length;      // input - essential attribute

   // Constructors, accessors, and modifiers remain the same as in Fig. 8.2.

} // class IntRectangle
```

Figure 8.7 Class IntRectangle redefined with package (default) visibility

If we define class DrawableRect to be in package figures, then method drawMe can access data fields width and length directly, as shown in Fig. 8.8.

```
/*    File: DrawableRect.java (with package-default-visibility)
      Developed for Problem Solving with Java, Koffman & Wolz.
      Appears in Fig. 8.8.
*/
package figures;
import java.awt.*;

public class DrawableRect extends IntRectangle {
   // Data fields
   private Point pos;
   private Color borderColor;
   private Color interiorColor;

   // Constructors, accessors, and modifiers, remain the same as in Fig. 8.4.

   // Operations
   public void drawMe(Graphics g) {
       g.setColor(interiorColor);
       g.fillRect(pos.x, pos.y, width, length);
       g.setColor(borderColor);
       g.drawRect(pos.x, pos.y, width, length);
   }

} // class DrawableRect
```

Figure 8.8 DrawableRect redefined with package (default) visibility

---

Package Declaration

Syntax Display

Form: package *packageName*;

Example: package figures;

Interpretation: This declaration appears at the top of the file in which a class is defined. The class is now considered part of the package.

Classes that are not part of a package can only access public **members** (data fields or methods) of classes in the package. The packaging of classes creates a higher degree of encapsulation than before. For example, assume that IntRectangle in Fig. 8.2 and DrawableRect in Fig. 8.8 are in package figures. Figure 8.9 shows an application class that is not in the figures package. It compares the areas of IntRectangle r1 and DrawableRect r2. Because it is not in the package, the application class must reference the classes by their complete names. The complete name of a class is *packageName . className*.

member:
a data field or method defined in a class.

```
/*   File: AnApp.java
     Developed for Problem Solving with Java, Koffman & Wolz.
     Appears in Fig. 8.9.
*/
// Not declared as part of package figures.

import java.awt.*;

public class AnApp {

    public static void main (String[] args) {
        figures.IntRectangle r1 = new figures.IntRectangle(5, 10);
        figures.DrawableRect r2 =
            new figures.DrawableRect(10, 20, new Point(0,3),
                                     Color.red, Color.blue);
        if (r1.computeArea() == r2.computeArea())
            System.out.println("same size");
        else
            System.out.println("different size");
    }
}
```

Figure 8.9 An application using package figures

You may wonder why we don't have to use the complete name when comparing the areas. Shouldn't the code look like the following?

```
if (r1.figures.IntRectangle.computeArea() ==
        r2.figures.DrawableRect.computeArea())
```

The compiler needs to know the complete name of the class to create the instance. But once the instance is bound to the variable name (such as `r1` or `r2`), the instance can be referred to by just the variable name. There is no longer any need to use the package name or the class name.

The `import` Statement

The `import` statement allows class members to be referred to directly by their class name. Contrast the code in Fig. 8.9 with Fig. 8.10. In Fig. 8.10, the `import` statement specifies that all the classes in `figures` are to be imported. In many operating systems * is a symbol for "everything." So `figures.*` means all of the classes in the package `figures`.

Note that the classes in a package must declare themselves to be in the package. If they use other classes in the package, they must also import the package. You will see examples of this throughout the chapter.

```
/*    File: AnApp2.java
      Developed for Problem Solving with Java, Koffman & Wolz.
      Appears in Fig. 8.10.
*/
// Not declared as part of package figures.
import figures.*;
import java.awt.*;

public class AnApp2 {
   public static void main (String[] args) {

      IntRectangle r1 = new IntRectangle(5, 10);
      DrawableRect r2 =
          new DrawableRect(10, 20, new Point(0,3),
                               Color.red, Color.blue);
      if (r1.computeArea() == r2.computeArea())
          System.out.println("same size");
      else
          System.out.println("different size");
   }
}
```

Figure 8.10 An application using `figures` with the `import` statement

`import` *statement*

Form: import *packageName*.*;

Example: import figures.*;

Interpretation: This statement imports the classes in package *packageName*. The classes may be referred to by their short names rather than by their complete names. For example, if `IntRectangle` is in the `figures` package, then without the `import` statement, you must say `figures.IntRectangle`. When the `import` statement is present, you can reference `IntRectangle` directly. More than one `import` specification may appear in a file.

The No Package Declared Environment

Throughout the previous chapters packages were not specified, yet objects of one class could communicate with objects of another class. How did this work? Just as there is a default visibility, there is a default package. Files that do not specify a package are considered part of the default package. If all three classes, `IntRectangle`, `DrawableRect`, and the application class did not contain a package declaration, then all three would be in the same package and could refer to each other using short names.

Program Style: *When to Package Classes*
The default package facility is intended for use during the early stages of implementing classes or for small prototype programs. If you are developing an application that has a few classes that will eventually be bundled into one package, then you may use the default. However, as soon as you begin exploiting default visibility in your design, you should declare packages. The declaration will keep you from accidentally referring to classes by their short name in other classes that are outside the package.

`protected` Visibility

Creating a package implies creating a **library** of classes for others to use. You have used libraries such as `simpleIO`, `java.awt`, and `java.applet` before. In fact, you have also used a library called `java.lang` that is automatically loaded without an explicit `import` statement. If your task is to create a library of classes that others will extend, then you need a bit more flexibility to properly encapsulate your classes.

In Fig. 8.8, `DrawableRect` can access the data fields `length` and `width` from the `IntRectangle` class definition in Fig. 8.7 because the

library:
a collection of classes organized into a package.

data fields in `IntRectangle` have `package` visibility. Classes outside the package that use `DrawableRect` or `IntRectangle` can only access the `public` members. If a user needs to extend either of these classes, it cannot refer to the members with `package` visibility.

A solution might be to include the new extension in the package. But that violates principles of modularity. A package that is fully debugged and available for general use should be viewed as a closed and completed entity. Imagine that a dozen methods were added to the `Math` package at your institution. You implement solutions using those methods, never knowing they were not part of the original package. At your first job in industry, you may write classes that rely on that specialized version of `Math` and nothing works because those additional methods are not available to you.

The `protected` visibility feature is intended to avoid this predicament. The designer of a library may declare some members to be `protected` rather than merely available in the package. These members may be accessed by classes outside the package that extend classes within the package.

EXAMPLE 8.3

Assume that the `figures` package is a completed library that consists of a set of geometric figures (rectangle, circle, triangle, etc.) as well as subclasses that allow these classes to be drawn using the AWT. An application requires a special kind of rectangle whose width is always twice its length. The library has been designed so that all essential data fields have `protected` rather than `package` visibility. Figure 8.11 shows the changes to the `IntRectangle` class, complete with package identification and `protected` `width` and `length`.

```
/*    File: IntRectangle.java (with protected visibility)
      Developed for Problem Solving with Java,
        Koffman & Wolz.
      Appears in Fig. 8.11.
*/
package figures;

public class IntRectangle {
    // Data Fields
    protected int width;          // input, essential
                                  //    attribute
    protected int length;         // input, essential
                                  //    attribute
```

Figure 8.11 *continued*

Figure 8.11 *continued*
```
        // Constructors, accessors, modifiers are same as
        //   in Fig. 8.2.


        . . .


    } // class IntRectangle
```
Figure 8.11 IntRectangle defined in figures with protected visibility

Figure 8.12 provides a definition of class DoubleWide. Although it is not in the figures package, it can reference the data members of class IntRectangle because they are declared as protected rather than just having package visibility. The modifiers for DoubleWide must reflect the fact that the length and width are dependent upon each other.

```
/*   File: DoubleWide.java
     Developed for Problem Solving with Java,
       Koffman & Wolz.
     Appears in Fig. 8.12.
*/
import figures.*;

public class DoubleWide extends IntRectangle {
    // Methods
    // Constructors
    public DoubleWide(int len) {
        super(2 * len, len);
    }

    // Modifiers
    public int setWidth(int w)
      {width = w; length = width / 2;}

    public int setLength(int l)
      {length = l; width = 2 * l;}
}
```
Figure 8.12 Class DoubleWide

Visibility Supports Encapsulation

The rules for visibility control how encapsulation occurs in a Java program. Table 8.2 summarizes the rules in order of decreasing protection.

Table 8.2 Summary of visibility rules

Visibility	Applied to class	Applied to members (data fields or methods) of the class
private	Not applicable	Accessible only within methods of this class.
package (default)	Only accessible to classes in this package.	Accessible only to classes in this package.
protected	Not applicable	Accessible only to other classes in this package and to classes outside the package that extend this class.
public	Accessible to all other classes.	Accessible to all other classes; the class defining the member must also be public.

Notice that `private` visibility is for members of a class that should not be accessible to anyone but the class, not even classes that extend it. It doesn't make sense for a class to be `private`. It would mean that no other class can use it.

Also notice that `package` visibility (the default) allows the developer of a library to shield classes and class members from classes outside the package. Typically such classes have a supporting role that the `public` classes within the package exploit.

Use of `protected` visibility allows the package developer to give control to other programmers who want to extend classes in the package. Protected data fields are typically essential to an object. Similarly, `protected` methods are those that an extending class needs to execute processes essential to its abstract definition.

Table 8.2 shows that `public` classes and members are universally available. Within a package, the `public` classes are those that are essential to communicating with objects outside the package.

EXERCISES FOR SECTION 8.3

Self-Check

1. Explain why accessors and modifiers must be `public`.
2. Make a case for why `public` and `private` visibility are not sufficient.
3. Why is it better for `DoubleWide` objects to directly access data fields of class `IntRectangle`?

4. In earlier chapters you have imported the `java.awt` package. Given your ability to access methods from that package, make a case for the need for `protected` visibility.

8.4 Polymorphism

In this chapter we haven't yet built a fully working program. Instead we have the basic components of an **Application Programmer's Interface** (API), which is an established set of rules for accessing a class. In Java the API is obvious: it is the `public` methods of a class. An application's programmer uses the class by creating class instances (objects) and then manipulating those objects through the `public` methods.

Application Programmer's Interface: the methods that allow a programmer to manipulate the data elements of a class.

The class `DrawableRect` provides a mechanism for a programmer to draw figures. Fig. 8.8 shows the minimal set of methods needed for a programmer to manipulate a `DrawableRect` class. These methods constitute the core API for class `DrawableRect`.

Core Versus Convenient Programmer's Interface

Although the methods in Fig. 8.8 are complete, they aren't necessarily convenient for the programmer. For example, to create an instance of a `DrawableRect` object, we must write something like:

```
DrawableRect myRect =
    new DrawableRect(10, 20, new Point(3,4),
                     Color.red, Color.white);
```

Assume that the vast majority of the time when the class is used the starting position will be `(0, 0)`, interior color will be white, and the border color will be black. Only the length and width vary often. The programmer should have the convenience of setting the length and width in a constructor without specifying the position and colors.

Another inconvenience is the use of the `Point` class for the position. The programmer writing the client program may find it very awkward to always specify a `Point` instance. For example:

```
myRect.setPos(new Point(15, 20));
```

It would be much more convenient to simply give two integers as arguments.

```
myRect.setPos(15, 20);
```

Figure 8.13 shows an expanded version of the class `DrawableRect` that includes convenience constructors and modifiers, as well as accessors that individually retrieve the x and y coordinate of the starting position. The new methods appear in color.

```
/*    File: DrawableRect.java (expanded version)
      Developed for Problem Solving with Java, Koffman & Wolz.
      Appears in Fig. 8.13.
*/
public class DrawableRect extends IntRectangle {
    // Data fields
    private Point pos = new Point(0, 0);
    private Color interiorColor = Color.white;
    private Color borderColor = Color.black;

    // Methods
    // Constructors
    public DrawableRect() {}

    public DrawableRect(int w, int l, Point p, Color i, Color b ) {
        super(w, l);
        pos = p;
        interiorColor = i;
        borderColor = b;
    }

    public DrawableRect(int w, int l) {
        super(w, l);
    }

    public DrawableRect(int w, int l, int x, int y) {
        super(w, l);
        pos = new Point(x, y);
    }

    public DrawableRect(int w, int l, Color i, Color b) {
        super(w, l);
        interiorColor = i;
        borderColor = b;
    }

// Accessors
    public Point getPos() {return pos;}
    public Color getBorderColor() {return borderColor;}
    public Color getInteriorColor() {return interiorColor;}
    public int getX() {return pos.x;}
    public int getY() {return pos.y;}
```

Fgure 8.13 *continued*

Fgure 8.13 *continued*

```
// Modifiers
public void setBorderColor(Color c) {borderColor = c;}
public void setInteriorColor(Color c) {interiorColor = c; }
public setPoint(Point p) {pos = p;}
public setPoint(int x, int y) {pos.x = x; pos.y = y;}
public setX(int x) {pos.x = x;}
public setY(int y) {pos.y = y;}


// Operations
public void drawMe(Graphics g) {
    g.setColor(interiorColor);
    g.fillRect(pos.x, pos.y, width, length);
    g.setColor(borderColor);
    g.drawRect(pos.x, pos.y, width, length);
}


} // class DrawableRect
```

Figure 8.13 Expanded version of DrawableRect

Polymorphism

The constructors that we added are examples of polymorphism. There is more than one shape for the constructors of the DrawableRect class. **Polymorphism** means many shaped. It captures the idea that methods may take on a variety of forms.

polymorphism:
the idea that methods may take on a variety of forms.

Visibility and packages are mechanisms that impose structure on a problem solution. They support encapsulation and help protect code from deliberate or accidental misuse. Polymorphism loosens constraints by allowing a number of classes to reference methods by the same name. We examine three kinds of polymorphism. In order of complexity they are polymorphism across classes, method overloading, and method overriding.

Polymorphism across Classes

A method can have a variety of meanings depending upon its class For example, in the real world a method for driving a car is a bit different than one for driving a bus. But we refer to both methods as "driving" because we can distinguish them by the object (car or bus) to which they refer.

Throughout the preceding chapters you have seen many examples of polymorphism across classes. Although these methods have the same name, they are uniquely defined within each class. Example 8.4 shows one more example.

> ### EXAMPLE 8.4
>
> We've defined an `IntRectangle` class and in Chapter 4 we defined a `Circle` class. Figure 8.14 recasts the `Circle` class in the more formal structure of OOD. The `main` method in Fig. 8.15 compares the areas and perimeters of a rectangle and a circle inscribed within the rectangle as shown in Fig. 8.16. In Fig. 8.15 the condition
>
> `(c.computeArea() == r.computeArea())`
>
> calls both methods `computeArea`. The method that executes is determined by the object which is asked to compute its area (`Circle c` on the left and `IntRectangle r` on the right). Each method is unique because each is defined in a separate class.

```java
/*    File: Circle (revisited)
      Developed for Problem Solving with Java,
        Koffman & Wolz.
      Appears in Fig. 8.14.
*/
package figures;

public class Circle {
    // Data Fields
    protected int radius; // Input, essential attribute

    // Methods
    // Constructors
    public Circle() {}

    public Circle(int r) {
        radius = r;
    }

    // Modifiers
    public void setRadius(int r) {radius = r}

    // Accessors:
    public int getRadius() {return radius;}

    // Operations
    public double computeArea() {
        return radius * radius * Math.PI;
    }

    public double computePerimeter() {
        return 2 * radius * Math.PI;
    }
} // class Circle
```

Figure 8.14 Circle class revisited

```
/*    File: Demo.java
      Developed for Problem Solving with Java,
        Koffman & Wolz.
      Appears in Fig. 8.15.
*/
import figures.*;

public class Demo {
      public static void main (String[] args) {

            IntRectangle r = new IntRectangle(10, 10);
            Circle c = new Circle(5);

            if (c.computeArea() == r.computeArea())
                System.out.println("same area");
            else
                System.out.println("different areas");

            if (c.computePerimeter() ==
                r.computePerimeter())
                System.out.println("same perimeter");
            else
                System.out.println
                              ("different perimeters");

      }
} // class Demo
```

Figure 8.15 Comparing areas of a rectangle and circle

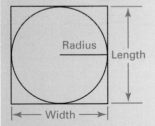

Figure 8.16 A circle inscribed within a rectangle

This is an example of polymorphism across classes. Both classes calculate areas and perimeters, but the calculations are different in each class.

Method Overloading and the Keyword this

Polymorphism also occurs when there is more than one way to express a method for a class. There would be a difference in the argument list for the method. This is the simplest kind of polymorphism, and, in fact, it can exist in languages that aren't object-oriented. You have seen some examples of method overloading in using methods of SimpleGUI. For example, displayResult can take an argument of any primitive type or type String. Similarly, method displayRow (see Section 7.8) has four different forms of argument lists.

There are many situations in which you need to have a method that has some flexibility in the number of arguments it takes. This is especially true for constructors (see Fig. 8.13).

Method overloading allows you to define an abstract task through more than one method definition. Each definition may have the same name provided each has a different argument specification. The **method signature** consists of the method's name, its return type, and its argument specification. Therefore, each method is unique and the compiler can determine which definition to use based on the signature, as determined from the method call.

method overloading:
providing multiple definitions with different argument specifications for the same abstract task.

method signature:
the form of a method as determined by its name, return type, and argument specification.

EXAMPLE 8.5

Figure 8.17 shows three constructors for an IntRectangle class, one that takes no arguments, one that takes two arguments, and one that takes a single argument that assigns the same value to an object's length and width, creating a square. When we allocate a new IntRectangle object, the Java compiler knows which constructor to execute based on the form of the argument list.

```
public class IntRectangle {
    // Data fields
    int width;      //input - essential attribute
    int length;     //input - essential attribute

    // Constructors
    public IntRectangle() {};

    public IntRectangle(int w, int l) {
        width = w;
        length = l;
    }

    public IntRectangle(int side) {
        this(side, side);
    }
    . . .
```

Figure 8.17 Three constructors for class IntRectangle

The body of the third constructor in Fig. 8.17 contains the statement

```
this(side, side);
```

The effect of this statement is to activate the IntRectangle constructor that has two arguments (the second constructor in Fig. 8.17), passing the value of side to each argument. Using the keyword this to activate a class constructor is analogous to using the keyword super to activate a super-class constructor.

The Keyword this   **Syntax Display**

Form: this.*memberName*
        this(...)

Example: this.x
        this(100, 100)

Interpretation: The keyword this refers to the recipient of the method in which the keyword appears. The form this.*memberName* provides a specific reference to a data field of the recipient object. The form this(...) refers to a constructor of the class.

Method Overriding

Polymorphism also occurs when one class extends another. By way of review, a subclass extends a superclass. The subclass can use many or all of the methods of the superclass, and it can also define its own. Sometimes the subclass needs a more refined method than the superclass. The method is said to **override the method** defined in the superclass. The setWidth and setLength methods in the DoubleWide class are examples of this kind of polymorphism.

overriding a method: providing separate definitions of a method in a subclass and a superclass.

When you extend a class you often must modify some of the methods of the superclass. Method overriding allows you to rewrite the method in the subclass. For example, the class definition of DoubleWide (Fig. 8.12) overrides methods setWidth and setLength in class IntRectangle (Fig. 8.11) by providing new definitions.

When the compiler sees a reference to a method in a class, it first checks that class to see if there is a method with the same signature. If not, it checks the object's superclass. It continues up the inheritance hierarchy until it finds a method with a matching signature or displays an error message if none is found.

EXAMPLE 8.6

So far we haven't been concerned with displaying the values of data fields. The creation of such methods for `IntRectangle` and `DrawableRect` illustrates the relationship between class and overridden methods. We add a display method to each class (see Fig. 8.18).

```java
public class IntRectangle {
    ...

    // Displays an IntRectangle object.
    public void display() {
        System.out.println("width is " + width);
        System.out.println("length is " + length);
        System.out.println("area is " +
                            computeArea());
        System.out.println("perimeter is " +
                            computePerimeter());
    }
    ...

} // class IntRectangle
```

```java
public class DrawableRect extends IntRectangle {
    ...

    // Displays a DrawableRect object.
    public void display() {
        super.display();
        System.out.println("x coordinate is " +
                            pos.x);
        System.out.println("y coordinate is " +
                            pos.y);
        System.out.println("interior color is " +
                            interiorColor);
        System.out.println("border color is " +
                            borderColor);
    }
    ...

} // class DrawableRect
```

Figure 8.18 display methods for `IntRectangle` and `DrawableRect`

Method `display` in class `DrawableRect` begins with the statement

```
super.display();
```

that calls the `display` method of its superclass (`IntRectangle`) to print out the values of the two original data fields and the area and perimeter calculations. Next, method `display` (class `DrawableRect`) prints out the values of an object's x–y position and colors. It is necessary to use the keyword `super` because both display methods have the same signature (`void display()`). If you omit the keyword `super`, method `display` in `DrawableRect` would attempt to call itself and would generate infinite recursive calls, leading to a run-time error.

`toString()`, overriding methods of the class `Object` All classes defined in Java are subclasses of the class `Object`. `Object` has a number of general-purpose methods that can be overridden to create powerful results. Method `toString` is the easiest to understand and perhaps the most useful.

The `toString` method is used by the `String` class concatenation operator to convert an object to a string. For example, a `toString` method for `IntRectangle` could be defined as follows:

```
public String toString() {
    return "length is " + length +
           ", width is " + width;
}
```

As shown above, method `toString` must have `public` visibility, it must return a string, and it can't have any arguments. Because the result is a string, it can be used with the concatenation operator. For example, the call to method `System.out.println` in the `main` method below

```
public static void main(String[] args) {

    IntRectangle r1 = new IntRectangle(5, 10);
    IntRectangle r2 = new IntRectangle(5, 15);

    System.out.println("r1 has data fields: " + r1 +
                    "\nr2 has data fields: " + r2);
}
```

produces the following output:

```
r1 has data fields: length is 5, width is 10
r2 has data fields: length is 5, width is 15
```

Java generates the first line when it reaches the operator + in the expression `"r1 has data fields: " + r1`. Because `r1` is an `IntRectangle` object, it applies the `toString` method for `IntRectangle` to "convert" `r1` to a `String` operand for the concatenation operator.

We introduced two `display` methods earlier (Fig. 8.18) to illustrate the `super` reserved word. These methods aren't nearly as useful as overriding `toString`, because `toString` can be used anywhere a string is required and it doesn't bind you to using `System.out` (or even `SimpleGUI`). When you write a `toString` method for a class, you should keep it as simple as possible so that the client method has more latitude in how to use it.

EXERCISES FOR SECTION 8.4

Self-Check

1. Explain the difference between overriding and overloading a method.
2. When do you use the reserved word `this`?
3. When do you use the reserved word `super`?

Programming

1. Modify the program in Fig. 8.15 to determine which figure is larger based on area and which is larger based on perimeter.
2. An ellipse is the mathematical term for an oval. Each ellipse has two radii. Write constructors for this class that (1) default the radii to 0, (2) set the radii to the same value, and (3) set the radii to different values.
3. In Fig. 8.13 the constructors were written without using the reserved word `this`. Try writing them with `this` and contrast your solution with the one presented in that figure. *Hint:* Define the constructor with the most arguments and have the other constructors call it.
4. Write `toString` methods for all of the classes defined in this section.

8.5   Another Look at Inheritance

You have now seen many examples of extending classes through inheritance. We've also said that inheritance is based on the "is a" relationship, that is, the subclass "is a" more refined version of the superclass. Typically, the extending class (the subclass) has added members, either data fields or methods, to create a class that contains more detail. We now consider a case where conceptually a subclass has more detail, but fewer data fields or methods.

Case Study

Is a Square a Rectangle?

Any kindergartner will tell you that yes, a square is a rectangle, but all the sides are the same. (Well, at least the kindergartners we talk to think so.)

Ironically, this simple answer proves to be perplexing from an object-oriented standpoint. Subclasses tend to have more data fields, not less than the superclass. A rectangle requires two essential data fields: a width and a length. A square requires only one: a side. The question is, Can we extend the class IntRectangle to the class Square? Is it worth it? We show you that it is possible if we are very careful when designing the IntRectangle class.

PROBLEM

Extend the IntRectangle class in Fig. 8.7 to support squares.

ANALYSIS

Analysis of the problem leads us to identify the following:

Data Requirements

Problem Inputs

the length of a side

Problem Output

area of a square
perimeter of a square

Relevant Formulas

area = side * side
perimeter = 4 * side

If length and width are both set to the value of side, then the formulas for IntRectangle also work for Square.

DESIGN

We can store the length of a side in both the length and width data fields that are inherited from the superclass, so we don't need to introduce any more data fields. We look at the new methods that we need next.

Constructors

The `Square` class needs two constructors, a default constructor and one that takes a single argument for the value of the side. This constructor sets both the width and length data fields to the value of the side.

Accessors

We can retrieve either the width or length of a square by using the methods of the `IntRectangle` class. So there is no work to do here.

Modifiers

This is tricky. A `setSide` modifier sets both the length and width data fields. The `setLength` and `setWidth` modifiers must be overridden in the `Square` class so that either one sets both data fields.

So what was so difficult about that? Well, in this case, it wasn't so bad because of our initial design for `IntRectangle`. Consider the problem we would have if we happened to create the following `setDimensions` method in `IntRectangle`:

```java
public void setDimensions(int w, int l) {
    width = w;
    length = l;
}
```

How do we override this method in class `Square`, so that a client method doesn't accidentally do something harmful like the following?

```java
Square s = new Square(10);
s.setDimensions(10, 20);   // Square with unequal sides.
```

Because `setDimensions` is a method of `IntRectangle`, it is inherited by `Square`. There is no good way to override it (see Self-Check Exercise 3). The best solution is to remove it from `IntRectangle`. The client program has a variety of other constructors and modifiers through which it can set the data fields. Although `setDimensions` is useful, it isn't necessary.

IMPLEMENTATION

The implementation of the `Square` class appears in Fig. 8.19.

```
/*   File: Squares.java
     Developed for Problem Solving with Java, Koffman & Wolz.
     Appears in Fig. 8.19.
 */
```

Figure 8.19 *continued*

Figure 8.19 *continued*

```
package figures;
public class Square extends IntRectangle {
     // Constructors
     public Square() {}
     public Square(int side) {
          length = side;
          width = side;
     }

     // Accessors
     public int getSide() {return width;}

     // Modifiers
     public void setSide(int s) {
          width = s;
          length = s;
     }

     public void setLength(int s) {
          setSide(s);
     }

     public void setWidth(int s) {
          setSide(s);
     }
} // class Square
```

Figure 8.19 Class Square **extends** IntRectangle

This case study raises the following design issues:

1. Is the "is a" relationship between the objects really natural, or is it contrived? Don't make a subclass if the relationship is contrived.

2. If the relationship is natural, then as you design both classes, take care to design the superclass in such a way that it maintains its own integrity and simultaneously supports the subclass.

3. If the relationship is natural but the superclass is part of a library, make sure you don't force the fit between superclass and subclass. It may turn out that some of the methods in the superclass do not fit in well with the subclass. In this case, you might be forced to re-implement a lot of functionality in the superclass and thus create problems for other clients of the superclass.

Self-Check

1. Why is extending `IntRectangle` to `Square` different from other solutions involving inheritance?
2. Consider the `DoubleWide` class in Fig. 8.12. Which kind of solution is it: one that creates more essential data or one that has less data than the parent class?
3. Design an implementation of `IntRectangle` with a `setDimensions` method. Can you find a way to override this method in a `Square` class that extends `IntRectangle`?

Programming

1. Design and implement an `Ellipse` and a `Circle` class so that one extends the other.
2. Design and implement a collection of `Triangle` classes, including a general triangle, an isosceles triangle (two sides are the same), equilateral triangle (all sides are the same) and right triangle (one angle is 90 degrees). Provide methods to calculate the perimeter of each kind of triangle.

8.6   Class Members and Instance Members: `static` and `final`

In previous chapters you were introduced to examples of constants and shared data. The `Math` class has constant `PI`, the `Color` class has a whole collection of colors such as `Color.black`. You did not need to create instances of the `Math` or `Color` class to use these. Similarly, you were able to use methods of the `Math` class such as `Math.sin` without creating an instance of class `Math`. Class members provide this flexibility.

Class Data Fields

class data field:
a data field that is shared by all instances of a class.

With the exception of the `main` method in the application object, all of the class members you have created so far have been instance members. Each instance of an object has its own set of data fields with possibly different values. However, some information is always the same for all objects of the class, so it would be wasteful for each instance to have its own copy. A data field that is shared by all instances of a class is called a **class data field**. You use the keyword `static` to identify a class data field.

EXAMPLE 8.7

In Fig. 8.20, all instances of class Sample share the data fields sum and count. The class Sample uses its data field count to keep track of the number of objects of type Sample that are allocated, and it accumulates in data field sum the sum of the values stored in each object's myValue data field. Note that the accessors getSum and getCount are declared static so that they can be referenced via the class name rather than via the instances. Figure 8.21 shows an application and Fig. 8.22 show the output from running the application.

```java
/*    File: Sample.java
      Developed for Problem Solving with Java,
        Koffman & Wolz.
      Appears in Fig. 8.20.
*/
public class Sample {
    // Class data
    private static int sum;
    private static int count;

    // Instance data
    private int myValue;

    public Sample(int x) {
        myValue = x;
        count++;
        sum += myValue;
    }

    // Class accessors
    public static int getSum() {
        return sum;
    }

    public static int getCount() {
        return count;
    }

    // Instance accessor
    public int getMyValue() {return myValue;}

    public String toString() {
        return (myValue + ", " + sum + ", " + count);
    }

} // class Sample
```

Figure 8.20 Example of class data fields

```
/*    File: TestSample.java
      Developed for Problem Solving with Java,
        Koffman & Wolz.
      Appears in Fig. 8.21.
*/
public class TestSample {

    public static void main(String[] args) {
        Sample s1 = new Sample(5);
        System.out.println("s1: " + s1);

        Sample s2 = new Sample(10);
        System.out.println("\ns1: " + s1);
        System.out.println("s2: " + s2);

        System.out.println("\nSum of myValues: "
                            + Sample.getSum());
        System.out.println("Number of Sample objects: "
                            + Sample.getCount());
    }
} // class TestSample
```

Figure 8.21 Application using class `Sample`

```
s1: 5, 5, 1

s1: 5, 15, 2
s2: 10, 15, 2

Sum of myValues: 15
Number of Sample objects: 2
```

Figure 8.22 Output from running `TestSample` application

In Fig. 8.20, the constructor modifies the class data fields `count` and `sum` through the statements

```
count++;
sum += myValue;
```

when it creates objects `s1` and `s2`. Method `toString` creates a string from the values stored in all three data fields of an object of type `Sample`.

In Fig. 8.21, method `main` can access class data fields through the class using its accessors (for example, `Sample.getSum()` and `Sample.getCount()`). Note that you cannot access the instance data field (`myValue`) of objects `s1` and `s2` through the class.

Data Fields as Constants

Some problems require data values that are set initially and then do not change throughout execution of the program. You use the modifiers `static final` to identify class data that contain constants. The keyword `final` indicates that the value of a class data field may be retrieved, but it may not be modified.

In earlier programs, you used predefined constants, for example `Math.PI` and `Color.blue`. These are declared `public static final` within their respective class definitions. Next we show how Java's `Color` class defines color constants such as `Color.blue`.

EXAMPLE 8.8

Sometimes a class provides specific instances of itself to clients as well as allowing clients to create their own instances. For example, the class `Color` (in package `java.awt`) defines 13 colors (see Table 4.2) as specific instances. It defines `yellow` as the `Color` instance

```
public static final Color yellow = new Color(255,255,0);
```

The class constructor "mixes" a color based on the values (0 through 255) passed to it arguments, which represent the three color components red, green, and blue. The color instance `yellow` is formed by mixing bright red (first argument is 255) and bright green (second argument is 255). A client can reference this color through the `Color` class (that is, `Color.yellow`).

Some graphics applications require a range of shades of a particular color. The class `Yellows` defined here provides six shades of yellow tending toward green. The constants (`y1` through `y6`) stored in the class `Yellows` are `Color` instances (objects), so they can be used anywhere colors are used. A client can reference the first one as `Yellows.y1`. Class `Yellows` contains no methods, but you can use the methods in class `Color` to manipulate its instances.

```
public class Yellows {
    public static final Color y1 = new Color(255,255,0);
    public static final Color y2 = new Color(230,230,0);
    public static final Color y3 = new Color(210,210,0);
    public static final Color y4 = new Color(170,170,0);
    public static final Color y5 = new Color(150,150,0);
    public static final Color y6 = new Color(100,100,0);
}
```

Class Methods

Like data fields, methods can be declared `static`, `final`, or both. A `static` method, or class method, belongs to the class rather than to a particular class instance. Class methods can manipulate only class data fields, not instance data fields. You may access a class method through either the class name (for example, `Math.sqrt`) or through a class instance. You may not access an instance method through the class name.

EXAMPLE 8.9

The class `Math` provides a method `random` that returns a random number between 0.0 and 1.0. This is useful for statisticians but it isn't much help for game developers who need random integers between 1 and 6 to simulate a roll of the dice, or between 1 and 52 to pick a card from a deck.

The class `Rint` (Random integer) (see Fig. 8.23) synthesizes a number of techniques from this chapter. The constants `MIN` and `MAX` control the range of the allowable values. Method overloading provides three types of functionality dependent upon the number of arguments. The method call `Rint.rand(1, 6)` returns an integer between 1 and 6; the method call `Rint.rand(100)` returns an integer between 0 and 100; the method call `Rint.rand()` returns an integer between 0 and 10000.

```
/*    File: Rint.java
      Developed for Problem Solving with Java,
        Koffman & Wolz.
      Appears in Fig. 8.23.
*/
public final class Rint {
    public static final int MIN = 0;
    public static final int MAX = 10000; // Arbitrary
                                         //    maximum

    private Rint() {};

    public static final int rand(int min, int max) {
        return (int) (Math.floor(Math.random() * max)
                                            + min);
    }

    public static final int rand(int max) {
        return rand(MIN, max);
    }
```

Figure 8.23 *continued*

Figure 8.23 *continued*

```
      public static final int rand() {
            return rand(MIN, MAX);
      }
} // class Rint
```

Figure 8.23 The class `Rint` (Random integer)

You cannot create instances of this class because the constructor has been declared `private`. Also, notice that the class itself is declared `final`. This prohibits anyone from extending the class.

`static void main` Explained

The Java interpreter needs a distinct starting point to begin an application. If you could extend your application class and override `main`, then the interpreter wouldn't know which `main` to choose. Using the reserved words `static void` before `main` specifies that there is exactly one entry point into your program, and when the program ends, nothing will be returned.

Summary of Class Members

At first glance the keywords `static` `final` seem intimidating, but their meaning is simple:

- `static`—there is only one occurrence of this member, and it resides in the class, not in an instance of the class.
- `final`—the member (or the class) cannot be modified.

Table 8.3 summarizes the relationships between classes, their members, and the keywords `static` and `final`.

Table 8.3 Summary of impact of `static` and `final`

	Class	**Data field**	**Method**
Neither `static` **nor** `final`	May contain both class and instance members	Denotes an instance data field; each class instance has its own version accessed only by instance methods; cannot be referenced by the class name.	Denotes an instance method; can access both instance and class data fields; cannot be referenced by the class name.

Table 8.3 *continued*

Table 8.3 *continued*

	Class	Data field	Method
static alone	Not applicable	One data field held by the class, shared by the instances; modifiable with proper visibility.	Operates on class data fields only; can be referenced by the class name.
final alone	Cannot be extended; may contain both class and instance members.	Value cannot be changed after initialization; allowed but not practical since it creates the same constant for each instance.	Denotes an instance method that can not be overridden. Used for trivial methods like accessors.
static final	Not applicable	Creates a constant for the class.	Denotes a class method that cannot be overridden.

EXERCISES FOR SECTION 8.6

Self-Check

1. In Fig. 8.20 who keeps track of the values of sum and count? Is there a way for the instances to access these values?

2. What does the following statement from Fig. 8.23 do?

```
return (int) (Math.floor(Math.random() * max) +
                                            min);
```

   If min is 10 and max is 100, what value is returned when Math.random() has the value 0.5? Does this seem correct to you?

3. For the application class in Fig. 8.21, write a statement that displays the myValue data field of object s1 or s2, depending on which is larger.

Programming

1. In the class definition given in Fig. 8.20, any method in the package can modify the value of count. Modify the class definition to protect the variable from misuse.

2. Create your own palette of colors as class instances.

8.7 Abstract Classes

Encapsulation provides structure to protect objects from one another. But in any system there is a delicate balance between too little and too much structure. Without enough structure, the rules (such as who can access a data item) can be broken too easily. With too much structure, simple tasks can become complicated and cumbersome as you attempt to negotiate the rules of interaction.

Furthermore, if some organizational structure is lacking, redundant attributes must be individually coded for many similar entities. Structures such as hierarchies simplify the interaction between entities by providing a way to capture essential information and operations. In other words, hierarchies provide a means for effective organization of abstractions.

Inheritance

Hierarchies and inheritance are rich concepts that appear often in science. In biology, hierarchical organizations capture essential information about relationships between living organisms. For example, living things can be divided into plants and animals. Animals in turn can be separated into vertebrates and invertebrates. Each level in the hierarchy is a refinement of the previous level (see Fig. 8.24).

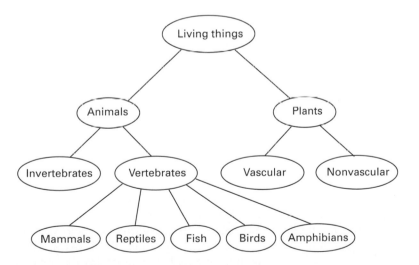

Figure 8.24 Hierarchical organizations in biology

Inheritance, in combination with hierarchical organizations, allows you to capture the idea that one thing may be a refinement or extension of another. For example, an animal is a living thing. Such an "is a" relationship creates the right balance between too much and too little structure. Think of inheritance as a means of creating a refinement of an abstraction. The entities farther down the hierarchy are more complex and less general than those higher up. The entities farther down the hierarchy may inherit data fields (attributes) and methods from those farther up, but not vice versa.

Contrast this viewpoint of a hierarchy with an organizational hierarchy. For example, a corporate hierarchy starts with the president or CEO of the company. Directors populate the next level, followed by section heads. A section head is not a director, but is subordinate to the director. This is not an "is a" relationship like the one between animals and living things. In object-oriented programming, "is a" relationships are used to support inheritance hierarchies. Do not confuse them with other kinds of organizational schemes such as those used to define corporate structure.

Another misuse of inheritance is confusing the "has a" relationship with the "is a" relationship. For example, a mammal has fur, or a car has wheels. Think of it this way. A car *is a* vehicle and it *has a* wheel. A vehicle has an engine, so by extension a car has an engine. But a wheel is not a refinement of a car, it is a *part* of a car. Consequently, it doesn't inherit the engine attribute from the vehicle. Note that not all vehicles have wheels; for example, snowmobiles do not!

Java allows you to capture both the inheritance relationship and the "has a" relationship. Inheritance is achieved by extending a class. We will explore this idea further in this section and the next. The "has part" relationship is achieved by declaring a data field with the part type. For example, a car class might be declared as follows:

```
public class Car extends Vehicle {
    Wheels[] w = new Wheels[4]; // cars have four
                                //    wheels.
```

One reason to use inheritance is that it allows you to reuse existing classes to build new classes. Another reason to use inheritance is that it allows you to cluster similar classes together. This clustering can help you design effective abstractions for large, complex systems. We illustrate this approach in the next case study, which takes advantage of Java's abstract class feature.

Areas of Different Geometric Figures

PROBLEM

Consider the problem of finding the total area of a collection of geometric figures. This problem has many practical applications. For example, in calculating the paint needed for a house, a painter might visualize the interior walls as a series of rectangular and triangular shapes. In calculating the amount of fertilizer to buy, a landscaper might represent a garden as a collection of oval and triangular shapes.

ANALYSIS

One way to solve this problem would be to create an array of rectangular objects and a separate array of triangular objects. Each object has an area, so we can calculate separately the sum of the areas of all objects in each array and then add the sums. However, what would happen if we needed to add a new geometric figure such as a circle? We would need to modify our code to define a new array of objects and to calculate the sum of the areas of the objects stored in this new array. Each new figure type would require us to define a new array type and to modify the area finding code.

There is a better way to add another geometric figure. If we could store objects of many different figure types in a single array, we would not need to modify our code when a new figure type was added. We can design a base class called `GeoFigure` and have all our figure types extend this class. We use this principle in the design discussed next.

DESIGN

Specification for `GeoFigure` class

Data Fields

There are no data fields in the general class.

Methods

`computePerimeter`—computes the perimeter of a `GeoFigure` object
`computeArea`—computes the area of a `GeoFigure` object

We know how to calculate the area or perimeter for a specific figure type but not for a generic `GeoFigure` object. One possible solution would be to leave the method bodies empty because each subclass of `GeoFigure` should define its own methods `computeArea` and `computePerimeter` that override the one in class `GeoFigure`. The programmer must ensure that each class that extends `GeoFigure` does indeed override these empty methods. However, if a programmer "forgets" to override the method, then this solution won't work.

abstract class:
a framework for a class that is completed in different ways by its subclasses.

Java provides a better solution—make class `GeoFigure` an abstract class. An **abstract class** provides an "outline" of a class, but leaves the complete definition to the subclasses that extend it. An abstract class contains methods that are properly defined by all of the classes that extend it. You cannot create an instance of an abstract class, but you can create instances of its subclasses.

Abstract classes support a very simple idea: put all of the common members (data fields and methods) as high up as you can in a hierarchy. All figures need methods for calculating area and perimeter. These class members are perfect candidates for inclusion in the abstract class.

IMPLEMENTATION

Figure 8.25 shows the definition of the abstract class `GeoFigure`. The reserved word `abstract` is used to identify the class as an abstract class and its methods as abstract methods (to be defined by the subclasses).

```
/*    File: GeoFigures.java
      Developed for Problem Solving with Java,
        Koffman & Wolz.
      Appears in Fig. 8.25.
*/
package figures;

public abstract class GeoFigure {
    public abstract double computePerimeter();
    public abstract double computeArea();
} // class GeoFigure
```

Figure 8.25 The abstract class `GeoFigure`

Figures 8.26 and 8.27 show new definitions of classes for a rectangle (`Rect`) and square (`Square`), which extend abstract class `GeoFigure`. Figures 8.28 and 8.29 show two new subclasses of `GeoFigure`, `Circle`, and `RightTriangle`. Each subclass implements the methods `computePerimeter` and `computeArea`. Also, each contains a method `toString`. Our new `Rect` and `Square` classes have type `double` data fields and accessors. (We use the name `Rect` instead of `Rectangle` to avoid conflict with the `Rectangle` class in library `java.awt`.)

Syntax Display

The Keyword **abstract**

Form: *visibility* abstract class *ClassName* {
    visibility abstract *type methodName* (*argumentList*) ;

Example: `public abstract class GeoFigure {`
    `public abstract double computeArea();`

Interpretation: The keyword `abstract` indicates that a class has at least one abstract method that must be defined by its subclasses.
Note: You can declare data members and also define real methods that are common to all subclasses in an abstract class.

```
/*    File: Rect.java
      Developed for Problem Solving with Java, Koffman & Wolz.
      Appears in Fig. 8.26.
*/
package figures;

public class Rect extends GeoFigure {
    // Data Fields
    protected double width;      // Input, essential attribute
    protected double length;     // Input, essential attribute

    // Methods
    // Constructors
    public Rect() {this(0, 0);}

    public Rect(double w, double l) {width = w; length = l;}

    // Modifiers
    public void setWidth(double w) {width = w;}
    public void setLength(double l) {length = l;}

    // Accessors
    public double getWidth() {return width;}

    public double getLength() {return length;}

    // Operations
    public double computeArea() {return length * width;}
```

Figure 8.26 *continued*

Figure 8.26 *continued*

```
        public double computePerimeter()
            {return 2 * (length + width);}

        public String toString() {
            return "Rectangle:" + length + ", " + width;
        }

    } // class Rect
```

Figure 8.26 Class Rect extending GeoFigure

```
/*      File: Square.java
        Developed for Problem Solving with Java, Koffman & Wolz.
        Appears in Fig. 8.27.
*/
package figures;

public class Square extends Rect {
        // Methods
        // Constructors
        public Square() {}

        public Square(double side) {super(side, side);}

        // Modifiers
        public void setSide(double side) {
            width = side;
            length = side;
        }

        public void setLength(double s) {setSide(s);}
        public void setWidth(double s) {setSide(s);}

        // Accessor
        public double getSide() {return width;}

        public String toString() {return "Square: " + width;}
} // class Square
```

Figure 8.27 Class Square extending Rect

```
/*    File: Circle.java
      Developed for Problem Solving with Java, Koffman & Wolz.
      Appears in Fig. 8.28.
*/
package figures;

public class Circle extends GeoFigure {
      // Data Fields
      protected int radius;            // Input, essential attribute

      // Methods
      // Constructors
      public Circle() {}

      public Circle(int r) {radius = r;}

      // Modifiers
      public void setRadius(int r) {radius = r;}

      // Accessors:
      public int getRadius() {return radius;}

      // Operations

      public double computeArea() {
          return radius * radius * Math.PI;
      }

      public double computePerimeter() {
          return 2 * radius * Math.PI;
      }

      public String toString() {
          return "Circle: " + radius;
      }
} // class Circle
```

Figure 8.28 Class Circle extending GeoFigure

```
/*    File: Triangle.java
      Developed for Problem Solving with Java, Koffman & Wolz.
      Appears in Fig. 8.29.
*/
package figures;

public class Triangle extends GeoFigure {
    // Data Fields
    protected double base;       // Input, essential attribute
    protected double height;      // Input, essential attribute

  // Methods
  // Constructor
  public Triangle() {}

  public Triangle(double b, double h) {base = b; height = h;}

  // Modifiers
  public void setBase(double b) {base = b;}

  public void setHeight(double h) {height = h;}

  // Accessors:
  public double getBase() { return base;}

  public double getHeight() { return height;}

  // Operations

  public double computeArea() {
      return height * base / 2;
  }

  public double computePerimeter() {
      return height + base +
              Math.sqrt(height*height + base*base);
  }

  public String toString() {
      return "Right Triangle: " + height + ", " + base;
  }

} // Class Triangle
```

Figure 8.29 Class Triangle extending GeoFigure

TESTING

To help you appreciate the real power of this design, Fig. 8.30 implements an application that uses class GeoFigure and its subclasses. Method main allocates storage for an array gf that contains four objects of different geometric types, each a subclass of abstract class GeoFigure. For example, array element gf[0] stores a right triangle with a base of 10 and a height of 20. In the first for loop, method main uses the method call gf[i].toString() to display the category of each object in the array. In the second for loop, method main displays each object's area (returned by geoFigure.computeArea()) and adds it to the total area (total). Figure 8.31 shows the output from running this simple test.

```java
/*   File: TestGeoFigure.java
     Developed for Problem Solving with Java, Koffman & Wolz.
     Appears in Fig. 8.30.
*/
import figures.*;

public class TestGeoFigure {

    public static void main(String[] args) {
        // Create an array of type GeoFigure
        GeoFigure[] gf = {new Triangle(10, 20),
                          new Circle(10),
                          new Rect(10, 20),
                          new Square(10)};

        double total; // Accumulator for total area of figures

        // Show that everything was properly created.
        for (int i = 0; i < gf.length; i++)
            System.out.println(gf[i].toString());

        // Calculate area of each figure and add it to total.
        total = 0.0;
        for (int i = 0; i < gf.length; i++) {
            System.out.println("\nObject area is " +
                                gf[i].computeArea());
            total += gf[i].computeArea();
        }

        System.out.println("\nTotal area is " + total);
    }
} // TestGeoFigure
```

Figure 8.30 Testing package figures

```
Right Triangle: 20, 10
Circle: 10
Rectangle: 10, 20
Square: 10

Object area is 100
Object area is 314.159
Object area is 200
Object area is 100

Total area is: 714.159
```

Figure 8.31 Output from application TestGeoFigure

The declaration of array `gf` with four different type `GeoFigure` elements perfectly balances flexibility and protection constraints. The ability to store objects of different types in a single array significantly simplifies the code. This kind of flexibility is not possible without inheritance mechanisms. You would be forced to declare one array for each geometric class (`Triangle`, `Square`, and so on).

The ability to declare an array of an abstract class type provides real protection for the programmer. Only instantiations of classes that extend the abstract class may be stored in the array. For example, if a class called `Ellipse` is defined that does not extend `GeoFigure`, then the compiler will not allow it to be included in the array:

```
GeoFigure[] gf = {new Triangle(10, 20),
                  new Circle(10),
                  new Ellipse(10, 20), // Compiler error
                  new Square(10)};
```

Abstract Classes with Data Fields and Implemented Methods

In the case study just shown, the abstract class acted as a place-holder for a collection of objects. We now show how a more "real" object can be viewed as abstract because of the need to refine one subclass method. In fact, this abstract class is a subclass of a regular class (`Triangle`).

EXAMPLE 8.10

The `Triangle` class in Fig. 8.29 calculates area. We now extend it so that it can be drawn by adding a starting position, a color (just the border color), and a `drawMe` method. We restrict our solution to the four possible ways to draw the `Triangle`, as shown in Fig. 8.32. (Two triangles are in color, and two are in gray.) We therefore need four subclasses of `DrawableTri` named for each corner of the bounding box in which its right angle appears. For example, the color triangle on the left has its right angle in the `Lower-Left` position, so it is a `LLTri` triangle and the four subclasses of triangle are `ULTri`, `URTri`, `LLTri`, and `LRTri`. For consistency with the `DrawableRect` class, the upper-left corner of the bounding box is the reference point for drawing.

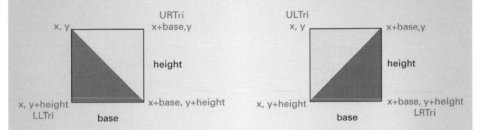

Figure 8.32 The four positions of a right triangle

The AWT class does not contain a method for drawing triangles. Instead we construct a `Polygon` object and use the `Graphics` class method `drawPoly`. A `Polygon` object is a vector of points. The `addPoint` method adds points to the vector. For example, the statements

```
Polygon p = new Polygon();
p.addPoint(0, 0);
p.addPoint(0, 10);
p.addPoint(20, 10);
g.drawPolygon(p);
```

construct a lower-left triangle starting at position `(0, 0)` that has a height of `10` and a base of `20`. The graphics object `g` can then draw it.

Figure 8.33 shows the class definition for `DrawableTri`. Fig. 8.34 shows its four subclasses. All of the triangles use the same `drawMe` method, but each has its own method for constructing the polygon. We indicate this by the line

```
abstract protected Polygon createPoly();
```

in class `DrawableTri`. Convenience methods for the `DrawableTri` class are left as an exercise. Each class in Fig. 8.34 should be saved as a separate file.

```
/*    File: DrawableTri.java
      Developed for Problem Solving with Java,
        Koffman & Wolz
      Appears in Fig. 8.33
*/
package figures;
import java.awt.*;
abstract public class DrawableTri extends Triangle {

    // Data fields
    protected Color color = Color.white;
    protected Point pos = new Point(0, 0);

    // Methods
    // Constructor
    public DrawableTri(double b, double h,
                       Point p, Color c) {
        super(b, h);
        pos = p;
        color = c;
    }

    public DrawAbleTri() {}

    // Modifiers
    public void setColor(Color c) {color = c;}
    public void setPos(Point p) {pos = p;}

    // Accessors:
    public Color getColor() {return color;}
    public Point getPos() {return pos;}

    // Operations
        public void drawMe(Graphics g) {
        g.setColor(color);
        g.fillPolygon(this.createPoly());
    }

    abstract protected Polygon createPoly();

} // class DrawableTri
```

Figure 8.33 Class DrawableTri

```
/*    Files: ULTri.java, URTri.java,
           LRTri.java, LLTri.java
      Developed for Problem Solving with Java,
        Koffman & Wolz
      Appears in Fig. 8.34
*/
package figures;
import java.awt.*;

public class ULTri extends DrawableTri {
    public ULTri(double b, double h,
                 Point p, Color c) {
        super(b, h, p, c);
    }

    final protected Polygon createPoly() {
        Polygon p = new Polygon();
        p.addPoint(        pos.x,          pos.y);
        p.addPoint((int)(pos.x+base), pos.y);
        p.addPoint(        pos.x,
                     (int)(pos.y+height));
        return p;
    }
} // class ULTri
```

```
//      File: URTri.java
package figures;
import java.awt.*;

public class URTri extends DrawableTri {
    public URTri(double b, double h,
                 Point p, Color c) {
        super(b, h, p, c);
    }

    protected Polygon createPoly() {
        Polygon p = new Polygon();
        p.addPoint(        pos.x,         pos.y);
        p.addPoint((int)(pos.x+base), pos.y);
        p.addPoint((int)(pos.x+base),
                     (int)(pos.y+height));
        return p;
    }
} // class URTri
```

```java
//      File: LRTri.java
package figures;
import java.awt.*;

public class LRTri extends Triangle {
    public LRTri(double b, double h,
                 Point p, Color c) {
        super(b, h, p, c);
    }

    protected Polygon createPoly() {
        Polygon p = new Polygon();
        p.addPoint((int)(pos.x+base),          pos.y);
        p.addPoint((int)(pos.x+base),
                                    (int)(pos.y+height));
        p.addPoint(        pos.x,
                                    (int)(pos.y+height));
        return p;
    }
} // class LRTri
```

```java
//      File: LLTri.java
 package figures;
 import java.awt.*;

public class LLTri extends Triangle {
    public LLTri(double b, double h,
                 Point p, Color c) {
        super(b, h, p, c);
    }

    protected Polygon createPoly() {
        Polygon p = new Polygon();
        p.addPoint(        pos.x,                  pos.y);
        p.addPoint(        pos.x,
                                    (int)(pos.y+height));
        p.addPoint((int)(pos.x+base),
                                    (int)(pos.y+height));
        return p;
    }
} // class LLTri
```

Figure 8.34 Four subclasses of class DrawableTri

EXERCISES FOR SECTION 8.7

Self-Check

1. Explain what makes a class abstract?
2. Why are abstract classes useful?
3. What may be declared in an abstract class?

Programming

1. Design a class hierarchy for the entire collection of drawable figures so far that includes a rectangle, a square, an ellipse, a circle, and the four triangles in Fig. 8.34. Pay special attention to where data fields go, what can be "moved up" the hierarchy and made abstract, and what is exclusively part of the subclasses.

8.8 Multiple Inheritance and Interfaces

Abstract classes can help you organize collections of classes. Under some circumstances you may want to organize classes in more than one way. You may want to have classes extend more than one superclass. This type of extension is called **multiple inheritance** and is not supported in Java.

Figure 8.35 shows a classic example of multiple inheritance. A toy elephant has some attributes of an elephant and some of a toy. The question is how to resolve conflicts between data fields and methods that belong to both superclasses. (For example, should method `isBreathing` be inherited from superclass `Elephant` or from superclass `Toy`?) Schemes for implementing multiple inheritance have been debated among designers of object-oriented languages for two decades. There are no easy answers.

multiple inheritance: the ability for a class to extend more than one superclass.

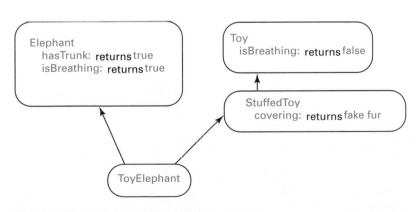

Figure 8.35 An Example of multiple inheritance

Interfaces

interface:
a Java construct for supporting limited multiple inheritance. It contains only abstract methods and final class data fields.

Java supports a simple form of multiple inheritance through a mechanism called an **interface**. An interface can be thought of as a highly specialized abstract class. The only members of an interface are abstract methods and final class data fields. Since all methods of an interface are abstract, they do not need to be explicitly declared abstract (with the keyword `abstract`).

EXAMPLE 8.11

We recast the problem of finding the areas of a figure to use an interface rather than an abstract superclass. In fact, since the abstract class `GeoFigure` does not implement methods or declare data types, an interface is a better choice for the implementation. On the other hand, the `DrawableTri` class cannot be recast as an interface because it contains data fields and implemented methods.

Figure 8.36 contrasts the `GeoFigure` class with a `NewGeos` interface.

```
/*    Files: NewGeos.java, GeoFigure.java
      Developed for Problem Solving with Java,
        Koffman & Wolz
      Appears in Fig. 8.36
*/
package figures;

public interface NewGeos {
  // Abstract methods
  // Operations
  public double getArea();
  public double getPerimeter();
} // interface NewGeos
```

```
//    File: GeoFigure.java
package figures;

public abstract class GeoFigure {
    public abstract double computePerimeter();
    public abstract double computeArea();
} // class GeoFigure
```

Figure 8.36 An abstract class contrasted with an interface

A class does not extend an interface, instead it *implements* it. For example, the class `Circle` is shown extending figures on the right, and implementing `NewGeos` on the left.

```
public class Circle          public class Circle
    extends GeoFigure {          implements NewGeos {
        // The class bodies are identical.
}                               }
```

An application class such as the one in Fig. 8.30 will execute properly regardless of whether the figures are implemented via an abstract class or an interface. A client cannot see any real difference. Encapsulation protects the client from the details of the implementation. The advantage of the interface implementation is that classes `Circle`, `Rect`, and so on, have all the benefits of the hierarchical structure needed here to calculate area and perimeter, but the classes are not tied to a superclass.

A class may extend only a single superclass, but it may implement any number of interfaces. Because the class must explicitly implement all the abstract methods, there is no potential conflict with methods defined outside the class.

Implementing an Interface

Syntax Display

Form: `class` *ClassName* `implements` *InterfaceName* `{`

Example: `public class Circle implements AreaPerimeter {`

Interpretation: The class *ClassName* extends the interface *InterfaceName* by defining all its abstract methods. The class may define other methods and data members.

Classes versus Interfaces

Be careful not to confuse interfaces with classes. An interface provides you with the ability to group classes together, but it is not a type of class. Note that an interface may contain only `static final` data members that a group of classes share. The practical use of any kind of interface is to create collections of objects (for example, to tightly control membership in an array). Interfaces may extend other interfaces, but since by definition their methods are abstract, they may not be instantiated (unlike abstract classes). Table 8.4 provides a summary of the rules for classes and interfaces.

We provide a large case study, the Patchwork Design Tool, on the website for this book. This case study illustrates object-oriented design and ties together many of the concepts introduced in this chapter. We recommend that you review it.

Table 8.4 Summary of classes and interfaces

	Ordinary class	final class	abstract class	Interface
May extend	Ordinary or abstract class, and implement numerous interfaces.	Same as ordinary class.	Same as ordinary class.	Other interfaces.
Can be extended by	Ordinary or abstract classes.	May NOT be extended.	Ordinary or abstract classes.	Other interfaces.
May implement	Numerous interfaces.	Same as ordinary class.	Same as ordinary class.	Nothing.
May be instantiated?	Yes, if abstract methods it inherits have been implemented.	Yes, same as ordinary class.	No.	No.
Has instance members?	Yes	Yes	Yes	No
Has class members?	Yes	Yes	Yes	Only public static final data fields.
Has abstract methods?	No	No	Yes	All methods are abstract.

EXERCISES FOR SECTION 8.8

Self-Check

1. Summarize the difference between an interface and an abstract class.

2. Explain why you can implement more than one interface, but only one abstract class.

3. Suggest reasons explaining why only static final class data fields may be declared in an interface. Give an example of name collision that would occur if a data field were not static final.

Programming

1. Extend a RightTriangle superclass to a RightIsoscelesTriangle subclass.

2. Implement the toy elephant example by using interfaces.

8.9 Common Programming Errors

Remember that you cannot access instance members from class methods. If you try, the compiler will tell you that you can't make a `static` reference. This error will occur if you create an instance method within an application class and try to reference it from `main` (a `static` method).

Try to clearly define packages when solutions start to exceed a few simple classes. Don't get lazy and leave all visibility at the default. It is dangerous to rely on the default package, especially if your application is merely testing the reliability of another class. Later, when you package the class, but not the application, you may get compiler errors indicating that the methods do not exist. The application class no longer can access them if you did not explicitly make them `public`.

Be conservative with the visibility of data fields. Think carefully about whether they should be something other than `private`. If you define them with more `public` visibility, the chances increase that a client will tamper with them. These kinds of errors are very hard to track down.

If you fail to implement all abstract methods in a subclass, the compiler will give you an error message saying your subclass should be declared abstract. It will tell you which method has not been implemented. If you think you properly defined the method in a subclass, check to make sure the method signature (the return type and the argument list) match the declaration in the abstract class.

Chapter Review

1. An abstraction provides a way of clustering data and methods. Traditionally, computer science views an *abstract data type* as one that collects the essential components of an entity in one place. Classes provide a mechanism for creating abstract data types in Java.

2. Encapsulation builds a wall around an object's private data, allowing users of an object to access its data only through the public methods of the object's class.

3. Inheritance, in combination with hierarchical organizations, allows you to capture the idea that one thing may be a refinement or extension of another. For example, an animal is a living thing. Such "is a" relationships create the right balance between too much and too little structure. Think of inheritance as a means of creating a refinement of an abstraction. The entities farther down the hierarchy are more complex and less general than those higher up. The entities farther down the hierarchy may inherit data members (attributes) and methods from those farther up, but not vice versa.

4. Encapsulation and inheritance impose structure on object abstractions. Polymorphism provides a degree of flexibility in defining methods. It loosens the structure a bit in order to make methods more accessible and useful. Polymorphism means many shaped. It captures the idea that methods may take on a variety of forms to suit different purposes.

5. Three types of polymorphism are possible. Polymorphism across classes occurs when two classes define the same method. Method overriding occurs when a subclass redefines a method of a superclass. Method overloading occurs when a method name within a class has more than one signature.

6. Visibility is influenced by the package in which a class is declared. You assign classes to a package by including the reserved word `package` at the top of the file. You can refer to classes within a package by their direct names when the package is imported through an `import` statement.

7. You can recognize class members by the keyword `static`. Final classes and members are those that cannot be redefined.

8. The keyword `abstract` defines an abstract class or method. The reserved word `interface` defines an interface. A class that uses an interface *implements* the interface. Interfaces provide a mechanism for multiple inheritance in Java.

Quick-Check Exercises

1. The _____ class is the sender of a message and the _____ class is the recipient.

2. List the five categories of methods.

3. Identify the category of methods that perform the following operations:
   a. Sets the value of a dependent variable.
   b. Eliminates a class instance.
   c. Creates a new class instance and defines its data fields.
   d. Calculates the value of a dependent variable.
   e. Retrieves the value of a dependent variable.

4. What does polymorphism mean? Describe the three kinds of polymorphism.

5. What is a method signature. Describe how it is used in method overloading?

6. Describe the use of the keywords `super` and `this`.

7. When would you use an abstract class and what should it contain?

8. When would you use an interface? Can a class have more than one interface? What does an interface contain?

9. Describe the difference between "is-a" and "has-a" relationships.

Answers to Quick-Check Exercises

1. application or client, support
2. accessors, modifiers, constructors, deconstructors, operations
3. modifier, destructor, constructor, operation, accessor
4. Polymorphism means many shaped. Three kinds of polymorphism are: polymorphism across classes, method overriding, method overloading. Polymorphism across classes means that the same method appears in different, unrelated classes. Method overriding means that the same method appears in a subclass and a superclass. Method overloading means that the same method appears with different signatures in the same class.
5. A signature is the form of a method determined by its return type, name, and arguments. For example, `void doIt(int, double)` is the signature for method `doIt` that has one type `int` argument and one type `double` argument and returns no result. If several methods in a class have the same name (method overloading), Java applies the one whose signature matches the signature implied by the method call.
6. The keyword `this` means use the member (data field or method) of the object to which the method referencing `this` has been applied. The keyword `super` means use the method with this name defined in the superclass of the object, not the one belonging to the object. Using `super` as a method call in a constructor tells Java to call the constructor for the parent class of the object being created.
7. Use an abstract class at the top level of a class hierarchy when the actual methods are defined in all the subclasses. The abstract methods defined in the abstract class act as placeholders for the actual methods. Also, you should define data fields that are common to all the subclasses in the abstract class.
8. An interface is an alternative to the use of abstract classes. It allows the definition of abstract methods for the subclasses of a hierarchy of classes. It provides all the advantages of using an abstract class without putting the classes that implement it in a subclass relationship. Therefore, a class can implement multiple interfaces and it is Java's form of multiple inheritance.
9. An "is a" relationship between classes means that one class is a subclass of a parent class. A "has a" relationship means that a class has members for representing the attribute being described.

Review Questions

1. Explain the differences between dependent variables and independent variables. Which would you normally declare as data fields?

2. Discuss the reason you do not want to declare too many data fields in a class.

3. Define the terms encapsulation and information hiding.

4. List the three kinds of visibility and explain the difference between them.

5. What is default or package visibility?

6. Explain how the compiler determines which method to use when a method definition is overridden in several classes that are part of an inheritance hierarchy.

7. Like a rectangle, a parallelogram has opposite sides that are parallel but it has a corner angle that is less than 90 degrees. Discuss how you would add parallelograms to the class hierarchy for geometric figures (see class `GeoFigure` in Fig. 8.25). Write a definition for class `Parallelogram` and make whatever modifications are required to the classes `GeoFigure` and `TestGeoFigure` (Fig. 8.30) to include parallelograms.

8. Explain what multiple inheritance means. Explain the way in which Java supports behavior that is similar to multiple inheritance.

Programming Projects

1. Redo the payroll program of Section 7.6 using more formal class definitions that include explicit constructors, modifiers and accessors. Separate the Graphical User Interface from the objects that support the payroll data structures.

2. A veterinary office wants to produce information sheets on the pets it treats. Data includes diet, whether the animal is nocturnal or not, whether its bite is poisonous (e.g., snakes), whether it flies, and so on. Use a superclass `pet` with abstract methods and create appropriate subclasses to support about 10 animals of your choice.

3. A student is a person and so is an employee. Create a person class that has the data attributes common to both students and employees (name, social security number, age, gender, address, and telephone number) and appropriate method definitions. A student has a grade-point average (GPA), major, and year of graduation. An employee has a department, job classification, and year of hire. In addition there are hourly employees (hourly rate, hours worked, and union dues) and salaried employees (annual salary). Define a class hierarchy and write an application class that you can use to first store the data for an array of people and then display that information in a meaningful way.

4. Define classes for the biology example in Fig. 8.24.

Applets, Graphical User Interfaces, and Threads

A major reason for the popularity of Java is that it allows you to program for the World Wide Web. This chapter introduces Web programming, focusing on the creation of applets. Applet programming is fun because applets include user interactivity as well as graphic animation, images, and sound.

Applet design provides concrete examples of how to solve problems from an object-oriented viewpoint, building on design concepts from Chapter 8. Because applets execute in the larger context of a Web browser, they also enable us to discuss multiprocessing: the simultaneous execution of more than one process.

This chapter provides an introduction to network programming (via applets) as well as an overview of Graphical User Interfaces (GUIs) and multiprocessing (through threads). A full discussion of real network and multiprocessing programming are beyond the scope of this textbook, but we will present the essential ideas. Chapter 10 provides more detail on GUI programming.

Although the material presented here may seem frivolous or inappropriate in a book on problem solving and programming, these topics address the very nature of how to organize and create program solutions in the modern context of programming. Few program solutions operate in complete isolation these days. For example, when you program for the Web, you do not have complete control of how your process is exe-

9.1 Web Programming and Client/Server Model

9.2 Applets, Panels, Containers, Components

9.3 The Basic Interactive Applet
Case Study: Click Me
Case Study: User-controlled Animation

9.4 Introduction to Threads

9.5 Threaded Animation (Optional)
Case Study: Two Animated Balls

9.6 Browser/Applet Interaction

Chapter Review

cuted. You must learn to think about how your small solution fits into a larger picture. You must also learn to think about how to fragment your solution so the processes that control the big picture can integrate your small part effectively and efficiently. These skills are essential to problem solving and programming in general, not just for Web programming.

9.1 Web Programming and Client/Server Model

Throughout this textbook we have stressed that a computer program consists of a process that creates output based on some input. For example, a method is given data via its arguments and returns a result. This input-process-output model is at the core of all programming. In the early days of computers, human interaction played a very minor part. Often the program and all its data were loaded into memory together before the program began execution.

The User Interface

With the advent of time-sharing and personal computers, it became more common for a user to interact with a running program and to enter data in response to prompts displayed by the program. This model promotes a "stop and wait" mindset. The program, and by extension, the CPU, stop and wait for input before proceeding with the steps that follow. This simple model is rapidly becoming obsolete.

The microcomputer industry dramatically changed the way software developers viewed the input and output of a program. Instead of just typing in data in response to prompts from the program (as in the old "stop and wait" model), the user controls what the program does by mouse clicks and other actions. Therefore, the effectiveness of the user interface becomes as important to the success of a program solution as the efficiency of its code.

event: a mouse-click or other action initiated by a program user to control its operation.

event handling: program interaction that occurs when a program responds to a user-generated event.

threaded processes: independent code fragments that run at the same time.

In the new world of programming, a good program solution must have mechanisms for communicating with users and with other processes. Therefore, the program must be able to handle arbitrary actions, or **events**, initiated by the user. **Event handling** and **threaded processes** support this shift in perspective. These concepts will be introduced in this chapter. Applets provide the perfect vehicle for studying them.

Thanks to the World Wide Web and Java, millions of people are interacting with a multitude of systems in many different locations. Many of the tasks that the systems do are not very sophisticated mathematically; that is, they do not "crunch" vast arrays of numbers. Instead, these computer systems spend most of their time managing the transfer of data. The Web and Java provide many excellent models for illustrating modern user interface design.

The Client/Server Model: The Browser and the Server

The World Wide Web solves a huge problem for individual computer users: it provides access to information on computers all over the world. The Web relies on two key technologies. The first is a GUI, the Web browser (for example, Netscape or Internet Explorer), which enables a user to specify what information is desired and where to get that information. The second technology is a set of **network protocols**. These are rules that ensure the accurate transmission and exchange of information between different kinds of computer systems.

network protocol: a set of rules that ensure the accurate transmission and exchange of information between computers on a network.

The programs developed in this text have generally involved a client object and a support object. The client supplies some data via arguments to the support object. The support object processes the data and returns results to the client. On the Web, the browser is a client object. Web servers are the support objects that supply HTML pages, graphics, sound, and video, as well as more sophisticated services such as database results to the browser.

The client/server model of Web communication is illustrated in Figure 9.1. The browser interacts with users and communicates with other computers. The browser interprets HTML (**HyperText Markup Language**, discussed in the next section) to make decisions about how to present the information received from the server. In this role, the browser acts as an output device, displaying results to the user.

The browser must respond to actions initiated by the user. The most common event occurs when a user selects a **hypertext link.** The browser takes user input and transforms it into a **Uniform Resource Locator** (URL). The URL is an identifying string that locates information on the Internet. The browser sends the URL to the Web server at that location. Most often the protocol of the URL is HTTP (**HyperText Transfer Protocol**). It allows the browser to request HTML pages, as well as graphics, sound, video, and applets.

hypertext link: a tag embedded in a document that connects to another document or to another place in the current document.

Uniform Resource Locator (URL): a string that identifies a particular document and the Web server where that document is located.

As an example, the URL for the home page for this book is:

```
http://www.awl.com/cseng/titles/0-201-35743-7
```

which identifies the Web server for the Addison Wesley Longman Publishing Company (named www.awl.com). This message tells the host computer to find the HTML document whose name follows the `.com/` part of the URL and to send that document back to your computer.

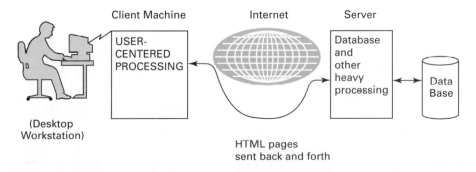

Client Machine Internet Server

USER-CENTERED PROCESSING

Database and other heavy processing

Data Base

(Desktop Workstation)

HTML pages sent back and forth

Figure 9.1 The interaction between a browser and a Web server

An Introduction to HTML

The browser interprets an HTML document or file and displays the information in the document in a readable form. An HTML file consists of text and HTML formatting tags. A tag is a delimiter that defines how a string of text should be interpreted. Figure 9.2 shows a small fragment of HTML code. Tags are shown in color. An explanation for each line appears on the right.

`<!--This file created 12/27/97 5:50 PM -->`	A comment
`<HTML>`	The actual HTML begins here.
`<HEAD>`	This is a header, it won't be displayed.
`<TITLE>`	Every HTML file should contain a title for web searches.
`Example for Problem Solving with Java, Chapter 9`	This is the actual title; it often appears in the browser.
`</TITLE>`	End of title
`</HEAD>`	End of header
`<BODY>`	Beginning of the HTML body (what will be displayed)
`<P ALIGN=CENTER>This text is centered</P>`	A new "paragraph," align it to the center.
`<HR>`	Insert a "bar" here.
`<B>THIS IS IN BOLD.</B>`	The text will appear in bold.
`<A HREF="java92.html">Go somewhere else</A>`	This declares a hyperlink to the file java92.html, it is stored in the same directory as this file.
`<IMG SRC="laugh.GIF"`	Insert an image called `laugh.GIF`. The image is also in the same directory as this file.
`  WIDTH=217 HEIGHT=162 ALIGN=bottom>`	The image has this width and height, it will be aligned at the bottom.
`</BODY>`	End of the body of the HTML
`</HTML>`	End of the HTML

Figure 9.2 HTML file `java91.html`

Figure 9.3 File `java91.html` displayed in a browser

Every tag in HTML begins with an open angle bracket "<" and ends with a close bracket ">". The tag name follows the open bracket and precedes the close bracket. The closing tag also contains a "/". For example, `<B>THIS IS IN BOLD</B>` declares that the text between tags should be in bold face. Although you can write HTML files by hand using a word processor, there are many software tools that allow you to create HTML files through a graphical user interface.

As shown in Fig. 9.2, an HTML document consists of two parts: a header and a body. The header is bracketed by the tags `<HEAD>`, `</HEAD>`. The header contains the document title (which appears in the browser top line) and is bracketed by `<TITLE>`, `</TITLE>`. Notice that this pair of tags is embedded within the tags that bracket the header.

Tags may contain attributes that further define the activity associated with the tag. For example, in one of the "P" tags, the `ALIGN` attribute with value `CENTER` specifies that the alignment of the text should be centered. The corresponding display in a browser is shown in Figure 9.3.

The file `java91.html` mixes both user input and output. Tags such as `<B>` and `<IMG SRC=>` provide directives to display or output information to the user. Tags such as `<A HREF>` provide a mechanism for receiving limited input from the user.

This is the essence of an HTML file. The more sophisticated interactivity you may have encountered in pages on the Web builds from these basic ideas. Table 9.1 lists some common tags. To learn more, see Appendix A.

Table 9.1   Basic HTML formatting tags

Start tag	End tag	Interpretation
<H#>	</H#>	Creates a heading that appears on a line by itself; H1 is the largest heading and H6 is the smallest.
 	None	Inserts a carriage return so that the text moves to the next line.
<P>	None	Inserts a carriage return and then a blank line for a new paragraph.
<HR>	None	Inserts a horizontal line or rule.
<B>	</B>	Bold text
<U>	</U>	Underlined text
<I>	</I>	Italicized text
<EM>	</EM>	Emphasized text
<CENTER>	</CENTER>	Centers text.
<A HREF = "*URLstring*">	</A>	Links to the URL in the string following the = sign.

Animation on the Web

Animation is the process of displaying a sequence of slightly varying images. The human eye interprets these changes as movement. Video and film technologies rely on the same principle. For example, Figure 9.4 shows a sequence of frames, which, if displayed in sequence in the same screen position, can be used to portray a stick figure doing a jumping jack. Computer-based animation uses the same basic technique. Timing is critical to animation. If the transition between frames is too fast or too slow, the animation will appear choppy.

Figure 9.4 A stick-figure animation

One approach to doing animation across the Web is through a file called an *animated GIF*. An animated GIF is a single file that contains a sequence of specially formatted images with instructions to display the sequence once, a fixed number of times, or to loop indefinitely. Although animated GIFs have become ubiquitous on the Web, they offer a very limited form of animation. They usually involve very large image files that can take an annoying amount of time to load onto a client system. Worse, there is no way for the browser to control them. For example, an animated GIF cannot be stopped, hidden, or moved about. In other words, it cannot be controlled by the user.

Distributed Processing

A crucial aspect of programming on the Web is determining which machine, server or client, should be responsible for different tasks. Ideally, a good balance is achieved when network traffic is minimized and resources are easily accessible.

Servers should be accessed for information that cannot easily be stored or calculated on client machines. Small throwaway tasks (such as verifying user input, or doing animation) should not directly involve server processing power. More to the point, processes should only be active on either end when they are needed. At the client end, the browser should not tie up resources while it waits for the server to respond. At the server end, a single request must be properly managed so that it does not prohibit other requests from being filled.

Three techniques have been developed to achieve distributed processing goals: HTML Forms with CGI scripts, plug-in applications, and applets.

HTML forms at the client side coupled with **CGI scripts** at the server side provide a rudimentary way for an HTML to pass user information to a server. A form is constructed using HTML tags. The user responses are sent to the server embedded in a request for a URL. The server responds by sending another URL to the browser. This technique is very inefficient because a lot of user-based processing occurs on the server. We discuss it further and give an example in the section on browser/applet interaction.

A **plug-in application** can be installed on the same machine as the browser (the client machine). The server has nothing to do with the plug-in; it simply assumes that the plug-in exists on the client side. A responsibly written HTML file will include links to other Web documents that facilitate installing the plug-in if it is not already on the client machine. Examples of plug-ins are Adobe Acrobat, which reads specially formatted files, and Shock Wave, which provides sophisticated control of multimedia activities.

An applet is a program embedded in an HTML file that is sent by a server to a client via a URL request. Like a plug-in, an applet executes on the client machine. When the user exits a browser, the plug-in remains resident on the client machine. However, an applet is removed from the client machine and must be reloaded from the server each time it is used.

HTML form:
a kind of tag that allows rudimentary user input within an HTML page.

CGI script:
a Common Gateway Interface script that runs on a server in response to user requests formulated through HTML forms.

plug-in application:
an application that resides on the client machine and is used by the browser to interpret data received through the Web.

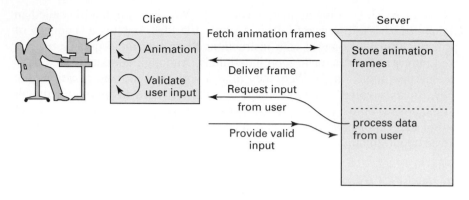

Figure 9.5 Managing client/server interaction with localized processes

Applets and plug-ins reduce the amount of processing that must occur at the server side. This efficiency is illustrated in Figure 9.5. Much of the data traffic between the server and client can be isolated at the client end. Plug-ins and applets each have their place. You can write plug-ins in Java by writing Java applications.

The remainder of this chapter explores issues pertaining to applets. Some ideas are just as valid for applications. In particular, any process, regardless of whether it is an applet, an application, or a plug-in, must know what input to expect, how it should process that input, what to send back as output, and where to send its output. Furthermore, programmers must keep in mind that data can come from (and go to) a variety of sources. As you will see in this chapter, communication between processes is key.

EXERCISES FOR SECTION 9.1

Self-Check

1. Characterize the difference between a client and a server.
2. For each of the following state whether it is stored on the client or server:

   application, HTML form, HTML page, CGIscript, plug-in, applet
3. What is an event?
4. What is a thread?
5. Explain why protocols are important.

Programming

1. If your institution allows it, create a Web page of your own.

9.2 Applets, Panels, Containers, Components

In Chapter 4 we introduced the Java `Applet` class. There are three ways to approach applets. You can see the effect of running an applet within an **applet context** such as a browser; you can study the methods and data fields of the `Applet` class definition; and you can examine its superclass definitions to see what additional properties applets have.

applet context:
a program such as a browser or applet viewer that can run applets.

Applets Are Executed by an Applet Context

An applet context is a program such as a browser or applet viewer. It may be written in Java or in some other programming language. You tell the applet context to run an Applet by providing it with an HTML document. The document must contain the tag "`applet`." Figure 9.6 shows an example.

```
<!--This file created 12/27/97 6:44 PM -->
<HTML>
<HEAD>
<TITLE>Simple Applet HTML, Problem Solving with Java,
  Chapter 9</TITLE>
</HEAD>
<BODY>
<applet code="FirstGUI.class" width=300 height=200>
</applet>
</BODY>
</HTML>
```

Figure 9.6 An HTML file that contains a minimal applet tag

In order for the applet to execute properly, the applet tag must contain the following attributes:

`code`—the class name of the applet to instantiate and execute

`width`—the width of the rectangle in the applet context in which the applet will appear

`height`—the height of the rectangle in the applet context in which the applet will appear

When the tag contains only these three attributes, the HTML file and the compiled `Applet` class must reside in the same directory. We list other attributes that provide more flexibility in Appendix A.

The applet context instantiates the specified `Applet` class (class `FirstGUI` in Fig. 9.6). It controls the execution of the applet by calling the applet's methods. When the applet context itself is a complex environment such as a browser, this level of control is essential. For example, when the user specifies an HTML page with an applet tag, the browser displays the entire page, and instantiates and displays the applet in the specified rectangle. It then starts up the applet and lets it run. When the user leaves the page, for example, by loading a different page or by overlaying the browser with a different application such as a word processor, the browser stops or suspends the applet. When the user returns to the page, the browser restarts the applet. Finally, when the user exits the browser, the browser must destroy the applet.

The scenario just described is an example of multiprocessing. At a minimum, three programs are running on the computer: the operating system, the browser, and the applet. The operating system monitors and controls the execution of the browser. The browser in turn controls the execution of the applet. The user, however, can move seamlessly between the background operating system, the browser, and the application. The GUI determines the process with which the user is interacting. For example, a user interacting with an applet might want to send e-mail to a friend about the applet. The user switches contexts, and tells the operating system to start up a mail program. The applet and the browser have no knowledge of, or responsibility for, the context switch. In order to run the mail program the user does not have to stop the applet, stop the browser, and then start the mailer. The browser and applet can continue running in the background, or may be suspended until the user returns to them.

The idea that a process, such as an applet should only be responsible for its own actions is extremely important. It has been around computer science for a long time. But examples that can be grasped by novice programmers are relatively new. Java is unique in its ability to make this perspective accessible to beginning programmers. The key is understanding how method calls work, and realizing that you can write methods without worrying about the details of who will call your method and in what context.

Methods Called by an Applet Context

When you define an applet, you extend the `Applet` class. This class has four methods that are called by the applet context. They are:

`init()`	Initializes the applet. You usually override this method when defining an applet.
`start()`	Makes the applet "active"; that is, it starts the applet running. You usually do not override this method.
`stop()`	Makes the applet "inactive"; that is, it stops the applet. You usually do not override this method.
`destroy()`	Destroys the applet so that its resources can be recycled. The applet context calls this method when the user exits the applet context.

Figure 9.7 shows how a browser calls these methods as a user visits and leaves a page. When you define an applet you do not need to concern your-

self with the order in which the applet's methods are called by the browser. Your job is to properly override the `Applet` methods so that your applet behaves properly.

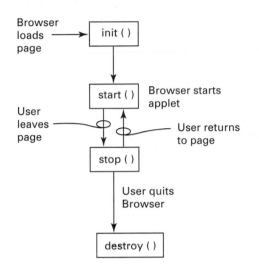

Figure 9.7 A browser calls the `Applet` methods

`Applet` Is a **GUI Component**

`Applet` is a class that extends a class called `Panel`, that in turn extends `Container` that extends `Component` (see Fig. 9.8). Applets therefore inherit properties from panels, containers, and components.

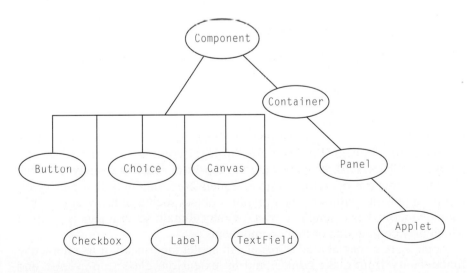

Figure 9.8 Class inheritance diagram

A `Component` is a GUI class defined in a Java package called `java.awt`. The `awt` stands for Abstract Window Toolkit (AWT). A component can act as both an input and an output device. Every component has a graphics context as well as a method `paint()` that defines how it appears on the screen.

Classes that extend `Component` include `Button`, `Textfield`, `Checkbox`, `Choice`, and `Label` (see Fig. 9.8). Figure 9.9 shows an applet that has some of these components: a textfield, a label, and three buttons. Components can be activated to notice user-initiated events. For example, a `Button` object notices that it has been pressed, and a `TextField` object notices that some text has been typed. Any component can notice properties of the mouse such as whether the mouse is being clicked or dragged. Any component can also notice whether keys have been pressed.

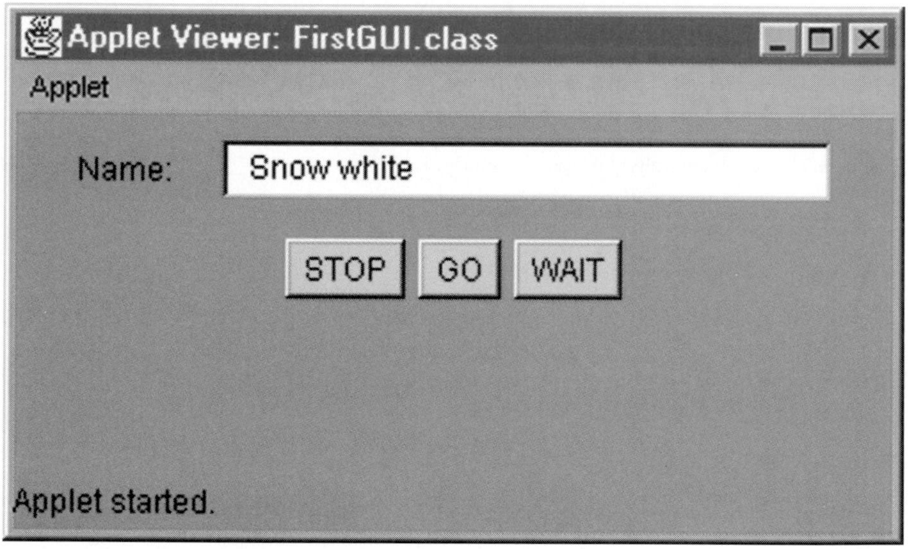

Figure 9.9 `FirstGUI` applet as seen through a browser

The `Container` class is a subclass of `Component`. Containers are components that can hold other components. There are two types of containers: panels and windows. Windows are top-level containers that will be described in Chapter 10. Windows are the top-level element displayed by the GUI for a modern operating system. Panels are containers that cluster related components within a larger graphics object such as a browser or application window. For example, a window may contain several panels, each of which may contain one or more components.

Applets are a special kind of panel. An applet inherits all of its interactive functionality from class `Panel`, and by extension, class `Container` and

`Component`. Because an applet is a panel rather than a window, it is contained within another window object, such as a browser. An applet is also a container, so it may include any number of other components such as buttons. It may also contain other panels that are used to group its components.

A container has an associated object called a `LayoutManager` that determines where the individual components will be displayed. In this chapter, we do not explicitly specify a `LayoutManager`, so the default is used; Chapter 10 will introduce other `LayoutManagers`. The `FlowLayout` manager is the default for applets. It displays components in a left-to-right, top-to-bottom order.

By grouping components within panels you tell the layout manager to keep them together. Figure 9.10 shows the *containment hierarchy* for the applet from Figure 9.9. As shown, the text field and its label are in a panel. The three buttons are also clustered within a panel. In Fig. 9.10, the panels have white backgrounds to highlight them for you. A panel can also be invisible to the user and act merely as a device to cluster other components.

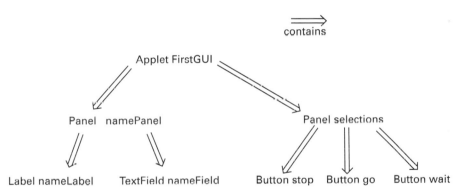

Figure 9.10 The containment hierarchy for Figure 9.9

Containers may recursively contain other containers. For example, a panel in a window may contain other panels that contain other panels. Just as the browser mediates the execution of the applet, a container mediates the behavior of its components. You will see examples of this in the remainder of this chapter and in the next.

Creating a Containment Hierarchy

The following procedure can be used to construct a containment hierarchy of components for any panel, including an applet. Remember that panels may be nested within other panels.

1. For each component in the panel (for example, a `Panel`, a `Button`, a `TextField`), create an object of the proper type.

2. For each object created in step 1 that is a panel, repeat this procedure (steps 1–3) for the components that will be contained in this subpanel.

3. Add all the components created in step 1 to the panel.

Figure 9.11 shows how this procedure was used to construct the display shown in Figure 9.9. Given your knowledge of objects you should be able to read this code without knowing the details of the components themselves.

`FirstGUI` extends `Applet`. It will inherit all the functionality of the `Applet` class. In this example, the `Applet` method `init` is overridden by `FirstGUI`'s `init`, which follows the procedure above to construct the containment hierarchy. Notice that the procedure is recursive because it applies to the applet as well as to the panels within the applet.

Typically, when you construct the containment hierarchy for an applet you will create all of its components in the `init` method regardless of whether they reside directly in the applet or in one of the subpanels. Be aware that any component referenced outside `init` must be declared as a data field rather than as a variable within `init`. You will see examples of this declaration in the next section.

Every container (such as a panel or applet) has an `add` method through which you add components. You must take care to place each component in the proper panel before you add that panel to its parent component. Layout managers rely on this order to determine how much space to allocate for the panel and its components as well as to determine the position of each component within a panel.

```
/*    File: FirstGUI.java
      Developed for Problem Solving with Java, Koffman & Wolz
      Appears in Figure 9.11
*/
import java.awt.*;
import java.applet.Applet;

public class FirstGUI extends Applet {

    public void init() {
        /* ******** Construct the name panel ******** */
        // Create the name panel, set background to white for visibility.
        Panel namePanel = new Panel();
        namePanel.setBackground(Color.white);

        // Create each component of the name panel
        //    and add it to the name panel.
        Label nameLabel = new Label("Name:");
        namePanel.add(nameLabel);
```

Figure 9.11 *continued*

Figure 9.11 *continued*

```
        TextField nameField = new TextField("Snow white",30);
        namePanel.add(nameField);

        // Add the name panel to the applet.
        add(namePanel);

        /* ******** Construct the selections panel ******** */
        // Create selections panel, set background to blue.
        Panel selections = new Panel();
        selections.setBackground(Color.blue);

        // Create each component of the name panel and
        //  add it to the selections panel.
        Button stop = new Button("STOP");
        selections.add(stop);

        Button go = new Button("GO");
        selections.add(go);

        Button wait = new Button("WAIT");
        selections.add(wait);

        // Add the selections panel to the applet.
        add(selections);
    }
} // class FirstGUI
```

Figure 9.11 A first applet that displays some GUI devices

Recall that the applet context (such as a browser) creates or instantiates the applet. This example does not allow the user to do anything yet. It merely assembles the GUI components of the applet. The construction must occur within the `init` method so that when the applet's `start` and `paint` methods are invoked, the components will be visible. Note that you may define a separate method to construct the component hierarchy, but you must call this method from within `init`.

Each component must first be instantiated before it is added to the panel in which it is contained. The simple components `Button`, `Label`, and `TextField` have constructors that take a string as an argument. This string is the text that will appear in the component (see Fig. 9.11). The `TextField` constructor may take a second argument; an integer that specifies how long (in characters) the text field should be. Appendix D summarizes the component classes including useful methods and constructors. Table 9.2 provides a summary of the component classes introduced in this section.

Table 9.2 Summary of classes in FirstGUI

Class	Parent class	Important methods	Purpose
Applet	Panel	init	init is used to construct component hierarchy here.
Panel	Container		Panels are used to contain other components, including other panels.
Container	Component	add	add is used to add components to this container.
Component	Object		All GUI objects rely on Components.
Button	Component	Button(String)	Buttons are user input devices; the constructor creates a button with String as its label.
Label	Component	Label(String)	Labels display simple information; the constructor creates a label with the String as its text.
TextField	Component	TextField(String, int)	TextFields are user-input devices; the constructor places the String in a text area of size int characters.

EXERCISES FOR SECTION 9.2

Self-Check

1. List the four methods of Applet called by the applet context and explain what they do.
2. What is a containment hierarchy?
3. List the steps in creating a containment hierarchy.

Programming

1. Modify the FirstGUI applet so that the panels are created in a method other than init.
2. Design a GUI interface that contains two text fields and three buttons. The text fields appear above and below a panel that contains the three buttons. The buttons are marked as red light, yellow light, blue light.

9.3 The Basic Interactive Applet

The previous section showed how to build up a container with components. This section shows you how to make those components respond to user-generated events. This is a wonderful example of how objects communicate with each other. It would be wasteful of CPU processing time to stop and wait for user input. Instead, modern computing is based on an **event model** in which processes are defined that respond to user events such as mouse

event model: a way to implement user interactivity based on events generated by the user.

clicks, button presses, or keystrokes. In this text we are only interested in events generated by a user. Each of these events is represented in Java by a class that extends the `AWTEvent` class.

The way events are handled in a programming language constitutes the event model for that language. Java 1.1 uses the model of event generators and event listeners. An **event generator** is an object that initiates an event. All GUI components are event generators. For example, a button has a visual representation on the screen. When a mouse click occurs within the area of the button, some action should take place in a program. The button therefore generates an "action event." An **event listener** is an object that listens for, and then responds to events of a particular type. For example, an applet will typically respond to events generated by its buttons. Note that an event listener need not be a component. For example, an applet could delegate its listening responsibilities to some other object.

event generator:
an object that initiates an event.

event listener:
an object that reacts to a specific event.

Registering as an Event Listener

The generator and listener must know about each other in order to establish their relationship. Usually, the listener creates the generator and can refer to it. Less often, an object will create both the listener and the generator. The event generator needs to know who is listening for the events it generates. In Java 1.1, all event generators have methods through which objects can register as listeners for the generator's events.

For example, an applet (the event listener) creates a button (the event generator). The applet can refer to the button through a variable. The applet then calls an add listener method of the button to register that the applet wants to listen for the button's events.

EXAMPLE 9.1

The following `init` method shows how an event listener registers with an event generator. The object that will do the listening is passed to the event generator as an argument. In English, the statement in color in the following code can be read as "tell the object `aButton` to add this object (the applet) as a listener for action events." Chapter 10 will describe the add listener methods for other components in the Java AWT.

```
public void init() {
    // Create the button.
        Button aButton = new Button();
        add(button);

    // Tell the button that this object (the applet)
    //   will be a listener for the button's
    //   action events.
        aButton.addActionListener(this);
}
```

The `EventListener` Interface

An event generator informs a listener of an event by sending the listener a message. In object-oriented languages such as Java, messages are sent by calling a method of the recipient of the message. In Example 9.1 the listener (the applet) sent a message to the generator (aButton). Therefore, the listener must have a standard method through which the generator (for example, aButton) can inform the listener of an event.

This is where Java interfaces come into play. For an object to behave as a listener, it must follow certain protocols. The Java compiler can guarantee that those protocols are being followed if the listener is of the proper type. Since most classes (such as applets) already extend some other class, the `EventListener` type is an interface rather than a class.

An add listener method such as `addActionListener` expects its argument to be of type `ActionListener`. Otherwise, it will not compile. This guarantees that only proper listeners can process events. For each type of `AWTEvent` there is a corresponding `EventListener` interface. Recall that interfaces may declare abstract methods. In order to be instantiated, a class that implements the interface must define method bodies for each abstract method. The methods of an event listener are used by event generators to inform the listener of an event. The compiler can therefore guarantee that the generator will have a method through which to communicate with the listener. The listener (such as an applet) will not compile unless it has defined the abstract methods of its event listener interface.

EXAMPLE 9.2

Figure 9.12 shows how an applet establishes communication with a button. The class `SimplestEvent` extends `Applet` and implements the interface `ActionListener`. It creates a button and registers itself (`this`) as the listener for action events from the button. `SimplestEvent` defines the body of the method `actionPerformed`, which is an abstract method of the `ActionListener` interface. The action performed is to display the message "Button clicked" as a label in the applet. The text of a label can be changed through the label's `setText` method. Other methods for the `Label` class can be found in Appendix D.

Notice that the label `aLabel` is declared as a data field rather than a variable in `init`. This is because both `init` and `actionPerformed` must reference it.

```
/*    File: SimplestEvent.java
      Developed for Problem Solving with Java,
        Koffman & Wolz
      Appears in Figure 9.12
*/
```

Figure 9.12 *continued*

Figure 9.12 *continued*

```
// The following must be imported for events to work
//   properly in Java.
import java.applet.Applet;
import java.awt.*;
import java.awt.event.*;

public class SimplestEvent extends Applet
                           implements ActionListener {
  // Label declared as a data field so it can be
  //  referenced in actionPerformed.
  Label aLabel = new Label("Button not clicked");

  public void init() {
        // Add components to Applet.
        Button aButton = new Button("Click Me");
        add(aButton);
        add(aLabel);

        // Register SimplestEvent as listener of aButton
        aButton.addActionListener(this);
  }

  public void actionPerformed(ActionEvent e) {
        aLabel.setText("Button clicked");
  }
} // class SimplestEvent
```

Figure 9.12 A very simple interactive Applet

When this applet is instantiated within an applet context, its `init` method will add a button and a label to the applet. The applet will be registered as a listener for events generated by the button. That's where the activity stops.

The operating system may do other things until the user moves the mouse over the button and clicks the mouse. The operating system then calls the button. The button creates an event object and uses the `actionPerformed` method to pass the event to the applet. The applet changes the message on the label from "Button not clicked" to "Button clicked" and the activity stops. If the user clicks on the button again, the button will create another event and call the applet. The applet will again set the text of the label, but the user will not notice a change. The applet and its button will continue in this cycle until the user quits the applet context.

The Steps in Designing a GUI Interface

You cannot start at one place in the applet definition and trace your way through all the steps. You must understand the processes working in the background in order to follow the flow of execution. This can be disconcerting for programmers, especially for those with experience in languages that are not object-oriented. However, this is a perfect example of programming for the task at hand. The `init` method sets things up. That's all it does. The `actionPerformed` method defines what should happen when an event occurs. That is all it does, too. These parts interact through an established protocol based on event listeners and event generators. In GUI and network programming, such background processes based on protocols are key to managing complicated tasks.

This situation raises some important issues from a design standpoint. Good design requires knowing how to organize an implementation so that all of the parts communicate properly. Designing a GUI interface involves the following steps:

1. Create the GUI components (as illustrated in Section 9.2).

2. Identify the input components that will act as event generators. Register event listeners for each.

3. Each event listener must define the abstract methods through which the generator will communicate its events. These are **event-handling methods**.

4. Check that you've identified all the input components by identifying the others as output components. These should only be accessed in event-handling methods.

event-handling method: a method that executes steps that handle or respond to an event. The abstract method of an event listener is a kind of event-handling method.

Two case studies illustrate the relationship between the design process and the implementation. The first shows you how to organize the process flow for a very simple applet that simply changes the color of a button when the button is clicked.

Case Study

Click Me

PROBLEM

In an applet display a green button that says "Click Me." When the button is clicked, change its color to red and change the text of the button to count the number of clicks. Every time the button is pressed, change its color, switching between red and green. The applet quits when the applet context quits.

ANALYSIS

The problem statement tells us that we will need to extend the `Applet` class. This problem has two parts: a GUI and an underlying process.

The underlying process is very simple. Every time the button is pressed the background color is changed and the button is given a new label that reports the number of clicks so far. We need a data field to keep track of the number of clicks.

The GUI can be developed using the steps described above. First, we identify the GUI objects. In this case there is only one button. It is both an input and an output device.

We know how to change the text of a button from Example 9.2 One problem we anticipate is that the label on the button after a click could be longer (contain more characters) than the initial button. If the button is initially sized by the layout manager based on the shorter string, the new label may not appear properly. The layout decisions may be invalid for the button. To fix this, we must mark the button as invalid and have the applet's layout manager make it valid again.

To change the color of the button we can use inherited methods from the `Component` class. The method `setBackground` takes a color as an argument and sets the component's background to that color. The method `getBackground` retrieves the current color of a component. Each time the button is clicked we retrieve the background color and set it to the other value.

These methods of the `Component` class are summarized here:

Method	Purpose
`void invalidate()`	Marks the component as invalid; that is, its layout may not be correct.
`void validate()`	Applies the layout manager to itself and any of its components. The size, shape, and position of components is recalculated.
`void setBackground(Color)`	Sets the color of the component to the color specified.
`Color getBackground()`	Retrieves the current background color of the component.

Because the button is also an input device, we will need to register a listener for its action. The applet will be the listener and must therefore implement the interface `ActionListener` and define the method `actionPerformed`.

Finally, as part of the analysis we should outline the major parts of the applet:

1. `init`—The applet must create the button and register as a listener for button actions.

2. `actionPerformed`—The method updates the color and label of the button.

DESIGN

The class specification follows:

Specification for `ClickMe` *class*

Data Fields

`Button aButton`—the button that will be pressed, declared as a data field because it is used in both methods of the class

`int clickCount`—initially 0

Methods

`init`—constructs the button, registers the action listener

`actionPerformed`—updates text and color of button

Next, we list the algorithms for the methods.

Algorithm for `init`

1. Construct the component hierarchy (see Section 9.2)

   1.1. Create an instance of a button. The button will be declared as a data field because it is referenced in `actionPerformed`.

   1.2. Add the button to the applet.

2. Establish that the applet will listen for action events from the button.

Algorithm for `actionPerformed`

1. If the current color is red, set it to green; otherwise set it to red.
2. Increment `clickCount`.
3. Change the label on the button.
4. Declare that the button has an invalid layout.
5. Have the applet validate the button.

IMPLEMENTATION

Figure 9.13 shows the implementation for the `ClickMe` class.

```
/*    File: ClickMe.java
      Developed for Problem Solving with Java, Koffman & Wolz
      Appears in Figure 9.13
*/

import java.applet.Applet;
import java.awt.*;
import java.awt.event.*;

public class ClickMe extends Applet implements ActionListener {

   private Button aButton = new Button("Click me");
   private int clickCount = 0;

   public void init() {
      // Add aButton to the Applet.
      aButton.setBackground(Color.green);
      add(aButton);
      // Register ClickMe as a listener for aButton
      aButton.addActionListener(this);
   }


   public void actionPerformed(ActionEvent e) {
      // Change color after each press.
      if (aButton.getBackground() == Color.red)
        aButton.setBackground(Color.green);
      else
        aButton.setBackground(Color.red);

      clickCount++;
      aButton.setLabel("Click count: " + clickCount);

      // Declare that the button layout is no longer valid.
      aButton.invalidate();
      // Have the applet validate the layout.
      validate();
   }
} // class ClickMe
```

Figure 9.13 Implementation of the ClickMe class

TESTING

Testing requires constructing an HTML file that can be loaded from an applet context. Construction of the HTML is left as an exercise. The button should be pressed at least twice to ensure that text and color change properly. Figure 9.14 shows a sequence of displays that result when the button is pressed.

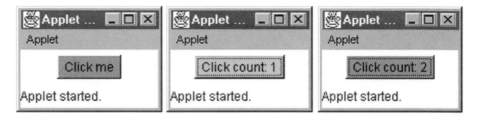

Figure 9.14 Example run of ClickMe

An important idea in this case study is using the applet's data fields to keep track of the state of the button. Since both methods of the ClickMe class can refer to these variables, the tasks associated with initializing the applet can be separated from those that occur after the button is clicked. Note that the applet had to store the click count, but not the color. Since the color was stored in the button itself, the applet could use methods to retrieve and change that value.

A second case study expands on the techniques just shown. Both the GUI layout and the event handler are more complicated. This case study illustrates how animation is achieved. By pressing a button, the user toggles between two drawings, causing a face to change from a smile to a frown and back again.

Case Study

User-controlled Animation

PROBLEM

Create an applet that displays a "smiley face" and that has two buttons. One button causes the face to smile, the other causes the face to frown.

ANALYSIS

The analysis of this problem proceeds in a manner similar to the previous case study. Once the idea of the underlying process is sketched, analysis switches to the GUI, and then back to the underlying process.

The underlying process is a graphic display. A `paint` method draws the face. It needs a way to distinguish between the happy and sad face. A `face` data field can signify whether a happy or sad face should be drawn. The `paint` method then must set a color, draw the eyes, and then draw the mouth based on the data field. The question, though, is: Who does the painting?

Analysis of the GUI helps determine what object should be responsible for painting. The applet will include two buttons that should be clustered together in a panel. If we draw the face directly on the applet, there is no guarantee that the buttons won't cover part of the face. To prevent this from happening, we will introduce another Java component, class `Canvas`, which is a component used for drawing pictures. We can draw the face on a `Canvas` object. The layout manager sets the size and position of the `Canvas` object. The containment hierarchy is shown in Figure 9.15.

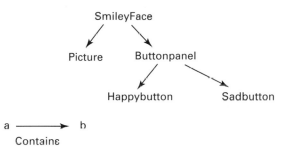

Figure 9.15 Containment hierarchy for the smiley face

The canvas is an output device.[1] In Section 4.6, you drew directly on the applet container using a graphics context (the class `Graphics`) within a `paint` method. To draw on a canvas you must extend the `Canvas` class and override the `paint` method. Unlike a button, a canvas must be given an explicit initial size. The `Component` method `setSize(int width, int height)` specifies the size of a component in pixels. Every time a button is pressed, the canvas will be redrawn. We will therefore need to invoke the `repaint` method on the canvas.

The buttons are input devices. The applet must therefore be a listener for action events. Its event-handler method will need to distinguish between the buttons. The event object that is passed to an event listener by a generator contains a data field that identifies the source of the event. This data field is accessed through the event's `getSource` method. The underlying process therefore determines which button has been pressed and repaints the canvas accordingly.

---

[1] The Java 1.1.2 release recommends that "lightweight components" replace `Canvas` as well as some uses of `Panel`. We chose to continue using these classes because of their simplicity compared to lightweight components. We also found that lightweight components did not yet behave reliably in some Java systems.

We identify two classes:

1. the applet—`SmileyFace`
2. the canvas—`FaceCanvas`

DESIGN

The class specification for the applet is as follows:

Specification for `SmileyFace` *class*

Data Fields

`Button happyButton, sadButton`—both are input devices and are used in both methods

Methods

`init`—constructs GUI components and registers the applet as a listener to both buttons

`actionPerformed`—updates the picture based on the button that was pressed

Specification for `FaceCanvas` *class*

Data Fields

`Boolean happyFace`—initially `true`, determines whether the face will be happy or sad

Methods

a constructor—creates an instance of the class, sets background color to blue, sets `happyFace` initially to `true`

`setHappyFace`—sets `happyFace` to `true`
`setSadFace`—sets `happyFace` to `false`
`paint`—draws the face depending on the face data field

Next, we list the algorithms for the methods.

Algorithm for `init`

We follow the steps from Section 9.2 for constructing the components of the applet.

1. For the `FaceCanvas`:
   1.1. Instantiate the `FaceCanvas` object picture.
   1.2. Add the picture to the applet.
2. For the `Button` panel:
   2.1. Create the button panel.

2.2. Create an instance of each button. The buttons will be declared as data fields because they are referenced in `actionPerformed`. Add each button to the button panel.

2.3. Add the button panel to the applet.

3. Establish that the applet will listen for action events from both buttons.

Algorithm for `actionPerformed`

1. If the source of the event was the `happyButton`, then set the picture's `happyFace` data field to `true`; otherwise, set the `happyFace` data field to `false`.

2. Repaint the picture.

Algorithm for `FaceCanvas` Constructor

1. Set background color to blue.

2. Set `happyFace` data field to `true`.

3. Set the size of the canvas.

Algorithm for `setHappyFace`

1. Set the `happyFace` data field to `true`.

Algorithm for `setSadFace`

1. Set the `happyFace` data field to `false`.

Algorithm for `paint`

1. Set the drawing color to red.

2. Draw the eyes.

3. If `happyFace` is `true`, draw the happy mouth; otherwise, draw the sad mouth.

Ovals can be used to draw the eyes. The mouths can be drawn with arcs.

IMPLEMENTATION

Figures 9.16 and 9.17 show the implementations. Notice the inclusion of two methods in `FaceCanvas`: `happy` and `sad`. These methods receive the graphics context from the `paint` method and then use the context to draw their respective arcs. This technique illustrates how you can pass support objects between other objects. The graphics context is given to `paint`, which in turn gives it to `happy` or `sad`.

```
/*    File: SmileyFace.java
      Developed for Problem Solving with Java, Koffman & Wolz
      Appears in Figure 9.16
*/
import java.awt.*;
import java.applet.Applet;
import java.awt.event.*;

public class SmileyFace extends Applet implements ActionListener {

  // Declared as data fields because they are used in both methods.
  private Button sadButton = new Button("Frown");
  private Button happyButton = new Button("Happy");
  private FaceCanvas picture = new FaceCanvas();

  public void init() {
    add(picture);

    Panel buttonPanel = new Panel();
    buttonPanel.add(happyButton);
    buttonPanel.add(sadButton);
    add(buttonPanel);

    happyButton.addActionListener(this);
    sadButton.addActionListener(this);
  }

  public void actionPerformed(ActionEvent e) {
    if (e.getSource() == happyButton)
      picture.setHappyFace();
    else if (e.getSource() == sadButton)
      picture.setSadFace();
    picture.repaint();
  }
} // class SmileyFace
```

Figure 9.16 Implementation of the SmileyFace class

```
/*    File: FaceCanvas.java
      Developed for Problem Solving with Java, Koffman & Wolz
      Appears in Figure 9.17
*/
// Only need awt, not other imports because there is no applet or
//    event here.
import java.awt.*;

public class FaceCanvas extends Canvas {
   private boolean happyFace;

   public FaceCanvas() {
      setBackground(Color.blue);
      happyFace = true;
      setSize(130, 130);
   }

   public void setHappyFace() {
      happyFace = true;
   }

   public void setSadFace() {
      happyFace = false;
   }

   public void paint(Graphics g) {
      g.setColor(Color.red);
      g.fillOval(10, 10, 30, 30);   // left eye
      g.fillOval(80, 10, 30, 30);   // right eye
      // Draw smile or frown.
      if (happyFace)
         happy(g);
      else
         sad(g);
   }

   public void sad(Graphics g) {
      g.drawArc(20, 60, 60, 30, 0, 180);
   }

   public void happy(Graphics g) {
      g.drawArc(20, 60, 60, 30, 180, 180);
   }
} // class FaceCanvas
```

Figure 9.17 Implementation of the FaceCanvas class

TESTING

Testing requires constructing an HTML and alternating button presses. Each button should also be pressed a few times repeatedly just to see what happens. Figure 9.18 shows a sequence of displays that result when the code is executed.

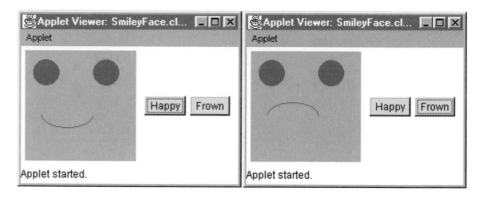

Figure 9.18 Example run of `SmileyFace`

EXERCISES FOR SECTION 9.3

Self-Check

1. What is an event generator? What is an event listener?
2. How is an event listener created?
3. If `aText` is an instance of the class `TextField`, what does the following statement do within a method in an applet:

   `aText.addEventListener(this);`
4. In an `actionPerformed` method, with argument `ActionEvent e`, what does `e.getSource()` return?

Programming

1. Modify `SmileyFace` so that the face appears within an oval rather than merely within the canvas.
2. Add a button to `SmileyFace` that shows a face that is neither happy nor sad.
3. Add to the picture eyebrows that change depending on which button is pressed.

9.4 Introduction to Threads

The animation in the previous section was controlled by the user. This section shows how a process can control animation. One simple technique involves writing a loop that repeatedly displays a sequence of pictures. One problem with this method is how to control the timing. If the transition between pictures is too rapid or too slow, you will not get the desired effect. A second problem is that the computer processor is tied up executing the loop, so it can't do anything else.

In Java, threads allow the programmer to control timing without involving the processor. Threads also enable a single processor to perform multiple processes. A **thread** is an independent sequence of steps in a program. The processor can appear to execute several different tasks simultaneously by executing one thread for a while, switching over to another thread, returning back to the first thread, and so on. We see how this is done in the next section.

thread:
an independent sequence of steps in a program.

The Thread Model

Most of the problems you have encountered so far in this text have focused on a single task at a time. But what if you wanted to do two or more things simultaneously? For example, while a user is entering information on a purchase you might want to look up her credit rating in a database. Without threads you would have to carefully orchestrate the timing so that the user would not perceive a delay as your program called the database access method.

Threads give the illusion that a number of activities are happening simultaneously. In truth, a process in the background takes responsibility for determining which thread is currently being processed by the CPU. Recall that the CPU can process statements significantly faster than the human eye can perceive.

The illusion that more than one activity is happening is a real advantage for the programmer. Each thread can be defined as if it were an isolated process. Before threads were invented, the programmer had to carefully orchestrate the sequence of steps. For example, integrating sound and animation was very difficult. A picture would be displayed, then a fragment of sound, then another picture. Timing was everything.

The Class Thread

In Java, the class `Thread` supports the illusion of simultaneous activities. Just like any other class, you can extend the `Thread` class and then instantiate the object. More significantly, after you have defined the process, you can create any number of instantiations.

EXAMPLE 9.3

A simple thread is created by extending the Thread class and overriding the run() method. Figure 9.19 defines two threads. AppleThread simply prints the message "Apple" 10 times. The thread OrangeThread prints the message "Orange" five times. The class DemoThread1 acts as a thread manager; it creates an instance of each thread and then starts each one.

```java
/*    File: AppleThread.java
      Developed for Problem Solving with Java,
        Koffman & Wolz
      Appears in Figure 9.19
*/
public class AppleThread extends Thread {
   public void run() {
      for (int i = 0; i < 10; i++)
         System.out.println("Apple" + i);
   }
} // class AppleThread
```

```java
/*    File: OrangeThread.java
      Developed for Problem Solving with Java,
        Koffman & Wolz
      Appears in Figure 9.19
*/
public class OrangeThread extends Thread {
   public void run() {
      for (int i = 0; i < 5; i++)
         System.out.println("Orange" + i);
   }
} // class OrangeThread
```

```java
/*    File: DemoThreads1.java
      Developed for Problem Solving with Java,
        Koffman & Wolz
      Appears in Figure 9.19
*/
```

Figure 9.19 *continued*

Figure 9.19 *continued*

```
public class DemoThreads1 {
   public static void main(String[] args) {
      AppleThread apple = new AppleThread();
      OrangeThread orange = new OrangeThread();
      apple.start();
      orange.start();
   }
} // class DemoThreads1
```

Figure 9.19 Two thread classes and a thread manager

When you run the `DemoThreads1` class you will see oranges and apples intermixed. Here is an example of what you might see:

```
Apple0
Apple1
Orange0
Orange1
Apple2
Orange2
Orange3
Orange4
Apple3
Apple4
Apple5
. . .
```

Depending on your operating system, you will see a variety of sequences. This illustrates that the processes are in fact not occurring simultaneously. The operating system determines when each thread should yield the CPU and when it should continue processing and, in this simple example, print its message.

Yielding the CPU Java provides a number of sophisticated mechanisms for allowing threads to interact. At the simplest level you can force threads to take turns by using the `yield` method. The `Thread` class contains a method called `yield`, which is called by the thread when it is willing to give up the CPU. Java contains a rich set of methods for controlling and synchronizing threads. These are listed in Appendix C.

EXAMPLE 9.4

This example shows how `yield` can be used. It also shows how a single definition can be used to spawn multiple threads. Figure 9.20 shows the `FruitThread` class that takes both the name and the number of times to execute as arguments to the class constructor. The loop includes a call for the thread to yield. The `DemoThread2` class creates two instantiations of this thread, one prints "`Apple`" 10 times, one prints "`Orange`" 10 times.

```
/*    File: FruitThread.java
      Developed for Problem Solving with Java,
        Koffman & Wolz
      Appears in Figure 9.20
*/
public class FruitThread extends Thread {

  private String fruit = "Fruit";
  private int times = 0;

  public FruitThread(String name, int execution) {
    fruit = name;
    times = execution;
  }

  public void run() {
      for (int i = 0; i < times; i++) {
          System.out.println(fruit + i);
          yield();
      }
  }
} // class FruitThread
```

```
/*    File: DemoThreads2.java
      Developed for Problem Solving with Java,
        Koffman & Wolz
      Appears in Figure 9.20
*/
public class DemoThreads2 {
  public static void main(String[] args) {
    FruitThread apple = new FruitThread("Apple", 10);
    FruitThread orange = new FruitThread("Orange", 10);
    apple.start();
    orange.start();
  }
} // class DemoThreads2
```

Figure 9.20 A single thread definition run as two independent threads

Because each thread yields, the messages alternate exactly if nothing else is happening on the computer. For example, if you run this applet on a desktop computer and don't do anything else, you will get the following display. However, if you even touch the mouse, you may cause other processes outside your program to take over the CPU and the perfectly alternating sequencing will not occur. The purpose of `yield` is to allow your process to pause. The method does not guarantee perfect synchrony. To accomplish that requires more sophisticated techniques beyond our scope.

```
Apple0
Orange0
Apple1
Orange1
Apple2
Orange2
Apple3
Orange3
Apple4
Orange4
Apple5
Orange5
Apple6
Orange6
Apple7
Orange7
Apple8
Orange8
Apple9
Orange9
```

Putting a thread to sleep   Another way to get a thread to yield the CPU is to put it to sleep, or to suspend its execution. You can do this by using a method call such as `sleep(sleepTime)`, where the argument `sleepTime` is the time to sleep measured in milliseconds. Note that the sleep time you specify is a minimum. For a variety of reasons, the operating system may decide not to resume the process right away.

EXAMPLE 9.5

This example shows a minor modification to Example 9.4. Instead of yielding, each thread sleeps for a specified amount of time. Sleep is measured in milliseconds. (See Appendix C for shorter periods of sleep.) The class `ThreadDemo3` (Fig. 9.21) starts up the two threads. Apples sleep for one second, oranges sleep for two. After an initial unsteady state, apples print approximately twice for every time an orange prints.

A sleeping process can be awakened by another process through an exception. The mechanics of this action are beyond the scope of this book. However, the compiler requires that any method, such as `run`, that contains a call to `sleep` must either throw the exception or handle it. In the following code, the exception is caught, but nothing is done with it. In more sophisticated solutions you should think through carefully what should happen if a sleeping thread is awakened prematurely. In this example, it is of no consequence.

```java
/*   File: FruitThread.java
     Developed for Problem Solving with Java,
       Koffman & Wolz
     Appears in Figure 9.21
*/
public class FruitThread extends Thread {

   private String fruit = "Fruit";
   private int times = 0;
   private int snooze = 1;

   public FruitThread(String name, int execution,
                        int sleepTime) {
      fruit = name;
      times = execution;
      snooze = sleepTime;
   }

   public void run() {
      for (int i = 0; i < times; i++) {
         System.out.println(fruit + i);
         try {sleep(snooze*1000);
         // do nothing if some exception
         //   managed to get through.
         } catch(InterruptedException e)  {}
      }
   }
} // class FruitThread
```

```java
/*   File: DemoThread3.java
     Developed for Problem Solving with Java,
       Koffman & Wolz
     Appears in Figure 9.21
*/
```

Figure 9.21 *continued*

Figure 9.21 *continued*

```
public class DemoThreads3 {
   public static void main(String[] args) {
      FruitThread apple = new FruitThread("Apple",
                                          20, 1);

      FruitThread orange = new FruitThread("Orange",
                                           20, 2);

      apple.start();
      orange.start();
   }
} // DemoThreads3
```

Figure 9.21 A sleeping thread

If you execute the `ThreadDemo3` class you will also notice that the printing hesitates. You can actually see this happen because the delay (at least one or two seconds) is long enough for the human eye to detect!

The `Runnable` Interface

Sometimes you need to extend a class and create a thread, too. Java provides a solution through the `Runnable` interface. This is an alternative way of creating a thread. The interface is a practical example of how objects can interact. It illustrates how interfaces, object instantiations, class methods, and objects as arguments can be used to solve a problem.

EXAMPLE 9.6

The idea is that you instantiate an object that implements the `Runnable` interface. The interface contains one abstract method `run` that you must define in your class. Figure 9.20 is rewritten here in Fig. 9.22 with a `Runnable` interface. The differences are shown in color.

```
/*   File: FruitThread.java
     Developed for Problem Solving with Java,
       Koffman & Wolz
     Appears in Figure 9.22
*/
public class FruitThread implements Runnable {

   private String fruit = "Fruit";
   private int times = 0;
```

Figure 9.22 *continued*

Figure 9.22 *continued*

```
  public FruitThread(String name, int execution) {
    fruit = name;
    times = execution;
  }


  public void run() {
    for (int i = 0; i < times; i++) {
      System.out.println(fruit + i);
      // Yield is static and can be called
      //   through the class name.
      // It is applied to the currently running thread.
      Thread.yield();
    }
  }
} // class FruitThread
```

```
/*   File: DemoThreads4.java
     Developed for Problem Solving with Java,
       Koffman & Wolz
     Appears in Figure 9.22
*/
public class DemoThreads4 {
  public static void main(String[] args) {
    Thread apple = new Thread(
                        new FruitThread("Apple", 10));
    Thread orange = new Thread(
                        new FruitThread("Orange", 10));
    apple.start();
    orange.start();
  }
} // class DemoThreads4
```

Figure 9.22 A thread implemented through the Runnable interface

There are three major differences. First, the FruitThread class does not need to extend Thread, so it could extend some other class. Second, because yield is a static method, we use the method call Thread.yield(). Third, the FruitThread object is passed as an argument to the Thread constructor. The two threads that are created will use the run method from the instances of the FruitThread class that were created.

Program Style: *Function Composition Versus Variable Reference*
The instantiations of the thread objects in Figure 9.22 use a technique called *function composition*. The result of one method is given as an argument to another. The newly instantiated `FruitThread` object is given as an argument to the `Thread` constructor. The `FruitThread` instance is not bound to any variable. There is no way to reference it further. Since we never need to reference it again, this is a very elegant way of instantiating it. Granted, you could write the statement:

```
Thread apple = new Thread(new FruitThread("Apple", 10));
```

as

```
FruitThread ft = new FruitThread("Apple", 10);
Thread apple = new Thread(ft);
```

but this is just an indirect way of saying the same thing. Because it involves less typing, and does not reference a variable, function composition is also less likely to introduce syntax errors.

EXERCISES FOR SECTION 9.4

Self-Check

1. What is a thread?
2. Explain the difference between subclassing the class `Thread` and implementing the `Runnable` interface.
3. What is the difference between yielding and sleeping in a thread?
4. Which method of the `Thread` class starts the thread? Which method do you override when you extend the thread class to define the thread process?

Programming

1. Write a program that starts a thread as a result of clicking a "start" button. Have the thread increment a counter that is displayed in a label. Clicking a "stop" button should stop the thread.
2. Extend your solution to Programming Problem 1 by allowing two threads to run simultaneously, each based on its own "start" and "stop" button.

9.5 Threaded Animation (Optional)

We now have all of the pieces to show you how to do animation in a multi-processing environment. The big difference between this kind of animation and animated GIFs and other HTML-based techniques is that the user can control threaded animation.

Case Study

Two Animated Balls

PROBLEM

Within an applet, display two balls. Each ball cycles through the colors red, green, and blue. One ball changes color every second, the other every five seconds. A button starts and stops the animation.

ANALYSIS

Once again we separate the GUI from the underlying process. An applet will include two GUI components: a button and a canvas. The button is an input device, the canvas an output device.

The underlying process is best accomplished with an object that extends `Thread`. When the button is pressed (handled by method `actionPerformed`), we determine whether the button is marked "start" or "stop." If the button is currently marked "start," both balls are created, the animation is started, and the button is changed to "stop." If the button is currently marked "stop," the animation is stopped, both balls are erased, and the button is changed to "start."

The balls themselves are best implemented as threads. In the previous section the `start` method was used to begin a thread. Threads can be stopped with the `stop` method.

The animation is accomplished within the `run` method of the thread. Drawing the balls requires changing the graphics color, then drawing an oval at the proper spot. A ball cycles through the three colors at the rate prescribed for each individual ball. The colors are stored in an array.

DESIGN

There will be two classes defined: `BlinkingBalls` is the applet that starts and stops the animation based on the button press. Class `Ball` extends `Thread` and implements the animation. The class specifications follow:

Specification for `BlinkingBalls` *class*

Data Fields

`Canvas display`—the canvas upon which the animation will take place

`Button startStop`—the button (input device)

`Ball fastBall`—the ball at position 50, 50, delaying 1 second

`Ball slowBall`—the ball at position 200, 50, delaying 5 seconds

Methods

`init`—adds the button and the canvas, gives a size to the canvas, registers the action listener

`actionPerformed`—controls the animation

Specification for `Ball` *class*

Data Fields

`Graphics g`—the graphics context for the canvas
(argument of the constructor)
`int x, y`—the position of the ball on the canvas
(argument of the constructor)
`int speed`—the rate, in seconds at which the ball changes color
(argument of the constructor)
`Color[] colors`—array of colors,
defined as {`Color.red, Color.green, Color.blue`}
`nextColor`—used as the array index, initially 0

Methods

`Ball(Canvas, x, y, speed)`—constructs a thread based on the arguments
`run`—shows a frame, then sleeps the specified amount of time
`drawNextFrame`—draws the next frame

Next, we list the algorithms for the methods.

Algorithm for `init` in `BlinkingBalls`

The steps follow in the usual order:

1. Create instances of the canvas and the button; put the proper label on the button. Add both to the applet.
2. Since the button is an input device, register the applet as a listener for the button's action event.

Algorithm for `actionPerformed` in `BlinkingBalls`

1. `if` the label on the button is "start"
    1.1 Instantiate and start the "fastball."
    1.2 Instantiate and start the "slowball."
    1.3 Change the label on the button.
2. `if` the label is not "Start"
    2.1 Stop the "fastball."
    2.2 Stop the "slowball."
    2.3 Change the label back to "start."
2.4 Repaint the display to erase the previous versions of the balls.

Algorithm for `Ball` constructor in `Ball`

1. Store the values of each of the `Ball` constructor arguments (`canvas, x, y, speed`) in the proper data field.
2. Get the graphics context from the canvas to enable drawing.

Algorithm for `run` in `Ball`

1. Draw the next frame for the first time
2. Loop forever. (The `stop` method will stop the thread!)
   2.1 Sleep for the specified time.
   2.2 Draw the next frame.

Algorithm for `drawNextFrame` in `Ball`

1. Set the color to the next color in the array.
2. Fill an oval at the proper position.
3. Update the color.

IMPLEMENTATION

Figure 9.23 shows the implementation for the `BlinkingBalls` class. Figure 9.24 shows the `Ball` class. In class `Ball`, the statement

```
nextColor = (nextColor + 1) % colors.length;
```

updates the color by incrementing the array index `nextColor`. The remainder division keeps the new value of `nextColor` within the array bounds (from zero to one less than the length of array `colors`).

```
/*    File: BlinkingBalls.java
      Developed for Problem Solving with Java, Koffman & Wolz
      Appears in Figure 9.23
*/
// Need these for buttons, etc.
import java.awt.*;
import java.applet.Applet;
import java.awt.event.*;

public class BlinkingBalls extends Applet
                           implements ActionListener {
   private Canvas display = new Canvas();
   private Button startStop = new Button("Start");
   private Ball fastBall, slowBall;

   public void init() {
     display.setSize(200,100);
     add(display);
     add(startStop);
     setSize(250,200);
```

Figure 9.23 *continued*

Figure 9.23 *continued*

```
      startStop.addActionListener(this);
   } // init()


   public void actionPerformed(ActionEvent e) {
      if (startStop.getLabel() == "Start") {
         fastBall = new Ball(display, 10, 10, 1);
         fastBall.start();

         slowBall = new Ball(display, 100, 10, 5);
         slowBall.start();

         startStop.setLabel("Stop");
      } else {
         fastBall.stop();
         slowBall.stop();

         startStop.setLabel("Start");
         display.repaint();
      }
   } // actionPerformed
} // class BlinkingBalls
```

Figure 9.23 Implementation of the `BlinkingBalls` class

```
/*   File: Ball.java
     Developed for Problem Solving with Java, Koffman & Wolz
     Appears in Figure 9.24
*/
import java.awt.*;

public class Ball extends Thread {
   private Graphics g;
   private int x;
   private int y;
   private int speed;

   private Color[] colors =
      {Color.red, Color.green, Color.blue};
   private int nextColor = 0;

   public Ball(Canvas c, int x, int y, int speed) {
      this.x = x;
      this.y = y;
      this.speed = speed;
      g = c.getGraphics();
   }
```

Figure 9.24 *continued*

Figure 9.24 *continued*

```
public void run() {
  drawNextFrame(); // Draw one initially.
  while (true) {
    try { sleep(speed*1000);
    } catch(InterruptedException e) {}
    drawNextFrame();
  }
}

public void drawNextFrame() {
  g.setColor(colors[nextColor]);
  g.fillOval(x, y, 50, 50);
  nextColor = (nextColor + 1) % colors.length;
}
} // class Ball
```

Figure 9.24 Definition of the Ball class

TESTING

Testing requires constructing an HTML file that can be loaded from an applet context. Construction of the HTML is left as an exercise. The button should be pressed at least twice to ensure that text and color change properly. Figure 9.25 shows an example display. Unfortunately, there is no good way to demonstrate the animated timing in a text. You can find these classes listed at the textbook Web site.

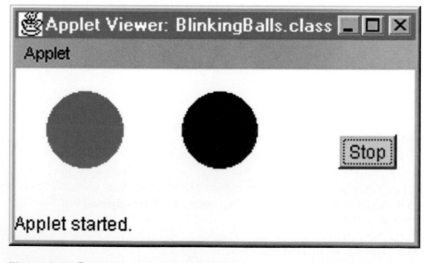

Figure 9.25 Example run of BlinkingBalls

EXERCISES FOR SECTION 9.5

Self-Check

1. What programming technique is being used to cause the balls to "blink"?
2. Explain why the `actionPerformed` method must explicitly stop the balls from blinking.
3. Why must the canvas object be passed to the balls that are created?

Programming

1. Add more balls to the animation.
2. Create a threaded animation in which a figure walks across the screen.
3. Create a "horse race" from two animated figures that walk across the screen. At the start of the race specify a random time for each figure to sleep.

9.6 Browser/Applet Interaction

In the last few sections we lost sight of the purpose behind applets. They are intended to provide a means of localizing program execution for Web sites. This section shows you how to pass information to an applet. The explanation of the reverse operation, in which the applet returns information to a server, is beyond the scope of this book. It requires using a class called `Socket` that establishes communication with a Web server. In order to program the `Socket` class, especially at the server side, you must have developed the skills to be a reliable programmer. Incorrect socket-based programs can impact not only the server, but the entire Web.

The Server Can Request Data from the User

Applets are useful to Web programming because HTML is not a programming language. HTML simply provides the browser with directives that describe where to place information on a page and where to look for potential user input (such as clicking on a hyperlink.) But if you have surfed the Web, you have probably encountered pages that ask for user input through forms. The browser does not process the user input. It bundles the input as variable name/value pairs and sends it off to a program on the server for processing. Figure 9.26 shows a simple HTML form in a browser. Figure 9.27 shows the corresponding HTML file.

Tags tell the browser what type of input devices to display and what to do with the results. The action tag specifies the program at the server side that will process the input. In this example, a text field waits for the user's name. The default name is "Snow White". Users can specify their sex (gender) through radio buttons. Because the two buttons have the same name attribute, the browser knows that only one may be selected. The HTML file shows that the Female button is checked by default. The Reset button tells the browser to reset the input devices to their original values.

The browser does not process the input, but merely ships it back to the server specified in the action tag. When the user selects the Submit button, the browser assembles the results from all the devices into an URL-encoded string that it sends to the server-side program.

Such programs are often referred to as CGI (Common Gateway Interface) scripts. (We introduced the concepts of HTML forms and CGI scripts in Section 9.1.) CGI is a protocol that can be interpreted by the server program. CGI programs are called scripts, and are beyond the scope of this text, although we provide an example of one that you can get through our Web site in Appendix A. You can imagine that the script at the server end takes the variable name/value pairs and processes them much as you processed payroll information in earlier chapters. Scripts often respond to the user by sending an HTML page back to the browser. The script can either send a preconstructed page or construct one dynamically based on user input. For example, search services such as Yahoo and Infoseek respond with dynamic pages built from database entries based on a user's keywords.

Figure 9.26 java92.html displayed in a browser

```
<!--This file created 12/27/97 6:44 PM -->
<HTML>
<HEAD>
    <TITLE>Forms example, Problem Solving with Java, Chapter 9</TITLE>
</HEAD>
<BODY>
<!-- This defines the form.  The action tag specifies the CGI script to run
        on the server. The method POST specifies a format for sending the
        form results. -->
<FORM
  action="http:/www.tcnj.edu/~mink/cgi-bin/pswj"
  method="POST">

<!-- Specifies three input devices, a text field and two radio buttons.
        Because the buttons have the same name, only one may be selected.-->
Name:<INPUT TYPE="text" NAME="name" VALUE="Snow White" SIZE-30>
<P>Sex:<INPUT TYPE="radio" NAME="sex" VALUE="male">Male
        <INPUT TYPE="radio" NAME="sex" VALUE="female" CHECKED>Female</P>

<!-- Every form must have a submit button and should also have a
        reset button. -->
<INPUT TYPE="reset" VALUE="Reset">
<INPUT TYPE="submit" NAME="name" VALUE="Submit">
</FORM>
</BODY>
</HTML>
```

Figure 9.27 The source file for `java92.html`

Real-Time or dynamic interaction   The interaction between the browser and the Web server as shown in Figure 9.1 is dependent upon the speed with which data can be moved on the network. For most situations, where the user sits quietly reading Web pages, data speed is not a problem. However, sometimes the data transfer rate will impact the interaction. At a minimum, a slow rate is annoying to the user. At its worst, it directly impacts the intent of the interaction. Web site designers must think carefully about how to manage the interaction so that users are not frustrated by delays.

The timing of the loop between browser and server can degrade to unacceptable levels for two reasons. First, many people still do not have very fast connections to the Internet. It can take hundreds of times longer for data to be transferred from server to browser than it took for that data to be processed by the server. A second problem is that a single server must process requests from potentially thousands of browsers simultaneously. When the server becomes flooded, each request must wait its turn in a queue, much as people wait in line for bank tellers or for store cashiers. When the service can't handle the load, delays occur.

These problems are particularly thorny for two types of interaction on the Web: animation and data verification. As you've seen in this chapter so far, both of these tasks can be done with applets at the client side. The only question that remains is how can an HTML page give information to an applet.

The Applet Parameter Tag

The applets shown so far do very specific tasks. You can make applets more general through parameter tags (`param` tags) in an HTML file. A Web page designer can use such an applet for a number of specific purposes. For example, an HTML page may allow a user to choose between two different pages. Both pages run the same applet, but with different settings, perhaps one for novices and one for more sophisticated users.

An even more exciting use of parameters can be seen when a server builds the parameter list. For example, a user might specify some preferences to a server via an HTML form. The server constructs a personalized applet for the user based on the form. The page returned to the user contains an applet and parameter settings that are personalized for the user.

The parameters form a protocol between Web pages and the applet they use. The Web page must supply the correct parameters to the applet. Recall that an HTML tag may have other tags embedded within it. The applet tag may include the parameter tag. The parameter tag must include two attributes:

`name`—the name of the parameter

`value`—a string that specifies the value of the parameter

Figure 9.28 shows an example HTML that includes an applet with parameters. Note that the value of the name attribute is not quoted, but the value of the value parameter is quoted. This is the protocol expected by the applet.

```
<!--This file created 12/27/97 6:44 PM -->
<HTML>
<HEAD>
   <TITLE>Generalized Applet HMTL, Problem Solving with Java, Chapter 9
   </TITLE>
</HEAD>
<BODY>
<applet code = "ManyBalls.class" width = 300 height = 200>
<param name = balls  value = "4">
<param name = color1 value = "red">
<param name = color2 value = "blue">
```

Figure 9.28 *continued*

Figure 9.28 *continued*

```
<param name = color3 value = "green">
<param name = color4 value = "yellow">
</applet>
</BODY>
</HTML>
```

Figure 9.28 An HTML that includes applet param tags

The Applet getParameter Method Fetches Parameter Values

An applet can retrieve parameter values by using the getParameter method. The method takes one argument, a string that specifies the parameter name. For example:

```
getParameter("color1")
```

retrieves the string "red" from the HTML file in Figure 9.28. The getParameter method sends a string to the applet context and receives a string back. String methods and operations can be used to construct the argument string and to translate the returned string into a number.

The examples that follow show how to generalize the BlinkingBalls applet from Section 9.5. The HTML file specifies the number of balls to create as well as the colors to be used. Example 9.7 shows how to convert a string parameter into a number. Example 9.8 shows how to retrieve an unknown number of parameters.

In both example applets, we are careful to perform error-checking on the parameter values retrieved. The applet should not generate run-time errors because the parameter specification in the HTML file was incorrect. The applet designer can take two approaches: either substitute default values if the parameters are not correct, or display error messages instead of running the expected applet. In these examples we have taken the first approach. The rationale is that the HTML file that uses the applet will have been thoroughly tested before being posted on the Web. Within HTML pages themselves, if the browser cannot interpret something, it simply ignores it rather than generating an error message. We explore the pros and cons of this approach in the exercises.

EXAMPLE 9.7

Consider the problem of generalizing the number of balls that will blink. We can store the ball objects that are created in an array. We can use method parseInt (from class Integer) to translate the string representing the number of balls into an integer.

Figure 9.29 shows the generalized `BlinkingBalls` applet. Method `parseBallCount` does all the work. It uses a `try-catch` statement to guarantee that a proper number was received from the HTML file. If the input was not an integer, the number of balls is set to 2. The statement

```
Integer.parseInt(getParameter("balls"));
```

applies method `parseInt` to the string retrieved by method `getParameter`.

We must generalize method `actionPerformed`. Instead of instantiating two threads, we instantiate an array of threads. The version shown in Figure 9.29 is rather primitive in the way it displays the balls. It places each ball 70 pixels to the right of the previous one and gives each ball a delay of five seconds more than the previous one. We explore other arrangements in the exercises.

```
/*   File: ManyBalls.java
     Developed for Problem Solving with Java,
        Koffman & Wolz
     Appears in Figure 9.29
*/
// Need these for buttons etc.
import java.awt.*;
import java.applet.Applet;
import java.awt.event.*;

public class ManyBalls extends Applet
                        implements ActionListener {
   private Canvas display = new Canvas();
   private Button startStop = new Button("Start");
   private Ball[] balls;


   public void init() {

      int numberOfBalls = parseBallCount();
      balls = new Ball[numberOfBalls];
      display.setSize(numberOfBalls*70, 70);
      add(display);
      add(startStop);
      setSize(numberOfBalls*70 + 100, 200);

      startStop.addActionListener(this);

   } // init()
```

Figure 9.29 *continued*

Figure 9.29 *continued*

```java
    public void actionPerformed(ActionEvent e) {
      if (startStop.getLabel() == "Start") {
        for (int i = 0; i < balls.length; i++) {
          balls[i] = new Ball(this, 70*i, 10, 1 + 5*i);
          balls[i].start();
        }
        startStop.setLabel("Stop");
      } else {
        for (int i = 0; i < balls.length; i++)
          balls[i].stop();

        startStop.setLabel("Start");
        display.repaint();
      }
    } // actionPerformed

    private int parseBallCount() {
      int numberOfBalls;
      try {numberOfBalls =
               Integer.parseInt(getParameter("balls"));
      } catch (NumberFormatException e)
          {numberOfBalls = 2;}
      return numberOfBalls;
    }

    public Canvas getDisplay() {return display;}

} // class ManyBalls
```

Figure 9.29 Implementation of the `BlinkingBalls` class

EXAMPLE 9.8

Getting the colors from the `param` tags presents a different problem. First, we need to read an indeterminate number of them. Second, we need to translate a string such as `"red"` into a standard color. The `for` loop in method `parseColors` (Figure 9.30) shows a technique for counting the number of colors. Each of the parameter names for color is of the form `colorN`. (This is a protocol of our applet that must be followed by any HTML page that uses it.) The `getParameter` method is called with the string `"color"` + `numColors` as its argument (actual arguments are: `"color1"`, `"color2"`, and so on) until it returns `null`. If `getParameter` retrieves a string that is not `null`, the statement

```
ballColors.addElement(parseAColor(getParameter("color" +
                                                i)));
```

calls method `parseAColor` to convert that string to a color value. It appends the color value to vector `ballColors`. Although method `parseAColor` can only recognize four color strings, we can easily extend it to handle more (see Programming Exercise 1 in this section).

Bad input for this problem comes in two forms. The HTML file may not contain color parameters, or the value of a color parameter may not be recognized by `parseAColor`. Method `ParseColors` handles the first problem by checking the count of colors found and storing the `Color` values `red` and `green` in vector `ballColors` if the count is less than 2. Method `parseAColor` handles the second problem by returning the `Color` value `black` if it does not recognize its argument string.

Notice that each individual ball has the same set of color values (vector `ballColors`). In this example, where the focus was on parsing the color strings, we've chosen an easy, but inefficient solution. Another approach would be to make `parseColors` a class method and call it once from the applet (see Programming Exercise 2). Another approach would be to allow each ball to have its own set of colors.

```
/*   File: Ball.java
     Developed for Problem Solving with Java,
       Koffman & Wolz
     Appears in Figure 9.30
*/
import java.awt.*;
import java.util.*;
import java.applet.*;
public class Ball extends Thread {
  private ManyBalls ap;
  private Graphics g;
  private int x;
  private int y;
  private int speed;
  private Vector ballColors = new Vector();
  private nextColor = 0;

  private void parseColors() {
    // Retrieve the value of each param tag that is of
    //    the form colorN
    //    & store the corresponding color in ballColors.
    for (int i = 1;
         ap.getParameter("color" + i) != null;
         i++)
      ballColors.addElement(parseAColor(ap.getParameter
                                        ("color" + i)));
```

Figure 9.30 *continued*

Figure 9.30 *continued*

```
   // At least 2 colors should be defined.
   if (ballColors.size() == 0) {
      ballColors.addElement(Color.red);
      ballColors.addElement(Color.green);
   } else if (ballColors.size() == 1) {
      ballColors.setElementAt(Color.red, 0);
      ballColors.addElement(Color.green);
   }
 }


  private Color parseAColor(String c) {
      if (c.equals("red"))        return Color.red;
      else if (c.equals("green"))  return Color.green;
      else if (c.equals("blue"))   return Color.blue;
      else if (c.equals("yellow")) return Color.yellow;
      else return Color.black;
  } // parseAColor

 public Ball(ManyBalls ap, int x, int y, int speed) {
   this.ap = ap;
   this.x = x;
   this.y = y;
   this.speed = speed;
   Canvas c = ap.getDisplay();
   g = c.getGraphics();
 }

 public void run() {
   parseColors();
   drawNextFrame(); // draw first one.
   while (true) {
      try {sleep(speed*1000);
      } catch(InterruptedException e) {}
      drawNextFrame();
   }
 }

 public void drawNextFrame() {
   g.setColor((Color)ballColors.elementAt(nextColor));
   g.fillOval(x, y, 50, 50);
   nextColor = (nextColor + 1) % ballColors.size();
 }
} // Class Ball
```

Figure 9.30 Generalized definition of the Ball class

EXERCISES FOR SECTION 9.6

Self-Check

1. Explain what the `getParameter` method does.
2. Which of the following is a proper HTML `param` tag? For the others, explain what is wrong.

   ```
   <param name = button value = "red">
   <param "figure" = color value = green>
   <param name = button "value" = 6.2>
   ```
3. How are multiple balls implemented in Example 9.7?

Programming

1. The `Ball` class in Fig. 9.30 parses four colors. Modify the method so that it handles any colors given as input. *Hint:* The `param` tags should encode values for the red, green, and blue components of a color object.
2. Re-implement the `parseBalls` method in the `Ball` class of Fig. 9.30 as a class method so that the color vector is initialized and stored only once.

Chapter Review

1. The World Wide Web allows novice programmers to get a feel for the client/server model of computing. Typically, a Web server provides HTML pages that can be accessed anywhere in the world through a Web browser. The computer on which the Web browser resides is the client machine.
2. The advent of microcomputing changed the focus of how users interact with a computer. Instead of the traditional "stop and wait" model, the event model allows the user to move between activities in a seamless manner.
3. HTTP is a protocol for moving information around the World Wide Web. HTML is a text-based set of directives that tell a browser how to display a page of text. Hyperlinks provide directives for loading new pages. A Web browser provides a "front end" through which a user can interact with servers on the Web. To some extent CGI scripts at the server side can customize what the user sees. The problem with programs based solely on HTTP and server access is that timing can be hard to control because data must be moved across the Web. Similarly, limited user interaction, including animation can be

achieved, but it cannot be controlled at a fine-grained level. Ideally, there should be a good distribution of responsibility between the server and the browser. Applets as well as applications in the form of plug-ins provide this kind of flexibility. Thus, they provide a form of distributed processing.

4. The `Component` class is the superclass of all AWT GUI objects. The `Container` class allows containment hierarchies to be created so that components can be organized. `Panels` are `Containers`. `Applets` are `Panels`. A `Panel` must reside in some kind of window. `Applets` reside within an applet context such as a browser.

5. Panels may be nested within other panels. Creating a containment hierarchy requires the following:

   1. For each component in the panel (for example, a `Panel`, a `Button`, a `TextField`), create an object of the proper type.

   2. For each object created in step 1 that is a panel, repeat this procedure (steps 1–3) for the components that will be contained in this subpanel.

   3. Add all the components created in step 1 to the panel.

6. An event generator is an object that creates events. An event listener is an object that listens for events that were generated and does something in response to the event. For example, a `Button` generates an `ActionEvent` and an `Applet` may initiate some action as a result. The Java 1.1 event model determines how Java deals with events and is based on this generator/listener interaction. All AWT components generate events. In order for a class to be a listener, it must implement the appropriate listener interface. This requirement guarantees that the class will have the proper method through which it is informed by the generator that an event has occurred.

7. Designing a GUI interface involves the following steps:

   1. Create the GUI components (see point 5 of the Chapter Review above)

   2. Identify the input components that will act as event generators. Register event listeners for each.

   3. For each event listener, define the abstract methods through which the generator will communicate its events. These are event-handling methods.

   4. Check that you've identified all the input components by identifying the others as output components. These should only be accessed in event-handling methods.

8. A thread is an independent sequence of steps in a program. Although threads may interact, the details of how to accomplish this interaction are beyond the scope of this text. A thread must be started, and if

it does not terminate on its own, it must be stopped by an outside agent, usually by a thread manager. Although a thread is started by calling its `start` method, the details of what it does are defined within its `run` method. A thread can yield the CPU, hoping to regain it at some future time, or a thread can go to sleep for a specified period of time.

9. A `Runnable` interface provides an alternative way to create a thread class. A `Thread` instance can be given an object that implements the `Runnable` interface. The thread instance will use that object's `run` method for its process. If the `run` method contains calls to the class method `yield`, then that method will be applied to this thread.

10. An applet can retrieve parameters from its HTML page through `param` tags and the `getParameter` method. The `param` tag specifies a name and a value for a parameter. The value must be a string. The `getParameter` method takes a string argument corresponding to the name of the parameter, and returns the string that is the value of the parameter. The applet is responsible for converting the string into other data types. For example, the `Integer` class can be used to convert the string to an integer.

Summary of AWT Classes and Methods

Class	Parent class	Important methods	Purpose
Applet	Panel	init	init is used to construct component hierarchy here.
Panel	Container		Panels are used to contain other components, including other panels.
Container	Component	add	add is used to add components to this container.
Component	Object		All GUI objects rely on Components.
		setBackground(Color)	Sets the color of the component to the color specified.
		getBackground()	Retrieves the current background color of the component.
		invalidate	Marks the component as invalid, meaning that its layout may not be correct.

		validate	Applies the layout manager to itself and any of its components. The size, shape, and position of components is recalculated.
Button	Component	Button(String)	Buttons are user input devices; the constructor creates a button with String as its label.
Label	Component	Label(String)	Labels display simple information; the constructor creates a label with the String as its text.
TextField	Component	TextFields(String, int)	TextFields are user-input devices; the constructor places the String in a text area of size int characters.
ActionEvent	AWTEvent	getSource()	Retrieves the source of the event. This method is called in the actionPerformed method to determine which event generator was the source of the event.

Interface

ActionListener	EventListener	actionPerformed (ActionEvent e)	This method must be implemented. It is called by the action event generator when an event has occurred.

Summary of the Thread Class

Thread	Purpose
start	Called by a "thread manager" object to start a thread. Usually not overridden.
run	Overridden by the class extending Thread. This method contains the statements that are to be executed within the thread.
yield	Yield the CPU; that is, stop processing until some outside source returns the CPU to this thread.
sleep(milliseconds)	Yield the CPU for at least the specified amount of time.

Quick-Check Exercises

1. Contrast the "stop and wait" model of user interaction with the event model.
2. What is the role of a browser in relation to a server?
3. Explain the difference between a component and a container.
4. What is a layout manager?
5. How do event generators and listeners interact?
6. What does the method `actionPerformed` do in an action event listener?
7. What is the difference between extending the class `Thread` and implementing the interface `Runnable`?
8. What does the `getParameter` method of the `Applet` class do?

Answers to Quick-Check Exercises

1. In the "stop and wait" model, the program and perhaps even the CPU literally stops and waits for the user to respond to a query. In the event model, the operating system informs processes that events have occurred.
2. A browser acts as a "front end" for user interaction to a server's programs.
3. A component is any GUI object that can be displayed. A container is a kind of GUI component that can contain other components. For example, a panel is a container.
4. A layout manager is a class attached to a container that determines how the components in the container will be arranged.
5. An event generator creates an event object when the user interacts with it. It calls a specific method of an event listener to inform the listener that the event has occurred. The event listener must register with the generator that it wants to be informed of events.
6. The `actionPerformed` method is called by the generator. The listener's `actionPerformed` method contains the statements that are to be executed as a result of the event.
7. A class that extends `Thread` overrides the `run` method that is to be executed when an instance of the thread is created. An instance of a class that implements the `Runnable` interface is passed as an argument to a thread constructor. The thread object created will use the `run` method of the instance as its process.
8. The `getParameter` method takes a string as an argument and returns another string. It asks the applet context for a parameter in the corresponding HTML with a name equivalent to its argument, and it returns the corresponding value string.

Review Questions

1. What is the difference between a single-process program and a threaded program?
2. Is HTML a programming language? What is a hypertext link?
3. Give an example of distributed processing.
4. What is the advantage of applets and plug-ins when compared with CGI scripts?
5. Describe the use of the `add` method of the `Container` class.
6. If `b1` and `b2` are `Buttons` declared within an applet, what do the following statements within a method of the applet do?

```
b1.addEventListener(this);
b2.addEventListener(this);
```

7. What is a thread and why are they needed within applets?
8. Explain the process of creating a thread by extending the class `Thread`.
9. What is the difference between having a thread yield versus sleep?
10. Why is the `Runnable` interface necessary?
11. What is the purpose of having `param` tags in an HTML? How can an applet access the information in these parameters?

Programming Projects

1. Create an animated figure by using drawing methods of the graphics class. The figure should wave its hands. Integrate your animation with the buttons in `FirstGUI` so that the figure responds to "stop," "go," and "wait."
2. Use the drawing methods of the graphics class to create a figure of your choice (for example, a monster, a dog, or a cat). Create a few frames that change the position of the figure. For example, have one figure standing still and one figure in a walking position. Implement an applet in which a Move button has the figure move, until a separate Stop button is pressed.
3. The animations throughout this chapter have not moved the picture being drawn. Create an animation in which a figure moves across the screen. *Hint:* You will have to "undraw" your figure by replacing its bounding box with a filled rectangle of the same color as the background color.
4. Create an applet in which independent threads control any (reasonable) number of animated figures. Allow the HTML to specify how many figures there will be, what shape they will have (e.g., oval, square, rec-

tangle, circle, triangle), what color each figure will be, as well as its starting position.

5. Using `TextFields`, write an applet that requests a name, street address, city name, and zip code from a user. A Submit button collects all the data from the text fields, stores it in a vector, and asks for data for another person. A Complete button ends the session and displays all of the information within the area of the applet (via labels).

10

GUIs as a Vehicle for Object-Oriented Design

This chapter will demonstrate how well-designed abstraction and encapsulation simplify programming. You will see how principles of re-use aid in solving problems. We study the Abstract Window Toolkit (AWT) as an example of how the complex problem of user input/output can be solved with the aid of a well-designed library. Our goal is to provide you with the basic ideas, so that you can successfully build rudimentary GUIs. The abstractions presented here should help you choose the most appropriate interface tools for the task at hand.

The entire AWT is much too large to be covered here. It is described in books such as *The Java Class Libraries (JCL), Vol. 2*," which devotes almost 1000 pages to its discussion. You can use reference sources such as the JCL and Appendix D to look up classes and methods that will help you fine-tune your design and implementation.

10.1 Abstraction Layers for User Input/Output

10.2 Output to the User—Label, Canvas, Fonts, and Layout Managers

10.3 Discrete User Input: Buttons, Boxes, and Lists

10.4 Continuous and Textual User Input

10.5 Low-Level User Input

10.6 Turn-Taking within the Event Model
Case Study: TicTacToe

10.7 Applications and Applets: Menus

Chapter Review

10.1   Abstraction Layers for User Input/Output

The key to object-oriented design is finding the right level of abstraction. You need to learn to achieve a balance between using existing classes and building your own. Nowhere is this principle as important as in managing user input/output. This section provides a discussion of user interface abstractions as well as an overview of parts of the AWT, their functions, and where they will be discussed.

Traditionally, programming languages give input/output short shrift. Some languages, such as Pascal, provide only very simple input/output techniques. Programmers use these to build up more elaborate tools. Some tools become part of a standard set that any programmer can access. Other sets are proprietary; that is, you can use them only if you belong to a particular organization. In other languages, such as C, the input/output tools consist of a set of standard libraries. Often these libraries are dependent upon particular platforms. For example, a library might work on a Macintosh, but not on a Sun computer. Regardless of what tools are available, they often require mastering a syntax that is different from the standard syntax of the language itself. It can be particularly difficult for novice programmers to master two different syntaxes.

Input/output is often divided between user interfacing and data transfer. At the machine level, bytes of data are moved about in both situations. But that is where the similarity ends.

data transfer:
the movement of data between machines or between machines and storage devices.

Data transfer between machines, or between machines and storage devices is usually implemented through a **stream model**. We introduced classes `SimpleReader` and `SimpleWriter` and the stream concept in Section 7.8. A stream of data flows from a source to a destination, just like a stream of water. You must open a stream, and either add data to the stream, or remove data from the stream depending on whether you are storing or fetching data. Finally, you must close the stream. A full range of data types can be moved using streams, everything from low-level bytes to whole objects. Stream filters do exactly what you would expect: they filter the data, often converting it from one form to another. For example, using function composition you can create a filter that will convert raw bytes into strings or into numbers. The `java.io` class summarized in Appendix C provides classes and methods that support this conversion. A full discussion of streams is beyond the scope of this text.

stream model:
a model for moving data between machines or between machines and storage devices.

user interface:
a mechanism for getting data from and presenting data to users.

The stream model is not a good model for **user interfaces**. Instead, GUIs now provide a vast array of techniques for getting data from a user and presenting results to the user. Design considerations for GUIs focus more on how to effectively communicate the data abstractions within a program to a user than on how to mechanically transfer data.

Although the Java language specification does not include input/output tools, the Java designers did build a package of classes, the AWT. These classes provide multiple layers of abstraction for handling user input and output. The programmer can control the interaction at a very fine-grained level or can delegate almost all the work to existing classes in the AWT. The AWT runs on any computer platform that conforms to the Java standard. Best of all, the way you use the AWT classes conforms to the same simple principles of object creation and method invocation of any other class in Java. And the classes and interfaces associated with user input/output can be extended and implemented just like any other class in Java.

So what does it mean to say there are levels of abstraction? A high level of abstraction means that a complicated concept has been captured. For example, in the programs in Chapter 9 a button was pressed through an action event. Both the button and the event are extremely sophisticated abstractions. A button doesn't really "exist" on a computer screen. It is simply a drawing composed of graphics pixels. The abstract activity of "clicking the button" actually involves noticing a click signal from the mouse device while simultaneously noticing that the cursor coordinates fall within the range of the button drawing. Without the high level of abstraction present in the `Button`, `ActionListener`, and `ActionEvent` classes you would have considerably more work to do to process a button click.

To further illustrate the differences between fine-grained and high-level abstractions, consider how a text-based program might get its input and produce its output. Program users type in a sequence of characters and the program displays a sequence of characters. In order to display a multidigit number such as 52.7 on the screen, the program would have to translate the internal representation of the real number into codes for the four characters 5, 2, . (period), and 7. In some languages, the programmer has to write the program to do the translation. In other languages a "Print" procedure provides a higher level of abstraction that does the translation automatically. Similarly, to receive input, a program would have to get the individual characters for a number and translate them into the internal representation of a real number.

Output Abstractions

When CRT screens first came into use, the sequential nature of output disappeared. The position of an output character was dictated by an *x,y* coordinate on the screen. Later, the ability to control the font, style, size, and color of a character further revolutionized the output display.

Abstractions provide mechanisms for describing objects on a screen, not just simple characters. These objects include strings of characters, graphics, and video images. But at their core, each of these output abstractions is merely a collection of pixels on the screen. If you were forced to program at the pixel level you would probably not get very far. First, you would have to write a lot of code, but more to the point, you wouldn't be thinking about the problem at the right level of abstraction. If your solution requires thinking about buttons, then you should be able to program buttons. You shouldn't have to worry about pixels and mouse movements.

Abstractions are essential for managing combined video and sound. Whereas visual images are handled by the CRT screen, sound requires a second output device that produces sound based on audio signals. Coordinating the sound production and graphic display requires thinking at a higher level than "change graphics pixel, and send audio signal." Even though coordinated signals for video and sound are sent simultaneously to the two output devices, multimedia output is not possible without layers of abstraction.

Input Abstractions

Once output was freed from being a sequential placement of characters, the next step was to enable two-dimensional input. Before pointing devices such as mice became popular, two-dimensional input was controlled through elaborate keystroke sequences. For example, in an editor called Emacs, you can move up the screen by typing <ctrl> p. This means hold down the Control key and press the "p" key. The abstraction "move up the screen" is captured in this keystroke sequence.

Pointing devices also dramatically changed the kind of abstractions required for programming user input. Most of us take the coordination of pointing device and screen cursor for granted. When you physically move the mouse, the cursor changes position. But at a less abstract level, as the physical device is moved, the output display must be updated to show the position of a cursor. Perhaps the shape of the cursor is changed, depending on the activity. The position of the cursor within a window provides a focus for the mouse movements and can attach deeper meaning to simple actions. For example, physically shifting the mouse a tiny bit may move it out of one window and into another.

Designing with Abstractions in Mind

low-level event:

the direct capture of a mouse or keyboard action.

semantic event:

a higher-level abstraction representing a user activity such as entering text or selection from a menu choice.

The AWT provides you with some standard high levels of abstraction to capture complex activities in simple user actions. The `Component` class is comprised of a set of subclasses (See Fig. 9.8) that constitute the essential entities for interacting with a user. The `LayoutManager` classes provide abstractions for organizing components within a container such as a window or panel. The `Menu` classes provide abstractions for managing activities within windows. `AWTEvents` are divided into low-level events and "semantic" events that capture different levels of abstractions of user activities. **Low-level events** directly capture mouse and keyboard actions; **semantic events** capture higher level abstractions such as "action occurred" or "text was entered."

The remaining sections of this chapter show how these abstractions can be used. The trick is to know what classes to pick for the task at hand. Two questions arise when choosing a level of abstraction:

- Does it simplify a programming task?
- Does it make the program more responsive to the user's needs?

These questions are related. Usually, if the answer to one of these questions is no, then the answer to the other question is also no. If you get the design right, then clean, usable interfaces as well as simple elegant code often follow.

The discussion so far has focused on abstractions that capture complicated actions. But another set of abstractions comes into play, namely, the kind of data we want from the user. Examples are listed in Table 10.1. The data might be a simple "do it" response. In Chapter 9 you saw how a button handles this type of response. Or you might require a yes/no response; that is, the user might have a discrete, binary choice. Perhaps you want the user to choose among a number of discrete choices. Perhaps the input falls along a continuum. Perhaps the input is uniquely textual, such as the user's name. Each of these abstractions for input type can be captured through AWT GUI components.

Table 10.1 shows that some components, such as scroll bars, are highly specialized, while others, such as text fields, can be used for a wider range of activities (indicated by X for all but one user data abstraction). This chapter introduces each of these components as well as some others. Just because a component can be used universally does not mean it is the best

Table 10.1 Relationship between components and user data abstractions

			Expected response from the user				
Component	Unary choice (e.g., do it)	Binary choice	Single selection from discrete values	More than one choice from discrete values	Continuous values (e.g., range from 0–1000)	Limited, open-ended text (e.g., name)	Open-ended text (e.g., notes or opinion)
Button	X						
Checkbox	X	X	X				
Choice	X	X	X	X	X		
List	X	X	X	X	X		
Menu				X			
MenuItem	X	X	X	X			
PopUpMenu			X	X			
Scrollbar					X		
TextArea	X	X	X	X		X	
TextField	X	X	X	X		X	X

choice. For example, you can have users type in "yes" or "no" in a text field. But then you have to make sure the response was correct. If you use a more restrictive device such as a checkbox, you may not only save yourself some programming, but the user interface will be "friendlier." In table 10.1, the most likely choices for a particular user task are in color. But, as you will see in later sections, these are merely suggestions.

The AWT Classes for Simple User Interfaces

Before jumping into the "how to" of input/output programming it is worthwhile to summarize the AWT classes that support simple user interface design. Six classes of objects are used to create a GUI interface. They are:

```
Components
MenuComponents
Events
EventListeners
LayoutManagers
Graphics
```

Overview of components and menu components   There are two kinds of components: simple components and container components. Both inherit properties from the class `Component` such as graphics context, layout manager, and low-level events. Section 10.3 shows how any component can be a source of low-level events. Recall from Chapter 9 that container components hold other components. The simple components are used primarily for input. Section 10.2 explores them in detail. The components and their use are as follows.

`Button`	Usually used to proceed with some action.
`Checkbox`	Used for binary values (for example, on/off).
`CheckboxGroup`	Not a subclass of `Component`; used to create a set of checkboxes.
`Choice`	Displays one of a list of choices.
`List`	Displays a list of choices.
`Scrollbar`	Allows fine gradations along a continuum.
`TextArea`	Allows a single line of text to be typed.
`TextField`	Allows multiple lines of text to be typed.

Two additional simple components are used primarily for output. But since both are components, they can also detect all events that the `Component` class detects, including mouse events and keystroke events. The classes are:

`Label`	Used for drawing a simple text identifier in a container.
`Canvas`	Used for drawing more complex graphics.

As described in Chapter 9, containers are divided into two classes: panels and windows. Section 10.7 explores this distinction further. In that section, we also introduce the `MenuComponent` class and its subclasses, which allow you to create menu objects that behave a bit differently from the simple components listed above.

Overview of layout managers and graphics In Chapter 9, the layout of components in applets happened automatically. As you might imagine, controlling all of the detail of how components appear is an extremely complex task. Recall from Chapter 4 how you placed graphics on the screen using `Graphics` objects in the `paint` method. Clearly, it would be an insurmountable task if you had to control even a simple button-based interface directly through such graphics commands.

Layout managers provide another example of abstraction. This time it is process abstraction. A layout manager has rules for positioning components within a container. It does all the work of calculating size and position and giving graphics directives to components. It also manages the repositioning of components if the container's size and position change. For example, a user may change the size of a browser window, that in turn affects the visible space of an applet, that impacts how the components appear. The layout manager removes the burden of responsibility for the appearance of the components. The Java AWT includes five layout managers:

`BorderLayout`	Contains five fixed positions: North, South, East, West, and Center.
`CardLayout`	Stacks components like a deck of cards so that only one is visible at a time.
`FlowLayout`	Positions components in a top-to-bottom, left-to-right order.
`GridLayout`	Displays components within cells of a grid of standard-sized columns and rows.
`GridBagLayout`	Creates a flexible grid in which columns and rows can have variable sizes and components can overlap more than one grid cell.

Section 10.2 will show you how to use all but the `GridBagLayout`, whose complexity is beyond the scope of this text. The abstractions provided by the layout managers constrain your ability to control position. But the constraints are for your benefit. In sophisticated solutions you might want more control. You can achieve this control by building your own layout manager, or by using methods of the `Container` and `Component` class to directly position components. Appendix D points you toward appropriate resources.

Overview of events The central class for user input is the `AWTEvent`. (Note that this is not the same class as `Event`, which is used by Java version 1.0.) The `AWTEvent` has five subclasses. Four are considered "semantic" events because they capture a high level of abstraction. Sections 10.2 and 10.3 show examples of the following semantic events:

`ActionEvent`	Describes simple actions such as a button press.
`AdjustmentEvent`	Describes a change on a scale such as movement on a scrollbar.
`ItemEvent`	Describes a selection within a list, choice, or checkbox.
`TextEvent`	Describes a change in the text area of a textual component (`TextField`, `TextArea`).

The fifth subclass of `AWTEvent` is `ComponentEvent`. It is described in Section 10.5 and includes subclasses that directly monitor mouse and keyboard activity.

We learned earlier, in Chapter 9, that every event has a generator and a listener. Sections 10.2 and 10.3 will provide detail on how to create listeners for each type of event. The Chapter Review contains tables that organize the relationship between components and events, and between events and listeners. Each of the component classes is summarized in Appendix D.

Exercises for Section 10.1

Self-Check

1. Explain why levels of abstraction are necessary for solving problems.
2. Which of the following can be an event generator?

   `Component   Container   TextField   Object   Graphics LayoutManager`

3. What does a layout manager do?
4. What is the difference between a semantic and a low-level event?

10.2 Output to the User—Label, Canvas, Fonts, and Layout Managers

In GUI-based systems, the distinction between input and output becomes a bit blurred. The user interacts with components in a window. Some of these components are enabled for input, and some are not. Two components are used primarily for output: the canvas and the label.

The layout of the screen can get complicated when input and output devices are intermixed. Four layout managers are presented in this section. They give you high-level ways of thinking about and implementing screen displays.

The Label, Canvas, and Font Classes

An output component must be a "drawable" space. You can place graphics or text (as well as images) on such drawable spaces using a graphics context (the class `Graphics`) within a `paint` method. This is a very low-level way of controlling a display. The examples in Section 4.6 show you the level of detail that must be considered when you attempt to customize something yourself.

The `Label` and the `Canvas` classes embody two abstract concepts for making displays. (A label is a text string that marks something or provides some information. A canvas is a space that can incorporate graphics as well as text.) Typically, you create instances of the `Label` class when you need labels. You rarely need to extend the `Label` class. On the other hand, you will often extend the `Canvas` class so that you can control the painting that takes place within the canvas.

We used labels in a number of examples in Chapter 9. A label is a text string. You can set the text of the label through the constructor or through the `setText` method.

EXAMPLE 10.1

Figure 10.1 shows a `Banner` class that extends `Canvas`. (A banner is a short line of colored text.) We build this class here to illustrate how class `Canvas` can be extended. The `Banner` class has four data fields:

message	Stores the message to be displayed.
pen	The color in which to display the text.
xSpace	The horizontal border between the edge of the banner and the text.
ySpace	The vertical border above and below the text.

The two constructors set up the attributes of a banner, including centering the banner within the canvas and determining the size of the canvas. The first constructor allows a high degree of control for the programmer. It sets attributes for font, color, and spacing as well as the actual string. The second constructor uses defaults for all but the most essential characteristic, the string. It calls the first constructor so that the proper size of the banner and the position of the text within it can be calculated. The width and height of the banner, as well as the position of the text within the banner, are dependent upon the font metrics that will be discussed shortly. Figure 10.3 shows an example banner that was created within the applet found in Fig. 10.2.

```java
/*    File: Banner.java
      Developed for Problem Solving with Java,
        Koffman & Wolz.
      Appears in Fig. 10.1.
*/
import java.awt.*;

public class Banner extends Canvas {
    // Data fields
    private String message;
    private Color pen;
    private int xSpace;
    private int ySpace;
    private FontMetrics fm;

    // Methods
    // Constructors
    public Banner(String s, Color p, Font font,
                  int x, int y) {
        message = s;
        pen = p;
        setFont(font);

        fm = getFontMetrics(font);
        int xSize = fm.stringWidth(message) +
                    2 * xSpace;
        int ySize = fm.getHeight() + 2 * ySpace;
        setSize(xSize, ySize);
    }

    public Banner(String b) {
        this(b, Color.black, new Font("Serif",
                          Font.PLAIN, 24), 10, 10);
    }

    // Operation
    public void paint(Graphics g) {
        g.setColor(pen);
        g.drawString(message, xSpace,
                     ySpace + fm.getAscent());
    }

} // class Banner
```

Figure 10.1   The simplified Banner class

```
/*    File: BannerApplet.java
      Developed for Problem Solving with Java,
        Koffman & Wolz.
      Appears in Fig. 10.2.
*/
import java.awt.*;
import java.applet.*;

public class BannerApplet extends Applet {
    public void init() {
        setBackground(Color.white);

        setLayout(new FlowLayout());
        Banner c = new Banner("This space for rent");
        add(c);
        c.setBackground(Color.blue);
    }
} // class BannerApplet
```

Figure 10.2 An applet that displays a banner

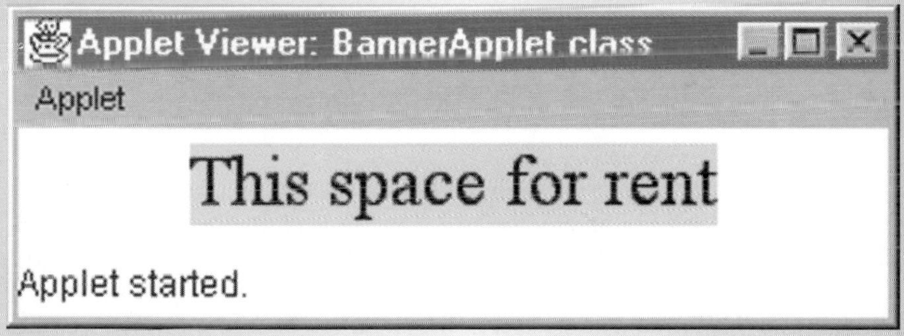

Figure 10.3 An example banner

The size of the canvas is dependent upon the font shape, style, and size of the lettering. In order for a canvas to appear, it must have a size greater than 0. The border around the lettering is also specified in arguments to the constructor. A single argument constructor chooses a standard-shaped banner that displays the message given as an argument.

The `paint` method does the work of displaying the string. It sets the pen color and then draws the message. The class shown in Figure 10.1 is not complete. It needs methods that allow the data fields of the banner to be manipulated after a banner is created. This task is left as an exercise.

Fonts   The font of a string (or character) characterizes the way it looks. Throughout this text, fonts are used to create visually informative distinctions. For example, most of the prose appears in one font and figure captions appear in another. The Java AWT supports a small set of standard font shapes (for example, the so-called serif fonts—see Appendix C for more examples). A font has a size and style as well as a shape. The size is an integer measured in a unit called a point. The style is characterized as italic and/or bold. The Java AWT contains a class `Font` that allows you to define a new `Font` object by providing it with a shape, style, and size. Table 10.2 shows some examples.

The style attributes are represented as bits that function as on/off signals. You turn on the bold style with the bit constant `BOLD`. You turn on the italic style with the bit constant `ITALIC`. The "`|`" operator combines the values of two bits, turning both on. So `BOLD | ITALIC` turns both on. The `PLAIN` bit constant represents the state where both bits are off.

Table 10.2 Examples of `Font` specifications

Call to `Font` Constructor	Effect
`new Font("Dialog", Font.BOLD | Font.ITALIC, 14)`	***An Example***
`new Font("SansSerif", Font.PLAIN, 10)`	An Example
`new Font("Serif", Font.BOLD, 12)`	**An Example**
`new Font("Monospaced", Font.ITALIC, 12)`	*An Example*

Font metrics   Every font that is created has a set of "font metrics" that define how much space a character occupies when it is displayed in that font. Figure 10.4 shows the metrics. The baseline refers to the bottom of most letters. The descent refers to the distance that letters such as "g" and "p" extend below the baseline. The ascent is the distance from the baseline to the top of capital letters. The leading is the space between the bottom of the previous line and the top of a capital letter. The height is the sum of the leading, ascent, and descent. Fonts also determine the horizontal space that a character will occupy. In the `Banner` class, we need six additional characteristics:

`x, y`	The lower-left starting position for drawing the first letter
`xSpace, ySpace`	The size of the horizontal and vertical borders, respectively
`xSize, ySize`	The width and height of the banner, respectively

Font metrics

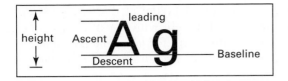

Calculation of position in a banner

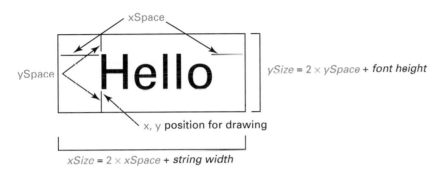

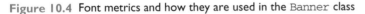

Figure 10.4 Font metrics and how they are used in the Banner class

The font metrics can be used to determine the size of the banner and the starting position for drawing the string as shown in Figure 10.3. The metrics of a font must be calculated by the component to which the font belongs (in our case, the Banner class). The first constructor in Figure 10.1 sets the font for the banner, then calculates the font metrics. A FontMetrics method stringWidth calculates the width of a string in the given font. From the font metrics, the Banner class can calculate the size (*ySize* = height, *xSize* = width) of the space needed to accommodate the message using the following formulas:

xSize = xSpace + string width + xSpace
ySize = ySpace + height + ySpace

The Banner calculates the starting position of the string using the formulas:

x position = xSpace
y position = ySpace + ascent

The FontMetric class contains other methods for determining the size and spacing of characters. Keep in mind that to determine font metrics you must set the font for a component, then request that the component give you the metrics (using method getFontMetrics). In the banner example, the Banner class inherited this capability from the Canvas class. Other methods for the FontMetrics class are listed in Appendix D.

Overview of Layout Managers

Most of the time you do not want to control layout at the level just described. It is tedious, time-consuming, and fraught with potential error. The AWT includes layout managers that do this work for you. The advantage is that you don't have to worry about petty detail. The disadvantage is that you sometimes get surprising results. Layout managers are especially useful for applet design, where you cannot predict how large an area will be given to your applet by its applet context.

You specify a layout manager for any container (window, frame, applet, panel) by calling the `setLayout()` method of the container. For example

```
setLayout(new FlowLayout());
```

creates a flow layout manager and associates it with the container.

FlowLayout   You've used the `FlowLayout` manager without knowing it in Chapter 9. This layout manager places the components of a container in left-to-right, top-to-bottom order, as determined by the sequence in which the components are added to the container. For example, the first component added is placed at the leftmost position of the top row, and the last component added is placed at the rightmost position of the bottom row. The `FlowLayout` manager gives you no control over position.

BorderLayout   The `BorderLayout` manager lets you specify five positions within a container as designated by the five constants: NORTH, SOUTH, EAST, WEST, and CENTER. Figure 10.5 shows how four buttons and a banner are added to an applet that has a `BorderLayout` manager. Notice how each `add` method specifies both a component to add to the container and a position at which to place it. The display is shown in Figure 10.6. The north and south components always take up the entire horizontal space of the container. You may have fewer than five components in a border layout, but you may not have more than five. If the east and west components don't exist, the center component will take up the space normally filled by them.

```
/*    File: BorderLayoutDemo.java
      Developed for Problem Solving with Java, Koffman & Wolz.
      Appears in Fig. 10.5.
*/
import java.awt.*;
import java.applet.Applet;
public class BorderLayoutDemo extends Applet {
   public void init() {
     setLayout(new BorderLayout());
```

Figure 10.5 *continued*

Figure 10.5 *continued*

```
      add(new Button("North"),BorderLayout.NORTH);
      add(new Banner("The Center"),
          BorderLayout.CENTER);
      add(new Button("East"),BorderLayout.EAST);
      add(new Button("West"),BorderLayout.WEST);
      add(new Button("South"),BorderLayout.SOUTH);
   }
} // class BorderLayoutDemo
```

Figure 10.5 An example of a border layout

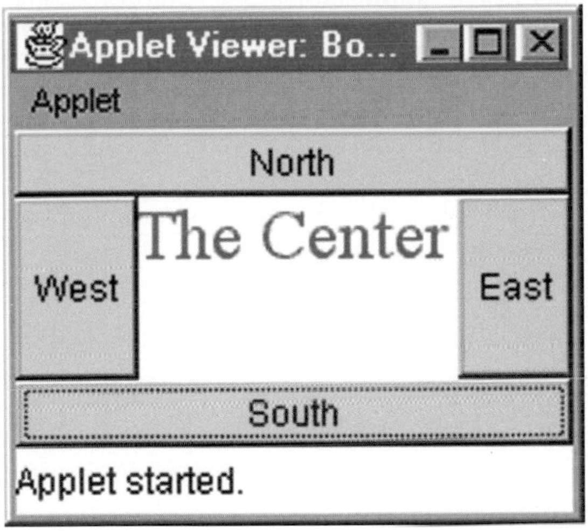

Figure 10.6 The display of a border layout

Notice in this example that the buttons and banner are not assigned to local variables or data fields. They are created and added to the container, but cannot be directly referenced in the class. This is another example of function composition, a technique that is particularly useful when variables would just clutter up the code. Finally, note that this class does not include events. The components are displayed, but they don't do anything.

GridLayout The `GridLayout` manager lets you specify a two-dimensional grid. Figure 10.7 shows how an array of buttons and a center banner may be added to a panel within an applet. The `for` loop constructs the buttons in left-to-right, top-to-bottom order, adding each button to the applet as it goes. The label on the button shows the position of the button in the grid. When the center of the grid is detected, a banner marked "TheCenter" is substituted for a button.

The display is shown in Figure 10.8. The constructor for the `GridLayout` class allows you to specify the size of the grid. If you do not give arguments to the constructor, it creates a grid with 1 row and 0 columns.

The components are always added to the grid in left-to-right, top-to-bottom order. If you want to leave space in the grid, then you must create a "dummy" component such as a label, and set its visibility to `false`:

```
Button b = new Button("Just a place holder");
b.setVisible(false);
```

This example also illustrates how you can specify the horizontal and vertical spacing between components in the constructor of `GridLayout`. The third and fourth arguments specify these gaps. You can also use other layout managers for this specification (See Appendix D). If you leave out the gaps in the constructor, then the gaps are assumed to be zero, and there will be no space between components.

```
/*    File: GridLayoutDemo.java
      Developed for Problem Solving with Java, Koffman & Wolz.
      Appears in Fig. 10.7.
*/
import java.awt.*;
import java.applet.Applet;

public class GridLayoutDemo extends Applet {
   public void init() {

      int rows = 3;
      int columns = 3;
      Panel gridP = new Panel();

      gridP.setLayout(new GridLayout(rows, columns, 5, 10));
      for (int r = 1; r <= rows; r++)
         for (int c = 1; c <= columns; c++)
            if (r == 2 && c == 2)
               gridP.add(new Banner("TheCenter"));
            else gridP.add(new Button(r + " , " + c));
      add(gridP);
   }
} //class GridLayoutDemo
```

Figure 10.7 An example of a grid layout

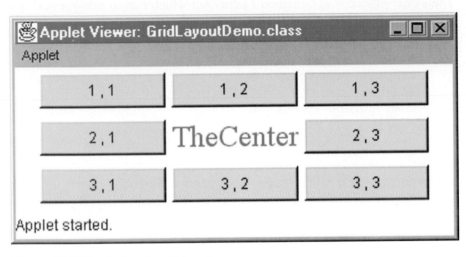

Figure 10.8 The display of a grid layout

CardLayout   The `CardLayout` manager lets you create a "stack of cards." When you add components to a container that has a card layout manager, only one component will appear at a time. The others are hidden, as if behind the visible component. The components are stacked in the order in which they are added. The `CardLayout` class has methods for viewing the "next", "previous", "first", and "last" components as well as for showing a specified component.

Figure 10.9 shows how an array of banners can be displayed. Figure 10.10 gives a sample display after the "first" button has been pressed. This example illustrates how two panels and the applet can each have their own layout manager. The applet has a border layout:

```
setLayout(new BorderLayout());
```

The button panel defaults to a flow layout, becasuse no explicit layout manager was created. The buttons themselves are added individually, exactly as we built buttons in Chapter 9.

In this example, the layout manager is assigned to a data field: `cLayout`. This object is tied to the card container. Its methods are used in the `actionPerformed` method to display banners:

```
cLayout = new CardLayout();
displays = new Panel(cLayout);
```

The panel `displays` contains five banners. The banners are built with a `for` loop, each banner is given the name `"Picture i"` where `i` is its position in the stack.

```
for (int i = 1; i <= 5; i++)
    displays.add(new Banner("Picture " + i));
```

The `actionPerformed` method figures out which button was pressed and tells the layout manager to display the appropriate banner:

```
Button b = (Button)e.getSource();
if (b == next)
    cLayout.next(displays);
else if (b == prev)
    cLayout.previous(displays);
    . . .
```

```java
/*   File: CardDemo.java
     Developed for Problem Solving with Java, Koffman & Wolz.
     Appears in Fig. 10.9.
*/
import java.awt.*;
import java.applet.Applet;
import java.awt.event.*;

public class CardDemo extends Applet implements ActionListener {
    private Button first, prev, next, last;
    private Panel displays;
    private CardLayout cLayout;

    public void init() {

        // The applet has a border layout.
        setLayout(new BorderLayout());

        // Create the buttons for controlling the card panel.
        // The button panel defaults to a FlowManager.
        Panel buttonP = new Panel();
        first = new Button("First");
        buttonP.add(first);
        prev = new Button("Previous");
        buttonP.add(prev);
        next = new Button("Next");
        buttonP.add(next);
        last = new Button("Last");
        buttonP.add(last);
        add(buttonP, BorderLayout.SOUTH);

        first.addActionListener(this);
        prev.addActionListener(this);
        next.addActionListener(this);
        last.addActionListener(this);
```

Figure 10.9 *continued*

Figure 10.9 *continued*

```
        // Create the card panel, and card layout.
        displays = new Panel();
        for (int i = 1; i <= 5; i++)
            displays.add(new Banner("Picture " + i));
        cLayout = new CardLayout();
        displays.setLayout(cLayout);
        add(displays, BorderLayout.CENTER);
    }

    public void actionPerformed(ActionEvent e) {
        Button b = (Button)e.getSource();

        if (b == next)
            cLayout.next(displays);
        else if (b == prev)
            cLayout.previous(displays);
        else if (b == last)
            cLayout.last(displays);
        else if (b == first)
            cLayout.first(displays);
    }
} // class CardDemo
```

Figure 10.9 An example of a card layout

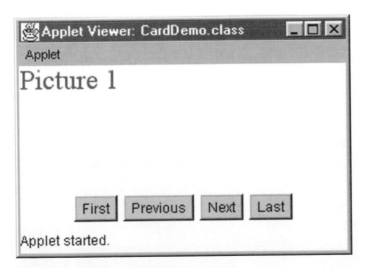

Figure 10.10 The display of a card layout

EXERCISES FOR SECTION 10.2

Self-Check

1. What is the difference between the `Font` class and the `FontMetric` class?

2. Under what circumstances would you use each of the following layout managers:

   `BorderLayout`

   `FlowLayout`

   `GridLayout`

   `CardLayout`

3. Why are layout managers useful?

4. How will the following buttons be displayed?

   ```
   setLayout(new GridLayout(3, 2));
   add(new Button("1"));
   add(new Button("2"));
   add(new Button("3"));
   add(new Button("4"));
   add(new Button("5"));
   add(new Button("6"));
   ```

5. How do you control the vertical and horizontal spacing between components in a container?

Programming

1. Add appropriate accessors and modifiers to the `Banner` class in Figure 10.1.

2. Add the ability to create italicized and bold text to the `Banner` class.

3. The `Banner` class assumes the text will fit on one line. Modify the class so that the width can be specified and the text is displayed on multiple lines within that text space.

4. Create an applet that includes three drawings. Use a card layout to "flip" through the pictures.

5. Create an applet that has a grid of buttons that looks like this:

   ```
                        red

           orange              purple
   yellow              white              blue

                       green
   ```

10.3 Discrete User Input: Buttons, Boxes, and Lists

The Java AWT characterizes four kinds of abstract input:

1. Actions
2. Item selections
3. Scale adjustments
4. Text changes

This section and the next describe situations in which these abstractions may be relevant and provide examples of their use. Also, we illustrate all of the simple input components as event sources. Table 10.3 shows the relationship between events and their sources.

Table 10.3 Semantic events and their component sources

Event generator	Event generated			
	ActionEvent	ItemEvent	Adjustment Event	TextEvent
Button	Unary choice			
Checkbox		Binary choice		
Checkbox Group	Single selection from small set of discrete values			
Choice		Single selection from a large set of discrete values		
List	(Double-click item) Unary choice	(Single-click item) Single or multiple selection from a set of discrete values		
Scrollbar			Continuum of values	

Table 10.3 *continued*

Table 10.3 *continued*

	Event generated			
Event generator	ActionEvent	ItemEvent	Adjustment Event	TextEvent
`TextField`	(After Return is pressed)			Limited, open-ended response
`TextArea`	(After Return is pressed)			Open-ended response

Actions

The action event captures the idea that something has happened and something should be done about it. `Buttons`, `Lists`, and `TextFields` are sources of `ActionEvents`. Section 9.3 shows how to execute actions based on buttons. The next example introduces `TextFields` and `Lists`. Section 10.5 describes how some of the subclasses of `MenuComponent` also generate `ActionEvents`.

EXAMPLE 10.2

We want to display a string in an applet in a particular font, style, size, and color. A default string is initially displayed in black. The font, style, and size are fixed. The color and text may be changed by the user. A Reset button restores the original black string.

The output component must be a "drawable" space such as the `Banner` class created in Example 10.1. Figure 10.11 shows the applet and Figure 10.12 shows a sample display. The class definition looks remarkably like the examples in Chapter 9. Two methods do all the work. The `init` method sets up the GUI layout, and the `actionPerformed` method handles the events generated by the button, the list, or the text field.

In the `init` method the display area is created first. The font and default message are given as arguments. Note that we assume here that the `Banner` class has been fully specified to include a constructor that takes just a message and a font. We also assume that the following methods have been defined for `Banner`:

```
void resetColor()        // Resets the text color to
                         //    black.
void setColor(Color)     // Sets the text color to the
                         //    argument.
void setMessage(String)  // Sets the message to the
                         //    string specified.
```

The button and text area are created in a manner exactly like the buttons in Chapter 9. The new component is the List. The statement

```
new List(3, false);
```

says to initially display three items in the list and only allow one item at a time to be selected. If the second argument were true, then more than one item in the list could be selected. The addItem method adds items to the list. The item can be referenced later by the string arguments of addItem.

```
/*    File: ColorText.java
      Developed for Problem Solving with Java,
         Koffman & Wolz.
      Appears in Fig. 10.11.
*/
import java.awt.*;
import java.applet.Applet;
import java.awt.event.*;
public class ColorText extends Applet
                        implements ActionListener {
    private Banner displayArea;
    private Button reset;
    private TextField message;
    private List colors;

    private final String
                defaultMessage = "Type a message";

    public void init() {
        // Create GUI layout.
        displayArea =
          new Banner(defaultMessage,
                    new Font("Serif", Font.BOLD |
                                Font.ITALIC, 14));
        add(displayArea);

        reset = new Button("Reset");
        add(reset);

        message = new TextField(defaultMessage);
        add(message);

        // Display three rows; don't allow
        //    multiple selections.
        colors = new List(3, false);
```

Figure 10.11 *continued*

Figure 10.11 *continued*

```
        colors.addItem("Red");
        colors.addItem("Green");
        colors.addItem("Blue");
        add(colors);

        setSize(350,400);

        reset.addActionListener(this);
        message.addActionListener(this);
        colors.addActionListener(this);
    }

    public void actionPerformed(ActionEvent e) {
        if (e.getSource() == reset) {
            displayArea.setMessage(defaultMessage);
            displayArea.resetColor();
            message.setText(defaultMessage);
        } else if (e.getSource() == message)
            displayArea.setMessage
                (message.getText());
        else { // Get the color from the list.
            String color =
                        colors.getSelectedItem();
            if (color == "Red")
                displayArea.setColor(Color.red);
            else if (color == "Green")
                displayArea.setColor(Color.green);
            else
                displayArea.setColor(Color.blue);
        }
        displayArea.repaint();
    }

} // class ColorText
```

Figure 10.11 ColorText applet demonstrates simple actions

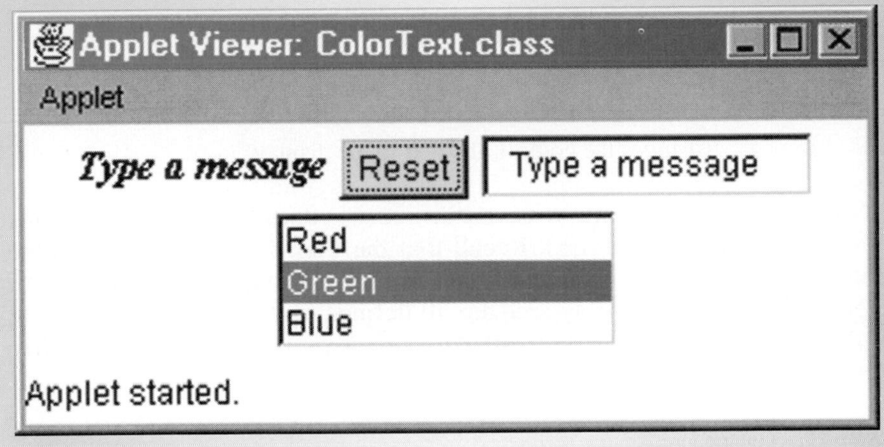

Figure 10.12 Initial display of the ColorText applet

TextField component can generate an action event   The TextField component provides the user with a one-line area in which to enter text. In Figure 10.12, the default string, which is given as an argument to the constructor, is initially displayed. The component handles all of the details that allow the user to enter and change the text. A text field generates an action event when the user presses the Return key. This is a useful action because usually pressing Return means "Do it." Text fields also generate text events. These will be described shortly. A summary of the methods of this component can be found in Appendix D.

List component can generate an action event   The List component can be used to generate simple actions when an item in the list is clicked twice. In this example, three buttons would have adequately done the job. We chose the list feature to visually highlight the difference in actions between the Reset button and the color selector. You can see this difference in Figure 10.12. Another advantage of the List component over Button is that lists will easily display a limited number of a very large set of choices. We will pursue this later in the discussion on selecting from a set.

Creating a listener for multiple action events   The init method contains three calls to addActionListener, one to each component that might produce an action event. A single actionPerformed method takes care of events generated by all three. The method uses the getSource method of an event to get the component that was the source. Based on the source, it determines what action to take (see Table 10.4).

Table 10.4 Event sources and actions

Event source	action
Reset button	Resets the color and text in the display, resets the text in the text field.
Text field	Changes the text in the display.
List	Changes the color of the text in the display.

Notice that the last thing `actionPerformed` does is repaint the display area (using method `repaint`). Recall that the `repaint` method erases the contents of a drawing surface and fills it with the background color. The other methods for the display area are all defined in the `TextCanvas` class. Table 10.5 shows the different `Component` methods used within `actionPerformed`.

Table 10.5 Components of `actionPerformed`

Component	Method	Explanation
TextField	setText(String)	Sets the text in the field to the string argument.
TextField	getText()	Retrieves the string that currently appears in the text field.
List	getSelectedItem()	Retrieves the string associated with item currently selected.

Binary Selections

The `Checkbox` component is used to make binary selections. A checkbox has a state that is either `true` (checked) or `false` (not checked). It generates an `ItemEvent` whenever its state is changed by the user. An object, such as an applet that wishes to listen for `ItemEvents` must register as an `ItemListener` and implement the method `itemStateChanged`. The `Checkbox` method `getState` can be used to retrieve the state of the box.

EXAMPLE 10.3

This example shows how to create an array of checkboxes where more than one may be selected at a time. This technique is particularly useful when a user wants to select a number of options from a set. This example shows a menu planner in which breakfast foods are presented as checkboxes. Each time a box is selected or deselected, the total number of calories for the meal is displayed. Figure 10.13 shows the `Food` class. Figure 10.14 shows the `CalorieCounter` applet class. Figure 10.15 shows a sample display. This example illustrates a number of important ideas:

1. A class `Food` is defined that associates a calorie amount with a checkbox.

2. An array of `Food` objects is created "in-line" in the applet as a demonstration. Other techniques from Chapter 9 could be used to fetch the object data field values from an external source.

3. The array of `Food` objects is traversed to set up the GUI display and simultaneously register the applet as the `ItemListener`.

4. In an applet, the GUI components may not be created before the `init` method is executed without causing unpredictable consequences. The array of `Food` objects is created when the applet is created, but the components are created within `init`.

5. Because of the constraint in point 4, the `makeBox` method illustrates how one object (a `Food` object) can set up the relationship between the source (a button) and the listener (the applet). This illustrates the elegant flexibility of the Java 1.1 event model.

```java
/*    File: Food.java
      Developed for Problem Solving with Java,
        Koffman & Wolz.
      Appears in Fig. 10.13.
*/
import java.awt.*;

public class Food {
    private String descrip;
    private int calorieAmount;
    private Checkbox box;

    public Food(String s, int c) {
        descrip = s;
        calorieAmount = c;
    }

    public void makeBox(CalorieCounter c) {
        // Create a new box.
        box = new Checkbox(descrip);
        // Add box to applet CalorieCounter.
        c.add(box);
        // Register container c as a listener.
        box.addItemListener(c);
    }
```

Figure 10.13 *continued*

Figure 10.13 *continued*

```java
    public Checkbox getBox() {
        return box;
    }

    public int getCalories() {
        return calorieAmount;
    }
} // class Food
```

Figure 10.13 The Food class for Example 10.3

```java
/*    File: CalorieCounter.java
      Developed for Problem Solving with Java,
        Koffman & Wolz.
      Appears in Fig. 10.14.
*/
import java.applet.Applet;
import java.awt.*;
import java.awt.event.*;

public class CalorieCounter extends Applet
                            implements ItemListener {
    Label calories;
    Food[] foods =
          { new Food("8 oz. orange juice", 80),
            new Food("1 cup black coffee", 0),
 new Food("1 serving cornflakes with 1/2 cup skim milk",
            120),
 new Food("1 delicious sugar coated donut", 600),
 new Food("8 oz. of skim milk", 70),
 new Food("2 slices white toast, lightly buttered", 200)
            };

    public void init() {
        setLayout(new GridLayout(0, 1));
        for (int i = 0; i < foods.length; i++)
            foods[i].makeBox(this);

        calories = new Label("Calories: 0           ");
        add(calories);
    }
```

Figure 10.14 *continued*

Figure 10.14 *continued*
```
    public void itemStateChanged(ItemEvent e) {
        int total = 0;
        for (int i = 0; i < foods.length; i++) {
            Checkbox box = foods[i].getBox();
            if (box.getState())
                total += foods[i].getCalories();
        }
        calories.setText("Calories: " + total);
    }

} // class CalorieCounter
```

Figure 10.14 The CalorieCounter applet for Example 10.3

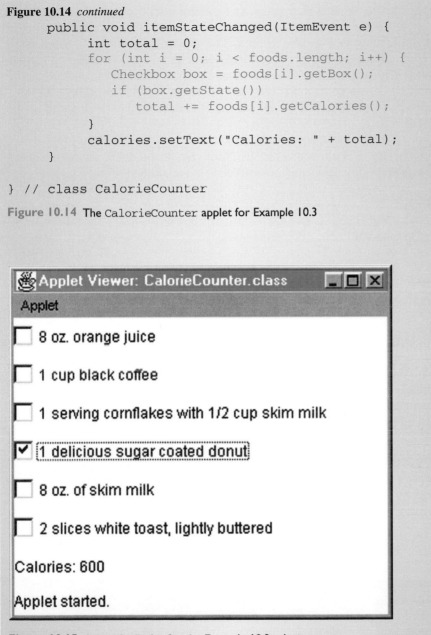

Figure 10.15 A sample display for the Example 10.3 calorie counter

The constructor in the Food class stores the food description and the calorie amount. The makeBox method is not called until the applet has been started. This procedure guarantees that the argument to `makeBox` (which is *this* applet) actually exists. In `init`, a grid layout of 0 rows and 1 column creates a display that is easy to read. The `for` loop goes through the array of `Food` objects, creating checkboxes for each one with the `makeBox` method. Within `makeBox`, a `Checkbox` object is created. It is added to the applet and the applet is registered as a listener for that checkbox. Finally, within `init`, a label for the total calories count is created and added to the applet.

The `itemStateChange` method recalculates the total calories every time a checkbox is clicked. The `for` loop goes through the array retrieving the `Checkbox` object associated with each `Food` object:

```
Checkbox box = foods[i].getBox();
```

If the box is checked (if its state is `true`), then the calories for this food are added to the total

```
if (box.getState())
   total += foods[i].getCalories();
```

and the label `calories` is updated to show the new total value.

Selecting One Item from a Set

There are three ways to select a single item from a set:

1. Use a `List` component that only allows a single choice. Use a list for very large sets where you don't want to view the whole list at once. Lists can also be used to select more than one item at a time.

2. Use checkboxes that are gathered within a `CheckboxGroup` when the set is very small and fixed in size.

3. Use a `Choice` component when the set is a bit larger, or you want to take up as little space as possible. `Choice` also works well in conjunction with text fields.

As you might have guessed, you select an item with an item event source and listener.

EXAMPLE 10.4

We want to show a simple multiple-choice question and evaluate the user's response. The user can select exactly one answer at a time. Messages are posted in response to wrong answers. When the right answer is selected, all the components are disabled so that they no longer generate events. Three techniques are implemented using each of the components listed above.

All three techniques reuse the label "report" to give feedback to the user based on the user's answer. A label's size is determined by the size of its initial string. If the initial string is replaced by a longer string, the new string may be clipped; that is, you may not see the whole string. One solution is to remove the label and create a new one. This process gets complicated, but is necessary in some instances. Alternatively, we can give the label an initial string—a sequence of underline characters that exceeds the length of the longest message. This guarantees enough space for each message.

Figure 10.16 shows how to use a CheckboxGroup. The display is shown in Figure 10.17. A CheckboxGroup is not a component. It is a class that allows you to cluster Checkbox components so that only one may be selected at a time.

The init method sets up the display, creating a label for the questions and a checkbox for each of the three possible answers. A CheckboxGroup is created that is given as an argument to each Checkbox component. This tells the checkboxes that only one of them may be selected at a time. All of the checkboxes are added to the panel and the applet is registered as a listener for each. The report label uses a graphics trick to create enough space for the longest anticipated response string. Programming Exercise 5 at the end of this section suggests another way to do this.

The itemStateChanged method checks to see if the user has selected the correct answer, that is, the one from checkbox 3. If so, it disables all of the checkboxes so that the test is complete. If the user selects either of the other two boxes, a response is displayed, and the user is allowed to try again.

```
/*    File: MultipleChoiceBox.java
      Developed for Problem Solving with Java,
        Koffman & Wolz.
      Appears in Fig. 10.16.
*/

import java.awt.*;
import java.applet.Applet;
import java.awt.event.*;

public class MultipleChoiceBox extends Applet
                                implements ItemListener {
    private Label question;
    private Checkbox a1, a2, a3;
    private CheckboxGroup answers;
    private Label report;
```

Figure 10.16 *continued*

Figure 10.16 *continued*

```
    public void init() {
        question = new
  Label("Which one is the best programming language?");
        add(question);

        answers = new CheckboxGroup();
        a1 = new Checkbox("Pascal", answers, false);
        a2 = new Checkbox("C++", answers, false);
        a3 = new Checkbox("Java", answers, false);

        Panel p = new Panel();
        p.add(a1);
        p.add(a2);
        p.add(a3);
        add(p);
        // Leave space for long string.
        report =
            new Label("_____");
        add(report);

        a1.addItemListener(this);
        a2.addItemListener(this);
        a3.addItemListener(this);
    }

    public void itemStateChanged(ItemEvent e) {
        if (a3.getState()) {
    report.setText("Of course!, Java is just right!");
            // Disable the buttons.
            a1.setEnabled(false);
            a2.setEnabled(false);
            a3.setEnabled(false);
        } else if (a2.getState())
            report.setText("No, C++ is too hard!");
        else
            report.setText("No, Pascal is too easy");
        repaint();
    }
} // class MultipleChoiceBox
```

Figure 10.16 A multiple-choice test using checkboxes and `CheckboxGroup`

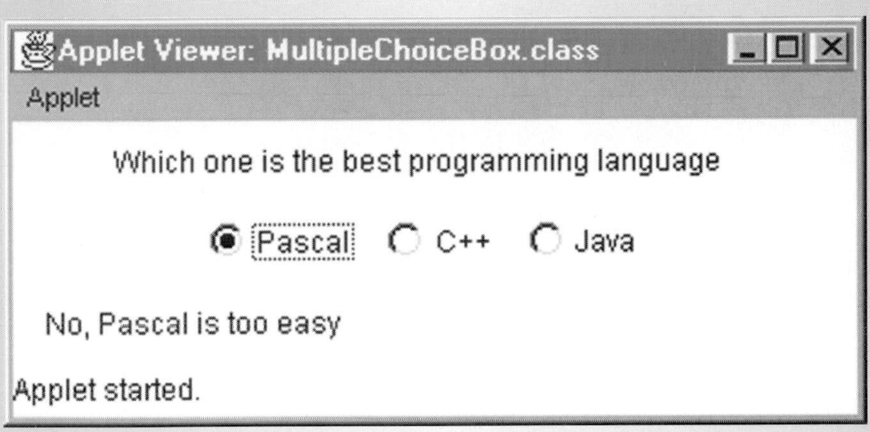

Figure 10.17 The CheckboxGroup multiple-choice test display

Figure 10.18 shows how the same problem is implemented using a list.
Figure 10.19 shows the display. Structurally, the solutions look very similar.

One difference is that a List is created rather than a CheckboxGroup
and the List method addItem is used to add each possible answer. In
itemStateChanged, the List method getSelectedItem is used to determine which answer was given. Based on the value returned, the display is
updated in a manner similar to the solution in class MultipleChoiceBox
in Fig. 10.16.

```
/*    File: MultipleChoice.java
      Developed for Problem Solving with Java,
         Koffman & Wolz.
      Appears in Fig. 10.18.
*/
import java.awt.*;
import java.applet.Applet;
import java.awt.event.*;

public class MultipleChoice extends Applet
                            implements ItemListener {
    private Label question;
    private List answers;
    private Label report;
```

Figure 10.18 *continued*

Figure 10.18 *continued*

```
    public void init() {
        question = new
  Label("Which one is the best programming language?");
        add(question);

        answers = new List(3,false);

        answers.addItem("Pascal");
        answers.addItem("C++");
        answers.addItem("Java");

        add(answers);
        answers.addItemListener(this);

        report =
         new Label("_____");
        add(report);
    }

    public void itemStateChanged(ItemEvent e) {
        if (answers.getSelectedItem() == "Java") {
    report.setText("Of course!, Java is just right!");
            answers.setEnabled(false); // Disable the
                                       //   choice.
        } else if (answers.getSelectedItem() == "C++")
            report.setText("No, C++ is too hard!");
        else report.setText("No, Pascal is too easy");
    }

} // class MultipleChoice
```

Figure 10.18 The multiple-choice test using the `List` component

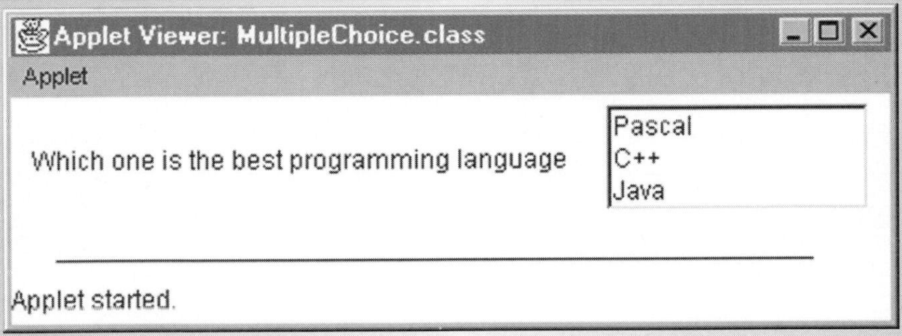

Figure 10.19 The List multiple-choice test display

Finally, Fig. 10.20 and 10.21 show how a Choice component can be used. The structure of the code is very similar to that of the List component. In init, the one difference is that a Choice component is created rather than a List. A second difference is that the first choice is a label that says "Pull down for choices." We used this label for visual effect; otherwise, only the first choice, "Pascal" would be visible. In itemStateChanged, the main difference is the need to account for the choice of "Pull down for choices." If the user selects it, the message "Try again" is displayed.

```
/*    File: MultipleChoice.java
      Developed for Problem Solving with Java,
         Koffman & Wolz.
      Appears in Fig. 10.20.
*/
import java.awt.*;
import java.applet.Applet;
import java.awt.event.*;


public class MultipleChoice extends Applet
                            implements ItemListener {
    private Label question;
    private Choice answers;
    private Label report;
```

Figure 10.20 *continued*

Figure 10.20 *continued*

```
    public void init() {
        question = new
  Label("Which one is the best programming language?");
        add(question);

        answers = new Choice();
        answers.addItem("Pull down for choices");
        answers.addItem("Pascal");
        answers.addItem("C++");
        answers.addItem("Java");

        add(answers);
        answers.addItemListener(this);

        // Leave space for long string.
        report =
            new Label("_____");
        add(report);

    }

    public void itemStateChanged(ItemEvent e) {
        if (answers.getSelectedItem() ==
                                "Pull down for choices")
            report.setText("Try again!");
        else if (answers.getSelectedItem() == "Java") {
    report.setText("Of course!, Java is just right!");
            answers.setEnabled(false); // Disable the
                                        //   choice
        } else if (answers.getSelectedItem() == "C++")
            report.setText("No, C++ is too hard!");
        else
            report.setText("No, Pascal is too easy");
    }
} // class MultipleChoice
```

Figure 10.20 The multiple-choice test using the Choice component

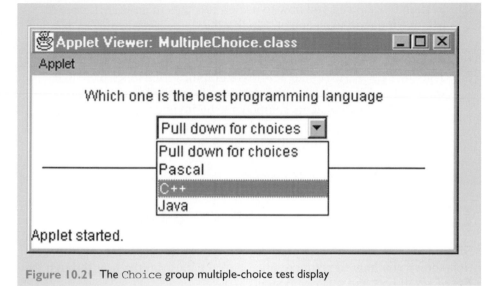

Figure 10.21 The Choice group multiple-choice test display

EXERCISES FOR SECTION 10.3

Self-Check

1. For each of the following, indicate whether it generates an action event or an item event:

    Button   TextArea   TextField   Choice   List   CheckBox

2. What is the difference between an action event and an item event?

3. What is the difference between putting a group of checkboxes in a panel and grouping them with a CheckboxGroup?

4. Under what circumstances is each of the following the best choice:

    Checkboxes, checkboxes in a CheckboxGroup, List, Choice

Programming

1. Using the calorie counting program as a guide, invent your own "select options" applet. For example, help someone figure out the cost of configuring a computer if you are given the components and their prices.

2. Write a multiple-choice question that asks users which of the following they would prefer to do on a Saturday night: go to the movies, go to a concert, read a book.

3. Write an applet that calculates someone's grade-point average. Provide a list of courses as well as the number of credits for each course. The user not only selects courses taken, but selects the grade received.

4. Section 9.6 showed you how to use `param` tags in an HTML page to pass information to an applet. Modify the `Calories` applet so that the food descriptions and corresponding calories are loaded from an HTML page.

5. The `MultipleChoice` applets use a graphics trick to save enough space for a change in label size. You can force the layout manager of a container to recalculate its components by invalidating the component and telling the container to validate itself using the `invalidate` and `validate` methods, respectively. Show how to use this technique in Fig. 10.16.

10.4 Continuous and Textual User Input

Section 10.3 showed a variety of ways of capturing discrete data. This section shows you how to get more open-ended data from the user through the use of scroll bars and text components.

Scrollbars

Scroll bars provide a mechanism for capturing a value within a range. Most user interfaces for word processors use scroll bars to enable the user to scroll through a document. Unlike discrete devices like buttons, scroll bars can be adjusted to catch very fine or very gross movements.

EXAMPLE 10.5

A color mixer lets you create new colors by mixing the basic red, green, and blue attributes of a `Color` object. Class `ColorBars` in Figure 10.22 creates a color mixer using the `Scrollbar` component. Three scroll bars are created, one to monitor each color. A `Scrollbar` component has five parameters that may be specified when it is instantiated:

```
new Scrollbar(orientation,  value,  visible-region,
                    minimum,  maximum);
```

A scroll bar can be oriented horizontally or vertically. The *value* is the current setting of the bar. The arguments *minimum* and *maximum* specify the range of values. The *value* must fall within the range. Set the *visible-region* argument to 1. (Other settings are needed only for `Scrollbar` applications that are beyond the scope of our book. (See Appendix D.) The scroll bars created in Figure 10.23 have a horizontal orientation, an initial value of 255, and range of values from 0 to 255. This range matches the possible values of color attributes in the `Color` class.

`Scrollbar` is the only component that is a source of `AdjustmentEvents`. Consequently, the applet implements `AdjustmentListener`, and defines the method `adjustmentValueChanged`. This method displays the current values of the color components and changes the color of the canvas.

The code in Fig 10.22 sets up an applet in which three labels are attached to three scroll bars within three panels through the following `for` loop.

```
for (int i = 0; i < 3; i++) {
    labels[i] = new Label(colorNames[i] + 255);
    barPanel.add(labels[i]);
    values[i] = new Scrollbar(Scrollbar.HORIZONTAL,
                              255, 1, 0, 256);
    barPanel.add(values[i]);
    values[i].addAdjustmentListener(this);
}
```

The array `labels` holds the three labels. The array `values` holds the `Scrollbar` objects. The variable `barPanel` is reused for each panel. First, each label is constructed. The label is based on the array `colorNames` initialized with literal names for the colors concatentated (joined) to the number 255 (the initial value of each scroll bar). Then each label is added to the panel. Next each scroll bar is created and stored in the `values` array. Each scroll bar is then added to the panel, and the applet is registered as a listener for each scroll bar's events.

Layout managers are exploited to create the display in Figure 10.23. Scroll bars take up as much space as the panel in which they reside. The combination of `GridLayout` and `BorderLayout` used here forces them to occupy the full width of the window. All the scroll bars and their labels are placed in a panel as a single column grid.

A canvas displays the color generated by the values of the three scroll bars. The color is the result of creating a new color from the red, green, and blue values that were selected by the user. The three array elements that store the scroll bars are each asked to retrieve their value, and their combination becomes the new background color for the canvas:

```
c.SetBackground(new Color(values[0].getValue(),
                          values[1].getValue(),
                          values[2].getValue()));
```

```
/*    File: ColorBars.java
      Developed for Problem Solving with Java,
        Koffman & Wolz.
      Appears in Fig. 10.22.
*/

import java.awt.*;
import java.applet.Applet;
import java.awt.event.*;

public class ColorBars extends Applet
                       implements AdjustmentListener {
    Canvas c;
    String[] colorNames = {"Red:    ", "Green: ",
                             "Blue:   "};
    Scrollbar[] values = new Scrollbar[3];
    Label[] labels = new Label[3];

    public void init() {
        setLayout(new BorderLayout());
        c = new Canvas();
        c.setSize(50,50);
        c.setBackground(new Color(255, 255, 255));
        add(c, BorderLayout.CENTER);

        Panel barPanel = new Panel();
        barPanel.setLayout(new GridLayout(0,1));
        for (int i = 0; i < 3; i++) {
            labels[i] = new Label(colorNames[i] + 255);
            barPanel.add(labels[i]);
            values[i] = new Scrollbar
                (Scrollbar.HORIZONTAL, 255, 1, 0, 256);
            barPanel.add(values[i]);

            values[i].addAdjustmentListener(this);
        }
        add(barPanel, BorderLayout.NORTH);
    }
```

Figure 10.22 *continued*

Figure 10.22 *continued*

```
public void adjustmentValueChanged
  (AdjustmentEvent e) {
  for (int i = 0; i < 3; i++)
    labels[i].setText(
              colorNames[i] + values[i].getValue());

  c.setBackground(new Color(values[0].getValue(),
                            values[1].getValue(),
                            values[2].getValue()));

  c.repaint();
  }

} // class ColorBars
```

Figure 10.22 A color mixer using Scrollbars

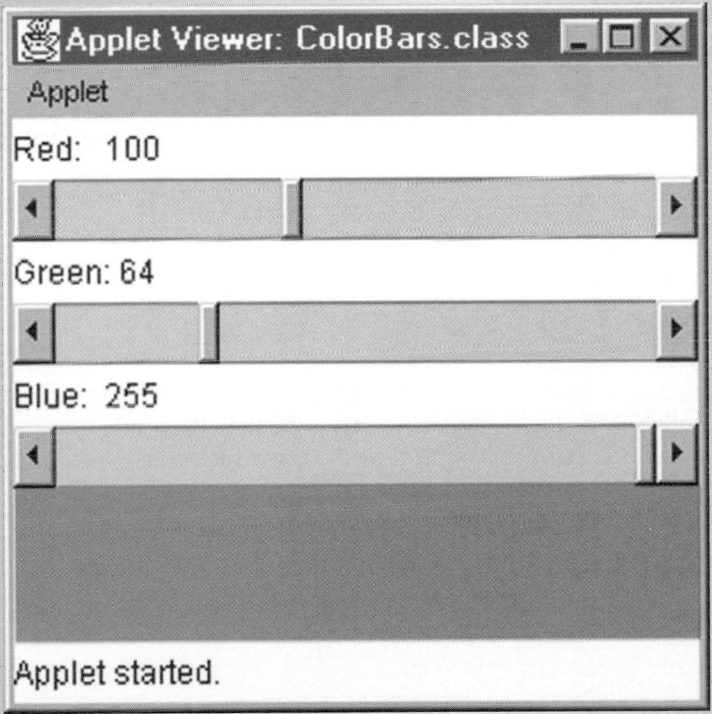

Figure 10.23 Display of the color mixer

TextComponents

Text components allow you a wider range of options for capturing textual data than do scroll bars. You should be aware that "back in the good old days" all user input came via text. As you might imagine, considerable error-checking was needed to guarantee that the user's response satisfied the constraints of the desired input. There are two `TextComponent` subclasses: `TextField` and `TextArea`. A `TextField` displays a single line of text; a `TextArea` displays an area of text. We illustrate this in our next implementation of a color mixer.

The applet in Figure 10.24 solves the color-mixer problem using `TextFields` and `ActionEvents`. The solution looks structurally similar to that of Figure 10.22, except that the `values` array stores `TextFields` instead of `Scrollbars`. A display appears in Figure 10.25. The major difference is in the `actionPerformed` method. `TextFields` store strings, not integers. Consequently, the string typed in by the user must be converted to an integer. Two potential input errors must be caught:

- Strings that are not numeric
- Numeric strings that are out of range

The `actionPerformed` method uses the `Integer` class to do the conversion. It catches an exception thrown by the conversion if the input string was nonnumeric. It then tests whether a numeric string is within range.

Admittedly, this is a complicated piece of Java code. In the `for` loop, the `try` block

```
try {intObj = Integer.valueOf(values[i].getText());
     numbers[i] = intObj.intValue();
}
```

gets a `String` from a `TextField` stored in the `values` array. The `Integer` class method `valueOf` attempts to convert the string into an integer. If it is successful, the integer is stored in the corresponding position in the `numbers` array. If the user entered nonnumeric characters, then the exception thrown by `valueOf` is caught:

```
catch(NumberFormatException except) {
     numbers[i] = 0;
     values[i].setText("0");
     System.err.println
               ("String entered is not a number");
}
```

and the value stored and displayed is set to 0. Similarly, if the integer entered lies outside the valid range (0–255):

```
if ((numbers[i] < 0) || (numbers[i] > 255)) {
    numbers[i] = 0;
    values[i].setText("0");
    System.err.println
                ("Number entered is not in range 0-255");
}
```

the value stored and displayed is set to 0. Notice that an out-of-range number does not throw an exception, so we use an `if` statement, not a `catch` block, to detect it.

Note that the response to a user error is not handled gracefully. The user may have no idea why the input was not accepted. Although there are some circumstances in which a user would rather enter text than manipulate a scroll bar, most of the time your interface should create constraints that prevent the user from making an error in the first place.

```
/*   File: ColorBars.java
     Developed for Problem Solving with Java, Koffman & Wolz.
     Appears in Fig. 10.24.
*/
import java.awt.*;
import java.applet.Applet;
import java.awt.event.*;

public class ColorBars extends Applet implements ActionListener {
    Canvas c;
    String[] colorNames = {"Red:    ", "Green: ", "Blue:   "};
    TextField[] values = new TextField[3];
    Label[] labels = new Label[3];

    public void init() {
        setLayout(new BorderLayout());
        c = new Canvas();
        c.setSize(50, 50);
        c.setBackground(new Color(255, 255, 255));
        add(c, BorderLayout.CENTER);
```

Figure 10.24 *continued*

Figure 10.24 *continued*

```
        Panel textPanel = new Panel();
        textPanel.setLayout(new GridLayout(0, 1));
        for (int i = 0; i < 3; i++) {
            labels[i] = new Label(colorNames[i]);
            textPanel.add(labels[i]);
            values[i] = new TextField("255");
            textPanel.add(values[i]);
            values[i].addActionListener(this);
        }
        add(textPanel, BorderLayout.NORTH);
    }

    public void actionPerformed(ActionEvent e) {
      Integer intObj;
      int[] numbers = new int[3];
      for (int i = 0; i < 3 ; i++) {
        try {intObj = Integer.valueOf( values[i].getText());
            numbers[i] = intObj.intValue();
        } catch(NumberFormatException except) {
            numbers[i] = 0;
            values[i].setText("0");
            System.err.println("String entered is not a number");
        }
        if ((numbers[i] < 0) || (numbers[i] > 255)) {
            numbers[i] = 0;
            values[i].setText("0");
            System.err.println("Number entered is not in range 0-255");
        }
      }

      c.setBackground(new Color(numbers[0],
                               numbers[1],
                               numbers[2]));
      c.repaint();
    }
} // class ColorBars
```

Figure 10.24 A color mixer using TextFields

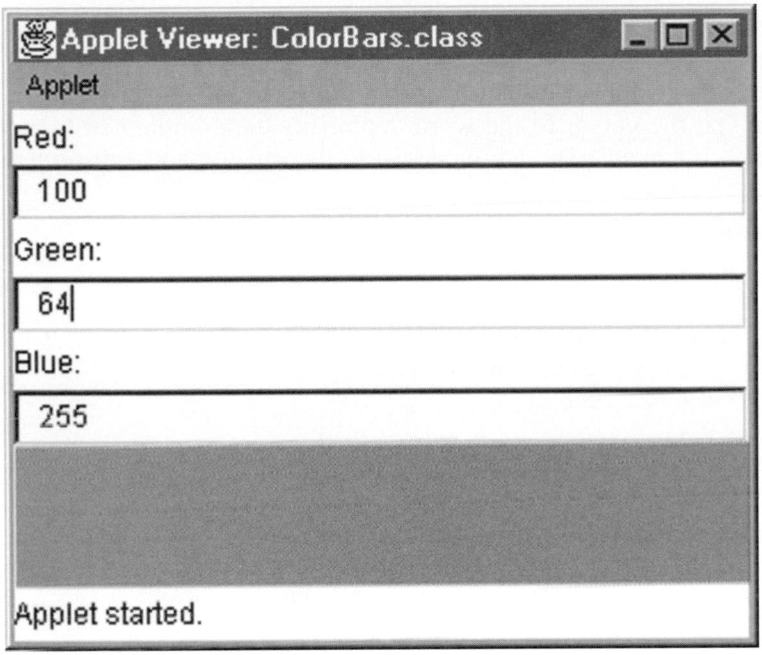

Figure 10.25 The display for color bars with `TextField`

TextEvent

Normally you don't need to capture a string until after the user is finished typing. However, if you were trying to do on-the-fly spell-checking, for example, you would need to monitor individual keyboard events. We show how to do this in the next example through low-level control of a `TextComponent`.

EXAMPLE 10.6

The problem now is to notice every time a character is pressed. In this example we create a text editor that censors words it doesn't like. Whenever there is a change in the contents of the `TextComponent` the entire text is reviewed, searching for words on a "bad" list. If the word is found, then it is replaced with the word "censored."

Figure 10.26 shows how to use a `TextEvent` for this purpose. The applet implements `TextListener` and defines the method `textValueChanged`. The component `TextArea` allows the user to type in multiple lines of text. `TextEvents` can also be used to detect text changes in `TextFields`. `TextEvents` are fired (initiated) when the actual text changes. `KeyEvents` (see Appendix D) are fired whenever any keystroke is detected. For example, the user might press successive Control keys that move the cursor to the left or right. These keystrokes do not change the text and therefore do not fire TextEvents. Figure 10.27 shows a before and after picture of a bad-word detection. The user typed in the text, then moved the cursor to the word "company" and attempted to replace it with "computer." The editor detected the change and substituted "censored."

```java
/*    File: CensorWords.java
      Developed for Problem Solving with Java,
         Koffman & Wolz.
      Appears in Fig. 10.26.
*/
import java.awt.*;
import java.applet.Applet;
import java.awt.event.*;

public class CensorWords extends Applet
                               implements TextListener {
    TextArea ta;

    String[] badWords = {"computer", "hack",
                         "program"};

    public void init() {
        add(tshow);
        ta = new TextArea();
        add(ta);
        ta.addTextListener(this);
    }

    public void textValueChanged(TextEvent evt) {
        String text = ta.getText();
        for (int i = 0; i < badWords.length; i++) {
            String word = badWords[i];
            int found = text.indexOf(word, 0);
            if (found >= 0) {
                ta.replaceRange("censored", found,
                                found + word.length());
                ta.setEnabled(false);
            }
        }
    }
} // class CensorWords
```

Figure 10.26 A censoring editor uses text events

The event handler `textValueChanged` uses the `String` class method `indexOf` to attempt to locate a "bad" word in the text. (See the `String` class in Appendix C.) This method returns -1 if the word is not found. If one of the words is in the text, then the `TextComponent` method `replaceRange` is used to substitute the word "censored" for that word. Method `replaceRange` requires a string, a start position (inclusive) and an end position (exclusive) for substitution. The component is disabled and cannot fire further events when the word is found. Disabling is accomplished with a call to `setEnabled(false)`. (To enable a component, you call `setEnabled(true)`.)

You can include as many `TextFields` and `TextAreas` in a GUI layout as will practically fit. You can also mix `ActionListeners` with `TextListeners` to determine which components have been changed. `Components` can be enabled and disabled, as well as made visible and invisible with the `setVisible(boolean)` method.

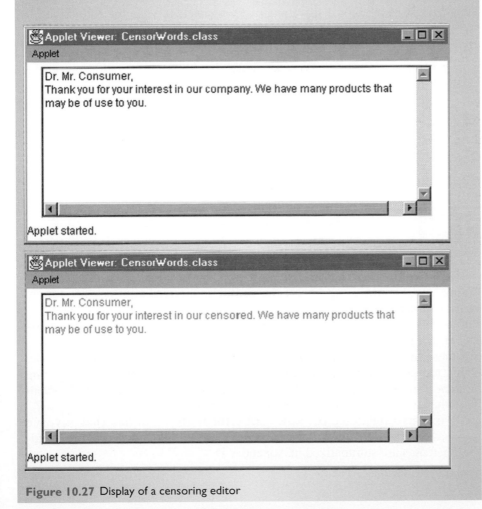

Figure 10.27 Display of a censoring editor

Self-Check

1. Under what circumstances are `Scrollbars` useful. Come up with an example in which you think `Scrollbars` would be inappropriate.

2. Explain the difference between what happens when an `ActionEvent` and a `TextEvent` are generated by a `TextComponent`.

3. What is the difference between a `TextField` and a `TextArea`?

Programming

1. Write a color mixer that allows a user to use either a scroll bar or a text field to mix the colors.

2. Write a text editor that automatically wraps text when the end of the line has been reached.

3. A classic program is to convert back and forth between Fahrenheit and Celsius temperatures. Write an applet that has two text fields, one each for Fahrenheit and Celsius temperature. If the user modifies one of these, the other must be updated with proper values.

4. Repeat Programming Exercise 3 using two scroll bars. *Hint:* You will need to study the documentation for `Scrollbar` in Appendix D to change the position of the bar.

10.5 Low-Level User Input

The events of the previous sections captured abstract actions. As a beginning programmer, you will probably be able to accomplish almost everything you want to using one of these. But sometimes you may need more fine-grained control. Every component responds to a set of basic input actions defined as `ComponentEvents`. Each of these events requires a listener that must define abstract methods of that particular listener class. Most of these listeners must implement a set of methods rather than a single one. This requirement can get annoying. Therefore, if you find yourself using `ComponentEvents`, step back from the problem and think carefully about whether some abstract event would suit your needs.

We illustrate `ComponentEvents` through examples that involve `MouseEvents`. The entire set of `ComponentEvents` and their corresponding listeners are summarized in Appendix D.

MouseEvents

A mouse event occurs whenever the mouse enters or leaves a component, when a mouse button is pressed or released, or when a mouse button is clicked. A click is defined as a mouse press/release sequence that happens "in close proximity." In other words, if the mouse is rapidly pressed and released without moving very far, it counts as a click. Appendix C summarizes how to figure out which button has been pressed as well as how many clicks might have occurred.

EXAMPLE 10.7

In this example we implement a drawable surface. Figure 10.28 shows a simple drawing surface created by running applet `MouseDemo` (Figure 10.29). When the mouse is detected outside the applet, the drawing surface has a black background color. When the mouse moves into the area, the drawing surface becomes white (see method `mouseEntered`). Notice that this is a way to clear the screen! The words "Mouse Pressed!" are displayed at the cursor position when the mouse is pressed (see method `mousePressed`). A line is drawn from the point of the initial press to the position where the mouse is released (see method `mouseReleased`). When a click occurs, the words "Mouse Clicked!" are drawn in the upper-left corner (see method `mouseClicked`). Illustrations in the text do not do justice to this example. You need to play with the mouse a bit. The programming exercises at the end of this section suggest ways to expand on the mouse demonstration program.

A `MouseEventListener` must define five methods:

- `mouseClicked()`
- `mouseEntered()`
- `mouseExited()`
- `mousePressed()`
- `mouseRelased()`

Even if your application is not interested in detecting one of these activities, you must define the method. A set of classes called `Adapter` classes are provided when you only want one or two methods. A brief summary of `MouseAdapters` appears in Appendix C.

In Figure 10.29 notice that some of the event handlers repaint the applet while others do not. Recall that the `repaint` method erases the contents of the drawing surface of a component (such as an applet, a button, or a panel) and fills it with the background color. Consequently, the methods that invoke the `graphics` object to draw lines or strings do not include `repaint` calls. Any drawing that is to be maintained between calls to `repaint` must occur within the `paint` method of a component. (See Self-Check Exercises 1 and 2 at the end of this section.)

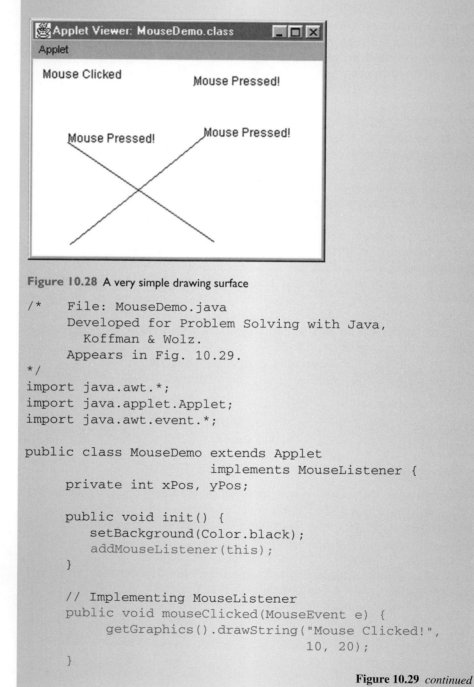

Figure 10.28 A very simple drawing surface

```
/*     File: MouseDemo.java
       Developed for Problem Solving with Java,
          Koffman & Wolz.
       Appears in Fig. 10.29.
*/
import java.awt.*;
import java.applet.Applet;
import java.awt.event.*;

public class MouseDemo extends Applet
                       implements MouseListener {
    private int xPos, yPos;

    public void init() {
        setBackground(Color.black);
        addMouseListener(this);
    }

    // Implementing MouseListener
    public void mouseClicked(MouseEvent e) {
        getGraphics().drawString("Mouse Clicked!",
                                 10, 20);
    }
```

Figure 10.29 *continued*

Figure 10.29 *continued*

```
    public void mouseEntered(MouseEvent e) {
        setBackground(Color.white);
        repaint();
    }

    public void mouseExited(MouseEvent e)  {
        setBackground(Color.black);
        repaint();

    }

    public void mousePressed(MouseEvent e) {
        Graphics g = getGraphics();
        xPos = e.getX();
        yPos = e.getY();
        g.drawString("Mouse Pressed!", xPos, yPos);
    }

    public void mouseReleased(MouseEvent e) {
        Graphics g = getGraphics();
        g.drawLine(xPos, yPos, e.getX(), e.getY());
    }
} // class MouseDemo
```

Figure 10.29 Detecting mouse events

MouseMotionListeners

The `MouseEvents` described so far were triggered by gross changes in mouse movement. `MouseEvents` also occur when minute changes in mouse position occur. The `MouseMotionListener` class is informed about such events. It can handle two types of events:

`mouseDragged`   The mouse moved while a button is being pressed.

`mouseMoved`   The mouse moved while no button is being pressed.

EXAMPLE 10.8

This example shows a slightly more sophisticated drawing surface. Figure 10.30 shows some rough sketches created by running the applet `MouseMotionDemo` (Fig. 10.31), which implements a `MouseMotionListener` as well as a `MouseListener`. The `mousePressed` method records the first position at which to draw. As the mouse moves, the `mouseDragged` method is called; it records the change in position and draws a line between the previously recorded position and the new one. It then resets the previous position to the current position. Drawing stops when the mouse is released, that is, when the mouse is no longer being "dragged."

Figure 10.30 A rough drawing surface

```
/*    File: MouseMotionDemo.java
      Developed for Problem Solving with Java,
         Koffman & Wolz.
      Appears in Fig. 10.31.
*/
import java.awt.*;
import java.applet.Applet;
import java.awt.event.*;

public class MouseMotionDemo extends Applet
         implements MouseListener, MouseMotionListener {
    private int xPos, yPos;

    public void init() {
        setBackground(Color.black);
        addMouseListener(this);
        addMouseMotionListener(this);
    }

    // Implementing MouseListener
    public void mouseClicked(MouseEvent e) {;}
```

Figure 10.31 *continued*

Figure 10.31 *continued*

```
    public void mouseEntered(MouseEvent e) {
        setBackground(Color.white);
        repaint();
    }

    public void mouseExited(MouseEvent e)  {
        setBackground(Color.black);
        repaint();
    }

    public void mousePressed(MouseEvent e) {
        xPos = e.getX();
        yPos = e.getY();
    }

    public void mouseReleased(MouseEvent e){;}

    // Implementing MouseMotionListener
    public void mouseDragged(MouseEvent e) {
        getGraphics().drawLine(xPos, yPos,
                               e.getX(), e.getY());

        xPos = e.getX();
        yPos = e.getY();
    }

    public void mouseMoved(MouseEvent e) {;}
} // class MouseMotionDemo
```

Figure 10.31 Using a `MouseMotionListener` to draw

Notice that the graphics context in `mouseDragged` is referenced directly, not through a local variable. Since it is referenced only once, there is no real need to first store it in a variable. Notice, too, that all of the abstract methods from `MouseListener` and `MouseMotionListener` must be implemented even if they don't do anything.

EXERCISES FOR SECTION 10.5

Self-Check

1. List the component events discussed in this section and explain what they do.

2. If every component can detect low-level events, why is there a need for semantic events?

Programming

1. Modify the `MouseDemo` program so that the mouse changes color between two colors every time a single click occurs. When a double click occurs, change the color to a third color.

2. Modify the `MouseDemo` program to include a text area adjacent to the drawing area. *Hint:* You will have to put the drawing area in a canvas and detect mouse events on the canvas. Instead of drawing the strings "Mouse Pressed!" and "Mouse Clicked!" on the drawing surface, display the words with the coordinates on a line in the text area.

3. Modify the `MouseMotionDemo` so that it draws on a canvas and the user can select the pen color in which to draw.

4. Create an applet that allows a user to put specified shapes such as squares anywhere on a canvas.

10.6 Turn-Taking within the Event Model

The hardest GUI concept for beginners to master is the event model. The event model is especially difficult to use when a complicated process flow is needed. This section synthesizes the ideas from the previous sections through a case study and shows how they can be used to develop a game in which players take turns.

At first glance the process flow for a computer game looks pretty simple:

Algorithm

1. Set up the game board.
2. Select an order of play (select who goes first).
3. Designate the first player.
4. `While` the game is not over.

   Current player takes a turn.

   Gives a turn to next player.
5. Determine who won.

This algorithm works for any number of players from a game of Solitaire to a game with numerous players such as Hearts or Bridge. Any of the players could be a human being or a computer.

The problem with this algorithm is that it assumes the "stop and wait" model of processing. When a human player takes a turn, the action stops until the player is finished. The case study presented here shows how to cast this algorithm into an object-oriented framework.

Instead of thinking of it as a "loop," think of the problem as involving two kinds of objects: a game-keeper and a player. The game-keeper sets up the board, keeps score, determines when the game is over, and decides whose turn it is. A player takes a turn. If the player is a machine (the computer), it simply determines its move, makes it, and reports to the game-keeper that it is done. If the player is a human, then that player must be given control of the GUI input devices. Event listener methods process the human player's move and then report to the game-keeper that the move is complete and control should be passed to the next player.

This perspective on turn-taking is shown through one of the simplest games around: TicTacToe. This version can be played as a two-person, or two-machine game, or a human can play a machine. The basic framework presented here can be extended to games with many more players.

Case Study

TicTacToe

PROBLEM

Within an applet, create a TicTacToe game in which either player can be a human or a machine. In TicTacToe two players take turns marking cells in a 3×3 grid. One player is "X" and the other is "O." When one player has three marks in a row, column, or diagonal, the game is over and that player has won. A draw (no winner) happens when all cells are filled and no player has "three in a row."

ANALYSIS

We use the framework described above to separate out responsibilities. Four classes will be needed:

A game-keeper for the TicTacToe game

A player (an abstract class)

A machine (extends the `Player` class)

A human (extends the `Player` class)

The game-keeper will be responsible for setting up the game. The game board can be represented by a 3×3 array of buttons. Players may only select enabled buttons. The GUI will therefore need a panel containing the buttons as well as a label that reports whose turn it is or whether the game is over. The game-keeper is also responsible for creating the players.

A player is an abstract object that can take a turn. Although we will try to ensure that a turn will only be offered when a turn is possible, our logic could go wrong. Therefore, any player, either machine or human, must have a recovery mechanism if a turn cannot be taken. This type of mechanism is called *error trapping*. It terminates the program in a "buggy state." Each player will report to the game-keeper, which will display the error. After an error, no more turns can be taken.

A machine player has an algorithm for selecting a button. Our version will use an extremely simple algorithm: Find the next available enabled button by searching from left to right, top to bottom.

To support moves for more than one human player we need to determine who pressed the buttons. In the sequential turn-taking used in TicTacToe, we effectively want to lock out all but the player whose turn it is. We can do this using event listeners. The instance of the player object whose turn it is registers as a listener for all enabled buttons. After the player has selected a button, the player object removes itself as a listener for button events and disables the button selected.

DESIGN

We elaborate on the specification of each object:

Specification for `TicTacToe` *Class*

Data Fields

`Button[3][3] board`—the game board
`Panel p`—to hold the board
`Label l`—to post game status
`Player p1, p2`—the players
`Player next`—the player who took the last turn, initially `p2` so that when `nextTurn` is called the first time, `p1` will be the first player.
`Player winner`—the player who won the game, initially null
`int turns`—the number of turns taken, initially 0

Methods

`init()`—constructs a game board, instantiates the players, starts play
`nextPlayer()`—passes play to the next player
`gameOver()`—determines whether the game is over
`findWinner(Player p)`—determines whether a player has won
`showWinner()`—displays the winner in the label
`position(int r, int c)`—returns button object at position `r`, `c` in the array
`errorFound()`—indicates that some object found a fatal error. Game ends.

Specification for `Player` *Class*

Data Fields

`String name`—the name of the player (`X` or `O`) (argument of the constructor)
`TicTacToe ap`–the game object (argument of the constructor)

Methods

`Player(String name, TicTacToe ap)`—constructs a player object

`getName()`—retrieves player's name

`abstract takeTurn()`—defined by `Machine` class or `Human` class, controls the turn

Specification for Machine Class

Methods

`Machine(String name, TicTacToe ap)`—creates an instance of a machine

`takeTurn()`—must be defined, uses `findMove` to locate a button, marks the button, and disables it

`findMove()`—algorithm to find next button

Specification for Human Class (implements ActionListener)

Methods

`Human(String name, TicTacToe ap)`—creates an instance of a human

`takeTurn()`—must be defined, registers `Human` object as event listener for enabled buttons

`actionPerformed`—must be defined, removes `Human` object as event listener for enabled buttons, marks button, and then disables it. Tells game-keeper to determine next player

We list the algorithms for the methods next.

Algorithm for `init` in `TicTacToe`

1. Create instances of the panel, buttons, and label. Add them to the applet. Don't register any listeners, however.

2. Create instances of two players. Here we will create one human and one machine.

Algorithm for `nextPlayer` in `TicTacToe`

1. `if` the game is over.

  1.1. Show winner.

  `else`

  1.2. Switch players.

  1.3. Set label to this player.

  1.4. Increment `turns`.

  1.5. Tell player to take a turn.

Algorithm for `gameOver` in `TicTacToe`

1. Return `true` if `p1` is a winner or `p2` is a winner or `turns >= 9`; otherwise, return `false`.

Algorithm for `findWinner` in `TicTacToe`

1. For this player determine:
    1.1. Is there a row in which the player has marked all buttons?
    1.2. Is there a column in which the player has marked all buttons?
    1.3. Is there a diagonal in which the player has marked all buttons?
2. Set winner to this player if any of the above are `true` and return `true`.

Algorithm for `takeTurn` in `Machine`

1. Call `findMove` to locate the next available button.
2. Mark the button with this object's name.
3. Disable the button.
4. Tell the game-keeper to pass the turn to the next player.

Algorithm for `findMove` in `Machine`

1. Starting at position `0, 0`, search the button array from left to right, top to bottom:
    1.1. Return the first button that is enabled.

Algorithm for `takeTurn` in `Human`

1. Starting at position `0, 0`, traverse the button array from left to right, top to bottom:
    1.1. `if` a button is enabled, register as a listener for that button.

Algorithm for `actionPerformed` in `Human`

1. Get the source of the event (the button that was pressed).
2. Put this object's name on the button.
3. Disable the button that was just pressed.
4. Starting at position `0, 0`, traverse the button array from left to right, top to bottom:
    4.1. `if` a button is enabled, remove this object as an event listener for that button.

IMPLEMENTATION

Figures 10.32–10.35 show the implementations for the different classes.

TESTING

Figure 10.36 shows a turn within a game. Note, in particular, that it is an easy modification to make this a two-person game or a two-machine-player game.

An interesting design feature is the ability to make a subclass of the machine class and override the `findMove` method. You could then implement a number of different algorithms for playing TicTacToe and let the machines battle it out!

```java
/*    File: TicTacToe.java
      Developed for Problem Solving with Java, Koffman & Wolz.
      Appears in Fig. 10.32.
*/
import java.awt.*;
import java.applet.*;

public class TicTacToe extends Applet {
   // GUI objects
    private Button[][] board = new Button[3][3];
    private Panel p;
    private Label l;

   // Game pieces
    private Machine p1;
    private Human p2;

   // Score-keeping devices
    private Player next = p2;       // p1 will go first (see nextTurn below).
    private Player winner = null;   // gameOver stores winning player here.
    private int turns = 0;          // Counts turns taken. Game ends when all
                                    // squares have been taken.

    public void init() {
       // Create applet layout.
       setLayout(new BorderLayout());

       // Create panel of buttons.
       p = new Panel();
       p.setLayout(new GridLayout(3, 3));
       for (int r = 0; r < 3; r++)
          for (int c = 0; c < 3; c++) {
             board[r][c] = new Button("");
             p.add(board[r][c]);
          }
       add(p, BorderLayout.CENTER);
```

Figure 10.32 *continued*

Figure 10.32 *continued*

```
      // Create label at the bottom.
      l = new Label();
      add(l, BorderLayout.SOUTH);

      // Create players; each player needs knowledge of THIS game.
      p1 = new Machine("X", this);   // p1 will be X.
      p2 = new Human("0", this);     // p2 will be 0.

      // Start play.
      nextPlayer();

   } // init


   // Check for winners FIRST! because the first
   //  player could win on the last move.
   // Theoretically, turns should never exceed 9, but you never know....
   public boolean gameOver() {
        int r, c;
        return (findWinner(p1) || findWinner(p2) || turns >= 9);
   }


   // This is not necessarily the best way to determine a winner.
   // It creates the side effect of registering the winner in the
   // data field winner. The method showWinner needs this!
   private boolean findWinner(Player p) {
        String name = p.getName();
        for (int r = 0; r < 3; r++) // Check rows.
             if ((board[r][0].getLabel() == name)
                 && (board[r][1].getLabel() == name)
                 && (board[r][2].getLabel() == name)
                 ) {winner = p; return true;}
        for (int c = 0; c < 3; c++) // Check columns.
             if ((board[0][c].getLabel() == name)
                 && (board[1][c].getLabel() == name)
                 && (board[2][c].getLabel() == name)
                 ) {winner = p; return true;}

        // Check diagonals.
        if ((board[0][0].getLabel() == name)
                 && (board[1][1].getLabel() == name)
                 && (board[2][2].getLabel() == name)
                 ) {winner = p; return true;}
```

Figure 10.32 *continued*

Figure 10.32 *continued*

```
        if ((board[0][2].getLabel() == name)
            && (board[1][1].getLabel() == name)
            && (board[2][0].getLabel() == name)
            ) {winner = p; return true;}
        return false; // No winner.
    }

    public void showWinner() {
        if (winner == p1) l.setText("X won");
        else if (winner == p2) l.setText("O won");
        else l.setText("It was a draw");
    }

    public void nextPlayer() {
        if (gameOver()) showWinner();
        else {
            if (next == p1) next = p2;          // Switch between players.
            else next = p1;
            l.setText("Player: " + next.getName());  // Display current
                                                 // player.
            turns++;                             // Count the number of turns.
            next.takeTurn();
        }
    }

    public void errorFound(String s) {
        l.setText("Fatal error, game terminated: " + s);
    }

    public Button position(int r, int c) {
        return board[r][c];
    }
}   // class TicTacToe
```

Figure 10.32 Implementation of the `TicTacToe` class

```
/*   File: Player.java
     Developed for Problem Solving with Java, Koffman & Wolz.
     Appears in Fig. 10.33.
*/
```

Figure 10.33 *continued*

Figure 10.33 *continued*

```
public abstract class Player {
    protected String name = "";
    protected TicTacToe ap;

    public Player(String na, TicTacToe a) {
        name = na;
        ap = a;
    }

    public abstract void takeTurn();

    public String getName() {
        return name;
    }
} // class Player
```

Figure 10.33 Implementation of the abstract Player class

```
/*    File: Machine.java
      Developed for Problem Solving with Java, Koffman & Wolz.
      Appears in Fig. 10.34.
*/
import java.awt.*;

public class Machine extends Player {

    public Machine(String name, TicTacToe ap) {
        super(name, ap);
    }

    public void takeTurn() {
        // findMove is the "guts" of decision making.
        Button b = findMove();
        if (b != null) {
            b.setLabel(name);
            b.setEnabled(false);
            ap.nextPlayer();
        }
        else ap.errorFound("machine player can't make a move!");
    }

    // This is a very simple decision maker. See if you can figure it out.
```

Figure 10.34 *continued*

Figure 10.34 *continued*

```
      private Button findMove() {
            for (int r=0; r < 3; r++)
                 for (int c=0; c < 3; c++) {
                       Button b = ap.position(r, c);
                       if (b.isEnabled()) return b;
                 }
            return null;
      }
} // class Machine
```

Figure 10.34 Implementation of the Machine class

```
/*    File: Human.java
      Developed for Problem Solving with Java, Koffman & Wolz.
      Appears in Fig. 10.35.
*/
import java.awt.*;
import java.awt.event.*;

public class Human extends Player implements ActionListener {

      public Human(String name, TicTacToe ap) {
            super(name, ap);
      }

      public void takeTurn(){
            // Activate all buttons that aren't claimed.
            for (int r=0; r < 3; r++)
                 for (int c=0; c < 3; c++) {
                       Button b = ap.position(r, c);
                       if (b.isEnabled()) b.addActionListener(this);
                 }
      }

      public void actionPerformed(ActionEvent e) {
            // Update label.
            Button b = (Button)e.getSource();
            b.setLabel(name);
            b.setEnabled(false);
            for (int r=0; r < 3; r++)
                 for (int c=0; c < 3; c++) {
                       Button bt = ap.position(r,c);
                       if (bt.isEnabled()) bt.removeActionListener(this);
                 }
            ap.nextPlayer();
      }
} // class Human
```

Figure 10.35 Implementation of the Human class

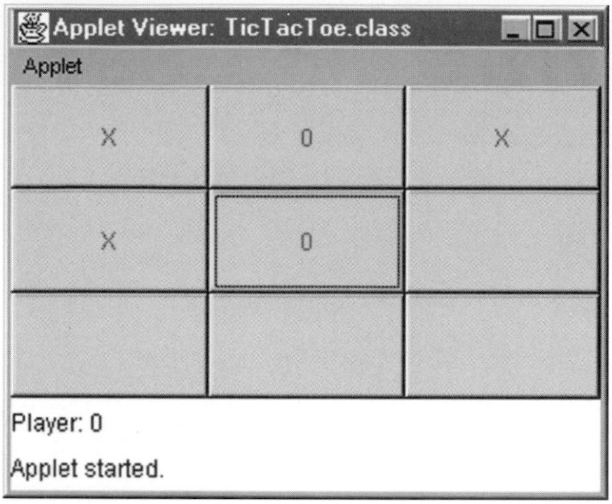

Figure 10.36 A turn during `TicTacToe`

EXERCISES FOR SECTION 10.6

Self-Check

1. Explain why four classes are needed to implement the solution. Why have the abstract class `Player`?
2. Design, but do not implement, an interface that would allow a user to select either a two-person game, or a game against the machine.

Programming

1. Implement your solution to Self-Check Exercise 1.
2. Modify the font on the buttons so that the displays are more visually appealing; for example, make the font larger, and use a different color for each player.
3. Design and implement a GUI that allows a player to select who will go first, the human or the machine.
4. Modify the `findMove` method so it picks a random space for its move.
5. Modify your solution to Programming Exercise 4 so that it first searches for a winning move and only picks randomly if there is none.
6. Modify your solution to Programming Exercise 4 so that a random move is selected only if it will not cause the other player to immediately win the game. *Hint:* You may have to account for the situation where there is *no* move you can make without forcing the other player to win.

10.7 Applications and Applets: Menus

Now we look at the differences between an application and an applet. Obviously, applications can also support GUIs. Doing so is more complicated because you must specify more of the detail. In particular, you must include methods that will cause the application to quit.

Recall that an applet is a panel that is a container that is a component. An applet can only exist within an applet context such as a Web browser. Consequently, it is the applet context's responsibility to provide space for the applet, show it, and mediate user activities that encompass activating and deactivating the applet as well as quitting the browser.

When you write an application that involves GUIs you are responsible for setting up and shutting down all of the processes within your application. In early chapters `SimpleGUI` took care of these actions for you.

To create an application that will contain a GUI you must:

1. Create a `Frame` component in which GUI activities will occur.

2. Explicitly show the `Frame`, if necessary.

3. Set up facilities for the user to leave and return to the application.

4. Set up facilities for the user to quit the application (terminating all of its processes).

Typically, you use `MenuComponents` to set up the facilities in steps 3 and 4 above. Much of the user activity that is special to applications is captured in `WindowEvents`. This section shows you how to integrate `Menu` and `WindowEvent` objects into applications.

The primary goal of this section is to give you another example of degrees of abstraction. Much of the activity you took for granted when you used `SimpleGUI` or extended applets required predefined abstractions. In this section we show how to build a few of those abstractions.

The `Frame` Component

An application needs an instance of a `Frame` in which to place its user input/output activities. Figure 10.37 shows how to construct a rudimentary frame. Be forewarned: On some systems with some compilers this code will not allow you to exit gracefully and can lock up your system. We, therefore, have not included this in the code that you can download from our Web site.

```
import java.awt.*;
import java.awt.event.*;

public class WinDemo extends Frame {
    public WinDemo() {
        super("Window Demo");
        setSize(200,200);
        show();
    }

    public static void main(String[] args) {
        new WinDemo();
    }
} // class WinDemo
```

Figure 10.37 A rudimentary frame application that does not exit gracefully

The `WinDemo` class supports the `main` method required to start up an application. That method does only one thing: It creates an instance of the `WinDemo` class. Consequently, there is no real reason to store this instance in a variable. This is a departure from the form we've been using, illustrating a technique used by GUI programmers. We didn't show you this approach in earlier chapters because it is rather sophisticated and takes some getting used to. The `WinDemo` class constructor sets the title bar of the `Frame` to "Window Demo," sets the size to 200×200 pixels, and then shows the `Frame`. Once the component is created it must be explicitly disposed of and the application exited. Presumably, some user event should trigger this action. Since the explicit exit doesn't happen in Figure 10.37, it is not clear how the application will exit.

Introduction to `Window` Events

`Window` events provide the mechanism for tracking user actions that affect windows. The `windowClosing` and `windowClosed` methods are of particular interest because we use them to shut down the window. In order to monitor window events, an application object must register as a `WindowListener`. A `WindowListener` must define the methods shown in Table 10.6. Each of these methods handles a different kind of window event.

Table 10.6 Abstract methods for `WindowListener`

Method	Take action because
windowClosed	Window has been disposed.
windowClosing	User-activated window-close mechanism is activated.
windowOpened	The window has been opened.
windowActivated	An activated window responded to mouse and key events.
windowDeactivated	Mouse focus has moved outside the window, some other window is active.
windowDeiconified	A window previously iconified has been opened, this is system-dependent.
windowIconified	Iconify the window action has been taken by the user, this is system-dependent.

Table 10.6 lists methods that iconify and deiconify a window. To **iconify a window** means to close it and to show an icon for it. You can **deiconify a window** that has been closed by clicking on the icon.

Figure 10.38 expands the `Frame` in Figure 10.37 to handle exits. This is still not the best way to handle exits, but it is a step in the right direction. When the user creates a "window-closing" event, the `windowClosing` method is called. It disposes of the frame, which triggers a call to the `windowClosed` method. This method calls `System.exit(0)` to stop execution of the object.

iconify a window:
close a window and show an icon for it.

deiconify a window:
open a window that has been iconified by clicking on its icon.

```
/*    File: WinDemo.java
      Developed for Problem Solving with Java,
        Koffman & Wolz.
      Appears in Fig. 10.38.
*/
import java.awt.*;
import java.awt.event.*;

public class WinDemo extends Frame
                     implements WindowListener {
    public WinDemo() {
        super("Window Demo");
        setSize(100, 100);
        show();

        addWindowListener(this);
    }
```

Figure 10.38 *continued*

Figure 10.38 *continued*

```
    public void windowClosing(WindowEvent e) {
        System.out.println(e);
        dispose();
    }
    public void windowClosed(WindowEvent e) {
        System.exit(0);
    }

    public static void main(String[] args) {
        new WinDemo();
    }
    public void windowActivated(WindowEvent e) {;}
    public void windowDeactivated(WindowEvent e) {;}
    public void windowDeiconified(WindowEvent e) {;}
    public void windowIconified(WindowEvent e) {;}
    public void windowOpened(WindowEvent e) {;}
} // class WinDemo
```

Figure 10.38 A rudimentary application

This application object, although rudimentary, will be adequate for your needs as you develop a program solution. The call to the constructor acts like the `init` method for an applet. It is the place to set things up. The application can implement whatever listeners you need. You may use other support objects as well. They can be called as needed from the constructor or from within the event-handling methods. Similarly, you may create `private` methods that support the constructor and the event handlers. For example, if the component layout is relatively complicated, you might want to do that in a method that is called by the constructor.

The two-stage shutdown may seem cumbersome but it delegates responsibility. Each platform has its own GUI mechanism for signaling that a window should be closed. This triggers an event that triggers a call to `windowClosing`. Before disposing of the window, any independent processes should be shut down too. These might include threads or other frames. This shutdown should happen in `windowClosing` before the call to `dispose`. The `dispose` method triggers the event process that calls `windowClosed`. Only then is it safe to quit the application.

Introduction to Menus

The "window-closing" mechanism is not the correct way to exit an application. You may have noticed that "real" applications have a menu bar and a quit choice under a menu. Java allows you to attach menu bars and menus to applications. Since applets are part of an applet context, they do not need menu bars. The applet context already has one. In fact, the applet context is an application. The HotJava browser is an applet context that was built entirely in Java.

A `MenuComponent` is used to implement various kinds of menus in Java. Menus are used to organize the actions that a user can take. Rather than cluttering a frame with buttons, programmers use menus to organize activities so that users can find them easily.

A `MenuComponent` differs from a `Component` in a number of crucial ways. With the exception of a `MenuItem`, a `MenuComponent` is never an event source. It cannot be painted and its layout is not controlled by layout managers. There are two types of `MenuComponent`s: `MenuBar`s and `MenuItem`s. A `Menu` is a kind of `MenuItem`.

A `MenuBar` is a list of menus. Typically, it is displayed as a strip across the top of a `Frame`. A `MenuBar` holds `Menu`s. `Menu`s in turn hold `MenuItem`s. The look and feel of `MenuComponent` manipulation is system-dependent. Figure 10.39 shows a `Frame` with a `MenuBar` that contains two `Menu`s that contain a few items. The "Calculate" menu is currently open, and lists two calculations that can be done: addition and subtraction. The "File" menu is used by convention as the place to have the "quit" function. Figure 10.40 shows how this `Frame` is implemented, complete with a quit function. Since a `MenuItem` generates an `ActionEvent`, the `Frame` must implement `ActionListener`.

Unlike an applet, the components of a `Frame` that are used in more than one method may be declared and initialized as data fields. The initialization does not have to take place within the constructor. In Figure 10.40 the `MenuItem`s will be used in `actionPerformed`. The remaining `MenuComponent`s are only referenced in the constructor and are therefore declared as local variables to that method.

The `MenuBar` component hierarchy is built up like a container hierarchy with one important difference. The `MenuBar` must be attached to the `Frame` with the `setMenuBar` method. Notice that the `MenuBar` is created and then each menu is constructed. The `MenuItem`s will be the event sources, so they are informed that the `WinDemo` object will be a listener for `ActionEvent`s. After each `MenuItem` is added to its menu, the menu is added to the `MenuBar`.

Conceptually, this is the simplest way to set up a `MenuBar`, even if the implementation looks rather intimidating. Other features of `MenuBar`s, `Component`s, and `Event`s, allow more concise expressions.

This version of `WinDemo` quits gracefully. If the user indicates that the window should be closed, then it is merely closed. Adding the functionality to re-open it is left as an exercise. To quit the application, the user must select the "quit" menu item. Note that we left a few `System.out.println` traces in this program so that we can confirm menu selections from the calculate menu.

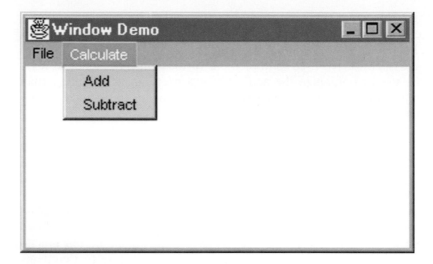

Figure 10.39 A Frame with MenuBars

```
/*    File: WinDemo.java
      Developed for Problem Solving with Java, Koffman & Wolz.
      Appears in Fig. 10.40.
*/
import java.awt.*;
import java.awt.event.*;

public class WinDemo extends Frame
                     implements WindowListener, ActionListener {
      private MenuItem quit = new MenuItem("Quit");
      private MenuItem add = new MenuItem("Add");
      private MenuItem subtract = new MenuItem("Subtract");

      public WinDemo() {
        super("Window Demo");

        // Create a menu bar.
        MenuBar bar = new MenuBar();
        // Add a "File" menu to it, add a "Quit" menu item to the menu.
        // Register as a listener, and add the menu to the bar.
        Menu m = new Menu("File");
        m.add(quit);
        quit.addActionListener(this);
        bar.add(m);
```

Figure 10.40 *continued*

Figure 10.40 *continued*

```
        // Add a second menu with two items, register the listeners
        //  and add the menu to the bar.
        Menu m2 = new Menu("Calculate");
        m2.add(add);
        add.addActionListener(this);
        m2.add(subtract);
        subtract.addActionListener(this);
        bar.add(m2);

        // Add the menubar to the frame.
        setMenuBar(bar);

        addWindowListener(this);
        setSize(300, 300);
        show();

    }

    public void actionPerformed(ActionEvent e) {
        System.out.println(e);
        if (e.getSource() == quit) {
            dispose();
            System.exit(0);
        }
    }

    public void windowClosing(WindowEvent e) {
        System.out.println(e);
        dispose();
    }

    public static void main(String[] args) {
        new WinDemo();
    }
    public void windowActivated(WindowEvent e) {;}
    public void windowClosed(WindowEvent e) {;}
    public void windowDeactivated(WindowEvent e) {;}
    public void windowDeiconified(WindowEvent e) {;}
    public void windowIconified(WindowEvent e) {;}
    public void windowOpened(WindowEvent e) {;}
} // class WinDemo
```

Figure 10.40 A frame with a MenuBar that quits gracefully

EXERCISES FOR SECTION 10.7

Self-Check

1. How is a window different from a frame? How is a frame different from a panel?
2. Which `MenuComponent` object can generate an `ActionEvent`?
3. Design a way for a window to be re-opened after it has been closed but before the application has been exited.

Programming

1. Implement your solution to Self-Check Exercise 3.
2. Create an application that lets you open as many windows as you want. Each window should identify itself by a count that is kept of open windows.

Chapter Review

1. AWT Components provide abstractions for user input and output. Six classes of objects interact to create GUI interfaces:
    1. `Component`
    2. `MenuComponent`
    3. `AWTEvent`
    4. `EventListener`
    5. `LayoutManager`
    6. `Graphics`
2. There are two kinds of events: semantic events and low-level events. Every `Component` can send low-level events. Semantic events capture high-level activities such as pressing a button, selecting an item from a set of choices, or adjusting a position on a scale.
3. Typically, the `Canvas` and `Label` classes are used for displaying output. Any component that displays text uses the `Font` class and `FontMetric` class to control the text's appearance at a fine-grained level. The font describes the shape and style that the text will have, whether it will be plain, bold, or italic. The font also describes the size of the text. The `FontMetric` class calculates the size of characters, including their height from the baseline, the ascent, and the descent. The `FontMetric` class can also calculate the amount of horizontal space that will be occupied by a string in a given font. You don't construct

font metrics directly. Instead you ask a font to construct the font metrics for you.

4. `ActionEvents` are abstractions that provide a way to capture specific actions of the user that include:

Executing an action based on a double-click on a list item

Pressing a button

Pressing return within a text component

5. An `ItemEvent` is an abstraction that provides a way to capture the fact that one of a group has been selected. An `ItemEvent` can be generated by a:

`Checkbox`

`List`

`Choice`

6. Low-level events capture direct actions by the mouse and at the keyboard. This chapter gave examples of mouse events that detected whether the mouse was pressed, released, clicked, entered, or exited a component. Low-level events give the programmer control over the user input at a very fine-grained level.

7. Writing a GUI for an application is more complicated than writing one for an applet. At a minimum, you must provide a means for the user to quit the application. Typically, this is done through a pull-down menu with a quit option. In an application you must also construct a parent frame that holds any other components you may need. Menu items generate action events, which provide a very nice mechanism for responding to user activities.

Summary of AWT Classes and Methods

The following classes from the AWT were introduced in this section. A full description of each class can be found in Appendix D.

Classes Used to Display Text

`Label`	Usually used to display a single line of text in a container.
`Canvas`	Usually used to display a mixture of graphics and text in a container.
`Font`	Controls the shape, style, and size of text in a component.
`FontMetric`	Constructed by the font; provides information on the size of characters.

Layout Managers

`BorderLayout`	Places components in a container in the positions North, South, East, West, and Center.
`CardLayout`	Displays only one component at a time, typically used in conjunction with other components that control actions on the stack of components: first, last, previous, next.
`FlowLayout`	Displays components in a top-to-bottom, left-to-right order.
`GridLayout`	Places components in a fixed-size grid, placing components in the grid from the upper-left corner to the lower-right corner of the grid.

AWT Semantic Events

(AWT semantic events capture abstract actions on the part of the user.)

`ActionEvent`	Occurs when:

- A button is pressed.
- A Return key is pressed in a text field.
- The mouse is double-clicked in a list.
- A menu item is selected from a menu.

`AdjustmentEvent`	Occurs when a scale such as a scroll bar is adjusted.
`ItemEvent`	Occurs when a checkbox, list item, or choice item is selected.
`TextEvent`	Occurs when the user changes the contents of a text component.

AWT Low-level Events

(AWT low-level events detect simple user events such as mouse movements.)

`mouseClicked()`	The mouse was pressed and released in rapid succession.
`mouseEntered()`	The mouse entered this component.
`mouseExited()`	The mouse exited this component.
`mousePressed()`	The mouse button was pressed down and held.
`mouseReleased()`	The mouse button was released.

Frames used in applications require more fine-grained programming than the panel that supports an applet. In particular, you must show the frame explicitly. You also need a way for the frame and, consequently, the application to be exited. Window events provide information on user activity within frames. They include:

`windowClosed`	Window has been disposed.
`windowClosing`	User activates window-close mechanism.
`windowOpened`	The window has been opened.
`windowActivated`	An activated window responds to mouse and key events.
`windowDeactivated`	Mouse focus is outside the window; some other window is active.
`windowDeiconified`	A window previously iconified has been opened, this is system-dependent.
`windowIconified`	Iconify the window action has been taken by the user, this is system-dependent.

Quick-Check Exercises

1. List three objects that interact to create a GUI interface.
2. What is an event?
3. What do the following statements do in the constructor of a component:

```
Font f = new Font("Monospaced",PLAIN,10);
setFont(f);
FontMetrics fm = getFontMetrics(f);
setSize(fm.stringWidth("hello"), fm.getHeight());
```

4. Match the layout manager with its distinctive characteristic:

`BorderLayout`	Stacks the items in the component so only one is visible at a time.
`CardLayout`	Places the components in a top-to-bottom, left-to-right order.
`FlowLayout`	Places the components in a matrix starting at the top left, ending at the bottom right.
`GridLayout`	Positions the components according to a compass: North, South, East, West, and Center.

5. Match each event type with the user action it captures:

`ActionEvent`	Detects that a selection from a discrete set was made.
`AdjustmentEvent`	Detects that characters were typed.
`ItemEvent`	Detects that a discrete action took place.
`TextEvent`	Detects that the value of a scale was changed.

6. If semantic events exist, why bother with low-level events?

7. Why do applications need code to control termination of the program and applets do not?

Answers to Quick-Check Exercises

1. Any of the following or their subclasses interact to create a GUI interface: `Component`, `Graphics`, `LayoutManager`, `AWTEvent`, `Container`.

2. An event occurs when an input abstraction such as a button is activated by the user. An event object holds the pertinent information for the event.

3. The component's font is set to the font "Monospaced PLAIN" with size 10. The size of the component is calculated by the width of the string `"hello"` in this font and the height of characters in this font.

4. `BorderLayout`   Positions the components according to a compass: North, South, East, West, and Center.

   `CardLayout`   Stacks the items in the component so only one is visible at a time.

   `FlowLayout`   Places the components in a top-to-bottom, left-to-right order.

   `GridLayout`   Places the components in a matrix starting at the top left, ending at the bottom right.

5. Match each event type with the user action it captures:

   `ActionEvent`   Detects that a discrete action took place.

   `AdjustmentEvent`   Detects that the value of a scale was changed.

   `ItemEvent`   Detects that a selection from a discrete set was made.

   `TextEvent`   Detects that characters were typed.

6. Low-level events give the programmer very fine control over the user input.

7. Applets are components of an applet context. The applet context takes care of exiting. An application is a standalone program that is responsible for all activity; hence, it must know how to quit.

Review Questions

1. Explain why abstractions are important in program design.

2. Why are semantic events useful?

3. What is the difference between a label and a canvas? What kind of abstraction does each capture?

4. What do layout managers do? Why are they useful?

5. Describe what each of the following semantic events represents:

   `ActionEvent   ItemEvent   AdjustmentEvent   TextEvent`

6. List the mouse events presented in this chapter and explain why they are necessary. Do you think they constitute a complete set, or can you think of other mouse events that might be useful?

7. Explain what window events are used for.

Programming Projects

1. Write a machine player for TicTacToe that plays more "intelligently." *Hint:* See the programming exercises at the end of Section 10.6.

2. A game similar to TicTacToe is Score Four. In this game you load disks from the top of a grid and they fall to the bottom. The object of the game is to create a complete row, horizontally, vertically, or on the diagonal. Write an applet for a Score Four game that can be played by two people.

3. Write a machine player for Score Four.

4. Implement a Checkers game.

5. Implement Black Jack. *Hint:* Use a `CardLayout` manager to stack the deck.

6. At AnyWhere College all computer science majors take four core courses: CS1, CS2, Discrete Math 1, and Discrete Math 2. Students may only continue in the major if they have received a grade of C or better in these four courses. Write an applet that determines whether a student may continue in the program.

7. Write an application that gives a multiple-choice test based on entries in a text file. The file contains a test question followed by four possible answers. Your application should load the test into an array or vector, display the test questions, and keep a tally of correct first answers.

8. Modify your solution to Programming Project 7 so that the exam questions are given in random order and the answers are presented in random sequence following the question.

9. Modify your solution to Programming Project 8 so that the exam is presented via an applet rather than an application. The test questions and answer choices should be loaded from the HTML page.

10. Modify the text editing program from Chapter 7 to use "real" GUI components rather than `SimpleGUI`.

Interview

Marc Andreessen

Marc Andreessen is co-founder and Executive Vice President of Products and Marketing for Netscape Communications Corporation. He received his B.S. in computer science from the University of Illinois-Champaign in 1993. While working at the university's National Center for Supercomputing Applications (NCSA), Marc helped to create the NCSA Mosaic browser prototype for the Internet.

On his introduction to computers ...

Marc studied computer science at the University of Illinois. Almost immediately after graduation he began working in a research lab at the university's physics research facility. It was here that he learned about high-end computing and networking. He took an internship at IBM and then returned to NCSA to do 3D work.

On the creation of Mosaic (now Netscape) ...

At the time of Mosaic's creation, the Internet was gaining popularity, but was still limited to a small group of skilled programmers. Marc and others decided to pull together the Internet's power with a graphical interface for the desktop PC. They designed Mosaic with the goal that multimedia would become an integral part of the Internet.

On a typical day ...

Marc begins his day at 9 A.M. with a number of meetings, project reviews, and customer visits. He spends the rest of the day talking with people about various issues affecting Netscape, such as product development status, marketing programs, and developer activities. At home, the work continues with product planning and e-mail follow-ups from his Thinkpad.

On the number of visitors to the Netscape homepage ...

Marc estimates that there are currently over 4 million members on Netcenter. All of these visitors are registered members, with digital Ids issued from the center. The Netscape Website has a far larger number of visitors; estimates place it at more than 6 million per day. And the number of Navigator (and Communicator) users totals over 65 million.

On Java and the future ...

Java is the programming language of the network, so Netscape is working hard to develop tools to increase its performance. One challenge is developing features to improve upon speed so that Java applets on Web pages load as quickly as HTML and

JavaScript. Another goal is working to reduce the amount of memory that Java applications use in download and start-up time. Java is a great language for the network because of its platform-independence and built-in security features. The long-term goal is to make network-based applications ubiquitous because the Java applications will become part of the network instead of living on a desktop or server.

C H A P T E R 11

Recursion

A recursive method is one that calls itself. Each time it is called, the recursive method can operate on different arguments. You can use recursion as an alternative to iteration (looping). Generally, a recursive solution is slightly less efficient, in terms of computer time, than an iterative one because of the overhead for the extra method calls. In many instances, however, recursion enables us to specify a natural, simple solution to a problem that otherwise would be difficult to solve. For this reason, recursion is an important and powerful tool in problem solving and programming. Recursion is used widely in solving problems that are not numeric, such as proving mathematical theorems, writing compilers, and in searching and sorting algorithms.

11.1 Recursive Methods

11.2 Recursive Mathematical Methods

11.3 Use of the Stack in Recursion

11.4 Recursive Methods with Arrays, Vectors, and Strings
Case Study: Summing the Values in an Array

11.5 Binary Search
Case Study: Recursive Binary Search

11.6 Solving Towers of Hanoi with Recursion
Case Study: Towers of Hanoi Problem

11.7 A Recursive Program with a GUI
Case Study: Counting Cells in a Blob

11.8 Common Programming Errors
Chapter Review

11.1   Recursive Methods

recursive method:
a method that calls itself.

In this section we demonstrate recursion using a simple method and we develop rules for writing **recursive methods**, or methods that call themselves. Consider the computer solution to the problem "Raise 6 to the power 3". A computer can multiply but it cannot perform the operation "Raise to the power." However, we know that 6^3 is 6 times 6^2, and 6^2 is 6 times 6. Therefore, the problem "Raise 6 to the power 3" can be split into the problems:

Subproblems generated from "Raise 6 to the power 3":

Problem 1   Raise 6 to the power 2.
Problem 2   Multiply the result of problem 1 by 6.

Because a computer can multiply, we can solve problem 2 but not problem 1. However, problem 1, is an easier version of the original problem. We can split it into two problems, 1.1 and 1.2, leaving three problems to solve (1.1, 1.2, and 2), two of which are multiplications:

Subproblems generated from "Raise 6 to the power 2":

Problem 1.1   Raise 6 to the power 1.
Problem 1.2   Multiply the result of problem 1.1 by 6.

You can program a computer to recognize that the result of raising any number to the power 1 is that number. Therefore, we can solve problem 1.1 (the answer is 6), and then solve problem 1.2 (the answer is 36) which gives us the solution to problem 1. Multiplying this result by 6 (problem 2) gives us 216 which is the solution to the original problem.

Figure 11.1 implements this approach to raising a number to a power as the recursive Java method `power`, which returns the result of raising its first argument, `m`, to the power indicated by its second argument, `n`. If `n` is greater than 1, the statement

```
return m * power(m, n-1);      // Recursive step
```

executes, splitting the original problem into the two simpler problems as desired:

Problem 1   Raise `m` to the power `n-1` (`power(m, n-1)`).
Problem 2   Multiply the result by `m`.

recursive step:
the step in a program or algorithm that contains a recursive call.

If the new second argument is greater than 1, there will be additional calls to method `power`. We call this case the **recursive step** because it contains a call to method `power`.

```
/* Part of class MyMath in package simpleMath.
   Developed for Problem Solving with Java,
     Koffman & Wolz.
   Appears in Fig. 11.1.


   Raises m to the power n.
   Precondition : m and n are defined and n > 0.
   Postcondition: Returns m raised to the power n.
*/
public static int power(int m, int n) {
    if (n <= 1)
        return m;                    // Stopping case
    else
        return m * power(m, n-1); // Recursive step
}
```

Figure 11.1 Recursive method power

The first case in Fig. 11.1 causes an immediate return from the method when the condition n <= 1 becomes true. We call this a **stopping case** because it ends the recursion. A condition that is true for a stopping case is called a **terminating condition**.

stopping case: the statement that causes recursion to terminate.

terminating condition: a condition that evaluates to true when a stopping case is reached

Program Style: *Preconditions and postconditions*

Method power illustrates a common convention for documenting methods. The precondition is a condition that must be true before the method is called in order to guarantee that the method will perform as expected. In this case, the precondition specifies that m and n should both be defined and that n is greater than zero. The postcondition summarizes the effect of executing the method. In this case, the method returns the desired result, m raised to the power n.

Tracing a Recursive Method

Hand-tracing an algorithm's execution demonstrates how that algorithm works. We can trace the execution of the method call power(6, 3) by drawing an activation frame that corresponds to each call of the method. An **activation frame** is a logical device that shows the argument values for each call and summarizes its execution.

Figure 11.2 shows the three activation frames generated to solve the problem of raising 6 to the power 3. The part of each activation frame that executes before the next recursive call is in color; the part that executes after the return from the next call is in gray.

The value returned from each call appears alongside each black arrow. The return arrow from each method call points to the operator * because the multiplication is performed just after the return.

activation frame: a logical device showing the argument values for each recursive call and its execution.

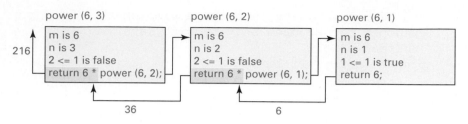

Figure 11.2 Trace of method power

Figure 11.2 shows that there are three calls to method power. Argument m has the value 6 for both calls; argument n has the values 3 , 2, and finally 1. Because n is 1 in the third call, the value of m (6) is returned as the result of that call. After the return to the second activation frame, the value of m is mulitiplied by this result, and the product (36) is returned as the result of the second call. After the return to the first activation frame, the value of m is multiplied by this result, and the product (216) is returned as the result of the original call to method power.

Properties of Recursive Problems and Solutions

Problems that can be solved by recursion have the following characteristics:

- One or more stopping cases have a simple, nonrecursive solution.
- The other cases of the problem can be reduced (using recursion) to problems that are closer to stopping cases.
- Eventually the problem can be reduced to only stopping cases, which are relatively easy to solve.

Follow these steps to solve a recursive problem:

1. Try to express the problem as a simpler version of itself.
2. Determine the stopping cases.
3. Determine the recursive steps.

The recursive algorithms that we write generally consist of an if statement with the form:

if the stopping case is reached
   Solve it.
else
   Split the problem into simpler cases using recursion.

Figure 11.3 illustrates these steps. Assume that for a particular problem of size *n,* we can split the problem into a problem of size 1, which we can solve (a stopping case), and a problem of size *n* – 1. We can split the problem of size *n* – 1 into another problem of size 1 and a problem of size *n* – 2, which we can split further. If we split the problem *n* times, we end up with *n* problems of size 1, all of which we can solve.

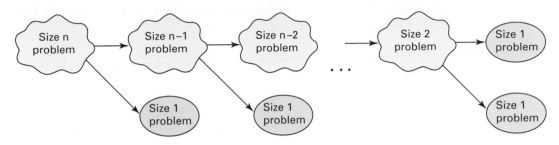

Figure 11.3 Splitting a problem into smaller problems

In some situations, we represent a recursive algorithm as an `if` statement whose consequent is the recursive step. The condition tests whether the stopping case has been reached. If not, the recursive step executes; otherwise, an immediate return occurs.

`if` the stopping case is not reached

   Split the problem into simpler cases using recursion.

EXERCISES FOR SECTION 11.1

Self-Check

1. Show how the problem generated by the method call `power(5, 4)` can be split into smaller problems as in Fig. 11.3.
2. Trace the execution of `power(5, 4)`.
3. Given the following method and the call `whatDo(4)`, what would be the output?

```
public static void whatDo(int i) {
    if (i > 1) {
        displayResult(i);
        whatDo(i - 1);
        displayResult(i)
    }
}
```

Programming

1. Write a recursive method `multiply(int a, int b)` to compute the same result as `a * b` without using the operator `*`.
2. Write a recursive method `divide(int a, int b)` to compute the same result as `a / b` without using the operator `/` or `%`.

11.2 Recursive Mathematical Methods

Many mathematical methods are defined recursively. An example is the factorial of a number n (represented as $n!$).

- 0! is 1
- $n!$ is $n \times (n-1)!$ for $n > 0$

This is the definition of $n!$. Thus, $4! = 4 \times 3! = 4 \times 3 \times 2!$, and so on. In Section 6.7 (see Fig. 6.23) you saw how to implement this recursive mathematics definition as a recursive method.

EXAMPLE 11.1

The *greatest common divisor* (gcd) of two integers is the largest integer that divides them both. A recursive definition of Euclid's algorithm for finding the greatest common divisor of two positive integers, m and n, follows.

- gcd(m, n) is gcd(n, m) if m < n.
- gcd(m, n) is n if n <= m and n divides m.
- Otherwise, gcd(m, n) is gcd(n, remainder of m divided by n).

This algorithm states the following. If m is the smaller number, then the gcd determination should be performed with the arguments transposed. If n is less than or equal to m and n divides m, the result is n. If n does not divide m, the answer is obtained by finding the gcd of n and the remainder of m divided by n. Figure 11.4 shows method gcd which is part of class MyMath (package simpleMath).

```
/*    Part of class MyMath in package simpleMath.
      Developed for Problem Solving with Java,
        Koffman & Wolz.
      Appears in Fig. 11.4.

      Finds the greatest common divisor of m and n.
      Precondition : m and n are defined and
                        both are > 0.
      Postcondition: Returns greatest common divisor
                        of m & n.
*/
public static int gcd(int m, int n) {
    if (m < n)
        return gcd(n, m);
```

Figure 11.4 *continued*

Figure 11.4 *continued*

```
      else if (m % n == 0)
          return n;
      else
          return gcd(n, m % n);
}
```

Figure 11.4 Method gcd

EXAMPLE 11.2

The Fibonacci numbers are a sequence of numbers that have varied uses. They were originally intended to model the growth of a rabbit colony. We will not describe the model here, but you can see that the Fibonacci sequence 1, 1, 2, 3, 5, 8, 13, 21, 34, . . . increases rapidly. The 15th number in the sequence is 610 (that's a lot of rabbits!). The Fibonacci sequence is defined as follows:

- Fib_1 is 1.
- Fib_2 is 1.
- Fib_n is $Fib_{n-2} + Fib_{n-1}$, for $n > 2$.

Verify for yourself that the sequence of numbers in the preceding paragraph is correct. Figure 11.5 shows a recursive method that computes the *n*th Fibonacci number.

```
/*    Part of class MyMath in package simpleMath.
      Developed for Problem Solving with Java,
         Koffman & Wolz.
      Appears in Fig. 11.5.

      Computes the nth Fibonacci number.
      precondition : n is defined and n > 0.
      postcondition: Returns the nth Fibonacci number.
*/
public static int fibonacci(int n) {
    if (n <= 2)
        return 1;
    else
        return fibonacci(n-2) + fibonacci(n-1);
}
```

Figure 11.5 Recursive method Fibonacci

Although easy to write, the `fibonacci` method is very inefficient because each recursive step generates two calls to method `fibonacci`. Also,
we must evaluate the two recursive calls independently. This means that
for a particular value of n, we cannot use the result of the earlier call to
`fibonacci(n-2)` to reduce the effort needed to calculate the value of
`fibonacci(n-1)`. We have to recalculate `fibonacci(n-2)` all over
again.

EXERCISES FOR SECTION 11.2

Self-Check

1. What does method `puzzle` compute? What is its result when n is 2?

```
public static int puzzle(int n) {
        if (n == 1)
                return 0;
        else
                return 1 + puzzle(n / 2);
}
```

2. If a program had the statement `f = fibonacci(5)`, how many calls
   to `fibonacci` would be performed?

3. Complete the following recursive method, which calculates the result of
   raising an integer (`base`) to a power (`power`). The value of `power` can
   be positive, negative, or zero. You should provide two stopping cases.

```
public static double powerRaiser(int base,
                                        int power) {
        if (base == 0)
                return _____;
        else if (power == 0)
                return _____;
        else if (power < 0)
                return 1.0 / _____;
        else
                return _____;
}
```

4. What would happen if the terminating condition for method `fibonacci`
   is n <= 1?

Programming

1. Write a recursive method, `findSum`, that calculates the sum of successive integers starting at 1 and ending at n (e.g., `findSum(n)` = 1 +
   2 + . . . + (n - 1) + n).

2. Write an iterative version of the `fibonacci` method. Hint: First determine the least number of calculations you need to remember.

3. Write an iterative method that calculates the greatest common divisor.

11.3 Use of the Stack in Recursion

Displaying Characters in Reverse Order

Method `reverse` in Fig. 11.6 is an unusual recursive method because it has no argument, and it does not return a value. It reads in a sequence of individual characters and displays the sequence in reverse order. If the user enters the data characters a, b, c, d, e, * (the sentinel), they will be displayed in the order e, d, c, b, a.

```
/*    File: Reverser.java.
      Developed for Problem Solving with Java, Koffman & Wolz.
      Appears in Fig. 11.6.
*/
import simpleIO.*;
public class Reverser extends SimpleGUI {

      // Method
      /*    Displays a sequence of characters in reverse
            of the order in which they are entered.
            precondition : none
            postcondition: displays characters in reverse order
      */
      public void reverse() {
            char next = getChar("Next character or * to stop");
            if (next != '*') {
                  reverse();
                  displayResult(next);
            }
      }
} // class Reverser
```

Figure 11.6 Method reverse in class Reverser

The body of method `reverse` first reads a data character into `next`. Then it executes the `if` statement. The stopping case is reached when `next` contains the character *. Otherwise, the recursive step executes:

```
reverse();
displayResult(next);
```

The character just read is not displayed until later. This is because the call to `displayResult` follows the recursive method call; consequently, `displayResult` is not called until after the recursive call to `reverse` is completed. For example, the first character that is read is not displayed until after the method execution for the second character is done. Hence, the first character is displayed after the second character, which is displayed after the third character.

To see why this is so, let's trace the execution of method `reverse` assuming the characters c, a, t, * are entered as data. The trace (Fig. 11.7) shows three activation frames for method `reverse`. Each activation frame shows the value of `next` for that frame. Note that the sentinel character * is not displayed.

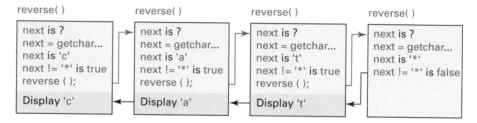

Figure 11.7 Trace of method `reverse`

The statements that execute for each frame are shown next. The statements in color are recursive method calls and result in a new activation frame, as indicated by the colored arrows. A method return is indicated by a black arrow that points to the statement in the calling frame to which the method returns. Tracing the colored arrows and then the black arrows in Fig. 11.7 gives us the sequence of events listed in Fig. 11.8. To help you understand this list, all the statements for a particular activation frame are indented to the same column.

Call `reverse`.

    Read the first character (c) into `next`.

    `next` is not *—Call `reverse`.

        Read the second character (a) into `next`.

        `next` is not *—Call `reverse`.

            Read the third character (t) into `next`.

            `next` is not *—Call `reverse`.

                Read the fourth character (*) into `next`.

                `next` is *—Return from fourth call.

            Display the third character (t).

            Return from third call.

Figure 11.8 *continued*

Figure 11.8 *continued*

        Display the second character (a).

        Return from second call.

    Display the first character (c).

    Return from original call.

Figure 11.8 Sequence of events for trace of `reverse()`

As shown, there are four calls to method `reverse`. The method returns always occur in the reverse order of the method calls; that is, we return from the last call first, then we return from the next to last call, and so on. After we return from a particular execution of the method, we display the character that was read into `next` just prior to that method call. The process of returning from a succession of recursive calls is called **unwinding the recursion**.

unwinding the recursion: the process of returning from a succession of recursive calls.

Stack for Method Calls

Java uses a special data structure called a **stack** to keep track of critical data for a recursive method as it changes from call to call. A stack is analogous to a stack of dishes or trays. In a stack of dishes in a buffet line, clean dishes are always placed on top of the stack. When you need a dish, you always remove the last one placed on the stack. This causes the next to last dish placed on the stack to move to the top of the stack.

Whenever a method call occurs (recursive or otherwise), a number of items are placed onto the stack. They include the argument values for that call, a storage location for each local variable during that call, and the instruction to return to after that call is finished. Whenever `next` is referenced in method `reverse`, Java accesses the top storage location for `next` allocated on the stack. When a method return occurs, the storage locations for that call at the top of the stack are removed, and the storage locations for the previous call "move" to the top.

stack: a data structure in which the last component stored is the first one removed.

Let's look at the stack right after the first call to `reverse`. To simplify our discussion, we consider only the storage locations for local variable `next` that are allocated on the stack. There is one storage location on the stack and the letter c is read into it:

Stack after first call to reverse:

    |c|

Right after the second call to `reverse`, another storage location for `next` is allocated on the stack and the letter a is read into it:

Stack after second call to reverse:

    |a|
    |c|

Right after the third call to `reverse`, another storage location for `next` is allocated on the stack and the letter `t` is read into it:

Stack after third call to reverse:

```
t
a
c
```

Right after the fourth call to `reverse`, another storage location for `next` is allocated on the stack and the character `*` is read into it:

Stack after fourth call to reverse:

```
*
t
a
c
```

Because next is `*` (the stopping case), an immediate return occurs. The method return causes the value at the top of the stack to be removed, as shown next.

Stack after first return from reverse:

```
t
a
c
```

Control returns to the statement that calls method `displayResult`, so the value of `next` (`t`) at the top of the stack is displayed. Another return from method `reverse` occurs, causing the value currently at the top of the stack to be removed.

Stack after second return from reverse:

```
a
c
```

Again, control returns to the statement that calls method `displayResult`, and the value of `next` (`a`) at the top of the stack is displayed. Another return from method `reverse` occurs, causing the value currently at the top of the stack to be removed.

Stack after third return from reverse:

Again, control returns to the statement that calls method `displayResult`, and the value of `next` (`c`) at the top of the stack is displayed. Another return from method `reverse` occurs, causing the value currently at the top of the stack to be removed. Now, the stack is empty and control returns to the statement in the application that follows the original call to method reverse.

Chapter 12 shows you how to declare and manipulate stacks yourself. Because these steps are all done automatically by Java, we can write recursive methods without worrying about the stack.

EXERCISES FOR SECTION 11.3

Self-Check

1. Assume the characters q, w, e, r,* are entered when method `reverse` is called. Show the contents of the stack immediately after each recursive call and return.

2. For the method call `power(5, 4)`, show the stack after each recursive call. Place a new pair of values on the stack for each call. Remove the top pair after returning from each call.

3. Modify method `reverse` so that it also displays the sentinel character.

Programming

1. Write an application that instantiates class `Reverser` and calls method `reverse`.

11.4 Recursive Methods with Arrays, Vectors, and Strings

So far our recursive examples have used arguments that are integers. Recursive methods also can process arguments that are data structures or objects.

Case Study

Summing the Values in an Array

PROBLEM

Write a recursive method that finds the sum of the values in an array x of size n (elements x[0] through x[n-1]).

ANALYSIS

The stopping case occurs when n is 1, that is, the sum is x[0] for an array with one element. If n is not 1, then we must add x[n-1] to the sum we get when we add the values in the subarray with indices 0 through n-2 (a simpler version of the problem).

Data Requirements

Problem Inputs

int[] x—array of integer values
int n—number of elements to be added

Problem Output

the sum of the array values

DESIGN

Algorithm for findSum

if (n is 1)
    The sum is x[0].
else
    Add x[n-1] to the sum of values in the subarray with indices 0 through
    n-2.

IMPLEMENTATION

Method findSum in Fig. 11.9 implements this algorithm.

```
/*   Part of class IntArray in package simpleMath.
     Developed for Problem Solving with Java, Koffman & Wolz.
     Appears in Fig. 11.9.

     Finds the sum of first n elements of array x.
     precondition : Array x is defined and n >= 1.
     postcondition: Returns sum of first n elements of x.
*/
public static int findSum(int[] x, int n) {
     if (n <= 1)
          return x[0];
     else
          return x[n-1] + findSum(x, n-1);
}
```

Figure 11.9 Using recursive method findSum

TESTING

Figure 11.10 traces the method call findSum(x, 3) for the array x shown
next.

x[0] x[1] x[2]

5	10	-7

As before, the colored part of each activation frame executes before the next recursive method call, and each colored arrow points to a new activation frame. The gray part of each activation frame executes after the return from a recursive call, and each black arrow indicates the return point (the operator +) after a method execution. The value returned is indicated alongside the black arrow. The value returned for the original call, findSum(x, 3), is 8, which is displayed.

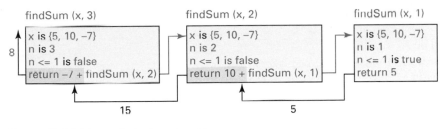

Figure 11.10 Trace of findSum(x, 3)

Method search in Fig. 11.11 returns the location (array index) where the argument target occurs in the array with elements x[0] through x[n-1]. If target is not found, method search returns the value -1. The target cannot be present if the array is empty, so the empty array (n == 0) is a stopping case. For nonempty arrays, the result is true if the last element, x[n-1], equals target (another stopping case). Otherwise, the result depends on whether target occurs in the subarray x[0] through x[n-2], as indicated by the recursive step:

```
return search(x, target, n-1)
```

```
/* Part of class IntArray in package simpleMath.
   Developed for Problem Solving with Java,
      Koffman & Wolz.
   Appears in Fig. 11.11.

   Searches array elements x[0] through x[n-1]
                 for target.
   precondition : target, n, and array x are defined &
                  n >= 0.
   postcondition: Returns position of its
                  last occurrence
```

Figure 11.11 *continued*

Figure 11.11 *continued*

```
                          if target is found in
                          array x; otherwise, returns -1.
*/
public static int search(int[] x, int target, int n) {
    if (n == 0)
        return -1;              // Target not in
                                //  empty array.
    else if (x[n-1] == target)
        return n-1;             // Found! - return
                                //  location.
    else  // Search rest of array.
        return search(x, target, n-1);
}
```

Figure 11.11 Recursive method search

Figure 11.12 traces the method call `search(x, 10, x.length)` for the array x shown next.

```
x[0] x[1] x[2]
```

5	10	−7

The value returned is `true`, because the expression `x[n-1] == target` is `true` when n is 1 (the second activation frame).

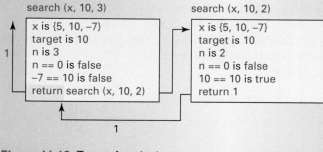

Figure 11.12 Trace of method search

Comparison of Iterative and Recursive Methods

In method `searchIt` (Fig. 11.13), the iterative version of `search`, a loop is needed to examine each array element, starting with the last. If `target` is found at element x[i], the array search terminates and the method returns the index i. If all array elements are examined without success, the method returns -1.

```
/* Part of class IntArray in package simpleMath.
   Developed for Problem Solving with Java, Koffman & Wolz.
   Appears in Fig. 11.13.

   Searches array elements x[0] through x[n-1] for target.
   precondition : target, n, and array x are defined & n >= 0.
   postcondition: Returns position of its last occurrence
                  if target is found in
                  array x; otherwise, returns -1.
*/
public static int searchIt (int[] x, int target, int n) {
    for (int i = n-1; i >= 0; i--)
        if (x[i] == target)
            return i;       // Found! - return location.

    // Assert: All elements examined & target not found.
    return -1;
}
```

Figure 11.13 Iterative method searchIt

The iterative method would execute a bit faster than the recursive version. However, many programmers would argue that the recursive version is aesthetically more pleasing. It is certainly more compact (a single if statement). Once you are accustomed to thinking recursively, the recursive form is somewhat easier to read and understand than the iterative form.

Some programmers like to use recursion as a conceptual tool. Once they have written the recursive form of a method, they can always translate it into an iterative version if run-time efficiency is important. In Section 11.5, we describe a much more efficient searching algorithm.

A Recursive boolean Method

Methods that return boolean values (true or false) also can be written using recursion. These methods do not perform a computation; however, the method result is still determined by evaluating an expression (type boolean) containing a recursive call.

EXAMPLE 11.4

The `boolean` method `isEqual` (Fig. 11.14) returns `true` if two arrays, say, x and y, of n elements are the same (e.g., `x[0] == y[0]`, `x[1] == y[1]`, ..., `x[n-1] == y[n-1]`). There are three stopping cases: If the array lengths are not equal, the result is false. For single-element arrays, the result depends on whether `x[0]` and `y[0]` have the same value. For larger arrays, the result is `false` if the last elements of each array have different values. If they are equal, we still have to compare the first n-1 elements of both arrays (a simpler version of the problem).

```
/* Part of class IntArray in package simpleMath.
   Developed for Problem Solving with Java,
     Koffman & Wolz.
   Appears in Fig. 11.14.

   Compares two n-element arrays.
   precondition : Arrays x & y are defined and n > 0.
   postcondition: Returns true if arrays
                  x & y are equal;
                     otherwise, returns false.
*/
public static boolean isEqual (int[] x, int[] y, int n)
{
    if (x.length != y.length)
        return false;              // Array sizes unequal.
    else if (n == 1)
        return (x[0] == y[0]); // Compare 1-element
                               //    arrays.
    else if (x[n-1] != y[n-1])
        return false;              // Found an unequal
                                   //    pair.
    else  // Compare rest of arrays.
        return isEqual(x, y, n-1);
}
```

Figure 11.14 Recursive method `isEqual`

A Recursive Vector Search

Figure 11.15 shows a recursive method, `searchVec`, that searches a vector. If names is a vector of strings, you can use the method call

```
searchVec(names, "Sally", names.size());
```

to search for the string `"Sally"` in vector names.

```
/* File: recursionDemo.java.
   Developed for Problem Solving with Java, Koffman & Wolz.
   Appears in Fig. 11.15.

   Searches vector elements v[0] through v[n-1] for target.
   precondition : target, n, & vector v are defined & n >= 0.
   postcondition: Returns position of its last occurrence
                     if target is found in
                     vector v; otherwise, returns -1.
*/
public static int searchVec(Vector v, Object target, int n) {
    if (n == 0)
        return -1;
    else if (v.elementAt(n-1).equals(target))
        return n-1;           // Found! - return location.
    else  // Search rest of vector.
        return searchVec(v, target, n-1);
}
```

Figure 11.15 Method searchVec

The stopping cases for searchVec are similar to recursive method search (Fig. 11.11). The first condition tests for an empty vector (n == 0). The second condition tests whether the last element matches target. The recursive step calls searchVec to search a smaller-sized vector. Note that method equals must be defined for the objects being compared.

Recursion with Strings

Figure 11.16 shows a recursive method, searchStr, that searches for a character in a string. It is very similar to the other search methods. Notice that we don't need to pass the string length as an argument. The statement

```
int posLast = s.length() - 1; // Index of last
                              //   character.
```

defines the position of the last character in the string when searchStr is entered. If the string is not empty (first stopping case) and the last character in string s does not match the target (second stopping case), the recursive step

```
return searchStr(s.substring(0, posLast), target);
```

searches for target in the substring of s that excludes the last character.

```
/* File: recursionDemo.java.
   Developed for Problem Solving with Java, Koffman & Wolz.
   Appears in Fig. 11.16.

   Searches for target in string s.
   precondition : target & string s are defined.
   postcondition: Returns position of its last occurrence
                  if target is located in
                  string s; otherwise, returns -1.
*/
public static int searchStr(String s, char target) {
    int posLast = s.length() - 1; // Index of last character.

    if (posLast == -1)
        return -1;                 // Empty string.
    else if (s.charAt(posLast) == target)
        return posLast;            // Found - return location.
    else  // Search rest of string.
        return searchStr(s.substring(0, posLast), target);
}
```

Figure 11.16 Method searchStr

EXAMPLE 11.5

Method `reverse` in Fig. 11.4 displayed a sequence of data characters in the reverse of the order in which they were entered. In this example, we show how to reverse a string that is already stored in a `String` object. The recursive algorithm follows.

Algorithm for `reverseStr`

`if` the string is empty
> Return the empty string.

`else`
> Return the string formed by concatenating (joining) the last character with the reverse of the rest of the string (all but the last character).

Figure 11.17 shows the implementation. For the method call

`reverseStr("Happy Birthday Dustin")`

the result is the string formed by concatenating the string "n" with the reverse of the string "Happy Birthday Dusti". After reversing all substrings and performing all concatenations, the result is "nitsuD yadhtriB yppaH".

```
/* File: recursionDemo.java.
   Developed for Problem Solving with Java,
     Koffman & Wolz.
   Appears in Fig. 11.17.

   Reverses string s.
   precondition : string s is defined.
   postcondition: Returns the reverse of string s.
*/
public static int reverseStr(String s) {
    int posLast = s.length() - 1; // Index of last
                                  //    character.

    if (posLast == -1)
        return "";                // Return the empty
                                  //    string.

    else
        return s.charAt(posLast) +
                reverseStr(s.substring(0, posLast));
}
```

Figure 11.17 Method reverseStr

EXERCISES FOR SECTION 11.4

Self-Check

1. Trace the execution of recursive method isEqual for the three-element arrays x (element values 1, 15, 10) and y (element values 1, 5, 7).

2. Trace the execution of the recursive method search on array x in Self-Check Exercise 1 when searching for 15 and for 3.

3. What does the following recursive method do? Trace its execution on array x in Self-Check Exercise 1. *Hint:* Method Math.min returns the smaller of its two arguments.

```
public static int mystery (int[] x, int n) {
    if (n == 1)
        return x[0];
    else
        return Math.min(x[n-1], mystery(x, n-1));
}
```

4. Trace the execution of the method call searchStr("happy", 'p').
5. Trace the execution of the method call reverseStr("tick").

Programming

1. Write a recursive method that returns the largest value in an array.
2. Write a recursive method that returns the *index of* the largest value in an array.
3. Answer Programming Exercise 1 for a vector of `Integer` objects.
4. Answer Programming Exercise 2 for a vector of `Integer` objects.

11.5 Binary Search

This section describes another recursive search algorithm called binary search. Binary search is an example of an $O(\log_2 n)$ algorithm—a significant improvement over the sequential search algorithm, which is $O(n)$ (see Section 7.5).

Case Study

Recursive Binary Search

Methods `search` and `searchIt` implement a *linear* or *sequential search* for a target key in an array, examining the elements in sequence from last to first. Because the method requires an average of $n/2$ comparisons to find a target in an array of n elements, and n comparisons to determine that a target is not in the array, sequential search is not very efficient for large arrays ($n > 100$). If the elements of the array being searched have been sorted and are in sequence by key value, we can make use of a more efficient search algorithm known as binary search.

PROBLEM

Write an improved search algorithm that takes advantage of the fact that the array is sorted.

ANALYSIS

The *binary search algorithm* uses the ordering of array elements to eliminate half the array elements with each probe into the array. Consequently, if the array has 1,000 elements, it either locates the target value or eliminates 500 elements with its first probe, 250 elements with its second probe, 125 elements with its third probe, and so on. For this reason, a binary search of an ordered array is an $O(\log_2 n)$ process. This means that you could use the binary search algorithm to find a name in a large metropolitan telephone directory using 30 or fewer probes (2^{30} is approximately equal to 1,000,000,000).

Because the array is sorted, we only need to compare the target value with the middle element of the subarray we are searching. If their values are the same, we are done. If the middle element value is larger than the target value, we should search the lower half of the subarray next; otherwise, we should search the upper half of the subarray.

The subarray being searched has indices `first` through `last`. The variable `middle` is the index of the middle element in this range. Figure 11.18 shows an example in which the target is 35, `first` is 0, `last` is 8, and `middle` is 4. The upper half of the array (indices `middle` through `last`) is eliminated by the first probe.

The argument `last` needs to be reset to `middle - 1` to define the new subarray to be searched, and `middle` should be redefined as shown in Fig. 11.19. The target value, 35, would be found on this probe.

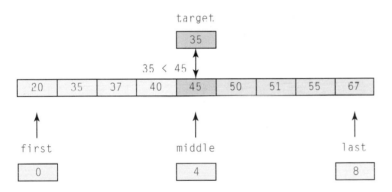

Figure 11.18 First probe of binary search

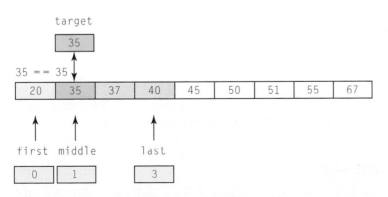

Figure 11.19 Second probe of binary search

Data Requirements

Problem Inputs

array to search
target value
index of first element in subarray
index of last element in subarray

Problem Outputs

location of target value in array if found, or -1

DESIGN

We can write the binary search algorithm without too much effort using recursion. The stopping cases are:

- The array bounds are improper (`first > last`).
- The middle value is the target value.

In the first case, the method returns -1 to indicate that the target is not present in the array. In the second case, `middle` is returned as the index of the target value. The recursive step is to search the appropriate subarray (a simpler problem).

Binary Search Algorithm

1. Compute the index of the middle element of the array.
2. `if` the array bounds are improper
       3. Target not present, return -1.
    `else if` target is the middle value
       4. Return `middle`.
    `else if` target is less than the middle value
       5. Search subarray with indices `first` through `middle-1`.
    `else`
       6. Search subarray with indices `middle+1` through `last`.

For each of the recursive steps (steps 5 and 6), the bounds of the new subarray must be listed as actual arguments in the recursive call. The actual arguments define the search limits for the next probe into the array.

IMPLEMENTATION

In the initial call to the recursive method, `first` and `last` should be defined as the first and last elements of the entire array, respectively. For example, you could use the method call

```
binSearch(x, 35, 0, 8)
```

to search an array x with nine elements for the target value 35. The position of the target element in array x will be returned as the method result if 35 is found. Method binSearch is shown in Fig. 11.20.

The statement

```
int middle = (first + last) / 2;
```

computes the index of the middle element by finding the average of first and last. The value has no meaning when first is greater than last, but it does no harm to compute it.

```
/* Part of class IntArray in package simpleMath.
   Developed for Problem Solving with Java, Koffman & Wolz.
   Appears in Fig. 11.20.

   Searches for target in elements first through last of
     array table.
   precondition : The elements of table are sorted &
                    first and last are defined.
   postcondition: If target is in the array, return its
                    position; otherwise, returns -1.
*/
public static int binSearch (int[] table,
                             int target,
                             int first,
                             int last) {
    int middle = (first + last) / 2; // Middle of array

    if (first > last)
        return -1;                          // Unsuccessful search
    else if (target == table[middle])
        return middle;                      // Successful search
    else if (target < table[middle])
        return binSearch(table, target, first, middle-1);
    else  // search upper half of array
        return binSearch(table, target, middle+1, last);
}
```

Figure 11.20 Recursive binary search method

TESTING

Check for targets in the first and last elements of the array. Check for targets that are not present. Check the algorithm for even- and odd-length arrays. Also check arrays with multiple target values. See what happens when the array size gets very large, say, 1,000.

EXERCISES FOR SECTION 11.5

Self-Check

1. Trace the execution of `binSearch` for the array shown in Fig. 11.18 and a `target` value of `40`.
2. What would happen if `binSearch` were called with the precondition of elements in increasing order violated? Would `binSearch` still find the item?

Programming

1. Sorting algorithms need to know where in a sorted array a new item should be inserted. Write a recursive method `insertLocation` that returns a location where `target` could be inserted into an array and still maintain correct ordering.

11.6 Solving Towers of Hanoi with Recursion

In this section, we develop an elegant recursive solution to a problem that would be very difficult to solve without recursion. Our analysis will show that the solution to the original problem can be expressed readily in terms of simpler versions of itself, so a recursive solution is called for.

Case Study

Towers of Hanoi Problem

PROBLEM

Solve the Towers of Hanoi problem for *n* disks, where *n* is an argument.

ANALYSIS

To solve the Towers of Hanoi problem you must move a specified number of disks of different sizes from one tower (or peg) to another. Legend has it that the world will come to an end when the problem is solved for 64 disks. You may be familiar with a children's game that is a three-disk version of this puzzle.

    In the version of the problem shown in Fig. 11.21, there are five disks (numbered 1 through 5) and three towers or pegs (lettered A, B, and C). The goal is to move the five disks from peg A to peg C subject to the following rules:

- Only one disk may be moved at a time, and this disk must be the top disk on a peg.
- A larger disk can never be placed on top of a smaller disk.

A stopping case of the problem is the movement of only one disk (e.g., "move disk 2 from peg A to peg C"). Simpler problems than the original would be to move four disks subject to the rules above, to move three disks, and so on. Therefore, we want to split the original five-disk problem into one or more problems involving fewer disks. Let's consider splitting the original problem into three problems:

1. Move four disks from peg A to peg B.
2. Move disk 5 from peg A to peg C.
3. Move four disks from peg B to peg C.

Step 1 moves all disks but the largest to tower B, an auxiliary tower. Step 2 moves the largest disk to the goal tower, tower C. Step 3 then moves the remaining disks from B to the goal tower, where they will be placed on top of the largest disk. Let's assume that we can perform steps 1 and 2 (a stopping case); Figure 11.22 shows the status of the three towers after completion of these steps. At this point it should be clear that we can solve the original five-disk problem if we can complete step 3 (Move four disks from peg B to peg C). In step 3, peg C is the goal tower and peg A becomes the auxiliary tower.

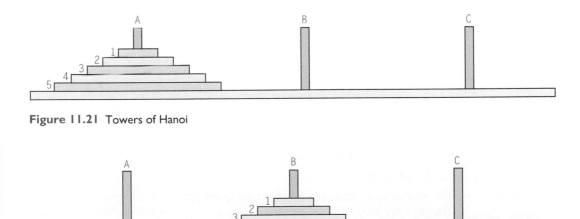

Figure 11.21 Towers of Hanoi

Figure 11.22 Towers of Hanoi after steps 1 and 2

Unfortunately, we still don't know how to perform step 1 or step 3. Both steps, however, involve four disks instead of five, so they are easier than the original problem. We should be able to split them into even simpler problems. In step 3 we must move four disks from peg B to peg C, so we can split it into two three-disk problems and a single one-disk problem:

3.1   Move three disks from peg B to peg A.

3.2   Move disk 4 from peg B to peg C.

3.3   Move three disks from peg A to peg C.

Figure 11.23 shows the towers after completion of steps 3.1 and 3.2. The two largest disks are now on peg C. Once we complete step 3.3, all five disks will be on peg C. Although we still do not know how to solve steps 3.1 and 3.3, they are at least simpler problems than the four-disk problem from which they are derived.

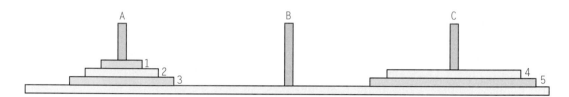

Figure 11.23 Towers of Hanoi after steps 1, 2, 3.1, and 3.2

By splitting each *n*-disk problem into two problems involving *n* − 1 disks and a one-disk problem, we eventually reach the point where all the cases manipulate only one disk, cases that we know how to solve. Next, we use this process to write a Java method that solves the Towers of Hanoi problem.

The solution to the Towers of Hanoi problem consists of a printed list of individual disk moves. We need a method to read the problem data. We also need a recursive method that moves any number of disks from one peg to another, using the third peg as an auxiliary. The role of each peg (source, destination, auxiliary) changes with each call.

Data Requirements

Problem Inputs

The source peg, destination peg, and spare peg
The number of disks

Problem Outputs

A list of individual disk moves

DESIGN

Specification for `TowersOfHanoi` *class*

Data Fields

`int numDisks`—input - the count of disks
`char sourcePeg`—input - the peg that has the disks
`char destinationPeg`—input - the peg where the disks will end up
`char sparePeg`—input - the peg that has no disks at the beginning or
        at the end

Methods

`readTowerData`—Reads the count of disks and the letter for each peg.
`tower`—Determines and displays the sequence of disk moves.
`showTower`—Reads the tower data (using `readTowerData`) and
       passes this information to method `tower`.

Algorithm for `tower`

1. `if n is 1`

   2. Move disk 1 from the *from* peg to the *to* peg.

  `else`

   3. Move n-1 disks from the *from* peg to the *auxiliary* peg using
     the *to* peg as an intermediary.

   4. Move disk n from the *from* peg to the *to* peg.

   5. Move n-1 disks from the *auxiliary* peg to the *to* peg using the
     from peg as an intermediary.

If n is 1, a stopping case is reached. If n is greater than 1, the recursive step splits the original problem into three smaller subproblems (steps 3, 4, and 5), one of which is a stopping case (step 4). Each stopping case displays a move instruction. Verify that the recursive step generates the three subproblems shown earlier and repeated below when n is 5, the *from* peg is A, and the *to* peg is C.

3. Move four disks from peg A to peg B.

4. Move disk 5 from peg A to peg C.

5. Move four disks from peg B to peg C.

IMPLEMENTATION

The implementation of this algorithm is shown as method `tower` in Fig. 11.24. Method `tower` has four arguments. The method call statement

```
tower('A', 'C', 'B', 5)
```

solves the problem posed earlier of moving five disks from peg A to peg C using B as an auxiliary peg.

The stopping case in method tower ("Move disk 1 from peg...") is written as a call to `displayResult`. Each recursive step consists of two recursive calls to `tower`, with a call to `displayResult` sandwiched between them. The first recursive call solves the problem of moving n-1 disks to the *auxiliary* peg. The call to `displayResult` displays a message to move disk n to the *to* peg. The second recursive call solves the problem of moving the n-1 disks back from the *auxiliary* peg to the *to* peg.

```
/*    File: TowersOfHanoi.java.
      Developed for Problem Solving with Java, Koffman & Wolz.
      Appears in Fig. 11.24.
*/
import simpleIO.*;

public class TowersOfHanoi extends SimpleGUI {

    // Data fields
    private int numDisks;          // input - number of disks
    private char sourcePeg;        // input - starting peg
    private char destinationPeg;   // input - ending peg
    private char sparePeg;         // input - other peg

    // Methods
    public void readTowerData() {
        numDisks = getInt("How many disks", 1, 8);

        // Get 3 different pegs.
        sourcePeg = getChar("Enter the source peg",'A','C');
        destinationPeg = getChar("Enter destination",'A','C');
        sparePeg = getChar("Enter the spare peg",'A','C');
    }
```

Figure 11.24 *continued*

Figure 11.24 *continued*

```
    /* Moves n disks from fromPeg to toPeg
       using auxPeg as an intermediary.
       precondition : fromPeg, toPeg, auxPeg, and n are defined.
       postcondition: Displays a list of move instructions that
                             transfer the disks.
    */
    public void tower(char fromPeg,
                      char toPeg,
                      char auxPeg,
                      int n) {
        if (n == 1)
            displayResult("Move disk 1 from peg " +
                                  fromPeg + " to peg " + toPeg);
        else { // Recursive step.
            tower(fromPeg, auxPeg, toPeg, n-1);
            displayResult("Move disk " + n +
                " from peg " + fromPeg + " to peg " + toPeg);
            tower(auxPeg, toPeg, fromPeg, n-1);
        }
    }


    public void showTower() {
        readTowerData();

        tower(sourcePeg, destinationPeg, sparePeg, numDisks);
    }

} // class TowersOfHanoi
```

Figure 11.24 Recursive method `tower`

TESTING

Figure 11.25 traces the solution to a simpler problem: move three disks from peg A to peg C. Figure 11.26 shows the output generated by method `tower`. Verify for yourself that this list of steps solves the problem.

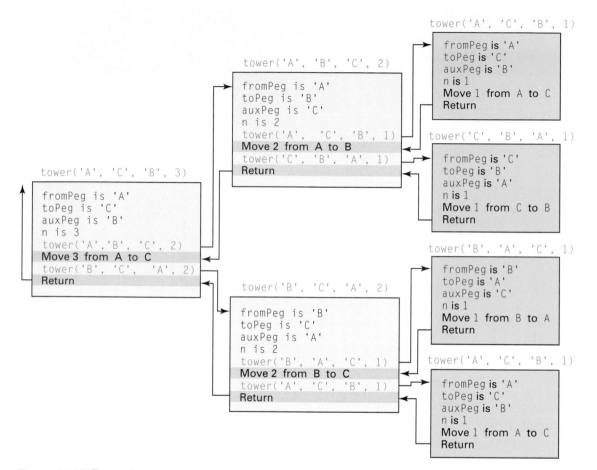

Figure 11.25 Trace of tower('A', 'C', 'B', 3);

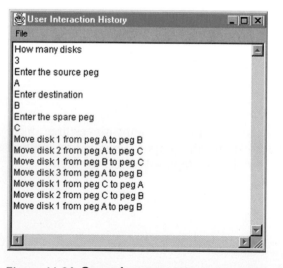

Figure 11.26 Output for tower('A', 'C', 'B', 3);

Comparison of Iterative and Recursive Methods

It is interesting to consider that method `tower` in Fig. 11.24 will solve the Towers of Hanoi problem for any number of disks. The three-disk problem results in a total of seven calls to method `tower` and is solved by seven disk moves. The five-disk problem would result in a total of 31 calls to method `tower` and is solved in 31 moves. In general, the number of moves required to solve the *n*-disk problem is $2^n - 1$. Because each method call requires the allocation and initialization of a local data area in memory, the computer time increases exponentially with the problem size. For this reason, be careful about running the program with a value of n larger than 10 (2^{10} is 1024).

The dramatic increase in processing time for larger numbers of disks results because of the problem, not because of recursion. In general, however, if there are recursive and iterative solutions to the same problem, the recursive solution requires a bit more time and space because of the extra method calls.

Although recursion was not really needed to solve many of the simpler problems in this chapter, it was extremely useful in formulating an algorithm for the Towers of Hanoi. For certain problems, recursion leads naturally to solutions that are much easier to read and understand than their iterative counterparts. In those cases, the benefits gained from increased clarity far outweigh the extra cost in time and memory of running a recursive program.

EXERCISES FOR SECTION 11.6

Self-Check

1. What problems are generated when you attempt to solve the problem "Move three disks from peg B to peg A"? Answer the same question for the problem "Move three disks from peg A to peg C."
2. How many moves are needed to solve the six-disk problem?

Programming

1. Write an application for the Towers of Hanoi problem.
2. There is no error checking in method `readTowerData`; consequently, a user may attempt to use a peg for more than one purpose. Discuss how you might incorporate error checking into `readTowerData` to eliminate this possibility.

11.7 A Recursive Program with a GUI

In this section, we develop a recursive solution to an image processing problem. We incorporate a GUI in the solution.

Case Study

Counting Cells in a Blob

PROBLEM

We have a two-dimensional array of cells, each of which may be empty or filled. The filled cells that are connected form a blob. There may be several blobs on the array. We would like a method (findBlob) that accepts as input the row and column of a particular cell and returns the size of the blob containing the cell. The filled cells might represent islands of land surrounded by water or malignant cells in a tissue sample.

There are three blobs in the sample array shown in Fig. 11.27. If the method arguments represent the row and column of a cell, the result of findBlob(0, 0) is 5; the result of findBlob(5, 1) is 2; the result of findBlob(5, 2) is 0; the result of findBlob(3, 4) is 5.

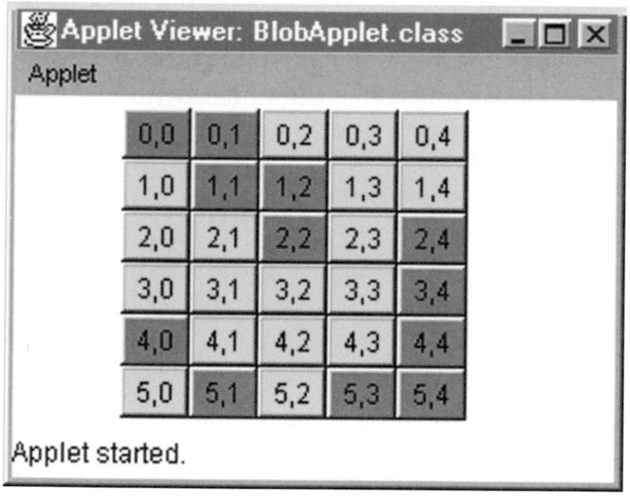

Figure 11.27 Applet with three blobs

ANALYSIS

Method findBlob must test the cell specified by its arguments to see whether it is filled. There are two stopping cases: the cell is not in the array or the cell is empty; in either case, the value returned by findBlob is 0. If the cell is in the array and filled, then the value returned is 1 plus the size of the blobs containing each of its eight neighbors. The recursive algorithm for findBlob follows.

Algorithm for findBlob

if the cell is not in the array
>   Return a count of 0.

else if the cell is empty then
>   Return a count of 0.

else
>>   Mark the cell as empty.
>>   Return 1 plus the size of the blob containing any of its 8 neighbors.

The recursive step (following else) marks the cell as empty before visiting its neighbors. If this were not done first, then a filled cell would be counted more than once since it is a neighbor of all its neighbors. A worse problem is that the recursion would not terminate. When each neighbor of the current cell is visited, findBlob is called again with the row and column of the current cell as arguments (the current cell is a neighbor of its neighbors). If the current cell had not been marked as empty, then the recursive step would be executed erroneously. Eventually all memory allocated to the stack would be used up (a stack overflow error).

DESIGN

Let's see how we can take advantage of Java's graphics capabilities to design a solution that incorporates a GUI. We will represent the array of cells as a two-dimensional grid of smart buttons. We will use the color gray (for land) to represent a filled cell and the color blue (for water) to represent an empty cell. These colors are stored as the background color of the button (defined in the Component class). A smart button also knows its row and column position in the grid and its current color. The current color of an empty cell is always the same as its background color; the current color of a filled cell should change temporarily to blue when it is marked empty.

Specification for SmartButton *class (extends* Button*)*

Data Fields

int row—row position of button
int column—column position of button
Color curColor—its current color

Methods

getRow—Gets row.
getColumn—Gets column.
getStoredColor—Gets current color.
setStoredColor—Sets current color.
toString—Returns its stored information as a string.

We also need an applet. The applet defines a two-dimensional grid of smart buttons (buttons) and a Label field (result). The applet has an init method that creates a panel. Method init allocates storage for the array of buttons and adds a grid to the panel with the same dimensions as this array. Method init must create each button, define its characteristics, and add it to the panel. It also registers the applet as a listener for actions from each button. Finally, init adds the panel and label to the applet.

The applet also needs an actionPerformed method. It determines the button that was pressed, finds the size of the blob containing that button (using method findBlob), resets any button colors that were changed (using method recolorMap), and defines the Label field result.

Specification for BlobApplet *class (extends* Applet*)*

Data Fields

smartButton[][] buttons—the grid of smart buttons
Label result—a label that shows the position and color of the button selected and the blob size

Methods

init—Sets up the applet and defines the array of buttons.
actionPerformed—Responds to the user selection, calls findBlob and recolorMap, and defines the result field.
findBlob—Finds the blob size, resetting the color of each button in the blob to blue.
recolorMap—Resets the current color of each button to its background color.

We showed the algorithm for findBlob earlier. The algorithms for init and actionPerformed follow.

Algorithm for init

1. Construct the panel.
    1.1. Create a two-dimensional array of smart buttons. Call the GridLayout constructor to build a grid with the same dimensions.
    1.2. Set the characteristics of each button. Add it to the panel and register the applet as an action listener for actions from the button.
2. Add the panel to the applet.
3. Add the label to the applet.

Algorithm for actionPerformed

1. Determine which button was selected.
2. Find the size of the blob that contains it.
3. Recolor the array of buttons.
4. Define the Label result.
5. Declare that the Label is invalid.
6. Have the applet redo the layout.

IMPLEMENTATION

Figure 11.28 shows class SmartButton and Fig. 11.29 shows the applet.

```java
/*   File: SmartButton.java.
     Developed for Problem Solving with Java, Koffman & Wolz.
     Appears in Fig. 11.28.
*/
import java.awt.*;

public class SmartButton extends Button {
    // Data fields
    private Color curColor;
    private int row;
    private int column;

    // Methods
    // Constructor
    public SmartButton(String s, Color col, int r, int c) {
        super(s);               // Call button constructor -
                                //    define label field
        curColor = col;
        row = r;
        column = c;
        setBackground(col);  // Define background color.
    }

    // Accessors
    public int getRow() {return row;}
    public int getColumn() {return column;}
    public Color getStoredColor() {return curColor;}

    // Modifier
    public void setStoredColor(Color col) {curColor = col;}

    // toString
    public String toString() {
        String col;
        if (curColor == Color.green)
            col = "green";
        else
            col = "blue";
        return row + "," + column + " (" + col + ")";
    }
} // class SmartButton
```

Figure 11.28 Class SmartButton

```
/*    File: BlobApplet.java.
      Developed for Problem Solving with Java, Koffman & Wolz.
      Appears in Fig. 11.29.
*/
import java.awt.*;
import java.applet.Applet;
import java.awt.event.*;

public class BlobApplet extends Applet
                    implements ActionListener {

    private SmartButton[][] buttons;    // array of buttons
    private Label result = new Label(); // label for result

    public void init() {
        Panel Map  = new Panel();

        // Define bitMap array
        int[][] bitMap = {   {1,1,0,0,0},
                             {0,1,1,0,0},
                             {0,0,1,0,1},
                             {0,0,0,0,1},
                             {1,0,0,0,1},
                             {0,1,0,1,1}
                         };

        // Create an array of the proper size.
        buttons = new
            SmartButton[bitMap.length][bitMap[0].length];

        // Create the grid.
        Map.setLayout(new
            GridLayout(buttons.length, buttons[0].length));

        // Traverse the array of buttons. Create each
        //    button, add it to the panel, and register it.
        for (int r = 0; r < buttons.length; r++)
            for (int c = 0; c < buttons[r].length; c++) {
                Color col;
                if (bitMap[r][c] == 1)
                    col = Color.green;
                else
                    col = Color.blue;
                // Make a new smart button
                buttons[r][c] = new SmartButton(r + "," + c,
                                                col, r, c);
```

Figure 11.29 *continued*

Figure 11.29 *continued*

```
                         // Add it to the panel and register the
                         //    applet as the listener.
                         Map.add(buttons[r][c]);
                         buttons[r][c].addActionListener(this);
               }

        add(Map);      // Add the grid to the panel
        add(result);   // Add the label to the panel
   }


   public void actionPerformed(ActionEvent e) {
        SmartButton b = (SmartButton) e.getSource();

        // Find the size of the blob.
        int count = findBlob(b.getRow(), b.getColumn());

        // Reset the colors.
        recolorMap();

        // display the result.
        result.setText("Button " + b +
                       ", cells in blob: " + count);
        result.invalidate();
        validate();
   }

   // For each button reset the current color field to
   //    the background color.
   private void recolorMap() {
        for(int r = 0; r < buttons.length; r++)
             for(int c = 0; c < buttons[r].length; c++)
                  buttons[r][c].setStoredColor
                         (buttons[r][c].getBackground());
   }

   // Find the size of the blob.
   private int findBlob(int r, int c) {
        if (r < 0 || c < 0 || r >= buttons.length ||
            c >= buttons[0].length)
               return 0;                     // Cell is not in array.
        else if (buttons[r][c].getStoredColor() == Color.blue)
               return 0;                     // Cell is empty.
```

Figure 11.29 *continued*

Figure 11.29 *continued*

```
        else {
            // Mark cell empty.
            buttons[r][c].setStoredColor(Color.blue);
            // Count it and its filled neighbors.
            return 1 + findBlob(r-1,c-1) +
                    findBlob(r,c-1) + findBlob(r+1,c-1) +
                    findBlob(r-1,c) + findBlob(r+1,c) +
                    findBlob(r-1,c+1) + findBlob(r,c+1) +
                    findBlob(r+1,c+1);
        }
    }

} // class BlobApplet
```

Figure 11.29 Class `BlobApplet`

Method `init` allocates storage for panel `Map` and defines a two-dimensional array (`bitMap`) of `0`s and `1`s. The `for` loops traverse the array of buttons, setting each button's background color to blue or green based on the value of the corresponding element of array `bitMap` (green for `1`, blue for `0`).

In method `findBlob`, if the cell being visited is off the grid or is empty (current color is blue), a value of zero is returned immediately. Otherwise, the recursive step executes causing method `findBlob` to call itself eight times. Each time a different neighbor of the current cell is visited. The method result is defined as the sum of all values returned from these recursive calls plus `1` (for the current cell). These problems are simpler than the original because the current cell has been marked as empty.

The sequence of operations performed in `findBlob` is very important. The `if` statement tests whether the current cell is on the grid before testing whether it is empty. If the order were reversed, an index-out-of-bounds error would occur whenever the current cell was off the grid.

TESTING

Earlier (Fig. 11.27) we showed a result of running the applet. Each time you click on a new button, the result changes. You should try clicking on buttons that are filled and empty and buttons that are near the borders of the grid. Also, make sure you click on two buttons that are in the same blob.

EXERCISE FOR SECTION 11.7

Self-Check

1. Trace the execution of method `findBlob` for the buttons at positions [1, 1] and [2, 1] in the sample grid in Fig. 11.27.

2. Is the order of the two tests performed in method `findBlob` critical? What happens if we reverse them or combine them into a single condition?

Programming

1. Instead of using the array `bitMap` to set the color of each button, consider how you would write a method that enabled the user to indicate a filled button by clicking on it. The initial color for each button would show that it was empty.

⊞⊞⊞ Common Programming Errors

The most common problem that occurs with a recursive method is that it may not terminate properly. For example, if the terminating condition is not correct or is incomplete, the method may call itself indefinitely or until all available memory is used up. Normally, a `stack overflow` run-time error indicates that a recursive method is not terminating. Make sure you identify all stopping cases and provide a terminating condition for each one. Also be sure that each recursive step leads to a situation that is closer to a stopping case and that repeated recursive calls eventually lead to stopping cases only.

When debugging, you may find it helpful to display the value of the argument that is supposed to be getting smaller during each call as the first statement in a recursive method. This will help you determine whether the method is being called correctly and whether it will eventually terminate.

Chapter Review

1. A recursive method is one that calls itself. You can use recursion to solve problems by splitting them into smaller versions of themselves.

2. Each recursive method has one or more stopping cases and recursive steps. The stopping cases can be solved directly; the recursive steps lead to recursive calls of the method.

3. Recursive methods can be used with arguments that are simple types or structured types. Recursive methods can implement mathematical operations that are defined by recursive definitions.

4. Binary search is a recursive search method that can search a large array in $O(\log_2 n)$ time.

Quick-Check Exercises

1. How are stacks used in recursion.
2. Can the stopping case also have a recursive call in it?
3. In Java, which control statement is always in a recursive method?
4. What is the relation between a terminating condition and a stopping case?
5. Returning from a series of recursive calls is called _____ the recursion.
6. What causes a `stack overflow` error?
7. What can you say about a recursive algorithm that has the following form?

   if (*condition*)
       Perform recursive step.

Answers to Quick-Check Exercises

1. The stack is used to hold all argument and local variable values and the return point for each execution of a recursive method.
2. No, if it did, recursion would continue.
3. `if` statement
4. A recursive method reaches a stopping case when a terminating condition is true.
5. unwinding
6. A stack overflow error occurs when there are too many recursive calls. Usually recursion doesn't terminate.
7. The method is exited immediately when the stopping case is reached.

Review Questions

1. Differentiate between a recursive step and a stopping case in a recursive algorithm.
2. Discuss the time and space efficiency of recursive methods versus iterative methods.
3. What basic characteristics must a problem have for a recursive solution to be applicable?
4. Write a recursive method that prints the accumulating sum of ordinal values corresponding to each character in a string. For example, if the string is `"a boy"`, the first value printed would be the ordinal number of a, then the sum of ordinals for a and the space character, then the sum of ordinals for a, space, b, and so on.

5. Write a recursive method that calculates an approximate value for *e*, the base of the natural logarithms, by summing the series

$$1 + \frac{1}{1!} + \frac{1}{2!} + \ldots + \frac{1}{n!}$$

until additional terms do not affect the approximation.

Programming Projects

1. The expression for computing *c(n,r)*, the number of combinations of *n* items taken *r* at a time, is

$$c(n, r) = \frac{n!}{r!(n - r)!}$$

Write and test a method for computing *c(n,r)*, given that *n*! is the factorial of *n*.

2. A palindrome is a word that is spelled exactly the same when the letters are reversed (for example, level, deed, and mom). Write a recursive method that returns the `boolean` value `true` if a word, passed as an argument, is a palindrome.

3. Write a recursive method that lists all subsets of pairs of letters for a given set of letters, for example,

```
['A','C','E','G']  =>  ['A','C'],  ['A','E'],
                       ['A','G'],  ['C','E'],
                       ['C','G'],  ['E','G']
```

4. Write a method that accepts an 8 × 8 array of characters that represents a maze. Each position can contain either an X or a blank. Starting at position `[0,0]`, list any path through the maze to get to location `[7,7]`. Only horizontal and vertical moves are allowed (no diagonal moves). Make sure your algorithm avoids retracing previously tried paths. If no path exists, write a message indicating this.

   Moves can be made only to locations that contain a blank. If an X is encountered, that path is blocked and another must be chosen. Use recursion.

5. The bisection method finds an approximate root for the equation *f(x)* = 0 on the interval `xLeft` to `xRight`, inclusive (assuming that function *f(x)* is continuous on this interval). The interval endpoints (`xLeft` and `xRight`) and the tolerance for the approximation (`epsilon`) are input by the user.

   One stopping criterion for the bisection method is the identification of an interval `[xLeft, xRight]` that is less than `epsilon` in length over which *f(x)* changes sign (from positive to negative or vice versa). The midpoint `[xMid = (xLeft + xRight)/2.0)]` of the interval will be an approximation to the root of the equation when `f(xMid)` is very close to zero. Of course, if you find a value of `xMid` such that `f(xMid)` = 0, you have found a very good approximation of the root, and the algorithm should also stop.

To perform the recursive step, replace either `xLeft` or `xRight` with `xMid`, depending on which one has the same sign as `xMid`. Write a program that uses the bisection method to determine an approximation to the equation

$$5x^3 - 2x^2 + 3 = 0$$

over the interval `[-1,1]` using `epsilon = 0.0001`.

6. Write a program which, given a list of up to 10 integer numbers and a sum, will find a subset of the numbers whose total is that sum if one exists or that will indicate that none exists, otherwise. For example, for the list: 5, 13, 23, 9, 3, 3 and sum = 28, your program should find: 13, 9, 3, 3.

7. A mergeSort is an $O(n \times \log n)$ sorting technique with the following recursive algorithm (*mergeSort*):

`if` the array to sort has more than one element

mergeSort the left half of the array.

mergeSort the right half of the array.

Merge the two sorted subarrays to form the sorted array.

For example, mergeSort the array 10, 20, 15, 6, 5, 40 by following these steps:

mergeSort the subarray 10, 20, 15, giving 10, 15, 20.

mergeSort the subarray 6, 5, 40, giving 5, 6, 40.

Merge the two sorted subarrays, giving 5, 6, 10, 15, 20, 40.

Of course, each call to mergeSort above will generate two more recursive calls (one for a one-element array and one for a two-element array). mergeSort for a one-element array is a stopping case.

8. Do project 4 using an array of smart buttons. Green buttons correspond to empty cells and red buttons correspond to cells that contain x. As the program traces out a path through the maze, it should select only buttons that are green and reset the color of the buttons on the path to white.

C H A P T E R 12

Linked Data Structures

In this chapter we focus on linked data structures that are also dynamic data structures. Unlike static structures, in which the size of the data structure is determined when the storage is initially allocated and remains unchanged throughout program execution (like an array), dynamic data structures expand and contract as a program executes.

12.1 Linked Lists

12.2 Stacks

12.3 Queues

12.4 Binary Trees

12.5 A Binary Search Tree Class

12.6 Efficiency of a Binary Search Tree

12.7 Common Programming Errors

Chapter Review

The first dynamic data structure we will study is called a *linked list*. A linked list is a collection of elements (called *nodes*) that are objects. Each node has a reference field, called a *link*, that connects it to the next node in the list.

Linked List

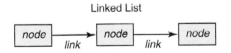

Linked lists are extremely flexible. It is easy to add new information by creating a new node and inserting it between two existing nodes. It is also relatively easy to delete a node.

In this chapter we study three special kinds of linked lists: stacks, queues, and trees. All three data structures have many applications in computer science. We will show how to implement them and how to use them.

12.1 Linked Lists

linked list:
a group of objects that are connected.

We can arrange groups of dynamically allocated nodes into a flexible data structure called a **linked list**. Linked lists are like chains of children's "pop beads." Each bead has a hole at one end and a plug at the other (see Fig. 12.1). We can connect the beads in the obvious way to form a chain. After a chain has been created, we can easily modify it. We can remove the color bead by disconnecting the two beads at both its ends and reattaching this pair of beads. We can add a new bead by connecting it to the bead at either end of the chain. Or we can break the chain somewhere in the middle (between beads A and B) and insert a new bead by connecting one end to bead A and the other end to bead B. We show how to perform these operations to rearrange the nodes in a linked list next.

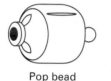

Pop bead   Chain of pop beads

Figure 12.1 Children's pop beads in a chain

Building a Linked List

Although a link to a node is a new term, it is not really a new concept. For example, the statement

```
Employee emp = new Employee();
```

link:
a storage location whose contents is a reference to an object stored elsewhere.

actually allocates a new `Employee` object and stores a reference to it in the memory cell named `emp`. We say that `emp` references this object or is a **link** to this object.

We can define a list node as a class with data fields that represent the data stored in the node and its link to the next node. Figure 12.2 shows a class `ListNode` that stores string data.

```
/*    File: ListNode.java.
      Developed for Problem Solving with Java, Koffman & Wolz.
      Appears in Figure 12.2.
*/
package linkList;

public class ListNode {
    // Data fields
    String info;          // Data stored in the node
    ListNode link;        // Link to next node
```

Figure 12.2 *continued*

Figure 12.2 *continued*

```
        // Methods
        // Constructors
        public ListNode() {info = ""; link = null;}

        public ListNode(String i) {info = i; link = null;}

        public ListNode(String i, ListNode l) {
            info = i;
            link = l;
        }
    }
}
```

Figure 12.2 Class ListNode

Because data field link has type ListNode, it can store a reference to another node of type ListNode. We give the data fields package visibility so
any class in package linkList can access them directly. The default constructor initializes info to the empty string and link to null. The second
constructor stores its single argument (a String) in the info field of a new
node (the link field is null). The third constructor stores its argument values
in both fields of a new node, thereby, linking the new node to another node.

Connecting Nodes

The statements

```
ListNode p = new ListNode("the");
ListNode q = new ListNode("hat");
```

allocate storage for two objects of type ListNode referenced by p and q. The
node referenced by p stores the string "the", and the node referenced by q
stores the string "hat" (see Fig. 12.3). The link fields of both nodes are null.

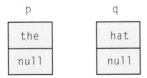

Figure 12.3 Nodes p **and** q

The statement

```
p.link = q;
```

stores the address of node q in the link field of node p, thereby connecting
node p to node q (see Fig. 12.4). The link field of node p is now a link to
node q. Because p.link references node q, we can use either q.info or
p.link.info to access the data in node q.

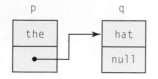

Figure 12.4 Connecting nodes p and q

Programmers often represent the value `null` by drawing a diagonal line in a `link` field (Fig. 12.5). The linked list contains the strings `"the"`, `"hat"`.

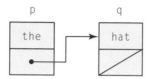

Figure 12.5 Linked list with two nodes

Inserting a Node in a List

To insert a new node between nodes p and q, we can use the statement

```
// Insert a new node between nodes p and q.
p.link = new ListNode("top", q);
```

This statement allocates a new node that is referenced by `p.link`. The new node stores the string `"top"` and its `link` field references node q. Figure 12.6 shows the effect of this statement. The color arrows show the new values of the link fields; the gray arrow shows an old value. The new linked list contains the strings `"the"`, `"top"`, `"hat"`.

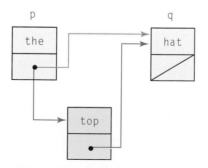

Figure 12.6 Inserting a new node in a list

We can access the data in each node directly or by following a trail of links. Table 12.1 shows some expressions that reference the list data in Fig. 12.6.

Table 12.1 References to list data in Fig. 12.6

Expression	Data Referenced
`p.info`	`info` field of first node (`"the"`)
`p.link.info`	`info` field of second node (`"top"`)
`q.info`, `p.link.link.info`	`info` field of third node (`"hat"`)

Insertion at the head of a list   We usually insert new data items at the end of an array or vector. However, it is normally easier to insert a new item at the front or **head of a list**. If we assume that `head` has been declared as type `ListNode`, the statement

```
// Insert a new node at head of list.
head = new ListNode("in", p);
```

links `head` to a new node with `info` field `"in"` and `link` field `p`, so the new node is connected to the list in Fig. 12.6. Node `head` becomes the first element of the expanded list containing the strings `"in"`, `"the"`, `"top"`, `"hat"` (see Fig. 12.7).

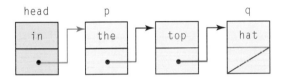

Figure 12.7 New list of four nodes

Insertion at the end of a list   The reason it is less efficient to insert an item at the end of a list is that we usually do not have a link to the last list element. Consequently, we often need to follow the trail of links from the list head to the last list node and then perform the insertion. However, in this example, `q` is a link to the last list node, so the statement

```
// Attach a new node to the end of the list.
q.link = new ListNode("box");
```

links the node referenced by `q` to a new node that stores the string `"box"` (see Fig. 12.8). The new list contains the strings `"in"`, `"the"`, `"top"`, `"hat"`, `"box"`. We have no direct reference to the node that contains `"box"`, but we can access its data using the expression `q.link.info`.

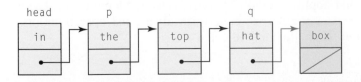

Figure 12.8 Insertion at the end of a list

Removing a Node

To remove or delete a node from a linked list, we simply change the `link` field of the node that references it (its *predecessor*). We want to link the predecessor to the node that follows the one being removed (its *successor*). For example, to remove the node referenced by p from the five-element list in Fig. 12.8, we change the `link` field of the first node so that it references the same node as the `link` field of node p:

```
head.link = p.link;      // Bypass node p.
```

Next, we use the statement

```
p.link = null;      // Disconnect p from the list.
```

to disconnect node p from the list. The new list (Fig. 12.9) contains the strings `"in"`, `"top"`, `"hat"`, `"box"`.

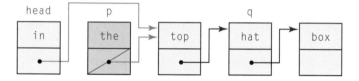

Figure 12.9 Removing a list node

Traversing a List

In many list-processing operations, we must process each node in the list in sequence; this is called **traversing a list**. To traverse a list, we must start at the list head and follow the trail of links.

A typical operation performed on a linked data structure is to display the data structure's contents. To display the contents of a list, we display only the data in its information fields, not the link fields. The recursive method `traverse` in Fig. 12.10 displays the information field for each node of a linked list. The recursive step

```
displayResult(next.info);
traverse(next.link);
```

displays the string stored at the head of the list referenced by `next` and calls `traverse` to display the information fields for the rest of the list (referenced by `next.link`).

To test this class, you need to write an application class that creates a `LinkList` object and applies method `showList` to it. Method `showList` first calls method `buildTestList` to perform all the list operations discussed in this section. Then, the method call

```
traverse(head);
```

initiates the list traversal.

```
/*  File: LinkList.java.
    Developed for Problem Solving with Java, Koffman & Wolz.
    Appears in Figure 12.10.
*/
package linkList;

import simpleIO.*;

public class LinkList extends SimpleGUI {

    private ListNode head;              // Reference to
                                        // first list node

    public void buildTestList() {
        // Build a list with nodes p and q.
        ListNode p = new ListNode("the");
        ListNode q = new ListNode("hat");
        p.link = q;

        // Insert a new node between nodes p and q.
        p.link = new ListNode("top", q);
        // Insert a new node at head of list.
        head = new ListNode("in", p);

        //Append a new node to the end of the list.
        q.link = new ListNode("box");
        head.link = p.link; // Bypass node p.
        p.link = null;      // Disconnect p from the list.
    }


    /*
        Displays the linked list to which it is applied.
        precondition : The last list node has a null link.
        postcondition: The data fields of each list node are displayed.
    */
    public void traverse(ListNode next) {
        if (next != null) {
            displayResult(next.info);
            traverse(next.link);
        }
    }
```

Figure 12.10 *continued*

Figure 12.10 *continued*

```
    public void showListTraverse() {
        buildTestList();

        traverse(head);
    }
}
```

Figure 12.10 Class LinkList

Circular Lists and Two-way Lists (Optional)

You can move in only one direction in a list, and you can't move past the last element. To get around these restrictions, programmers sometimes use circular lists or two-way lists.

circular list:
a list in which the last list node contains a link to the first list node.

Circular lists A **circular list** is a list in which the last list node references the list head. In the circular list below, you can start anywhere in the list and still access all list elements.

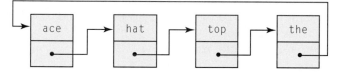

two-way (doubly linked) list:
a list in which each node has a link to its predecessor and successor.

Two-way lists In a **two-way** or **doubly linked list**, each node has two links: one to the node's successor and one to the node's predecessor. The node next below has two link fields named left and right. The statement

```
next = next.right;
```

resets link next to the successor node, and the statement

```
next = next.left;
```

resets link next to the predecessor node.

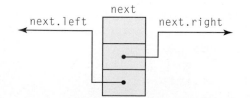

EXERCISES FOR SECTION 12.1

Self-Check

1. For the four-element list in Fig. 12.7, explain the effect of each fragment. Assume the list is restored to its initial state before each fragment executes.

a. `p.link = q;`

b. `head.link = q;`

c. `head = p.link;`

d. `p.info = p.link.info;`

e. `p.info = p.link.link.info;`

f. `q.link = new ListNode("zzz");`

g. `p.link = q.link;`

h. `p.info = q.info;`

i. `p.link.link = null;`

j.
```
ListNode next = head;
int count = 0;
while (next != null) {
    count++;
    next = next.link;
}
```

2. How would you delete the node at the head of a list?

3. How would you delete a node if you were given only a reference to the node to be deleted and a reference to the list head?

Programming

1. Write a method for class `LinkList` that returns the length of a list.

2. Write a method `insert` for class `LinkList` that inserts a string passed as an argument at the beginning of a list. Make sure your method handles correctly the special case of an empty list (`head` is `null`).

3. Write a method `insertAtEnd` for class `LinkList` that inserts a string passed as its argument at the end of a list. Make sure your method handles correctly the special case of an initially empty list (`head` is `null`).

4. Write a method `readListData` for class `LinkList` that reads in some strings and stores them in a linked list in the order in which they were read. The first list node should contain the first data string, the second list node the second data string, and so on.

12.2 Stacks

A **stack** is a data structure in which only the top element can be accessed. The plates stored in the spring-loaded device in a buffet line perform like a stack. A customer always takes the top plate; when a plate is removed, the plate beneath it moves to the top.

stack:
a data structure in which only the top element can be accessed.

The diagram below shows a stack of three characters. The letter C is the character at the top of the stack and is the only character that we can access.

We must remove the letter C from the stack in order to access the symbol +. Removing a value from a stack is called **popping the stack**. Storing a data item in a stack is called **pushing** it onto the stack.

popping the stack:
removing the top element of a stack.

pushing the stack:
placing a new top element on the stack.

Implementing Stacks as Linked Lists

We can think of a stack as a linked list in which all insertions and deletions are performed at the list head. A list representation of the stack containing C, +, and 2 follows:

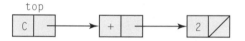

Variable top is a reference to the list head (the top of the stack). We can access only the character referenced by top, the letter C. Next we draw the stack after we push the symbol * onto it. Now the only character we can access is the symbol *:

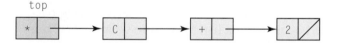

last-in-first-out (LIFO):
a data structure in which the last element stored is the first to be removed.

If we pop this stack, we retrieve the symbol * and restore the stack to its earlier state. A stack is called a *last-in-first-out (LIFO)* structure because the last element stored in a stack is always the first one removed.

Specification for Class `StackList`

Next we provide a specification for class `StackList`. Besides operators push and pop, we include operators peek and isEmpty. Operator peek accesses the top element on a stack without removing it. Operator isEmpty determines whether or not a stack has any elements.

Specification for `StackNode` class

Data Fields

`Object info`—the node's data
`StackNode link`—a link to the next node

Specification for StackList class

Data Fields

StackNode top—a reference to the top of the stack

Methods

void push(x)—the object x is placed at the top of the stack

Object pop()—returns the object at the top of the stack and removes
it

Object peek()—returns the object at the top of the stack without removing it

boolean isEmpty()—returns true if the stack is empty; otherwise,
returns false.

Implementing StackNode and StackList

Figure 12.11 shows class StackNode and Fig. 12.12 shows class
StackList. A StackNode object has an information field (info) and a
link field. Declaring the info field as type Object enables us to store
any object type in a stack.

```
/*  File: StackNode.java.
    Developed for Problem Solving with Java,
       Koffman & Wolz.
    Appears in Figure 12.11.
*/
package stackList;

public class StackNode {
    // Data fields
    Object info;
    StackNode link;

    // Methods
    // Constructors
    public StackNode() {};

    public StackNode(Object i) {info = i; link = null;}

    public StackNode(Object i, StackNode l) {
        info = i;
        link = l;
    }
} // class StackNode
```

Figure 12.11 Class StackNode

```
/*  File: StackList.java.
    Developed for Problem Solving with Java, Koffman & Wolz.
    Appears in Figure 12.12.
*/
package stackList;

public class StackList {
   // Data fields
   private StackNode top;          // Reference to
                                   // top of stack

   // Methods
   /* push - pushes an item onto a stack
      precondition : item is defined.
      postcondition: item is at the top of the stack.
   */
   public void push(Object item) {
      // Allocate a new node, store item in it, and
      //  link it to old top of stack.
      top = new StackNode(item, top);
   }


   /* pop - pops an item from a stack
      precondition : Stack is defined and is not empty.
      postcondition: Returns item at top of stack and removes it from the
                     stack. Old second stack element is at top of stack.
   */
   public Object pop() {
       StackNode oldTop = top; // Reference to top of stack.

       Object item = peek();    // Retrieve item at top.

       //Remove old top of stack
       top = top.link;         // Link top to second element.
       oldTop.link = null; // Disconnect old top of stack.

       return item;            // Return data at old top.
   }


   /* peek - retrieves an item from a stack
    * precondition : Stack is defined and is not empty.
    * postcondition: Returns item at top of stack without removing it.
    */
```

Figure 12.12 *continued*

Figure 12.12 *continued*

```
    public Object peek() {
        if (isEmpty())
            throw new NullPointerException();
        return top.info;        //Return top item.
    }


    /* isEmpty - tests whether a stack is empty
     * precondition : None
     * postcondition: Returns true if stack is empty;
     *                otherwise, return false.
     */
    public boolean isEmpty() {
        return (top == null);
    }
} // class StackList
```

Figure 12.12 Class StackList

In method push, the statement

```
top = new StackNode(item, top);
```

creates a new node at the top of the stack, copies item into its info field, and links the new node to the old top of the stack.

Method peek returns the information at the top of a stack without changing the stack. Method peek uses the condition (isEmpty()) to test whether the stack is empty before returning the data in its top element (accessed by top.info). Method isEmpty returns true when the boolean expression top == null is true. Method peek throws a NullPointerException if the stack is empty.

Method pop uses the statement

```
Object item = peek();           // Retrieve item at top.
```

to retrieve the item at the top of the stack. Next, it removes the current top of the stack by executing the statements

```
top = top.link;        // Link top to second element.
oldTop.link = null;    // Disconnect old top of stack.
```

Notice that the order of these statements is critical. If you reverse the order, then you will also set top to null (Why?)

Displaying a Collection of Strings in Reverse Order

Next we write a class StackOfStrings (Fig. 12.13) with methods readStringStack and showStringStack. Method readStringStack reads each string through the sentinel (`"***"`) and pushes it onto its stack argument, excluding the sentinel. Method `showStringStack` creates a stack, calls `readStringStack` to fill it with data, and then pops each string off the stack and displays it. Because the last string stored on the stack is the first one removed, the strings are displayed in reverse order.

Method `main` in Fig. 12.14 creates a `StringsInReverse` object and calls method `showStringStack` to read a group of strings and display them in reverse order. Figure 12.15 shows a sample run.

```java
/*  File: StringsInReverse.java.
    Developed for Problem Solving with Java, Koffman & Wolz.
    Appears in Figure 12.13.
*/
package stackList;

import simpleIO.*;

public class StringsInReverse extends SimpleGUI {

    // Methods
    // Reads a group of strings & pushes them onto a stack.
    public void readStringStack(StackList s) {
        String next = getString("Enter a string or ***:");
        while (!next.equals("***")) {
            s.push(next);
            next = getString("Enter a string or ***:");
        }
    }

    // Pops strings off the stack and displays them.
    public void showStringStack() {
        StackList s = new StackList();   // Create a stack.

        readStringStack(s);                    // Read data into stack.

        // Pop each string and display it.
        while (!s.isEmpty()) {
            String next = (String) s.pop();
            displayResult(next);
        }
    }
} // class StringsInReverse
```

Figure 12.13 Class StringsInReverse

```
/*   File: StringsInReverseApp.java.
     Developed for Problem Solving with Java,
       Koffman & Wolz.
     Appears in Figure 12.14.
*/
package stackList;

public class StringsInReverseApp {

    public static void main(String[] args) {
        StringsInReverse myStr =
                          new StringsInReverse();

        myStr.showStringStack();
    }
} // class StringsInReverseApp
```

Figure 12.14 Class StringsInReverseApp

Figure 12.15 Sample run of StringsInReverseApp

In method showStringStack (Fig. 12.13), the statement

```
String next = (String) s.pop();
```

pops a string from stack s and stores it in next. Because next is type String, we must cast the object popped to type String before assigning it to next.

Implementing a Stack Using a Vector

You may be wondering why we called our class StackList instead of just Stack. We chose StackList because Java provides a Stack class (in package java.util). Instead of using a linked list, Java implements class

Stack as an extension of a vector. This is quite natural because the size of a vector automatically increases as elements are appended. In a vector representation of a stack, the element with subscript size() - 1 is considered the element at the top of the stack.

Figure 12.16 sketches stack myStrings using a vector representation. Stack myStrings contains the three data strings "first", "is", "last", and the top of the stack (element with index 2) contains the string "last". Figure 12.17 shows class StackVector.

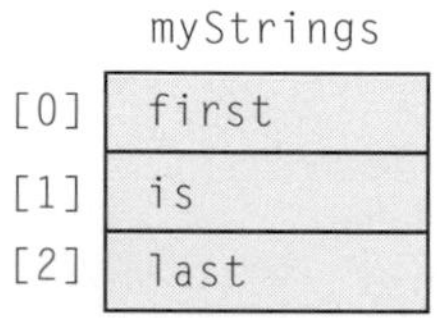

Figure 12.16 Stack myStrings as a vector

```
/*   File: StackVector.java.
     Developed for Problem Solving with Java, Koffman & Wolz.
     Appears in Figure 12.17.
*/
import java.util.*;

public class StackVector extends Vector {
  /* push - pushes an item onto a stack
     precondition : item is defined.
     postcondition: item is at the top of the stack.
   */
  public void push(Object item) {
    addElement(item);
  }


  /* pop - pops an item from a stack
   * precondition : Stack is defined and is not empty.
   * postcondition: Returns item at top of stack and removes it from the
   *                stack. Old second stack element is at top of stack.
   */
  public Object pop() {
     Object item;

     item = peek();                      // Retrieve item at top.
     removeElementAt(size() - 1);  // Remove top element.
     return item;
  }
}
```

Figure 12.17 *continued*

Figure 12.17 *continued*

```
/* peek - retrieves an item from a stack
 * precondition : Stack is defined and is not empty.
 * postcondition: Returns item at top of stack without removing it.
 */
public Object peek() {
  if (isEmpty())
      throw new NullPointerException();
  return elementAt(size() - 1);
}


/* isEmpty - tests whether a stack is empty
 * precondition : None
 * postcondition: Returns true if stack is empty; otherwise, returns
 *                false.
 */
public boolean isEmpty() {
  return (size() == 0);
}
} // class StackVector
```

Figure 12.17 Class StackVector

Our class StackVector differs from class Stack in folder java.util in two ways. Class Stack has a method empty instead of isEmpty. Also, method push in class Stack returns as its result the item pushed onto the stack. Hence, method push in class Stack is type Object (instead of type void).

EXERCISES FOR SECTION 12.2

Self-Check

1. Explain the difference between methods pop and peek.
2. Assume stack s is a stack of characters. Perform the following sequence of operations. Indicate the result of each operation and the new stack if it is changed. Rather than draw the stack each time, use the notation |2+C/ to represent a stack of four characters, where the last symbol on the right (/) is at the top of the stack.

```
StackList s = new StackList();
s.push("$");
s.push("-");
nextCh = (String)s.pop();
nextCh = (String)s.peek();
boolean success = s.isEmpty();
```

3. It is helpful to include a field, `numItems`, in type `StackList`, which contains a count of the number of elements on the stack. What changes would be required to the data fields and methods if field `numItems` were included?

4. How could a stack be implemented using an array instead of a linked list or vector? What are two disadvantages to this approach?

Programming

1. Write a method `copyStack` for class `StackList` that uses the stack operators to make a copy of an existing stack. The new stack will contain a duplicate of each node in the original stack. *Hint:* You will need to pop each node and store its data in a temporary stack.

12.3 Queues

queue:
a data structure in which elements are inserted at one end and removed from the other end.

A **queue** (pronounced "Q") is a list-like structure in which items are inserted at one end and removed from the other end. In contrast, stack elements are inserted and removed from the same end (the top of the stack).

A queue consists of a collection of elements that are all the same data type. The elements of a queue are ordered according to time of arrival. The element that was inserted first is the only one that may be removed or examined. Elements are removed from the front of the queue and inserted at the rear of the queue.

first-in-first-out (FIFO):
a data structure in which the first element stored is the first to be removed.

Because the element that was stored first is removed first, a queue is called a ***first-in-first-out (FIFO)*** structure. A queue can be used to model a line of customers waiting at a checkout counter or a stream of jobs waiting to be printed by a printer.

Figure 12.18a shows a queue of three customers waiting for service at a bank. The name of the customer who has been waiting the longest is `McMann` (referenced by `front`); the name of the most recent arrival is `Carson` (referenced to by `rear`). Customer `McMann` in the node referenced to by `front` will be the first one removed from the queue when a teller becomes available, and link `front` will be reset to reference `Wilson` (Fig. 12.18b). Any new customers will be inserted after `Carson` in the queue, and link `rear` will be adjusted accordingly (Fig. 12.18c).

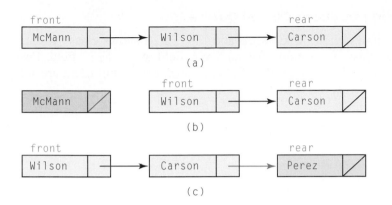

Figure 12.18 Queue of customers (a), after insertion (b), and removal (c)

Specification for Class Queue

Next we provide the specification for class Queue. A queue is a class with two reference fields, front and rear. Variable front references the node at the front of the queue, and variable rear references the node at the rear of the queue. Because we might also want to know how many elements are in a queue, we will add a third data field, size. Each queue node (object of class QueueNode) has an information field and a link to the next queue node. The only methods are constructors.

Specification for Class QueueNode

Data Fields

Object info—the node's data
QueueNode link—a link to the next node

Specification for Class Queue

Data Fields

QueueNode front—a reference to the front of the queue
QueueNode rear—a reference to the rear of the queue
int size—the size of the queue

Methods

void insert(item)—inserts item at the rear of the queue
Object peek()—returns the element at the front of the queue without removing it
Object remove()—returns the element at the front of the queue and removes it
boolean isEmpty()—returns true if the queue is empty; otherwise, returns false
int getSize()—returns the size of the queue

Implementing QueueNode and Queue

Figure 12.19 shows class QueueNode and Fig. 12.20 shows class Queue. Each object of class QueueNode has an info field and a link field. For each new object of class Queue, data fields front, rear, and size are set to their defaults (null, null, and 0).

```
/*   File: QueueNode.java.
     Developed for Problem Solving with Java,
       Koffman & Wolz.
     Appears in Figure 12.19.
*/
package queue;

public class QueueNode {
      // Data Fields
      Object info;
      QueueNode link;

      // Methods
      // Constructors
      public QueueNode() {};

      public QueueNode(Object i) {info = i; link = null;}

      public QueueNode(Object i, QueueNode l) {
          info = i;
          link = l;
      }
} // class QueueNode
```

Figure 12.19 Class QueueNode

```
/*   File: Queue.java.
     Developed for Problem Solving with Java, Koffman & Wolz.
     Appears in Figure 12.20.
*/
package queue;

public class Queue {
    // Data Fields
    private QueueNode front;   // Reference to front of queue
    private QueueNode rear;    // Reference to rear of queue
    private int size;          // Size of queue
```

Figure 12.20 *continued*

Figure 12.20 *continued*

```
// Methods
/* Inserts item in a queue.
   precondition : None
   postcondition: Inserts item in a new node and resets
       rear to reference the new node. If the queue has
       1 element, front references the new node also.
*/
public void insert(Object item) {

    if (isEmpty()) { // Empty queue
        // Link rear and front to only node.
        rear = new QueueNode(item);
        front = rear;
    } else { // extend a nonempty queue
        rear.link = new QueueNode(item);
        rear = rear.link;   // Move rear to new node.
    }

    size++;                      // Increment queue size.
}


/* Returns the element at the front of the queue
   precondition : The queue has been created.
   postcondition: If the queue is not empty, returns its
    first element & front references new first element.
*/
public Object remove() {
    QueueNode oldFront = front; // Reference to front

    Object item = peek();        // Retrieve first item.

    // Remove first element.
    front = front.link;          // Delete first node.
    oldFront.link = null;        // Disconnect it from queue.
    size--;                      // Decrement queue size.

    return item;
}
```

Figure 12.20 *continued*

Figure 12.20 *continued*

```
    /* Returns the element at the front of the queue
       precondition : The queue has been created.
       postcondition: If the queue is not empty, returns its
                      first element.
    */
    public Object peek() {
        if (isEmpty())
            throw new NullPointerException();
        return front.info;
    }


    /* Tests for an empty queue.
       precondition : None
       postcondition: Returns true if queue is empty; otherwise, returns
                      False.
    */
    public boolean isEmpty() {
        return (size == 0);
    }


    public int getSize() {
        return size;
    }
} // class Queue
```

Figure 12.20 Class Queue

Method `insert` treats insertion of a node in an empty queue as a special case. For an empty queue, it uses the statements

```
rear = new QueueNode(item);
front = rear;
```

to create a new node (with `item` in its info field) and to link both `front` and `rear` to this node. If the queue is not empty, the statements

```
rear.link = new QueueNode(item);
rear = rear.link;   // Move rear to new node.
```

link `rear` to a new node (with `item` in its info field) and reset `rear` to reference the new node (Fig. 12.18c). Next, the statement

```
size++;                      // Increment queue size.
```

increments the queue size.

If a queue is empty, method `peek` throws a `NullPointerException`. Otherwise, it returns the data at the front of the queue (`front.info`).

Method `remove` uses method `peek` to retrieve the queue data. Next, the statements

```
front = front.link;     // Delete first node.
oldFront.link = null;   // Disconnect it from queue.
size--;                 // Decrement queue size.
```

reset `front` to reference the second node in the queue (Fig. 12.18b), disconnect the old first node from the queue, and decrement its size.

Testing the Queue Class

Figure 12.21 shows an application program that tests the queue class. It begins by storing four names in the queue and then removes and displays the first name stored (`Chris`), stores a new name (`Dustin`), and removes and displays the second name stored (`Robin`). Finally it displays the queue size (3) after a total of five insertions and two removals.

```
/*  File: QueueTest.java.
    Developed for Problem Solving with Java, Koffman & Wolz.
    Appears in Figure 12.21.
*/
package queue;

public class QueueTest {

    public static void main (String[] args) {
        Queue q = new Queue();
        String name;

        // Insert 4 names
        q.insert("Chris");
        q.insert("Robin");
        q.insert("Debbie");
        q.insert("Richard");

        name = (String) q.remove();
        System.out.println(name);    // Displays Chris.
```

Figure 12.21 *continued*

Figure 12.21 *continued*

```
        q.insert("Dustin");

     name = (String) q.remove();
     System.out.println(name);    // Displays Robin.

     System.out.println("size of q is " + q.getSize());
   }
} // class QueueTest
```

Figure 12.21 Class QueueTest

EXERCISES FOR SECTION 12.3

Self-Check

1. Redraw the queue in Fig. 12.18 after the insertion of customer Harris and the removal of one customer from the queue. Which customer is removed? How many customers are left? Show links first and rear after each operation.

2. Trace the operation of methods insert and remove as the operations in Self-Check Exercise 1 are performed. Show before and after values for all links.

3. What changes would be made to method insert to create a new rudeInsert method that inserts at the front of the queue rather than the end?

4. A circular queue is a queue in which the node at the rear of the queue references the node at the front of the queue. (See circular lists in Section 12.1.) Draw the queue in Fig. 12.18 as a circular queue with just one link field named rear. Explain how you would access the queue element at the front of a circular queue.

Programming

1. Add a new method display() that displays the data stored in a queue.

2. Is it possible to simulate the operation of a queue using two stacks? Write a class QueueStacks assuming two stacks are used for storing the queue. What performance penalty do we pay for this implementation?

12.4 Binary Trees

In Section 12.1 we briefly discussed a doubly linked list—a list whose nodes have two link fields. Another more important data structure whose nodes have two link fields is a **binary tree** (or **tree**). Because one or both links can be `null`, each node in a binary tree can have 0, 1, or 2 successor nodes.

Figure 12.22 shows two binary trees. For the tree (a), each node stores a three-letter string. The nodes on the bottom of the tree have 0 successors and are called **leaf nodes**. All other nodes have two successors. For tree (b), each node stores an integer. The nodes containing `40` and `45` have a single successor; all other nodes have 0 or two successors.

In the definition for binary tree, the phrase *disjoint subtrees* means that a node cannot be in both a left and right subtree of the same root node. For the trees shown in Fig. 12.22, the values `"FOX"` and `35` are stored in the root nodes of each tree. The node with `info` field `"DOG"` is the root of the left subtree of the tree whose root has the `info` field `"FOX"`; the node with `info` field `"CAT"` is the root of the left subtree of the tree whose root has the `info` field `"DOG"`; the node with `info` field `"CAT"` is a leaf node because both its subtrees are empty trees.

A binary tree resembles a family tree and the relationships among the members of a binary tree are described with similar terminology. In Fig. 12.22 the node with `info` field `"HEN"` is the *parent* of the nodes with `info` fields `"HAT"` and `"HOG"`. Similarly, the nodes with `info` fields `"HAT"` and `"HOG"` are *siblings*, because they are both *children* of the same parent node. The root of a tree is an *ancestor* of all other nodes in the tree, and they in turn are *descendants* of the root node.

binary tree: (a recursive definition) a binary tree is either empty (no nodes) or it consists of a node, called the **root node**, and two disjoint binary trees called its **left subtree** and **right subtree**, respectively.

root node: the first node in a binary tree.

left subtree: the part of a tree referenced to by the left link of the root node.

right subtree: the part of a tree referenced by the right link of the root node.

leaf node: a binary tree node with no successors.

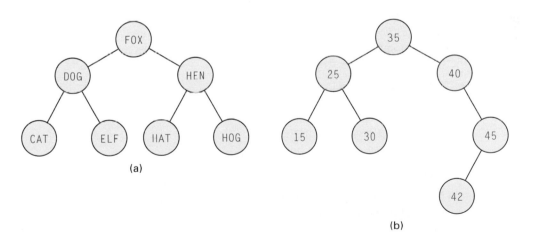

(a)

(b)

Figure 12.22 Binary trees

For simplicity, we did not show the link fields in Fig. 12.22. Be aware that each node has two link fields and that the nodes in (b) with `info` fields `45` and `42` are stored as follows.

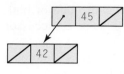

Binary Search Tree

In the rest of this chapter, we focus our attention on a particular kind of binary tree called a binary search tree. A **binary search tree** is a tree structure which stores data in such a way that it can be retrieved very efficiently. Every item stored in a binary search tree has a unique key.

The trees in Fig. 12.22 are examples of binary search trees; each node has a single data field that is its key. For tree (a), the string stored in every node is alphabetically larger than all strings in its left subtree and alphabetically smaller than all strings in its right subtree. For tree (b), the number stored in every node is larger than all numbers in its left subtree and smaller than all numbers in its right subtree. Notice that this must be true for every node in a binary search tree, not just the root node. For example, the number 40 must be smaller than both numbers stored in its right subtree (45, 42).

binary search tree:
a binary tree that is either empty or has the property that the item in its root has a larger key than each item in its left subtree and a smaller key than each item in its right subtree. Also, its left and right subtrees must be binary search trees.

Searching a Binary Search Tree

Next we explain how to search for an item in a binary search tree. To find a particular item, say `target`, we compare `target`'s key to the root item's key. If `target`'s key is smaller, we know that `target` can only be in the left subtree, so we search it. If `target`'s key is larger, we search the root item's right subtree. We write this recursive algorithm in pseudocode below; the first two cases are stopping cases.

Algorithm for searching a binary search tree

`if` the tree is empty

    The target key is not in the tree.

`else if` the target key is in the root item

    The target key is found in the root item.

`else if` the target key is smaller than the root's key

    Search the left subtree.

`else`

    Search the right subtree.

Figure 12.23 traces the search for 42 in a binary search tree containing integer keys. The argument `root` indicates the root node whose key is being compared to 42 at each step. The color arrows show the search path. The search proceeds from the top (node 35) down to the node containing 42.

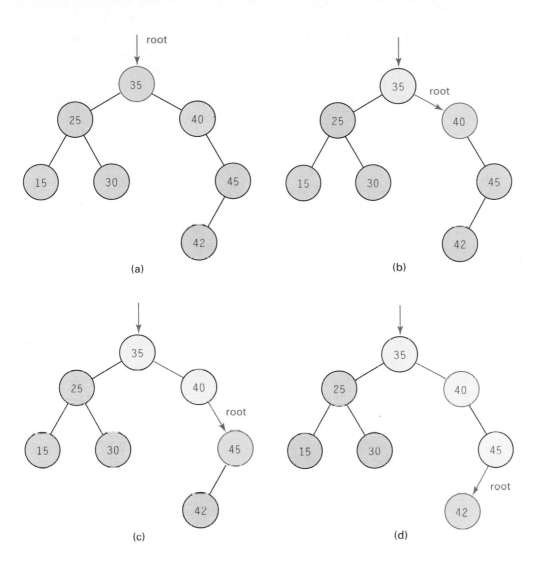

Figure 12.23 Searching for key 42

Building a Binary Search Tree

Before we can retrieve an item from a binary search tree, we must, of course, build the tree. To do this, we must process a collection of data items that is in no particular order and insert each one individually, making sure that the expanded tree is a binary search tree. We build a binary search tree from the root node down, so we must store the first data item in the root node. To store each subsequent data item, we must find its parent node in the tree, attach a new node to the parent, and then store that data item in the new node.

When inserting an item, we must search the existing tree to find that item's key or to locate its parent node. If the item's key is already in the tree, we will not insert the item (duplicate keys are not allowed). If the item's key is not in the tree, the search will terminate at a `null` reference in the parent node of the item. If the item's key is smaller than its parent's key, we attach a new node as the parent's left subtree and insert the item in this node. If the item's key is larger than its parent's key, we attach a new node as the parent's right subtree and insert the item in this node. The recursive algorithm below maintains the binary search tree property; the first two cases are stopping cases.

Algorithm for insertion in a binary search tree

`if` the tree is empty

    Insert the new item in the tree's root node.

`else` `if` the current node's key matches the new item's key

    Skip insertion—duplicate key.

`else` `if` the new item's key is smaller than the current node's key

    Insert the new item in the left subtree of the current node.

`else`

    Insert the new item in the right subtree of the current node.

Figure 12.24 builds a tree from the list of keys: 40, 20, 10, 50, 65, 45, 30. The search path followed when inserting each key is shown in color.

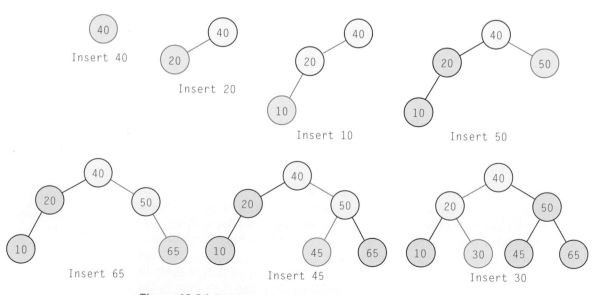

Figure 12.24 Building a binary search tree

The last node inserted (bottom-right diagram) contains the key 30 and it is inserted in the right subtree of node 20. Let's trace how this happens. Target key 30 is smaller than 40, so we insert 30 in the left subtree of node 40; this tree has 20 in its root. Target key 30 is greater than 20, so we insert 30 in the right subtree of node 20, an empty tree. Because node 20 has no right subtree, we allocate a new node and insert target 30 in it; the new node becomes the root of 20's right subtree.

Be aware that we would get a very different tree if we changed the order in which we inserted the keys. For example, if we inserted the keys in increasing order (10, 20, 30, ...), each new key would be inserted in the right subtree of the previous key and all left links would be null. The resulting tree would resemble a linked list. We will see later (Section 12.6) that the insertion order also affects search efficiency.

Displaying a Binary Search Tree

To display the contents of a binary search tree so that its items are listed in order by key value, use the recursive algorithm below.

Algorithm for displaying a binary search tree

1. if the tree is not empty
    2. Display left subtree.
    3. Display root item.
    4. Display right subtree.

For each node, the items in its left subtree are displayed before the item in its root; the items in its right subtree are displayed after the item in its root. Because the root key value lies between the key values in its left and right subtrees, the algorithm displays the items in order by key value as desired. Because the nodes' data components are displayed in order, this algorithm is also called an **inorder traversal**.

Table 12.2 traces the sequence of calls generated by applying the display algorithm to the last tree in Fig. 12.24. The trace so far displays the item keys in the sequence: 10, 20, 30, 40. Completing the sequence of calls for the last step shown in Table 12.2—"Display right subtree of node 40."—is left as an exercise.

inorder traversal: the display of items in a binary search tree in order by key value.

Table 12.2 Trace of tree display algorithm

Display left subtree of node 40.
      Display left subtree of node 20.
            Display left subtree of node 10.
                  Tree is empty—return from displaying left subtree of node 10.

Table 12.2 *continued*

Table 12.2 *continued*

> Display item with key 10.
>
> Display right subtree of node 10.
>
>> Tree is empty—return from displaying right subtree of node 10.
>
> Return from displaying left subtree of node 20.

Display item with key 20.

Display right subtree of node 20.

> Display left subtree of node 30.
>
>> Tree is empty—return from displaying left subtree of node 30.
>
> Display item with key 30.
>
> Display right subtree of node 30.
>
>> Tree is empty—return from displaying right subtree of node 30.
>
> Return from displaying right subtree of node 20.

Return from displaying left subtree of node 40.

Display item with key 40.

Display right subtree of node 40.

EXERCISES FOR SECTION 12.4

Self-Check

1. Are the trees below binary search trees? Show the list of keys as they would be displayed by an inorder traversal of each tree. If the trees below were binary search trees, what key values would you expect to find in the left subtree of the node containing key 50?

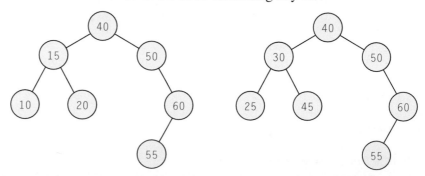

2. Complete the trace started in Table 12.2.

3. Show the binary search trees that would be created from the lists of keys below. Which tree do you think would be the most efficient to search? What can you say about the binary search tree formed in parts (b) and (c)? What can you say about the binary search tree formed in part (d)? How do you think searching it would compare to searching a linked list with the same keys?

a. 25, 45, 15, 10, 60, 55, 12

b. 25, 12, 55, 10, 15, 45, 60

c. 25, 12, 10, 15, 55, 60, 45

d. 10, 12, 15, 25, 45, 55, 60

4. What would be displayed by an inorder traversal of each tree in Self-Check Exercise 3?

12.5 A Binary Search Tree Class

A binary search tree is a collection of elements (nodes) such that each element has a unique key value. Each node of a binary tree has zero, one, or two subtrees connected to it. The key value in each node of a binary search tree is larger than all key values in its left subtree and smaller than all key values in its right subtree.

Next, we write the specification for a binary search tree class. Besides the methods discussed so far (`search`, `insert`, and `display`), we include a method `peek` that returns the tree item whose key matches a target key. Each binary search tree node (object of class `TreeNode`) has an information field and two link fields (`left` and `right`).

Specification for `TreeNode` class

Data Fields

`info`—the node's key
`TreeNode left`—a reference to the left subtree of this node
`TreeNode right`—a reference to the right subtree of this node

Specification for `SearchTree` class

Data Fields

`TreeNode root`—a reference to the root of the tree

Methods

`boolean search(target)`—searches a tree to find a node with the same key as `target`. If found, returns `true`; otherwise, returns `false`.

`boolean insert(item)`—inserts `item` into the binary search tree and returns `true`. If there is already an element with the same key as `item`, returns `false` and no insertion is performed

`Object peek(item)`—returns the tree element with the same key as `item`. If there is no tree element with the same key as `item`, returns `null`

`boolean isEmpty()`—returns `true` if the tree is empty; otherwise, returns `false`

Implementing Class TreeNode

Figure 12.25 shows class TreeNode with two constructors and method insertNode. Method insertNode is called by method insert of SearchTree to perform steps 2 through 4 of the recursive tree insertion algorithm illustrated in Fig. 12.24. We explain why insertNode is needed shortly.

```java
/*  File: TreeNode.java.
    Developed for Problem Solving with Java, Koffman & Wolz.
    Appears in Figure 12.25.
*/
package searchTree;

public class TreeNode {
    // Data Fields
    Object info;
    TreeNode left;
    TreeNode right;

    // Methods
    // Constructors
    public TreeNode() {};

    public TreeNode(Object i) {
        info = i;
        left = null;
        right = null;
    }

    public boolean insertNode(Object item) {
        if (item.toString().compareTo(info.toString()) == 0)
            return false;
        else if
            (item.toString().compareTo(info.toString()) < 0)
            // target key < root key - check left subtree
            if (left == null) {
                left = new TreeNode(item); // Insert item.
                return true;
            } else  // Insert in left subtree.
                return left.insertNode(item);
        // target key > root key - check right subtree
```

Figure 12.25 *continued*

Figure 12.25 *continued*

```
            else if (right == null) {
                right = new TreeNode(item);      // Insert item.
                return true;
            } else  // Insert in right subtree.
                return right.insertNode(item);
    }
} // class TreeNode
```

Figure 12.25 **Class** TreeNode

Implementing Class SearchTree

Figure 12.26 shows class SearchTree with methods insert and isEmpty (returns true if root is null).


```
/*  File: SearchTree.java.
    Developed for Problem Solving with Java, Koffman & Wolz.
    Appears in Figure 12.26.
*/
package searchTree;

import simpleIO.*;

public class SearchTree extends SimpleGUI {
    // Data fields
    private TreeNode root;

    //Methods
    /* Inserts item into a binary search tree.
       precondition : None
       postcondition: Returns true if the insertion is performed. Returns
                      false if there is a node with the same key as item.
    */
    public boolean insert(Object item) {
        if (isEmpty()) { // Empty search tree
            root = new TreeNode(item); // Insert item in root.
            return true;
        } else  // Find insertion point and insert item.
            return root.insertNode(item);
    }
```

Figure 12.25 *continued*

Figure 12.25 *continued*

```
public boolean isEmpty() {
    return (root == null);
}


// Insert methods search and display (Fig. 12.28) here.


} // class SearchTree
```

Figure 12.26 Class SearchTree with methods insert and isEmpty

Methods insert and insertNode   Method insert (Fig. 12.26) tests for an empty tree (a stopping case). If so, it uses the statement

```
root = new TreeNode(item); // Insert item in root.
```

to create a root node and insert item in it. If the tree is not empty, method insert calls insertNode (Fig. 12.25) to find the insertion point for item and to insert item in the tree.

The first condition of insertNode

```
(item.toString().compareTo(info.toString()) == 0)
```

tests whether the root of the current tree contains item, a stopping case. If so, insertNode returns false (no insertion) because we don't allow duplicate items in the tree.

If a stopping case is not reached, method insertNode must determine whether to insert in the left subtree or the right subtree of the current node. The condition

```
(item.toString().compareTo(info.toString()) < 0)
```

is true if the target key is less than the key in the current node. In this case, we must insert in its left subtree. Before doing this, we test whether the left subtree is empty using the condition left == null. If the left subtree is empty, the statement

```
left = new TreeNode(item); // Insert item.
```

links a new node to the left subtree and inserts item in it. If the left subtree is not empty, the statement

```
return left.insertNode(item);
```

causes the insertion path to follow the left subtree of the current node. There are similar statements for inserting in the right subtree that execute when the target is greater than the current node's key.

Figure 12.27 illustrates the insertion of `"same"` in a binary search tree. The left subtree of the node containing `"smoke"` is empty before the insertion takes place.

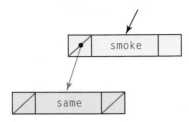

Figure 12.27 Inserting a node in a tree

Method `toString` converts the tree data to a string. You need to provide this method for any object you store in a search tree. Method `compareTo` compares two strings in the following way:

Method call	Effect
`a.compareTo(b)`	Returns a negative value if string a is lexically less than string b; returns 0 if the strings are equal; returns a positive value if string a is lexically greater than string b.

Methods `search` and `display`   Method `search` (Fig. 12.28) implements the recursive search algorithm illustrated in Fig. 12.23. Notice that there are two methods named `search`. The first method would be called in an application class to initiate the search. The public `search` method calls the private `search` method, passing it the tree root and target as arguments, and returns the result of the private `search` method to the application.

The private `search` method actually performs the recursive search. The first two conditions test for stopping cases. If the tree is empty, `search` returns `false`. If the root node contains the target key, the condition

```
(target.toString().compareTo(root.info.toString()) == 0)
```

is `true`, and method `search` returns `true`.

If either stopping case above is not reached, method `search` must determine whether to search the left subtree or the right subtree. The condition

```
(target.toString().compareTo(root.info.toString()) < 0)
```

is `true` if the target key is less than the key in the root node. In this case, we must search the left subtree. Before doing so, we test whether the left subtree is empty using the condition `root.left  ==  null` and return `false` if it is. Otherwise, the statement

```
return search(root.left, target);
```

applies method `search` to the left subtree and returns the result of this search.

If the condition shown earlier is `false`, the target key is greater than the key in the current node, so we must search the right subtree. If it is empty, we return `false`; otherwise, we search it.

We also provide two `display` methods. The public one is called by the application object and it, in turn, calls the private `display` method, which performs the recursive inorder traversal discussed earlier.

```
/* Methods search and display for class SearchTree:
   Searches for the tree item that matches target.
   precondition : None
   postcondition: Returns true if target's key is found;
                  otherwise, returns false.
*/
public boolean search(Object target) {
     return search(root, target);
}


private boolean search(TreeNode root, Object target) {
     if (isEmpty())
          return false;                 // Tree is empty.
     else if
     (target.toString().compareTo(root.info.toString()) == 0)
          return true;                  // Target is found.
     else if
     (target.toString().compareTo(root.info.toString()) < 0)
          // target key < root key - check left subtree
          if (root.left == null)
               return false;        // Left subtree empty.
          else  // Search left.
               return search(root.left, target);
     // target key > root key - check right subtree
     else if (root.right == null)
          return false;               // Right subtree empty.
     else  // Search right.
          return search(root.right, target);
}
```

Figure 12.28 *continued*

Figure 12.28 *continued*

```
    /* Displays a binary search tree in key order.
       precondition : None
       postcondition: Displays each node in key order.
    */
    public void display() {
         display(root);
    }

    private void display(TreeNode root) {
         if (!isEmpty()) {
              // Display left subtree.
              if (root.left != null)
                   display(root.left);

              // Display root key.
              displayResult((root.info).toString());

              // Display right subtree.
              if (root.right != null)
                   display(root.right);
         }
    }
```

Figure 12.28 Methods search and display (part of SearchTree)

You may be wondering why we didn't provide a recursive insert method in class `SearchTree` instead of writing method `insertNode` (in class `TreeNode`). A recursive insertion method in `SearchTree` would require the root of the current tree as its argument. The root would change as we moved down the tree and would eventually become `null` when we reached the insertion point (the parent node). Next, we need to link the parent node to a new node containing `item`. However, Java does not allow us to change a method's argument, so the parent node's actual link would remain `null`.

Method `peek` (see Programming Exercise 1) returns the tree element with the same key as `target`. Its implementation would be similar to `search`. When `peek` locates the `target`'s key, use the statement

```
return root.info;      // Return tree data with same key.
```

to return the tree data instead of returning `true`.

Testing the `SearchTree` Class

Figure 12.29 shows an application class that tests class `SearchTree`. Method `main` stores 12 strings in the tree and then displays the tree. Figure 12.30 shows that the names are displayed in lexicographical order even though they were not entered that way.

```
/*  File: TreeTest.java.
    Developed for Problem Solving with Java,
      Koffman & Wolz.
    Appears in Figure 12.29.
*/
package searchTree;

public class TreeTest {

    public static void main (String[] args) {
        SearchTree t = new SearchTree();

        // Insert 12 names and nicknames in the tree.
        t.insert("Richard");
        t.insert("Debbie");
        t.insert("Robin");
        t.insert("Chris");
        t.insert("Jacquie");
        t.insert("Jeff");
        t.insert("Dustin");
        t.insert("Richie");
        t.insert("Deborah");
        t.insert("Jeffrey");
        t.insert("Jacqueline");
        t.insert("Christopher");

        // Display the tree contents.
        t.display();
    }
} // class TreeTest
```

Figure 12.29 Application class `TreeTest`

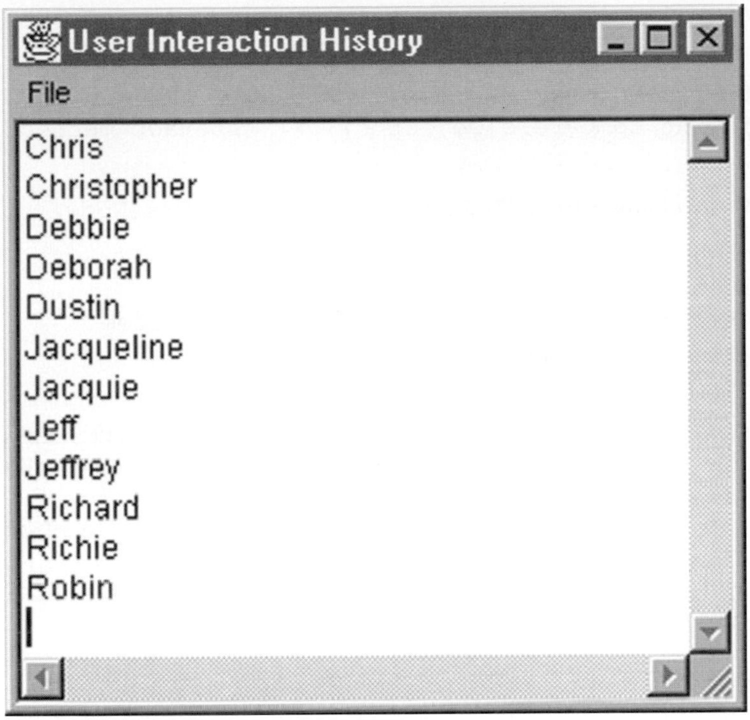

Figure 12.30 Output from Running TreeTest

Using a Comparable Interface

Even though you can store objects of any type in the binary search tree implemented in the previous section, the tree is not completely generic. Because we use String method compareTo to determine the relative ordering of two objects, we must convert each object to a String using its toString method before we can insert it in the tree. The objects in our search tree will be in correct order only if the toString method defined for a class returns values that represent correctly the relative order of each object. This may not always be the case.

A more general approach is to define a Comparable interface with an abstract compareTo method. Then we can use our search tree with any object class that defines its own compareTo method. The result returned by method compareTo can be based on any attributes of the objects being compared, not just their string representations. We define the Comparable interface as follows.

```
package searchTree;

public interface Comparable {
    public int compareTo(Object c); // Abstract method
}
```

Next we show the changes to method `insertNode` in class `TreeNode`.

```
public boolean insertNode(Comparable item) {
    if (item.compareTo(info) == 0)
        return false;      // Item already in tree.
    else if (item.compareTo(info) < 0)
    ...
```

The `if` statement uses method `compareTo` defined in the object's class to determine the object's position in the tree. The rest of this method and class `TreeNode` would not change.

We would need to change methods `search` and `insert` in class `SearchTree` in a similar manner. Wherever the argument `Object target` appears, it becomes `Comparable target`. In the recursive `search` method, we would use the method call

```
target.compareTo(root.info)
```

to determine the relationship between the keys in the target item and the root node.

We can then use our `SearchTree` and `TreeNode` classes to build and maintain a tree of objects for any class that implements the `Comparable` interface.

EXERCISES FOR SECTION 12.5

Self-Check

1. Explain the effect of each statement in the following fragment if `myTree` is type `SearchTree`. Draw the tree built by the sequence of insertions. What values would be displayed?

    ```
    myTree.insert("hit");
    myTree.insert("apple");
    myTree.insert("toy");
    myTree.insert("this");
    myTree.insert("cat");
    myTree.insert("dog");
    myTree.insert("goat");
    myTree.insert("can");
    myTree.insert("tin");
    myTree.insert("cat");
    myTree.display();
    ```

2. Draw the tree created by the sequence of insertions in Fig. 12.29.

3. Deletion of an entry in a binary tree is more difficult than insertion. Given any node in a tree that is to be deleted, what are the three cases for deletion and what must be done in each case? Be sure your approach preserves the binary search tree order.

Programming

1. Write method `peek`.

2. Write an application class that stores a sequence of integers in a binary tree. You will need to wrap each integer value in an `Integer` object.

3. Define a student class that implements the `Comparable` interface. Assume that a student has a name field (a string), an `id` (an integer), and `gPA` (grade-point average). Let the relative order of two student objects be determined by their names. If their names are the same, use their `id`'s as a tie-breaker.

12.6 Efficiency of a Binary Search Tree

Searching a linked list for a target data value is an $O(n)$ process. This means that the time required to search a list increases linearly with the size of the list. Searching a binary search tree can be a much more efficient process. If the left and right subtrees of every node are exactly the same size, each move to the left or the right during a search eliminates the elements of the other subtree from the search process. Because they need not be searched, the number of nodes we do have to search is cut in half in each step. This is a *best-case analysis* because, in reality, it is unlikely that a binary search tree will have exactly the same number of nodes in the left and right subtrees of each node. But, this best-case analysis is useful for showing the power of the binary search tree.

As an example, if n is 1,023 it will require searching 10 trees ($n = $ 1,023, 511, 255, 127, 63, 31, 15, 7, 3, 1) to determine that a target is missing. It should require fewer than 10 probes to find a target that is in the tree. The number 1,024 is a power of 2 (1,024 is 2 raised to the power 10), so searching such a tree is an $O(\log_2 n)$ process ($\log_2 1024$ is 10). Keep in mind that not all binary search trees will have left and right subtrees of equal size!

What difference does it make whether an algorithm is an $O(n)$ process or an $O(\log_2 n)$ process? Table 12.3 evaluates $\log_2 n$ for different values of n. A doubling of n causes $\log_2 n$ to increase by only 1. Since $\log_2 n$ increases much more slowly with n, the performance of an $O(\log_2 n)$ algorithm is not as adversely affected by an increase in n.

Table 12.3 Values of n versus $\log^2 n$

n	$\log_2 n$
32	5
64	6
128	7
256	8
512	9
1,024	10

EXERCISES FOR SECTION 12.6

Self-Check

1. Given the binary tree below, how many comparisons are needed to find each of the following keys or to determine that the key is not present? List the keys compared to the target for each search.

   a. 50   **d.** 65

   b. 55   **e.** 52

   c. 10   **f.** 48

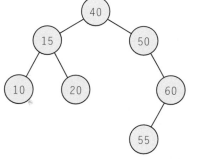

2. Why is it unlikely that a given binary tree will have exactly the same number of elements in the left and right subtrees of every node? For what numbers of nodes is this possible?

3. If the elements of a binary tree are inserted in order, what will the resulting tree look like? What is the Big-O notation for searching in this tree?

4. The binary search introduced in Chapter 11 also performed searches in $O(\log_2 n)$ time. Name two advantages of a binary tree over the binary search. Name one disadvantage.

12.7   Common Programming Errors

Several run-time errors can occur when traversing linked data structures. For example, if link `next` is supposed to reference each node in the linked list, make sure `next` is initialized to reference the list head.

Watch out for infinite loops caused by failure to advance a link down a list. The `while` statement

```
while (next != null)
  System.out.println(next.info);
  next = next.link;
```

executes forever. That happens because the link assignment statement is not included in the loop body, so `next` is not advanced down the list.

A `NullPointerException` can occur when the link `next` is advanced too far down the list and `next` takes on the value `null`, indicating the end of the list. If link `next` has the value `null`, the `while` condition

```
while ((next.info != "9999") && (next != null))
```

causes a run-time error because `next.info` is undefined when `next` is `null`. The `while` condition should be rewritten as

```
while ((next != null) && (next.info != "9999"))
```

Problems with heap management can also cause run-time errors. If your program gets stuck in an infinite loop while you are creating a linked data structure, your program could consume all memory cells on the storage stack. This situation leads to a `stack overflow` error.

Similar problems can occur with recursive methods. If a recursive method does not terminate, you can get a `stack overflow` error.

Make sure your program does not attempt to reference a list node after the node is disconnected from the list. All links to a node being disconnected should be set to `null` so that the node can never be accessed unless it is reallocated.

Debugging Tips

When writing driver programs to test and debug linked data structures, you can create small linked structures by allocating several objects and linking them together using assignment statements (see Section 12.1). You also can use assignment statements to store information in the nodes.

Chapter Review

1. If object p contains a link field, you can connect it to another object of the same type, thereby building a linked data structure. We considered linked lists, stacks, queues, and binary search trees.

2. Linked lists are flexible data structures that shrink and expand as a program executes. It is relatively easy to insert and delete nodes of a linked list.

3. A stack is a LIFO (last-in-first-out) structure in which all insertions (push operations) and deletions (pop operations) are done at the list head. Stacks have many varied uses in computer science, including saving argument lists for recursive methods and for translation of arithmetic expressions.

4. A queue is a FIFO (first-in-first-out) structure in which insertions are done at one end and deletions (removals) at the other end. Queues are used to save lists of items waiting for the same resource (e.g., a printer).

5. A binary tree is a linked data structure in which each node has two link fields leading to the node's left and right subtrees. Each node in the tree belongs to either the left or right subtree of an ancestor node, but it cannot be in both subtrees of an ancestor node.

6. A binary search tree is a binary tree in which each node's key is greater than all keys in its left subtree and smaller than all keys in its right subtree. Searching for a key in a binary search tree is an $O(\log_2 n)$ process.

Quick-Check Exercises

1. If a linked list contains the three strings "him", "her", and "its" and h is a reference to the list head, what is the effect of the following statements? Assume the data field is info, the link field is link, and n and p are links.

   ```
   n = h.link;
   n.info = "she";
   ```

2. Answer Quick-Check Exercise 1 for the following fragment.

   ```
   p = h.link;
   n = p.link;
   p.link = n.link;
   ```

3. Answer Quick-Check Exercise 1 for the following fragment.

   ```
   n = h;
   h = new ListNode("his");
   h.link = n;
   ```

4. When is it advantageous to use a linked list data structure? When would an array be a better choice?

5. If A, B, and C are inserted into a stack and a queue, what would be the order of removal for the stack? For the queue?

6. Often computers allow you to type characters ahead of the program's use of them. Should a stack or a queue be used to store these characters?

7. Write a fragment that removes the element just below the top of a stack s. Use the stack operators.

8. Assume each left link of the tree below is null. Is it a binary search tree? What would be displayed by its inorder traversal? Write a sequence for inserting these keys that would create a binary search tree whose null links were all at the lowest level. Is there more than one such sequence?

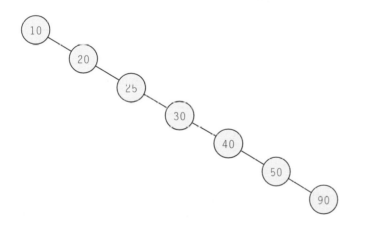

9. If a binary search tree has an inorder traversal of 1, 2, 3, 4, 5, 6, and the root node contains 3 and has 5 as the root of its right subtree, what do we know about the order that numbers were inserted in this tree?

10. Each node in a binary search tree has two children. True or false?

11. What is the relationship between the left child and the right child in a binary search tree? Between the left child and the parent? Between the right child and the parent? Between a parent and all descendants in its left subtree?

12. When is searching a binary search tree more efficient than searching an ordered linked list?

Answers to Quick-Check Exercises

1. `"her"` is replaced by `"she"`.
2. The third list element is deleted.
3. A new list node with value `"his"` is inserted at the front of the list.
4. It is advantageous to use a linked list data structure when the number of elements is variable and there are frequent insertions and deletions. An array is a better choice when elements must be accessed in random order.
5. For stack: C, B, A; for queue: A, B, C.
6. A queue should be used.
7. `String x = (String)s.pop();`
   `s.pop();`
   `s.push(x);`
8. yes; 10, 20, 25, 30, 40, 50, 90;
   30, 20, 10, 25, 50, 40, 90; yes
9. 3 was inserted first and 5 was inserted before 4 and 6.
10. False, one or more of its links can be null.
11. left child < parent < right child; parent > all descendants in left subtree
12. Search of a binary search tree is more efficient when the left and right subtrees of each node are similar in size.

Review Questions

1. Why are recursive methods often used for processing linked data structures?
2. Why is it more efficient to insert at the front of a list than at the end? What is the time in Big-O notation for insertion at the front of a list? The end of a list? How can insertion at the end of a list be made more efficient?
3. If a linked list of data elements is in sorted order, could we perform a binary search on that list in $O(\log n)$ time? Why or why not.
4. Show the effects of each of the following operations on stack s.
   ```
   s.push("hit");
   s.push("hat");
   displayResult(s.peek().toString());
   displayResult(s.pop().toString());
   s.push("top");
   while (!s.isEmpty())
        displayResult(s.pop().toString());
   ```
5. Write a stack operator that reverses the order of the top two stack elements if the stack has more than one element. Use `push` and `pop`.

6. Answer Review Question 4 for a queue q of characters. Replace `push` with `insert` and `pop` with `remove`.

7. Write a queue method `moveToRear` that moves the element currently at the front of the queue to the rear of the queue. The element that was second in line will be at the front of the queue. Do this using methods `insert` and `remove`.

8. Write a queue method `moveToFront` that moves the element at the rear of the queue to the front of the queue. Do this using `insert` and `remove`.

9. Discuss the differences between a simple linked list and a binary tree. Consider the number of link fields per node, search technique, and insertion algorithm.

10. How can you determine if a binary tree node is a leaf?

11. Trace an inorder traversal of the following tree as it would be performed by method `display` of class `SearchTree`.

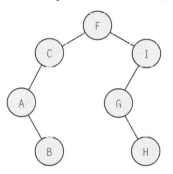

12. What happens when all the elements in a binary search tree are inserted in order. In reverse order? How does this affect the future performance of search and insertion methods?

Programming Projects

1. Write an application program that uses a queue to simulate a typical session for a bank teller. Store the customer's name, the transaction type, and the amount in a customer record. After every five customers are processed, display the size of the queue and the names of the customers who are waiting.

2. Carry out Programming Project 1 using a stack instead of a queue.

3. Write a program to monitor the flow of an item into and out of a warehouse. The warehouse will have numerous deliveries and shipments for this item (a widget) during the time period covered. A shipment out is billed at 50 percent over the cost of a widget. Unfortunately, each shipment received may have a different cost associated with it. The accountants for the firm have instituted a last-in, first-out system for filling orders. This means that the newest widgets are the first ones sent out to

fill an order. This method of inventory can be represented using a stack. The `push` method will insert a shipment received. The `pop` method will delete a shipment going out. Each data record will consist of the following items:

`shipIn`: shipment received (`true`) or order to be sent (`false`)

`quantity`: quantity received or shipped out

`cost`: cost per widget (for a shipment received only)

`vendor`: string that names company sent to or received from

Write the necessary methods to store shipments received and to process orders. The output for an order will consist of the quantity and the total cost for all widgets in the order. *Hint*: Each widget price is 50 percent higher than its cost. The widgets used to fill an order may come from multiple shipments with different costs.

4. Redo Programming Project 3 assuming widgets are shipped using a first-in, first-out strategy. Use a queue to store the widget orders.

5. A *dequeue* might be described as a double-ended queue, that is, a structure in which elements can be inserted or removed from either end. Write and test class `Dequeue`.

6. The radix sorting algorithm uses an array of 10 queues (numbered 0 through 9) to simulate the operation of the old card-sorting machines. The algorithm requires one pass to be made for every digit of the numbers being sorted. For example, a list of three-digit numbers would require three passes through the list. During the first pass, the least significant digit (the ones digit) of each number is examined and the number is inserted at the rear of the queue whose subscript matches the digit. After all numbers have been processed, the elements of each queue, beginning with the first queue, are copied one at a time to the end of an eleventh queue prior to beginning the next pass. The process is repeated for the next most significant digit (the tens digit) using the order of the numbers in the eleventh queue. Repeat the process for the third most significant digit (the hundreds digit). After the final pass, the eleventh queue will contain the numbers in sorted order. Write a program that implements radix sort using class `Queue`.

7. Use a binary search tree to maintain an airline passenger list. Each passenger record should contain the passenger name and number of seats. The main program should be menu driven and allow the user to display the data for a particular passenger, display the entire list, create a list, insert a node, delete a node, and replace the data for a particular passenger. When deleting a node, simply change the number of assigned seats to zero and leave the passenger's node in the tree.

8. Save each word appearing in a block of text in a binary search tree. Also save the number of occurrences of each word and the line number for each occurrence. Use a stack for the line numbers. After all words

have been processed, display each word in alphabetical order. Along with each word, display the number of occurrences and the line number for each occurrence.

9. The fastest binary tree is one which is as close to balanced as possible. However, there is no guarantee that elements will be inserted in the right order. It is possible to build a balanced binary tree if the elements to be inserted are in order in an array. Write a method and test program that, given a sorted array of elements, builds a balanced binary tree. Augment the binary search tree to keep a count of the number of nodes that are searched to find an element and display the number of nodes that are searched to find each item in the tree. *Hint:* The root of the tree should be the middle (median) of the array. This project is easier to do if you use recursion.

10. Write a method that performs an inorder traversal of a binary tree without using recursion. It will be necessary to use a stack. Write a suitable test program for your method.

11. Write a method that uses the selection sort strategy to create a sorted copy of a linked list.

12. A polynomial can be represented as a linked list, where each node contains the coefficient and the exponent of a term of the polynomial. The polynomial $4x^3 + 3x^2$ 5 would be represented as the following linked list:

Write a class `Polynomial` that has operators for creating a polynomial, reading a polynomial, and adding and subtracting a pair of polynomials. *Hint:* To add or subtract two polynomials, traverse both lists. If a particular exponent value is present in either one, it also should be present in the result polynomial unless its coefficient is zero.

13. There are many programs which create multiple, overlapping windows on the screen. With overlapping windows comes the concept of a window being on top and a front-to-back ordering of windows. If windows are drawn from back to front, their appearance matches the expected results. Write a program which maintains a linked list of colored rectangles representing windows in back-to-front order. Your program should have a menu which allows the user to enter a letter for a rectangle, the color of the rectangle, and its screen location. Other menu options should allow the screen to be redrawn and any window to be moved to the top.

Interview

Laura Groppe

Laura Groppe is the president and CEO of Girl Games, Inc., an interactive entertainment company that creates entertainment for girls. Their products include Planetgirl.com, an online environment for girls, and three CD-ROMs: Let's Talk About Me, Let's Talk About Me Some More, and Clueless. Laura spent eight years in Hollywood as an assistant director and coproducer of feature films and music videos before starting Girl Games, Inc.

What is your educational background? How did you first become interested in computer science/computers?

I received a B.A. in philosophy from Sweetbriar College. I became interested in computers through entertainment. I viewed computers as a vehicle for entertainment and as a way to spread information to girls.

You worked for many years in Hollywood as a co-producer; why did you decide to found Girl Games and become involved in the software industry?

I noticed that there was a lack of entertainment products for girls. With the entertainment industry moving in an interactive direction, this was the obvious market opportuntiy.

How does Planet Girl differ from other online games/environments that are currently on the market? What other types of interactive software does Girl Games operate?

Planetgirl.com is not an online game, it is an environment dedicated to girls. It is primarily a window for us into their lives. Based on their interactions and feedback, we gain a lot of insight into their world. We have three CD-ROM's on the market: Let's Talk About Me, Let's Talk About Me Some More, and Clueless.

How would you describe a typical day for you at Girl Games?

My day involves building new relationships, finding new partners, and developing new product ideas and fleshing them out. I also spend time managing the overall operations of people, coming up with strategies for the direction of Girl Games, and implementing them.

What is the most challenging part of your job?

The most challenging part of my job is that I must balance all of these responsibilites and continually prioritize on a daily basis.

With advances in Java and online technology, where do you see Girl Games heading over the next few years?

Technogical advances will allow us to link together the different worlds that girls live in: radio, televsion, film, online, print, CD-ROM, fashion.

Do you have any advice for beginning computer science students who might be interested in the software industry?

You will need to better understand possible innovative applications of the technologies that are developed. Once you do, learn how to link the applications to what the consumer market prefers and wants.

Getting Started, Going Further

This appendix provides information on resources available both as print materials and on the World Wide Web. It tells you where to find information on:

- The optional CD that contains the Java™ on Campus with Borland® JBuilder™ University edition version of Java.
- Where to find the simpleIO package as well as the example code in this text.
- Where to find resources on Java compilers and interpreters.
- Resources for learning more about the Java language and the Java Class Libraries.
- Resources for learning more about HTML.

Java and the World Wide Web are constantly being improved and updated. Although we have made an effort to provide reliable sites that are unlikely to change drastically in the near future, we cannot guarantee that they won't.

The place to start, and the place to return to if things fail, is our Web site at:

http://www.awl.com/cseng/titles/0-201-35743-7

This is the place to learn how to retrieve the class definitions given in the text as well as the simpleIO package.

While developing the text we tested our classes and the package simpleIO on Sun, Intel/Windows, and Macintosh computers. The code "ran the first time" as we moved from platform to platform. However, installing a version of Java, creating a project and accessing packages requires detailed instructions impossible to include here, in part because the Java environments are constantly being updated. Our Web site provides some hints for those environments with which we have experience.

The JBuilder CD

If your book comes with the optional CD, it will enable you to install INPRISE™'s Java™ on Campus with Borland® JBuilder™ environment. This is an integrated programming environment (IPE) that contains an editor, debugger, code browser as well as the Java 1.1 compiler and interpreter. The environment also contains tools for building graphical user interfaces as well as extensive documentation and tutorials on both the JBuilder environment and Java.

To install JBuilder, simply insert the CD into your CD-rom drive and follow the directions. Unless you have experience with other IPEs, select the "typical" install. We suggest that you spend time exploring the help facility and the online documentation. Learn how to create a project, browse through classes, "make" and run a project. Our text does not expect you to know how to create Java Beans or develop graphical user interfaces (GUIs) with the JBuilder tools. A brief tutorial is available at our Web site.

Online information on JBuilder may be found at

```
http://www.borland.com/jbuilder
```

The `simpleIO` Package and Example Code

We have provided a package of class definitions that simplify the task of building user interfaces. Although JBuilder contains a sophisticated tool for building complex interfaces we believe that attempting to use it in conjunction with the early chapters detracts from our focus on problem solving.

The `simpleIO` package is introduced in Chapter 2, and is used in Chapters 3–7, and 11–12. You can retrieve both the source code (the `.java` files) as well as the object code (the `.class` files) from

```
ftp://ftp.aw.com/cseng/authors/Koffman/psjava
```

Instructions on how to download and install the package are available at our Web site

```
http://www.awl.com/cseng/titles/0-201-35743-7
```

We recommend that you follow our structure when you develop projects. Place all of the class definition files (source files or `.java` files) as well as the resulting class files (object files or `.class` files) for a project in a single directory (folder).

If you need `simpleIO` classes, then place the statement "`import simpleIO.*;`" at the top of your file. In order for the compiler and interpreter to find those classes the directory `simpleIO` must reside within the `classpath` structure. The specifics of how you do this differs on every platform and with every IPE. Please see the download instructions on our Web site for platform-dependent details. In general you must place the `simpleIO` package directory with the compiled class files within the path defined by the system variable `CLASSPATH`. In many, but not all, cases the simplest way to do this is to place the `simpleIO` folder inside your current project.

The simpleIO Package

This package of classes was developed by the authors and their students to support very simple graphical user interface programming and text file handling.

SimpleGUI

public class SimpleGUI extends Frame implements WindowListener, ActionListener

Used to create very simple dialog-based interactivity. Includes methods for querying for text input, Boolean values (checkboxes), and menus. Includes methods for displaying int, char, double, boolean, and string values as well as arrays of these types. Includes functionality for supporting graphics displays. A "history" window is displayed.

SimpleGUI display and get methods are discussed in Chapter 3. Menu creation is discussed in Chapter 5. SimpleGraphic appears in Chapter 6. The displayRow() method, SimpleReader, and SimpleWriter are discussed in Chapter 7.

Constructors:

public SimpleGUI()

Creates a SimpleGUI object.

Methods:

public void addChoice(String label)

Adds a choice with the given label to the current menu. See createMenu().

public void createMenu()

Creates a menu object for displaying multiple options. See addChoice.

```
public void displayRow(char a[])
public void displayRow(char a[], int length)
public void displayRow(char a[], int offset, int length)
public void displayRow(char a[], int offset, int length,
                       char delimiter)
public void displayRow(int a[])
public void displayRow(double a[])
public void displayRow(boolean a[])
public void displayRow(String a[])
```

Displays an array of the specified type on a line. If offset and length are specified, begins at offset continuing for length items; tab (\t) is the default delimiter. All the optional arguments shown for arrays of characters may be provided with the other array types (not shown).

```
public void displayResult(String text)
```

Displays a text string in the history window.

```
public void displayResult(char ch)
```

Displays a character in the history window.

```
public void displayResult(int i)
```

Displays an integer in the history window.

```
public void displayResult(double d)
```

Displays a real number in the history window.

```
public void displayResult(boolean b)
```

Displays a `boolean` value in the history window.

```
public boolean getBoolean(String prompt, String yes,
                                         String no)
```

Displays the prompt and two radio buttons with corresponding labels in a dialog window; prompt and response (a string) are displayed in the history window.

```
public boolean getBoolean(String prompt)
```

Displays the prompt with a checkbox; prompt and response (true or false) are displayed in the history window.

```
public char getChar(String prompt)
public char getChar(String prompt,char lowerBound,
                                       char upperBound)
```

Displays the prompt in a dialog window. Filters response for a valid `char` value with bounds if specified; prompt and response are displayed in the history window.

```
public int getChoice(String prompt)
```

Displays a prompt in a dialog window with the menu built by `createMenu()` and `addChoice()`; prompt and choice (a string) are displayed in the history window.

```
public double getDouble(String prompt)
public double getDouble(String prompt, double lowerBound,
                                         double upperBound)
```

Displays the prompt in a dialog window. Filters response for a valid `double` value with bounds if specified; prompt and response are displayed in the history window.

```
public int getInt (String prompt)
public int getInt (String prompt,  int lowerBound,
                                    int upperBound)
```

Displays the prompt in a dialog window. Filters response for a valid `int` value with bounds if specified; prompt and response are displayed in the history window.

```
public String getString (String prompt)
```

Displays the prompt in a dialog window; prompt and response are displayed in the history window.

```
public void removeMenu ()
```

Clears the menu object of choices. See `createMenu ()`, `addChoice ()`.

```
public void showGraphic (SimpleGraphic ds)
```

Displays the drawing `ds` in the history window.

SimpleGraphic

public class `SimpleGraphic` extends `Canvas`

Extend this class and override the `paint ()` method to display graphics in the `SimpleGUI` history window. See Chapter 6.

Constructors:

```
public SimpleGraphic ()
```

Methods:

```
public void setSize (int w,  int h)
```

Sets the size of the `SimpleGraphic` area.

```
public int getWidth ()
```

Gets the height of the `SimpleGraphic` area.

```
public int getHeight ()
```

Gets the width of the `SimpleGraphic` area.

SimpleReader

public class `SimpleReader` extends `BufferedReader`

Reads input from a text file. Each "get" retrieves the contents of one line and attempts to parse characters into the proper type.

Constructors:

```
public SimpleReader(String fileName)
                    throws FileNotFoundException
```

Opens the file specified for reading. Note that the file name format is system dependent.

Methods:

```
public double getDouble() throws IOException
```

Gets the next value from the file as a `double`.

```
public int getInt() throws IOException
```

Gets the next value from the file as an `int`.

```
public boolean getBoolean() throws IOException
```

Gets the next value from the file as a `boolean`.

```
public char getChar() throws IOException
```

Gets the next value from the file as a `char`.

```
public String getString() throws IOException
```

Gets the next value from the file as a `String`.

```
public boolean EOF() throws IOException
```

Checks whether the end of file has been reached.

```
public void close() throws IOException
```

Closes the file (inherited from superclass).

SimpleWriter

public class `SimpleWriter` extends `BufferedWriter`

Writes output to a text file. Each item appears on a single line.

Constructors:

```
public SimpleWriter(String fileName) throws IOException
public SimpleWriter(String fileName, boolean append)
                                     throws IOException
```

Opens the file specified for writing. Note that the file name format is system dependent. If `append` is true, data is appended to the end of the file; otherwise, the file is written over.

Methods:

```
public void putData(double d) throws IOException
public void putData(int i) throws IOException
public void putData(boolean b) throws IOException
public void putData(char c) throws IOException
public void putData(String s) throws IOException
```

Puts the data of the specified type on a line in the file.

The Java Development Kit

The Java Development Kit (JDK) is the standard collection of tools authorized by Sun Microsystems. As of this writing, versions of the JDK are available free from Sun. The advantage of the JDK is that it contains only the essentials and doesn't take up a lot of space. It is also relatively easy to learn how to create a project with the JDK. The disadvantage is that it is easier to manage a project within an IPE such as JBuilder.

The following sites as well as other `java.sun.com` sites are worth exploring to learn more about Java, Java resources, and Java products.

Information on available JDKs can be found at:

```
http://java.sun.com/products/
```

Information on Java documentation can be found at:

```
http://java.sun.com/docs/
```

Java Resources

We cannot begin to provide adequate coverage of the Java language and the Java Class Libraries in an introductory text. Your local institution may have set up resources for you such as the Java API Web structure. Ask your instructor or systems administrator whether such resources have been installed. The following two Web sites provide extensive Java documentation and tutorials.

Online Documentation

This site provides documentation of all of the Java Class Libraries:

```
http://java.sun.com/products/jdk/1.1/docs/api/
```

This site provides information on how to navigate through the Class Libraries:

```
http://java.sun.com/products/jdk/1.1/docs/api/API_users_
guide.html
```

Online Tutorial

This site provides an online tutorial of Java that goes beyond the introduction in this text:

```
http://java.sun.com/docs/books/tutorial/
```

See the related book in the Java Series below.

Resource Books on Java

The Java Series is the authoritative collection of resources on Java, written by members of the JavaSoft team at Sun Microsystems, Inc. These books provide extensive information and examples on programming in Java. These books are not computer science textbooks, but are resource books that describe the Java language and the Java Class Libraries. Up-to-date information on the series can be found at the following two sites:

```
http://java.sun.com/docs/books/
http://www.awl.com/cseng/javaseries/
```

The following titles are a subset of the Java Series and may form the core of a reference library for a Java programmer:

The Java™ Tutorial, Second Edition: Object-Oriented Programming for the Internet (Book/CD) Mary Campione, Kathy Walrath; Addison-Wesley, 1998, ISBN: 1998 0-201-31007-4 (A tutorial that covers Java programming beyond the scope of this text.)

The Java™ Class Libraries: Second Edition, Volume 1: java.lang, java.io, java.math, java.net, java.text, java.util, Patrick Chan, Rosanna Lee, and Doug Kramer; Addison-Wesley, 1998, ISBN: 0-201-31002-3. (Well organized coverage of the Java Class Libraries, with excellent code examples that provide models of solutions as well as coding style. Includes coverage of threads.)

The Java™ Class Libraries: Second Edition, Volume 2: java.applet, java.awt, java.beans, Patrick Chan and Rosanna Lee; Addison-Wesley, 1998, ISBN: 0-201-31003-1. (The second volume of the Java Class Libraries, with wonderful examples of GUI programming)

The Java™ Language Specification, James Gosling, Bill Joy, and Guy Steele; Addison-Wesley, 1997, ISBN 0-201-63451-1. (Provides the complete technical definition of the Java Language.)

The Java™ Programming Language, Second Edition, Ken Arnold, James Gosling; Addison-Wesley; 1998, ISBN 0-201-31006-6. (The Java Class Libraries describe the many classes defined as part of the standard language. This book covers the details of the language itself.)

HTML Resources

You can learn about HTML from many sources. There are a multitude of "how to" books. Many browsers such as Internet Explorer and Netscape Communicator allow you to construct HTML pages through icons and menus. The JBuilder environment contains some resource material as well as support for building HTML files. A general primer can be found at:

```
http://www.ncsa.uiuc.edu/General/Internet/WWW/HTMLPrimer
.html
```

Tags related to applets are summarized here.

`<applet> </applet>`	Defines the boundaries of the applet tag.
`<param name =` *unquoted string* `value =` `"`*quoted string*`" />`	Appears within applet boundaries; specifies parameters for the applet (see Chapter 9).
`code`	The class name of the applet
`height`	The initial height of the applet in pixels
`object`	The filename containing a serialized version of the applet; see resource materials for details
`width`	Specifies the initial width of the applet in pixels
`align`	The alignment of the applet within the browser, value may be: `left`, `right`, `top`, `texttop`, `middle`, `absmiddle`, `baseline`, `bottom`, and `absbottom`
`alt`	Text to display if the browser understands the applet tag but cannot run Java applets
`archive`	A list of comma-separated archive files in JAR format; see resource materials for details)
`codebase`	The applet's code base (where the applet class file is stored)
`hspace`	Horizontal space to the left and right of the applet
`name`	The applet's name
`vspace`	Vertical space on the top and bottom of the applet

Java Language Summary

Basic Syntax and Structure of the Java Language

Although the Java Class Libraries make Java a huge language, the basic forms and syntax of Java are simple. They are summarized here within the context of (1) class definitions, (2) variable and method declarations and object instantiations, (3) statements and control structures, (4) array declarations and element reference, and (5) package declarations.

Class Definitions

A class definition consists of a class declaration and a body. The body contains data field and method declarations.

The declaration consists of keywords and identifiers. Optional parts are underlined. Detailed summaries of their meaning can be found in Chapter 8. Reserved words appear in color. Examples of identifiers appear in plain text.

```
/* The simplest form of a class definition */

class simplestClass {

    // Data field and method declarations go here.

} // class simplestClass

/* A simple class that extends anotherClass */

public class simpleClass extends anotherClass {

    // Data field and method declarations go here.

} // class simplestClass

/* A complicated object with all the options */
```

```
public abstract class myObject extends anotherClass
       implements interfaceOne, interfaceTwo {

    // Data field and method declarations go here.

} // class myObject
```

Variable and Method Declarations, and Object Instantiations

In Java, variables may be declared (1) as data fields of a class, (2) as arguments to a method, or (3) as local variables within a block.

Data field and method variable declarations   You declare a variable by giving its type and its identifier. The type may be one of the primitive types or it may be a class. Data field and local variable declarations may include assignment of an initial value. Arguments get their initial value when the method is called.

```
// Examples of data field or method variable declaration

int x;                    // Identifier x is of type int
char myInitial = 'C';     // myInitial is of type char
                          //  with initial value 'C'
String answer = "Hello";  // Answer is of type String
                          //  with initial value "Hello"
boolean flag = true;
```

Creating an instance of a class   To create an initial value for a variable whose type is an object you must create an instance of the class. The reserved word new, followed by a constructor for the class allocates space for the object and initializes the data fields of the object.

```
SomeClass x = new SomeClass(); // x is an instance of a
                               //  SomeClass object.
```

Visibility of data fields and methods   Data fields are accessible from any method within the class. Depending on the declared visibility, other objects may also access the data fields (see Chapter 8). Data fields that are not given an explicit initial value are set to the appropriate default (see the data type summary below).

```
/* Examples of data field declarations */
public class Example1 {
    // Data fields
    public int y = 10;      // Will be accessible to any
                            //  other class
```

```
    AnotherObject x;    // Default visibility, accessible
                        //   within package
                        // Set to the default value null.

    protected int x;    // Accessible within the package
                        //   and by subclasses
                        // Set to the default value 0.

    private SomeObject y = new SomeObject();
                        // Only accessible within the class.
                        // Creates an instance of a
                        //   SomeObject.
} // class Example1
```

Method declarations   Simple method declarations, also called method signatures, consist of a return type, an identifier, and an argument list. The return type may be a valid type (including a class) or the type void if nothing will be returned. The argument list consists of type declarations (without initial values) separated by commas. The argument list may be empty. Methods may also be given an explicit visilibity.

```
public class Example2 {
    // No data fields declared

/* The simplest method declaration: returns nothing, is
    not passed any arguments */
    private void calculateX() {
        // Method body
    }

/* A method with a single argument of type double that
returns an integer */
    public int calculateY(double x) {
        // Method body
    }

/* A method that returns an object of type MyObj, given
    an integer and string as input */
    protected MyObj translateIT(int x, String y) {
        // Method body
    }
} // class Example2
```

Method calls   When these methods are called, arguments of the proper type must be provided. The returned value must be handled properly:

```
// Within a method:
{ calculateX();        // A simple statement (returns
                       // void), no arguments required.

  int w = calculateY(15.7); //Returns an int, requires a
                            //  double as an argument.

  MyObj x = translateIT(5, "Hello"); // Returns a MyObj.
                                     // Requires an int and a
                                     //  string.
  ...
}
```

Constructor declarations   The declaration of a constructor differs in one important way from an ordinary method. It does not include a return type. If no constructors are declared for a class, then a default constructor is automatically created. If any constructors are declared, then the default constructor is not automatically generated. For example:

```
public class SimpleClass {
    int x;
    void incrementX() { x = x + 1;}
}
```

This class may be instantiated and used as follows:

```
{ SimpleClass anObj = new SimpleClass();
    // An object is created, x is initially set to 0.
  anObj.incrementX();
    // The value of anObj.x will be 1.
 }
```

```
public class ConstructorClass {
    int x;

    public ConstructorClass(int s) { x = s;}

    void incrementX() { x = x + 1;}
}
```

This class may be instantiated and used as follows:

```
{ ConstructorClass anObj = ConstructorClass(10);
  // This is not allowed:
  //  ConstructorClass anObj = ConstructorClass();
  //  because the default constructor
  //  has not been built.
```

```
      anObj.incrementX();
      // The value of anObj.x will be 11.
}
```

The reserved words `this` and `super`   When used within a constructor the reserved words `this` and `super` refer to this class and the superclass, respectively. The reserved word `this` may also be used to refer to the current object, for example to pass this object as an argument. See Chapter 8.

Summary of default data field values

Type	Value
number (integer or real)	0
boolean	false
char	' '
String	null
Object	null

Instance vs. class members, final members   Data fields or methods may be instance or class members. Instance members are unique to each instance, class members are shared by all instances of the class. Both data fields and methods may be declared final. Final data fields may not have their initial value changed. Final methods may not be overridden by a subclass.

```
// All members have default visibility.
public class Example3 {
    int x = 3;              // Instance data field,
                            //   may be modified.

    final int y = 10;       // Instance data field,
                            //   may not be modified.

    static int z = 4;       // Class data field,
                            //   shared by all instances,
                            //   may be modified.

    static final int w = 7; // Final class data field,
                            //   shared by all instances,
                            //   may not be modified.

} // class Example3
```

A `static` method may be referenced by the class name as well as by an instance of the class.

Abstract class and interface declarations   An abstract class is one in which at least one method is declared abstract. See Chapter 8 for details. For example:

```
public class anAbstractClass {

    int x; // An abstract class may have data fields.
    // The method fillInLater will be defined by
    //   a subclass of this class.
    public abstract void fillInLater();

}
```

An interface only contains abstract method definitions and final class data fields. See Chapter 8 for details. For example:

```
public interface anInterface {
    public static final x = 3; // Only final class data
                               //   fields allowed.

    public void fillInLater(); // Doesn't need to be
                               //   declared abstract.
}
```

Method declarations that throw exceptions   A method may either handle an exception or "throw it" to the method that called it. See the discussion of `try-catch` below for exception handling and Appendix C for the standard exception types. A method throws an exception by adding the reserved word `throws` and the exception to throw to the end of the method declaration. For example:

```
public void myFileMethod(int x) throws IOException {
    // method body
}
```

Statements and Control Structures

A method body consists of one or more program statements. Statements contain identifiers, reserved words, and expressions. Variable declarations are the simplest kind of statement.

Assignment statements   An assignment statement assigns the value of the expression on the right-hand side to the variable on the left-hand side. For example:

```
x = (5 + y) * 21;  // The sum of 5 and y is multiplied
                   //   by 21 and assigned to variable x.
```

Return statements   Return statements provide an exit from a method with a nonvoid return value. Return statements may not appear in a method with return type `void`. Return statements may appear anywhere in a control structure; they cause an immediate return from the method. The value of the expression following the return must match the return type of the method. All possible paths (for example, in a selection statement) through the method must contain a valid return value. For example:

```
public int calculateSum(int x, int y) {
        return x + y;
}
```

Compound statements   Compound statements are enclosed in { }, and cause sequential execution of the statements within the block. For example:

```
{ int x = 5;       // Assigns the value 5 to x.
  int y = 10;      // Assigns the value 10 to y.
  int z = x + y; // Assigns the value 15 (10 + 5) to z.
}
```

The `if` and `if-else` statements   Selection statements provide control over alternative paths based on the `boolean` value of an expression. In general:

- `if` Statement (One Consequent)

   ```
   if (condition) // Only do statement if
                  //   condition is true.
       statement_T;
   ```

   For example:

   ```
   if (x > 0.0)
       posProd = posProd * x;
   ```
- `if` Statement (Two Alternatives)

   ```
   if (condition)        // If condition is true,
                         //   then do statement_T'
       statement_T;
   else                  //   otherwise do statement_F'
       statement_F;
   ```

   Example:

   ```
   if (x >= 0.0)
       displayResult("Positive");
   else
       displayResult("Negative");
   ```

The `switch` statement   In a `switch` statement the *selector* expression is evaluated and compared to each *case label*. Each *case label* is a single, constant value, and each *case label* must be different from the others. If the value of the *selector* expression matches a *case label*, then execution begins with the first statement following that *case label*. To prevent executing the statements associated with another *case label*, you must place a `break` statement before each new set of *case label*s. Control passes out of the `switch` statement when a `break` statement executes. If the value of the *selector* does not match any *case label*, no *statement* is executed unless a `default` case label is provided. If present, the `default` statements (*statement*$_d$) are executed. Each *case label* must be a unique value. The type of each *case label* must correspond to the type of the *selector* expression. Any ordinal data type is permitted as the *selector* type. If a `break` statement is missing, execution "falls through" to the statements associated with the next set of *case label*s.

```
switch (selector) {
        case label₁:
                statements₁;
                break;
        case label₂:
                statements₂;
                break;
                     . . .
        case labelₙ:
                statementₙ'
                break;
        default:
                statement_d'
} // End switch
```

For example:

```
switch (n) {
        case 1:
        case 2:
                displayResult("1, 2, Buckle my shoe");
                break;
        case 3:
        case 4:
                displayResult("3, 4, Shut the door");
                break;
        case 5:
        case 6:
                displayResult("5, 6, Pick up sticks");
                break;
        default:
                displayResult(n + " is out of range");
} // End switch
```

The `try-catch` block sequence The `if` and `switch` statements handle normal program flow. Occasionally, exceptions to normal flow occur. These may be handled with try-catch blocks as follows:

1. Create a `try` block containing *statements* that may cause an exception. A `try` block has the form:

```
try {
      // Statements that may cause an exception
      statements;
}
```

2. Follow the `try` block by one or more `catch` blocks. Each `catch` block contains *statements* that handle a particular exception. A `catch` block has the form:

```
catch (exceptionType exceptionIdentifier) {
      // Statements that handle an exception
      statements;
}
```

   For example:

```
public void delete() {
      String out = getString("Enter string to delete:");
      int posOut = text.indexOf(out);

      try {
              text = text.substring(0, posOut) +
                  text.substring(posOut +
                                        out.length());
      } catch (StringIndexOutOfBoundsException e) {
              displayResult("String not found " +
                      " - no deletion performed");

      }
}
```

where the part in parentheses is like an argument list. The first item is the type of the exception being handled. The second item is a name that can be used to refer to the exception by the statements that handle it. Appendix C lists the standard exception types.

The `while` statement The `while` statement is used to create repetition in the program flow. The *repetitionCondition* is tested; if it is true, the *loop-body* is executed and the *repetitionCondition* is retested. When the *repetitionCondition* becomes false, the loop is exited, and the next program statement after the `while` statement is executed. If *repetitionCondition* evaluates to `false` the first time it is tested, *loop-body* is not executed. The `while` statement has the following form:

```
while (repetitionCondition)
      loop-body
```

For example:

```
countStar = 0;
while (countStar < n) {
     displayResult("*");
     countStar = countStar + 1;
}
```

The do-while statement   The do-while statement is used for repetition when the loop-body should be executed at least once. After each execution of loop body, the *repetitionCondition* is evaluated. If the *repetitionCondition* is true, the loop-body is repeated. If the *repetitionCondition* is false, loop exit occurs and the next program statement is executed. The do-while statement has the following form:

```
do {
      loop-body
} while (repetitionCondition);
```

For example:

```
do {
     ch = getChar("Enter a digit");
} while (ch < '0' || ch > '9');
```

The for statement   The for loop header summarizes the loop-control operations. The *initialization statement* executes when the for statement begins execution. Prior to each loop repetition, including the first, the *repetitionCondition* is tested. If it is true, the *loop-body* executes. If it is false, loop exit occurs. The *update statement* executes right after each repetition of the *loop-body*. The for statement has the following form:

```
for (initialization statement;  repetitionCondition;  update statement)
      loop-body
```

For example:

```
sum = 0;
for (int n = 0; n < 5; n++) {
     nextNum = getInt("Enter an integer:");
     sum += nextNum;
}
```

Scope of variables

The scope of a data field is determined by its visibility.

The scope of a method argument is the method.

The scope of a local variable is the block in which it is declared. A block is delimited by {}.

For example:

```java
public int myMethod(int arg) { // arg may be accessed
                              // anywhere in the method.
    int x = 10;        // Can be accessed anywhere in
                       //  the method.
    if (x > 3) {
        int y = 3; } // y can only be accessed within
                     //  this clause.
    } else {
        x = 15; }    // y cannot be accessed here.
    }
    for (int w = 0; w < 10; w++)   { // The scope of w
                                     //  is the for loop.
        if (w > 5)
            x = x + 1;
    }
}
```

Array Declarations and Element Reference

Arrays provide a data structure in which elements of the same type may be stored.

Array element reference   The index of an array must be an integer expression. If the expression value is not in the allowable range of values, an Out of bounds error occurs during run-time. The form is:

```
array[index]
```

For example:

```
x[3 * i - 2]
```

Multidimensional arrays are referenced with the following form:

```
array[index₁][index₂].....
```

For example:

```
matrix[5][3]        // This refers to position 5, 3 in the
matrix.
```

Array declaration   An array declaration may take one of three forms:

elementType [] *arrayName* ;
elementType [] *arrayName* = new *elementType* [*size*] ;
elementType [] *arrayName* = {*list-of-values*} ;

The identifier *arrayName* represents a collection of array elements; each element can store an item of type *elementType*. In the first example, the identifier is declared, but no space is allocated for the array. In the second example, enough space for an array of *size* is allocated, but the elements themselves are not specified. In the third form, the array size is not explicitly specified, but is implied by the size of the *list-of-values* enclosed in braces. These values are stored sequentially (one after the other) in the array elements and their data type must be *elementType*. The *elementType* can be any primitive type or class. If the element type is a class, the array elements contain references to objects, each of which must be separately instantiated. For example:

```java
public class ArrayExample {
    int totals[]; // Totals will be an array,
                  //  with no size specified.

// salary will contain 50 double values,
//  the array contents is undefined.
    double[] salary = new double[50];

// coinValues contains 5 integers,
//  the values shown are stored in order.
    int[] coinValues = {1, 5, 10, 25, 50};

    Person[] employees; // employees will be an array
                        //  of class Person.

// managers will contain two people, "Fred" and "Ethel"
    Person[] managers = { new Person("Fred"),
                          new Person("Ethel")
                        }

    public void loadPeople(int number) {
    // Allocate enough space for the number
    //  of people specified.
        Person[] people = new Person[number];
    // Load each array element with an
    //  unnamed Person object.
        for (int i = 0; i < people.length; i++) {
            people[i] = new Person();
        }
    }
}
```

Multidimensional arrays are declared by adding [ ] for each dimension. Note that Java supports arrays of arrays rather than true multidimensional arrays. See Chapter 7.

Package Declarations

A package is a collection of classes that reside in the same structure. The source file for each class must contain the following statement at the top of the file:

package *packageName*;

Other classes may import the classes in the package by including the following statement at the top of the source file. The * indicates that all classes may be referenced.

import *package.Name*.*;

Any classes defined in source files that do not include the package reserved word are considered part of the default package. All such default classes that reside in the same folder (directory) are considered to be part of the same package and may access each other's protected and default visibility data fields and methods.

Reserved Words

The following reserved words may not be used as identifiers. Words in italics have no meaning in current versions of Java but are reserved for future use.

abstract	else	int	static
boolean	extends	interface	super
break	false	long	switch
byte	final	native	synchronized
byvalue	finally	new	this
case	float	null	throw
cast	for	*operator*	throws
catch	*future*	*outer*	transient
char	*generic*	package	true
class	*goto*	private	try
const	if	protected	*var*
continue	implements	public	void
default	import	*rest*	volatile
do	*inner*	return	while
double	instanceof	short	

Operator Precedence

The following table summarizes operators used in this text in order of precedence.

Operator	Description
method call	
type cast	
!, + (unary), – (unary)	Logical not, unary plus, unary minus
*, /, %	Multiplication, division, modulus
+, –, +	Addition, subtraction, string concatenation
<, <=, >=, >	Relational inequality
==, ! =	Equal, not equal
&&	Logical and
||	Logical or
+, +=, –=, etc.	Assignment, addition then assignment, subtraction then assignment, etc.

The Unicode Character Set

Java uses the Unicode character set for representing characters and strings. Unicode supports characters in many languages. A Unicode character is encoded as a 16-bit unsigned numeric value. This means there are 2^{16} possible characters, or approximately 65,000 of them. A subset of Unicode is ASCII, the American Standard Code for Information Interchange. ASCII is based on an 8-bit representation. The table below lists the first 128 Unicode characters with their corresponding numeric values. These are also ASCII characters. Only printable characters are listed as well as some standard nonprintable ones such as carriage return. These nonprintable characters appear in italics.

0 *null*	32	64 @	96 `
1	33 !	65 A	97 a
2 1	34 "	66 B	98 b
3	35 #	67 C	99 c
4	36 $	68 D	100 d
5	37 %	69 E	101 e
6	38 &	70 F	102 f
7 *bell*	39 '	71 G	103 g
8 *backspace*	40 (	72 H	104 h
9 *tab*	41)	73 I	105 i
10 *line feed*	42 *	74 J	106 j
11	43 +	75 K	107 k
12 *form feed*	44	76 L	108 l
13 *carriage returrn*	45 –	77 M	109 m
14	46 .	78 N	110 n
15	47 /	79 O	111 o
16	48 0	80 P	112 p
17	49 1	81 Q	113 q
18	50 2	82 R	114 r
19	51 3	83 S	115 s
20	52 4	84 T	116 t
21	53 5	85 U	117 u
22	54 6	86 V	118 v
23	55 7	87 W	119 w
24	56 8	88 X	120 x
25	57 9	89 Y	121 y
26	58 :	90 Z	122 z
27 *escape*	59 ;	91 [	123 {
28	60 <	92 \	124	
29	61 =	93]	125 }
30	62 >	94 ^	126 ~
31	63 ?	95 _	127 *delete*

Primitive Types

The eight primitive types are listed here with their corresponding sizes.

	Type	Bits Used	Minimum Value	Maximum Value
Integers	`byte`	8	–128	127
	`short`	16	–32,768	32,767
	`int`	32	–2,147,483,648	2,147,483,647
	`long`	64	–9,223,372,036,854,755,808	–9,223,372,036,854,755,807
Real numbers	`float`	32	Approximately -3.4^{38} with 7 significant digits	Approximately 3.4^{38} with 7 significant digits
	`double`	64	Approximately -1.7^{308} with 15 significant digits	Approximately 1.7^{308} with 15 significant digits
Text characters	`char`	16		65,534 unique characters
Boolean	`boolean`			`true` or `false`

Class Wrappers for the Primitive Types

The following classes correspond to the primitive types. These classes are useful when a data type must be an object, for example, to be stored in a vector. Methods associated with these classes can be used to convert between primitive types.

Not all data fields and methods associated with each class are listed here. For complete definitions see your online documentation or one of the resources listed in Appendix A. We describe only the wrapper classes for the primitive numeric types discussed in this book (`int` and `double`).

Boolean

The Boolean class wraps a value of the primitive type `boolean` in an object.

`public final class Boolean extends Object implements Serializable`

Data fields:

`public static final Boolean TRUE`

Corresponds to the primitive value `true`.

`public static final Boolean FALSE`

Corresponds to the primitive value `false`.

Constructors:

```
public Boolean(boolean value)
public Boolean(String s)
```

Creates a Boolean object representing the value `true` if the string argument is not `null` and is equal (ignoring case) to the string "true"; otherwise, a `false` value is represented.

Methods:

```
public boolean booleanValue()
```

Returns the value of this Boolean object as a `boolean`.

```
public boolean equals(Object obj)
```

Returns true if and only if the argument is not null and is a Boolean object that contains the same boolean value as this object.

```
public String toString()
```

Returns either the string `"true"` or `"false"` depending on the Boolean value of this object.

```
public static Boolean valueOf(String s)
```

Returns the boolean value represented by the specified string using the same rules as the constructor with a string argument.

Double

```
public final class Double extends Number
```

Data fields:

```
public static final double POSITIVE_INFINITY
```

positive infinity of type double.

```
public static final double NEGATIVE_INFINITY
```

negative infinity of type double.

```
public static final double NaN
```

represents "not a number."

```
public static final double MAX_VALUE
```

largest positive value of type double.

```
public static final double MIN_VALUE
```

smallest positive value of type double.

Constructors:

```
public Double(double value)
```
constructs a newly allocated `Double` object from a primitive double.

```
public Double(String s) throws NumberFormatException
```
constructs a newly `Double` object represented by the string.

Methods:

```
public byte byteValue()
```
returns the value of this `Double` as a byte (by casting to a `byte`).

```
public double doubleValue()
```
returns the `double` value of this `Double`.

```
public boolean equals(Object obj)
```
compares this object against the specified object

```
public float floatValue()
```
returns the `float` value of this `Double`.

```
public int intValue()
```
returns the value of this `Double` as an int (by casting to an `int`).

```
public boolean isInfinite()
```
returns true if this `Double` is infinitely large.

```
public static boolean isInfinite(double v)
```
returns true if the number is one of the infinite values.

```
public boolean isNaN()
```
returns true if this `Double` is the `NaN` value.

```
public static boolean isNaN(double v)
```
returns true if the specified number is `NaN`.

```
public long longValue()
```
returns the long value of this `Double` (by casting to a `long`).

```
public short shortValue()
```
returns the value of this `Double` as a `short` (by casting to a `short`).

```
public String toString()
```
returns a string representation of this `Double` object

```
public static String toString(double d)
```

creates a string representation of the double argument.

```
public static Double valueOf(String s) throws
NumberFormatException
```

returns a new `Double` value based on the string.

Integer

public final class `Integer` extends `Number`

Data fields:

```
public static final int MIN_VALUE
```

smallest value of type `int`.

```
public static final int MAX_VALUE
```

largest value of type `int`.

Constructors:

```
public Integer(int value)
```

constructs an `Integer` object that represents the primitive `int` argument.

```
public Integer(String s) throws NumberFormatException
```

constructs an `Integer` object for the value represented by the string.

Methods:

```
public byte byteValue()
```

returns the value of this `Integer` as a `byte`.

```
public double doubleValue()
```

returns the value of this `Integer` as a `double`.

```
public boolean equals(Object obj)
```

compares this object to the specified object.

```
public float floatValue()
```

returns the value of this `Integer` as a `float`.

```
public int intValue()
```

returns the value of this `Integer` as an `int`.

```
public long longValue()
```

returns the value of this `Integer` as a `long`.

```
public static int parseInt(String s)
                    throws NumberFormatException
```

parses the string argument as a signed decimal integer.

```
public static int parseInt(String s, int radix)
                    throws NumberFormatException
```

parses the string argument as a signed integer in the radix (base) specified by the second argument.

```
public short shortValue()
```

returns the value of this `Integer` as a `short`.

```
public static String toBinaryString(int i)
```

creates a string representation of the integer as an unsigned integer in base 2.

```
public static String toHexString(int i)
```

creates a string representation of the integer as an unsigned integer in base 16.

```
public static String toOctalString(int i)
```

creates a string representation of the integer as an unsigned integer in base 8.

```
public String toString()
```

returns a string object representing this `Integer`'s value.

```
public static String toString(int i)
```

creates a string representation of the integer.

```
public static String toString(int i, int radix)
```

creates a string representation of the first argument in the radix (base) specified by the second argument.

```
public static Integer valueOf(String s)
                        throws NumberFormatException
```

returns an `Integer` object initialized to the value of the string, assumes base 10.

APPENDIX C

Classes for Program Abstraction

This appendix contains brief summaries of classes from the Java Class Libraries that support program abstraction. Only methods and datafields relevant to novice programming are included. See the on-line and text support materials listed in Appendix A for more complete coverage.

Classes Supporting Program Abstraction

The Math Class

public final class Math extends Object

Datafields:

```
public static final double E
```

The base of all natural algorithms, it is represented as 2.7182818284590452354.

```
public static final double PI
```

The ratio of the circumference of a circle to its diameter; it is represented as 3.14159265358979323846.

Constructors:

None. The class Math may not be instantiated.

Methods:

```
public static double abs(double d)
public static float abs(float f)
public static int abs(int i)
public static long abs(long l)
```

Returns the absolute value of the argument.

```
public static native double acos(double d)
```

Returns the arc cosine of an angle, in the range of 0.0 through pi.

```
public static native double asin(double d)
```

Returns the arc sine of an angle, in the range of –pi/2 through pi/2.

```
public static native double atan(double d)
```

Returns the arc tangent of an angle, in the range of –pi/2 through pi/2.

```
public static native double atan2(double y, double x)
```

Converts rectangular coordinates (y, x) to polar (r, θ), returning θ, r. Can be calculated from the square root of the sum of the squares of x and y.

```
public static native double ceil(double d)
```

Returns the smallest whole number greater than or equal to d.

```
public static native double cos(double d)
```

Returns the trigonometric cosine of d.

```
public static native double exp(double d)
```

Returns e^d

```
public static native double floor(double d)
```

Returns the largest whole number less than or equal to x.

```
public static native double IEEEremainder(double x,
                                          double y)
```

Computes the remainder of dividing x by y as defined by the IEEE 754 standard.

```
public static native double log(double x)
```

Returns $\log_e x$

```
public static double max(double x, double y)
public static float  max(float x, float y )
public static int    max(int x, int y)
public static long   max(long x, long y)
```

Returns the greater of the two values.

```
public static double min(double x, double y)
public static float  min(float x, float y )
public static int    min(int x, int y)
public static long   min(long x, long y)
```

Returns the lesser of the two values.

```
public static native double pow(double x, double y)
```

Returns x^y. If $x=0$, y must be greater than 0. If $x <= 0$, y must be a whole number.

```
public static syncronized random()
```

Returns a random number between 0.0 and 1.0.

```
public static native double rint(double d)
```

Returns a `double` that is the closest integer to *d*.

```
public static long round(double d)
```

Returns a `long` that is the closest `long` to *d*.

```
public static int round(float d)
```

Returns an `int` that is the closest `int` to *d*.

```
public static native double sin(double d)
```

Returns the trigonometric sine of angle *d* measured in radians.

```
public static native double sqrt(double d)
```

Returns the square root of *d*.

```
public static native tan(double d)
```

Returns the trigonometric tangent of angle *d* measured in radians.

The Object Class

public class Object

Class `Object` is the root of the class hierarchy. Every class has `Object` as a superclass. All objects, including arrays, implement the methods of this class.

Constructors:

public Object()

Methods:

public final native Class getClass()

Returns the runtime class of an object.

public boolean equals(Object obj)

Compares two `Objects` for equality.

public String toString()

Returns a `String` representation of the object.

The Runnable Interface

public interface `Runnable`

This interface is used to implement a thread when a class already extends another class. See Chapter 8.

Methods:

public abstract void run()

Used by a `Thread` object to create a process.

The String Class

public final class `String` extends `Object` implements `Serializable`

The `String` class represents character strings. All string literals in Java programs, such as `"abc"`, are implemented as instances of this class.

Constructors:

public String()

Allocates a new `String` containing no characters.

public String(String s)

Allocates a new `String` that contains the same sequence of characters as s.

public String(char a[])

Allocates a new `String` that represents the sequence of characters in the array a.

public String(char a[], int offset, int count)

Allocates a new `String` that contains count characters from a, beginning at position offset.

public String(StringBuffer buffer)

Converts a `StringBuffer` to a `String`.

Methods:

public char charAt(int index)

Returns the character at the specified index.

public int compareTo(String anotherString)

Compares two strings lexicographically.

```
public String concat(String str)
```

Concatenates `String str` to the end of this string.

```
public static String copyValueOf(char data[])
public static String copyValueOf
                    (char data[], int offset,int count)
```

Returns a `String` that is equivalent to `data`, beginning at `offset` for `count` characters. If `offset` and `count` are not specified, the entire array is used.

```
public void getChars(int sourceOffset,int sourceEnd,
                     char destination[], int dstOffset)
```

Copies characters from `sourceOffset` to `sourceEnd` into the character array `destination`, beginning at position `dstOffset`.

```
public boolean endsWith(String suffix)
```

Tests if this `String` ends with the suffix.

```
public boolean equals(Object anObject)
```

Compares this `String` to the specified object.

```
public boolean equalsIgnoreCase(String anotherString)
```

Compares this `String` to another, ignoring case.

```
public int indexOf(int ch)
public int indexOf(int ch, int offset)
public int indexOf(String str)
public int indexOf(String str, int offset)
```

Returns the index of the first occurrence of the character or string within this `String`. If `offset` is not specified, search begins at position 0 and returns −1 if not found.

```
public int lastIndexOf(int ch)
public int lastIndexOf(int ch, int offset)
public int lastIndexOf(String str, int offset)
public int lastIndexOf(String str)
```

Returns the index of the last occurrence of the character or string within this String. If `offset` is specified, search begins from there proceeding to the front of the string and returns −1 if not found.

```
public int length()
```

Returns the length of this string.

```
public boolean regionMatches(int offset1, String str2,
                             int offset2, int length)
public boolean regionMatches(boolean ignoreCase,
                             int offset1, String str2,
                             int offset2, int length)
```

Compares two string regions of length, beginning with `offset1` of this string, and `offset2` of `str2`. If `ignoreCase == false`, then case matters.

```
public String replace(char oldChar, char newChar)
```

Returns a new `String` in which all occurrences of `oldChar` are replaced by `newChar`.

```
public String trim()
```

Removes white space from both ends of this String.

```
public String toLowerCase()
```

Converts this `String` to lowercase.

```
public String toUpperCase()
```

Converts this `String` to uppercase.

```
public char[] toCharArray()
```

Converts this `String` to a new character array.

```
public String toString()
```

Returns this object.

```
public boolean startsWith(String prefix)
public boolean startsWith(String prefix, int offset)
```

Tests if this `String` starts with the specified prefix. If `offset` is not specified, start at position 0.

```
public String substring(int offset)
public String substring(int offset, int endIndex)
```

Returns a new `String` that is a substring of this string, beginning at `offset` and ending at the length of the string if `endIndex` is not specified.

```
public static String valueOf(boolean b)
public static String valueOf(char c)
public static String valueOf(int i)
public static String valueOf(long l)
public static String valueOf(float f)
public static String valueOf(double d)
```

Returns the `String` representation of the argument.

```
public static String valueOf(Object obj)
```

Returns the `String` representation of the object (returns the `toString()` value).

```
public static String valueOf(char data[])
```

Returns the `String` representation of the `char` array.

```
public static String valueOf(char data[],int offset,
                             int count)
```

Returns the `String` representation of the subarray `data`, beginning at `offset` for a length of `count`.

The System Class

public final class `System` extends `Object`

The `System` class contains some general methods and datafields.

Datafields:

```
public static final InputStream in
```

The "standard" input stream.

```
public static final PrintStream out
```

The "standard" output stream.

```
public static final PrintStream err
```

The "standard" error output stream.

Constructors:

None. The class System may not be instantiated.

Methods:

```
public static native void arraycopy (Object source,
                            int sourceStart,
                            Object dest, int destStart,
                            int length)
```

Copies array `source` beginning at position `sourceStart` to array `dest` beginning at position `destStart`, copying `length` array elements.

```
public static native long currentTimeMillis()
```

Returns the current time in milliseconds.

```
public static void exit(int status)
```

Terminates the currently running Java Virtual Machine; a zero argument indicates normal termination.

```
public static void gc()
```

Runs the garbage collector.

```
public static void setErr(PrintStream err)
```

Resets the "standard" error output stream.

```
public static void setIn(InputStream in)
```

Resets the "standard" input stream.

```
public static void setOut(PrintStream out)
```

Resets the "standard" output stream.

The Thread Class

public class Thread extends Object implements Runnable

A process (a program) can have multiple threads of concurrent flow of control. Threads may have priorities. There are user threads and daemon threads. The Java Virtual Machine terminates when all user threads are stopped. There can be synchronization between threads. Thread datafields and methods are summarized here. For more detailed information on threads see Chapter 9 and the resources in Appendix A.

Datafields:

```
public static final int MIN_PRIORITY
```

The minimum priority that a thread can have.

```
public static final int NORM_PRIORITY
```

The default priority that is assigned to a thread.

```
public static final int MAX_PRIORITY
```

The maximum priority that a thread can have.

Constructors:

```
public Thread(ThreadGroup group,
              Runnable target, String name)
public Thread()
public Thread(Runnable target)
public Thread(ThreadGroup group,Runnable target)
public Thread(String name)
public Thread(ThreadGroup group,String name)
public Thread(Runnable target, String name)
```

A thread has three arguments, a group, a target, and a name. If a name is not supplied, one is automatically generated. The run method of the target is executed by the thread. If a `run` method is not supplied, then the `run` method of this class is used. The thread `group` allows threads to interact. If you do not supply a `group`, then the group of the currently executing threads is used. Threadgroups are beyond our scope; see reference materials in Appendix A.

Methods:

```
public void checkAccess()
```

Determines if the currently running thread has permission to modify this thread.

```
public static native Thread currentThread()
```

Returns a reference to the currently executing thread object.

```
public void destroy()
```

Destroys this thread, without any cleanup.

```
public final String getName()
```

Returns this thread's name.

```
public final int getPriority()
```

Returns this thread's priority.

```
public void interrupt()
```

Interrupts this thread.

```
public static boolean interrupted()
```

Tests if the current thread has been interrupted.

```
public final native boolean isAlive()
```

Tests if this thread is alive (thread has started and has not yet died).

```
public final boolean isDaemon()
```

Returns `true` if this thread is a daemon thread.

```
public boolean isInterrupted()
```

Tests if this instance of a thread has been interrupted.

```
public final void join() throws InterruptedException
public final synchronized void join(long millis)
                            throws InterruptedException
public final synchronized void join(long millis,
                                int nanos)
                            throws InterruptedException
```

Waits at most `millis` milliseconds + `nanos` nanoseconds (if specified) for this thread to die. If time is not specified or is set to 0, then wait forever.

```
public final void resume()
```

Resumes a suspended thread.

```
public void run()
```

The method to override to define a thread process; see Chapter 9.

```
public final void setDaemon(boolean on)
```

Marks this thread as either a daemon thread (on == true) or a user thread.

```
public final void setName(String name)
```

Changes the name of this thread.

```
public final void setPriority(int newPriority)
```

Changes the priority of this thread.

```
public static native void sleep(long millis)
                              throws InterruptedException
public static void sleep(long millis, int nanos)
                              throws InterruptedException
```

The currently executing thread sleeps for the specified number of milliseconds (plus nanoseconds, if specified).

```
public native synchronized void start()
```

This thread to begins the execution; the Java Virtual Machine then calls the run method of this thread.

```
public final void stop()
```

The thread stops executing.

```
public final void suspend()
```

Suspends this thread.

```
public String toString()
```

Returns a string representation of this thread.

```
public static native void yield()
```

The currently executing thread is temporarily paused, allowing other threads to execute.

The Vector Class

public class Vector extends Object implements Cloneable, Serializable

The size of a vector is the number of elements it currently holds. The capacity of a vector is the number of elements it may hold before the capacity must be increased.

Constructors:

```
public Vector()
public Vector(int initialCapacity)
public Vector(int initialCapacity,
              int capacityIncrement)
```

Constructs an empty vector; default capacity is 10. If `initialCapacity` is not specified, the capacity is doubled whenever the capacity is reached; otherwise, the capacity is incremented by `capacityIncrement`.

Methods:

```
public final synchronized void addElement(Object obj)
```

Adds `obj` to the end of this vector.

```
public final int capacity()
```

Returns the current capacity of this vector.

```
public final synchronized void copyInto(Object
                                                anArray[])
```

Copies the elements of this vector into the specified array.

```
public final boolean contains(Object elem)
```

Tests if the specified object is an element in this vector.

```
public final synchronized Object elementAt(int index)
```

Returns the element at the specified index.

```
public final synchronized void ensureCapacity(int
                                         minCapacity)
```

Increases the capacity of this vector, if necessary, to ensure that it can hold at least the number of elements specified by `minCapacity`.

```
public final synchronized Object firstElement()
```

Returns the first element in this vector.

```
public final int indexOf(Object elem)
public final synchronized int indexOf(Object elem,
                                      int offset)
```

Returns the index of the first occurrence of `elem` in the vector, and returns −1 if it is not found. Begins at the offset (if specified).

```
public final synchronized void insertElementAt
                                   (Object obj,
                                    int index)
```

Inserts `obj` at position `index` in this vector, shifting right all elements whose index is greater than or equal to `index`.

```
public final boolean isEmpty()
```

Tests if this vector has no elements.

```
public final synchronized Object lastElement()
```

Returns the last element in this vector.

```
public final int lastIndexOf(Object elem)
public final synchronized int lastIndexOf(Object elem,
                                          int offset)
```

Returns the index of the last occurrence of `elem` in the vector, and returns −1 if it is not found. Begins at the `offset` (if specified), searching forward in the vector.

```
public final synchronized void removeAllElements()
```

Removes all elements from this vector and sets its size to zero.

```
public final synchronized boolean removeElement
                                   (Object obj)
```

Removes the first occurrence of `obj`, shifting left all elements to the left of `obj`.

```
public final synchronized void removeElementAt
                                   (int index)
```

Deletes the element at the specified index, shifting left all elements to the right of the removed element.

```
public final synchronized void setElementAt(Object obj,
                                            int index)
```

Places the object at position `index` in this vector, discarding the element previously in that position.

```
public final synchronized void setSize(int newSize)
```

Sets the size of this vector, adding null items or discarding elements in positions beyond `newSize` as necessary.

```
public final int size()
```

Returns the number of elements in this vector.

```
public final synchronized String toString()
```

Returns a string representation of this vector.

```
public final synchronized void trimToSize()
```

Trims the capacity of this vector to be the vector,'s current size.

Overview of the java.io Package

Data transfer in Java is handled through *streams*. Input streams bring data into a process, output streams send data out. The data may be bytes or characters. The classes InputStream, OutputStream, and their subclasses provide rich functionality for handling bytes of data. See the resources in Appendix A for more detail. The Reader class provides basic methods for reading characters. The Writer class provides basic methods for writing characters. Selected subclasses of Reader and Writer are presented here. Note that only the classes and methods that might be relevant to a first-semester course are included. Others may be found in the resource materials listed in Appendix A.

The Reader Class and Selected Subclasses

The Reader Class

public abstract class Reader extends Object

This Abstract class is used for reading character streams. Subclasses must implement read(char[], int, int), and close().

Methods:

```
public abstract void close() throws IOException
```

Closes the stream.

```
public void mark(int readAheadLimit) throws IOException
```

Marks the present position in the stream. Later calls to reset() will attempt to reposition the stream at this point.

```
public boolean markSupported()
```

Tells whether this stream supports the mark() operation.

```
public int read() throws IOException
```

Reads a single character.

```
public int read(char cbuf[]) throws IOException
```

```
public abstract int read(char cbuf[], int offset,
                         int length) throws IOException
```

Reads characters into an array, starting at `offset` and reading `length` characters, if specified.

```
public boolean ready() throws IOException
```

Tells whether this stream is ready to be read.

```
public void reset() throws IOException
```

Resets the stream to either the mark or the starting point. Position is dependent upon the type of character input stream.

```
public long skip(long n) throws IOException
```

Skips n characters.

Buffered Reader

public class `BufferedReader` extends `Reader`

Reads text from a character-input stream, buffering characters for the efficient reading of characters, arrays, and lines.

Constructors:

```
public BufferedReader(Reader in)
public BufferedReader(Reader in, int size)
```

Creates a buffered reader for in. If size is not specified, then size is 8K characters.

Methods (that do not override Reader methods):

```
public String readLine() throws IOException
```

Reads a line of text (a line terminates by line feed (`'\n'`), a carriage return (`'\r'`), or a carriage return followed immediately by a linefeed).

CharArrayReader

public class `CharArrayReader` extends `Reader`

Creates a character buffer so that you can read from an array of characters as if it was a buffered input stream.

Constructors:

```
public CharArrayReader(char buf[])
public CharArrayReader(char buf[], int offset,
                                   int length)
```

Creates a `CharArrayReader` from the specified array of chars, starting at `offset` and continuing for `length`, if specified.

Methods:

All methods override Reader methods.

FileReader

public class `FileReader` extends `InputStreamReader`

Used for reading character files.

Constructors:

```
public FileReader(String fileName)
                              throws FileNotFoundException
public FileReader(File file)
                              throws FileNotFoundException
public FileReader(FileDescriptor fd)
```

Opens the file specified by the (1) system-dependent filename, (2) the file object, or (3) the file descriptor. See resources in Appendix A for a discussion of file objects and descriptors.

Methods:

No methods are defined.

InputStreamReader

public class `InputStreamReader` extends `Reader`

Allows conversion from a byte stream to a character stream. The character encoding scheme may be specified.

```
public InputStreamReader(InputStream in)
public InputStreamReader(InputStream in, String enc)
                         throws UnsupportedEncodingException
```

Creates an `InputStreamReader` that uses the character encoding scheme specified. If none is specified, then uses the default.

Methods:

```
public String getEncoding()
```

Returns the name of the encoding being used by this stream.

LineNumberReader

public class `LineNumberReader` extends `BufferedReader`

A buffered character-input stream keeps track of line numbers (terminated by a line feed (`'\n'`), a carriage return (`'\r'`), or a carriage return followed immediately by a linefeed).

Constructors:

```
public LineNumberReader(Reader in)
public LineNumberReader(Reader in,int size)
```

Creates a new line-numbering reader, using the default input-buffer size, or size specified.

Methods: (that do not override BufferedReader or Reader)

```
public void setLineNumber(int lineNumber)
```

Sets the current line number.

```
public int getLineNumber()
```

Returns the current line number.

StringReader

public class `StringReader` extends `Reader`

Converts a string to a character input stream.

Constructors:

```
public StringReader(String s)
```

Creates a new string reader.

Methods:

There are none that do not override `Reader` methods.

The Writer Class and Selected Subclasses

The Writer Class

public abstract class `Writer` extends `Object`

An abstract class for writing to character streams. Subclasses must implement `write(char[], int, int)`, `flush()`, and `close()`.

Methods:

public void `write(int c)` throws `IOException`

Writes a single character based on the 16 low-order bits of the integer `c`.

public void `write(char cbuf[])` throws `IOException`
public abstract void `write(char cbuf[], int offset,`
                               `int length)` throws `IOException`

Writes an array of characters, starting at `offset` for `length` specified; writes the entire array otherwise.

public void `write(String str)` throws `IOException`
public void `write(String str, int off,int len)`
                               throws `IOException`

Writes a string, from `offset` for `length`, if specified; writes the entire string otherwise.

public abstract void `flush()` throws `IOException`

Flushs the stream, that is, empties it of characters.

public abstract void `close()` throws `IOException`

Closes the stream, flushing it first.

BufferedWriter

public class `BufferedWriter` extends `Writer`

Writes text to a character-output stream, buffering characters.

Constructors:

public `BufferedWriter(Writer out)`
public `BufferedWriter(Writer out, int size)`

Creates a new buffered character-output stream. If `size` is not specified, buffer is 8K characters.

Methods (that do not override Writer methods):

```
public void newLine() throws IOException
```

Writes a line separator defined by the system property `line.separator`.

CharArrayWriter

public class `CharArrayWriter` extends `Writer`

Implements a character buffer that can be used as a `Writer`. The data can be retrieved using `toCharArray()` and `toString()`.

Constructors:

```
public CharArrayWriter()
public CharArrayWriter(int initialSize)
```

Creates a new `CharArrayWriter`. If size is not specified, default buffer is 32 characters.

Methods (that do not override Writer methods):

```
public void writeTo(Writer out) throws IOException
```

Writes the contents of the buffer to another character stream.

```
public void reset()
```

Resets the buffer so that it can be used again.

```
public char[] toCharArray()
```

Returns a copy of the input data.

```
public int size()
```

Returns the current size of the buffer.

```
public String toString()
```

Converts data in array buffer to a string.

FileWriter

public class `FileWriter` extends `OutputStreamWriter`

Used for writing characters to a file.

Constructors:

```
public FileWriter(String fileName) throws IOException
public FileWriter(String fileName, boolean append)
                                   throws IOException
public FileWriter(File file) throws IOException
public FileWriter(FileDescriptor fd)
```

Opens the file specified by the (1) system-dependent filename, (2) the file object, or (3) the file descriptor. See the resources in Appendix A for a discussion of file objects and descriptors. If append is true, then append to rather than overwrite the file.

Methods:

No methods defined.

PrintWriter

public class PrintWriter extends Writer

Prints formatted representations of objects to a text-output stream.

Constructors:

```
public PrintWriter(Writer out)
public PrintWriter(Writer out, boolean autoFlush)
public PrintWriter(OutputStream out)
public PrintWriter(OutputStream out, boolean autoFlush)
```

Creates an output stream. Automatic flushing occurs after println if autoFlush is true.

Methods (that do not override Writer):

```
public boolean checkError()
```

Flushes the stream and checks its error state.

```
protected void setError()
```

Indicates that an error has occurred.

```
public void print(boolean b)
public void print(char c)
public void print(int i)
public void print(long l)
public void print(float f)
```

```
public void print(double d)
public void print(char s[])
public void print(String s)
public void print(Object obj)
```

Prints the specified object using its toString method.

```
public void println()
public void println(boolean x)
public void println(char x)
public void println(int x)
public void println(long x)
public void println(float x)
public void println(double x)
public void println(char x[])
public void println(String x)
public void println(Object x)
```

Prints the specified object, then finishes the line.

APPENDIX

AWT for Graphical User Interfaces

This appendix contains brief summaries of classes from the Java Class Libraries that support graphical user interface programming including applets. Only methods and data fields relevant to novice programming are included. See the online and text support materials listed in Appendix A for more complete coverage.

The Applet Class and AppletContext Interface

Based on the principles introduced in this text some rather sophisticated programming may be accomplished using the `Applet` class and the `AppletContext` interface.

The Applet Class

public class `Applet` extends `Panel`

An applet is a small program that is embedded in an applet context (another application such as a Web browser or appletviewer).

Constructors:

public `Applet()`

Creates an instance of an applet.

Methods:

public void `destroy()`

Called by the applet context to inform this applet that it is being reclaimed and that it should destroy any resources (such as threads) that it has allocated.

public AppletContext `getAppletContext()`

Gets the applet context for this applet (the browser or appletviewer in which it is embedded).

```
public String getAppletInfo()
```

Returns information about this applet. It should be overridden by sub-classes to include information about the author, version, and copyright of the applet.

```
public AudioClip getAudioClip(URL url)
public AudioClip getAudioClip(URL url,String name)
```

Returns the `AudioClip` object specified by the URL argument. This method returns immediately even if the URL is not completely loaded. See resources in Appendix A for more information on how to use audio clips.

```
public URL getCodeBase()
```

Gets the base URL of the applet itself.

```
public URL getDocumentBase()
```

Gets the document URL in which the applet is embedded.

```
public Image getImage(URL url)
public Image getImage(URL url, String name)
```

Returns an `Image` object that can then be painted on the screen. This method returns immediately even if the URL is not completely loaded. See resources in Appendix A for more information on how to use images.

```
public String getParameter(String name)
```

Returns the value of the named parameter in the HTML tag.

```
public String[][] getParameterInfo()
```

Returns an array of strings corresponding to information about the applet's parameters. It should be overridden by subclasses that are understood by this applet. The form is { { *"parameterName1"* , *"description1"*}, { *"parameterName2"*, *"description2"*} ...}.

```
public void init()
```

Called by the browser or applet viewer to inform this applet that it has been loaded into the system. It should be overridden by `Applet` subclasses to perform initializations.

```
public boolean isActive()
```

Determines if this applet is active; an applet is active just before `start()` is called and is inactive immediately after `stop()` is called.

```
public void play(URL url)
public void play(URL url, String name)
```

Plays the audio clip at the specified absolute URL.

```
public void resize(Dimension d)
public void resize(int width, int height)
```

Requests that the applet context resize this applet.

```
public void showStatus(String msg)
```

msg should be displayed in the "status window" of the applet context.

```
public void start()
```

Called by applet context to inform this applet that it should start its execution. It is called after the init method and each time the applet is revisited in a Web page.

```
public void stop()
```

Called by the applet context to inform this applet that it should stop its execution.

AppletContext Interface

public interface `AppletContext`

Corresponds to the document (the HTML) that contains the applet.

Methods:

```
public abstract Applet getApplet(String name)
```

Finds and returns the named applet if it exists in the applet context document. Note that an HTML page may contain more than one applet.

```
public abstract AudioClip getAudioClip(URL url)
```

Creates an audio clip.

```
public abstract Image getImage(URL url)
```

Returns an Image object that can then be painted on the screen.

```
public abstract void showDocument(URL url)
```

Replaces the Web page currently being viewed with the given URL.

```
public abstract void showStatus(String status)
```

Requests that the status string be displayed in the "status window."

Graphics Classes

This section contains classes that are used for creating graphics. They include:

```
Color    Font    FontMetric    Graphics    Point
```

The Color Class

public class `Color` extends `Object` implements `Serializable`

This class represents colors using the RGB (red, green, blue) format in which each color is represented by a range 0–255 (absense of color to complete saturation of that color). Note that HSB (hue, saturation, brightness) conversion methods are also available. See the resources in Appendix A for more detail.

Data fields:

Numbers in parentheses are the red, green, blue values for each color.

```
public static final Color black        (0,0,0)
public static final Color blue         (0,0,255)
public static final Color cyan         (0,255,255)
public static final Color darkGray     (64,64,64)
public static final Color gray         (128,128,128)
public static final Color green        (0,255,0)
public static final Color lightGray    (192,192,192)
public static final Color magenta      (255,0,255)
public static final Color orange       (255,200,0)
public static final Color pink         (255,175,175)
public static final Color red          (255,0,0)
public static final Color white        (255,255,255)
public static final Color yellow       (255,255,0)
```

Constructors:

public `Color(int r, int g, int b)`

Creates a color with the specified red, green, and blue components. The integers must be in the range 0–255.

public `Color(int rgb)`

Creates a color with the specified RGB value, where the red component is in bits 16–23 of the argument, the green component is in bits 8–15 of the argument, and the blue component is in bits 0–7.

public `Color(float r, float g, float b)`

Creates a color with the specified red, green, and blue values, where each of the values is in the range 0.0–1.0. This is *not* a HSB constructor.

Methods:

public `Color brighter()`

Creates a brighter version of this color.

```
public Color darker()
```

Creates a darker version of this color.

```
public boolean equals(Object obj)
```

Determines whether another object is equal to this color.

```
public int getBlue()
```

Gets the blue component of this color.

```
public int getGreen()
```

Gets the green component of this color.

```
public int getRed()
```

Gets the red component of this color.

```
public int getRGB()
```

Gets the RGB value representing the color. Bits 16–23 are for the red value, bits 8–15 are for the green value, and bits 0–7 are for the blue value.

```
public String toString()
```

Creates a `String` representation of this color.

The Font Class

public class `Font` extends `Object` implements `Serializable`

This class creates `Font` objects that control the shape, size, and texture of characters.

Data fields:

```
public static final int PLAIN
```

The `PLAIN` style constant.

```
public static final int BOLD
```

The `BOLD` style constant can be combined with `ITALIC`.

```
public static final int ITALIC
```

The italicized style constant can be combined with `BOLD`.

Constructors:

```
public Font(String name, int style, int size)
```

Creates a new font with the specified name, style, and point size.

Methods:

```
public static Font decode(String str)
```

Gets the specified font, parsing `str` as follows: *logicalFontName-style-point-size.* For example, `Monospaced-bolditalic-14` is equivalent to `new Font("Monospace", Font.BOLD|Font.ITALIC, 14)`.

```
public boolean equals(Object obj)
```

Compares this object to the specifed object.

```
public String getFamily()
```

Gets the platform-specific family name of the font.

```
public String getName()
```

Gets the logical name of the font.

```
public int getSize()
```

Gets the point size of the font.

```
public int getStyle()
```

Gets the style of the font, by applying the `&` operator and the appropriate style constant the user can determine the style: e.g., (`getStyle()  & Font.BOLD`) is `true` if the font style is bold.

```
public boolean isBold()
```

Returns whether the font's style is bold.

```
public boolean isItalic()
```

Returns whether the font's style is italic.

```
public boolean isPlain()
```

Returns whether the font's style is plain.

```
public String toString()
```

Converts this object to a `String` representation.

The FontMetric Class

public abstract class `FontMetrics` extends `Object`
                                          implements `Serializable`

A font metrics object gives information about the rendering of a particular font on a particular screen.

Constructors:

```
protected FontMetrics(Font font)
```

Creates a new `FontMetrics` object for finding out height, width, and so forth about that font.

Methods:

```
public int charWidth(int ch)
public int charWidth(char ch)
```

Determines the advance width of the specified character in this `Font`, the amount by which the current point is moved from one character to the next in a line of text.

```
public int charsWidth(char data[], int off, int len)
```

Returns the total advance width for showing the specified array of characters in this `Font`.

```
public int getAscent()
```

Determines the font ascent, the distance from the font's baseline to the top of most alphanumeric characters.

```
public int getDescent()
```

Determines the font descent, the distance from the font's baseline to the bottom of most alphanumeric characters having descenders.

```
public Font getFont()
```

Gets the font described by this font metric.

```
public int getHeight()
```

Determines the standard height of a line of text, that is, the distance between the baseline of adjacent lines of text (leading + ascent + descent).

```
public int getLeading()
```

Determines the standard leading of the font described by this font metric, that is, the logical amount of space to be reserved between the descent of one line of text and the ascent of the next line.

```
public int getMaxAdvance()
```

Determines the maximum advance width of any character in this `Font`, that is, the amount by which the current point is moved from one character to the next in a line of text.

```
public int getMaxAscent()
```

Determines the maximum ascent of the font.

`public int getMaxDescent()`

Determines the maximum descent of the font described by this font metric.

`public int stringWidth(String str)`

Returns the total advance width for showing the specified `String` in this `Font`, that is, the amount by which the current point is moved from one character to the next in a line of text.

`public String toString()`

Returns a representation of this `FontMetric` object's values as a string.

The Graphics Class

public abstract class `Graphics` extends `Object`

A Graphics object encapsulates state information needed for the basic rendering operations that Java supports. This class contains many sophisticated methods for graphics. See the resources in Appendix A for more detail.

Constructors:
Since `Graphics` is an abstract class, applications cannot call this constructor directly. Graphics contexts are obtained from other graphics contexts or are created by calling `getGraphics` on a component.

Methods:

```
public abstract void copyArea(int x, int y, int width,
                              int height, int dx, int dy)
```

Copies an area of the component by a distance specified by *dx* and *dy*.

`public abstract Graphics create()`

Creates a graphics object that is a copy of this object.

`public abstract void dispose()`

Disposes of this graphics context and releases any system resources that it is using.

```
public void draw3DRect(int x, int y, int width,
                                     int height,
                                     boolean raised)
```

Draws a 3D highlighted outline of the specified rectangle. The edges of the rectangle are highlighted so that they appear to be beveled and lit from the upper-left corner. The `boolean raised` determines whether the rectangle appears to be raised above the surface or sunk into the surface.

```
public abstract void drawArc (int x, int y, int width,
                  int height, int startAngle, int arcAngle)
```

Draws the outline of a circular or elliptical arc covering the specified rectangle.

```
public abstract void drawLine (int x1, int y1,
                        int x2, int y2)
```

Draws a line, using the current color, between the points (*x1*, *y1*) and (*x2*, *y2*)

```
public abstract void drawOval (int x, int y, int width,
                                      int height)
```

Draws the outline of an oval.

```
public void drawRect (int x, int y,
                  int width, int height)
```

Draws the outline of the specified rectangle.

```
public abstract void drawRoundRect (int x, int y,
                              int width,
                  int height, int arcWidth, int arcHeight)
```

Draws an outlined round-cornered rectangle.

```
public abstract void drawPolyline (int xPoints[],
                              int yPoints[],
                              int nPoints)
```

Draws a sequence of npoints connected lines defined by arrays of *x* and *y* coordinates, where each pair of (*x*, *y*) coordinates defines a point.

```
public abstract void drawPolygon (int xPoints[], int
yPoints[],
                              int nPoints)
```

Draws a closed polygon defined by arrays of *x* and *y* coordinates using nPoints – 1 pairs and closing the first and last points.

```
public abstract void drawString (String str, int x,
                              int y)
```

Draws the text given by the specified string starting at position (*x*, *y*).

```
public void drawPolygon (Polygon p)
```

Draws the outline of a polygon defined by the specified Polygon object.

```
public void fill3DRect(int x,  int y,  int width,
                            int height, boolean raised)
```

Paints a 3D highlighted rectangle filled with the current color. The edges of the rectangle will be highlighted so that it appears as if the edges were beveled and lit from the upper-left corner. The argument raised determines whether the rectangle appears to be raised above the surface or etched into the surface.

```
public abstract void fillArc(int x,  int y, int width,
                          int height, int startAngle, int arcAngle)
```

Fills a circular or elliptical arc covering the specified rectangle.

```
public abstract void fillOval(int x,  int y,  int width,
                                            int height)
```

Fills an oval bounded by the specified rectangle with the current color.

```
public void fillPolygon(Polygon p)
```

Fills a closed polygon based on *p*.

```
public abstract void fillPolygon(int xPoints[],
                                        int yPoints[],
                                        int nPoints)
```

Fills a closed polygon defined by arrays of *x* and *y* coordinates. See drawPolygon.

```
public abstract void fillRect(int x,  int y,  int width,
                                            int height)
```

Fills the specified rectangle.

```
public abstract void fillRoundRect(int x,  int y,
                                      int width,
                    int height, int arcWidth, int arcHeight)
```

Fills the specified rounded-corner rectangle with the current color.

```
public abstract Color getColor()
```

Gets this graphics context's current color.

```
public abstract Font getFont()
```

Gets the current font.

```
public FontMetrics getFontMetrics()
```

Gets the font metrics of the current font.

```
public abstract FontMetrics getFontMetrics(Font f)
```

Gets the font metrics for the specified font.

```
public abstract void setColor(Color c)
```

Sets this graphics context's current color to the specified color.

```
public abstract void setFont(Font font)
```

Sets this graphics context's font to the specified font.

```
public abstract void setPaintMode()
```

Sets the paint mode of this graphics context to overwrite the destination with this graphics context's current color. Sets the logical pixel operation function to the paint or overwrite mode.

```
public abstract void setXORMode(Color c1)
```

Sets the paint mode of this graphics context to alternate between this graphics context's current color and the new specified color. The logical pixel operations are performed in the XOR mode, which alternates pixels between the current color and *c1*.

```
public String toString()
```

Returns a `String` object representing this `Graphics` object's value.

```
public abstract void translate(int x, int y)
```

Translates the origin of the graphics context to the point (x, y) in the current coordinate system.

The Dimension Class

public class `Dimension` extends `Object` implements `Serializable`

The Dimension class encapsulates the width and height of a component.

Data fields:

```
public int width
```

The width dimension.

```
public int height
```

The height dimension.

Constructors:

`public Dimension()`

Creates a `Dimension` with a width of zero and a height of zero.

`public Dimension(Dimension d)`

Creates a `Dimension` whose width and height are the same as for the specified dimension.

`public Dimension(int width, int height)`

Creates a `Dimension` and initializes it to the specified width and height.

Methods:

`public Dimension getSize()`

Gets the size of this `Dimension` object.

`public boolean equals(Object obj)`

Checks whether two `Dimension` objects have equal values.

`public void setSize(Dimension d)`
`public void setSize(int width, int height)`

Sets the size of this `Dimension` object.

`public String toString()`

Returns a string that represents this `Dimension` object's values.

The Point Class

`public class Point extends Object implements Serializable`

The `Point` class represents a location in a two-dimensional (*x*, *y*) coordinate space.

Data fields:

`public int x`

The *x* coordinate.

`public int y`

The *y* coordinate.

Constructors:

`public Point()`

Constructs and initializes a point at the origin (0, 0) of the coordinate space.

```
public Point(Point p)
```

Constructs and initializes a point with the same location as *p*.

```
public Point(int x, int y)
```

Constructs and initializes a point at the specified (*x*, *y*) location.

Methods:

```
public boolean equals(Object obj)
```

Determines whether two points are equal.

```
public Point getLocation()
```

Returns the location of this point

```
public void move(int x, int y)
```

The same as `setLocation(int, int)`.

```
public void setLocation(Point p)
public void setLocation(int x, int y)
```

Changes the point to have the specified location.

```
public String toString()
```

Returns a representation of this point and its location.

```
public void translate(int dx, int dy)
```

Translates this point, at location (*x*, *y*), by *dx* along the *x* axis and by *dy* along the *y* axis so that it now represents the point (*x* + *dx*, *y* + *dy*).

The Polygon Class

public class `Polygon` extends `Object` implements `Shape, Serializable`

The `Polygon` class describes a closed, two-dimensional region within a coordinate space, bounded by an arbitrary number of line segments, each of which is one side of the polygon.

Data fields:

```
public int npoints
```

The total number of points.

```
public int xpoints[]
```

The array of *x* coordinates.

```
public int ypoints[]
```

The array of *y* coordinates.

Constructors:

```
public Polygon()
```

Creates an empty polygon.

```
public Polygon(int xpoints[], int ypoints[], int npoints)
```

Constructs and initializes a polygon from the specified parameters where each *x,y* pair represents a point.

Methods:

```
public void addPoint(int x, int y)
```

Appends a point to this polygon.

```
public boolean contains(Point p)
public boolean contains(int x, int y)
```

Determines whether the specified point is inside the `Polygon`.

```
public void translate(int deltaX, int deltaY)
```

Translates the vertices by `deltaX` along the *x* axis and by `deltaY` along the *y* axis.

The Component Class and Subclasses

The `Component` class is the superclass of all AWT components and containers. This section also includes the base-level components. Separate sections are included for the `Container` class and subclasses, and the `MenuComponent` class and subclasses.

The Component Class

```
public abstract class Component extends Object
         implements ImageObserver, MenuContainer, Serializable
```

A component is an object that has a graphical representation and can interact with a user. The `Component` class is the abstract superclass of the nonmenu-related Abstract Window Toolkit components.

Data fields:

```
public static final float TOP_ALIGNMENT
public static final float CENTER_ALIGNMENT
public static final float BOTTOM_ALIGNMENT
public static final float LEFT_ALIGNMENT
public static final float RIGHT_ALIGNMENT
```

Specifies an alignment of the component.

Methods:

`public synchronized void` `add(PopupMenu popup)`

Adds the specified popup menu to the component.

`public synchronized void`
        `addComponentListener(ComponentListener l)`

Adds the specified component listener to receive component events from this component.

`public synchronized void`
        `addFocusListener(FocusListener l)`

Adds the specified focus listener to receive focus events from this component.

`public synchronized void` `addKeyListener(KeyListener l)`

Adds the specified key listener to receive key events from this component.

`public synchronized void`
        `addMouseListener(MouseListener l)`

Adds the specified mouse listener to receive mouse events from this component.

`public synchronized void`
        `addMouseMotionListener(MouseMotionListener l)`

Adds the specified mouse motion listener to receive mouse motion events from this component.

`public boolean` `contains(int x, int y)`
`public boolean` `contains(Point p)`

Checks whether this component "contains" the specified point, where x and y are defined to be relative to the coordinate system of this component.

`public void` `doLayout()`

Prompts the layout manager to lay out this component. Usually called when the component (more specifically, container) is validated.

`public Color` `getBackground()`

Gets the background color of this component.

`public Rectangle` `getBounds()`

Gets the bounds of this component. A `Rectangle` object has fields width, height, x, and y.

```
public Component getComponentAt(Point p)
public Component getComponentAt(int x, int y)
```

Determines if this component or one of its immediate subcomponents contains the (x, y) location, and if so, returns the containing component.

```
public Font getFont()
```

Gets the font of this component.

```
public FontMetrics getFontMetrics(Font font)
```

Gets the font metrics for the specified font.

```
public Color getForeground()
```

Gets the foreground color of this component.

```
public Graphics getGraphics()
```

Creates a graphics context for this component.

```
public Point getLocation()
```

Gets the location (top-left corner) of this component relative to the parent's coordinate space.

```
public Point getLocationOnScreen()
```

Gets the location (top-left corner) of this component relative to the screen's coordinate space.

```
public Dimension getMaximumSize()
```

Gets the maximum size of this component. A `Dimension` object x has public width and height fields: e.g., `x.width`, `x.height`.

```
public Dimension getMinimumSize()
```

Gets the minimum size of this component. A `Dimension` object x has public width and height fields: e.g., `x.width`, `x.height`.

```
public String getName()
```

Gets the name of the component.

```
public Container getParent()
```

Gets the parent of this component, the container in which this component resides.

```
public Dimension getPreferredSize()
```

Gets the preferred size of this component. A `Dimension` object x has public width and height fields: e.g., `x.width`, `x.height`.

`public Dimension getSize()`

Returns the size of this component. A `Dimension` object *x* has public width and height fields: e.g., `x.width`, `x.height`.

`public void invalidate()`

Invalidates this component, so that its parent will lay it out again.

`public boolean isEnabled()`

Determines whether this component is enabled. Can respond to user input and generate events.

`public boolean isShowing()`

Determines whether this component is showing on screen.

`public boolean isValid()`

Determines whether this component is valid. Components are invalidated when they are first shown on the screen.

`public boolean isVisible()`

Determines whether this component is visible.

`public void paint(Graphics g)`

Paints this component and defines the "picture" that you see.

`public void paintAll(Graphics g)`

Paints this component and all of its subcomponents.

`protected String paramString()`

Returns the parameter string representing the state of this component. Useful for debugging.

`public synchronized void remove(MenuComponent popup)`

Removes the specified popup menu from the component.

`public synchronized void
        removeComponentListener(ComponentListener l)`

Removes the specified component listener so that it no longer receives component events from this component.

`public synchronized void
        removeFocusListener(FocusListener l)`

Removes the specified focus listener so that it no longer receives focus events from this component.

```
public synchronized void
                     removeKeyListener(KeyListener l)
```

Removes the specified key listener so that it no longer receives key events from this component.

```
public synchronized void
                     removeMouseListener(MouseListener l)
```

Removes the specified mouse listener so that it no longer receives mouse events from this component.

```
public synchronized void
          removeMouseMotionListener(MouseMotionListener l)
```

Removes the specified mouse motion listener so that it no longer receives mouse motion events from this component.

```
public void repaint()
```

Repaints this component. Called by update.

```
public void repaint(int x, int y, int width, int height)
```

Repaints the specified rectangle of this component.

```
public void requestFocus()
```

Requests that this component get the input focus.

```
public void setBackground(Color c)
```

Sets the background color of this component.

```
public void setBounds(Rectangle r)
public void setBounds(int x, int y,
                      int width, int height)
```

Moves and resizes this component.

```
public void setEnabled(boolean b)
```

Enables or disables this component.

```
public synchronized void setFont(Font f)
```

Sets the font of this component.

```
public void setForeground(Color c)
```

Sets the foreground color of this component.

```
public void setLocation(int x, int y)
public void setLocation(Point p)
```

Moves this component to a new location (top-left corner).

```
public void setName(String name)
```

Sets the name of the component to the specified string.

```
public void setSize(Dimension d)
public void setSize(int width, int height)
```

Resize's this component.

```
public void setVisible(boolean b)
```

Shows or hides this component.

```
public String toString()
```

Returns a `String` representation of this component and its values.

```
public void validate()
```

Ensures that this component has a valid layout.

```
public void update(Graphics g)
```

Updates this component: clears this component by filling it with the background color, sets the color of the graphics context to be the foreground color of this component, calls this component's paint method to completely redraw this component.

The Button Class

public class `Button` extends `Component`

This class creates a labeled button.

Constructors:

```
public Button()
public Button(String label)
```

Constructs a `Button`. If the label is specified, it will appear on the button.

Methods:

```
public synchronized void
                addActionListener(ActionListener l)
```

Adds the specified action listener to receive action events from this button.

```
public String getActionCommand()
```

Returns the command name of the action event fired by this button.

```
public String getLabel()
```

Gets the label of this button.

```
public synchronized void
            removeActionListener(ActionListener l)
```

Removes the specified action listener so that it no longer receives action events from this button.

```
public void setActionCommand(String command)
```

Sets the command name for the action event fired by this button. By default this is the label on the button.

```
public synchronized void setLabel(String label)
```

Sets the button's label to be the specified string.

The Checkbox Class

public class Checkbox extends Component
                implements ItemSelectable

A checkbox can either be "on" (true) or "off" (false).

Constructors:

```
public Checkbox()
public Checkbox(String label)
public Checkbox(String label, boolean state)
public Checkbox(String label, boolean state,
                CheckboxGroup group)
```

Creates a checkbox, with the label, if specified. The default state is false.

Methods:

```
public synchronized void addItemListener(ItemListener l)
```

Adds the specified item listener to receive item events from this checkbox.

```
public CheckboxGroup getCheckboxGroup()
```

Determines this checkbox's group.

```
public String getLabel()
```

Gets the label of this checkbox.

```
public boolean getState()
```

Determines whether this checkbox is in the "on" or "off" state.

```
public synchronized void
                    removeItemListener(ItemListener l)
```

Removes the specified item listener so that the item listener no longer receives items.

```
public void setCheckboxGroup(CheckboxGroup g)
```

Sets this checkbox's group to be the specified checkbox group.

```
public synchronized void setLabel(String label)
```

Sets this checkbox's label to be the string argument.

```
public void setState(boolean state)
```

Sets the state of this checkbox to the specified state.

The CheckboxGroup Class

```
public class CheckboxGroup extends Object
                        implements Serializable
```

The `CheckboxGroup` class is used to group together a set of `Checkbox` buttons, so that exactly one checkbox button is on at a time.

Constructors:

```
public CheckboxGroup()
```

Creates a new instance of `CheckboxGroup`.

Methods:

```
public Checkbox getSelectedCheckbox()
```

Gets the current choice from this `CheckboxGroup`.

```
public synchronized void
                    setSelectedCheckbox(Checkbox box)
```

Sets box to be the currently selected checkbox in this group.

The Choice Class

```
public class Choice extends Component implements ItemSelectable
```

The `Choice` class shows a pop-up menu of choices with the selected choice displayed.

Constructors:

```
public Choice()
```

Creates a new choice menu with no items in it. The first item added is marked as the selected item.

Methods:

`public synchronized void addItemListener(ItemListener 1)`

Adds the specified item listener to receive item events from this `Choice` menu.

`public synchronized void add(String item)`
`public synchronized void addItem(String item)`

Adds an item to this `Choice` menu.

`public int getItemCount()`

Returns the number of items in this `Choice` menu.

`public String getItem(int index)`

Gets the string at the specified index in this `Choice` menu.

`public int getSelectedIndex()`

Returns the index of the currently selected item.

`public synchronized String getSelectedItem()`

Gets a representation of the current choice as a string.

`public synchronized void insert(String item, int index)`

Inserts the item into this choice at the specified position.

`public synchronized void remove(int position)`

Removes an item from the `Choice` menu at the specified position.

`public synchronized void remove(String item)`

Removes the first occurrence of item from the `Choice` menu.

`public synchronized void removeAll()`

Removes all items from the `Choice` menu.

`public synchronized void`
`                    removeItemListener(ItemListener 1)`

Removes the specified item listener so that it no longer receives item events from this `Choice` menu.

`public synchronized void select(int pos)`

Sets the selected item in this `Choice` menu to be the item at the specified position.

`public synchronized void select(String str)`

Sets the selected item to be the item whose name is equal to the specified string.

The Label Class

public class `Label` extends `Component`

A label displays a single line of text that can be changed by the application, but not by the user.

Data fields:

public static final int `LEFT`

The label should be left justified.

public static final int `CENTER`

The label should be centered.

public static final int `RIGHT`

The label should be right justified.

Constructors:

public `Label()`
public `Label(String text)`
public `Label(String text, int alignment)`

Creates a `Label` with text and alignment, if specified. Default alignment is `LEFT`.

Methods:

public int `getAlignment()`

Gets the current alignment of this label.

public synchronized void `setAlignment(int alignment)`

Sets the alignment for this label to the specified alignment.

public String `getText()`

Gets the text of this label.

public synchronized void `setText(String text)`

Sets the text for this label to the specified text.

The List Class

public class `List` extends `Component` implements `ItemSelectable`

The `List` component presents the user with a scrolling list of text items from which the user can select either a single item or multiple items.

Constructors:

```
public List()
public List(int rows)
public List(int rows, boolean multipleMode)
```

Creates a new scrolling list with specified rows visible. Four rows are visible by default. Only one item may be selected.

Methods:

```
public void add(String item)
public synchronized void add(String item, int index)
public void addItem(String item)
public synchronized void addItem(String item, int index)
```

Adds the specified item to the end of scrolling list, if index isn't specified.

```
public synchronized void
                    addActionListener(ActionListener l)
```

Adds the specified action listener to receive action events from this list. (Action events occur when a user double-clicks on a list item.)

```
public synchronized void addItemListener(ItemListener l)
```

Adds the specified item listener to receive item events from this list.

```
public synchronized void delItem(int position)
```

Removes the item at the specified position from this list.

```
public synchronized void deselect(int index)
```

Deselects the item at the specified index.

```
public String getItem(int index)
```

Gets the item associated with the specified index.

```
public synchronized String[] getItems()
```

Gets the items in the list.

```
public int getItemCount()
```

Gets the number of items in the list.

```
public Dimension getMinimumSize()
```

Determines the minimum size of this scrolling list.

```
public Dimension getMinimumSize(int rows)
```

Gets the minumum dimensions for a list with the specified number of rows.

```
public Dimension getPreferredSize()
```

Gets the preferred size of this scrolling list.

```
public Dimension getPreferredSize(int rows)
```

Gets the preferred dimensions for a list with the specified number of rows.

```
public int getRows()
```

Gets the number of visible lines in the list.

```
public synchronized int getSelectedIndex()
```

Gets the index of the selected item on the list.

```
public synchronized int[] getSelectedIndexes()
```

Gets the selected indexes on the list.

```
public synchronized String getSelectedItem()
```

Gets the selected item on this scrolling list.

```
public synchronized String[] getSelectedItems()
```

Gets the selected items on this scrolling list.

```
public int getVisibleIndex()
```

Gets the index of the item that was last made visible by the method `makeVisible`.

```
public boolean isIndexSelected(int index)
```

Determines if the specified item in this scrolling list is selected.

```
public boolean isMultipleMode()
```

Determines whether this list allows multiple selections.

```
public synchronized void makeVisible(int index)
```

Makes the item at the specified index visible.

```
public synchronized void remove(int position)
```

Removes the item at the specified position from this scrolling list.

```
public synchronized void remove(String item)
```

Removes the first occurrence of an item from the list.

```
public synchronized void removeAll()
```

Removes all items from this list.

```
public synchronized void
                    removeActionListener(ActionListener l)
```

Removes the specified action listener so that it no longer receives action events from this list.

```
public synchronized void replaceItem(String newValue,
                                     int index)
```

Replaces the item at the specified index in the scrolling list with the new string.

```
public synchronized void
                    removeItemListener(ItemListener l)
```

Removes the specified item listener so that it no longer receives item events from this list.

```
public void select(int index)
```

Selects the item at the specified index in the scrolling list.

```
public synchronized void setMultipleMode(boolean b)
```

Sets the mode to multiple selections allowed if b is true.

The Scrollbar Class

public class `Scrollbar` extends `Component` implements `Adjustable`.

The `Scrollbar` allows a user to select from a range of values by sliding a bar.

Data fields:

```
public static final int HORIZONTAL
```

A horizontal scroll bar.

```
public static final int VERTICAL
```

A vertical scroll bar.

Constructors:

```
public Scrollbar()
public Scrollbar(int orientation)
```

Constructs a new scroll bar. If orientation is not specified, it will default to VERTICAL.

```
public Scrollbar(int orientation, int value,
                 int visible, int minimum, int maximum)
```

Constructs a new scroll bar with the specified orientation, initial value, page size, and minimum and maximum values.

Methods:

```
public synchronized void
            addAdjustmentListener(AdjustmentListener l)
```

Adds the specified adjustment listener to receive instances of `AdjustmentEvent` from this scroll bar.

```
public int getMaximum()
```

Gets the maximum value of this scroll bar.

```
public int getBlockIncrement()
```

Gets the block increment of this scroll bar. The value that is added (subtracted) when the user activates the block increment area of the scroll bar.

```
public int getMinimum()
```

Gets the minimum value of this scroll bar.

```
public int getOrientation()
```

Determines the orientation of this scroll bar.

```
public int getValue()
```

Gets the current value of this scroll bar.

```
public int getVisibleAmount()
```

Gets the visible amount of this scroll bar.

```
public int getUnitIncrement()
```

Gets the unit increment for this scrollbar, that is, the value that is added (subtracted) when the user activates the unit increment area of the scroll bar.

```
public synchronized void
            removeAdjustmentListener(AdjustmentListener l)
```

Removes the specified adjustment listener so that it no longer receives instances of `AdjustmentEvent` from this scroll bar.

```
public synchronized void setBlockIncrement(int v)
```

Sets the block increment for this scroll bar, that is, the value that is added (subtracted) when the user activates the block increment area of the scroll bar.

`public synchronized void` `setMaximum(int newMaximum)`

Sets the maximum value of this scroll bar.

`public synchronized void` `setMinimum(int newMinimum)`

Sets the minimum value of this scroll bar.

`public synchronized void` `setOrientation(int orientation)`

Sets the orientation for this scroll bar.

`public synchronized void` `setValue(int newValue)`

Sets the value of this scroll bar to the specified value.

`public synchronized void` `setValues(int value,`
`int visible,`
`int minimum, int maximum)`

Sets the values of the four properties of a scroll bar.

`public synchronized void` `setVisibleAmount(int newAmount)`

Sets the visible amount of this scroll bar.

`public synchronized void` `setUnitIncrement(int v)`

Sets the unit increment for this scroll bar, that is, the value that is added (subtracted) when the user activates the unit increment area of the scroll bar.

The TextComponent

public class `TextComponent` extends `Component`

The `TextComponent` class is the superclass of any component that allows the editing of some text.

Methods:

`public synchronized void` `addTextListener(TextListener l)`

Adds the specified text event listener to receive text events from this text component.

`public int` `getCaretPosition()`

Gets the position of the text insertion caret for this text component.

`public synchronized String` `getSelectedText()`

Gets the selected text from the text that is presented by this text component.

`public synchronized int getSelectionEnd()`

Gets the end position of the selected text in this text component.

`public synchronized int getSelectionStart()`

Gets the start position of the selected text in this text component.

`public synchronized String getText()`

Gets the text that is presented by this text component.

`public boolean isEditable()`

Indicates whether or not this text component is editable.

`public void removeTextListener(TextListener l)`

Removes the specified text event listener so that it no longer receives text events from this text component.

`public synchronized void`
`        select(int selectionStart, int selectionEnd)`

Selects the text between the specified start and end positions.

`public synchronized void selectAll()`

Selects all the text in this text component.

`public void setCaretPosition(int position)`

Sets the position of the text insertion caret for this text component.

`public synchronized void setEditable(boolean b)`

Sets whether or not this text component is editable.

`public synchronized void`
`            setSelectionEnd(int selectionEnd)`

Sets the selection end for this text component to the specified position.

`public synchronized void`
`            setSelectionStart(int selectionStart)`

Sets the selection start for this text component to the specified position.

`public synchronized void setText(String t)`

Sets the text that is presented by this text component.

The TextArea Class

`public class TextArea extends TextComponent`

A `TextArea` object is a multiline region. It displays text that can be set to allow editing or to be read only.

Data fields:

`public static final int` SCROLLBARS_BOTH

Creates and displays both vertical and horizontal scroll bars.

`public static final int` SCROLLBARS_VERTICAL_ONLY

Creates and displays vertical scroll bar only.

`public static final int` SCROLLBARS_HORIZONTAL_ONLY

Creates and displays a horizontal scroll bar only.

`public static final int` SCROLLBARS_NONE

Does not create or display any scroll bars for the text area.

Constructors:

`public` TextArea()
`public` TextArea(String text)

Constructs a new text area, with both scroll bars, and with text, if specified.

`public` TextArea(int rows, int columns)
`public` TextArea(String text, int rows, int columns)

Constructs a new text area with the text, rows, and columns, as specified.

`public` TextArea(String text, int rows,
                  int columns, int scrollbars)

Constructs a new text area with the specified text, rows, columns, and scroll bar visibility as specified.

Methods:

`public synchronized void` append(String str)

Appends the given text to the text area's current text.

`public int` getColumns()

Gets the number of columns in this text area.

`public Dimension` getMinimumSize()

Determines the minimum size of this text area.

`public Dimension` getMinimumSize(int rows, int columns)

Determines the minimum size of a text area with the specified number of rows and columns.

```
public Dimension getPreferredSize()
```

Determines the preferred size of this text area.

```
public Dimension getPreferredSize(int rows, int columns)
```

Determines the preferred size of a text area with the specified number of rows and columns.

```
public int getRows()
```

Gets the number of rows in the text area.

```
public int getScrollbarVisibility()
```

Gets a value that indicates which scroll bars the text area uses.

```
public synchronized void insert(String str, int pos)
```

Inserts the specified text at the specified position in this text area.

```
public synchronized void
          replaceRange(String str, int start, int end)
```

Replaces text between the indicated start and end positions.

```
public void setColumns(int columns)
```

Sets the number of columns for this text area.

```
public void setRows(int rows)
```

Sets the number of rows for this text area.

The TextField Class

public class TextField extends TextComponent

A TextField object is a text component that allows a single line of text to be edited.

Constructors:

```
public TextField()
public TextField(String text)
```

Constructs a new text field with text if specified

```
public TextField(int columns)
public TextField(String text, int columns)
```

Constructs a new TextField with the specified number of columns and text, if specified.

Methods:

```
public synchronized void
                    addActionListener(ActionListener l)
```

Adds the specified action listener to receive action events from this text field.

```
public int getColumns()
```

Gets the number of columns in this text field.

```
public char getEchoChar()
```

Gets the character that is to be used for echoing (for example, to hide a password).

```
public Dimension getMinimumSize()
```

Gets the minimum dimensions for this text field.

```
public Dimension getMinimumSize(int columns)
```

Gets the minimum dimensions for a text field with the specified number of columns.

```
public Dimension getPreferredSize()
```

Gets the preferred size of this text field.

```
public Dimension getPreferredSize(int columns)
```

Gets the preferred size of this text field with the specified number of columns.

```
public boolean echoCharIsSet()
```

Indicates whether or not this text field has a character set for echoing.

```
public void setColumns(int columns)
```

Sets the number of columns in this text field.

```
public void setEchoChar(char c)
```

Sets the echo character for this text field.

```
public synchronized void
                    removeActionListener(ActionListener l)
```

Removes the specified action listener so that it no longer receives action events from this text field.

The Container Class, Subclasses, and LayoutManagers

The Container Class

public abstract class `Container` extends `Component`

A generic Abstract Window Toolkit (AWT) that can contain other AWT components.

Methods:

public Component `add`(Component comp)

Adds the specified component to the end of this container.

public Component `add`(Component comp, int index)

Adds the specified component to this container at the given position.

public synchronized void
                        `addContainerListener`(ContainerListener l)

Adds the specified container listener to receive container events from this container.

public Component `getComponent`(int n)

Gets the nth component in this container.

public int `getComponentCount`()

Gets the number of components in this panel.

public Component[] `getComponents`()

Gets all the components in this container.

public Insets `getInsets`()

Determines the insets of this container, which indicate the size of the container's border.

public LayoutManager `getLayout`()

Gets the layout manager for this container.

public boolean `isAncestorOf`(Component c)

Checks if the component is contained in the component hierarchy of this container.

public void `paintComponents`(Graphics g)

Paints each of the components in this container.

```
public void remove(int index)
```

Removes the component, specified by index, from this container.

```
public void remove(Component comp)
```

Removes the specified component from this container.

```
public void removeAll()
```

Removes all the components from this container.

```
public void removeContainerListener(ContainerListener l)
```

Removes the specified container listener so it no longer receives container events from this container.

```
public void setLayout(LayoutManager mgr)
```

Sets the layout manager for this container.

```
protected void validateTree()
```

Recursively descends the container tree and recomputes the layout for any subtrees marked as needing it (those marked as invalid).

The Dialog Class

public class Dialog extends Window

Produces a dialog window that takes input from the user.

Constructors:

```
public Dialog(Frame parent)
public Dialog(Frame parent,String title)
public Dialog(Frame parent, boolean modal)
public Dialog(Frame parent, String title, boolean modal)
```

Constructs a Dialog, (without title if not specified) that is initially invisible. A modal dialog prevents the user from interacting with any other AWT window.

```
public String getTitle()
```

Gets the title of the dialog.

```
public boolean isModal()
```

Indicates whether the dialog is modal.

```
public boolean isResizable()
```

Indicates whether this dialog window is resizable.

```
public void setModal(boolean b)
```

Specifies whether this dialog is modal.

```
public synchronized void setResizable(boolean resizable)
```

Sets the resizable flag.

```
public synchronized void setTitle(String title)
```

Sets the title of the dialog.

```
public void show()
```

Shows the dialog.

The FileDialog Class

public class `FileDialog` extends `Dialog`

The `FileDialog` class displays a dialog window that allows the user to select a file.

Data fields:

```
public static final int LOAD
```

Indicates that the file to locate will be read in.

```
public static final int SAVE
```

Indicates that the file to locate will be written out.

Constructors:

```
public FileDialog(Frame parent)
public FileDialog(Frame parent, String title)
public FileDialog(Frame parent, String title, int mode)
```

Creates a file dialog. Default mode is LOAD.

Methods:

```
public String getDirectory()
```

Gets the directory of this file dialog.

```
public String getFile()
```

Gets the selected file of this file dialog.

```
public int getMode()
```

Indicates whether this file dialog is for loading from or saving to a file.

`public synchronized void` `setDirectory(String dir)`

    Sets the directory of this file dialog window to be the specified directory.

`public synchronized void` `setFile(String file)`

    Sets the selected file for this file dialog window to be the specified file.

`public void` `setMode(int mode)`

    Sets the mode of the file dialog.

The Frame Class

`public class` `Frame` `extends` `Window` `implements` `MenuContainer`

    A `Frame` is a top-level window with a title and a border.

Constructors:

`public` `Frame()`
`public` `Frame(String title)`

    Constructs a new `Frame` that is initially invisible.

Methods:

`public` `Image` `getIconImage()`

    Gets the icon image for this frame.

`public` `MenuBar` `getMenuBar()`

    Gets the menu bar for this frame.

`public` `String` `getTitle()`

    Gets the title of the frame.

`public boolean` `isResizable()`

    Determines whether this frame is resizable.

`public synchronized void` `setIconImage(Image image)`

    Sets the image to display when this frame is iconized (not supported by all platforms).

`public synchronized void` `setMenuBar(MenuBar mb)`

    Sets the menu bar for this frame.

`public synchronized void` `setResizable(boolean resizable)`

    Sets this frame to be resizable when argument is true.

`public synchronized void` `setTitle(String title)`

    Sets the title for this frame.

The Panel Class

public class `Panel` extends `Container`

`Panel` is the simplest container class. A panel provides space in which an application can attach any other component, including other panels.

Constructors:

public `Panel()`
public `Panel(LayoutManager layout)`

Creates a new panel. The default layout manager is `FlowLayout`.

The Window Class

public class `Window` extends `Container`

A `Window` object is a top-level window with no borders and no menu bar.

Constructors:

public `Window(Frame parent)`

Constructs a new invisible `Window`.

Methods:

public synchronized void
                    `addWindowListener(WindowListener l)`

Adds the specified window listener to receive window events.

public `Component getFocusOwner()`

Returns the child component of this `Window`. The child component has focus if and only if this `Window` is active.

public `Toolkit getToolkit()`

Returns the toolkit of this frame.

public void `pack()`

Causes subcomponents of this window to be laid out at their preferred size.

public synchronized void
                    `removeWindowListener(WindowListener l)`

Removes the specified window listener.

public void `show()`

Shows this window and brings it to the front.

```
public void toBack()
```

Sends this window to the back.

```
public void toFront()
```

Brings this window to the front.

The BorderLayout Class

public class BorderLayout extends Object
                            implements LayoutManager2, Serializable

A border layout lays out a container, arranging and resizing its components to fit in five regions: North, South, East, West, and Center. [Variables]

Data fields:

```
public static final String NORTH
public static final String SOUTH
public static final String EAST
public static final String WEST
public static final String CENTER
```

Constructors:

```
public BorderLayout()
```

Constructs a new border layout with no gaps between components.

```
public BorderLayout(int hgap, int vgap)
```

Constructs a border layout with the specified gaps between components.

Methods:

```
public int getHgap()
```

Returns the horizontal gap between components.

```
public int getVgap()
```

Returns the vertical gap between components.

```
public void setHgap(int hgap)
```

Sets the horizontal gap between components.

```
public void setVgap(int vgap)
```

Sets the vertical gap between components.

The CardLayout Class

public class CardLayout extends Object
                           implements LayoutManager2, Serializable

A `CardLayout` object treats each component in the container as a card with only one card visible at a time.

Constructors:

`public CardLayout()`

Creates a new card layout with gaps of size zero.

`public CardLayout(int hgap, int vgap)`

Creates a new card layout with the specified horizontal and vertical gaps.

Methods:

`public void first(Container parent)`

Flips to the first card of the container.

`public int getHgap()`

Gets the horizontal gap between components.

`public int getVgap()`

Gets the vertical gap between components.

`public void last(Container parent)`

Flips to the last card of the container.

`public void next(Container parent)`

Flips to the next card of the specified container (first follows last).

`public void previous(Container parent)`

Flips to the previous card of the specified container (last precedes first).

`public void setHgap(int hgap)`

Sets the horizontal gap between components.

`public void setVgap(int vgap)`

Sets the vertical gap between components.

`public void show(Container parent, String name)`

Flips to the component that was added to this layout with the specified name.

The FlowLayout Class

`public class FlowLayout extends Object`
                  `implements LayoutManager, Serializable`

A flow layout arranges components in a left-to-right flow, text in a paragraph.

Data fields:

`public static final int LEFT`

Each row of components should be left-justified.

`public static final int CENTER`

Each row of components should be centered.

`public static final int RIGHT`

Each row of components should be right-justified.

Constructors:

`public FlowLayout()`

Constructs a new `Flow Layout` with a centered alignment and a default 5-unit horizontal and vertical gap.

`public FlowLayout(int align)`

Constructs a new `Flow Layout` with the specified alignment and a default 5-unit horizontal and vertical gap.

`public FlowLayout(int align, int hgap, int vgap)`

Creates a new flow layout manager with the given alignment and horizontal and vertical gaps.

Methods:

`public int getAlignment()`

Gets the alignment for this layout.

`public int getHgap()`

Gets the horizontal gap between components.

`public int getVgap()`

Gets the vertical gap between components.

`public void setAlignment(int align)`

Sets the alignment for this layout.

`public void setHgap(int hgap)`

Sets the horizontal gap between components.

`public void setVgap(int vgap)`

Sets the vertical gap between components.

The GridBagLayout Class

public class `GridLayout` extends `Object`
                    implements `LayoutManager`, `Serializable`

The `GridLayout` class lays out a container's components in a rectangular grid.

Constructors:

public `GridLayout()`

Creates a grid layout in a single row with a default of one column per component.

public `GridLayout(int rows, int cols)`

Creates a grid layout with the specified number of rows and columns.

public `GridLayout(int rows, int cols,
                int hgap, int vgap)`

Creates a grid layout with the specified number of rows and columns and horizontal and vertical gaps.

Methods:

public int `getColumns()`

Gets the number of columns in this layout.

public int `getHgap()`

Gets the horizontal gap between components.

public int `getRows()`

Gets the number of rows in this layout.

public int `getVgap()`

Gets the vertical gap between components.

public void `setColumns(int cols)`

Sets the number of columns in this layout to the specified value.

public void `setHgap(int hgap)`

Sets the horizontal gap between components to the specified value.

public void `setRows(int rows)`

Sets the number of rows in this layout to the specified value.

public void `setVgap(int vgap)`

Sets the vertical gap between components to the specified value.

Events and Listeners

Events and Listeners go hand in hand. Therefore, the events and listeners are paired in this section.

The ActionEvent and ActionEventListener

public class `ActionEvent` extends `AWTEvent`

> The action semantic event.

Data fields:

public static final int `SHIFT_MASK`

> The shift modifier constant.

public static final int `CTRL_MASK`

> The control modifier constant.

public static final int `META_MASK`

> The meta modifier constant.

public static final int `ALT_MASK`

> The alt modifier constant.

Constructors:

```
public ActionEvent(Object source, int id,String command)
public ActionEvent(Object source, int id,
                   String command, int modifiers)
```

> Constructs an `ActionEvent` object with the object where the event originated, the type of event, the command string for this action event, and if present, the modifiers held down during this action.

Methods:

public String `getActionCommand()`

> Returns the command name associated with this action.

public int `getModifiers()`

> Returns the modifiers held down during this action event.

The ActionListener

public interface `ActionListener` extends `EventListener`

> The listener interface for receiving action events.

Methods:

public abstract void actionPerformed(ActionEvent e)

The method is invoked when an action occurs.

The AdjustmentEvent and AdjustmentEvent Listener

public class AdjustmentEvent extends AWTEvent

The adjustment event that is emitted by Adjustable objects.

Constructors:

public AdjustmentEvent(Adjustable source, int id,
                       int type, int value)

Constructs an AdjustmentEvent object with the specified Adjustable source, id, type, and value.

Methods:

public Adjustable getAdjustable()

Returns the Adjustable object where this event originated.

public int getAdjustmentType()

Returns the type of adjustment that caused the value changed event.

public int getValue()

Returns the current value in the adjustment event.

The AdjustmentListener

public interface AdjustmentListener extends EventListener

The listener interface for receiving adjustment events.

Methods:

public abstract void
            adjustmentValueChanged(AdjustmentEvent e)

Is invoked when the value of the adjustable has changed.

The ItemEvent and ItemListener

The ItemEvent

public class ItemEvent extends AWTEvent

The item event emitted by `ItemSelectable` objects. This event is generated when an item is selected or deselected.

Data fields:

`public static final int ITEM_FIRST`

Marks the first integer id for the range of item event ids.

`public static final int ITEM_LAST`

Marks the last integer id for the range of item event ids.

`public static final int ITEM_STATE_CHANGED`

The item state changed event type.

`public static final int SELECTED`

The item selected state change type.

`public static final int DESELECTED`

The item deselected state change type.

Constructors:

```
public ItemEvent(ItemSelectable source, int id,
                 Object item, int stateChange)
```

Constructs an `ItemEvent` object with the specified `ItemSelectable` source, type, item, and item select state.

Methods:

`public Object getItem()`

Returns the item where the event occurred.

`public ItemSelectable getItemSelectable()`

Returns the `ItemSelectable` object where this event originated.

`public int getStateChange()`

Returns the state change type that generated the event.

The ItemListener

`public interface ItemListener extends EventListener`

The listener interface for receiving item events.

Methods:

`public abstract void itemStateChanged(ItemEvent e)`

Is invoked when an item's state has been changed.

The TextEvent and TextEventListener

public class `TextEvent` extends `AWTEvent`

The text event emitted by `TextComponents`.

Data fields:

public static final int `TEXT_FIRST`

Marks the first integer id for the range of adjustment event ids.

public static final int `TEXT_LAST`

Marks the last integer id for the range of adjustment event ids.

public static final int `TEXT_VALUE_CHANGED`

The adjustment value changed event.

Constructors:

public `TextEvent(Object source, int id)`

Constructs a `TextEvent` object with the specified `TextComponent` source and type.

The TextListener

public interface `TextListener` extends `EventListener`

The listener interface for receiving adjustment events.

Methods:

public abstract void `textValueChanged(TextEvent e)`

Is invoked when the value of the text has changed.

The InputEvent, Subclasses, and Listeners

This event is generated by low-level keystrokes and mouse movements. The subclasses follow:

The InputEvent

public abstract class `InputEvent` extends `ComponentEvent`

The root event class for all component-level input events.

Data fields:

public static final int `ALT_MASK`

The Alt key modifier constant.

`public static final int BUTTON1_MASK`

  The mouse button1 modifier constant.

`public static final int BUTTON2_MASK`

  The mouse button2 modifier constant.

`public static final int BUTTON3_MASK`

  The mouse button3 modifier constant.

`public static final int META_MASK`

  The Meta key modifier constant.

`public static final int CTRL_MASK`

  The Control key modifier constant.

`public static final int SHIFT_MASK`

  The Shift key modifier constant.

Methods:

`public int getModifiers()`

  Returns the modifiers flag for this event.

`public long getWhen()`

  Returns the timestamp of when this event occurred.

`public boolean isAltDown()`

  Returns whether or not the Alt modifier is down.

`public boolean isControlDown()`

  Returns whether or not the Control modifier is down.

`public boolean isMetaDown()`

  Returns whether or not the Meta modifier is down.

`public boolean isShiftDown()`

  Returns whether or not the Shift modifier is down.

The KeyEvent

public class `KeyEvent` extends `InputEvent`

  The component-level keyboard event. See resources in Appendix A for data fields and constructors.

Methods:

`public char getKeyChar()`

Returns the character associated with the key in this event.

`public void setKeyChar(char keyChar)`

Sets the character associated with the key in this event.

`public int getKeyCode()`

Returns the integer key-code associated with the key in this event.

`public void setKeyCode(int keyCode)`

Sets the key in this event to the key-code.

`public static String getKeyModifiersText(int modifiers)`

Returns a `String` describing the modifier key(s), such as "Shift" or "Ctrl+Shift".

`public static String getKeyText(int keyCode)`

Returns a String describing the `keyCode`, such as "HOME", "F1", or "A".

`public void setModifiers(int modifiers)`

Changes the modifiers for a `KeyEvent`.

The KeyListener

public interface `KeyListener` extends `EventListener`

The listener interface for receiving keyboard events.

Methods:

`public abstract void keyTyped(KeyEvent e)`

Is invoked when a key has been typed (pressed and released).

`public abstract void keyPressed(KeyEvent e)`

Is invoked when a key has been pressed.

`public abstract void keyReleased(KeyEvent e)`

Is invoked when a key has been released.

The MouseEvent

public class `MouseEvent` extends `InputEvent`

The mouse event.

Data fields:

`public static final int MOUSE_FIRST`

Marks the first integer id for the range of mouse event ids.

`public static final int MOUSE_LAST`

Marks the last integer id for the range of mouse event ids.

`public static final int MOUSE_CLICKED`

The mouse clicked event type.

`public static final int MOUSE_PRESSED`

The mouse pressed event type.

`public static final int MOUSE_RELEASED`

The mouse released event type.

`public static final int MOUSE_MOVED`

The mouse moved event type.

`public static final int MOUSE_ENTERED`

The mouse entered event type.

`public static final int MOUSE_EXITED`

The mouse exited event type.

`public static final int MOUSE_DRAGGED`

The mouse dragged event type.

Constructors:

```
public MouseEvent(Component source, int id, long when,
                  int modifiers, int x, int y,
                  int clickCount, boolean popupTrigger)
```

Constructs a MouseEvent object with the specified source component type, modifiers, coordinates, and click count.

Methods:

`public int getClickCount()`

Returns the number of mouse clicks associated with this event.

`public Point getPoint()`

Returns the *x,y* position of the event relative to the source component.

`public int getX()`

Returns the *x* position of the event relative to the source component.

```
public int getY()
```

Returns the *y* position of the event relative to the source component.

```
public boolean isPopupTrigger()
```

Returns whether or not this mouse event is the popup-menu trigger event for the platform.

```
public synchronized void translatePoint(int x, int y)
```

Translates the coordinate position of the event by *x,y*.

The MouseListener

public interface MouseListener extends EventListener

The listener interface for receiving mouse events on a component.

Methods:

```
public abstract void mouseClicked(MouseEvent e)
```

Is invoked when the mouse has been clicked on a component.

```
public abstract void mouseEntered(MouseEvent e)
```

Is invoked when the mouse enters a component.

```
public abstract void mouseExited(MouseEvent e)
```

Is invoked when the mouse exits a component.

```
public abstract void mousePressed(MouseEvent e)
```

Is invoked when a mouse button has been pressed on a component.

```
public abstract void mouseReleased(MouseEvent e)
```

Is invoked when a mouse button has been released on a component.

The MouseMotionListener

public interface MouseMotionListener extends EventListener

The listener interface for receiving mouse motion events on a component.

Methods:

```
public abstract void mouseDragged(MouseEvent e)
```

Is invoked when a mouse button is pressed on a component and then dragged.

```
public abstract void mouseMoved(MouseEvent e)
```

Is invoked when the mouse button has been moved on a component (with no buttons down).

The WindowEvent and WindowListener

public class `WindowEvent` extends `ComponentEvent`

The window-level event.

Data fields:

```
public static final int WINDOW_ACTIVATED
```

The window activated event type.

```
public static final int WINDOW_DEACTIVATED
```

The window deactivated event type.

```
public static final int WINDOW_CLOSED
```

The window closed event type.

```
public static final int WINDOW_CLOSING
```

The window closing event type.

```
public static final int WINDOW_DEICONIFIED
```

The window deiconified event type.

```
public static final int WINDOW_FIRST
```

Marks the first integer id for the range of window event ids.

```
public static final int WINDOW_ICONIFIED
```

The window iconified event type.

```
public static final int WINDOW_LAST
```

Marks the last integer id for the range of window event ids.

```
public static final int WINDOW_OPENED
```

The window opened event type.

Constructors:

```
public WindowEvent(Window source, int id)
```

Constructs a WindowEvent object with the specified source window and type.

Methods:

```
public Window getWindow()
```

Returns the window where this event originated.

The WindowListener

public interface `WindowListener` extends `EventListener`

The listener interface for receiving window events.

Methods:

```
public abstract void windowActivated(WindowEvent e)
```

Is invoked when a window is activated.

```
public abstract void windowClosed(WindowEvent e)
```

Is invoked when a window has been closed.

```
public abstract void windowClosing(WindowEvent e)
```

Is invoked when a window is in the process of being closed.

```
public abstract void windowDeactivated(WindowEvent e)
```

Is invoked when a window is deactivated.

```
public abstract void windowDeiconified(WindowEvent e)
```

Is invoked when a window is deiconified.

```
public abstract void windowIconified(WindowEvent e)
```

Is invoked when a window is iconified.

```
public abstract void windowOpened(WindowEvent e)
```

Is invoked when a window has been opened.

The MenuComponent Class and Subclasses

Menus have some fundamentally different behavior than Components, consequently a separate class structure exists.

The MenuComponent Class

public abstract class `MenuComponent` extends `Object`
                                 implements `Serializable`

The abstract class `MenuComponent` is the superclass of all menu-related components.

Methods:

```
public Font getFont()
```

Gets the font used for this menu component.

```
public String getName()
```

Gets the name of the menu component.

```
public MenuContainer getParent()
```

Returns the parent container for this menu component.

```
public void setFont(Font f)
```

Sets the font to be used for this menu component to the specified font.

```
public void setName(String name)
```

Sets the name of the component to the specified string.

The Menu Class

public class Menu extends MenuItem implements MenuContainer

A Menu object is a pull-down menu component in a menu bar.

Constructors:

```
public Menu()
public Menu(String label)
public Menu(String label, boolean tearOff)
```

Constructs a new menu with the label, if specified. The default is not tearOff.

Methods:

```
public synchronized MenuItem add(MenuItem mi)
```

Adds the specified menu item to this menu.

```
public void add(String label)
```

Adds an item with the specified label to this menu.

```
public void addSeparator()
```

Adds a separator line, or a hyphen, to the menu at the current position.

```
public MenuItem getItem(int index)
```

Gets the item located at the specified index of this menu.

```
public int getItemCount()
```

Gets the number of items in this menu.

```
public synchronized void insert(MenuItem menuitem,
                                int index)
```

Inserts a menu item into this menu at the specified position.

```
public void insert(String label, int index)
```

Inserts a menu item with the specified label into this menu at the specified position.

```
public void insertSeparator(int index)
```

Inserts a separator at the specified position.

```
public boolean isTearOff()
```

Returns whether this menu is a tear-off menu.

```
public synchronized void remove(int index)
```

Removes the menu item at the specified index from this menu.

```
public synchronized void remove(MenuComponent item)
```

Removes the specified menu item from this menu.

```
public synchronized void removeAll()
```

Removes all items from this menu.

The CheckboxMenuItem Class

```
public class CheckboxMenuItem extends MenuItem
                          implements ItemSelectable
```

This is a checkbox that can be included in a menu.

Constructors:

```
public CheckboxMenuItem()
public CheckboxMenuItem(String label)
public CheckboxMenuItem(String label, boolean state)
```

Creates a checkbox menu item with the specified label and state. Default state is false or "off."

Methods:

```
public synchronized void addItemListener(ItemListener l)
```

Adds the specified item listener to receive item events from this checkbox menu item.

```
public boolean getState()
```

Determines whether the state of this checkbox menu item is "on" or "off."

```
public synchronized void
                  removeItemListener(ItemListener l)
```

Removes the specified item listener so that it no longer receives item events from this checkbox menu item.

```
public synchronized void setState(boolean b)
```

Sets this checkbox menu item to the specified state.

The MenuBar Class

public class `MenuBar` extends `MenuComponent`
                      implements `MenuContainer`

The `MenuBar` class binds a menubar to a frame via the frame's `setMenuBar` method.

Constructors:

```
public MenuBar()
```

Creates a new menu bar.

Methods:

```
public synchronized Menu add(Menu m)
```

Adds the specified menu to the menu bar.

```
public Menu getHelpMenu()
```

Gets the help menu on the menu bar.

```
public Menu getMenu(int i)
```

Gets the specified menu.

```
public int getMenuCount()
```

Gets the number of menus on the menu bar.

```
public synchronized void setHelpMenu(Menu m)
```

Sets the help menu on this menu bar to be the specified menu.

```
public synchronized void remove(int index)
```

Removes the menu located at the specified index from this menu bar.

```
public synchronized void remove(MenuComponent m)
```

Removes the specified menu component from this menu bar.

The MenuItem Class

public class MenuItem extends MenuComponent

All items in a menu belong to the class MenuItem.

Constructors:

```
public MenuItem()
public MenuItem(String label)
```

Constructs a new MenuItem with the label, if specified.

Methods:

```
public synchronized void
                    addActionListener(ActionListener l)
```

Adds the specified action listener to receive action events from this menu item.

```
public String getActionCommand()
```

Gets the command name of the action event that is fired by this menu item.

```
public boolean isEnabled()
```

Checks whether this menu item is enabled.

```
public String getLabel()
```

Gets the label for this menu item.

```
public synchronized void
                removeActionListener(ActionListener l)
```

Removes the specified action listener so it no longer receives action events from this menu item.

```
public void setActionCommand(String command)
```

Sets the command name of the action event that is fired by this menu item.

```
public synchronized void setEnabled(boolean b)
```

Sets whether or not this menu item can be chosen.

```
public synchronized void setLabel(String label)
```

Sets the label for this menu item.

The PopupMenu

public class PopupMenu extends Menu

A menu that can be dynamically popped up at a specified position within a component.

Constructors:

```
public PopupMenu()
public PopupMenu(String label)
```

Creates a new popup menu with the name, if specified.

Methods:

```
public void show(Component origin,int x, int y)
```

Shows the popup menu at the *x,y* position relative to an origin component.

Answers to Self-Check Exercises

Chapter 1

Section 1.1

1. Microcomputer, minicomputer, mainframe, supercomputer.

Section 1.2

1.

Address	Contents
0	75.625
2	0.005
999	75.62

3. Bit, byte, memory cell, main memory, secondary memory.

Section 1.3

1. File servers, print servers, gateways, and workstations.

3. Its platform-independence, and its ability to embed applets inside a Web document.

Section 1.4

1. The values in memory cells a, b, and c are added, and the value is stored in the memory cell represented by x.

The value in memory cell y is divided by the value in memory cell z, and the result is stored in the memory cell represented by x.

The value in memory cell b is subtracted from the value in memory cell c, the value in a is added, and the result is stored in memory cell d.

The value in the memory cell represented by z has 1 added to it, and is stored back in the same location.

3. Methods and data.

5.

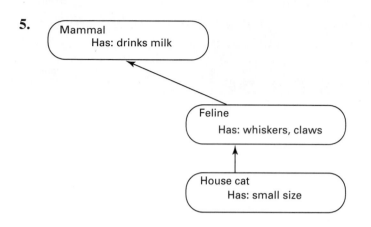

Section 1.5

1. A C program is compiled specifically for the underlying machine (IBM PC, Apple Macintosh, UNIX, etc.). A Java program is compiled to byte code, which is platform-independent.

3. A virtual machine allows cross-platform transparency by allowing many different models of computers to emulate a standard "Java computer."

Section 1.6

1. Spending a few minutes tracing your program to make sure it's working correctly can save you hours of wasted time trying to debug a program that wasn't designed well to begin with.

Section 1.7

1. The editor is used to create the source program.

3. The debugger can be used to identify errors when the program is run. You will probably need to go back to the editor to fix them.

Chapter 2

Section 2.1

1. 1. Specify the problem requirements.
   2. Analyze the problem.
   3. Design the classes to solve the problem by:
      a. Locating relevant classes in existing libraries.
      b. Modifying existing classes where necessary.

    c. Designing new classes where necessary.

    4. Implement the new and modified classes.

    5. Test and verify the completed program.

    6. Maintain and update the program.

3. Algorithms are developed in the Design phase. Problem inputs and outputs are identified in the Analysis phase.

Section 2.2

1. You would need a method to read square yards, a method to convert square yards to square meters, and a method to display the problem input (in square yards) and output (in square meters). You would also need a variable for the yards-to-meters conversion factor.

Section 2.3

1. Start by reading the steps of the main method in the application class.

3. A library is a file structure that contains definitions for standardized classes. A package is a named collection of classes.

5. An input statement reads data into memory. An output statement displays data stored in memory.

Section 2.4

1. Reserved words are words that have some special meaning to the Java compiler and that you are not allowed to use as identifier names.

3. **a.** `new`, `private`, `extends`, `static`

    b. `Bill`, `program`, `Rate`, `Start`, `XYZ_123`, `ThisIsAlongOne`

    c. `Sue's`, `123_XYZ`, `Y=Z`, `Prog#2`, `'MaxScores'`

Section 2.5

1. Integers (type `int`), real numbers (type `double`), Boolean (`true`/`false`) (type `boolean`), characters (type `char`).

3. Valid: `15` (int), `'*'` (char), `25.123` (double), `15.` (double), `-999` (int), `.123` (double), `'x'` (char), `"X"` (String), `'9'` (char), `true` (boolean)

    Invalid: `'XYZ'`, `$`, `'-5'`, `'True'`

5. The integer type (`int`) represents numbers, while the character type (`char`) represents characters.

7. `char` and `String` types are needed for processing text.

Section 2.6

1. A header declaration, the data field declarations of the class, and the method definitions of the class.
3. Initializing a data field means you assign it an initial value.
5. So they can be distinguished from reserved words and identifiers.

Section 2.7

1. An argument list is a means of passing data to a method as input.
3. Passing an argument means providing a method with input via its argument list.
5. The word `void` signifies that a method returns no data.

Chapter 3

Section 3.1

1. Data declarations and executable statements.
3. `x = 0, y = 0.0, z = 'a', testResult = false.`
5. A constructor is a class method used to initialize an instance of the class. We don't need one in `PieceOfFabric`, because we are going to rely on the default constructor.

Section 3.2

1. Because `displayFabric` and `readSqMeters` are both of type `void`, while `toSqYards` is type `double`.
3. Because `true` is not a valid return type for a function that needs to return a `double` (a floating-point value).
5. **a.** `x = getDouble("Enter number between -5.5 & 7.7:", -5.5, 7.7);`

    b. `ch = getChar("Type your first initial:", 'A', 'Z');`

    c. `n = getInt("Enter positive integer less than 100", 0, 99);`

    d. `str = getString("Enter your astrological sign:");`

Section 3.3

1. **a.** valid; `r = 8.5`   **f.** invalid
   b. valid; `i = 10`   **g.** invalid
   c. invalid   **h.** valid; `r = 10.0`
   d. invalid   **i.** invalid
   e. invalid   **j.** valid; `r = 20.0`

Section 3.4

1. **a.** $22/7 = 3$ $7/22 = 0$ $22\%7 = 1$ $7\%22 = 7$
   b. $15/16 = 0$ $16/15 = 1$ $15\%16 = 15$ $16\%15 = 1$
   c. $3/23 = 0$ $23/3 = 7$ $3\%23 = 3$ $23\%3 = 2$
   d. $-4/16 = -1$ $16/-1 = -4$ $-4\%16 = 12$ $16\%-4 = 0$

3.

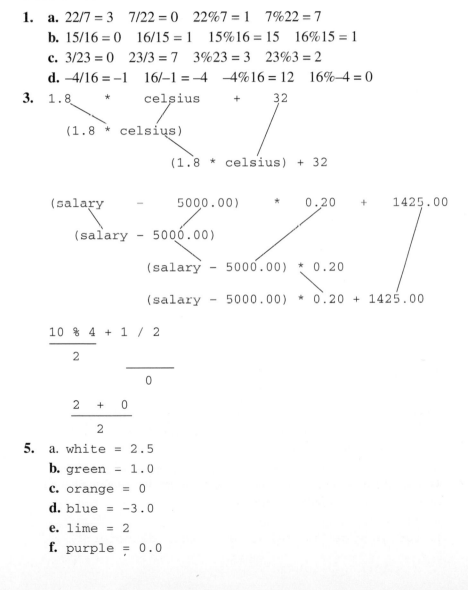

```
1.8        *        celsius        +        32

     (1.8 * celsius)

                     (1.8 * celsius) + 32


(salary      -      5000.00)      *      0.20      +      1425.00

    (salary - 5000.00)

                  (salary - 5000.00) * 0.20

                  (salary - 5000.00) * 0.20 + 1425.00


10 % 4 + 1 / 2
──────────────
     2
               ───
                0

    2  +  0
    ───────
       2
```

5. **a.** `white = 2.5`
   b. `green - 1.0`
   c. `orange = 0`
   d. `blue = -3.0`
   e. `lime = 2`
   f. `purple = 0.0`

7. **a.** `"value of x is 35"`

   b. `"value of x is 57"`

   c. `"value of x is 12"`

   d. `"T"`

   e. `"T"`, `ERROR`, `"This string"`, `" strin"`

9. **a.** `word2 = word1.substring(0, 4);`

   b. `word2 = "A" + word1.substring(2, 4) + "z";`

   c. `word2 = word1.substring(4, (word1.length() - 1));`

   d. `word2 = word1.substring((word1.length() / 2), (word1.length() - 1));`

Section 3.8

1. **a.** not invalid.

   b. Because `displayResult()` is not a method in class `PieceOfFabric`.

   c. Because the data member `sqMeters` is private.

   d. Again, data member `sqMeters` is private.

   e. We need to have the parentheses: `aPiece.readSqMeters();`

   f. There is no object called "`Piece`".

   g. The function needs to be called using the name of an object of type `PieceOfFabric`, followed by a dot (`.`).

Chapter 4

Section 4.1

1. The process of creating an outline clarifies your thought process and helps you plan what classes, data, methods, and algorithms you will need to use in writing your program. It also provides you with program documentation and comments.

3. The easiest approach is to keep `radius` as our only circle attribute. Because the user is providing the circle diameter, we need to change method `readRadius` as follows:

```
public double readRadius() {
    radius = getDouble("Enter circle diameter:") / 2;
}
```

Section 4.2

1. Problem Inputs:
hours worked
hourly rate

Problem Output:
`salary`—employee's gross salary

Specification for `Employee` class
Data Fields
`double numHours`
`double rate`

Need methods: `readEmpData`, `showEmp`, and `computeSalary`
Algorithm for `computeSalary`:
Compute `salary = numHours * rate`.

3. Add another Data Field:
`OTHours`—number of overtime hours

Algorithm for `computeSalary`:
1. Compute `salary = numHours * rate`
2. Add `OTHours * rate * 1.5 to salary`.

Section 4.3

1. Because a `PricedCircle` object is an extension of a `Circle` object, it inherits its properties, including its protected data. If the data fields in `Circle` were private, `PricedCircle` could not access them at all. We would then have to rewrite `PricedCircle` so it had many of the same data fields and methods as `Circle`, which would be redundant and a waste of time and memory.

Section 4.4

1. **a.** `u + v * Math.pow(w, 2)`

b. `Math.log(Math.pow(x, y))`

c. `Math.pow((x - y), 3)`

d. `Math.abs(x * y - w/z)`

e. `Math.sqrt(x * x + y * y)`

3. Class methods are methods that you reference directly, not through an instance of the class. Class methods are accessed by prefixing the name of the method with the name of the class. Instance methods are methods that must be called via an instance of the class. They are accessed by prefixing the name of the method with the name of an instance, or object, of that class.

Section 4.5

1. An accessor is a method that returns the value of one object's data field to another object.

3. Because an object might need to pass initial values to a new object it is creating.

5.
```java
public class Box {

    // Data Fields
    private int height;
    private int width;
    private int length;

    // constructors
    public Box()
       {height = 1; width = 1; length = 1;}
    public Box(int s)
       {height = s; width = s; length = s;}
    public Box(int squareBase, int h) {
         height = h;
         width = squareBase;
         length = squareBase;
    }

    public Box(int h, int w, int l)
       {height = h; width = w; length = l;}

    public double computeVolume () {
         return height * width * length;
    }

    public double computeSurfArea() {
         return 2 * width * length + 2 * height *
                          length + 2 * width * height;
    }

    // accessors
    public double getWidth() {return width;}
    public double getLength() {return length;}
    public double getHeight() {return height;}

    public void readCube() {
         height = getInt("Enter height:");
         width = getInt("Enter width:");
         length = getInt("Enter length:");
    }
```

```
    public void showCube() {
        displayResult("Volume is " +
                                computeVolume());
        displayResult("Surface area is " +
                                computeSurfArea());
    }

} // Box
```

7. If data fields are declared public, it is true that accessors and constructors are not needed. But these data fields then become subject to accidental modification by other classes. If you are writing long,
   complicated programs, or working with other programmers, this is a
   risk you won't want to take.

9. You may want to force classes to establish initial values for data fields
   when they establish a new instance of your class. By not providing a
   default constructor, you force other classes to use one of your constructors with arguments.

Section 4.6

1. Because most computer screens are in landscape orientation, which
   means that their height (*y*-value) is smaller than their width (*x*-value).

3. It represents an instance of the graphics class, so that we may call the
   methods of that class.

5. `g.drawRect(150, 250, 50, 50);`
   `g.drawRect(400, 250, 50, 50);`

7. Method `setColor` sets the drawing color. It is in effect until changed
   by another call to that method.

Chapter 5

Section 5.2

1. **a.** true
   b. false
   c. true
   d. true
3. **a.** true
   b. true
   c. true

    d. false

    e. true

5.   **a.** true

    b. true

    c. false

    d. false

    e. true

    f. positive

    g. negative

    h. false

    i. true

Section 5.3

1.   **a.** `Not less`

    b. `>`

3.   **a.** `Hi kiddo`
        `How was your day?`

    b. `Hi kiddo`

Section 5.4

1.
```
if (x > y) {
      x = x + 10.0;
      displayResult ("x bigger");
}
else
      displayResult ("x smaller");
displayResult ("y is " + y);
```
The last line will always execute.

3. Placing braces around the last two lines would make both lines be part of the `else` statement. Then, the last line would be executed only when `x <= y`.

Section 5.5

1. net pay = gross pay
    `if` union dues
        subtract union dues from net pay

3. If `gross` were declared as a data field of the `Employee` class, there would be no guarantee that it had been assigned a value by `computeGross` before another class method referenced it. For example, if `computeNet` were called before `computeGross`, the value of `gross` used by `computeNet` wouldn't have been properly assigned. The way the program example has been written guarantees that `gross` will have been assigned the proper value before other methods can access it.

Section 5.6

1. If hours is 50 and rate is 1, the condition in `computeGross` will be false, and gross pay will be assigned 55, which will make the condition in `computeNet` true.

Section 5.7

1. salary   tax

   | 13500 | | ? |

   All conditions are false until `salary < 15000.0` is evaluated.

   `tax` is `(13500 - 8000) * 0.25 + 1425.00 = 5500 * 0.25 + 1425 = 2800`

Section 5.8

1. ```
if (x == 2)
      displayResult ("Snake Eyes!");
else if (x == 7 || x == 11)
      displayResult ("Win!");
else
      displayResult ("Try again.");
```

3. ```
public String showGrade (char grade) {
      switch (grade) {
            case 'A':
            case 'B':
            case 'C':
                  return "Passing";
            case 'D':
            case 'F':
                  return "No credit";
            default:
                  return "Invalid grade";
      }
}
```

Chapter 6

Section 6.1

1. The loop is repeated three times.

   Here is the output:

   ```
   9
   27
   81
   81
   ```

3. If the last statement in the loop body were deleted, the condition for ending the loop would never be met, and it would repeat "forever."

Section 6.2

1.
   ```
   1
   5
   25
   125
   ```

3.
   ```
   int x = getInt("Enter an integer:");
   int product = 1;
   int count = 0;
   while (count < 4) {
         displayResult(product);
         product *= x;
         count++;
   }
   ```

5. After the end of `displayPayTotals`, add the statements:
   ```
   displayResult("The average gross salary is " +
                           totalGross / numberEmp);
   displayResult("The average net salary is " +
                           totalNet / numberEmp);
   ```

Section 6.3

1. 0

3.

Step	balance	bill	Effect
	150.00		
Is balance positive?			Yes, execute loop.
Get the next bill.		75.00	
Pay it in full.			150 >= 75, pay $75
Deduct payment from balance.	75.00		

Step	balance	bill	Effect
Is balance positive?			Yes, execute loop.
Get the next bill.		50.00	
Pay it in full.			75 >= 50, pay $50
Deduct payment from balance.	25.00		
Is balance positive?			Yes, execute loop.
Get the next bill.		25.00	
Pay it in full.			25 >= 25, pay $25
Deduct payment from balance.	0		
Is balance positive?			No, exit loop.

Section 6.4

1. Because you only want to add the score to the sum if the score read in during the current loop iteration was not the sentinel. If the assignment statement was moved, the score would be added to sum, even if it was −1. This is not a data value, but is the signal that there is no more data. Also, the first score read in (before the loop was entered) would not be counted in the total!

3.
```
nextBill.readBill();
while (balance > 0 && nextBill.getAmount() != 0) {
    balance = nextBill.payBill(balance);
    nextBill.readBill();
}
```

Section 6.5

1.

Step	j	i	Output	
j = 10	10	?		
for ()	10	1		
displayResult()			1	10
j -= 2	8	1		
for ()	8	2		
displayResult()			2	8
j -= 2	6	2		
for ()	6	3		
displayResult()			3	6
j -= 2	4	3		
for ()	4	4		

Step	j	i	Output	
displayResult()			4	4
j -= 2	2	4		
for ()	2	5		
displayResult()			5	2
j -= 2	0	5		
for ()		<loop terminates here>		

3. **a.** for (int celsius = -10; celsius <= 10; celsius++)
   b. for (int celsius = 100; celsius >= 1; celsius--)
   c. for (int celsius = 15; celsius <= 50; celsius++)
   d. for (int celsius = 50; celsius >= -75; celsius--)

Section 6.6

1. A series of 10 ovals would be drawn, each of a different color as defined by method defineColor(). Each oval will be drawn to the right and overlapping the one drawn immediately before it.

Section 6.7

1.

Step	m	n	Effect
if ()	4	3	Condition is false.
else	4	3	Call mystery(4, 2).
if ()	4	2	Condition is false.
else	4	2	Call mystery(4, 1).
if ()	4	1	Condition is true.
return m			Return 4.
return m * m			Return 4 * 4 or 16.
return m * m * m			Return 4 * 16 or 64.

mystery returns the value of m raised to the power n.

Section 6.8

1.
```
count = 0;
while (count <= n) {
    System.out.println("***** count is " + count);
    sum += count;
    count++;
    System.out.println("***** sum is " + sum);
}
```

Chapter 7

Section 7.1

1.
```
double y;
double x3;
double[] x = new double[4];
```

3. **a.** `double[] roomSize = new double[5];`

   b. `int[] numStu = new int[6];`

   c. `char[] color = new char[30];`

   d. `String[] javaColors = {"black", "gray", "magenta", "red", "blue", "green", "orange", "white", "cyan", "lightGray", "pink", "yellow", "darkGray"}`

   e. `String[] daysOfWeek = {"Saturday", "Sunday", "Monday", "Tuesday", "Wednesday", "Thursday", "Friday"}`

   f. `String[] familyNames = {"Mom", "Dad", "Bill", "Fred", "Helen"}`

Section 7.2

1.
```
x[i] = x[i] + 10.0;   // adds 10.0 to x[3],
                      // making it 36.0
x[i - 1] = x[2 * i - 1];   // changes value of x[2]
                           // to 12.0
x[i + 1] = x[2 * i] + x[2 * i + 1];   // changes
                           // value of x[4] to -40.5
for (i = 5; i <= 7; i++)
    x[i] = x[i + 1];   // copies x[6] through x[8]
                       // into x[5] through x[7]
for (i = 3; i >= 1; i--)
    x[i + 1] = x[i];   // copies x[1] through x[3]
                       // into x[2] through x[4]
```

Section 7.3

1. **a.** Creates an array of 10 integers and assigns them the values 1 through 10.

   b. Creates an array of 10 integers.

   c. Creates another array of 10 integers.

   d. Copies the first half of the array in x to the array in y, starting with y[5].

   e. Copies half of the elements in x, starting with x[5], to the beginning of array y.

   f. Creates a new array z, whose elements are the sums of the corresponding elements in x and y.

Section 7.4

1. a. The index of the last score is returned.

   b. The index of the first score that matches the target is returned.

3. In each pass through the subarray, look for the biggest value instead of the smallest, and exchange it with the first element in the subarray.

Section 7.5

1. n	n^2	n^3	2^n
1	1	1	2
2	4	8	4
3	9	27	8
4	16	64	16
5	25	125	32
10	100	1000	1024
100	10,000	1,000,000	1.26765060023E 30
1000	1,000,000	1,000,000,000	too large to compute

Section 7.6

1. To avoid an error of trying to divide by zero.

Section 7.7

```
1. for (int i = 0; i < employees.size(); i++)
       (Employee) employees.elementAt(i).showEmpData();
3. Vector n = new Vector();   // creates an empty vector
                               // called n
   n.addElement(new Integer(5));   // adds the value 5
                                   // at element 0
   n.addElement(new Integer(8));   // adds the value 8
                                   // at element 1
   n.setElementAt(new Integer(6), 0); // changes
                                       // element 0 to 6
```

```
n.insertElementAt(new Integer(3), 2);   // inserts
                             // new element at index
                             // 2 with the value 3
int k = ((Integer)n.ElementAt(2)).intValue();
                             // assigns 3 to variable k
n.removeElementAt(1);   // deletes the element at
                    // position 1,
                    // and moves the remaining elements
                    // forward to fill its space
displayResult("Size is " + n.size());   // displays
                         // the size of the vector
                         // i.e., "Size is 2"
```

Section 7.8

1.
```
try {
    SimpleWriter outFile = new
                            SimpleWriter("MyStats");
    outFile.putData("Bill Jones");
    outFile.putData(26);
    outFile.putData('M');
    outFile.putData("139-55-4567");
}
```

Section 7.9

1. **a.** 20

    b. `displayResult(matrix[2] [3]);`

    c. `matrix[4][3]`

Chapter 8

Section 8.1

1. The sender is the object that is requesting some operation be performed. The receiver is the object that is being asked to perform this task.

3. Accessors provide public access to private data members in a way that preserves encapsulation and protection. Modifiers allow another object to change the value of the private data. A constructor is invoked in order to create a new class instance or object. A destructor does what its name implies, destroying objects and freeing memory once the objects are no longer needed.

Section 8.2

1. Because `width` and `length` are private data members of class `IntRectangle`, they cannot be accessed directly by other classes. They could be accessed directly if they were defined as `public`, or perhaps `protected`, data members.

Section 8.3

1. If accessors and modifiers were not defined as `public`, it would defeat their whole purpose, because objects of other classes would not be able to access them.

3. Data fields `width` and `length` represent essential attributes of a `DoubleWide` object as well as an `IntRectangle` object, so they should be directly accessible. It would be awkward for a `DoubleWide` object to have to use accessors and modifiers to manipulate its attributes.

Section 8.4

1. Overloading occurs when two methods have the same name, but different argument lists. Overriding occurs when a subclass modifies a method of its parent class to adapt it for its purposes.

3. `super` is used by a subclass in order to call the superclass. This is the only way to call a superclass constructor without actually creating an object of the superclass.

Section 8.5

1. Because a square is a special type of rectangle, but unlike most subclasses, it requires fewer data members, not more, than its parent class. In other words, we need to know two things about a rectangle: its length, and its width. For a square, we only need to know one thing: the length of any side.

3. If `IntRectangle` contained the following method definition:

```
public void setDimensions(int w, int l) {
     width = w;
     length = l;
}
```

`Square` should contain the following overridden method definition:

```
public void setDimensions(int s) {
     width = s;
     length = s;
}
```

Section 8.6

1. All instances of class `Sample` share the data fields `sum` and `count` because they are defined as `static`, so they are maintained by the class. These data fields can be accessed through accessors that are also defined as `static`.

3.
```
if (s1.getMyValue() > s2.getMyValue())
     system.out.println(s1.getMyValue());
else
     system.out.println(s2.getMyValue());
```

Section 8.7

1. A class is abstract when it includes only the most basic, general data and methods that all its subclasses will be able to use without modification, and declarations for methods that will be implemented differently in each subclass.

3. Methods that will be implemented in subclasses, as well as data members and methods common to all subclasses, may be declared in an abstract class.

Section 8.8

1. An interface is even more specialized than an abstract class, in that it only allows abstract methods and `final` class data fields (data fields that cannot be redefined). A class may extend only one class but it may implement many interfaces.

3. Because an interface cannot be instantiated, a data field is like a class data field, so it should be static. If a data field were not `static` `final`, it would be possible for each class that implements the interface to change the data field's value. The new value may not be what is expected by another class that implements the interface.

Chapter 9

Section 9.1

1. A client is a piece of software running on a number of distributed computers. It requests information from a server or servers that are kept at a central location.

3. An event is a mouse-click or other action performed by a computer user to control a program's operation.

5. Protocols are important so that systems may communicate with one another in a way that ensures accurate transfer of information between computers that "speak a different language" from one another.

Section 9.2

1. `init()`—initializes the applet; `start()`—starts the applet running; `stop()`—stops the applet; and `destroy()`—destroys the applet.
3. **1.** For each component, create an object of the proper type.
   2. For each object created in step 1 that is a panel, repeat this procedure for the components contained in this subpanel.
   3. Add all the components created in step 1 to the panel.

Section 9.3

1. An event generator is an object that generates events. An event listener is an object that listens for, and responds to, certain types of events.
3. It makes the applet a listener of object `aText`.

Section 9.4

1. A thread is an independent sequence of steps in a program.
3. Yielding causes a thread to give up control of the CPU to another thread until the other thread yields or finishes what it is doing. Putting a thread to sleep causes the thread to suspend execution for a minimum length of time, whether other threads are ready to occupy the CPU or not.

Section 9.5

1. The balls are redrawn in the same position but in different colors, giving them the appearance of blinking.
3. Because the graphics context `g` used for drawing in class `Ball` is derived from the `Canvas` object in `BlinkingBall`.

Section 9.6

1. Method `getParameter` allows an applet to retrieve parameter values from an HTML file.
3. It creates an array of balls. The size of the array is specified as a parameter in the HTML file, and if invalid, the applet defaults to 2 balls.

Chapter 10

Section 10.1

1. Working with different levels of abstraction allows a programmer to solve problems in a structured way, and to leave the implementation of details to subclasses, or to classes and methods already defined as part of the Java class libraries.

3. A layout manager controls the size and position of elements in a container. It calculates size and position and gives graphics directives to components. It manages the repositioning of components if the container's size and position change.

Section 10.2

1. The `Font` class contains methods that allow you to define a new `Font` object by providing it with a shape, style, and size. The `FontMetric` class contains methods for determining the size and spacing of characters.

3. The advantage of layout managers is that you don't have to worry about managing the low-level details of a user interface; you can leave these decisions to the layout manager methods.

5. You can specify the horizontal and vertical spacing of elements through the layout manager's argument list.

Section 10.3

1. ```
Button: ActionEvent
TextArea: TextEvent
TextField: TextEvent
Choice: ItemEvent
List: ItemEvent
Checkbox: ItemEvent
```

3. For a `CheckboxGroup`, only one checkbox may be enabled at a time. Any number of checkboxes may be enabled for a group of individual checkboxes in a panel.

## Section 10.4

1. Scroll bars are useful when you want to make more text available to a user than can be displayed in a single window, or where you want the user to be able to select from a continuum of values. Scroll bars would be inappropriate for an interface in which you will only be displaying a
```

few lines of text, or where a user will enter either discrete values or textual information. For example, a scroll bar would be inappropriate if you wanted the user to select one choice from a menu of choices.

3. A text field displays only a single line of text and allows only one line of text to be entered, while a text area allows multiple lines of text to be displayed.

Section 10.5

1. `mouseClicked()`—the mouse button was clicked
`mouseEntered()`—the mouse entered the component
`mouseExited()`—the mouse left the component
`mousePressed()`—the mouse button was pressed
`mouseReleased()`—the mouse button was released
`mouseMoved()`—the mouse was moved with no button pressed
`mouseDragged()`—the mouse was moved with a button pressed

Section 10.6

1. The four classes are needed for the scorekeeper, the abstract player class, the human player, and the computer player. The abstract player class is used because the human player and the computer player have so much in common. This way, all the methods they share only need to be written once, and only need to be loaded into memory once.

Section 10.7

1. A frame is derived from a window, but is resizable and has a title bar. Also, you can add menus to a frame. Panels are containers that are used to hold applets and other containers.

3. You could write a new `windowClosing()` method that does not call the `dispose()` method, but merely deactivates the window.

Chapter 11

Section 11.1

1. Calculate 5^4 ⟶ Calculate 5^3 ⟶ Calculate 5^2 ⟶ Calculate 5^1

Multiply 5^3 by 5   Multiply 5^2 by 5   Multiply 5^1 by 5

3. 4
3
2
2
3
4

Section 11.2

1. Method `puzzle` computes the log (base 2) of *n* or the number of times *n* can be divided by 2. When *n* is 2, the result is 1.

3. Complete the following recursive method, which calculates the result of raising an integer (`base`) to a power (`power`). The value of `power` can be positive, negative, or zero. You should provide two stopping cases.

```
public static double powerRaiser(int base,
                                 int power) {
    if (base == 0)
        return 0;
    else if (power == 0)
        return 1;
    else if (power < 0)
        return 1.0 /
                (double) powerRaiser(base, -power);
    else
        return power *
                powerRaiser(base, power - 1);
}
```

Section 11.3

1. Stack after first recursive call: |q
Stack after second recursive call: |qw
Stack after third recursive call: |qwe
Stack after fourth recursive call: |qwer
Stack after fifth recursive call: |qwer*
Stack after first return: |qwer, so r is popped and displayed.
Stack after second return: |qwe, so e is popped and displayed.
Stack after third return: |qw, so w is popped and displayed.
Stack after fourth return: |q, so q is popped and displayed.

3. Change the `if` statement as follows:

```
if (next == '*')
    displayResult(next);
else {
    reverse();
    displayResult(next);
}
```

Section 11.4

1. `int[] x = {1, 15, 10}; int[] y = {1, 5, 7};`
`isEqual(x, y, 3)`—returns `false` from the initial call, `x[2] != y[2]` is `true`.

2. `int[] x = {1, 15, 10};`

`search(x, 15, 3)`—generates the recursive call `search(x, 15, 2)`. Because `x[1] == 15` is `true`, returns 1. This result is passed up unchanged.

`search(x, 3, 3)`—generates the recursive call `search(x, 3, 2)`, which generates the recursive call `search(x, 3, 1)`. Because `x[0] == 3` is `false`, returns −1. This result is passed up unchanged.

3. It returns the smallest value in elements 0 through *n* − 1 of its array argument.

5. `reverseStr("tick")`—generates the following sequence of recursive calls: `'k' + (reverseStr("tic"))` →
`'k' + ('c' + reverseStr("ti"))` →
`'k' + ('c' + ('i' + reverseStr("t")))` →
`'k' + ('c' + ('i' + 't')))`. The resulting string is: `"kcit"`.

Section 11.5

1. `binSearch(table, 40, 0, 8)`, middle value is 45 →
`binsearch(table, 40, 0, 3)`, middle value is 35 →
`binsearch(table, 40, 2, 3)`, middle value is 37 →
`binsearch(table, 40, 3, 3)`, middle value is 40, so method call returns 3, which is passed all the way up.

Section 11.6

1. Problems generated from "Move three disks from peg B to peg A."
 1. Move two disks from peg B to peg C.
  1.1 Move 1 disk from B to A.
  1.2 Move disk 2 from B to C.
  1.3 Move 1 disk from A to C.

2. Move disk 3 from B to A.

3. Move two disks from peg C to peg A.

    3.1 Move 1 disk from C to B.

    3.2 Move disk 2 from C to A.

    3.3 Move 1 disk from B to A.

Problems generated from "Move three disks from peg A to peg C."

1. Move two disks from peg A to peg B.

    1.1 Move 1 disk from A to C.

    1.2 Move disk 2 from A to B.

    1.3 Move 1 disk from C to B.

2. Move disk 3 from A to C.

3. Move two disks from peg B to peg C.

    3.1 Move 1 disk from B to A.

    3.2 Move disk 2 from B to C.

    3.3 Move 1 disk from A to C.

Section 11.7

1. The button at grid point [1, 1] is filled, so we generate calls to `findBlob` for each of its eight neighbors. Four of them are filled: [0, 0], [0, 1], [1, 2], and [2, 2]. In visiting each filled cell, we come across no other cells that are filled, so the final answer will be 5.

The button at grid point [2, 1] is empty, so we return 0.

Chapter 12

Section 12.1

1. **a.** Deletes node containing `"top"`.

    b. Deletes two middle nodes. List contains `"in"`, `"hat"`.

    c. `head` references node containing `"top"`.

    d. Node referenced by `p` contains `"top"`, not `"the"`.

    e. Node referenced by `p` contains `"hat"`, not `"the"`.

    f. Appends a new node with `"zzz"` to the end of the list.

    g. Stores `null` in the link field of the node referenced by `p`. List now has just two nodes.

    h. Stores `"hat"` in the node referenced by `p`.

i. Deletes the last list element.

j. Counts the number of nodes (4) in the list.

3. Traverse the list, starting at the list head. If the link field of the current node references the node to be deleted, then copy the link field of the node to be deleted into the current node's link field.

```
ListNode next = head;
while (next.link != toDelete)
    next = next.link;
next.link = toDelete.link;
```

Section 12.2

1. Method `pop` retrieves the value at the top of the stack and removes it from the stack, whereas method `peek` just retrieves the value at the top of the stack without removing it.

3. Add a data field:

   private int `numItems`;

   Method `push` should increment `numItems` by 1 and method `pop` should decrement `numItems` by 1. There should be an accessor for field `numItems`.

Section 12.3

1. After insertion, queue contents is `McMann`, `Wilson`, `Carson`, `Harris`; `first` references `McMann` and `rear` references `Harris`. After removal (of `McMann`), queue contents is `Wilson`, `Carson`, `Harris`; `first` references `Wilson` and `rear` references `Harris`. There are three customers in the queue.

3. ```
public void insert(Object item) {

        if (isEmpty()) { //empty queue
            // Link rear and front to only node.
            front = new QueueNode(item);
            rear = front;
        } else // insert at front of a non-empty queue
            front = new QueueNode(item, front);

        size++;   //Increment queue size.
    }
```
```

Section 12.4

1. The tree on the left is a binary search tree, the tree on the right is not. Inorder traversal of left tree: 10, 15, 20, 40, 50, 55, 60. Inorder traversal of right tree: 25, 30, 45, 40, 50, 55, 60.

   You would expect to find key values less than 50 in the left subtree of the node containing key 50.

3.
```
        25
       /  \
     15    45
    /        \
  10          60
    \        /
    12      55
```

```
        25
       /  \
     12    55
    / \    / \
  10  15 45  60
```

```
       25
      /  \
    12    55
   / \   / \
 10  15 45  60
```

```
    10
      \
      12
        \
        15
          \
          25
            \
            45
              \
              55
                \
                60
```

   Trees (b) and (c) would be most efficient to search because they are full binary trees (no holes). Searching these trees is an $O(\log n)$ process. Each node in the tree in (d) has an empty left subtree. Searching it would be an $O(n)$ process, the same as for a linked list.

Section 12.5

1. Each method call would insert its string argument in the tree, except for the second attempt to insert string `"cat"`.

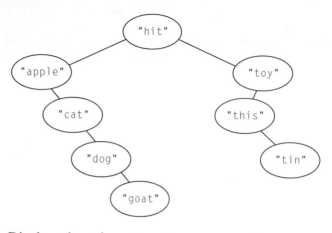

Displays the strings: `"apple"`, `"cat"`, `"dog"`, `"goat"`, `"hit"`, `"this"`, `"tin"`, `"toy"`.

3. The first case is deleting a node with no subtrees—just delete the node. The second case is deleting a node with only one subtree—the link from the parent node to the node being deleted should be changed to connect the parent node to the subtree of the node being deleted. The third case is deleting a node with two subtrees—overwrite the key in the node to be deleted with the value in the leftmost node of the right subtree and delete that node instead.

Section 12.6

1. Given the binary tree below, how many comparisons are needed to find each of the following keys or to determine that the key is not present? List the keys compared to the target for each search.

   a. 40 < 50, 50 == 50 (two comparisons)

   b. 40 < 55, 50 < 55, 60 > 55, 55 == 55 (4 comparisons)

   c. 40 > 10, 15 > 10, 10 == 10 (3 comparisons)

   d. 40 < 65, 50 < 65, 60 < 65 (3 comparisons)

   e. 40 < 52, 50 < 52, 60 > 52, 55 > 52 (4 comparisons)

   f. 40 < 48, 50 > 48 (2 comparisons)

3. Each node will have a right subtree only. The search time is $O(n)$.

Index

A

abs 136
abstract class 425, **428, 429,** 434, 561
abstract data type **382**
abstract object 35
Abstract Window Toolkit (AWT) 17, 150, 458, 508-510
abstraction **37, 381-382,** 508
abstraction layer 508
accessor 386
accessor method **143**
accumulate a sum 250
accumulator **250**
acos 136
action event 531
ActionEvent 509, 514, 528, 548, 575
ActionListener 464, 509, 553, 575
actionPerformed 465, 531, 548, 622
activation frame **589**
addActionListener 464, 531
addChoice 224
addItem 539
address **5,** 14
AdjustmentEvent 514, 545
AdjustmentListener 545
adjustmentValueChanged 545
algorithm **34,** 198, 208, 671
algorithm refinement **37**
algorithm simplification 344
Altair 2
analog signal **11**

analysis of an algorithm 336
analyzing the problem 36
anatomy of memory 5
ancestor 655
and operator && 181
animated balls 486
animated GIF 453, 485
animation 13, 452, 470, 485
Apple 2
Applet 13, 21, 150, 448, 455, 457, 462, 491, 571
applet context **455,** 461, 571
applet parameter tag 494
applet tag 455
appletviewer 150
application 21, 41, 150, 571
Application Programmer's Interface (API) **405**
application software **15**
argument 62, 325
  correspondence 327
  list **61,** 77
arithmetic expression 86
  operation 86
  overflow **111**
array **307**
  argument 325, 327
  assignment 323
  declaration 307
  element **307,** 311
  index **309**
  length 313
  of arrays 359
  of objects 339
  search 330

size 308, 313
arraycopy 324, 325
asin 136
assignment compatible **85**
  operator **83**
  statement **83,** 188
atan 136
Atanasoff, Dr. John 2
AWTEvent 463, 510, 513

B

Banner 515, 516
BASIC 15
best-case analysis 671
Big-O notation 336, 671
Bill class 259-263
binary search 608
  search tree **656**
  string 13
  tree 654, **655**
bit **6**
blank space 107
BlinkingBalls 486, 488
blob 620
BlobApplet 622
block **73**
BOLD 518
boolean 52, 53, 348,
  assignment 188
  expression 178, 180, 189, 247
  flag 269
  operator 181
  variable 178
booleanValue 348

boot instructions 7
BorderLayout 513, 520
BorderLayout manager 520
break 220
browser 12, 21, 150, 449, 453,
    461, 491, 493, 571
browser/applet interaction 453,
    491
button **10**
Button 150, 457, 462, 509, 512,
    521, 527
byte **6**
byte 52
byte code **20**, 25

C

C 15
C++ 15
calling method 76
CalorieCounter 534
Canvas 457, 471, 512, 514
CardLayout 513, 523
case 220
case label 220
    sensitive 50
casting 91
catch block 234, 351
CD-ROM 8
ceil 136, 141, 142
CENTER 520
central processor unit (CPU) **8**
Cerf, Vinton **174**
CERN 12
CGI script 492
char 52, 54
char comparison 185
character 52, 185
Character 348
charAt 94, 199
charValue 348
check box 179
Checkbox 457, 458, 512, 527,
    532, 536
CheckboxGroup 512, 527, 536

CheckingAccount 258-263
children 655
Choice 457, 512, 527, 536, 541
circular list **638**
class **16**
    data field **418**
    definition 56, 58
    member 418
    method **133**, 422
    path error 111
    reuse 23
    versus interfaces 441
classpath **47**, 111
ClickMe 468–469
client **383**, 453
client/server model 449
close 354
COBOL 15
Color 152, 286, 498, 544-550
color mixer 421
comment **46**, 107, 108, 110, 120
Common Gateway Interface (CGI)
    453, 492
communication between objects
    383
Company 253
Comparable interface 669
compareTo 187, 665, 669
comparison 180
    of if and while 248
compiler 20, **25**
complement 180
Component 455, 457, 458, 462,
    467, 471, 510, 512
ComponentEvent 514, 554
compound
    operator 251
    statement **177**, 195
computer chip **2**
    graphics **149**
    network **11**
concatenate **93**
condition 184
connecting nodes 633
consequent 191

constant 207, 421
constructor **75**, 145, 386, 393
    definition 388
    method 145
container 455
Container 455, 457, 458, 462
containment hierarchy 459
contents **6**
control structure **177**
control timing 477
convention **106**
copying an array 324
cos 136
counter **246**
counter-controlled loop **246**
counting cells 620
counting loop **246**
createMenu 224
creating a data file 354
cross-platform transparency 19
cursor **9**

D

dangling comment 110
data
    declaration 59, 60, **73**
    entry error 111
    field 49, 58, 394
    file **350**
    structure **307**
    transfer **508**
    type **52**, 110
debugger 25
debugging **108**, 111, 290
decision steps 198
declaring data field 389
declaring counter variables 276
decrement operator 251
default 222
default
    constructor **75**, 388
    initialization 75
    package **47**
    values for data fields 394

visibility 397
defensive programming 232
defining class methods 146
deiconify a window **573**
delimiter **46**
dependent variable **385**, 389
descendants 655
design consideration 257
designing a GUI 466
desk check 24, 37, 208
destroy 456
destructor 386
diagnostic output 111, 290
digital signal **11**
disabling 553
disjoint subtrees 655
disk drive **7**
display
    array 350
    binary search tree 659
    boolean value 178
    two-dimensional array 361
displayResult 80, 178
displayRow 350
dispose 574
division 86
documentation 120
double 52
Double 348
DoubleValue 348
doubly linked list 654
do-while 271
DrawableRect 391
drawing surface **149**
drawLine 152
drawRect 152
drawString 155, 161

E

EAST 520
EditableString 226, 229
editor **25**
efficiency
    algorithm 336, 671

binary search tree 671
elementAt 346
else 191
Employee 201-205
encapsulation **381**, **396**, 403
ENIAC 2
EOF 354
equality operator **180**
equals 186
error trapping 562
escape sequence **54**
essential data 102
Euclid's algorithm 592
European Laboratory for Particle
    Physics (CERN) 12
event **448**, 527, 531
    generator **463**
    handling **448**
    listener **463**
    model **462**, 560
event-driven programming 273
event-handling method **466**
Event 512
EventListener 512
    interface 464
Exam class 317
exception **233**, 351
executable statement **73**
exit 574
exp 137
expression **73**, 86
extend 17, 130
extending
    class 58
    problem solution 125

F

FaceCanvas 472
factorial 288
false 52, 178
fetching an instruction **8**
Fibonacci numbers 593
file **7**
file server **12**

FileNotFoundException 351
fillArc 161
filled figure 159
filter the data 508
final 421
findBlob 620
findMedian 335
FirstGUI 460
first-in-first-out (FIFO) **648**
fixed disk 7
flag **269**
float 52
floor 137, 141, 142
floppy disk **7**
flowchart **191**
FlowLayout 459, 513, 520
Font 518
font metrics 518
for 274
formatting tag 450
formula 92
FORTRAN 15
Frame 150, 571, 575
full name 47
function composition 485
function key **9**

G

garbage collector **386**
gateway **12**
general graphics program 159
generator 463
GeoFigure 427
geometric figure 427
geometric pattern 281
getBackground 467
getBoolean 178, 354
getChar 81, 354
getChoice 225
getDouble 81, 354
getFontMetrics 516, 519
getInt 81, 354
getParameter 495
getSelectedItem 532, 539

getSource 471, 531
getState 532
getString 80, 354
getText 532
GIF 453
Graphical User Interface (GUI)
    10, 447, 466, 507
graphics 13, 149, 281
Graphics 149, 471, 512, 515
graphics context **149**, 515
Graphics in SimpleGUI 284
greatest common divisor 592
grid 621
GridBagLayout 513
GridLayout 513, 521
growth rate 336
GUI 10, 447, 466, 507
    programming 150
    window 80

H

hand-tracing 208
hard disk **7**
hardware **4**
"has a" relationship 426
head of a list **635**
hierachical organization 425
high-level language **14**
home page 150, 449
HTML 491, 495
    form **453**
    tag 494
hypertext link **449**
HyperText Transfer Protocol
    (HTTP) 449

I

icon **9**
iconify a window **573**
identifier **49**
if 191, 192
    one consequent 193

two alternatives 193
image processing 619
implementation 38
implementing an interface 441
implements 441
import **47**, 400
incorrect data type 110
increment operator 251
independent variable 389
index 309
indexed variable **309**
indexOf 200, 227
infinite loop **249**
information hiding **397**
Infoseek 492
inheritance 16, **58**, 130, **381**, 414,
    425
init 456, 461, 622
initializing
    array 307
    data field **59**, 394
    two-dimensional array 361
inorder traversal **659**
input 36
    abstraction 510
    data 48
    file **351**
    operation **48**
input/output 508
insertElementAt 346
inserting node
    in binary search tree 658
    in list 634
instance 16
    member 418
    method **133**
int 52, 97
IntArray **600**
integer **52**, 97
    division 87
Integer 348
integrated programming environ-
    ment (IPE) **25**
interactive applet 462

interface **440**
Internet **11**
    Explorer 150
interpreter **20**, 25
IntRectangle 385
intValue 348
invalidate 467
IOException 351, 358
"is a" relationship 426
ITALIC 518
item event source 536
ItemEvent 514, 532
itemStateChanged 532, 537

J

Java 13
Java Virtual Machine **20**, 21, 25
java.awt 150

K

keyboard 9
keyboard event 551

L

Label 457, 462, 512, 514
language standard **15**
last-in-first-out (LIFO) **640**
layout manager 467, 513, 520
LayoutManager 459, 510, 512
leaf node **655**
left
    associative 89
    subtree **655**
length 94, 313
level of abstraction 509
lexicographic order **187**
library **47**, **401**
line break 107
link **12**, **632**
linked list **632**, 640
Lisp 15

List 512, 527, 539
    component 531, 536
listener 463, 531, 536
literal **59**, 207
local-area network (LAN) **11**
log 137
logic error **111**
long 52
loop **246**
    body **246**
    boundary 291
    control 266
    control variable **249**
    design 266
    repetition condition **246**
lower-level user input 554
low-level event **510**

M

Mac OS 26
machine language **13**
main 41, 423
main memory 5, 6
mainframe 2
maintenance 38, 207, 264
matching else with if 212
Math 133
mathematical formula 92
max 137
median value 334
member **399**
memory cell **5**
menu **10**, 220, **224**, 571
Menu 510, 575
MenuBar 575
MenuComponent 512, 528, 571,
    575
menu-driven loop 271
MenuItem 575
message **383**, 464
message passing 384
method **15**, 72
    body **73**

call 78
    overloading **410**
    overriding 411
    signature **410**
microcomputer 2
min 137
minicomputer 2
mixed-type assignment 87, **88**
mixed-type expression **87**
mixing break statements 223
modem (modulator/demodulator)
    11
modifier **143**, 385
modular programming **390**
monitor 9
mouse **9**, 458
mouse event 555
mouseClicked 555
MouseDemo 555
mouseDragged 557
mouseEntered 555
MouseEvent 554, 557
MouseEventListener 555
mouseExited 555
MouseMotionListener 557
mouseMoved 557
mousePressed 555
mouseReleased 555
multidimensional array **359**
multimedia **13**
multiple
    inheritance **439**
    operators 89
    processes 477
    alternative decision 211, **213**
multiplication 92
multiprocessing 456, 485

N

name/value pair 491
negation 181
nested if **211**
    compared to switch 223

nested loop 362
Netscape 150
network 11, 19
network protocol **449**
NewCompany class 341
no object file error 111
no package declared 401
node 632
NORTH 520
not operator ! 181

O

object **16**, 339
    creation 85
    instance 41, 74
    instantiation **74**
    program **19**
object-oriented 102
    design 381, 508
    language 15
    programming 15, **34**
off-by-one error 291
operating system **25**
operation code **14**
operator precedence 89, 182
or operator || 181
order of conditions 215
ordinal data type **220**
output 36
    abstraction 509
    data 48
    device 10
    file **351**
    operation **48**

P

package **47, 397**
package declaration 399
paint 461, 471, 515, 517
Panel 150, 455, 457-459, 462,
    471
param 494

parameter tag 494
parent class **16**
parent of node 655
parentheses rule 89
Pascal 15, 34
    triangle 363
passing an argument **62**
payroll computation 252
picture element 149
pie slice 161
Pig Latin 102, 198
pixel **149**
PLAIN 518
platform independence **13**
plug-in application **453**
polymorphism **381**, 405, **407**
    across classes 407
popping the stack **640**
postcondition 589
pow 137
power 588
precedence 89, 182
precondition 589
predefined method 133
priming read 268
primitive type **52**
print server **12**
printer **10**
println 111
printStackTrace 351
private **57**, **123**
problem solving 23
program **4**
    documentation **107**
    flag **269**
prompting message **10**
protected **123**
protected visibility 130, 401
protocol 464
pseudocode **202**
public **57**
public data field 395
pull-down menu **10**
pushing the stack **640**
putData 353

Q
quadratic sort 337
queue **648**
Queue 649
QueueNode 649
Quilt 282

R
raise to the power 588
random 137, 139
random access 368
random access memory (RAM)
    7
rational operators 180
readability 207
reading
    boolean value 178
    data into an array 316
    from a file 353
    programs 46
read-only memory (ROM) **7**
real number 52
recipient of message **383**
rectangle 152
recursion 287, 588
    as a conceptual tool 603
    with strings 605
recursive
    algorithm 591
    mathematical method 592
    method **287**, **588**
    problem 590
    step **588**
referencing data and methods 78
remainder operator 87
removeElement 347
removing a node 636
repaint 532
replaceRange 553
reserved word **49**
result type 61
retrieve
    array of values 355
    data from a file 353

single value **6**
return statement **79**, 223
return value **61**, 79
returning an array 327
reuse 133, 257, 390, 426
right subtree **655**
rint 137
root node **655**
round 137
row length 363
Runnable interface 483
run-time error **110**
Russo, Anthony **377**

S
scope of a variable **206**
Scrollbar 512, 527, 544, 548
search 331
search service 492
searching
    array 330
    binary search tree 656
    string 198
    vector 604
SearchTree class 661
secondary
    memory 5, 7
    storage device 7
selecting one item 536
selection control structure **178**
selection sort 331
selector expression 222
selectSort 333
semantic event **510**
sender of a message **383**
sentinel value **267**
sentinel-controlled loop 267
sequence control 177
sequence of ifs 212
sequential access 313
sequential search 608
server **11**, 453, 491, 493
setBackground 467
setColor 152

setElementAt 346
setEnabled 553
setLayout 520
setMenuBar 575
setSize 471
setText 532
setVisible 553
short 52
short-circuit evaluation 189
showGraphic 285
siblings 655
SimpleGUI 34, 47, 80, 178, 571
SimpleGraphic 284, 286
simpleIO 47
simpleMath 319, 335, 600
SimpleReader 48, 350, 353
SimpleWriter 48, 350, 352
sin 136
size 347
sleep 481
sleeping process 482
Smalltalk 34
SmartButton 621
SmileyFace 472
Socket 491
socket-based program 491
software 4
    development method 35, 120
sorting an array 330
sound 13
source program 19
SOUTH 520
specifying problem 35
spell-checking 551
sqrt 133
Square 416
stack 594, 597, 639
    as linked list 640
    as a vector 645
StackList 640
StackNode 640
StackVector 646
standard deviation 318
standard font 518
start 456, 461

state-controlled loop 258
statement 73
static 418, 421
statistics 316
stop 456
stopping case 287, 589
storage allocation 308
store value 6
stored-program concept 6
stream model 508
string 93, 102, 185
    comparison 186
    method 94
String 54
structured programming 38
style 106
subclass 16, 58
substring 94, 187, 228
super 161, 393
superclass 16, 58
supercomputer 2
support
    class 383
    object 150
switch 220
syntax error 25, 109
system documentation 120
system software 15
System.exit 573
System.out 112

T

tag 450
tan 136
temperature table 277
template for
    counter-controlled loop 267
    menu-driven loop 271
    sentinel-controlled loop 267
TempTable class 277
terminating condition 589
testing 38, 290, 292
text
    component 548

editor 225
text to drawing 155
TextArea 512, 528, 548, 553
TextComponent 548, 551
TextEvent 514, 552
TextField 457, 462, 512, 528,
    531, 548, 553
TextListener 553
textValueChanged 553
this 409, 411
Thread 477
thread 477
    animation 485
    model 477
    put to sleep 481
threaded processes 448
three-dimensional array 365
throws 351, 358
TicTacToe game 561
time sharing 3
time-space tradeoff 337
top-down design 37
toString 348, 413, 665, 669
Towers of Hanoi 612
tracing recursive method 589
traversing a list 636
TreeNode class 661
true 52, 178
try block 233, 351
turn-taking 560
two-dimensional array 359
two-way list 638
type casting 88

U

unary minus 92
Unicode 186
Uniform Resource Locator (URL)
    449
UNIX 25
unwinding recursion 289, 597
user
    input/output 508
    interface 448, 508

V

validate 467
variable 49, **74**
vector 345, 646
  search 604
video 13
visibility 57, **123**, 403
void **61**
volatile memory **7**

W

Web 2, 12, 19, 21, 448, 493
  browser **12**
  client/server model 448
  page 494
  programming 448

WEST 520
while 246, 248
whole array 322
WinDemo class 572
window **10**, 458
Window 150
  event 572
windowActivated 573
windowClosed 572
windowClosing 572
windowDeactivated 573
windowDeiconified 573
WindowEvent 571
windowIconified 573
WindowListener 572
windowOpened 573
Windows (Microsoft) 25

Wirth, Nicklaus 34
workstation 3, 12
World Wide Web (see Web) 2
wrapper class **348**

Y

Yahoo 492
year-2000 problem 38
yield 479
yielding CPU 479

Z

zero-iteration loop **264**, 269
Zip disk 8